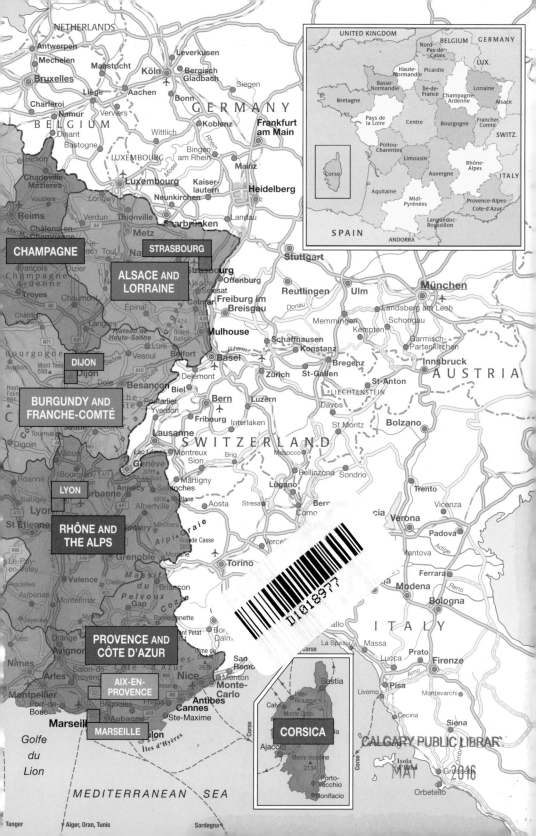

NETHERLANDS
Antwerpen
Mechelen
Maastricht
Bruxelles
Köln
Leverkusen
Bergisch Gladbach
Liège
Charleroi
Aachen
Siegen
Namur
Verviers
GERMANY
Dinant
Bonn
Koblenz
BELGIUM
Bastogne
Wittlich
Frankfurt am Main
LUXEMBOURG
Bingen am Rhein
Mainz
Charleville-Mézières
Longwy
Luxembourg
Kaiserlautern
Heidelberg
Vouziers
Neunkirchen
Landau
Reims
Verdun
Thionville
Saarbrücken
Châlons-en-Champagne
Metz
Stuttgart

CHAMPAGNE

STRASBOURG

ALSACE AND LORRAINE

Troyes
Chaumont
Offenburg
Sélestat
Reutlingen
Ulm
München
Colmar
Freiburg im Breisgau
Donau
Landsberg am Lech
Schongau
Épinal
Plateau de Haute-Saône
Mulhouse
Memmingen
Kempten
Garmisch-Partenkirchen
Vesoul
Belfort
Schaffhausen
Konstanz

DIJON

Besançon
Basel
Bregenz
Innsbruck
Dole
Biel
Zürich
St-Gallen
St-Anton
AUSTRIA

BURGUNDY AND FRANCHE-COMTÉ

Pontarlier
Bern
Luzern
LIECHTENSTEIN
Davos
Fribourg
Interlaken
St Moritz
Bolzano
Yverdon
Lausanne
SWITZERLAND
Digoin
Tournus
Lac Léman
Montreux
Sion
Brig
Mesocco
Sondrio
Mâcon
Genève
Martigny
Salnches
Bellinzona
Trento
Roanne
Bourg-en-Bresse
Annecy
Aosta
Lugano
Como
Vicenza

LYON

Albertville
Stresa
Verona
St-Étienne
Lyon
Padova
Chambéry
Méutiers
Grande Casse
Vercelli

RHÔNE AND THE ALPS

Grenoble
Torino
Ferrara
Modena
Valence
Briançon
Bologna
Aubenas
Gap
ITALY
Montélimar
La Spezia
Massa
Prato

PROVENCE AND CÔTE D'AZUR

Orange
San Remo
Lucca
Firenze
Nîmes
Avignon
Côte d'Azur
Nice
Monte-Carlo
Pisa
Montevarchi

AIX-EN-PROVENCE

Arles
Salon-de-Provence
Antibes
Cannes
Cecina
Montpellier
Ste-Maxime
Siena
Marseille

MARSEILLE

Aubagne
Îles d'Hyères
Golfe du Lion

CORSICA

Bastia
Île-Rousse
Calvi
Monte Cinto
Ajaccio
Monte Incudine 2134
Porto-Vecchio
Bonifacio
Isola d'Elba
Grosseto
Orbetello

MEDITERRANEAN SEA

Tanger
Alger, Oran, Tunis
Sardegna

UNITED KINGDOM
BELGIUM
GERMANY
Nord-Pas-de-Calais
LUX.
Haute-Normandie
Picardie
Lorraine
Basse-Normandie
Île-de-France
Champagne-Ardenne
Alsace
Bretagne
Franche-Comté
Pays de la Loire
Centre
Bourgogne
SWITZ.
Poitou-Charentes
Corse
Limousin
Rhône-Alpes
ITALY
Auvergne
Aquitaine
Midi-Pyrénées
Provence-Alpes-Côte-d'Azur
Languedoc-Roussillon
SPAIN
ANDORRA

CALGARY PUBLIC LIBRARY
MAY 2016
D10189??

INSIGHT ⊙ GUIDES

FRANCE

www.insightguides.com/France

◉ Walking Eye App

Your Insight Guide now includes a free app and eBook, dedicated to your chosen destination, all included for the same great price as before. They are available to download from the free Walking Eye container app in the App Store and Google Play. Simply download the Walking Eye container app to access the eBook and app dedicated to your purchased book. The app features an up-to-date A to Z of travel tips, information on events, activities and destination highlights, as well as hotel, restaurant and bar listings. See below for more information and how to download.

MULTIPLE DESTINATIONS AVAILABLE

Now that you've bought this book you can download the accompanying destination app and eBook for free. Inside the Walking Eye container app, you'll also find a whole range of other Insight Guides destination apps and eBooks, all available for purchase.

DEDICATED SEARCH OPTIONS

Use the different sections to browse the places of interest by category or region, or simply use the 'Around me' function to find places of interest nearby. You can then save your selected restaurants, bars and activities to your Favourites or share them with friends using email, Twitter and Facebook.

FREQUENTLY UPDATED LISTINGS

Restaurants, bars and hotels change all the time. To ensure you get the most out of your guide, the app features all of our favourites, as well as the latest openings, and is updated regularly. Simply update your app when you receive a notification to access the most current listings available.

Shopping in Oman still revolves around the traditional souks that can be found in every town in the country – most famously at Mutrah in Muscat, Salalah and Nizwa, which serve as showcases of traditional Omani craftsmanship and produce ranging from antique khanjars and Bedu jewellery to halwa, rose-water and frankincense. Muscat also boasts a number of modern malls, although these are rare elsewhere in the country.

TRAVEL TIPS & DESTINATION OVERVIEWS

The app also includes a complete A to Z of handy travel tips on everything from visa regulations to local etiquette. Plus, you'll find destination overviews on shopping, sport, the arts, local events, health, activities and more.

HOW TO DOWNLOAD THE WALKING EYE

Available on purchase of this guide only.

1. Visit our website: www.insightguides.com/walkingeye
2. Download the Walking Eye container app to your smartphone (this will give you access to both the destination app and the eBook)
3. Select the scanning module in the Walking Eye container app
4. Scan the QR code on this page – you will be asked to enter a verification word from the book as proof of purchase
5. Download your free destination app* and eBook for travel information on the go

* Other destination apps and eBooks are available for purchase separately or are free with the purchase of the Insight Guide book

Contents

Introduction

The Best of France.....................6
Vive La France...........................19
La Belle France 21

History

Decisive Dates..........................28
The Early Years 31
The Age of Absolutism.............35
Revolutions and Republics 38
War and Peace 43
Postwar France.........................47
Modern France 50

Features

The French 57
La Cuisine 69
Wine 79
Art...85
Architecture 91

Insights

MINI FEATURES

The Outsiders 53
French Cinema 66
Paris Fashion 130
D-Day 194
Post-Impressionists 334

PHOTO FEATURES

French Cheeses........................76
French Design...........................96
The Louvre 140
France's Festivals..................182

Châteaux Country....................228
The Golden Age of Canals.....250
Wildlife 324

Places

Introduction 105
Paris and Surroundings......109
Paris 113
Around Paris 143
The North 155
Le Nord....................................157
Champagne 162
Lorraine....................................166
Alsace......................................171
The West 187
Normandy 189
Brittany....................................203
Loire Valley.............................214
Poitou-Charentes 230
**Central France and
    the Alps**.............................239
Burgundy.................................240
The Rhône Valley....................253
The French Alps 260
Auvergne.................................269
Limousin 276
The Southwest 281
Aquitaine.................................283
Midi-Pyrénées........................297
The South.............................315
Languedoc and Roussillon ...316
Provence 327
The Côte d'Azur 341
Corsica 356

Travel Tips

TRANSPORT
Getting There 362
Getting Around.......................364

EATING OUT
How to Choose 368
Wine – Reading the Label 368
Restaurant Listings 368
Paris 369
Around Paris (Ile de France)..371
Le Nord..................................371
Champagne 371
Lorraine.................................372
Alsace....................................372
Normandy 373
Brittany..................................373
Loire Valley............................374
Poitou-Charentes 375
Burgundy & Franche-Comté..376
Rhône Valley and the Alps 376
Auvergne 378
Aquitaine...............................378
Midi-Pyrénées........................379
Languedoc and Roussillon ...380
Provence and Côte d'Azur 381
Corsica 382

ACTIVITIES
The Arts 383
Festivals and Events 385
Nightlife.................................386
Shopping................................387
Sport 389
Children's Activities...............392

A – Z
Admission Charges 393
Budgeting for Your Trip 393
Children..................................393
Climate..................................394
Crime and Safety 394
Customs Regulations............394
Disabled Travellers 394
Electricity 395
Embassies and Consulates ..395
Etiquette 395
Gay and Lesbian Travellers ...395
Health and Medical Care 395
Lost Property.........................396
Media 396
Money 397
Opening Hours......................397
Postal Services 398
Student Travellers.................398
Telephones 399
Tourist Information 399
Visas and Passports.............400

LANGUAGE 401

FURTHER READING 404

Maps
France 106
Paris 110
Montmartre............................134
Outer Arrondissements.........138
Around Paris 144
Le Nord..................................158
Lille..161
Champagne 163
Alsace and Lorraine...............167
Strasborg 174
Normandy 190
Rouen.....................................198
Brittany..................................204
Loire Valley............................216
Poitou-Charentes 232
Burgundy and
    Franche-Comté.................242
Dijon......................................245
Rhône and the Alps...............254
Lyon.......................................257
Auvergne and the
    Massif Central 270
Limousin 277
Bordeaux................................284
Aquitaine...............................286
Midi-Pyrénées........................298
Toulouse.................................305
Languedoc-Roussillon 317
Provence and the
    Côte d'Azur 328
Aix-en-Provence....................336
Marseille 338
Corsica 357
Inside front cover France
Inside back cover Paris Metro

THE BEST OF FRANCE: TOP ATTRACTIONS

From art and architecture to festivals, food and châteaux, here is the rundown of France's most spectacular attractions.

▷ **Champagne**. Celebrations all over the world are incomplete without a bottle of Champagne which can only come from France's most northern vineyards. See page 162.

△ **Mont-St-Michel**. The medieval abbey stands on an isolated rock rising out of a vast tidal bay. It is reached from the mainland by a brand new bridge. See page 196.

▽ **Versailles**. Louis XIV's Palace of Versailles, within easy reach of a day trip from Paris, takes regal excess to a new limit. Its splendid interiors are matched by its formal gardens. See page 143.

△ **Alsace**. On the German border between the Vosges mountains and the Rhine, the region of Alsace has picture-perfect villages and waterfront city quarters, as here in Petite France in Strasbourg. See page 174.

△ **The Dordogne**. This *département* is picturesque at every turn, with old castles, fortified hilltop villages, colourful markets, forests, river banks and caves with prehistoric paintings to explore. See page 287.

△ **Loire Valley châteaux**. The lower valley of the River Loire is home to a string of elegant Renaissance châteaux, especially Villandry, Azay-le-Rideau, Chambord, Blois and Chenonceau – which is built on piers over the water. See page 214.

△ **Provence**. An inspiration for artists such as Van Gogh and Picasso, Provence not only has a beautiful coastline (the Riviera) but also historic towns and cities in abundance including Avignon and Arles. See page 327.

▷ **Medieval gems**. There are more medieval towns and villages in France than anyone could hope to visit in a lifetime. Among them is the pretty St Cirq-Lapopie in the Lot valley. See page 309.

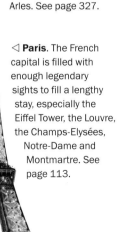

◁ **Paris**. The French capital is filled with enough legendary sights to fill a lengthy stay, especially the Eiffel Tower, the Louvre, the Champs-Elysées, Notre-Dame and Montmartre. See page 113.

▽ **French cuisine**. The exquisitely varied food of France is a highlight of any visit. Every region has its own distinctive cuisine and nothing beats a leisurely meal on the terrace of a celebrated restaurant. See page 69.

THE BEST OF FRANCE: EDITOR'S CHOICE

A gourmet's paradise where you'll also find elegant cities of culture, historic sites, medieval clifftop villages, landscapes that have inspired some of the world's best artists and much more – here are the editor's top tips for your stay.

EXQUISITE TOWNS AND VILLAGES

Riquewihr. Alsace's prettiest village is also a wine town. See page 179.

St-Emilion. An attractive old town renowned for its red Bordeaux wines that has a subterranean rock church dug into the hillside. See page 285.

St-Paul-de-Vence. Contained within 16th-century walls, this village in the hills behind Nice has long been a mecca for both artists and tourists. See page 349.

Carcassonne. The restored medieval citadel. See page 318.

Rocamadour. Shrine clinging to the side of a valley whose many levels are connected by lifts and steps. See page 310.

Cordes sur Ciel. Preserved hill town in the Tarn that looks little different today than it did in the Middle Ages. See page 304.

St-Paul-de-Vence.

MOST INTERESTING CITIES

Rouen. The capital of Normandy and birthplace of novelist Gustave Flaubert has many preserved half-timbered houses in the streets around its Great Clock. See page 198.

Lille. This Flemish city on the border with Belgium has both delightful architecture and a plethora of excellent shops and restaurants. See page 161.

Nancy. Lorraine's main city is 18th-century architecture and town planning at its most elegant, along with fine examples of Art Nouveau. See page 169.

Lyon. The old quarter is characterised by its secretive *traboules* (covered passageways)

and its *bouchons* (bistros) where you are guaranteed to eat well. See page 256.

Toulouse. A lively, easy-going Midi city on the Garonne River built of red brick, with a great Romanesque cathedral at its heart. See page 305.

Marseille. France's second city and its busiest seaport is a delightful mixture of communities and cultures, and has some great new museums to visit. See page 337.

Avignon. As well as the truncated bridge from the children's song, the massive 14th-century Palace of the Popes is a must-see. See page 329.

Avignon's famous bridge.

INSPIRING ARTISTS' HAUNTS

The Musée Matisse.

Albi. This town in Tarn was once home to Henri de Toulouse-Lautrec, and the museum in the bishop's palace next to the cathedral contains a great collection of his works. See page 303.

Auvers-sur-Oise. On the outskirts of Paris, this is where Van Gogh spent his last days, days during which he painted the church before tragically dying from a self-inflicted gunshot wound. See page 145.

Giverny. Bolthole of Monet, the originator of Impressionism. The lily pond and wooden bridge he painted are still here to see. See page 198.

Antibes. The castle here was used as a studio by Picasso and has since been turned into a museum of his works. See page 351.

Nice. The Musée Matisse, one of four major art galleries in the resort, is a reminder of the artist's time here. See page 351.

Montmartre. Occupying the highest spot in Paris, this *quartier* has always provided studio space and inspiration for visiting artists, not least Salvador Dalí. See page 135.

BEST ATTRACTIONS FOR KIDS

Disneyland. The inimitable European Disney theme park is divided into five zones and needs time and planning to explore. See page 147.

Parc Astérix. A theme park on a more Gallic theme, built around the exploits of the famous comic book hero and his companions. See page 146.

Futuroscope. Attractions, shows, rides and screenings explore all things cosmo, eco, cyber, digital and robotic – anything to do with the future. See page 235.

Vulcania. The Auvergne's introduction to the volcanoes of the surrounding countryside. Partly entertainment and partly educational, with the tour kicking off underground. See page 272.

Cité de l'Espace. Toulouse's "space city" is as enjoyable as it is informative, covering real space exploration but with lots of stuff on aliens thrown in for good measure. See page 306.

Cité des Sciences (La Villette). Paris's popular science museum includes a planetarium, the story of the universe, a submarine, interactive exhibits and an IMAX/3D entertainment dome, La Géode. See page 138.

Astérix and his big buddy Obélix.

BEST WINE REGIONS

Champagne. The main producers, most of whom do tours for visitors, are concentrated in Reims (also worth visiting for its cathedral) and Epernay. See page 162.

Burgundy. Time your visit if you can for the annual charity wine auction held in the beautiful surroundings of the Hôtel-Dieu in Beaune. See page 240.

Bordeaux. The city that claims to be the world's

wine capital is the hub of a vast region of vineyards dotted with famous-name châteaux. See page 283.

Armagnac. This region in northern Gascony, around the town of Condom, is less well known than Cognac but makes just as good brandies. See page 309.

Alsace. An established wine route takes you north–south through the vineyards producing dry

white wines, stopping at pretty towns on the way. See page 171.

Cognac. The distillers of the world's best brandy,

which must conform to strict quality controls, are in the town of the same name. See page 231.

Burgundy vineyards.

The salt flats of the Camargue.

BEST SCENERY

Alps. With their majestic peaks and three national parks, the scenery in France's highest mountain range is unbeatable. See page 260.

Pyrénées. They may not be as high as the Alps but they are easily accessible on day trips from the lowlands below. See page 297.

Corsica. Whether you stick to the coast or drive inland, the landscapes on the island are varied, surprising and often dramatic. See page 356.

Marais Poitevin. A warren of shady green man-made waterways and wetlands that can be explored by boat, by bike or on foot. See page 234.

Camargue. Coastal lagoons, salt flats, grazing land and marshes in the delta of the Rhône make up a landscape inhabited by flocks of pink flamingos. See page 335.

Gorges du Tarn. A dramatic canyon between cliffs, which are sometimes 600m (2,000 ft) high, beneath the limestone hills and plateaux of the Cévennes. See page 322.

Omaha Beach Memorial commemorates the American soldiers who landed there in 1944.

BEST HISTORICAL SITES

Carnac. Over 3,000 upright stones were placed in alignments here by prehistoric man thousands of years ago, for reasons no one knows. See page 207.

Lascaux. The original painted caves are closed to the public but a replica, Lascaux II, is almost as good as the real thing. See page 289.

Bayeux. The famous tapestry tells the story of William the Conqueror's invasion of England in 1066 almost like a strip cartoon. See page 193.

Somme Battlefields. The horrors of World War I are remembered in memorials and cemeteries in towns in the middle of now-peaceful Picardy. See page 160.

D-Day Beaches. The north coast of Normandy has several museums recalling the events of 6 June 1944. Begin at Caen's Peace Museum. See page 192.

GREAT VIEWPOINTS

Pic du Midi. A cable car ascends from La Mongie to the observatory on top of this Pyrenean peak for a view of Gascony below. See page 301.

Puy-de-Dôme. This small mountain above Clermont-Ferrand has views all round over the city and the volcanoes of the Massif Central chiefly over other. See page 269.

Ballon d'Alsace. Alsace's highest summit is easy to climb. It looks down on the Rhine Valley and across country to the Alps. See page 172.

La Rhune. A delightful old-fashioned cog-railway ascends the Basque country's sacred hill. From the top you look over the Basque region and Spain. See page 294.

Eiffel Tower. It may be over a hundred and twenty years old, but this iconic monument still provides the best view of the capital. See page 124.

Moonrise over the Pic du Midi.

Taking the Dune du Pilat, Europe's largest sand dune, at a run.

BEST SHORT AND EASY CLASSIC WALKS

Cirque de Gavarnie. A long but rewarding walk from a village at the head of the valley takes you to this enormous natural amphitheatre with a waterfall. See page 300.

Etretat. Footpaths north and south from the town lead to the summit of dramatic cliffs of chalk towering above the English Channel. See page 200.

Puy Mary. Park below at the Pas de Peyrols and take the flight of steps up to the summit of the Cantal's emblematic volcanic peak. See page 274.

Dune du Pilat. Europe's largest sand dune hovers over one of the longest beaches on the Atlantic coast, just south of the Bay of Arcachon. See page 292.

MONEY-SAVING TIPS

Menu du jour. Almost all restaurants serve a *menu du jour* at midday on weekdays which is cheaper than ordering à la carte. It will include a limited number of choices or just the one, and may or may not include wine. Some restaurants offer a *plat du jour* (dish of the day) with either starter or dessert.

Roadside hotels. If you just want an overnight stop, France has many prefab hotels, such as the rudimentary Formule 1 chain, on its city outskirts. Rooms are functional and there are no public spaces but formalities are minimal: you can book online and check out when you want.

Motorways. Tolls can add up, but some sections around the cities come free. With a good map or sat nav you can clock up a few kilometres quickly and leave before the start of the next toll section.

What's On. Ask in the tourist information office or check the local paper for places and events with free admission. Most monuments and museums have free visiting days and wine producers often offer free tastings in autumn after the grape harvest. Such events are often called *portes ouvertes* (open day).

Positive thinking at Le Touquet.

Place des Vosges, Paris.

Dining out in Lyon's old town.

Freshly baked bread in this St-Jean-de-Luz bakery, Basque Country.

VIVE LA FRANCE

Its capital may be one of the world's most celebrated cities of culture and a hard act to follow, but France's visitor appeal goes well beyond the charms of Paris.

Flying Le Tricolore under the Arc de Triomphe, Paris.

"Everyone has two countries – their own and France". So pronounced Benjamin Franklin, and there are good reasons why France is the most visited country in the world, attracting more than 84 million visitors a year – 15.5 million of them drawn to Paris alone.

This is a land of extraordinary variety, largely without harsh extremes of geography or climate. Within a hexagon of coasts and frontiers lies a bit of everything, from forbidding Atlantic cliffs to pretty Provençal villages overlooking Mediterranean beaches; from austere Alpine and Pyrenean peaks to bucolic, wooded valleys; from busy street markets to patchworks of fields and forests where the sounds of civilisation just don't filter through. History (and prehistory) are everywhere. No country does sumptuous châteaux, exquisitely carved Romanesque churches, towering cathedrals and picturesque medieval villages quite as well. It's easy to see why artists throughout the centuries have found France to be a haven and inspiration, the works they created now lovingly displayed in France's museums, major and minor.

A game of boules.

And it is an easy country to travel in, with superb motorway and high-speed rail networks. But should you want to take it slow you'll find that rural France is backroad heaven, with any number of meandering but well sign-posted scenic routes to explore by car or on bicycle. Alternatively, you could navigate through the country on its extensive network of rivers linked up by canals. If you prefer to take off on foot, long-distance walking routes are plentiful.

France is a hospitable country with a long experience of catering to tourists. The choice of places to stay and eat is legendary, and children are universally welcomed. Which brings us to the country's most powerful but least tangible allure: its way of life as epitomised by the national attitude to food and wine. Both are to be savoured at length and at leisure. A long lunch enjoyed on a shady restaurant terrace overlooking some slow-flowing river or picturesque medieval village – what more could life have to offer?

Sunflowers nodding in the Loire Valley breeze.

LA BELLE FRANCE

From the windswept coastline of Brittany to the scented, sun-baked hills of Provence, France is a rich and beautiful amalgam of landscapes.

With preordained natural boundaries provided by the English Channel, North Atlantic, Pyrenees, Mediterranean, Alps and River Rhine, France is often described by its inhabitants as a divinely shaped hexagon that absorbs and unites all the different parts of Europe. Indeed, France is at once a northern and southern European country, connecting the cold Atlantic Ocean with the warm Mediterranean Sea, and the empyreal Pyrenees with the Flemish flatlands.

At approximately 550,980 sq km (212,741 sq miles), France is Western Europe's largest nation and the 47th largest country in the world. Three quarters of the population of almost 64 million live in towns and cities but outside the major urban industrial areas, the population is spread thinly over huge areas with an average density of just under 100 people per square kilometre (260 per square mile).

> "England is an empire, Germany is a nation, a race, France is a person." Jules Michelet, Histoire de France 1833–67.

Rolling hills and fertile plains

The territory of modern France escaped the gouging glaciers of the Ice Age, so its landscape is generally mellow and pastoral, characterised by gentle hills and plateaus, carved by deep river valleys. Imposing mountains lie only along the eastern and southern frontiers.

Later geophysical development in the large southeastern Garonne region left profound impressions between younger and older hills, providing perfect conditions for the formation of valuable minerals as well as oil and natural gas.

The cliffs at Etretat, Normandy.

To add to France's fortune, an extensive network of rivers irrigates the landscape and ensures that France is a heavily forested country with 29 percent of its surface covered in trees, many of them deciduous.

A nation of farmers

Some 35 percent of the land is divided into 545,000 farms. Although agriculture employs only about 3 percent of the country's workforce, France is still Europe's leading agricultural producer and exporter. Its main crops include cereals, wine, sugar beet, maize and sunflowers.

Its vineyards are important both economically and culturally. Champagne, Bordeaux and Burgundy are known the world over and immense pride is taken in maintaining their reputations. Livestock include beef and dairy cattle (particularly in Normandy), pigs, sheep in upland regions (which supply milk for cheese as well meat) and goats (again for cheese) mainly in the south.

Many regions have their speciality crop or item of farm produce. The southwest raises ducks and geese for producing foie gras. Olives are grown in Provence. The east is known for its chickens and snails. Exquisite fish and seafood are landed on the Atlantic coast where sheep are raised on the salt flats. Bayonne and the Ardennes produce dry-cured hams.

A slag heap typical of the Pas-de-Calais serves as backdrop to this field near Lens.

A varied climate

The French climate is temperate and varied, as one might expect in a country with so many different faces. In the northwest, the Atlantic Ocean is the dominant influence, bringing high winds and driving rain as well as warm winters and cool summers. Eastern France, closer to the heart of Continental Europe, has marked seasonal changes, with cold winters and very warm summers, while the west enjoys a high proportion of sunshine, particularly along the Atlantic coast. The south has a Mediterranean climate, its winters mild, its summers hot, characterised by sudden fierce winds and dramatic storms.

Regions and départements

Politically, the country is divided into 22 regions, which group together 96 *départements*. The largest region is Ile de France, which incorporates Paris. The other regions are: Alsace, Aquitaine, Auvergne, Brittany (Bretagne), Burgundy (Bourgogne), Centre, Champagne-Ardenne, Corsica (Corse), Franche-Comté, Languedoc-Roussillon, Limousin, Lorraine, Midi-Pyrénées, Nord-Pas-de-Calais, Lower Normandy (Basse Normandie), Pays de la Loire, Picardy (Picardie), Poitou-Charentes, Provence-Alpes-Côte d'Azur, Rhône-Alpes and Upper Normandy (Haute Normandie).

There are also five *départements* overseas – Guadeloupe, Martinique, Guyane, Mayotte and Réunion – as well as other scattered territories.

Although the modern regions and *départements* are the most convenient way to divide up the country, other divisions are sometimes used for the purposes of promoting tourism or defining a region of agricultural production. Thus, for example, the "Loire Valley" refers to a geographical feature, a wine region and a tourist destination which crosses two official regions and several *départements*.

Border country

The northern border with Belgium, Luxembourg and Germany is the least well-defined of the hexagon's natural frontiers and the regions here blend into their foreign neighbours. Historically, this was France's mining and manufacturing belt and some heavy industry remains. The landscapes are often flat in Nord-Pas-de-Calais, Picardy and Champagne. Only when in

NATIONAL PARKS

France has seven mainland national parks: the Cévennes, Ecrins (Hautes-Alpes/Isère), Mercantour (Alpes-Maritimes), Port-Cros (one of the îles d'Hyères), the central Pyrenees, Vanoise (in Savoie) and the Calanques. There are a further three parks overseas, in Guyane and on the islands of Réunion and Guadeloupe. Their aim is protect the country's most fragile wildlife while ensuring controlled access to the public.

There are also 49 natural regional parks (*parcs naturels régionaux*) where the focus is not so much on protecting wildlife as safeguarding rural ways of life.

The French département of Guyane appears on the euro bank notes in circulation in the European Union even though it is in South America.

Lorraine do hills of any size appear: the beautiful, wooded Vosges mountains separate Lorraine from Alsace.

The Rhine valley in the northeast forms the Franco-German border. For a long time these were disputed territories and the region of Alsace passed back and forth between the two

peak crowns the highest mountain in Europe, impressive at 4,810 metres (15,780ft), and its broad-shouldered shape, once seen, is never forgotten. Three of France's seven mainland national parks are here in the eastern mountains.

Western peninsulas

The northwest of the country is made up of the two Atlantic peninsulas of Brittany and Normandy, each with independent-minded peoples and traditions dating back millennia. The thatched cottages, bent apple trees and locally produced cheeses and ciders of Normandy con-

Swathes of lavender.

Vineyards near St-Emilion.

countries; it retains a German feel in its architecture and in its culinary specialities. The city of Strasbourg, however, is a resolutely international metropolis which houses the European Parliament and the Council of Europe.

Eastern mountains

The east of the country is shaped by lows and highs. The river Rhône flows through France's third largest city, Lyon, and its valley creates an artery for north-south communications along which the country's first high-speed rail route runs. The mountains of the Jura and the French Alps rise steeply into Switzerland and Italy, and stretch almost to the Mediterranean in the south. In the Alps, Mont Blanc's imposing icy white

tribute to its popularity as a place to visit. Many painters have understandably been drawn to the gentle green countryside, dotted with fields of black and white cows under dramatic and often stormy skies, as well as to the colourful fishing ports along the coast.

The craggy coastline and harsh landscape of Brittany still evoke the druidical presence of the region's Celtic past. Particularly intriguing are the mysterious fields of megaliths and the pink granite rocks of the Corniche Bretonne. Fishing is a major industry in this area.

Moving south down the coast, the landscapes become much gentler in the subdued Loire valley, one of the country's chief tourist attractions dug out by France's longest river (980km/609 miles). The splendid châteaux and gardens of Touraine are still redolent of the glory of the Ancien Régime and its aristocratic pleasures.

Several islands embellish the Atlantic coastline. The largest, connected to the mainland by road links, are the Ile de Ré and the Ile d'Oléron.

The volcanic heartland

A great brooding bulk of upland occupies the centre of the country, the enormous Massif Central, which supplies France with much of its grain. The *puys* or volcanoes of the Auvergne create their own unmistakeable landscape

The Ardèche, popular with kayak enthusiasts.

around the industrial city of Clermont-Ferrand. Centuries past their tough lava was used to build black-stone churches and cathedrals.

As the Massif Central merges into the Rhône Valley to the east it creates beautiful canyons in the Ardèche. It does the same to the south in the Gorges du Tarn, near which are the austere hills of the Cévennes.

The Midi

A crude location for the Midi would be the area under a line drawn between Bordeaux and Grenoble; but a better way of defining it is linguistically. The Midi is, effectively, the area where, before the unification of France, the *langue d'oc* (Occitan) was spoken as opposed to the *langue d'oil*, which became standard French.

The name Midi evokes a dry Mediterranean landscape basking in the sunshine, pantiled farmhouses and a slower pace of life. As such, it is best applied to the southeast: the Languedoc (an old name recycled for a new region) and above all legendary Provence, which revolves around France's second metropolis, the port city of Marseille. Provence is a repository of all things associated with easy southern living: corniche coastal drives, smart resorts on the Côte d'Azur, jet-setting elegance in the principality of Monaco (independent of France but intimately connected to it), exquisite villages, wines, olives and historical cities, notably Avignon. Provence has dramatic scenery both inland and on the coast where the marshlands of the Camargue, in the Rhône delta, are home to flocks of pink flamingos. It has also always attracted and inspired artists and writers.

PROVINCES, PAYS AND TERROIRS

The French are extremely proud of their local identities – connected to lifestyle, cuisine and culture. To understand this you have to look beyond the regions and *départements* to the country's "emotional" geography.

Along with their *département*, most people identify with the *province* in which they live or were born. These territorial units without precise boundaries and of only quasi-official status hark back to pre-Revolutionary days. The provinces derive from the medieval counties that became administrative divisions of the *Ancien Régime*.

Another way they divide up territory is by *pays*. A *pays* is a swathe of the country in which the food, architecture, traditions etc. are part of a shared heritage, as

perceived by the inhabitants. As Elsie Burch Donald puts it in *The French Farmhouse*: "A *pays* was generally the distance a man could travel in a day and return home – roughly 20 miles; and within this area lay his entire world [...] and probably all his relations, for many peasants never travelled beyond the boundaries of their own *pays*. As a result the *pays* engendered a feeling of belonging and loyalty that amounted to a concentrated form of nationalism."

The word *terroir*, meanwhile, is often used for food and wine to denote an area of common agricultural production influenced by the same soil and microclimate. It emphasises the locality of dishes and their ingredients.

But the south can be deceptive. There may still be corners where traditional peasant life crawls along, but wealthy immigrants, many of them foreign, have transformed choice parts of Provence into a tourist playground. Also in existence is a very modern, functional side to the south of France. The city of Montpellier, especially, has reinvented itself as a dynamic place with a thriving university and cutting-edge industries.

The Southwest

Where the Atlantic supplies wind and rain, the countryside is much greener. Some of the lushest and most beautiful landscapes are to be found where the Massif Central peters out and the river valleys of the Dordogne and Lot take over.

The Dordogne has been the site of human settlements for thousands upon thousands of years, as evidenced by the prehistoric cave paintings found in its grottoes, particularly the enigmatic depictions of horses, elk and bison surrounded by arrows and strange symbols in the Lascaux cave complex, discovered in 1940 by two boys out walking their dog.

Two major cities dominate the southwest. Bordeaux is synonymous with wines – and claims to be the wine capital of the world. Toulouse, France's fourth largest city, is built of handsome brick and has an important aerospace industry building Airbus jets. The southwest comes to an abrupt and impressive halt at the Pyrenees, a range of high mountains blocking the way from the Atlantic to the Mediterranean. Two singular communities occupy the extremes of the Pyrenees: Basques at one end, Catalans at the other.

Corsica

The Mediterranean island of Corsica not only *seems* like a separate country to the northerner, it would become one if the independence movement had its way. Its wild, barren landscape, steep cliffs and mountains and lovely beaches make it an interesting destination for the traveller and the sun-seeker, though a difficult one to traverse.

Eye of the hurricane

At the centre of everything – not topographically but politically, connecting and administering the whole – is Paris, which has been called everything from a "whore" by Henry Miller to

Southern France is sometimes referred to as the Midi, although this name has no precise geographical meaning, referring to a land where the midday sun is due south.

"one of the most noble ornaments of the world" by Montaigne. It sits in a natural basin formed by the meandering River Seine and, taking in all the satellite dormitory settlements which surround it in the Ile de France region, plays home to approximately 12 million people.

The dune du Pilat, in the bay of Arcachon.

Paris is the energy centre, the political, economic, cultural, transport and tourist hub of France. It is the home of government; a reservoir of French culture; the nexus of French transport (all distances are measured from the square in front of Notre-Dame Cathedral). Motorways and railways radiate from here and it has the country's two principal international airports.

The city is growing daily both in size and stature, sucking in people and resources from the provinces as if by right. At times its inhabitants like to think that they *are* France and everything outside the Ile de France only of secondary importance. But, of course, that is not true. France is a country of diversity and all its ingredients go to make up the rich whole.

Revolutionary mural in metro station.

DECISIVE DATES

Representation of Charlemagne flanked by popes Gregor I and Gelasius I.

Pre-Roman and Gallo-Roman Era

600 BC
Greeks found Massalia (Marseille).

58 BC
Beginning of Roman occupation of Gaul under Julius Caesar.

AD 3rd–5th century
Barbarian invasions of Roman Gaul by Goths, Vandals and Franks.

The Dark Ages

496
Clovis the Frank, first ruler of the Merovingian Dynasty, having driven out the Romans, converts to Christianity.

751
Pepin the Short initiates the Carolingian dynasty.

800
Pepin's son, Charlemagne, is crowned Holy Roman Emperor.

843
Treaty of Verdun splits the Carolingian Empire into three.

The Middle Ages

987
Hugh Capet becomes the first ruler of the Capetian Dynasty.

1066
Norman conquest of England.

1152
Henry Plantagenet (future Henry II of England) marries Eleanor of Aquitaine. A third of France falls into English hands.

1305
The Papacy is transferred from Rome to Avignon.

1337
Beginning of the Hundred Years' War.

The Renaissance

1415
French defeat by Henry V of England at the Battle of Agincourt.

1429
Joan of Arc leads French troops against the English at

The battle of Crécy – from the illuminated chronicles of Jean Froissart.

Orléans. Charles VII is crowned at Reims.

1431
Joan of Arc burned at Rouen.

1453
End of the Hundred Years' War.

1562–98
Wars of Religion setting Huguenots (Protestants) against Catholics.

1594
Henry of Navarre, having converted to Catholicism, is crowned Henry IV.

1624
Cardinal Richelieu represses Protestants and involves France in the Thirty Years' War.

1643
Accession of Louis XIV, the "Sun King".

1756–1763
The Seven Years' War; France loses her North American colonies.

1769
Annexation of Corsica.

1778–1783
French support for the 13 colonies in the American War of Independence.

The First Empire and Restoration

1789
Storming of the Bastille.

1792
Overthrow of Louis XVI. Declaration of the First Republic.

The storming of the Bastille, 1789.

1793
Execution of Louis XVI; Robespierre's Reign of Terror, ending in his execution in 1794.

1804
Napoleon crowned as emperor; introduction of the Code Napoleon. First Empire.

1815
Napoleon's One Hundred Days; he is defeated at the Battle of Waterloo and exiled to St Helena.

1830
Revolution deposes Charles X in favour of the July Monarchy of Louis-Philippe.

1848
Louis-Philippe, the Citizen King, deposed. Second Republic.

The Second Empire and Third Republic

1851
Coup d'état by Louis Napoleon Bonaparte, Napoleon's nephew. Second Empire.

1870
Franco-Prussian War; overthrow of Louis Napoleon Bonaparte (Napoleon III).

1871
Uprising by Paris Commune with 25,000 people killed. Third Republic.

Third Republic

1889
Universal Exhibition of Paris; construction of the Eiffel Tower.

1897–99
The Dreyfus Affair.

1914–18
World War I, concluded by Treaty of Versailles in 1919.

1939
Outbreak of World War II.

1940
France falls to Nazi armies and is occupied.

Fourth Republic

1944
Allied landings in Normandy on D-Day. Paris is liberated.

1945
End of World War II.

1946
Fourth Republic is declared. War commences in Indochina.

1954
France withdraws from Indochina. Start of the Algerian insurrection.

1958
Algerian crisis topples the Fourth Republic.

The Fifth Republic

1959
General de Gaulle elected the first president of the Fifth Republic.

1962
Algerian independence.

1968
Strikes and student riots in Paris threaten to bring down the de Gaulle government.

1981
François Mitterrand elected president.

1995
Jacques Chirac elected president.

2002
The euro becomes official currency. Chirac wins a second term after a surprise showing for the Front National.

2007
Nicolas Sarkozy wins the presidential elections, promising tough reforms.

2012
Socialist François Hollande is elected president.

2015
Paris terrorist attacks leave 17 dead.

Clovis I in the battle of Soissons
(detail from a tapestry, c.1440).

THE EARLY YEARS

As fossil finds and cave paintings attest, France has been inhabited for millennia. The Gauls settled it, the Romans usurped it and the French made it a nation.

After the great glaciers receded from Europe, c.450 BC, France was populated from the east by a large influx of Celtic peoples. These were the Gauls, reputedly a strong and independent people, who left an indelible stamp on the French character and are celebrated since in every French language classroom, from Paris to Martinique, as "nos ancêtres les Gaulois" (our ancestors the Gauls).

The southern part of the country, meanwhile, received the attention of the classical civilisations. The coast was Hellenised by Greek merchants who founded the port of Massalia (Marseille) c.600 BC. In 121 BC the Roman Senate assumed a protectorate over the region, expanding its influence into Provence. Then in 58 BC, the Gallic tribes were invaded by an ambitious Roman proconsul seeking prestige through conquest, Julius Caesar. The Gauls, under Vercingétorix, put up a brave fight, but in the end Caesar triumphed.

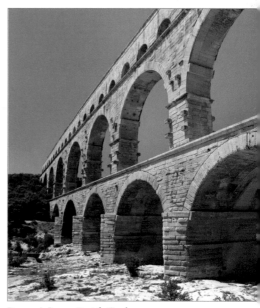

Provence's Roman Pont du Gard.

France has a rich legacy of intriguing but often enigmatic prehistoric remains, including cave paintings in the southwest, the megalithic alignments of Carnac in Brittany, and dolmens, statues and artefacts in many museums.

The Romans

The Roman occupation of Gaul brought refinements such as roads, architecture and urbanisation, especially to the southern Midi in towns like Nîmes and Arles. Lyon became a capital of sorts, and the French language started to develop from Celtic and Latin. On the Seine a small town called Lutetia sprang up – the germ of what would grow into the great metropolis of Paris.

Attracted by relative peace and prosperity, many "barbarian" peoples migrated to Roman Gaul from the 3rd to the 5th century. Among these were the Franks (from whom France derived its name), the Burgundians, the Goths (Visi and Ostro), the Vandals and the Alans.

In 451, the growing town of Lutetia narrowly escaped total destruction by Attila the Hun, allegedly through the intervention of its patron saint, Genevieve. In the 5th and 6th centuries Britons from Cornwall and Wales emigrated, giving the peninsula of Brittany its name.

The incoming barbarian presence began to undermine flagging Roman authority and, in 486, a Frankish king, Clovis, attacked and defeated the Gallo-Romans at Soissons.

He consolidated his power by defeating the Alemanni at Tolbiac in 496 and the Visigoths near Poitiers in 507. Converting to Christianity and moving his capital to Paris the same year, Clovis effectively brought into being the French state, which he called "Francia". His descendants, however, were weak leaders, and when Charles Martel led the French troops to victory over the invading Muslims at Poitiers (732), the groundwork was laid for a new dynasty. His son, Pepin the Short, crowned himself King of the Franks, beginning the Carolingian succession.

The taking of Jerusalem by Sultan Saladin – Third Crusade.

Pepin's offspring was Charlemagne, whose papal coronation at Rome in 800 created the Holy Roman Empire. Charlemagne doubled his domain to include what later became Germany by fighting the pagans of Western Europe in the name of Christianity. He is also known for unifying the Franks and Gallo-Romans under his leadership and encouraging education in his court. The *Chanson de Roland*, France's oldest poem written *c.*1100, later celebrated the bravery of his knights.

The problem of succession plagued Charlemagne, as it had Clovis before him, and in 843 the Treaty of Verdun split the empire into three. After a weak and unstable period, the Count of Paris, Hugh Capet, declared himself king

> *The Chanson de Roland is the epic tale of the death of one of Charlemagne's brave knights. The work traditionally marks the conception of both French literature and the chivalrous ideal of noble self-sacrifice for France.*

in 987, although at that time his jurisdiction extended only to the region around Paris. He was, however, the founder of a long-surviving dynasty: 806 years later, his descendant Louis XVI was addressed as "Citizen Louis Capet" just before his execution.

The Middle Ages

Religious fervour inspired a frenzy of church building in what is now known as the Romanesque style and led to the erection of some of France's most impressive monuments. A driving force was monasticism and two of the greatest orders were based in Burgundy – the Benedictines at Cluny and the Cistercians at Cîteaux. Although it was destroyed during the French Revolution, the abbey church at Cluny was the largest of its kind until the construction of St Peter's in Rome. Another marvel of the age, the church on the island of Mont-St-Michel was built from 1024 to 1144, although later added to.

French participation in the Crusades (1096–1291) bolstered nationalism (*Gloria Dei per Francos*, or the Glory of God through the French, was the motto of French crusaders) and worldliness, and the Romanesque style was strongly influenced by Eastern architecture. The 1066 invasion of England also expanded French influence, although more as a result of Norman than French foreign policy.

French fortune was checked, however, by the marriage in 1152 of Eleanor of Aquitaine to England's Henry II, and his consequent possession of this huge chunk of France. The accession of Philip II (Augustus) to the throne in 1180 greatly strengthened the monarchy, and his victory at Bouvines in 1214 helped win back from England some of its French possessions as well as some sense of a national identity. Philip much improved the status of his capital by advancing the construction of Notre-Dame Cathedral (1163–1320), the University of Paris (founded in 1120) and the Louvre fortress.

In 1253 the Sorbonne was established. The growth of cities and universities was complementary, and signalled a shift away from the dominance of monasteries and feudalism. New rational thinkers such as Pierre Abélard (1079–1142) emerged, although the castration he was subjected to after secretly marrying and having a son by his student Héloïse illustrates the precariousness of the intellectual's position versus the orthodoxy of the established Church. Nevertheless, his now legendary example also proves the zeal with which the French pursued scholarship and romance. In parallel with the growth of cities was the construction of majestic Gothic cathedrals. Those at Chartres, Rouen, Reims and Amiens are among the most impressive buildings in the world.

The monarchy and kingdom grew stronger under forceful leaders such as Louis IX (St Louis, 1226–70), who established the Parliament, built Sainte-Chapelle and fought the infidel, and Philip IV (the Fair, 1285–1314). Yet France remained a confusing hotchpotch of independent duchies for some time. The southern region of Languedoc suffered vigorous repression at the hands of northerners ostensibly angered by the Albigensian and Waldensian heresies.

> The First Crusade was launched from the county of Champagne by Pope Urban II, who in 1095 exhorted clergymen and nobles at the Council of Clermont (in the Massif Central) to raise an army to fight the Muslims in the Holy Land.

The Hundred Years' War

A protracted struggle to remove the English presence in France began in 1337. Supported by the Burgundians, the English tried to get a continental foothold. It was not until 1558 that they were finally kicked out of Calais, and only in 1802 did British sovereigns relinquish the title "King of France and England". Internal matters were complicated by the Black Death (1337–50) and by the so-called Babylonian Captivity (1309–78), when the papal seat was transferred to Avignon to escape the petty intrigues of Rome. To make matters worse, in 1392 Charles VI (son of Charles the Wise) began to lose his mind, managing only to increase the bitterness of

the dukes of Burgundy and the dukes of Orléans rather than temper the growing conflict between them.

In 1415, the English Army under Henry V, composed largely of archers and light infantry, routed the more numerous but less mobile French at Agincourt. Seven years later, when Charles VI died, the French crown was awarded to his grandson, the English King Henry VI, rather than the French Dauphin. The end of the Hundred Years' War (which actually lasted 116 years) in 1453 essentially marks the end of the medieval period.

Joan of Arc's entry into Orléans.

JOAN OF ARC

The tide of French affairs during the Hundred Years' War against the English seemed at its lowest ebb when a peasant girl from Lorraine appeared on the scene. Inspired by heavenly voices and an angelic vision, Joan of Arc (or Jeanne d'Arc) led the French troops to raise the siege of Orléans and crown the Dauphin king at Reims in 1429. She was captured by the English and burned at the stake in Rouen in 1431 (at the age of just 19) but Joan's defiant patriotism captured the people's growing sense of national identity. The words which were spoken at her trial, "God will send victory to the French", inspired the whole nation.

Louis XIV, the Sun King.

THE AGE OF ABSOLUTISM

The 17th and 18th centuries saw the rise and apogee
of the monarchy, and a golden age of learning
before the storm clouds of revolution set in.

The reign of shrewd Louis XI (1461–83) prepared the way for the French Renaissance.
It saw the elimination of much opposition
to royal authority, adding Maine, Provence and
Burgundy to the realm, thereby uniting most of
present-day France (the duchy of Brittany was
annexed in 1491 on the marriage of Anne of
Brittany to Charles VIII).

The 16th century brought important changes
to France in almost every area. The discovery and
absorption of the Italian Renaissance inspired
great artistic activity at the courts of François
I (1515–47) and Henri II (1547–59). Explorer
Jacques Cartier (and later Samuel de Champlain)
carried the fleur-de-lis (symbol of France) into
the North American wilderness. The reformed
teachings of Martin Luther and John Calvin took
hold, especially in the south of France. Even more
important was the general rise in knowledge, particularly outside the aristocracy and church.

Henri IV outside the besieged city of Paris in 1590, during the
Wars of Religion.

> Leonardo da Vinci himself spent his final
> years at the royal château of Amboise in the
> Loire Valley, and writers such as the poet
> Ronsard, the essayist Montaigne and the
> bawdy Rabelais all contributed to the growth
> of French literature.

The latter part of the 16th century was
marred by fierce religious wars between the
Protestants, called Huguenots, and the Catholics, culminating in the St Bartholomew's Day
Massacre (1572), when thousands of Protestants
were slaughtered by royal troops as they prayed.
The blame for this has been laid at the door
of Catherine de Medici, the scheming Floren-
tine who exerted power through her husband

Henri II and her sons, François II, Charles IX
and Henri III.

A strange sequence of deaths and assassi-
nations among Catholic rivals to the throne
brought the crown to the Protestant Henri
of Navarre (Henri IV), destined to be one of
France's greatest kings. To appease the worried
citizenry, he converted to Catholicism with the
memorable declaration that "Paris is worth a
Mass." The womanising Henri, whose tongue
had been sprinkled with wine and garlic at his
baptism to give him proper spirit, endeared
himself to France with his leadership and bois-
terous behaviour. He declared "There should be
a chicken in every peasant's pot every Sunday",

and improved the religious climate with the Edict of Nantes (1598), granting some tolerance to the Protestants. France mourned when he was murdered in 1610 by the fanatic Ravaillac.

The rigorous Richelieu

The tender age of Louis XIII (1610–43) at succession made his reign vulnerable to the wily machinations of interlopers such as Cardinal Richelieu, a humourless and strong-minded man who got his daily exercise jumping over the furniture of his apartments. Richelieu, nonetheless, did much to strengthen the central

somewhat inauspiciously with a regency presided over by his mother, Anne of Austria, and Richelieu's successor, Cardinal Mazarin. The nobility sought to regain its former power during the rebellion of the Fronde (1648–53), but was ultimately subdued. Yet, in spite of these difficulties, the reign of *Le Roi-Soleil* (the Sun King) marks the apogee of the French monarchy, and tales of the luxury with which Louis surrounded himself are legion.

Determined to escape the complications of Paris, which was rapidly gaining in importance and becoming independent of all authority,

Cardinal Richelieu, first minister of France, on the sea wall of La Rochelle during the siege of 1628.

authority of the monarchy. Indeed, the combination of royal power and longevity that characterised the 17th and 18th centuries led this period to be known as the Age of Absolutism.

As Grand Master of Navigation and Commerce, Richelieu also bolstered France's mercantile status, expanded its American holdings and founded the Académie Française. At the same time, the wars and intrigues he pursued, such as the expensive and inconclusive Thirty Years' War (1618–48), brought great misery to the people.

The Sun King

The death of Louis XIII left his five-year-old son Louis XIV on the throne. Destined to rule longer than any king of France, his reign began

THE ENLIGHTENMENT

The Enlightenment spawned unprecedented cultural activity, and Paris saw itself as a beacon illuminating the rest of civilisation. The fight for intellectual progress took place on several fronts. Montesquieu argued for representative law and political reform. Diderot and d'Alembert directed the mammoth Encyclopédie from 1750 to 1780. Buffon studied natural history, and the Montgolfier brothers recorded the first balloon flight in 1783. Rousseau suggested sweeping changes in society and education and Voltaire, perhaps the brightest light of all, virulently satirised oppression and intolerance wherever he saw it.

Louis decided that he needed a royal court so magnificent that it would require the presence and consequent submission of the aristocracy. The construction of the palace at Versailles perfectly achieved this aim.

Louis judiciously chose his ministers from the bourgeoisie and petty nobility to keep the nobles in their place. He gave France the largest army in Europe. He was indeed the state, as he boasted. Yet under him the "state" also grew somewhat distant from the people. The bourgeoisie became envious of the opulence of Versailles, while workers and peasants grew jealous

and Descartes all brought to French literature a refinement that it had not known before.

Louis's death in 1715 left on the throne his five-year-old great-grandson Louis XV, who reigned until 1774. Despite Louis XV's personal mediocrity, France's reputation as the most sophisticated nation on earth grew steadily in an age known as the Enlightenment.

The acquisition of knowledge apparently did not quite extend to military matters, for France lost its North American possessions to England following the Seven Years' War (1756–63). The French did, however, later gain a sort of revenge

Queen Christina of Sweden watches a geometry demonstration by the philosopher Descartes.

of the bourgeoisie. The revocation of the Edict of Nantes (1685) renewed hostility towards the Protestants, many of whom left the country for good (including 200,000 artisans France could scarcely afford to lose). There was a renewal of hostilities between the sects in the Cévennes to the south (1702–05), and a brief peasant uprising in Brittany was crushed. The famines of 1662 and 1693 underscored vast differences in the distribution of wealth.

In spite of these ethnic problems, the age of Louis XIV witnessed a great revival of popular interest in classical learning and art. The theatre of Corneille and Racine, the fables of La Fontaine, the comedies of Molière, the oratory of Bossuet, and the brilliant thought of Pascal

when they supported the American rebels in their subsequent War of Independence, seeing parallels between American idealism and their own Enlightenment.

Discontent brewing

The success of the relationship between France and America was offset by the war's enormous cost, and the taxation proposed by Louis XVI's ministers during his reign (1774–1793) grated on a populace that had become less tolerant of inequality. Discontent was fuelled by the bad harvests of the 1780s, and for a complex combination of reasons that are still debated today, France plunged into a revolution that changed the course of history.

REVOLUTIONS AND REPUBLICS

The Ancien Régime had to be overthrown but no one could agree on a system of government to replace it. There followed a century of constitutional experiment.

Napoleon Bonaparte at the alpine Great St Bernard Pass.

What is generally referred to as the French Revolution began in 1789, and actually consisted of several different power struggles that overlapped and fed off one another. To settle the fiscal crisis, Louis XVI convened an assembly of deputies elected by the nobility, clergy and Third Estate (everybody else). The bourgeoisie seized the occasion to create an alternative assembly charged with electing a new constitutional government.

On 14 July 1789 a Parisian mob stormed the Bastille prison, long a symbol of royal power. Inspired by this audacity, peasants organised themselves across the country and the bour-

> *The Revolution officially did away with the provinces of the Ancien Régime, replacing them with 83 methodically drawn départements; but the archaic names are still used today to evoke traditional areas which people identify with.*

geois National Assembly abolished the privileges of the nobility and clergy. The Declaration of the Rights of Man and the Citizen, signed on 26 August, was the culmination of a century of enlightened thought.

In this spirit of reform, France was reorganised into a constitutional monarchy and the republican *tricolore* replaced the royal fleur-de-lis as national flag. Meanwhile however, Queen Marie-Antoinette had secretly requested intervention from her brother, the Emperor of Austria, and so war was declared. Counter-revolutionary activity in Brittany, the Vendée and Lyon challenged the fragile revolutionary order further.

A new assembly, called the Convention, abolished all royal authority, instituted the metric system, adopted the "Marseillaise" as national anthem, and declared 1793 to be Year One of the Republic, replacing the Julian calendar with a new system of months and dates. Louis and his family were arrested and on 21 January 1793 the King of France was guillotined.

To maintain control, the Convention, under Robespierre, assumed draconian powers and executed anyone who challenged its authority. An estimated 40,000 people died during this period, known as the Terror, which ended only after the execution of Robespierre himself in 1794.

Napoleon Bonaparte

A young Corsican general who had distinguished himself in battle – one Napoleon

Bonaparte – took advantage of the climate of confusion by seizing power in 1799. He quickly consolidated his power by enacting a sweeping body of civil legislation known as the Code Napoleon. This code remains the backbone of the French legal system even today.

In addition, Napoleon reformed the French educational and monetary systems, founded the Bank of France, appeased French Catholics frightened by the revolution and reunited the divided country. In 1803 he sold off a large chunk of middle America to Thomas Jefferson. His popularity enabled him to crown himself emperor in 1804.

Unfortunately, these early successes led Napoleon to believe he could create an empire of the order of Charlemagne's, and, although he almost succeeded, France became embroiled in an unending succession of wars that culminated in the disastrous expedition into Russia in 1812. Defeated and exiled to Elba, Bonaparte escaped and made a dramatic return during the so-called "Hundred Days", but the alarmed European powers defeated him once and for all in the Battle of Waterloo in 1815. Napoleon's wars had reduced France to poverty.

Victors of the Bastille, 1789.

ROMANTICISM AND ITS INFLUENCES

Feeling restless with the complacency of the Restoration, in the late 18th and early 19th centuries a new generation of writers sparked rejuvenated interest in literature and sought to stage an intellectual revolution to parallel the political ones that had taken place. Led by the young Victor Hugo, these writers emphasised the power of the imagination in distinct contrast to the rationality of the Enlightenment's *philosophes*, such as Jean-Jacques Rousseau.

The most important literary form of the romantic period was that best equipped to describe and appeal to the now-powerful bourgeoisie: the *roman* (the French word for novel corresponds closely to the French word

romantisme). Allowing free expression, the novel was well-suited both to paint exotic pictures of foreign lands and less flattering ones of a progressively industrial and aggressive French society. Authors such as Stendhal and Honoré de Balzac disparagingly exposed the rapacity and snobbery of their fellow citizens and subjected them to minute analyses of character and appearance.

Later, Gustave Flaubert built on the legacy of the Romantics in his *Madame Bovary* (1857), which shocked readers with its graphic account of provincial adultery and avarice. His contemporary, the poet Charles Baudelaire, too, excited indignation by his celebration of sensuality and the morbid attraction of death.

Restoration and rebellion

The Bourbon kings were placed back on the throne by the victors at Waterloo but the restoration of the monarchy was not universally welcomed. The bourgeoisie were unhappy to serve a king once again after the great expansion of their importance under the Revolution and Napoleon.

When Charles X (1824–30) unwisely curtailed the freedom of the press in July 1830, students and workers erected barricades in Paris and began three days of rioting in protest. The king was forced to flee, and his cousin Louis-Philippe, who claimed to support republican principles,

The National Assembly, 1848.

was appointed to replace him. France became a constitutional monarchy again.

The emotions that precipitated the "July Days" of 1830 were in many ways the legacy of the unfinished Revolution. Under the "July Monarchy" social changes accelerated and Paris became the capital not only of Europe but of the 19th century. Technological innovation and urban growth consolidated the dominance of the bourgeoisie and fostered the development of a large, urban working class. Photography was invented by Joseph Niepce in 1816 and advanced by Louis Daguerre in the 1830s. The railways (1832) revolutionised transportation in France as they enhanced the capital city.

Complicated class doctrines were advocated

by philosophers such as Saint-Simon that were later to serve as an inspiration to Karl Marx. History writing, as exemplified by Jules Michelet and others, became a newly respected mode of expression. The caricatures of cartoonist Auguste Daumier also reflected the changing times.

In spite of 17 assassination attempts in 18 years and several serious urban riots (Paris, 1831 and 1834; Lyon, 1831), opposition from extremists of the left and right, and growing class tension, the "July Monarchy" was at least able to avoid foreign conflict. Moreover, the government, led by Louis-Philippe's minister Guizot, presided over steady economic growth.

The Second Republic

The downfall of Louis-Philippe remains as difficult to explain as the previous revolutions. Again, one of the issues at stake was the discontent of those who felt strangled by society. The 1847 fiscal crisis and unfair voting laws combined to remind workers of their inferior status. In February 1848, Guizot forbade an anti-government banquet to be held in Paris and provoked public rioting and barricades similar to those of 1830. The National Guard supported the demonstrators, and suddenly Louis-Philippe had to flee the country just as unceremoniously as his predecessor.

The poet Lamartine proclaimed the founding of the Second Republic, and a provisional government was formed that shortened the working day, declared universal male suffrage and abolished slavery. After initial elections were won by moderate republicans, workers of the far left rioted during the so-called "June Days" of 1848. Barricades again went up in Paris, but this time the insurrectionists were crushed and 4,000 of them killed. A presidential election conferred power upon the surprisingly popular nephew of Napoleon, Louis Napoleon Bonaparte. A man without the dynamism that his name suggested, Bonaparte declared himself emperor and arrested his opponents in a coup on 2 December 1851. The idealistic republic had ended where it had started, with yet another monarchy.

The Second Empire continued much of the expansion, both industrial and intellectual, that had taken place under Louis-Philippe. France annexed Savoy and Nice from Italy in 1860. The Crimean War against Russia (1854–55) was inconclusive, but nevertheless France began to extend its influence into other regions, including China, Mexico and northern Africa.

For a long time after its brief existence, the Paris Commune was looked back on by both anarchists and Marxists as the first true assertion of the revolutionary power of the working classes.

The *grands boulevards*

One of Louis Napoleon's more lasting achievements was the urban redesign of Paris. Wishing to build a more salubrious and graceful capital, and having noted the significance of street bar-

whereupon a provisional republican government was formed that tried in vain to perpetuate the war against the better-equipped Prussians. Wounded French pride was assuaged somewhat by leader Léon Gambetta's escape from besieged Paris in a balloon. Victory for Bismarck was inevitable, however, and the French were forced to cede the provinces of Alsace and Lorraine.

The Commune

In Paris, a feeling of patriotic indignation, combined with resentment of the extreme hardship inflicted upon the capital during the Prussian

Massacre of Monseigneur Darboy, archbishop of Paris.

ricades in overturning governments, he entrusted Baron Haussmann with the task of modernising the city. Haussmann changed the shape of Paris by widening avenues, eliminating congested areas and creating large public parks. The result was a truly grand, international metropolis – and a far harder place in which to stage an effective riot.

The status of the Second Empire ended abruptly in 1870. Tricked into a hasty declaration of war against Prussia by the insulting Ems Telegram, which allegedly made sport of his moustache, an overconfident Bonaparte established his lack of military ability once and for all by leading his troops to a cataclysmic defeat at Sedan.

Following this debacle, the entire super-structure of the Second Empire promptly collapsed,

war, created a climate of bitter discontent. When the provincial government, temporarily seated at Bordeaux, surrendered to Prussian demands, exasperated Parisians declared the formation of an independent workers' committee – the Commune. With the support of its National Guard, the Commune refused to comply with orders to surrender to the French Army based at Versailles. The result was a bloody two-month civil war in which Paris was again besieged and which only ended after 20,000 *communards* gave their lives to protect the city from their fellow countrymen. The northeast wall of the Père Lachaise cemetery, Mur des Fédérés, where the last insurgents were gunned down, has since become a site of pilgrimage for members of the left.

French soldiers in a trench at Verdun, 1916.

WAR AND PEACE

The Belle Epoque gave way to the nightmare of a "war to end all wars". Two decades later France again became an international battleground.

O ut of the debacle of the Prussian war and the hope and then disillusionment of the Commune was born a much longer lived constitution. In spite of the disastrous conditions which spawned it, the Third Republic would survive for 70 years and escort France confidently into the 20th century.

In the aftermath of the violent Commune, the republicans chose to concentrate on stability both at home and abroad. Basing its power among the enormous petty bourgeoisie, the Republic nevertheless made important concessions to workers, such as allowing unions in 1884. The Ferry Laws (1880–81), moreover,

> The 1,792 steps of the new Eiffel Tower served as a painful reminder to visitors of the weight of France's history. Some thought the tower ugly; others hailed it as a sign of the country's energy.

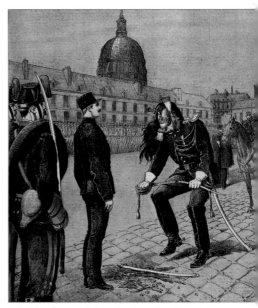

Alfred Dreyfus, branded a traitor in Le Petit Journal.

granted free public education across France. The Republic also managed to atone somewhat for the loss of Alsace and Lorraine by developing an enormous colonial empire in Africa and Asia. At its greatest extent, the French network of overseas possessions was second only to that of Britain.

Measured against the industrial and military standards of Germany, Britain and the United States, France's worldwide importance diminished somewhat during this period. There are many other indices of a nation's greatness, however, and during this Belle Epoque the French inspired the envy of the world with their ebulliance and *joie de vivre*. It was about this time that Paris began to acquire the racy, risqué

image which has always been more to do with fantasy than reality.

Paris reminded the world of its more serious import with Universal Expositions in 1855, 1867 and 1889, in which year the chief attraction was the new Eiffel Tower.

The Dreyfus affair

The status quo of Belle Epoque France was severely shaken by a military scandal which broke in 1894 and split the country into two camps. Suspected of assisting German spies, and convicted in part because of his Jewish background, Captain Alfred Dreyfus was dispatched to a prison island for a life sentence but later found to have been wrongly charged. The army was accused by the volatile intelligentsia of framing Dreyfus and covering up its mistake. The mood was summed up in an incendiary open letter to a newspaper by the novelist Emile Zola's entitled *J'Accuse!*. The after-effects of the affair reverberated through society for decades afterwards.

> "So there is such a thing as anti-semitism among the young? Youthful brains, fresh souls that have been distorted by that poison? How sad and disturbing for the 20th century that is about to begin." Emile Zola (1897)

The Great War

The outbreak of World War I in 1914 was a traumatic event. Quick German penetration of France was stopped by the Allies at the Marne. Protracted trench warfare followed, with tremendous losses sustained by both sides in the muddy fields of Northern France and Belgium. Abortive campaigns in Champagne and Artois were followed by the costly victory of Verdun, in which there were 700,000 casualties. Ironically, Verdun was also the site of the partition of the Carolingian Empire that had originally created France and Germany. The Battle of Verdun is still remembered as France's heroic moment of resistance and sacrifice. The British, however, remember the catastrophic battles of the Somme in Picardy.

While most of the war was a bloody stalemate, the harsh terms imposed on Germany by President Georges Clémenceau in the Treaty of Versailles (1919) allowed the French to perceive it as a victory in the grand.

Besides claiming reparations, the French were able to reunite Alsace and Lorraine under the *tricolore*. The heavy price of the victory, however, may still be seen in the lengthy list of names inscribed on the solemn memorials you find in every French village.

Entrenched Canadian soldiers going "over the top".

EXPATS IN PARIS

The emergence of Paris in the 1920s as a hothouse of literary talent was in great part due to the large expatriate colony whose attention had been called to France by the Great War. Ernest Hemingway, F. Scott Fitzgerald, Gertrude Stein, James Joyce and Henry Miller all spent considerable time imbibing French culture and enjoying a bohemian lifestyle away from the glare of publicity at home.

French writers, too, were well represented during the interbellum. The novel profited from the craftsmanship of old masters like Marcel Proust and André Gide, while André Malraux injected adventure.

The années folles

France emerged from the catastrophe with characteristic élan and the decade which followed proved to be lively and prosperous. Unfortunately, the ebullience of the 1920s, known in France as *les années folles* (the crazy years), did not serve as an accurate barometer of the rough weather ahead. The depression of the 1930s hit France hard. The collapse of the European money markets, accelerated by the unstable cycle of reparation payments following the war, wreaked havoc on the French economy and political structure.

Peace, meanwhile, was considered to be too fragile to be left to diplomacy, an impression reinforced by the military build-up in Germany and Italy under Hitler and Mussolini. From 1930 onwards a series of fortifications, together known as the Maginot line (named after a Minister of Defence), were built along the border with Germany to give the French several tactical advantages if attacked. The Line seemed especially necessary after Nazi Germany's repossession of the demilitarised Rhineland in 1936, the same year in which the Spanish Civil War broke out just across France's southern frontier.

At home, meanwhile, politics were becoming increasingly polarised and the Communists had joined forces with the Socialists as the Popular Front under Léon Blum to stand up to fascism and facilitate social reforms at home.

In 1938, France joined Britain in appeasing Hitler at Munich, and, after Poland was invaded on 3 September 1939, World War II was declared.

France at war

For eight months during the so-called "Phoney War" (the "drôle de guerre") little happened except the half-hearted Saar Offensive launched by the French to assist Poland but making no great gains. Then, on 10th April 1940, the German army launched a new kind of battle, the swift-moving *blitzkrieg* which penetrated through Belgium deep into northern France, rendering the vaunted Maginot Line irrelevant. The British Expeditionary Force was forced back to the sea and evacuated from Dunkerque. Paris was occupied on 14th June and an armistice signed eight days later creating a German occupation zone in the north and a nominally autonomous region in the south with its capital at Vichy.

France was united in its astonishment that its armies could have been beaten so swiftly and decisively. The country was divided, however, by the question of how best to respond to this defeat – submission and co-operation or resistance at whatever cost? The answer often came down to personal circumstances and conscience. Officially, however, there was little left to decide: France had been subjugated by its old enemy, Germany.

The famous World War I general Marshal Henri Philippe Pétain was given full leadership powers in the "Free Zone", the region under Vichy's control, and the constitution of the Third Republic was abrogated. In hindsight, everything to do with Vichy has become tainted with national shame, collaboration and anti-semitism; but at the time many saw Marshal Pétain as one of the country's most respected men, who at a difficult time personified the strengths and values of France: tradition, family and Catholicism. Collaboration with the Nazis was deemed the least painful means of coexistence, even if it implied the deportation of Jews and other French citizens. This question still has ramifications of almost unbearable delicacy for the French conscience, and it has been agonisingly debated.

De Gaulle and the Resistance

Meanwhile, General Charles de Gaulle, Undersecretary of State for National Defence, had fled to London to organise Free French forces from abroad. The British took the difficult decision to scuttle the French fleet moored in Algeria lest it fall into German hands, although this action produced painful hostility between the allies.

De Gaulle in Bayeux, 18 May 1944.

In France, the Resistance became active in opposition to the Nazi occupiers. If Vichy has become demonised, the Resistance has, in contrast, been turned into heroic myth. What is certain is that its activities often involved great bravery, led to loss of life and helped boost national morale among those Frenchmen and women who felt that Vichy was not so much an accommodation with reality as a sell-out.

On 6 June 1944 the Allied armies launched their long awaited invasion of continental Europe on the beaches of Europe against heavy resistance. Paris was liberated after two and half more months of fighting and the rest of France later the same year.

World War II Freedom poster.

POSTWAR FRANCE

Emerging from the misery of war, France
needed to overcome internal instability and
become a cohesive nation at ease with itself.

France's position in the world of 1945 was more precarious than it had been for many centuries. Its cities and most precious architectural treasures had been razed by German invaders and Allied bombs. Worse, the fragile national ego had been shattered by defeat and the collaboration of Vichy; and France now surveyed a world dominated by the US and the Soviet Union in which it had to find a new role.

After a brief period of intense self-analysis and recrimination, during which thousands of convicted and suspected collaborators were publicly shamed and in many cases executed, France began to look towards the future. The immediate priorities were to recreate a system of government to replace the one lost in 1940; to undertake massive urban rehabilitation projects, particularly in the north and in Normandy; to build a stable modern economy; and to ensure the peace and security of France within its borders.

The Fourth Republic, set up in the aftermath of war, proved itself fragile and instable, as testified by the succession of 24 ministries (1945–58).

In a 1962 speech to the French people, de Gaulle appeals for support of his Algerian policy in the national referendum.

The "common market" created in 1957 was to become the EEC, and later the European Union, an attempt to ensure peace and prosperity on the continent but with a long-term goal of economic – and increasingly political – integration.

In this period French Indochina was lost to the Viet Minh at the battle of Dien Bien Phu (1954).

Meanwhile a "new European order" was taking shape, with France forming the central axis along with West Germany. The Treaties of Rome, signed in 1957, created a "common market".

France's main preoccupation in the late 1950s, however, was the conflict in Algeria – only acknowledged to be a "war" much later. An inability of politicians to deal with the conflict prompted the imperial return of de Gaulle, who had withdrawn from the political stage a decade earlier. Summoning up all of his prestige he bulldozed the National Assembly into giving him what he had always wanted: a new constitution vesting unquestioned authority in the presidency. Thus the Fifth Republic was born in 1958 with General de Gaulle at its head.

General de Gaulle urged France to "marry the century" and adapt to the modern world. In spite of his militaristic appeal and his staunch nationalism, he presided over a gradual withdrawal from Algeria which was completed in 1962. This left a deep scar in the national psyche, particularly among the one million *pied-noir* settlers who returned to France feeling betrayed by their country. De Gaulle was the target of more than one assassination attempt.

Despite his past allegiances, de Gaulle in office distanced himself from the leaders of the United States and Great Britain, ejecting NATO from Paris (1967), vetoing Britain's membership of the European Economic Community (1963) and strengthening the *rapprochement* with Germany.

Burned out vehicles testify to the riots in the Latin Quarter, May 1968.

May 1968

During the 1950s and 60s French culture underwent a resurgence. The existentialist philosophy of Jean-Paul Sartre, Simone de Beauvoir and Albert Camus electrified the world, and French film-makers led world cinema with the *nouvelle vague*, New Wave. Pop culture might have been an Anglo-American invention, but Paris was the hippest, most counter-cultural city on the planet.

In May 1968, a general feeling of malaise erupted into aggressive demonstrations against the Vietnam War, government control of the media and the stagnant values of the adult generation. The insurrection, which seemingly

> *"I have tried to lift France out of the mud. But she will return to her errors and vomitings. I cannot prevent the French from being French." Charles de Gaulle*

came from nowhere, began with students protesting. Soon they were removing paving stones in the Latin Quarter, building barricades and occupying the Sorbonne. Joined by the workers of the left, the demonstrations escalated into a national crisis that threatened to bring down the government. Badly shaken by these events and by his failing foreign and economic policy, de Gaulle relinquished power to his former prime minister Georges Pompidou the following year.

Giscard d'Estaing

In the presidential election following Pompidou's death in 1974 Valéry Giscard d'Estaing, representing the Gaullists, beat Socialist François Mitterrand. Although an élitist patrician, Giscard d'Estaing was also a modernist and technocrat with an international outlook. His seven-year presidency incorporated reforms desired by the left: less restrictive divorce laws, legalised abortion and widely available contraception, and an 18-year-old voting age.

However, world economic forces were not in his favour and France was hit by the effects of the 1973/4 oil crisis. A period of 30 years of more or less uninterrupted economic growth matched by an explosion of French cultural and intellectual talent, known as the *trente*

COHABITATION

The Fifth Republic was designed to deliver strong government but in the 1980s and 90s a flaw in the constitution was exposed. What happened if the president and national assembly were of different political colours and couldn't agree on policy? The chances of stalemate were high. The nominally Socialist François Mitterrand faced this challenge from 1986, when right-wing parties formed the majority in the assembly and Jacques Chirac became prime minister. Later, in 1997, Chirac confronted the same problem in reverse when a backlash against his policies produced a left-wing parliament under Lionel Jospin.

glorieuses, came to an end in the mid-1970s. France entered what can alternatively be seen as a long, slow period of decline, or a period of adjustment – in which France has had to learn that it resembles other developed countries more than it would like to admit.

The Mitterrand Years

In 1981, the Fifth Republic faced the challenge of accommodating its first left-wing president when Mitterrand defeated Giscard d'Estaing. As an experienced but hitherto unremarkable politician with a highly distinguished war record, François Mitterrand spoke to a new generation. Yet at heart he was not a man of the people, rather an urbane intellectual of the old school with a literary bent and philosophical outlook.

Mitterrand arrived in office invested with the hopes of the left – and the Communists in tow – who felt they had been effectively barred from office by de Gaulle's 1958 constitution. He was to become the longest serving president in French history but only by departing from the radical programme of social and economic reform that many of his supporters expected, and which was partly thwarted by recession.

Mitterrand proved himself a wily politician whose ideals could be tempered by a principled pragmatism. Although he remains much admired as a president his time in office is associated with austerity programmes and the introduction of the market economy in France. He was not helped by having to endure a period of "cohabitation": working with a parliament and prime minister (the right of centre Jacques Chirac) of a different political stamp to himself.

Mitterrand is also remembered for his *grands projets* or *travaux*: major public works that shaped 20th-century French society, transformed the Paris skyline and boosted the country's self-esteem.

Abroad, Mitterrand played a significant role on the world stage, from the Falklands to the Gulf War and Bosnia. In foreign policy, he cemented the Franco-German axis at the heart of the European Union. The relationship with Chancellor Helmut Kohl was forged on common defence interests, a dread of war and a shared enthusiasm for full European integration.

In 1989 France celebrated the bicentenary of the Revolution with an orgy of self-congratulation but also used the occasion for more introspection on its past, present and future. Six

years later, the right regained the presidency in the shape of the avuncular Jacques Chirac.

Tackling cohabitation

Almost immediately Chirac was faced with the challenge of a big wave of strikes, and a pattern crystallised in which a government would attempt reforms but withdraw them under pressure from a sector of the public. Chirac also had to endure his own ordeal of "cohabitation" when a left-wing national assembly, under Lionel Jospin, was elected in 1997.

This second period of conflict-ridden politics

Mitterrand and Chirac, 1994.

forced the political class to think the unthinkable: that there might be a flaw in the constitution of the Fifth Republic. Cohabitation could easily lead to deadlock and it might one day be impossible for a president, whatever his personal popularity, to effectively govern the country. Between them, Jospin and Chirac steered through legislation to make the presidency a five-year rather than a seven-year term. With Chirac coasting and Jospin riding high in the public esteem, the latter seemed certain to become the next president. But, whether through the left's eternal inability to rally round a candidate (Mitterrand excepted) or through his own miscalculations, things were to go disastrously wrong for Jospin.

MODERN FRANCE

The 21st century has brought with it the challenges of market liberalisation, environmental crisis, a diverse society and the threat of terrorism.

If modern France has a defining moment it is not the handover of power from Mitterrand to Chirac in 1995, but the presidential election of April 2002. On the evening that the results of the first round were announced a sense of disbelief ran around the country. Jean-Marie Le Pen, leader of the far-right Front National party, renowned for its strong stance on immigration, had won 16 percent of the national vote – beating the left's candidate, Lionel Jospin, into third place. Subsequently, many voters felt they were left with no choice come the second round: either the incumbent, Chirac, or a man considered by the French as beyond the pale of Republican values.

It was a time which has been hyperbolically compared to 1940. Shock quickly gave way to indignation and the media was apoplectic. How could the Fifth Republic, which had even accommodated Communist ministers in the government under Mitterrand, throw up such an unacceptable situation? The Revolutionary principles of Liberty, Equality and Fraternity seemed at stake.

To "save France" from shame and disgrace even extreme left-wingers dutifully turned out to vote for the lesser evil, their arch-enemy Chirac. In reality, there was never any doubt that Chirac would beat Le Pen in the play-off, with or without the support of the left; but the mere possibility of him losing was enough to rouse his most vehement critics into awarding him a second term as president by a landslide. Most people agreed: this was not a vote of personal confidence in Chirac but done for the survival of the republic itself.

It was surely this episode that caused Nicolas Sarkozy, appointed Minister of the Interior in the wake of the election, to think carefully before planning his own bid for the presidency.

Campaign posters spelling out an anti-EU message in the run-up to the May referendum, 2005.

In May 2005, France, up till this point one of the leading movers of the EU, delivered a surprising rebuttal to further European integration when the French electorate voted in a referendum against the proposed EU constitution.

While the disunity of the left could be counted on, he reasoned he would have to appeal to Le Pen's constituency, voters of the far-right, to be sure of victory. He thus increasingly presented himself as the candidate conservatives could trust on law and order, and immigration. His outspoken and controversial comments on the

2005 riots which involved disaffected Muslim youth, broke out in Paris's run-down housing estates and spread throughout the country, outraged moderate opinion. However his standing in his own party was raised enough to beat Chirac's protégé, Dominique de Villepin, for the centre-right presidential nomination in 2007.

Sarkozy offered voters a break with the "old politics", a closer relationship with the US, greater control of illegal immigration, the repeal of a highly controversial measure passed by Jospin in 2000 to limit the working week to 35 hours and a spate of further economic liber-

ageing population who are living longer for which there are relatively fewer younger people to contribute to those early and long retirements.

The fourth area of policy was the environment. In line with EU objectives, the French government's stated aim was, and still is, to encourage sustainable development and implement renewable energies. Despite some vociferous opposition the number of proposed wind farms was greatly increased during Sarkozy's presidency.

Sarkozy billed himself as a new kind of politician for France, appealing directly to his supporters and constituents, and promoting himself as

Former president Nicolas Sarkozy and his wife Carla Bruni on an official visit to South Africa, February 2008.

alisation under the slogan "work more to earn more". During the campaign, Sarkozy proved a commanding media player who could promise all things to every Frenchman and woman.

Reform Agenda

In office, Sarkozy pursued an agenda of reforms in four key areas. One major goal was to slim the large and expensive state. In a similar vein, Sarkozy took steps to rationalise the multi-tiered system of local government, each tier adding to costs; and to reduce the power of the regions – the majority of which happened to be in the hands of the left wing.

Another target for reform was the pensions system. Like other countries, France has an

JE SUIS CHARLIE

On 7th January 2015 a huge police operation was implemented in Paris after the shocking shooting of 11 people at the offices of the satirical magazine Charlie Hebdo, leaving 12 others injured. The two gunmen, belonging to an Islamist terrorist group, waged war against the magazine for publishing cartoons of the prophet Mohammed. Several related attacks saw a further six people killed and 11 wounded. The gunmen were finally shot by police. On 11th January 2 million people and 40 world leaders joined a Paris march of national unity, plus 3.7 million more across France. Their slogan went viral across the world, – "Je suis Charlie".

The sporadic desecration of Jewish graves, as well as attacks on Jewish cemeteries, synagogues, schools and shops, all show that anti-Semitism remains a serious and persistent problem for France.

a media player, camera-friendly but unafraid to court controversy. Another way in which Sarkozy differed from previous presidents was that his private life was always very much a part of his public and political story. Six months after his election,

President François Hollande.

he met the former model turned singer-songwriter, Carla Bruni. In Februrary 2008 she became Sarkozy's third wife and immediately began turning the heads of the international media.

From Sarkozy to Hollande

From 2008 President Sarkozy was beset with problems as the global and European financial crisis tightened its grip. As a result of his planned cuts in pay and jobs, plus reform of the pension benefits and pressure from the EU to inject money into France's largest banks, he was losing popularity. In March 2010 his UMP party suffered heavy defeats in the regional elections and opposition to his policies continued to grow. His government then announced public spending cuts of 45 billion euros in an effort to reduce the high level of public debt and by the autumn thousands came out on the streets in a wave of anti-government feeling against the plans to raise the retirement age to 62.

Austerity measures continued in the following year, which also saw France's credit rating fall. Sarkozy had also to face growing problems of racism and immigration. The wearing of the niqab or full-face veil had been banned in public places to prevent individuals from hiding their identity and to attempt to integrate all sectors of society.

Further problems arose with the scandal surrounding Dominique Strauss-Kahn, backed by the president to become head of the IMF in 2007. Allegations of sexual harassment and assault surrounding DSK resulted in his retirement in 2011, and despite a case against him being dropped, the damage to the establishment had been done.

By the 2012 election Sarkozy's popularity had further waned. France is a modern prosperous country and its people expect to work less but be well looked after by the state. Socialist François Hollande beat Sarkozy at the polls but he too had his work cut out with zero growth in 2012 and a second recession in 2013. Although there were tensions over the euro crisis between France and Germany, Hollande managed to secure a closer Franco-German partnership with Angela Merkel, the German Chancellor. This remains particularly strong in areas of defence and diplomacy in foreign conflicts, such as in Ukraine.

By 2014, however, the far-right Front National party were making significant gains in both the municipal and European elections and finally won a seat in the French senate, with the Socialists losing their majority in the upper chamber.

By the end of the year President Hollande announced yet more cuts in public spending and the number of people seeking work climbed to a record high of over three and a half million. In January 2015 the French, along with the rest of the world, were outraged by the shocking Charlie Hebdo terrorist attack and internal politics were put on hold, increasing Hollande's popularity short term. The president has indicated he will not stand for a second term if unemployment is not reduced and Sarkozy, despite being subject to a formal investigation into insider dealings, has resumed his old job as head of the UMP party, which made significant gains in the 2015 local elections. France will have to wait until 2017 to see which party will form the next government.

The Outsiders

Dictionaries translate *banlieue* as "suburbs", but whereas its English counterpart is a relatively unproblematic word, the French term is loaded with nuance.

Banlieue means "outskirts". Historically, it was the loop of land within a distance of one league (*lieue*) from a city's perimeter; nowadays the word applies to any residential area in the orbit of Paris, Lyon, Toulouse or any other large city. Whereas some *banlieues* are affluent and picturesque complexes of middle-class detached and semi-detached houses, mostly the term puts French people in mind of *cités*: estates of high-rise blocks of flats, often built as HLMs (*habitation à loyer modéré*, that is, social housing at affordable prices for tenants on low incomes).

Most were built in the 1960s and '70s to provide cheap housing for a growing workforce. In particular, immigrants from Algeria, Morocco and former French colonies in Africa moved into these new *banlieues*, arriving at a time when France was booming and there was demand for labour.

The first arrivals lived in the *banlieues* long enough only to earn the means to move on to somewhere better. But when industry slumped from the mid-1970s and employment became less easy to come by, life changed for the children and grandchildren of the migrants who could not accumulate the wealth to move out as their predecessors had done.

And so began a vicious circle whereby disadvantaged people with similar social, economic and educational handicaps accumulated in out-of-town ghettos, ignored by policy makers who had no clear idea of how to tackle the problem. Poor facilities have fuelled local resentment, and chronic vandalism given the state the perfect excuse not to further invest in these neglected communities. Some *banlieues* developed their own submerged, parallel economies while a few sinkholes of endemic delinquency and burned-out cars became no-go areas for the police.

In October 2005, the subject that many politicians and middle-class voters preferred to ignore punched its way to the top of the news. Trouble had started in the Paris *banlieue* of Clichy-sous-Bois, where two teenagers, running from the police,

climbed into an electricity substation and died. The resulting riots spread across the country. France experienced 23 nights of violence, 9,000 cars were torched, and a state of emergency declared. Presidential hopeful, Nicolas Sarkozy, then interior minister, faced criticism but also made a name for himself by talking about the problem in confrontational rather than comprehending language.

Still, not all of France was in denial. It's a measure of how heavy the topic weighs on the national conscience that it has even spawned a cinematic sub-genre, the "*banlieue* film" – of which the best-known is Matthieu Kassovitz's incendiary 1995 hit

Hanging out at the entrance of a run-down block on an estate in the northeast suburb of Paris.

La Haine; reportages such as the Taverniers' *De l'autre côté du périph'* are frequent; and occasionally a film "from the inside" gets made, like *Wesh Wesh, qu'est-ce qui se passe?* by Rabah Ameur-Zaïmeche (2001). On the fashion front, the "*banlieue* look" has entered the mainstream.

Where the worst *banlieues* are concerned little has improved since 2005, but at least the problem has come more to the fore. The January 2015 attacks have seen François Hollande promise to spend more on education and urban renewal; with an increase in social housing. He emphasises the need for solidarity of the republic, for integration and an end to ghettoisation. Is this just more talk or will the French people finally see action?

Like much of Europe, France prizes its café culture.

THE FRENCH

The French way of life is the envy of many, but France is having to learn to adapt to the challenges of living in a competitive world.

Never was there a country more commented on by the rest of the world than France. Everyone has an opinion on the place and its people. France does not incite indifference. It may no longer be one of the most powerful nations on earth; it may not be the cultural trend-setter it once was; and it may, as is often said, be in decline; but France *matters* out of proportion to its size and circumstances.

The French have a reputation for not much caring what the world thinks of them, but they do (understandably) share the fascination with asking what makes their country special or at least different; and why and how it works. In the media, they endlessly pick over the traits of their identity, celebrate their achievements or wonder how they got into their present state; and always end with a Gallic shrug of *tant pis* or *tant mieux* (so what, too bad).

Partly, the universal interest in all things French lies is in history. For centuries, France was a cultural beacon to the world. Under the

Exuding that je ne sais quoi...

> "I believe only in French culture, and regard everything else in Europe which calls itself "culture" as a misunderstanding." Nietzsche Ecce Homo 1888

absolutist Ancien Régime, during the Enlightenment and in the wake of its multiple spasms of revolution, it sent out ideas and influences to sympathisers and admirers everywhere. If you were anyone, you spoke French to distinguish you from the riff-raff; if you could afford it, you built yourself a château in the French style; and if you were a penniless romantic you headed straight for France. "As an artist," said

Nietzsche, "a man has no home in Europe save in Paris."

An innate charm

France may have changed greatly since its historical hey-day, but it hasn't lost much of its old charm. Other nationalities regard the French as a people with an open secret; an innate knowledge about the art of living that they are not always willing to share.

Not that France gets a universally good press. For every Francophile ready to gush about pavement cafés and corner *boulangeries*, there is at least one francophobe ready to remind the world of France's shortcomings and failures. It is not uncommon for the two attitudes to be combined: to regard the French with a mixture of envy for their way of life and derision for their arrogance and underachievement.

Geographical divisions

Even if it's not easy to brush preconceptions aside and approach the subject with an open mind, there are some questions worth asking here. Who are the French today and why are they as they are? What do you need to know to get the best out of them and what, if anything, do they still have of value to offer the rest of the world? Any country is defined as much by its internal dichotomies as its homogeneity, and this is especially true of France. Yet only by appreciating these differences, is it possible to arrive at any tentative generalisations.

To begin with, France is a megacephalic nation. Paris (and the Ile de France region in which it lies) is an oversized, ever-swelling head quite out of proportion to the body of its provinces. It is not unusual to hear foreigners refer to Paris and France as if they were the same thing. It would almost be true to say that there are two countries to talk about: France and the Ile de France, as if the latter were a country within a country. Move away from Paris and suddenly things look very different. In the southwest, for instance, Paris is a far-away place and Parisians are looked down upon as intruders who know nothing about rural affairs.

Paris is of course in the north and France has a classic north/south split. The north is more populated and was, until recently at least, industrialised. The south has never had any heavy industry; its population is scattered; and its economy is rural.

A further nuance is to be teased out between the growing urban areas and the increasingly marginalised countryside. The inhabitants of any provincial *grande ville* do not see life quite in the same way as people living in isolated houses or market towns. The picture of settlement pattern is complicated by the *banlieues* – out of town ghettoes of socially and economically disadvantaged people who do not feel as if they have the same stake in society as their fellow man – and by *rurbanisation*, the morphing of rural-urban fringes into dormitory estates.

In addition to these divisions, it must be remembered that France is a composite country of sometimes quasi-nationalistic regions. So, for example, a Breton living on the Atlantic coast and an Alsatian living within walking distance

Flea market finds in Granville, Normandy.

Boys from the Pays Basque in traditional berets.

> "The French point of view [is] that the law is an instrument designed to prevent one's neighbour from enjoying one iota more of any benefit than one's self." Eugene Fodor

of the German border, do not have quite the same view of France.

Age and class

Overlaid on to these geographical divisions, are social and demographic factors, not always

finishing off the monarchy and aristocracy in favour of a society in which birth did not guarantee privilege.

In theory, and to some extent in practice, anyone in France can succeed whatever his background. As in any country, there are always rich and poor people; and certainly wealthy and powerful families – including some with residual aristocratic titles – who know how to look after their own. But these people do not constitute a definable caste and there is no discernible pecking order of deference. A sociologist would certainly try to

Setting off for the wedding, Strasbourg.

obvious to an outsider. Inevitably, age divides the French. The older generations remember the war and not just the Fourth Republic but the one before that. The young, on the other hand, have grown up as hypermarket shoppers and internet users. In between are middle-aged people some of whom took to the barricades as bona fide old school Communists before history came to an end with the fall of the Berlin Wall and the collapse of the Soviet Union.

The question of class divisions is more complicated. It is both true and not true to say that France is a classless society. The French certainly think of themselves as such. The 19th-century was a staccato process of

tease out strata in French society according to income levels and employment status, beginning with the unemployed, unskilled worker and progressing through the *petite* and *grande bourgeoisie*, but his report would not be very enlightening.

There is, though, only one class that needs to be singled out and that is the *élite* that keeps the country functioning. France deliberately nurtures this elite and refreshes it with new talent through the system of *grandes écoles* (universities which take only the highest flyers). However, the important point is that the elite largely identifies its interest with that of the country as a whole and so does not constitute a class in the strict Marxist sense.

For all the differences, there is a single, continuous France, inhabited by people who share something in common, a binding force which could be called "Frenchness". It is impossible to define this term accurately and fully – and it would be politically contentious to do so in France – but according to the journalist Anthony Peregrine it is *"an accumulation of their history, thought, arts and food – all wrapped up into a sort of "Project France". This is imbibed with the mother's milk, taught in schools and underlined in newspapers and on television…Backed by a myth of magnificence, Project*

Frenchness and republican values are at least nominally respected by all for the good of all. Across the English Channel, Margaret Thatcher once famously declared that there was no such thing as society; for the French there is nothing else *but* society. France is a nation of individuals but not a nation of individualists, as can be seen in the scrupulous unwritten rules on saying hello.

As a counterpoint to the emphasis on public formality, personal privacy is largely respected and this accounts for the freedom of the individual to do what he wants in his

A Ribeauville (Alsace) couple at their window.

Making the famous Laguiole knives in Cordes-sur-Ciel.

France co-opts most people most of the time, keeping them moving in broadly the same direction."

Republican values

Underpinning "Frenchness" are the republican values established by the Revolution. The outward symbols of these – the cock, Marianne, the Marseillaise and the portrait of the incumbent president on the wall of the town hall – may look faintly ridiculous to an outsider but they represent the deep and enduring slogans of liberty, equality and fraternity. These principles are the glue, or necessary myth, that the people need to live by; qualities to aspire to and against which to compare the performance of their fellow man.

DON'T ASK MY NAME

Wherever two French people meet they begin with a formal salutation. To fail to greet someone, even a shop check-out assistant, is considered rude. The average French person is capable of kissing, or shaking hands with, a whole room of people before starting a conversation or conducting urgent business. The number of kisses given varies from two to four, depending on the region.

Everyone scrupulously respects the distinction between *vous* (polite and distant) and *tu* (intimate) and is careful not to ask personal questions of a new acquaintance, not his name nor his occupation – questions that undermine the notion of equality.

own bedroom. The rest of the Western world has always been pruriently shocked by the "liberated" French attitude to sex – the story of François Mitterrand's mistress turning up to his funeral is regularly dragged out – but now that the rest of the West has caught up with France in this respect there is no longer much difference between the sexual mores of young people in Orléans and New Orleans.

A fundamental dollop of social glue is applied daily in the use of the French language, a source of pride to its owners, who are often pedantic about its correct use. It is a mistake, however, to assume you have to speak perfect French or else keep your mouth shut. Parisian waiters may have a reputation for being brusque with customers who get their genders wrong or fail to annunciate their vowels correctly, but almost every other French person is extremely grateful to any foreigner who takes the trouble to speak French, however appallingly.

The rules of French are rigidly defined by the venerable Académie Française, watchdog of the language, which often steps in to provide a "proper" French word in place of some creeping American import. The anglophone world often finds this puritanical linguistic policy incomprehensible, if not amusing, but it offers an insight into the fundamental premise of French culture.

"No foreigner should ever mock the French language," warns Theodore Zeldin in his classic study, *The French*: "first because he does not understand it properly, and secondly because it has divine status in France…If one forced the French to strip-tease, discarding one by one all the outward disguises that give them their national identity, the last thing one would be left with would be their language."

Making an exception

Language forms a key component of the *exception culturelle française*, a concept which underpins the country's idea of itself. This is the assumption that France is different, unique, and has something vital to contribute to the world; and that its culture must be preserved and promoted at all cost not just for the benefit of the world's 180 million francophones but as an alternative world view to stand up to the globalised culture of the English language.

To leave French culture to the mercy of market forces would not be the French way, and so it is actively championed by the government. The state imposes – for now – a quota of French pop music that must be played on the nation's radio stations, and it collects a levy from cinema tickets to subsidise film production. The Ministry of Foreign Affairs, meanwhile, is charged with disseminating French culture as far and wide as it can.

It would be wrong to see this as cultural imperialism on the part of a nation in a huff; and it is certainly not anti-Americanism. If anything, the French are pro-American culture

The French police force.

whatever they think about US fast food and foreign policy. Deauville in Normandy hosts an American film festival and Mirande in the Gers has a week of country and western music. The French simply regard *all* culture as important. The more diversity, the more international exchange, the better.

The state of the nation

It could be said that the work of all French governments is to uphold the *exception culturelle* abroad and to secure its source at home. "Frenchness" has almost been legislated into the duty of a citizen and much political *angst* is spent in worrying about how to go about safeguarding it.

The agreed starting point of French politics is that there is only one legitimate power in the land, the state, and it exists for the good of all. The state in France is not seen as suspect, intrusive, a necessary evil to be reined in, but as an institution for preserving and applying the values of the Republic.

As the novelist Adam Thorpe puts it: "France is a secular republic achieved by an Enlightenment revolution…the French republic is not merely a political construct but, for good or ill, an embodiment of reason, justice and the will to carry out enlightened policies. One of the most cherished values of the republic [is] to care materially for its citizens."

The French state provides its citizens with a high standard of living; through systems of health, education and transport that generally work well. The populace is well educated and the average life expectancy at birth of 77.8 years for men 84.5 for women is well above the EU average.

Obedience and conformity

The price for this – which most people consider worth paying – is a centralised and highly

The French love their dogs.

Colourful street performers.

IN PRAISE OF THE FARMER

France looks with adoration on its countryside and on farmers as the providers of edible wealth. The French word for peasant, *paysan*, has none of the belittling connotations it has in English. "Tilling and grazing are the two breasts by which France is fed," wrote the Duc de Sully in 1638, and the French maintain their produce is as good as ever.

Food is considered too important to be left to the whims of economic theory, but in truth the French know that liberalism is hard to resist. Modern farming practices have done away with many labour-intensive forms of cultivation and preparation that French cuisine holds inviolable. Shoppers may eulogise about the small

farmer and his old-fashioned way of growing vegetables but they are happy to buy imported tomatoes out of season from hypermarkets. And however much they may praise their own wines, they drink ever smaller quantities of them in favour of New World upstart vintages. McDonald's too is doing brisk business all over France.

French farmers have never been slow to protest to highlight their plight or to celebrate their world and in May 2010 they filled the Champs Elysées with their produce. They brought 8,000 plots of earth and 150,000 plants including 650 mature trees. The two-day event had private backing and cost 4.2m euros to stage, attracting crowds of 2 million supporters.

controlled state which demands obedience and conformity of its citizens; and that they should suppress their centrifugal tendencies in the interests of a greater good. Like Alexander Dumas' Three Musketeers, it is all for one and one for all. France must work together or it may not work at all.

In the light of this, politicians are not expected to pursue divisive policies, however good the reason, or take the country in new directions "We don't like change in France," says Jacques Reland, head of European Research at the Global Policy Institute. "We

importance – and it does not believe that this precludes toleration. It is instead a melting pot and new arrivals are expected to fit in. Caribbeans living in the French departments of Martinique and Guadeloupe, Algerians, legalised immigrants from sub-Saharan Africa – all are expected to appreciate the value of French civilisation, to treat their distinguishing marks (ethnicity and religion) as of secondary importance, and not beg to be treated preferentially.

"You [the English] celebrate the differences; we celebrate the resemblance..." says the writer and nouveau *philosophe* Pascal Bruckner. "We

Young fruit seller.

Immigrant communities are considered French before all.

are revolutionary conservatives. We take to the streets to safeguard hard-won rights but in general, French politicians have a wait and see attitude to change. We adapt rather than abolish...Thanks to our wait-and-see approach we still have decent public services, good health care and a fully functioning national transport network."

Assimilation

It is this obsession with keeping the country together and moving in a single direction that explains France's approach to its immigrant communities. France is not and does not aspire to be a multicultural society – a society in which diverse elements are given equal

think a French citizen whether North African, African, Asian is French before all...that explains our attitude towards Islam and the Muslims."

France has vast experience of immigration, even more, perhaps, than the United States, and many of its citizens are themselves relative newcomers. Historically, this was a relatively underpopulated country, a net receiver of immigrants who were drawn by the demands of industry. One in four French people are statistically considered of foreign origin, going by the nationality or one or more of their grandparents, and many of them have foreign-sounding surnames. It is not uncommon to meet people who claims to be Italian or Spanish when what they really mean is that they have a spiritual affinity to an ancestral culture but much prefer to have French nationality, something akin to being Irish-American.

Perhaps because of this, and because of the way post-colonial France operates, with its overseas territories (the "DOM-TOMs") intimately linked to the mother country, French people have always offered hospitality to political and artistic exiles. But only on condition that they do not destabilise French society. The existence of a populous minority that considers itself a rival to the values France stands for would be entirely different.

it assistance, could be a way of branding it as non-French and leaving it open to persecution. However, anger among the French people has been apparent in the recent attacks on Jewish cemeteries and synagogues, instigated by terrorist extremists.

There is not much about religion that 21st-century France can agree on except that it must be kept inconspicuous and well away from anything to do with the state, including public schools. This explains the furore over Muslim girls wearing head scarfs to school which prompted the government to reiterate the rules

Attending synagogue in Paris's Marais district.

Ethnicity and religion

Officially, there are no ethnic or religious minorities in France, just French people and foreign residents who have their own beliefs and notions of self-identity. In 1872 it was decided that the state had no right to keep data about the faith or racial origin of its citizens. This policy was reinforced at the birth of the Fifth Republic in 1958, which preached the virtues of inclusivity and assimilation for good reason. Between 1940 and 1944 all Frenchmen and women had not been equal and the stigma of what happened to Jews – who in all other respects were as French as their neighbours – has hung heavy over society ever since. To identify a minority, even in order to give

RELIGION

France is an overwhelmingly Catholic country. While 25 percent say that they don't practise any religion and only 13 percent say they do, an average of 65 percent of the population claims to be at least nominally Catholic. Protestantism accounts for just 2 percent. For most people, Catholicism is part of the background fuzz of French culture. It caters for most funerals, but otherwise there's no need to go to church. For every three marriages celebrated there are two civil partnership agreements.

The second religion is Islam, at 6 percent and growing. France has the highest populations in Europe of Muslims, Buddhists and Jews.

requiring all things religious to be kept in the private domain.

In other countries, this looked anti-libertarian but in France there was little debate or disagreement because the national consensus is clear. To most French people it was a necessary measure to assert the virtue of equality through conformity over the right to diversity and self-expression. Far from being racist or discriminatory, the banning of head scarfs in school was seen as a way of deactivating these forces. The January 2015 terrorist atrocities may lead to a more defining agenda on

High spirits in the Parc des Buttes Chaumont, Paris.

Muslim extremism but the state's answer is for more integration through education and improved housing.

The invasion of liberalism

A far more insidious threat to France than the changing ethnic and religious composition of society within comes from "perfidious Albion" and the United States. Politicians of both right and left have always been agreed on the need for the interventionist state to do what is necessary to uphold the job security and living standards of the populace. But Anglo-Saxon neoliberalism is introducing uncomfortable changes that threaten the essence of the French way of life.

For many people, the downsides of naked free market competition are not worth risking for the sake of any supposed rewards. A full 28.5 percent of the working population – 7.5 million people – are employed by the public sector, and many more work for companies that supply the state, in hospitals, schools, social service departments, transport networks and the military. They consider their jobs safe and do not see any benefit in changing the arrangement.

In the new global economic reality, and under directives from the EU, France must get used to a life less subsidised. For the young this means less job security; for the old it means working longer before retiring; for parents less teachers in their children's schools; and for everyone it will mean a more restricted range of free health care.

Liberalism also militates against some very fundamental principles such as a long lunch break in the middle of the day and opening hours for shops that suit employees rather than the whims of consumers – most shops do not open at all on Sundays.

France after France?

The French regard themselves as standing up to the *un*-civilisation of the modern world, a bit like Asterisk and his fellow villagers who defy the entire Roman civilisation because they can't see what they stand to gain by letting it in. But an increasingly common attitude these days is to shrug the heads and lament the inevitability of French decline in the face of superior forces and hence the "banalisation" of their beloved France.

Their greatest fear is that their country will become just like any other and the *exception française* worthless currency. "You know, the French remind me a little bit of an aging actress of the 1940s who was still trying to dine out on her looks but doesn't have the face for it," the US senator and presidential candidate John McCain told Fox News.

The unutterable question is: what happens if France ceases to be French? Could there be such a country, without a recognisable, homogenising culture to sustain it? Would it be worth living in or visiting? Wouldn't it just become a caricature of itself? The answers are not just of significance to the French. What happens to France matters to the rest of us as well.

French Cinema

More films are made in France per head of population than in any other country. Some of them turn out to be classics.

As the birthplace of cinema and host of the world's most famous film festival, France has long given movies a special place in its cultural life. They first flickered into the light at a private screening given by

Jean-Paul Belmondo and Jean Seberg in A bout de souffle.

Auguste and Louis Lumière, brothers from Besançon in eastern France, at a café near the place de l'Opéra in Paris in 1895. Two years later the production companies of Pathé and Gaumont appeared.

Developing technology was put to experimental use in the 1920s by avant-garde directors such as René Clair (*Entr'acte/Interlude*) and Germaine Dulac (*La coquille et le clergyman/The Seashell and the Clergyman*) but it was Abel Gance who most demonstrated what the medium could do in his epic silent biopic *Napoleon*. Its restored, 1980 version lasts for five hours.

The following decade was dominated by the undisputed master of French cinema, Jean Renoir, son of the Impressionist Pierre-Auguste Renoir. His best-known film, *La règle du jeu* (*The Rules of the Game*) caused outraged because it depicted a corrupt upper

class on the eve of World War II.

After the war, diverting entertainment was required and it brought both the inventive, comic Monsieur Hulot (*Les vacances de Monsieur Hulot*) and Brigitte Bardot, whose sex-kitten image was launched by her husband, Roger Vadim, in the 1956 film *Et Dieu... créa la femme* (*And God Created Woman*). Symbolising all that was desirable about France, her appearances at Cannes were a major boost to the French film industry.

Cinema worldwide was given a jolt by the next generation of French film-makers who emerged in the Nouvelle Vague, or New Wave. Claude Chabrol, Jean-Luc Godard, Alain Resnais, François Truffaut and Louis Malle kicked against mainstream cinema and went out into the streets as self-conscious *auteurs* with small crews and hand-held cameras to make films as they thought they should be. Godard's *A bout de souffle* (*Breathless*, reissued on its 50th anniversary in 2010) and Truffaut's *Jules et Jim* are required viewing for anyone interested in the development of film as an art form. Other French films of the 1960s did not travel abroad so well but the 1964 *Les parapluies de Cherbourg* (*The Umbrellas of Cherbourg*), a musical in which all the dialogue, even the most trivial, throwaway comment, is sung, is a classic.

In the 1970s Eric Rohmer sets the tone of the decade with his six "Moral Tales", which include *Le genou de Claire* (*Claire's Knee*), shot around Lake Annecy where a young diplomat becomes obsessed with the desire to caress a teenage girl's knee.

The birthplace of surrealism, France has also been home-from-home for foreign film-makers. Luis Buñuel, in self-imposed exile from Franco's dictatorship in Spain, made his best films in French in the late 1960s and early '70s: *Belle de Jour* and *Le charme discret de la bourgeoisie* (*The Discreet Charm of the Bourgeoisie*).

Cinéma du Look

A new generation of French film-makers, active since the 1980s, has introduced the concept of *cinéma du look*, in which style is judged as important, if not more important, than plot. Jean-Jacques Beineix is one of its leading exponents in *Diva*, the tale of an opera singer and a postman fan, and more so in his cult road movie set in the Languedoc *37°2 le matin* (*Betty Blue*). Another example of look is Luc Besson, as seen in *Subway* and *The Fifth Element*, a film marking his shift from France to mainstream Hollywood.

Contemporary France has a strong indigenous cinema culture with more films produced per head of population than any other country.

Government backing

This immense productivity is partly due to government policy. Cinema is considered a leading part of the *exception culturelle française*, to be encouraged and promoted by the state. All aspects of film production in France and in French are aided by a levy on cinema tickets, while television channels have quotas to fill. This means that the wider public gets a chance to see a great number of films.

Although French cinema sets out to provide a cultural alternative to the mainstream American film industry, there is a considerable flow of talent across the Atlantic. Directors and actors often cross the language divide to make it in both countries – Gérard Depardieu used his accent and his unreconstructed French-male personality to good effect in *Green Card*, bringing him Golden Globe award. Hollywood probably doesn't feel threatened with competition from Paris but it keenly watches out for films that it can remake in its own way, such as Coline Serreau's *Trois hommes et un couffin* which became *Three Men and a Baby*.

Animation and Amélie

Although France has a great tradition of cartoon art, *bande dessinée*, it doesn't make many highly-rated animated films. Two exceptions are *Persepolis*, co-directed by Marjane Satrapi and based on her own autobiographical *bande dessinée* about growing up in Iran, and Sylvain Chomet's *Les triplettes de Belleville (Belleville Rendezvous)*, which achieved great success abroad.

Jean-Pierre Jeunet takes the spirit of *bande dessinée* and makes it flesh in *Delicatessen* (co-directed with Marc Caro) and, later, *Le fabuleux destin d'Amélie Poulain (Amélie)*, a love letter to Paris that introduced the world to Audrey Tautou.

Of an entirely different nature and mood are French documentaries. *Etre et avoir (To Be and to Have)* by Nicolas Philibert, observes the life of children and their teacher in a small village school in the Auvergne. With a bigger picture, the aerial photographer Yann-Arthus Bertrand put together the visually stunning *Home*, intended to drive home the message about global warming. Around 20,000 turned up for its open-air premier screening on the Champ de Mars in June 2009, and opening in 181 countries it broke the world record for the biggest film release in history.

Filmmakers to look out for today include Mathieu Kassovitz, actor and director of the black-and-white *La Haine (Hate)*, which pits a gritty realism against the cinema du look in its depiction of life in the multi-ethnic *banlieues* of Paris; Michael Haneke, an Austrian working in French, who's *Caché (Hidden)*, Funny Games and The White Ribbon have all received high acclaim and numerous awards; and Jacques Audiard, director of *De battre mon cœur s'est arrêté (The Beat that My Heart Skipped)*, the Oscar-nominated *Un prophète (A Prophet) and De rouille et d'os (Rust and Bone)*. That said, the movie that put French cinema back in the spotlight in recent years is without a doubt Michel Hazanavicius' *The Artist* (2011), a black-and-white silent film about the relationship between an ageing silent film star and a rising young actress as silent cinema falls out of fashion. It won awards throughout the world, notably

Marion Cotillard as Edith Piaf, the role that won her an Oscar.

five AcademyAwards, including Best Picture, Best Director and Best Actor for Jean Dujardin.

Meanwhile a vogue for biopics looks set to continue promoting French celebrities. It began with *La môme (La Vie en Rose)* by Olivier Dahan and starring Marion Cotillard, who won the first Oscar for a French actress performing in her own language for her portrayal of Edith Piaf. *Coco avant Chanel (Coco before Chanel)* followed with Audrey Tautou, then *Gainsbourg (Vie Héroïque)* about singer Serge Gainsbourg, though the premiere was overshadowed by the suicide of Lucy Gordon, the British actress who played singer Jane Birkin. Rival biopics, both made in 2014, Yves Saint Laurent and Saint Laurent, about the infamous fashion designer, battled for the box office and brought mixed acclaim from the critics.

Indoors or out, the French love good food.

LA CUISINE

For the French, eating is as much a way of life as of keeping alive. The purchase and preparation of the country's abundant produce is all part of the "art de vivre".

Food and wine are the subject of constant interest, assessment and discussion in France. The French are gastronomic chauvinists – but then they have good reason to be. True, the perfidious microwave and pre-prepared chilled products have been a boon to more than a generation of lazy restaurateurs; and those who forecast that fast food would never catch on in France have had to eat their words, particularly in Paris. Even so, French standards of cooking, both in restaurants and in the home, are still comfortably ahead of those in most countries.

The French nation's love of good food is only natural, for France offers an enormous variety of produce. It is able to do so because it is a land of great climatic and agricultural diversity, from the dairy lands of the north to the olive oil regions of the south. And with coastlines washed by both the Atlantic Ocean and the Mediterranean, there is a temptingly wide variety of seafood.

Regional strengths

Each region has its specialities, both animal and vegetable. With its high concentration of res-

> Restaurant guides are an industry in France. The best are Michelin Red Guide, Gault Millau, Bottin Gourmand and Champérard. Look out, too, for Routard's Petits Restos des Grands Chefs, and Le Fooding's online guide: www.lefooding.com.

taurants and demand for fine produce, Paris is surrounded by a belt of top-quality market gardens. They provide the capital with many early vegetables, from tender green peas and carrots to crisp spinach and new potatoes.

Michelin-starred chef Nicolas Masse at Les Sources de Caudalie.

The Loire valley offers fresh salmon from its river, cultivated mushrooms from the caves around Saumur, and a rich variety of game and wild mushrooms from the lake-studded woods of Sologne, in addition to a host of fruit and vegetables – plump asparagus, cherries, plums – as befits "the garden of France". The full-flavoured specialities of the southwest include *foie gras* (goose or duck liver) from Gascony, truffles from Périgord, smoked ham from Bayonne and cured anchovies from Collioure, while Provence is the home of fragrant Cavaillon melons, sun-gorged tomatoes and pungent basil, which gives *pistou* soup its distinctive flavour.

One of the delights of visiting small restaurants and bistros all over France is tracking down unusual regional specialities found only rarely in Paris, let alone the rest of the world. In the Pyrenean town of Castelnou, for example, you may find a dish called *cargolada*, a grill of local snails, sausages and lamb chops cooked over a fire of vine cuttings and eaten in the open air.

Some restaurants in Nice still feature *estocaficada*, a pungent dish of stockfish (dried cod), tomatoes, peppers, potatoes and black olives. In the Auvergne, salt pork is poached in wine and served with tiny Puy lentils. *Baeckeoffe*, an unusual stew of mixed meats (beef, lamb and pork) and potatoes, can still be found in the local country inns of Alsace, washed down, of course, with fine Alsace wine.

The French calculate freshness in hours, not days, which is why French markets are such good sources for local specialities. This also shows in dishes such as *plateau de fruits de mer*, a huge platter of raw shellfish and cooked crustaceans that brings with it the tang of the sea. If you eat at restaurants in seaside resorts like Deauville in Normandy and Bouzigues (near Sète) or Cassis on the Mediterranean, you are quite likely to see fishermen wandering in with buckets of fresh seafood for the chef.

Top tables

It is always a good idea, when sizing up an unfamiliar restaurant from the menu posted outside, to see if any attempt has been made by the chef to give his dishes a regional touch: pride in one's origins can often stimulate that extra bit of care.

Nowadays even France's grandest restaurants – Georges Blanc in the Burgundy village of Vonnas, Troisgros in Roanne, Paul Bocuse outside Lyon and L'Oustau de Baumanière in Les Baux-de-Provence – will provide their own versions of regional fare alongside the more sophisticated *haute cuisine* their customers expect.

Blanc's menu regularly features snails from the Burgundy vineyards and frog's legs from the nearby Dombes lakes, while Bocuse offers France's finest (and most expensive) poultry, chicken from Bresse, in various guises. The famed local Alpilles lamb at L'Oustau de Baumanière is accompanied by vegetables and herbs full of Provençal scents and flavours.

Fresh sardines from Brittany.

COOKING COURSES

There is a gourmet cookery course to suit everyone in France, but decide first on your ability level.

Cook in France, www.cookinfrance.com, holds a five-day residential cookery course in the Dordogne, in English, for around €845 with accommodation, food and classes.

Cours de Cuisine Olivier Berté, www.cookingclassesinparis.com, is one of the most affordable options in Paris. It offers friendly beginner's classes by a professional chef in a *hôtel particulier*. Classes take place from Wednesday to Saturday and cost around €100 for a morning or afternoon session.

Kerrouet House, French Dining School, www.frenchdiningschool.com, runs five-day courses in a beautiful 16th-century château in Brittany. Tutor Michelin-star chef Poul Jensen demonstrates all the techniques of French cooking, both traditional and modern at an inclusive cost of €995 for your stay.

Les Petits Farcis, www.petitsfarcis.com, based in Nice and run by Rosa Jackson, offers a day course in English, on the preparation of Niçois and Provençal cuisine, plus a guided tour of the local food market, for a cost of €195.

Promenades Gourmandes, www.promenadesgourmandes.com, offers cookery classes and gourmet walking tours in the heart of Paris. Paule Caillat will guarantee a friendly, relaxed approach to the serious subject of French cuisine. From €290 per person.

More perhaps than in any other country, French specialities of food and drink are named after the towns and villages that produce them, rather than the producer, as defined by the *appellation*. Many a cheese carries the name of the place where it originated – Camembert, Roquefort and Munster, for example. The highly prized *belon* oyster is named after the Belon river in Brittany. Cognac is a town as well as a world-famous brandy, Calvados an administrative department as well as a prized apple brandy. And of course many a fine wine, including Champagne, reveals its place of origin in its name.

village café, over a glass of *pastis* or wine.

Food merchants take a loving interest in their wares. The fishmonger does not just sell fish – he or she may offer a recipe for, say, grilling sardines in vine leaves. The fruit and vegetable merchant knows which potato variety is best suited to a *gratin*, and if you ask whether the peaches are ripe, the seller will often let you taste one, free of charge, so that you can decide for yourself.

Seasonal fare

A common, but dwindling, sight along major roads are the roadside stands that sell just-

Supermarkets may be a part of 21st-century living, but the French still honour their weekly markets.

You'll find a wider variety of produce in specialist markets.

Buying local

Anyone driving through France, where each region is defined by the local speciality and produce, cannot fail to be struck by the overwhelming importance of food. Although a weekly supermarket shop is now part of modern life, the French still prefer local produce when possible.

Outdoor markets selling anything from fruit and vegetables to meat, fish and cheese are regular weekly events in towns both large and small. They are also social occasions which give people a chance to catch up on the latest gossip and talk about the weather (which the French do just as much as the British). Such exchanges usually take place in the neighbourhood or

picked peaches, apples and plums, homemade preserves, home-cured olives, or honey from local hives, all of which are worth applying the brakes for. There are also large signs pointing enticingly to nearby farms, where eggs, poultry, goat's cheese or homemade *foie gras* and *confits* are available. Some petrol stations even offer customers a selection of surplus vegetables (tomatoes, young white onions, shallots) from the owner's garden. And of course wine estates and cider producers also put up signs to make their presence known. Look out for the *agriculture biologique* label on wine and produce, which means it is organically grown.

The glorious appearance of much French produce available is not unrelated to the fact that France is the second greatest user of agricultural pesticides in the world, after the United States. Political awareness is growing, however, resulting in a growing demand for more organic produce.

Each food has its season. When asparagus from the Loire valley appears in the shops you can be certain that spring is in the air. The charming Roussillon town of Céret produces the first-of-the-season cherries in mid-April. Come May, juicy new garlic arrives on the market – garlic lovers like to roast the cloves, then spread them like butter on toast.

celebrated in the Roussillon village of Ille-sur-Têt. In August the entire spa town of Digne, in the Alpes-de-Haute-Provence, turns out for a lavender festival, while in November the inhabitants of the Normandy village of Beuvron-en-Auge sample the new crop of apple cider.

Wine, too, has its season. On the third Thursday of November, at tables all over France, the first wine of the season, Beaujolais Nouveau, is eagerly tasted. At its best it is a light, fruity, uncomplicated tipple, ideal for washing down an improvised meal of dry pork sausage and buttered country bread.

French bread usually comes in the form of the baguette.

If driving through France in the month of June, you may find the road blocked by a herd of cows or a flock of sheep with clanging bells round their necks. They are being led up to their summer pastures in the mountains, where they will feast on sweet grasses and wild flowers.

In Savoie, the milk of Tarine cows is best for the finest cheese of the region, Beaufort d'Alpage, which is made into huge wheels such as Gruyère. At local markets, merchants discuss the age of a Beaufort as seriously as wine buffs compare vintages. As a Beaufort matures (over a period of anything up to eight months), its flavour gets better, nuttier and more profound.

By July, towns and villages come alive with the first of the harvest festivals. The peach is

The daily diet

The French spend about 20 percent of their income on food and wine. There is no absolutely typical meal, though there are typical local eating patterns. The biggest dividing line is between city and country.

Although generalisations are always suspect, it's fair to say that most French begin the day with a large bowl or mug of white coffee and a *tartine* (a slice of bread spread with butter and jam). Farmers and other country-dwellers who get up early and engage in manual work will usually follow this with a *casse-croûte* (snack) of bread and sausage or pâté at about 9.30am. A substantial three- or four-course lunch comes next, often beginning with soup, and almost always including a meat course. Supper is usually a light meal followed by cheese.

However, for many office workers, leisurely lunches are a thing of the past, and they make do with a sandwich and a glass of wine. Fast-food restaurants are also popular, especially with young people, despite counter-attacks from protestors such as José Bové, France's high-profile anti-globalisation activist.

With more and more working mothers, the evening meal will often consist of something simple like *bifteck frites* (steak and chips, one of France's favourite dishes) or frozen fish (sold

> The French consume 101 kilos (222 lbs) of meat per person per year (only slightly less than the Americans) 24 kilos (53 lbs) of cheese, 56 kilos (124 lbs) of bread and 43 litres (11 gallons) of wine.

or an apéritif on the way home from work, are the best places to soak up the atmosphere of everyday French life. However, the food served may only amount to a *croque monsieur* or a sandwich. Though city cafés such as Paris's Deux

Dining out in Alsace might involve tarte flambée – a type of cream-based pizza (right).

complete with its sauce), followed by cheese or a fruit yoghurt.

As in many countries, Sunday lunch provides an opportunity to let rip with a big meal. The fare is likely to be straightforward and traditional – roast chicken or leg of lamb, often with a tart or cake bought from the local *pâtisserie* for dessert.

Eating out

The French are proud of their gastronomic culture, and eating well is quintessential to their lifestyle. The range of eating places is vast and varies from ordinary street cafés to temples of *haute cuisine*. Corner cafés, where the locals meet for a quick morning coffee and croissant,

Magots and Café de Flore are institutions, the village café struggles to stay open.

Bistros are classic small restaurants, serving inexpensive meals, often slow cooked, with daily menus scrawled on a board and wine often coming in carafes.

Originating from Alsace, *brasseries* (meaning breweries) serve full meals and drinks – especially beer on tap – and are usually open from mid-morning to late at night. Some wonderful Art Deco buildings were built as brasseries, serving seafood, grilled meats, salads and traditional *choucroute*. Near the Bastille in Paris, Bofinger is famed for its seafood *choucroute*. Dating from 1864, it was one of the first brasseries to open in the capital. Brasserie Lipp is an upmarket, chic brasserie in the St-Germain-des-Prés district. Other notable brasseries are La Cigale in Nantes which has wonderful Belle Epoque décor, and Brasserie Georges in Lyon.

Bistronomie has been developing over the past years. This is a new breed of bistro, sometimes an annexe of a more famous establishment, where quality cuisine is served at more affordable prices. The leader in this field is the mythic chef Yves Camdeborde at Le Comptoir in the Odéon *quartier*, Paris. Further afield the acclaimed Pic restaurant in Valence has opened an annexe bistro to the main restaurant, and

Alain Llorca has branched out with a trendy bistro in St Paul-de-Vence, Provence.

Modern molecules

Although France is not the front runner in fusion and molecular cuisine, it does have its followers. French chemist Hervé first demonstrated molecular cuisine in 1992. He compared recipes to a series of chemical reactions and explained how different ingredients were transformed into food. This developed into a highly original cuisine that combines molecules using new cooking methods, often at extremely cold temperatures. Never

Showing off some skills at brasserie La Coupole in Paris.

VEGETARIAN DINING

Vegetarian restaurants are few and far between in France, even in Paris. Some progress has been made in recent years, and as more and more restaurants are offering vegetarian dishes, and with some vegetarian hotels opening, you are less likely to be met with a quizzical stare. Most gastronomic restaurants will prepare a vegetarian meal if notified in advance. Traditional Breton crêperies with a vast choice of fillings are a good option. Pizzerias – *socca* in Nice – salad bars and North African and oriental restaurants are other places to look out for. Large cities and university towns are more likely to have a selection of genuine vegetarian places.

In Paris, Le Grenier de Notre Dame, 18 rue de la

Bûcherie, 5th, is a quaint left-bank restaurant that proposes "Zen" vegetarian lunch and dinner menus; and both Soya Cantine and Pousse-Pousse in the 11th and 9th *arrondissements* respectively are proof that Paris can do vegetarian gourmet. And while not strictly vegetarian Le Paradis du Fruit is a chain of restaurants that has a good choice of meat-free dishes. For a picnic option La Vie Claire is a national chain of over 200 stores that specializes in health foods, including organic foods. Naturalia is another health food chain based mainly in Paris and the outskirts.

When invited to dinner in a French home, inform your hosts that you are vegetarian, as they are unlikely to ask.

New foodie talent to watch: Laurent Rigal at L'Alexandrin, Lyon; Stéphane Froidevaux at Fantin Latour, Grenoble; Grégory Marchand at Frenchie, Paris and Mauro Colagreco at Mirazur, Menton.

dull, this type of cuisine is definitely an interesting experience. The famous Parisian chef Pierre Gagnaire is the undisputed master of molecular cuisine. He uses molecular techniques which lend themselves more to the structural, and less

light innovative dishes, which are low in cream and butter and use spices instead of salt. There is no menu as such and diners make their own choices on the day; booking well in advance is essential. Another notable Paris-based fusion food restaurant is Market where Jean-Georges Vongerichten creates innovative dishes based on French, Italian and Asian cooking cultures.

Joël Robuchon is the biggest of the empire builders, with his chain of L'Atelier restaurants in Paris, Bangkok, Hong Kong, Las Vegas, London, Singapore, Taipei and Tokyo. Launched in 2003, the concept is an informal sushi-style

Chef Mauro Colagreco at Mirazur in Menton.

chemical aspect of the food. A less expensive alternative in Paris that creates decent molecular dishes is Chez Léna et Mimile in the Latin Quarter. Other restaurants that specialise in molecular cuisine are Le Cristal at the Futuroscope science park near Poitiers, and the Aphrodite restaurant at Nice where chef David Faure has a "techno-emotional" approach to cooking.

Fusion food is a speciality at L'Astrance in rue Beethoven in Paris. Established by two former employees of the highly regarded Alain Passard of L'Arpège fame this is a restaurant with a difference. Chef Pascal Barbot brings an oriental twist to his unique dishes, while Christophe Rolat is dedicated to front-of-house. With time spent cooking in the South Pacific Barbot creates

eating counter surrounding an open kitchen so that diners can watch their food being prepared. Robuchon now has a total of 20 restaurants world-wide and has the most Michelin stars, leading the world with 25.

Le Fooding is an anti-elitist movement which was founded in 2000 by two food journalists, Alexandre Cammas and Emmanuel Rubin. The name is derived from "food" and "feeling"' and is meant to reflect its disdain for "fossilised gastronomy" in favour of more soul and personality in French cuisine. Le Fooding publishes a guide, an antithesis to the Michelin guide, which lists around 900 less refined eating places, embracing even fast food establishments. Fooding events and giant picnic style dine-ins are also organised.

FRENCH CHEESES

"Nobody can bring together a nation that has 265 types of cheese," complained General de Gaulle. In fact France has more than 365 cheeses.

Cheeses are one of the crowning glories of France. They come in all shapes and sizes: square, pyramid, heart-shaped or in round discs. Certain cheeses are often displayed on straw mats (*paillons*), while others are wrapped in walnut or chestnut leaves. Classic cheeses are given *appellation d'origine* labels, which are as prestigious as those accorded to wine.

Regionalism is everything, as the concept of *terroir* (the quality and individual characteristic of the land) prevails in French cheese, as it does in wine. The regional repertoire is formidable, from creamy Camembert to cheeses rind-washed in beer, or the blue-veined champions, Roquefort and Bleu d'Auvergne. Given such splendours, it is easy to overlook the piquant discs of goat's cheese, the Swiss-style cheeses from the Alps (such as Emmenthal français and Raclette) or the monastic cheeses from Cîteaux in Burgundy or the Trappist Abbaye de Belval.

Blue cheeses, made from cow's or ewe's milk, are blue-veined, with a sharp, spicy aroma. Bleu d'Auvergne is similar to Roquefort, but made from cow's milk, while Bleu de Bresse is a factory-made blue cheese. Certain cheeses with a rind develop an edible crust and become runny as they age. Apart from Camembert, characteristic examples are Brie de Meaux and Chaource, both from Champagne. By contrast, rind-washed cheeses are more pungent: these unpressed cheeses have rinds soaked in beer or *eau de vie*. Maroilles, Munster, Epoisses and Livarot all have distinctive flavours. Hard, pressed cheeses, like Cantal and other alpine cheeses, are made from cow's and ewe's milk. Such cheeses are mild but acquire a crust and a pungent flavour.

Fourme d'Ambert, with its characteristic cylindrical shape, takes centre-stage on this French cheeseboard.

Cantal cheese – here undergoing its maturing process in a tunnel – made by curdling milk and separating the curds from the whey, hails from Auvergne.

Saint-Nectaire marries well with a light and fruity red wine, such as Beaujolais.

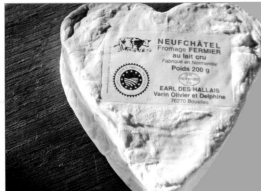

Neufchâtel is a soft, slightly crumbly cheese from Normandy usually sold in heart shapes.

FARMHOUSE FROMAGE

"Fromage fermier" is a mark of quality, a farmhouse cheese made from *lait cru* (unpasteurised milk). Compared with cheeses from large-scale dairies, the taste of these cheeses is infinitely deeper and subtler. Each cheese has its own time-honoured traditions and process. The cheese-makers use milk from their own or neighbouring herds. Brie de Meaux from Champagne takes 20 litres (4 gallons) of milk to produce one cheese 35cm (14 inches) in diameter. To produce Cantal in the Auvergne, curds are traditionally turned and pressed through cheese-cloth by hand. After being curdled, drained and hard-pressed, Cantal is aged for more than a year. Unlike mass-produced Camembert, Camembert *fermier* is moulded by ladle. Unpasteurised milk is heated and coagulated with rennet before the rich curds are ladled into Camembert moulds. Then the cheeses are removed from their moulds, dry-salted, and sprayed with a bacterium to encourage the ripening process. After a month, they develop their ripe bloom.

Chèvre fermier (farmhouse goat's cheese) can be flavoured in a range of ways – such as with herbs, peppercorns or ash.

Ewe's milk cheese from the Basque country.

Normandy is quintessential dairy country. The brown and white herds give the creamiest milk, ideal for Camembert.

A Saumur wine cellar, in the Loire Valley region.

WINE

Wine is more than a drink in France; like bread, it is inseparable from life and fine wines are a civilising pleasure, which speak to the palate and to the mind.

A visit to France is an opportunity to gain a real appreciation of wine. It is omnipresent: it fills shop windows, is served at every meal and is offered as a gift. Vineyards line the roads, not only in Burgundy and Bordeaux but along the Mediterranean coast, the length of the Loire, near the German border, and can be found even in Paris itself. Visitors are struck not only by the vast amounts of land devoted to grape growing but to the quality and diversity of the wines produced.

The stain on the map

A map of France showing the grape-growing regions looks as if someone has spilled a glass of wine on it. A large ring-shaped stain covers roughly two-thirds of the country. The ring starts just below Paris, extends westward to the Atlantic, curves inland along the Mediterranean then swings up north again to where it began. Being a stain, it is far from regular. Indeed, portions are very thick, particularly towards the

The pick of the bunch.

As a general rule, most wines are best savoured in or near the vineyards of their origin – usually not a problem in France, where vineyards feature in most regions.

top and western half of the ring, and numerous dribbles seep out along the lower rim covering most of the Mediterranean coast. A large drop just east of Paris (Champagne) and a streak near the German border (Alsace) are clearly visible.

This spill does not touch the north of the country. The Brittany peninsula, the area along the English Channel and most of the Belgian border is stain-free, as is the very centre of the

ring roughly equidistant from La Rochelle in the west and Grenoble in the east.

Few regions are otherwise spared. The island of Corsica is touched, especially in the north, with large patches on the southeast coast and inland from Ajaccio as well as on the extreme southern tip near Bonifacio.

Wherever you are in France, you will never be more than 160km (100 miles) from an area in which wine is being made. The range and density of vineyards account for the huge variety of French wines. Given the diversity of climates and soils, it is not surprising that France produces wines with "personalities" as different as those of the people who tend the vines. The flavour of an Alsatian Riesling is as different from that of a

> *Laws forbid the use of grape varieties in appellation d'origine protégée wines other than those traditionally grown in that region. The emphasis is on producing a distinctive wine in every region rather than the highest-quality wine.*

white Graves as the ruddy-faced Alsatian farmer is from an austere château-owner in Bordeaux.

This said, similarities exist, and though the average wine-drinker can quickly learn

or repeatedly purchase a rubbery baguette, deserve their fate.

In terms of quality, you can confidently purchase wine in France and expect it to be fairly decent, without much knowledge of how it is made or where it comes from: you can't go far wrong because good wine is produced throughout the country. This said, do not conclude that all French wines are fine wines – far from it. Within regions such as Burgundy and Bordeaux the truly fine wines form only a small percentage of the total production.

Indeed, most French wine comes from nei-

A display of Saint-Emilion reds.

to recognise wines with very strong personalities, only those who have taken the subject seriously enough to participate in many wine tastings can distinguish one Bordeaux from another or pin a name on a glass of fine Burgundy.

Familiar as bread

Wine is so much a part of French life that people could no more imagine studying wine than studying how bread is made – both products are so readily available and so frequently consumed, they believe that through the sheer extent of their exposure they know how to evaluate both. The consensus is that those who drink poor-quality wine,

ther of these regions (production is most heavily concentrated along the western half of the Mediterranean coast), and part of the pleasure of exploring France is discovering the many wines that are rarely exported and often have remarkably specific tastes. Anyone, for instance, who has not sampled the sherry-like whites of the Jura is in for a surprise.

France possesses 11 major wine-producing regions: Alsace, Beaujolais, Bordeaux, Burgundy, Champagne, Franche-Comté, Languedoc-Roussillon, Loire Valley, Provence, Rhône Valley, and the Southwest. Although the fame of Beaujolais Bordeaux, Burgundy, and Champagne is well established, the rest enjoy varying degrees of celebrity.

Also, the produce of some regions has only a limited market even within France itself, so it may be excellent but not well known. For the average wine-buyer, the main questions are: what differentiates each of these regions; and how to choose between hundreds of bottles bearing similar names?

Local variations

Though grape varieties are part of the key to understanding and identifying wines, many fine French wines are made by blending varieties to temper their individual tastes (this is

given *appellation*, some plots of land are better than others and some wine-makers are more talented than others. In short, the name of the wine-maker is as important as the wine itself.

The contrast is even greater when the same grape variety is used in different regions of France. The same Pinot Noir grape, for example, used in all the finest red Burgundies, is also used to make the still red wines of Champagne and Alsace. Though the former can produce sublime bottles, the latter two regions make simply pleasant red wines which are as much curiosities as anything else.

Checking out the crop.

The mechanics behind champagne production.

systematically the case in Bordeaux). Even in regions where only one grape variety is employed, results can vary enormously from vineyard to vineyard.

France is a country of micro-climates and this, combined with variable soil quality and strong Gallic personalities, means that neighbours often produce wines bearing similar labels but with strikingly different flavours.

This is particularly evident in Burgundy. The Clos de Vougeot vineyard, for example, is archetypical in that it counts over 80 owners, so there are potentially 80 different Clos de Vougeot wines to choose from. Hence, the quality of a bottle of Clos de Vougeot depends on which individual owner or shipper made it. Within a

NEW LABELLING

In 2008 the Government launched a five-year plan to modernise the industry in line with EU reforms, including changes to the labelling. There are now three categories of wine rather than four. The first, **Vin de France** replaces Vin de Table and allows both the grape variety and vintage to appear on the label. Cheaper winemaking technique has also been permitted, for example, the use of oak chips, the additions of tannins and sweetening with grape juice must. **Indication Géographique Protégée (IGP)** replaces Vin de Pays, and **Appellation d'Origine Protégée (AOP)** supersedes Appellation d'Origine Contrôlée.

Despite the emphasis on tradition, French wines have evolved and continue to change, generally for the better. Champagne, for instance, was one of the great red wines of France until the 18th century when the method for making sparkling wines was perfected. And in the 17th century, the *clairet* (claret) wines of Bordeaux were not ruby red but pale, almost rosé.

In recent years, changes have occurred in the far south where the wines of Languedoc-Roussillon (a vast area extending from the Spanish border all the way to Montpellier) have attained "name wine" status. This has occurred thanks to the proliferation of new *appellations protégées* (wine legislation controlling the way in which wines with specific place names are made). A bottle of Côtes de Roussillon, Minervois, Fitou or Corbières may not bring tears of joy to your eyes but are excellent value and particularly good when served with local food.

Matching with food

It remains a truism to say that local wines are at their best with local food. But why do certain wines marry well with specific foods? It all depends on the characteristics of the wine,

The cellars harbouring Veuve Clicquot champagne.

TASTING WINE

Throughout the country, French vineyards are planted not only with grapes but with signs inviting travellers to stop and sample their produce. Accepting such invitations is the best way to learn what French wines are all about, but both tact and caution are required.

A French proverb warns: *à bon vin, pas d'enseigne* (good wine, no sign). In other words, wines of high quality don't need to advertise. Indeed, many of the best growers (particularly in Burgundy) live in unpretentious homes with little or no indication that their wine is for sale. However, most will receive visitors, but don't consider such a visit a simple occasion for a free drink. Serious tasters don't even swallow the wine they are

offered – they politely spit it out onto the floor of the cellar or into a spittoon. Wine cellars are for tasting not drinking and, as long as the language is not a barrier, listening as well.

Owners and growers will invariably taste their wines with you and you will quickly discover the respect that wine receives in the depths of these French caves, though it is only at the table that wine blossoms into taste experiences that make bottles memorable.

If you are travelling by car, a spare canister for wine by the barrel may prove useful. If you want to visit one of the better known estates, contact them in advance, and be prepared to pay a good price for a box of wine.

such as body, acidity, tannin, fruitiness, grape variety and barrel ageing. All these factors create the overall flavour of a wine. Full-bodied reds, like a Rhône, will overpower a delicate sauce, yet a *boeuf bourguignon* needs a rich heady wine to complement the dish. In general, the fuller wines come from a hotter climate in the south, and the lighter fruity wines from the cooler north. The acidity in wine is important since it uplifts rich buttery dishes or oily fish, so Muscadet is the ideal partner for the butter sauce that accompanies many Loire fish dishes, Champagne is the best match with

In general, if you follow the golden rule – local wine with local food – you won't go far wrong. And this doesn't only apply to wine; a glass of local cider is a must with a *tarte tatin* in Normandy, and a glass of beer goes down well with a *choucroute* in Alsace.

The wine list

When confronted with a list of wine names, producers and vintages, the choice can be daunting. The best restaurants and those located in the larger cities will have extensive wine lists covering all the regions of France,

Choose a wine that marries well with the dish it is to accompany.

A simple red.

oysters, and Alsace whites accompany perfectly the region's sausages.

Tannins in red wines also have a similar cutting effect. Wines with strong tannins, such as red Bordeaux, are enhanced by local dishes such as the delicious but fatty *confit de canard*. But not all red wines are tannic: Loire red and Beaujolais, for example, are fruity and accompany fish well, and can even be drunk chilled. Young wines tend to have more upfront fruit and are a good choice for dishes such as duck *à l'orange*. Sweet wines combine well with both sweet and savoury foods – a glass of chilled Sauternes, or the less expensive Barsac, is delightful with *foie gras*, Roquefort cheese or fruit.

but smaller restaurants will usually offer a selection of local wines. The basic wines will be local *vins de pays* often sold by the carafe. These, although never great wines, at best can be pleasant and quaffable, but if your budget allows try a regional *appellation* wine from a good vintage. Some bistros offer wine by the glass, which gives you the chance to experience different wines throughout your meal.

Lastly, grower-bottled (*propriétaire*) wines are usually of higher quality than shipper-bottled (*négociant*) wines and, in better restaurants, don't hesitate to ask your *sommelier* (wine steward) for a recommendation. Remember, wine is not just a drink – each sip contains a drop of French culture.

Artist at work in Montmartre.

ART

French painters have been at the vanguard of most important artistic movements since the 17th century, from rococo to Impressionism and beyond.

The writer Emile Zola defined a work of art as "a corner of nature seen through a temperament". As befits their revolutionary sensibilities, French temperaments have been at the forefront of most major artistic movements since the 17th century. Since then French artists have forwarded the causes of rococo, neoclassicism, Romanticism, Realism, Impressionism and Cubism. Gustave Courbet (1819–77) declared, "There can be no schools; there are only painters..."

A golden age

The 17th century was a golden age for European art and it produced France's first great artist, Nicolas Poussin (1594–1665). Since the Renaissance, Rome had become the artistic capital of Europe. This was where Classical and Christian worlds collided, and since his mind was at home in antiquity, the "philosophical painter" chose the grand manner, a nostalgic vision of calm, dignified landscapes and dreamland pas-

Assumption of the Virgin by Nicolas Poussin (1594–1665).

> Poussin was the third artist to be appointed Premier Peintre du Roi, a post created by the popular King Henri IV, who added the Grande Galerie to the Louvre and invited hundreds of artists to live and work in the building.

torals. As Poussin intended: "The subject-matter shall be grand, as are battles, heroic actions and divine things." His search for structure and form concealed great power and deep reserves of emotion. As a result, Poussin influenced French artists from David and Ingres to Cézanne.

Claude Lorrain (1600–82) was equally enamoured of Rome but more dedicated to the pursuit of the picturesque. Whereas Poussin was passionately rational, Lorrain's landscapes were poetic and poignant. By contrast to these voluntary exiles, artists fêted in France were enslaved by the courtly tradition. Charles Le Brun (1619–90) acted as master of ceremonies to Louis XIV and produced portraits of great pomp. His successor, Pierre Mignard (1612–95), painted the court of Versailles with considerably more charm.

The flighty spirit of rococo flourished in 18th-century France. Jean-Antoine Watteau (1684–1721) reflected the decorative tastes of the aristocracy, painting a fantasy world of court revelries and bucolic bliss. In this shimmering, artificial society, even shepherdesses wore silk. Yet Watteau's gift is great enough to infuse the genre with delicacy, refinement and a soft melancholy, perfectly expressed in his *Pierrot* (1719). As the art historian Ernst Gombrich said, "His awareness of the transience of beauty gave his art that intensity which none of his many admirers and imitators could equal."

François Boucher (1703–70), the celebrated court painter, was influenced by the Flemish artist Rubens and patronised by Madame de Pompadour, but is best known for his creamy, voluptuous nudes. Jean-Honoré Fragonard (1732–1806) conveys a silken charm with his

Le serment de La Fayette à la fête de la fédération le 14 juillet 1790 by Jacques Louis David (1748–1825).

dancing, cavorting, amorous figure, but he outlived his era, and, reduced to poverty after the Revolution, he died forgotten.

Revolutionary art

The erotic games of the Ancien Régime were swept away by the political correctness of 1789. Jacques-Louis David (1748–1825) was the official artist of the Revolutionary government. An ardent supporter of Robespierre, David acted as a glorious propagandist, revelling in patriotic themes that befitted such heroic times. He claimed his elevated neoclassical style celebrated "a people guided by reason and philosophy; a reign of liberty, equality and law." In

truth, his austere and academic art was as much a reaction against rococo excesses.

The neoclassical tradition was also embraced by Jean-Auguste Ingres (1780–1867), a follower of David. Noted for his cool clarity, technical assurance and academic precision, Ingres was a conservative who decried the conflicting current of the age, Romanticism. In response to entreaties to "follow our century", Ingres retorted: "But suppose my century is wrong?"

Eugène Delacroix (1798–1863), the high priest of Romanticism, was convinced that he and his century were as one. "I see in painters prose writers and poets," he declared. "Cold exactitude is not art; ingenious artifice, when it pleases or when it expresses, is art itself." His passionate canvases rebelled against bloodless perfection. Instead of classical nobility, fine draughtsmanship and restraint, his creed was colour, exoticism and giving free reign to the imagination. *Liberty on the Barricades* is widely considered the last successful allegory ever painted.

Delacroix's visionary, melodramatic style is echoed by the energy and exoticism of Théodore Géricault (1791–1824). His fondness for spectacular effects and natural restlessness predisposed him to a revulsion against the rational. His Romantic masterpiece, *The Raft of Medusa* (1819), created a scandal with its gruesome depiction of grieving, hysteria and doom. Indeed, with the triumph of the Romantic movement the artistic baton definitively passed to France, a pre-eminence the country still claims.

Realism

The Revolution was slow to radicalise the hierarchical nature of public art. Hitherto, pride of place was given to dignitaries and heroic figures while peasants were relegated to genre scenes. Only after the 1848 Revolution was there a concomitant revolution in subject matter: painting began to portray the people. Although considered the architect of Realism, Gustave Courbet (1819–77) demurred: "the title of realist has been imposed upon me." Instead, he saw his instinctive naturalism as a quest for truth, at one with his desire to challenge staid conventions and shake the people.

François Millet (1814–75), who is best known for his paintings of peasants, worked in the same genre of Realism. *The Gleaners* (1857) is his quintessential work: a dignified composition of heavy-limbed women toiling in the cornfields. Millet was a member of the Barbizon School, a group of landscape painters who, reacting against pretension, were drawn to the glades of Fontainebleau.

Edouard Manet (1832–83) heralds 20th-century art and was a precursor of Impressionism. Manet was not afraid to discard outmoded conventions, trusting his eyes rather than traditional ways of seeing. His forceful pictures focused on social life and pleasure, exposing his subjects to harsh sunlight without the moral lessons expected by a bourgeois public. His most famous painting, which shocked at the time, is *Déjeuner sur l'herbe* (1863), in which a nude model picnics on the grass with two formally dressed gentlemen, holding the onlooker in her frank stare. The picture is a bold assertion of the right of the artist to depict whatever he pleases for the sake of aesthetic effect.

Impressionism

"Since the appearance of Impressionism, the official salons, which used to be brown, have become blue, green and red." Claude Monet (1840–1926), the master of colour and light, and founder of the new movement, focused on

L'Atelier du peintre, by Gustave Courbet (1819–77).

Portrait de Pierre-Joseph Proudhon avec ses enfants en 1853, also by Courbet.

IN THE ARTISTS' STUDIOS

There is no better way to feel close to understanding a painter than to visit his studio. The following house-museums are open to the public:

Paul Cézanne His house and studio is on the outskirts of Aix-en-Provence (see page 336).

Eugène Delacroix His Parisian house and atelier from 1857 until his death in 1863 (see page 121).

Claude Monet The famous studio and garden at Giverny, north of Paris, is a delight (see page 198).

Jean-Auguste Renoir His home outside Cagnes has a beautiful olive grove (see page 350).

Auguste Rodin The rose garden in the sculptor's Paris mansion is very romantic (see page 123).

the changes in colour brought about by this return to nature. Monet's *Water Lilies* series are reveries of colour and light, a shimmering restlessness of atmospheric effects and beautifully balanced tones and colours.

La Gare Saint-Lazare (1877) depicts a locomotive belching against a background of golden light streaming through the roof. The movement's preoccupation with the fleeting moment exposed painters to the charge of neglecting the solid forms of nature.

A new view

Although this lack of finish was dismissed as slapdash, Monet took comfort from the fact that Delacroix, Courbet and Millet had all been scorned in their day. In time, the public was won over by these puzzling pictures, retraining their eyes to appreciate Camille Pissarro (1831–1903). The painter tried to see his bird's-eye views of Parisian boulevards with the shock that first stunned his contemporaries: "If I walk along the boulevard, do I look like this? Do I lose my legs, my eyes and my nose and turn into a shapeless blob?"

Although sympathetic to Impressionism, Edgar Degas (1834–1917) was drawn more to movement, space and spontaneity. His off-centre

> "Young people today who prefer the later works of Degas and Renoir hardly realise how much of its looser character was due to their failing sight." Art historian William Rothenstein

Fauvism and Cubism

Two major movements came in with the 20th century: Fauvism and Cubism. The Fauvists, the first avant-garde movement in European art, believed colour to be an emotional force. Fauve artists first exhibited at the Salon d'Automne,

Considering Monet at the Musée de l'Orangerie, Paris.

The 'optical art' of Victor Vasarely (1906–97) at the Fondation Vasarely, Aix.

compositions captured the atmosphere of cafés, circuses, the races and ballet. His dispassionate studies of dancers in a range of unexpected postures cannot be dismissed as mere prettiness.

Pierre-Auguste Renoir (1841–1919) began as an Impressionist but later came under the more classical influence of Cézanne. Like Degas, his penchant for the picturesque often blinded critics to the artistry of his ravishing forms dissolving into sunlight and air. With Paul Cézanne (1839–1906), French art almost came full circle. The "father of modern art" aimed at painting "Poussin from nature", capturing in his canvases the balance, harmony, grandeur and serenity of the previous painter without losing any of the colour or modelling of the Impressionists.

at Paris in 1905 where *Open Window, Woman in a Hat* by Henri Matisse (1869–1954) met with derision, one critic describing it as 'a pot of paint that has been flung into the face of the public.' Georges Braque (1882–1963) was a Fauve who went on to discard colour in favour of shape, developing Cubism, which sought to flatten space. Working side by side in the same studio with the Spaniard Pablo Picasso (1881–1973) he produced *Houses at L'Estaque*, a work remarkably similar to Picasso's *Landscape with Bridge*, both produced in 1909. Moving on from this they introduced collaged objects into their paintings – newspapers, musical instruments, cigarettes, wine.

In 1916, in a bar in Zurich, Switzerland, the Dada philosophical movement was created, and it was swiftly taken up by André Breton (1896–1966) in Paris where it thrived. The provocative anti-art of Dada was a protest against the atrocities of war, but in 1923 Breton split with the Dadaists to form the Surrealist movement, issuing manifestos and influencing all the arts.

Klein blue

The next major art movement in France did not occur until after World War II. This was New Realism created in 1960 by Yves Klein (1928–62)

Museum of Modern, Contemporary and Outsider Art (LaM) re-opened after a major reconstruction. In 2012, the glass-panelled Louvre-Lens was inaugurated, bringing the wealth of the Louvre collections to the industrial north. In late 2014, the richest man in France, Bernard Arnault, head of the LVMH luxury brand empire, opened his Fondation Louis Vuitton at the edge of the Bois de Boulogne in Paris. This gigantic, all-glass-sails museum of contemporary art was designed by Frank Gehry and boasts the odd angles of his trademark deconstructivist style.

Graffiti artist in the Belleville neighbourhood of Paris.

and Pierre Restany (1930–2003) and often compared with Pop Art. The members of this group wanted to bring art and life closer together. Yves Klein had nude women roll around in blue paint, and then throw themselves onto the canvas – in fact his use of blue paint became famous as a colour: International Klein Blue (IKB).

Daniel Spoerri (b.1930) used meals and food as his medium, and Niki de Saint-Phalle (1930–2002) worked with plastic figures.

Contemporary art has a high profile in France, and favourite artists include Fabrice Hybert, Sophie Calle, and Daniel Buren. To meet the increasing interest in the art scene, in 2010 the amazing futurist Centre Pompidou-Metz opened its doors and the Lille Métropole

FABRICE HYBERT

Fabrice Hybert, born in 1961 at Luçon, is perhaps the best known artist working in France. The philosophy behind his multi-media works is "to draw from the impossible reservoir of the possible". He has produced a series of prototypes of functionless objects, or POF, such as POF No.10 Roof-Ceiling, a device that vacuums up rubbish and deposits it in a transparent ceiling. His first permanent sculpture, *Le cri, l'écrit*, is a 3.7-metre (12ft) high polychrome bronze erected in 2007 in the Jardins du Luxembourg. Hybert's works can also be seen at the CAPC, Bordeaux, the Musée des Beaux Arts, Nantes, and the Centre Pompidou, Paris.

ARCHITECTURE

Romanesque churches and Gothic cathedrals, Renaissance châteaux and Classical palaces, half-timbered cottages, medieval castles and motorway bridges all fit into a history of feverish experimentation.

For 2,000 years France has been adding to the canon of western architecture, often leading the way for other countries to follow. Sometimes it has built on home-grown inspiration; at other times ideas have been imported from abroad and adapted.

In any history of architecture it is tempting to look for a single, evolving narrative but few buildings embody a pure style; most have been added to over their lifetimes so that with a little insight it is possible to read their history literally written in stone.

Prehistoric inhabitants left no permanent structures behind them other than alignments,

> The amphitheatres at Nîmes and Arles, and the theatre at Orange, are some of the finest examples of Roman architecture. The towns lie on the Via Domitia, the road through Provence (Roman Province) to Spain.

Alsatian architecture as exemplified in Colmar.

dolmens and chamber tombs, and the earliest surviving architecture in the true sense is therefore Roman, as especially seen in the south.

Roman to Romanesque

The barbarian tribes, who settled Gaul from the 3rd century AD, adopting Christianity, continued to build in the familiar Roman style with only a little variation, and they left behind them baptisteries, oratories and crypts. Some of these survive; others have been incorporated into later churches.

Then, shortly after the turn of the first millennium, something dramatic happened. A building boom began that would last three centuries and be as rich in innovation as in the quantity

of magnificent buildings created. Between 1050 and 1350 France quarried more stone than Ancient Egypt in any equivalent period and used it to build 80 cathedrals and 500 large churches, as well as thousands of smaller ones.

Conventionally, the buildings of the Middle Ages are classed as Romanesque and Gothic, terms applied in hindsight to denote the start and finish of a continuum. As its name suggests, Romanesque builders were inspired by the remains of Roman buildings. It spread to France from Italy by means of master-craftsmen from Lombardy who provided the essential skills.

The Roman basilica was the prototype, a simple structure with radiating aisles. However, in fertile French soil, it soon developed its own vernacular forms. If the architecture itself is simple, the decoration is not: it is in its stone carving that the Romanesque excels. Capitals, tympanums and corbels show religious scenes and also an inscrutable bestiary of real and imagined animals straight out of the mind of medieval man.

A stimulus for the development and spread of Romanesque was the rise of monasticism in the 11th century. As the Benedictine abbey of Cluny in Burgundy grew ever wealthier its influence reached beyond France. Subordinate houses were established, particularly on the routes of pilgrimage, creating a demand for itinerant

A succession of technical breakthroughs – including pointed arches, buttresses and rib vaulting – enabled Gothic naves to be stretched upwards and continued skywards by means of slender spires. Experiments with the new methods can be seen already in several otherwise Romanesque churches but St Denis in the northern suburbs of Paris is considered the first Gothic building proper. But if the great Gothic cathedrals of France seem almost miraculously perfect today, at the time they were built they seemed positively risky. Structures could and did collapse as glitches in theory were ironed

The Gothic interior of Troyes Cathedral.

builders and ancillary tradesmen. The Cistercian order also originated in Burgundy and established abbeys in remote parts of the country. In line with its spiritual philosophy, its buildings tend to be simple and austere, free from adornment that could distract from prayer.

Gothic and its risks

Romanesque had essentially come from the south, growing out of the civilization of the Mediterranean, where there was a need to keep excess light *out* of a building. In the north, the goal was the opposite: to draw scarce sunlight in to illuminate the interior. The challenge was to create larger windows without the walls losing rigidity and strength.

out by trial and modification.

The stone structure established, windows could now expand within the slimmer walls to become features rather than pathways of light. A new skill developed to fill them with stained glass, as can be seen in all its glory in Chartres.

Peace and the Renaissance

The frenzy of Gothic building and innovation began to slow down around 1277 and there was no significant development in French architecture between the end of the 13th century and the turn of the 15th when, as before, new inspiration came from Italy, brought back by the returning armies of Louis XII, to be adapted to French tastes. It found particular favour during the reign of François I and was mainly applied to secular rather than religious uses.

The Renaissance style with its ideals of order, harmony and symmetry appealed to a new age casting off medieval preoccupations. It suited the hedonistic tastes of the wealthy and conditions were right for its implantation. Now that warfare had all but ceased on French territory, there was no need to build for siege and the château fort could become the château in the sense of stately home.

The best examples of the Renaissance in France are along the lower valley of the Loire.

At first classical motifs were added as ornament to existing buildings; interiors were updated; and Renaissance elements were grafted on to Gothic walls. The magnificent staircase added to the Château de Blois in 1515, for example, is one of the first accomplished works of the French Renaissance. Soon, everyone with the means wanted to have a Renaissance newbuild or at least re-build, resulting in such great houses as Chaumont, Azay-le-Rideau and Chambord.

Pretentious palaces

In Italy, the Renaissance was followed by a reac-

The Musée Alsacien (Alsatian Museum) in Strasbourg.

Staircase detail at Chaumont.

MEDIEVAL CASTLES

The castle of the high Middle Ages, *château fort*, was the home of the local seigneur. In times of war it served as the key defence of a town or village, and as a refuge for the people. A castle was sited on a defensive position: a spot from which visibility was good and the approach of a besieging army rendered difficult on one or more sides. Returning Crusaders brought back with them oriental design improvements. Thick walls with few openings – a few loopholes or arrow slits – made for a strong castle and these were topped by battlements where overhanging galleries were built to drop missiles on attackers.

tion against it in the form of Baroque, which favoured drama and ornamentation over simplicity, reason and restraint. In France, however, there was little taste for dramatic buildings, and a home-grown Classicism, an evolution of Renaissance ideas that is sometimes called French Baroque, became dominant.

It was pioneered by François Mansart who gave his name to a peculiarly French roof of double pitch (gentler in its upper part, steep below) but it reached its apogee during the reign of the Sun King, Louis XIV in the *grand siècle* of the 17th century.

The divergence between Baroque and French Classicism is well illustrated by the visit of the great genius of Italian art and architecture, Gian

Lorenzo Bernini, to Paris in 1665. He was invited by the king to lay out his plans for rebuilding the Louvre. These were rejected in favour of a less daring French project for the building overseen by Charles Perrault. Another architect, Louis Le Vau, also contributed to the revamped Louvre but he is best remembered for his role in creating the palace of Versailles, the epitome of the new style.

For at least the next century, French civilisation was at its height, both politically and culturally, and the royally-approved style of architecture was emulated by aristocrats and monarchs across Europe.

Mérimée, author of the novel on which the operetta Carmen is based, became Inspecteur Général des Monuments Historiques and he commissioned his old schoolfriend Eugène Viollet-le-Duc to restore some of France's most eloquent ruins. The results, notably at Carcassonne, Notre-Dame and the Château de Pierrefonds, have been criticised for their fanciful "enhancements" but at least these buildings were preserved for posterity.

Under the Third Republic, born in 1871, formal architecture began to filter down to the ordinary people. The introduction of compulsory primary education in the 1880s meant provincial

Brasseries and their outdoor seating areas line Lille's Grand Place.

Only later in the early 18th century did France develop a variant of Baroque, rococo – derived from *rocaille* (stone) and the *coquilles* (shells) used as motifs in its exuberant decoration.

Empire style

The vogue for French Classicism continued up until the Revolution only to be supplanted, after the upheavals, by neoclassicism or the Empire style, a harking back to antiquity favoured by Napoleon Bonaparte as a way of emulating the glory of his Roman predecessors.

The 19th century similarly looked backwards for its inspiration, reviving and mimicking lapsed and archaic styles. This was also the period in which heritage was discovered. In 1834, Prosper

RURAL CHARM

All across France, farmers and villagers constructed houses that were not designed on any aesthetic grounds. Far more important was to make the best use of materials to hand. They built according to the needs of their families, crops and livestock and in response to the local climate, with a windowless wall against the prevailing wind, adding personalised details where they could. The common medieval half-timbered house is found in Normandy, Alsace, Champagne and Gascony, its walls filled up with brick or wattle and daub. Some buildings cluster together in groups classified as among the *plus beaux villages* of France.

towns and villages acquired town halls incorporating elementary schools: dignified eclectic buildings impregnated with civic pride.

Into the modern age

French architecture of the 20th century is indebted to the work, but mostly the thought, of the Swiss-born Charles-Édouard Jeanneret-Gris, better known as Le Corbusier. A leading exponent of the Modern style, he famously described the house as "a machine for living" and illustrated his "five principles for a new architecture" in Villa Savoye in Poissy, near

France has over 42,000 classified monuments historiques, 100 of them owned and managed by the state. A further 147,000 other buildings are listed as of architectural value.

space and flexibility.

The 1980s saw more *grands projets*, this time credited to the *dirigisme* of François Mitterrand. The Louvre was transformed by the addition of I.M. Pei's pyramid in 1989 and in the same year the Great Arch at La Défense was erected.

The striking Fondation Louis Vuitton.

Paris, built during the interwar years.

After the destruction of World War II the most pressing need was to reconstruct the shattered cities of the north, which had lost irreplaceable medieval houses. The only quick and economic solution was to build with reinforced concrete in the modern style. The rebuilt port of Le Havre, by Auguste Perret, is often held up as the exemplary achievement.

The security of the Fifth Republic and sustained decades of prosperity meant great state projects could once again be envisaged. The most controversial and the best-loved of these is the Pompidou centre, the result of a collaboration between Renzo Piano and Richard Rogers. Their "inside out" design makes for light,

The 21st century has seen two innovative structures, the motorway viaduct at Millau and the Pompidou Centre at Metz, both involving foreign architects. In 2014, Frank Gehry's gigantic Fondation Louis Vuitton 'landed' in Paris' Bois de Boulogne, all glass sails and trademark odd angles.

After her stint as European Capital of Cutlure in 2013, Marseille has been regenerated with its waterfront now playing host to new glass pavilions and state-of-the-art museums.

The best-known French architect of today, Jean Nouvel, has built his most stunning buildings abroad but his work can be seen in Paris in the Institut du Monde Arabe, the Fondation Cartier, the Musée du quai Branly and the new Philharmonie de Paris concert hall.

FRENCH DESIGN

'Made in France' has a cachet – it describes an object that is not merely functional, but one that has a subtle panache and sense of style.

France has always been celebrated for its sense of style, which continues to fascinate the rest of the world. It can be seen in its architecture, domestic interiors, gardens and fashion, but also in more modest, often inconspicuous, everyday objects, in the form of design.

Until industrialisation in the late 19th century, things were made in the only way they could be, with form dictated by function. Gradually, however, the lofty ideals of fine art and the more mundane aspirations of commercialism converged with the aim of making objects which were utilitarian as well as being beautiful. Sensuous appeal and saleability, it was realised, could be mutually enhancing.

As the 20th century wore on, design acquired ever greater prestige and designers became regarded as celebrity artists in their own right. As new materials appeared and design crept into unexplored corners of everyday life, form and function drifted apart and no one seemed to care whether an object worked well as long as it looked good. We now live in an age dominated by design and manufacturers strive to catch and keep our attention with any visual trickery we can.

From out of a century and a half of fevered creativity, certain objects stand out as design classics. Pictured on these two pages are some legendary designs which are all unmistakeably made in France.

The Bauhaus-inspired lines of the Citroën 2CV, intended as an economy car.

The lemon-squeezer with attitude known as Juicy Salif (by Philippe Starck for Italian firm Alessi) is considered an icon of industrial design.

Pathé gramophone with its glorious Morning Glory horn.

Hector Guimard's Art-Nouveau entrance to the Abbesses Métro station in Paris.

ART NOUVEAU

At the end of the 19th century a new, fluid and infectious artistic movement spread across Europe. Although known by other names in other countries (*Jungendstil* in Germany, *Secession* in Austria, *Modernismo* in Spain), it is universally identified as "Art Nouveau", after a trend-setting shop of that name which opened in Paris in 1895. It was called a "new" style because it was a conscious reaction to the academic, rule-bound art that preceded it.

Art Nouveau delights in ornament, drawing inspiration particularly from nature as seen in its emblematic sensuous curves. It is instantly recognisable by its graceful, organic forms and its inventive use of industrial materials including mass-produced wrought iron and stained glass. After 1900, new approaches to art and decoration took its place but *fin de siècle* buildings have been preserved and restored all over France, particularly in the capital and in the city of Nancy. Many art historians would argue that the creations of Art Nouveau do not seem to date and that the style has never really gone out of fashion, its influences living on as strong as ever today.

Simple and unobtrusive, the Bic biro – design at its most universal.

The Opinel pocket knife, the classic, functional, French folding knife since the 1890s.

The Michelin Man, aka Monsieur Bibendum, is the mascot of the Michelin tyre company, introduced to the general public in 1894.

Rocamadour, nestled against its cliff.

Brasserie in Bergues, in Flanders country.

Perfect symmetry: the Louvre and its glass pyramid.

The unmistakably southern hues of St-Tropez.

INTRODUCTION

A detailed guide to the entire country,
with principal sites clearly cross-
referenced by number to the maps.

Sunflowers.

The hardest part of any visit to France is deciding where to start and how much to pack in. Getting about is no problem. In spite of an often empty landscape, here you will find high-speed trains and rapid motorways that make up the densest road network in the world.

If you just want to stop and relax there are 5,000km (3,000 miles) of coastline, from the wild, rocky Breton coast in the north to the sandy beaches of the Mediterranean in the south. Inland you are never far from water either. Its longest river is the Loire, where some 300 glorious châteaux spread out along its lazy length. France is also surprisingly mountainous. Mont Blanc in the French Alps is the highest mountain in Europe at 4,810m (15,780ft), with excellent ski resorts beneath it. Its other main ranges are the Pyrenees, the Vosges, the Jura and the Massif Central.

And yet, despite these nationwide statistics, France is essentially a country made up of regions, each with its own individual personality. Therein lies the nation's charm for the traveller, and the following pages attempt to do justice to the character of each region.

For convenience, these regions are grouped into seven sections. The obvious place to start is of course the romantic city of Paris and its hinterland, the Ile de France. The North takes you around Nord-Pas-de-Calais, Picardy, Champagne, Lorraine and Alsace. The West is Normandy, Brittany, the Loire Valley and Poitou-Charentes. The Centre covers Burgundy, Franche-Comté, the Rhone Valley, the Alps, the Auvergne and the Limousin. The Southwest is divided up into Aquitaine (including the Bordeaux wine region and the Basque Country) and Midi-Pyrénées. The South explores Provence (especially the Côte d'Azur) and the lesser known region of Languedoc-Roussillon. Finally comes the Mediterranean holiday island of Corsica.

Limousin geese, synonymous with foie gras.

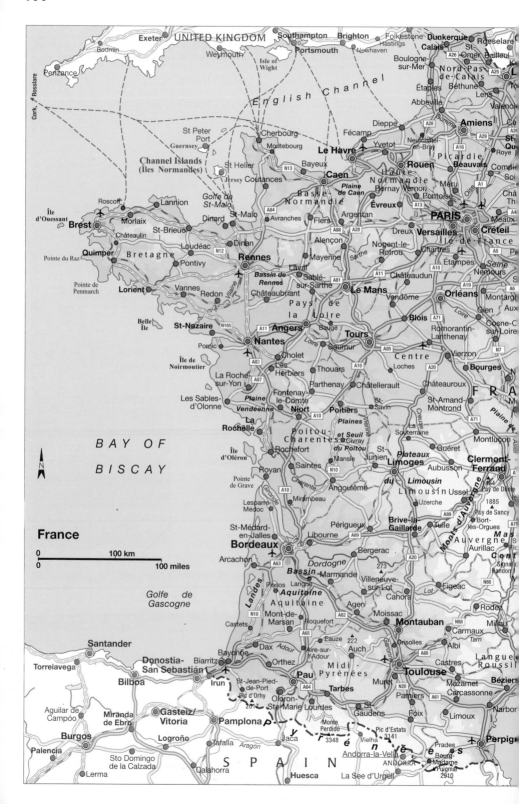

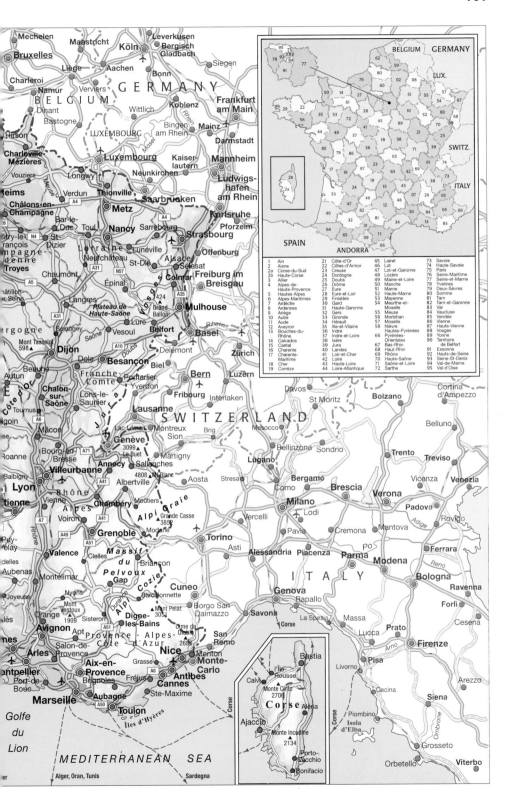

The Thinker sculpture is a highlight at the Musée Rodin.

PARIS AND SURROUNDINGS

The city of romantics and art enthusiasts is fascinating at every turn, while easy day trips take you to magnificent palaces and other historic monuments.

Métro sign.

As Victor Hugo put it: "It is in Paris that the beating of Europe's heart is felt. Paris is the city of cities." Certainly, it is at the heart of France. In terms of urban sprawl, in Europe it is second only to London. Where matters of French administration, politics and cultural life are concerned, it plays an absolutely dominant role. It is also the world capital of chic. For all these reasons and more, Paris is so unlike much of the rest of France that it has been described as a city-state in its own right.

Largely undamaged by two world wars, Paris has been created by centuries of inspired planning. Its street corners reek of history, its monuments and museums are well-known to people from all over the world and its inhabitants are an endless source of controversy. Every pavement is a theatre on which daily life is played out.

Place de la Concorde.

Perfectly preserved though it is, Paris is a city unafraid of change. I.M. Pei's glass pyramid in front of the Louvre and the massive development at La Défense financial district are evidence of that. But there are regrets in this process of evolution – in the city where Voltaire was reputed to drink 40 cups of coffee a day at Le Procope, the café culture is threatened by the fast-food invasion, and the number of cafés has fallen drastically. But Paris remains a city of romance, a city of arts *par excellence* and a city of fun. There's endless entertainment here for the observant, who will learn as much about Paris and its inhabitants from walking the streets as from visiting the great museums.

A superb public transport system is based on the metro, and the RER and SNCF rail lines. This extends into the further reaches of the Ile-de-France, making it easy to visit charming towns and beautiful swathes of countryside. Essential sights include Chartres, the palaces at Versailles and Fontainebleau and France's biggest tourist attraction, Disneyland Paris. All these are profiled in the Around Paris chapter (see page 143).

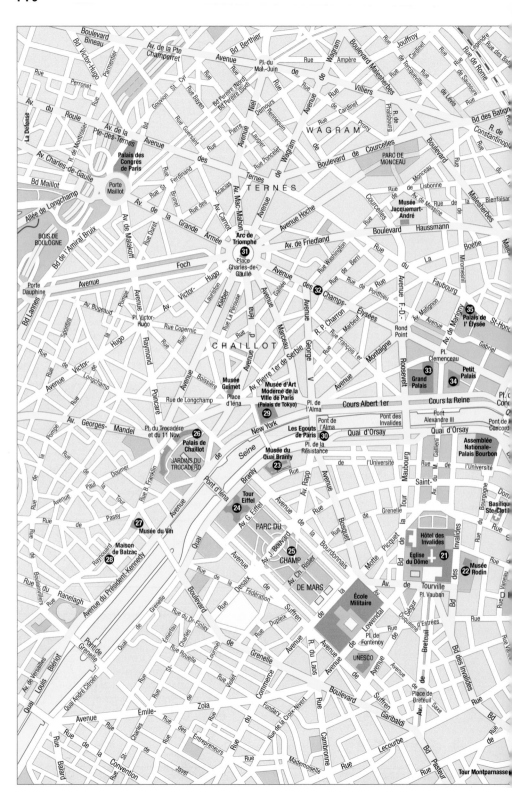

Boulevard Bineau
Bd Victor-Hugo
Parmentier
Av. de la Pte Champerret
Bd Berthier
Avenue
Pl. du Mal.-Juin
Rue
Ampère
Rue
Jouffroy
Cardinet
Rue de Torqueville
Rue
Legendre
Rue de Rome
Rue des Bat.

Rue
Perronet
St. Cyr
Rue Bayen
Bd Pereire (Nord)
Bd Pereire (Sud)
Rue
Gouvion
Av. de la Pte-des-Ternes
Avenue
de
de
Villiers
Rue de Torqueville
Rue de Saussure
R. de Levis
Bd des Batign

Av. du Roule
La Défense
R. de Montressier
Av. de Montbrison
Av. Charles-de-Gaulle
Palais des Congrès de Paris
Porte Maillot
Rue Guersant
St. Ferdinand
Rue
Niel
Demours
Rennequin
Rue
Cardinet
Prony
WAGRAM
R. de Phalsbourg
Bd des Batign
R. de Constantinop

Bd Maillot
Porte Maillot
Avenue
des
Acacias
Rue des
Av. Carnot
TERNES
de
Wagram
Boulevard de Courcelles
PARC DE MONCEAU
de
Monceau
de Lisbonne
Rue de Messine
Bienfaisa

BOIS DE BOULOGNE
Allée de Longchamp
Av. de l'Amiral Bruix
Bd de Malakoff
Av. de la Grande Armée
Av. Mac-Mahon
Arc de Triomphe
T E R N E S
Avenue Hoche
Courcelles
Boulevard
Courcelles
Musée Jacquemart-André
Av. de Messine
Malesherbes
Bienfaisa
Boëtie

Porte Dauphine
Bd Lannes
Foch
Place Charles-de-Gaulle
31
Av. de Friedland
Av. de Wagram
Rue Washington
Boulevard Haussmann
du
La
Miromesnil
Boëtie

Avenue
Victor-Hugo
Kléber
Laursion
La Pérouse
Avenue des
32
Champs-
Elysées
Rue de Berri
Rue de Ponthieu
Avenue
F-D-
Avenue de Marigny
Palais de l'Elysée
35
St-Hon

Av. Bugeaud
Pompe
Avenue
Raymond
Rue Copernic
Galilée
Marceau
George
R. P. Charron
Marbeuf
Rue François 1er
Rond Point
Roosevelt
Montaigne
Pl. Clemenceau
Gabriel

Pl. Victor-Hugo
Rue Copernic
d'
CHAILLOT
Av. Pierre 1er de Serbie
Musée Guimet
Musée d'Art Moderne de la Ville de Paris (Palais de Tokyo)
Grand Palais
33
Petit Palais
34
Pl. d.
Con

Hugo
Victor-
Longchamp
Avenue
Poincaré
Boissière
Place d'Iéna
29
Pl. de l'Alma
Cours Albert 1er
Cours la Reine
Pont Alexandre III
Pont de Concor

Av. Georges- Mandel
Pompe
Rue de Longchamp
de
New York
Seine
Pont de l'Alma
Quai d'Orsay
Quai d'Orsay
Assemblée Nationale- Palais Bourbon
l'Université

Pl. du Trocadéro et du 11 Nov.
26
Palais de Chaillot
JARDINS DU TROCADÉRO
Les Egouts de Paris
30
Pl. de la Résistance
Musée du Quai Branly
23
Branly
Av. Rapp
de
l'Université
Gallieni
l'Université

Rue
Avenue
Rue Paul
Passy
Rue B. Franklin
Pont d'Iéna
Tour Eiffel
24
Av. G. Eiffel
Av. J. Bouvard
de
Grenelle
Maubourg
Saint-
Dom.
Basiliqu Ste-Clotil

27
Musée du Vin
Doumer
Avenue
Quai
PARC DU
Av. Ch. Risler
25
de
Bosquet
Motte
la
Picquet
Hôtel des Invalides
Invalides
Rue S
Rue

Maison de Balzac
28
Raymond
Avenue du Président-Kennedy
CHAMP
DE MARS
Suffren
de
la
Bourdonnais
Eglise du Dôme
21
Musée Rodin
22
des
Tourville
D

Rue
Boulevards
Rue du
Ranelagh
Pont de Grenelle
Quai
Grenelle
Rue du Dr-Finlay
Desaix
Rue
de
Fédération
Av.
Ecole Militaire
Pl. Vauban
Ségur
d'Estrées
Bd des Invalides
Rue

Boulevard
Blériot
Av. de Versailles
Quai Louis
Quai André Citroën
Emerdau
Charles
Rue Rouelle
Journal
de
Rue
Dupleix
Suffren
de
Lowendal
Pl. de Fontenoy
Breteuil
Duquesne
Bd des Invalides
Rue
Bd
Bd

Émile-
Zola
Avenue
Rue
Rue
St-
de
la
Convention
Javel
Violet
Commerce
Rue
du
Fondary
Rue de la Croix-Nivert
UNESCO
Boulevard
Garibaldi
Suffren
Av.
de
Pl. de Breteuil
Saxe
Bd
Pasteur
Tour Montparnasse

Paris

0   500 m
0   500 yds

The most iconic and photographed monument in Paris.

PARIS

Perhaps the grandest and certainly one of the
most beautiful cities in the world, Paris is
loved for its inimitable atmosphere and its
many pleasures, from culture to cuisine.

One-fifth of France's 66 million people live in and around the capital, along with immigrants, students, artists, teachers, business people and political refugees from around the world. The expatriate community is active; theatre, cinema, arts and news publications abound in various languages, including English. So many of the people living in the cosmopolitan region come from foreign lands and the provinces of France that the native *parisien* is a rare beast.

The first to arrive in this enchanted spot on the River Seine were the Parisii, a tribe of Gaulish fishermen and boatmen. The ensuing Roman Empire brought about the strange mixture of Latin and northern civilisation that gives France its special flavour. Though the Romans imposed their tongue, their official name for the city, Lutetia, had disappeared by the time the Franks made it their capital in AD508. Since then the number of emperors, philosophers, ambassadors, adventurers and outcasts who have arrived in this city is as uncountable as the lights bedecking it by night.

Strollers' city

Lovers know the city best. Silent green courtyards, the river's edge, the misty air are all accomplices to seduction. Some visitors never see the inside of a

museum or monument, yet they know and love Paris deeply.

It is a city ideal for strolling, tucked inside a 34km (21-mile) perimeter. It is divided into 20 *arrondissements*, or districts, which are used in postal codes and which begin in the centre with the *premier* (1er) *arrondissement* and spiral out in a clockwise direction. Some arrondissements are better known by other names: Montmartre, Montparnasse, St-Germain, Quartier Latin and so on, each with its own distinct style and character.

Main Attractions
Cathédrale Notre-Dame
Conciergerie
Quartier Latin
Musée d'Orsay
Tour Eiffel
Arc de Triomphe
Champs-Elysées
Musée du Louvre
Centre Pompidou
Montmartre

Stylish Montmartre locals.

The River Seine, which begins near the Swiss Alps and empties into the English Channel at Le Havre, meanders through the city, dividing the north from the south of Paris into what is known as the *rive droite* (right bank), where the city's main institutions lie, and *rive gauche* (left bank), the upstart, bohemian side.

Everything in the city centre is accessible by public transport, and although work continues to make public transport more user-friendly, the elderly and those in wheelchairs may encounter difficulties. Free maps are widely available, but they won't show you the lanes of Montmartre or the key outer districts such as La Défense or La Villette.

Island beginnings

Paris was founded on the **Ile de la Cité**, the river island at the heart of the city and its primitive cradle. Some of the ancient soul remains in its celebrated monuments.

Most distinguished of all is the **Cathédrale Notre-Dame ❶** (www.notredamedeparis.fr; Mon–Fri 8am–6.45pm, Sat–Sun 8am–7.15pm, visits limited during religious services, free; charge for towers, tours Wed, Thu 2pm, Sat 2.30pm). It was built during the 12th and 13th centuries, and after the ravages of the Revolution, during which it had been the "Temple of Reason" it was extensively restored in the 19th century. The original Madonna to whom the Cathedral is dedicated was a "black virgin", a popular ancient fertility figure. This dark, hooded lady was already credited with several miracles before disappearing during the Revolution. A 14th-century statue of unknown origin stands in the same place (to the right of the choir) and is venerated still.

The building is a masterpiece of Gothic art. The tall central spire (82 metres/270ft) is flanked by two square towers. Visitors may climb all the way up during daylight hours and see the **Bourdon**, the 16-ton brass bell that the hunchback Quasimodo rang in Victor Hugo's novel, *Notre-Dame de Paris (The Hunchback of Notre-Dame)*. The view from the top, alongside the devilish stone gargoyles, is a heavenly reward after the

Notre-Dame's Portal of the Last Judgement.

SARKOZY'S GRAND PARIS

The capital sucks in inhabitants with a seemingly insatiable appetite, and the built-up area expands in all directions. Yet even if Paris looks like a vast city, technically it is quite small in comparison with other major European cities. The Ville de Paris is a commune of just 105 sq km (58 sq miles) and it hasn't expanded its borders since 1860. It is surrounded by the *petite couronne*, a circle of 123 communes in three *départements*, each with its own mayor. Beyond them is the *grande couronne* of the other four Ile-de-France départements bringing a great many more suburbs and satellite towns into the *agglomération parisienne*. All this makes a metropolitan region of more than 11 million people divided into 1,500 independent but interrelated communes.

In 2007, to inject some future cohesion into this huge and growing urban area, Nicolas Sarkozy announced a project for a "Grand Paris" to take shape over the next 30 or 40 years. This led to a new transportation master plan and laws passed in 2014 to create a Métropole du Grand Paris, a vision on a par with Greater London. Implementation will start in 2016 and will see an area of 762 sq km (294 sq miles) with a population of some 6.7 million undergo total modernisation and integration. It is to improve the quality of all aspects of life, from the environment, transport – with better links from the suburbs to the centre – housing and social cohesion.

long climb up the spiralling stone staircase.

Between the towers stretches a long gallery, and below this the central **Rose Window** has a diameter of 9 metres (31ft), forming a halo above a statue of the Virgin Mary. The window surmounts the **Galerie des Rois**, 28 statues of the kings of Judah and Israel rebuilt under Viollet-le-Duc during his 19th century reconstructions. The statues had all been decapitated during the Revolution, and in 1977 the heads were discovered in a nearby construction site. They are now on display at the Cluny Museum (see page 119).

On a level with the *parvis*, the paved terrace in front of the cathedral, the three doorways of Notre-Dame are, left to right, the **Virgin's Portal**, the **Judgment** and **St Anne's Portal**. Each one is covered with intricate carvings relating biblical tales and the lives of the saints.

Great Cathedral events

A number of events from French history took place both on the *parvis* and inside the cathedral. In 1430,

the young Henry VI of England was crowned King of France. In 1752, the French King Henri IV, a Protestant, stood outside the church and shouted his marriage vows at his bride, Marguerite de Valois, a Catholic, who stood at the altar. He was back 37 years later, having renounced Protestantism to be crowned here. His rumoured remark that "Paris is well worth a Mass" caused the population to doubt the sincerity of his belated conversion. Nevertheless "Henri le Grand" rode fearlessly to the altar, surrounded by troops in full battle dress.

Coronation in 1804 of Napoleon Bonaparte as Napoleon I, Emperor of France, was certainly the most grandiose ceremony witnessed. The gilded imperial coach materialised out of the snow. The gathered crowd saw nothing more than the curtained windows – Josephine and Napoleon drove to the back of the building to put on their coronation robes in the wings. In the rear of the cathedral nave they mounted the specially constructed double staircase to their thrones. The privileged guests, ladies bursting out of their

The Rose Window, seen from inside the cathedral.

Riverside view of the cathedral.

TIP

Every Sunday at 4.30pm, the organ master fills Notre-Dame with classical music, soaring to paradise out of the 112-stop instrument. Classical concerts are also given in Sainte-Chapelle.

low-cut gowns, gentlemen in uniform and high black boots, were accommodated on tiers of seats. Pope Pius VII agreed, for diplomatic reasons, to be present at the three-hour ceremony, but balked at performing the actual crowning. In fact, after the Pope's blessing, Napoleon simply crowned himself as the crowd cried *"Vive l'Empereur!"*

More recently, on the liberation of Paris in 1944, Charles de Gaulle came to give thanks at Notre-Dame, while the Bourdon bell tolled joyously and sniper shots rang out.

Lining the walls of the cathedral are 29 chapels. The large main altar represents the **Offering of Louis XIII**. It commemorates the birth of the king's heir. To the left and right of the Nicolas Coustou *Pietà* are statues of Louis XIV (who completed the memorial) and Louis XIII.

The **Trésor de Notre-Dame** (daily 9.30am–6pm; charge) contains richly ornamented robes and chalices. In the **Crypte Archéologique** (Tue–Sun 10am–6pm; charge), underneath the *parvis*, are excavations of buildings dating back to the 3rd century and later

foundations, giving a sense of the inns and churches that once stood here.

Behind the cathedral is the **Hôtel-Dieu**, the city's oldest hospital, and the **Préfecture de Police**, and, opposite, in Place Louis-Lépine, the colourful **Marché aux Fleurs**, an array of small glasshouses selling flowers and plants. On Sundays the stalls become a market for caged birds. In 2014, Queen Elizabeth II visited the market as part of her state visit to France to commemmorate the 70th anniversary of the D-Day landings. In her honour, the market was renamed Marché aux Fleurs Reine-Elizabeth-II.

On the eastern tip of the Ile de la Cité, a small park was inaugurated in 1962. It houses a monument by Pingusson honouring the 200,000 French martyrs who died in concentration camps in World War II. The **Mémorial de la Déportation** (daily), moving in its simplicity, marks an unknown grave.

The Conciergerie

The western end of the island is almost entirely occupied by the **Palais de Justice ❷** (Mon–Fri 8.30am–6pm,

The vaulted hall at the Conciergerie.

occasionally closed to the public), part of the huge Gothic structure (much restored and rebuilt) where the first 12 Capetian kings lived. At the corner of the Quai de l'Horloge, the **Tour de l'Horloge** (clock tower) dates from the 15th century and is echoed on the river facade by three round towers. On Boulevard du Palais, the **Concier- gerie** (daily Mar–Oct 9.30am–6pm, Nov–Feb 9am–5pm, closed some pub- lic hols; charge) is another part of the Capetian palace, with a magnificent Gothic vaulted hall.

It later became an infamous prison, where many a death sentence was pro- nounced during the French Revolu- tion. In one dark room the prisoners ate (the more fortunate had dinners sent in) and slept, struggled to keep warm and clean in the general squalor, and sometimes died of fear before reaching the guillotine. One of the last to go was Fouquier-Tinville, president of the Revolutionary Tribunal, who had sent 2,278 men and women to the guillotine before him.

Queen Marie-Antoinette was held here. Her cell has been reconstituted,

while the actual cell is now the Chapelle des Girondins, with royal relics of her last days. She left the Conciergerie, hair shorn and wrists bound, in a dirty cart, sitting with her back to the horse so that the crowd might insult her to her face.

Next to the Conciergerie, an ornate 18th-century gate opens onto the **Cours de Mai**. Rising up amid the stark walls of the high court is a glittering jewel of Gothic art, **Sainte-Chapelle** ❸ (daily Mar–Oct 9.30am–6pm, Nov– Feb 9am–5pm, closed some public hols; charge). The church was constructed in 1246 by Louis IX, Saint Louis, to hold the Crown of Thorns and other purported relics, which he purchased from the Emperor of Constantinople on his return from his Crusades in the Holy Land. The lower chapel was fre- quented by the palace servants and the upper by the royal household. Above, 15 great stained-glass windows fill the room with the precious coloured light that has given the chapel its renown. The walls soar to 31 metres (102ft) and seem to be made of sparkling glass held by the scantiest skeleton of ornately carved stone.

FACT

Vedettes du Pont Neuf (tel: 01 46 33 98 38) run cruises along the Seine lasting about one hour. Boats leave from Square du Vert-Galant at the western tip of the Ile de la Cité every half hour in high season.

The Pont Neuf spanning the Seine.

A wealth of medieval sculpture is on show at the Thermes de Cluny.

The café experience is an integral part of a visit to Paris.

Bridges

Several bridges link the island to both river banks. **Pont Neuf** (New Bridge) is, despite its name, the oldest bridge standing in Paris, completed in 1607. Connecting with both the left and right banks at the tapering downstream end of the island, it was the first bridge to be built entirely in stone. At the time it was also the widest, and the only one to be equipped with raised pedestrian walkways. These qualities, plus its central location, made the Pont Neuf a popular meeting place for pedlars, acrobats, tooth-pullers, musicians, pickpockets and prostitutes. From the lower *quai* or aboard a *bateau mouche* tour boat, you can see the 900 faces carved along the sides of the bridge, each one of them unique, and some of them particularly expressive.

The **Petit Pont** beside Notre-Dame leads directly from Ile de la Cité into the Latin Quarter of the Left Bank. The shortest bridge in town has the longest history, reaching back to the origins of Roman Lutetia. Originally a wooden bridge, it was burned down many times in the course of numerous battles. In 1718, the bridge and its surroundings blazed up once more, under strange circumstances. A custom of the times was to seek the repose of a loved one's soul by casting a bowl containing bread and a candle into the river. The mother of a drowned child did so, setting a barge piled with straw afire, and the bridge, packed with wooden houses, blazed out of control. This led to a law banning all buildings on bridges, changing the face of the city.

An iron bridge connects the Ile de la Cité with a smaller island upstream, the **Ile St-Louis** ❹, soaked in 17th-century calm. Along the quiet streets are small art galleries, intimate restaurants and tea rooms, and **Berthillon**, home of what is reputed to be the best ice cream in Paris. The poet Charles Baudelaire lived for a couple of years on the ground floor of the Hôtel de Lauzon on the Quai d'Anjou.

The Latin Quarter

On the left bank of the Seine, adjacent to the two islands is the **Quartier Latin** (**Latin Quarter**). Close to the

CAFÉS, THE FABRIC OF LIFE

Humorist George Mikes once wrote: "You sit in a café and watch people walking up and down in front of it. Then you walk up and down in front of the café and give other people a chance to watch you. As a member of that strolling or surging crowd you have become one of the sights of Paris; you have become a rival of the Eiffel Tower."

The café has always been the Parisian's decompression chamber, easing the transition between *Métro-boulot-dodo* – commuting, working and sleeping. It provides a welcome pause in which to savour a *petit noir (espresso)* or an *apéritif*, to empty the mind of troublesome thoughts and to watch the people go by. The café is also the place to meet friends, have a romantic tryst or even to do business in a relaxed atmosphere. There may be less authentic cafés than there once were, as Americanised coffee shops take their place, but there are still plenty to choose from. Several famous ones trade on past glories, such as Le Procope (13 Rue de l'Ancienne-Comédie) which has moved upmarket since it started serving customers in 1686 thanks to its reputation as a meeting place for the literati. Other cafés are more shabby and authentic, remaining closer to the notion of the neighbourhood "zinc" (named after its metal counter), which have always been such an important part of the fabric of French life.

river bank is the church **of St-Julien-le-Pauvre** . Begun in 1170 it is small and squat, and tucked into a corner of its little garden where it looks like a humble country church that has somehow been transported to the city. It is now a Greek Catholic church. Round the corner, **St-Séverin** ❻, another magical medieval church, harmoniously proportioned and delicately decorated, stands in a cluster of streets dubbed **Little Athens** because of their numerous Greek restaurants.

At the corner of boulevards St-Michel and St-Germain is the **Musée National du Moyen Age/Thermes de Cluny** ❼ (Wed–Mon 9.15am–5.45pm; closed some public hols; charge), built onto and over Lutetia's **Roman Baths**. The *hôtel*, with a tranquil garden, is one of the few medieval mansions remaining in Paris and was once the city residence by the Abbots of Cluny. The museum has one of the world's finest collections of artefacts from medieval castle and church life, most notably the exquisite tapestries of *La Dame à la Licorne* (The Lady and The Unicorn).

Seat of learning

At the heart of the Quartier Latin is **La Sorbonne** ❽, one of the most celebrated and distinguished institutes of learning in the world, which was founded in 1253 as a college for poor theological students. A few blocks down Boulevard St-Germain to the right, the Baroque facade of the **chapel of La Sorbonne** welcomes the curious. Cardinal Richelieu is buried in here with his hat suspended above his tomb: it will fall, so legend has it, when he is released from hell.

Uphill from wherever you are in the Latin Quarter is the **Panthéon** ❾ (daily Apr–Sept 10am–6.30pm, Oct–Mar 10am–6pm, closed public hols; charge), an 18th-century monument which sits on the top of **Montagne Ste-Geneviève**, the heart of the Roman city. The Panthéon is where illustrious French citizens are laid to rest in its crypt, and these include Victor Hugo, Voltaire, Rousseau, Zola and Resistance leader Jean Moulin.

Close by, the attractive church of **St-Etienne-du-Mont** ❿, with a superb rood screen, contains the remains of Racine and Pascal, commemorated by plaques. It also has an ornate shrine to St Geneviève, patron saint of Paris. Life is less serious on the **Place de la Contrescarpe**, ringed by cafés, and the **Rue Mouffetard**, a long, winding street with a thriving daily morning market (except Mon).

Besides the Baths at Cluny, the only other Roman vestige in Paris proper is the **Arènes de Lutèce** ⓫, the ancient arena. Tough Roman combatants have been replaced by *boulistes*, playing France's most celebrated game. *Pétanque* is a good spectator sport too, and the Arènes is a lovely park in which to rest.

Nearby, the **Jardin des Plantes** ⓬ is a good place for a stroll. Within the garden is the **Musée National d'Histoire Naturelle**, including the Grande Galerie de l'Evolution (Mon, Wed–Sun 10am–6pm, closed 1 May; charge) and the Menagerie zoo. Down the Rue

TIP

For a wonderful panoramic view of Paris, and a relatively easy ascent, climb to the dome of the Panthéon, the city's most rewarding tall building.

La Dame à la Licorne tapestry in the Musée National du Moyen Age.

KIDS

Attractions in the Luxembourg Gardens include boating, model sailboating, a bandstand, shady outdoor café, bee-keeping school, donkey rides, puppet theatre and an adjacent horse-riding centre.

Quatrefages, is **La Grande Mosquée de Paris** ⓭, the largest mosque in France, built in 1926 and open to visitors. It includes Turkish baths and courtyard Café Maure, a tranquil place where you can have baklava and tea.

The Luxembourg Gardens

The Sixth *arrondissement* lies on the opposite side of the Boulevard St-Michel from the Latin Quarter. It has a more formal atmosphere, beginning with the **Jardin du Luxembourg** ⓮ (daily, dawn to dusk). The **Palais du Luxembourg** ⓯, constructed in the 17th century for Marie de Medici, today houses the French Senate. In the park, children are more in evidence than politicians, sailing boats on the carp-filled pond.

Sacré Parnasse

The southern end of the Left Bank is dominated by **Tour Montparnasse** ⓰ (www.tourmontparnasse56.com), a shiny black skyscraper shooting up above the Montparnasse train station. The 59-floor complex, completed in 1973, transformed the rather down-at-heel

quarter in which itinerant artists and writers had settled in the 1920s. In the tower, a lift will whisk you to the top floor in 38 seconds to enjoy a panorama of Paris from the terrace or the rooftop restaurant.

Modern Montparnasse may have lost some of its old-fashioned charm but it has replaced it with a sense of dynamism, and it's possible to get the flavour of the past in its surviving cafés. A favourite hang-out of both Ernest Hemingway and Jean-Paul Sartre, the **Closerie des Lilas**, is still operating at 171 Boulevard Montparnasse and serves excellent meals inside or on the terrace. The 19th-century poet Gérard de Nerval used to take his pet lobster on a lead to La Rotonde (No. 105). **La Coupole (No 102)** is a spacious, popular café-brasserie with a low-key dance hall. Other former literary haunts are the **Select (No 99) and the Dôme (No 108)**.

As for art, the intimate **Musée Zadkine** (www.zadkine.paris.fr; 100bis rue d'Assas, Tue–Sun 10am–6pm, closed public hols; charge) was renovated in 2012 and displays the Cubist work

Jardin des Plantes.

of the émigré Russian sculptor, Ossip Zadkine, in his former house, studio and garden.

The extensive **Cimetière du Montparnasse** accommodates the remains of Baudelaire, Sartre, Simone de Beauvoir, Samuel Beckett and Alfred Dreyfus. Continuing the theme of death, under the lion at Place Denfert-Rochereau, stretch the **Catacombes** (Tue–Sun 10am–8pm, closed public hols; charge), miles of underground tunnels containing six million skeletons, stacked against the walls.

Chic St-Germain

Heading back towards the river from Montparnasse is a quarter of the city that has always seemed to have a quality of charm, bohemianism and privilege, **St-Germain-des–Prés**.

North of the Jardin du Luxembourg, the great bulk of **St-Sulpice ⑰** looms among the narrow streets, harmonious except for its ill-matching towers.

The crossroads at the 11th–12th-century church of **Saint-Germain-des-Prés ⑱**, which once belonged to one of the most powerful abbeys in

The Orsay museum clock, and a glimpse of the Sacré-Coeur.

the land, is another gathering place, the most chic on the left bank. Here the cafés **Flore** and **Deux Magots**, favoured by well-dressed intellectuals, face the **Brasserie Lipp**, where (rumour has it) only the most famous politicians and authors are invited to sit by the windows. There are a number of fine shops in the streets around here. Behind the abbey, is the delightful **Rue de Furstenberg**, and at No. 6 the **Musée Delacroix ⑲** (www.musee-delacroix.fr; Wed–Mon 9.30am–5pm; charge) shows that painter's work in his apartment and atelier

Lively and stylish streets abound in St-Germain. **Rue de Buci** is thronged with people shopping in its colourful daily market (except Mon). **Rue de Seine, Rue Bonaparte, Rue Jacob and Rue des Beaux-Arts** (where Oscar Wilde expired in a seedy hotel at No 13, now L'Hôtel, a luxury establishment), are full of modern art galleries and high-end shops. The **Ecole des Beaux-Arts**, facing the river, is the country's foremost school of art. In between here and the Musée d'Orsay, **Quai Voltaire** is lined with antique

View of the Eiffel Tower from the top of Tour Montparnasse.

shops and was once home to Wagner, Sibelius, Baudelaire and Voltaire.

Orsay

The long-abandoned train station, Gare d'Orsay, was given a new purpose in the 1980s when it became one of the city's foremost art galleries, **Musée d'Orsay** ⑳ (www.musee-orsay.fr, Tue–Sun 9.30am–6pm, Thu until 9.45pm; charge). Preserving the building's belle-époque architecture, Gae Aulenti redesigned the inner space into several exhibition levels, while keeping the airy majesty of the original train station. Devoted to works of the last half of the 19th century, it includes famous canvases by Monet, Manet, Renoir, Van Gogh and Cézanne. Major renovations completed in 2012 have rendered the gallery less a railway station and more an impressive display space; particularly striking is the revamped Impressionist Gallery. Do not miss the opulent restaurant.

The emperor's tomb

Most people who visit the **Hôtel des Invalides** ㉑ approach this impressive monument from the north side, facing the river, but a less sterile and imposing first view offers itself from the perspective of the **Avenue de Breteuil**. Laid out in 1680, this avenue rolls forth like a long green carpet to the **Place Vauban**. As one nears the dome, its vast proportions become evident.

Louis XIV ordered the construction of the Hôtel des Invalides in 1671, to serve as a home for disabled soldiers. In fact, it functioned as a clearing house for war veterans, many of whom, despite their infirmities, were sent to guard fortified places all over France. The regimen was strict: those who arrived late for meals sat at isolated tables in the middle of the refectory, drinking only water.

The graceful dome, topped by a spire reaching 102 metres (336ft), originally capped the Royal Church. Today, the building houses the tombs of French military heroes, including Vauban, Turenne and Foch.

It also contains the **Musée de l'Armée** (www.musee-armee.fr; daily Apr–Oct 10am–6pm, Nov–Mar 10am–5pm, closed first Mon of each month and

Musée d'Orsay: from the museum's upper level visitors get a strong sense of the original railway station layout.

public hols; charge), the world's largest military museum. In the former dining hall, now the **Salle des Armures**, magnificent suits of armour are displayed, and in the same wing is a fine collection of early arms and battle dress. The facing wing is dedicated to the world wars, and includes some of the famous Marne Valley taxis – cabs that were mobilised in World War I and contributed to the key victories in the valley.

The Invalides is probably most widely known for the **Tomb of Napoleon I** (charge). In 1840, King Louis-Philippe gave permission to bring the emperor's remains back to Paris from St Helena, the island where the fallen emperor had died in exile. A roaring crowd greeted the funeral chariot on 15 December. According to Victor Hugo, it resembled a "mountain of gold". Decorated with eagles, golden bees and 14 statues of victory carrying the symbolic coffin, the gilded creation weighed 11,818kg (26,000lbs). The coffin was then set in the church of the **Dôme** for 10 days as admirers filed through. The present sarcophagus in red porphyry rock was designed shortly afterwards by Visconti and has since stood directly under the dome.

Eve in the garden

A more peaceful spot is the nearby **Musée Rodin** ⑫ (www.musee-rodin.fr; Tue–Sun 10am–5.45pm, closed some public hols; charge) in the recently renovated **Hôtel Biron**, where the sculptor lived and worked. The setting is sublime, and visitors can admire a number of Rodin's most celebrated works (including *The Thinker*, *The Gates of Hell*, *Eve* and *The Burghers of Calais*) in the charming garden of roses, trees and ponds. Inside, the various models for his statue of Balzac, which shocked the city officials, are alongside the collection of drawings, etchings and studies. Early critics accused the artist of making plaster-casts of real bodies and pouring his bronze into them. The museum is a magical place to savour the master sculptor's work.

A short walk away is the popular **Musée du Quai Branly** ⑬ (www.quaibranly.fr; Tue–Wed and Sun 11am–7pm, Thu–Sat 11am–9pm; charge), a fabulous collection of artefacts, interactive

Looking up into the dome of Les Invalides.

Speeding up the Eiffel Tower by lift.

Taking in the spectacular view from the top of the tower.

displays and audiovisual installations on tribal arts from all over the world. The colourful building was designed by Jean Nouvel.

Just along the quai is Paris's most famous monument, the **Tour Eiffel ㉔** (www.toureiffel.paris/en.html; daily mid-June–Aug 9am–midnight, Sept–mid-June 9.30am–11pm; charge, booking in advance is advisable). Erected for the Universal Exhibition of 1889, the 300-metre (985ft) tower designed by Gustave Eiffel was snubbed by intellectuals. But ordinary people grew fond of it as it rose up slowly, and cheered when Eiffel himself climbed up to plant a French flag on the top. The aesthetic debate raged on for years. Ultimately, telegraphic communications saved the tower, which became a relay station and it is still used for radio.

You have a choice of being whisked up by lift or taking the 704 steps to the second floor. The view is spectacular, whether you stand at the bottom and watch the iron framework whooshing up, or look down at Paris from above. You can then go by lift or up further steps to the viewing platform. The

newly designed first floor features a transparent floor, which is not for the faint-hearted but is perfectly safe. Here you will find touch screens and the Eiffel Tower experience. The second floor has shops and restaurants. The best city-gazing is an hour before sunset. A modern lighting system provides stunning illumination after dark.

The rectangular park at the foot of the tower is the **Champ de Mars ㉕**. The former military parade ground has been used for popular celebrations (the first Bastille Day commemoration was held here on 14 July 1790) and military exercise. The park runs from the Seine to the **Ecole Militaire**, an 18th-century edifice designed by Jacques-Ange Gabriel.

Trocadéro

As you stand at the foot of the Eiffel Tower, your eye is carried across the river by the elegant span of the **Pont d'Iéna**. The buildings and terraces spread along the riverside on the far side of the bridge are known as the **Trocadéro**. The site was a wooded hill when Catherine de Medici built

a palace there, and Napoleon planned to build an imperial city, "a Kremlin a hundred times more beautiful than that of Moscow," on the spot. In 1827, Charles X had a fantastic stage-set installed to re-enact the battle of Fort Trocadéro in Cádiz, in which the French had intervened in Spain against the liberal government to restore the absolutist monarch Ferdinand IV, who had been held in the fort.

The **Palais de Chaillot** 26 dates from the International Exhibition of 1937. One wing holds the **Théâtre National de Chaillot**, devoted to monumental productions of both classical and modern plays. The **Musée de la Marine** (www.musee-marine.fr; Wed–Mon Apr–Sept 10am–6pm, Oct–Mar 1.30–6.30pm; charge) is also here. One of France's oldest museums, it has an extensive collection of model ships and marine items.

In the east wing are the **Musée de l'Homme** (closed for renovation until autumn 2015) covering mankind's origins, history and future, and the **Musée National des Arts Asiatiques – Guimet** (www.guimet.fr; Wed–Mon 10am–6pm; charge), which has a superb collection of Asian art and artefacts, notably Cambodian sculpture from Angkhor Wat. Here, too, is the **Cité de l'Architecture et du Patrimoine** (www.citechaillot.fr; Wed, Fri–Mon 11am–7pm, Thu until 9pm), which has three galleries showing developing architectural styles, and temporary exhibitions.

Grande bourgeoisie

Behind the Trocadéro is the ultra-chic **16th *arrondissement***, home to the *grande bourgeoisie* of Paris, as a quick look around at the sumptuous apartment buildings, expensive boutiques and exotic food markets will confirm.

Cut into the hillside near Passy Métro station on Square Charles Dickens are ancient wine cellars, today home to the **Musée du Vin** 27 (www.museeduvinparis.com; Tue–Sat 10am–6pm; charge), where visitors can study the tools of wine-making and the evolution of different bottles and glasses. The walls are covered with engravings, posters, sketches and watercolours, some of them quite funny. There is a

TIP

The best and certainly most romantic place to see the Eiffel Tower is from Trocadéro at night, when it is gloriously lit up and in full view at the end of Champ de Mars.

The Art Nouveau entrance to Abbesses metro station.

METRO STATIONS

It may sometimes be noisy, crowded, smelly and stuffy but Parisians have an unconcealed affection for, and pride in, their underground. For visitors it's usually a quick way to get around but it's worth taking a breath en route and looking at your surroundings.

Several stations have been turned into authentic works of art. Abbesses has a mosaic by Montmartre artists down its staircase. Arts et Metiers is like being in a steam punk submarine. Concorde spells out the *Declaration of the Rights of Man and of the Citizen*. Other stations given a cultural makeover include Louvre-Rivoli, Bastille, Hôtel de Ville, Tuileries, Parmentier, Pont-Neuf and Cluny-La Sorbonne. If you have nothing better to do, you could forget about the overground sights and spend a day exploring the Métro.

TIP

The Champs-Elysées is made for parades and it looks its best during the Bastille Day (14 July) parade, and at night when the Arc de Triomphe and Place de la Concorde are impressively floodlit.

shop with mouth-watering merchandise, and you can taste wines and have a light meal at Les **Echansons**.

On the top of the Passy hillside, the **Maison de Balzac ㉘** (Tue–Sun 10am–6pm, closed public hols, free entrance for the permanent collection only) has been converted into a museum where visitors can see mementos and manuscripts of Honoré de Balzac, whose many novels were set in early 19th-century Paris. The house was ideally suited for the ever-indebted author; while creditors knocked at the main entrance on Rue Raynouard, he slipped out the back on to Rue Berton.

Back on the river bank, another monumental vestige of the 1937 Exhibition is the **Palais de Tokyo ㉙** which contains in one wing, an adventurous space devoted to young international contemporary artists, and in the other the underrated municipal modern art collection, the **Musée d'Art Moderne de la Ville de Paris** (www.mam.paris.fr; Tue–Sun 10am–6pm, Thu until 10pm; charge).

Adjacent is the Pont de l'Alma. The road tunnel beneath the bridge is where Diana, Princess of Wales, had her fatal accident.

On the opposite side of the bridge at 93 Quai d'Orsay are **Les Egouts de Paris, The Paris Sewers ㉚** (Sat–Wed May–Sept 11am–5pm, Oct–Apr 11am–4pm; charge). This surprisingly entertaining experience includes a museum and an excursion through the city's sewer system.

Famous promenade

From the Place de l'Alma, the Avenue Marceau leads up to the **Arc de Triomphe ㉛**, in the centre of **Place Charles de Gaulle-Etoile**, which was completed in 1836 to commemorate the victories of the Napoleonic Empire. In 1920, an unknown soldier was buried beneath the arch and a flame marks his grave. If you want to climb to the top for the view and **museum** (daily Apr–Sept 10am–11pm, Oct–Mar 10am–10.30pm, closed public hols; charge) take the underground passage to the arch – the roundabout is notorious for heavy traffic.

The world's most famous street, the **Champs-Elysées ㉜**, leads you

Heartfelt graffiti mark the spot where the Princess of Wales and Dodi al-Fayed lost their lives.

DIANA AND DODI

The Pont de l'Alma was just another bridge across the Seine until the early hours of 31 August 1997 when a Mercedes travelling at high speed crashed in the underpass here. Three of its occupants died, including Diana, Princess of Wales and her boyfriend, Dodi al-Fayed, son of Mohammed Al Fayed, owner of The Ritz. The crash has been meticulously investigated by the French and British authorities, but is still the subject of fierce debate. The official version is that Henri Paul, the driver from the Ritz, was drunk and lost control of the car in a tragic accident. Sceptics point to inconsistencies in the evidence and allege that a more suspicious explanation is being covered up. The Flame of Liberty on the north side of the bridge has become an unofficial shrine to her memory.

elegantly back towards the city centre, people watching and window shopping on the way. Half-way down is the elegantly restored **Hôtel George V** (on the avenue of the same name), a dignified luxury hotel with beautiful sitting rooms and a fine courtyard restaurant.

The lower half of the avenue runs through majestic chestnut trees with several fine theatres and restaurants set among the trees. Here the **Grand Palais** ❸ (www.grandpalais.fr; Wed–Mon 10am–8pm; charge for temporary exhibitions) and the **Petit Palais** ❹ are two distinctive glass- and steel-domed museums built for the 1900 World Fair. They have changing exhibitions of 19th- and 20th-century paintings.

Across the other side of the avenue, at the end of Avenue de Marigny, is the **Palais de l'Elysée** ❺. Built as a country mansion, it is the official residence of the President of the Republic.

Continue walking and you emerge onto the **Place de la Concorde** ❻. The central **Obelisk**, which graced the tomb of Ramses II at Luxor 3,000 years ago, was erected on this spot in 1836. The greatest drama seen on the square was on 17 January 1793 when King Louis XVI was guillotined here. At 10am, the king arrived in a cart with his confessor and two *gendarmes*. He took off his coat and tie and mounted the scaffold. As the terrible roar of soldiers' drums filled the air, the king cried out *"Je suis perdu!"* (I am doomed!). His severed head was then held up for the crowd's inspection.

The Louvre

The **Jardin des Tuileries** ❼ continues the line of the Champs-Elysées towards the Louvre. The Tuileries were designed by landscape artist André Le Nôtre, who also conceived the park at Versailles and other royal gardens. The wide paths and small lawns in the midst of trees are dotted with stately stone statues.

At the Concorde end of the gardens, the small **Jeu de Paume** ❽ (www.jeu

depaume.org; Tue 11am–9pm, Wed–Fri noon–7pm, Sat–Sun 10am–7pm; charge) puts on exhibitions of photography. Just opposite is the **Musée de l'Orangerie** ❾ (www.musee-orangerie. fr; Wed–Mon 9am–5.45pm; charge), which contains Monet's magnificent "Water Lilies" series, as well as Cézannes and Renoirs.

Between the two wings of the palace which houses the Louvre is the **Jardin du Carrousel** ❿, ending in a square of the same name. Looking back you have one of the longest architectural vistas in the world, stretching all the way from this small arch past the obelisk and Concorde, through the Arc de Triomphe to the Grande Arche at La Défense, ghost-like in the distance.

The **Musée National du Louvre** ⓫ (www.louvre.fr; tel: 01 40 20 53 17; Wed–Mon 9am–6pm, Wed, Fri until 9.45pm; closed some public hols; charge; see page 140 for highlights of the galleries) revolves around a modern pyramid conceived by the Sino-American I.M. Pei and inaugurated in 1989. The design ingeniously disperses daylight around the ancient courtyard

Finding relaxation in the Jardin des Tuileries.

Fountain at Place de la Concorde.

and the foyer below, as well as providing multiple entrances to the Louvre's mighty galleries.

The original 13th-century palace was a royal residence until the Revolution in 1793, when it was turned into the world's largest museum. The collections are seemingly infinite, from Roman, Greek and Egyptian artefacts to Renaissance painting, and without a floor-plan it is easy to get lost. Getting lost may actually be a good way to find unexpected gems, but wander for too long without direction and you might miss even the major collections. You can pick up a map showing current exhibitions at the information desk on your way in. If it all gets too much, you can leave the museum and return on the same day, or you can rest and get a bite to eat at one of the Louvre's cafés and restaurants (try the Café Mollien, which overlooks the Cour Napoléon and the Carrousel Gardens). The museum also has some excellent shops selling souvenirs – but don't try to see everything in one day; go back again, and get lost in a different place.

One of the most dramatic features of the ongoing renovation of the Louvre is the Richelieu wing with two splendid light-flooded sculpture courts. Spectacular, too, are the Islamic Arts galleries in the lower ground floor, featuring a stunning undulating glass ceiling. The old favourites, however, are well signposted – *Mona Lisa* ("La Joconde" in French), *Winged Victory* and *Venus de Milo*.

In the wing along the Rue de Rivoli are the independently run **Musée de la Publicité**, devoted to advertising; the **Musée de la Mode et du Textile**, which is a fashion museum; and the **Musée des Arts Décoratifs** (all three open Tue–Sun 11am–6pm, Thu until 9pm, closed some public hols; charge).

At the Ritz

The medieval city that succeeded ancient Roman Lutetia huddled close about the walls of the Louvre. The maze of lanes and dead-end streets was so confusing that Queen Marie-Antoinette, preparing to flee Paris, wandered lost for two hours before discovering the royal coach waiting on the Rue de l'Echelle. Bonaparte made clearing the area an important part

Daniele da Volterna's two-sided David and Goliath (c.1555) takes pride of place in the centre of the Louvre's Grande Galerie.

of his ambitious urban programme. Nowadays, it is one of the most elegant parts of the city.

Across the Rue de Rivoli from the Louvre, overlooking two squares named after famous French writers, Colette and Malraux, is the **Comédie Française** ⓸, the revered classical theatre founded by Molière.

Beside it, the **Palais Royal** ⓺ was built by Cardinal Richelieu in the 17th century and willed to the king at his death. Anne of Austria moved here with her son, the future Louis XIV, because she preferred it to the gloomy Louvre.

The **Jardin du Palais Royal** ⓻ behind the palace is a tranquil park, surrounded by arcades with small, unusual shops. In the shaded gallery at the north end is the **Grand Véfour** restaurant, perhaps the most beautiful in Paris, its 18th-century listed interior and its food highly renowned. At the far end of the park, cross the street to enter two Parisian *galeries*, covered streets lined with shops. The **Galeries Colbert** and **Vivienne**, spacious and quiet, covered with high glass roofs,

are an oasis in the crush of midtown. Tea or lunch at **A Priori Thé** in the Vivienne Gallery is guaranteed to soothe the most jangled nerves.

The Grands Boulevards

The **Place Vendôme** ⓺, a short way up the Rue des Petits Champs, is a 17th-century marvel of harmony and now lined with luxury jewellers. The **Hôtel Ritz** is well suited to its surroundings. Its opulence created the word "ritzy". Hemingway once hoped that heaven would be as good as the Ritz; his ghost still haunts the bar that is named after him. Since then the hotel has earned notoriety through being where Diana, Princess of Wales and Dodi al-Fayed, spent their last hours before their fateful car journey. The Ritz was closed for refurbishment from 2013 to 2015; the grand re-opening is scheduled for the end of 2015.

The area north of here is known as the Grands Boulevards after its elegant avenues which were built straight and wide in the 19th century to replace untidy, crowded slums. The main axis is formed by streets running into

TIP

Each evening, one hour before curtain-rise at the Comédie Française, seats with reduced visibility of the stage are sold at low prices from the booth under the arches of Rue Richelieu behind the theatre. On the first Monday of the month under 28s get in free.

Reading in the Jardin du Palais-Royal.

Paris Fashion

French has traditionally been the language of fashion, and Paris its capital, where generations of designers have set the style for what every woman should be wearing.

The first of the style gurus in France was **Paul Poiret** (1879–1944). Born in the poor Les Halles neighbourhood, he worked for couture houses until 1903, when he opened his own house, and became famous as the man who released women from the corset – not for their comfort but in search of a look. After World War I, however, his clothes had begun to look dowdy in comparison with sleek and simpler creations of his new competitor, Gabrielle "**Coco" Chanel** who dominated fashion in the inter-war years.

World War II inevitably disrupted the world of fashion and after the conflict the world looked for change rather than a return to former styles. When **Christian Dior** presented his first collection (known as the "New Look") in 1947, he captured the mood of the post-war world, using extravagant yards of

Models pose in minidresses on the streets of Paris, 1969.

material after years of rationing and restraint. He shot to fame, becoming, some would say, a dictator of fashion. Other designers of his generation were **Pierre Balmain**, with an instinct for sophistication and elegance, and the tall aristocrat **Hubert de Givenchy** who dressed Audrey Hepburn in *Breakfast in Tiffany's*. Their success coincided with the rise of *Elle* magazine, founded in France in 1945, which would go on to be the largest fashion magazine in the world. It now prints 43 foreign editions in over 60 countries.

French fashion was to face another shake up in the 1960s, this time in response to the importation of youth culture from the US and Britain. **Yves St-Laurent**, groomed as a successor by Christian Dior, is considered the man of the 1960s and the inventor of *prêt a porter* – ready to wear. He once declared: *"the most beautiful way to dress a woman is with the arms of the man she loves,"* adding: *"but for those who haven't been lucky enough to find that happiness, I am here"*. **Pierre Cardin**, another doyen of French haute couture who started with Dior, is credited with the concept of unisex clothes and was instrumental in the 1960s vogue for futuristic fashion. **Paco Rabanne**, born in Spain but raised in France because of the civil war, is sometimes called the "enfant terrible" of the decade because of his use of unconventional materials.

The 1970s and '80s brought with them the omnipresence of the mass media and consequently the overarching importance of image and branding. **Jean-Paul Gaultier**, sometime TV personality and also a friend of the camera-friendly Madonna, knew how to project the necessary new kind of cool: controversial, provocative and attention-grabbing.

In the past three decades, the world of French fashion has seen three fundamental changes. The first is globalisation. French fashion is now led by big business rather than maverick creativity: a French name and slogan are all that is needed to imbue any product with the kind of insouciant cachet, and hence profitability, that marketing people cannot invent.

Simultaneously, Paris has seen the arrival of non-French designers at the head of its major fashion houses. The third change is that Paris has become only one among several international capitals of fashion. It still has major fashion shows that attract the elite, but it takes its place in the calendar alongside its equals, London, New York and Milan.

each other, Boulevard de la Madeleine (beginning at the squat 19th-century "Greek temple" of **La Madeleine**), Boulevard des Capucines and Boulevard des Italiens.

The beautiful **Palais Garnier – Opéra National de Paris** ⑯ (www. operadeparis.fr; daily 10am–5pm; charge), designed by Charles Garnier, completed in 1875 and now superbly renovated, occupies the central point where the great boulevards converge. This is a favourite quarter for strolling, shopping or sitting on a café terrace. The opera house is glorious. Inside, the majestic staircase and rich marble decorations evoke visions of swirling gowns, tuxedos and top hats. On rehearsal days, you can only peep through small portals at the auditorium and stage. But if it's possible, go in to look at the surprising **Marc Chagall ceiling**.

You may be irresistibly drawn to the pavement of the **Café de la Paix**, the most attractive café in town, also designed by Garnier and a frequent haunt of Oscar Wilde. Nearby are the top department stores **Galeries Lafayette** and **Printemps**.

Les Halles

South of the Place Vendôme, meanwhile, is the **Rue St-Honoré**, one of the city's surviving old streets and now an exclusive place to shop. Eastward, it extends past the Palais Royal to the Place Marguerite de Navarre.

Adjacent to it is the **Forum des Halles** ⑰ on the site of the old Paris market. The area has been undergoing renovation since 2011 and is due for completion in 2016. With larger metro and regional stations, revitalised shopping centre and a public garden it is designated to become the 'new heart of Paris.' Some of the old atmosphere does still exist, for example at **Pied de Cochon** (Rue Coquillière), which serves meals and hot onion soup night and day; and in pedestrianised **Rue Montorgueil**, where a colourful daily street market still operates.

The **Square des Innocents** on the southeast corner of the Forum occupies the site of the city's oldest cemetery, dating from the Gallo-Roman period. A ghastly spot surrounded by charnel houses, the cemetery absorbed some two million corpses before it was

The grand staircase at the Palais Garnier, perfect for making an entrance.

The glories of the Palais Garnier, home to the Paris opera.

FACT

In the Quartier de l'Horloge, a pedestrianised area just north of the Pompidou Centre, is a huge Defender of Time clock in brass and steel. On the hour, a life-size soldier does battle with either the dragon of earth, the bird of air or the crab of the sea. At 6 and 12, all attack.

emptied in 1786. The monumental Renaissance fountain here is the oldest fountain in Paris.

Contemporary culture

There's always a colourful crowd around the **Centre National d'Art et de Culture Georges Pompidou** ㊽ (www.centrepompidou.fr; Wed–Mon 11am–9pm, closed 1 May; charge), known locally as Beaubourg. Designed by an Italian-British team of architects (Renzo Piano and Richard Rogers), the building presents a glass facade supported totally by an external skeleton. Though some Parisians claim to detest it, the inside-out museum rapidly became one of the most visited attractions in town.

Within the Centre Pompidou, the galleries of the Musée National d'Art Moderne have a massive collection of Surrealists, Abstract Expressionists, early moderns and contemporary art. There are underground performance spaces, restaurants and a splendid view of Paris from the top floor, though you have to pay for it. The precinct below buzzes with crowds and performers of all kinds. On the square is the **Atelier**

Brancusi (Wed–Mon 2–6pm; charge included in Musée National d'Art Moderne), a reconstruction of the Romanian sculptor's studio.

The Marais

The **Marais** (literally, "swamp"), was *the* place for nobles to live in the 16th and 17th centuries. The charming streets were then neglected for 300 years, and the grand residences crumbled. Since the early 1960s the quarter has been renovated and the old mansions, the *hôtels particuliers*, renovated, and the area is now a mixture of rough charm and refined elegance. The character of Le Marais is today defined by its designer boutiques, trendy bars and cafés, and a thriving gay community.

The ornate neo-Renaissance **Hôtel de Ville** ㊾ (City Hall) on the Rue de Rivoli is the most monumental reminder of the neighbourhood's heyday. The original 16th-century structure was burned to the ground on 24 May 1871 by angry *communards* (see page 41). One year later, architect Viollet-le-Duc directed a scrupulous (though much enlarged) restoration.

The "inside-out" Centre Pompidou, aka Beaubourg.

THE LAST GRAND MASTER

The order of Knights Templar was founded in the Holy Land around 1119 and grew to be both rich and powerful. In 1307, however, its 23rd and last Grand Master, Jacques de Molay, was arrested without warning while he was in Paris. This was on the orders of King Philip the Fair who had grown jealous of the wealth of the Templars to whom he had become deeply in debt. Under torture Molay confessed to heresy, but he later retracted his confession. The order was suppressed in 1312, and Molay was burned at the stake two years later. According to legend, Molay declared from his pyre that his persecutors, Philip and Pope Clement V, would soon stand judgment with him before God. Clement died the month after and seven months later Philip was killed in a hunting accident.

Behind the Hôtel de Ville and off Rue de Rivoli, **Rue Vieille du Temple** winds into the oldest section of the Marais. The street takes its name from the Knights Templar, a medieval order of warrior monks, which was suppressed by the king of France in 1312. The knights either disappeared or went underground and their huge fortress continued to be used as a prison. In 1793, Louis XVI went to the guillotine from here and his son, Louis XVII, stayed on but mysteriously disappeared, aged 10, in 1795. It subsequently became a place of pilgrimage for royalists, so Napoleon I had it pulled down. The little that remains can be seen in Square du Temple, a tree-lined garden with outdoor table tennis.

The **Rue des Rosiers** is the heart of the Jewish quarter. The excellent kosher restaurants and shops sell products from Eastern Europe and the Middle East. The history of France's Jewish community, along with items from all over the Jewish diaspora, are displayed in the beautiful Hôtel St-Aignan at 71 Rue du Temple, now the **Musée d'Art et d'Histoire du Judaïsme** ⑤⓪ (www.mahj.org; Mon–Fri 11am–6pm, Sun 10am–6pm, closed some Jewish holidays; charge). At 17 Rue Geoffrey l'Asnier is the **Mémorial de la Shoah** (www.memorialdelashoah. org; Sun–Fri 10am to 6pm, Thu until 10pm), the most important centre in Europe devoted to the holocaust, with a permanent exhibition and a Wall of Names – 76,000 of them, which took six archivists two years to complete.

The story of Paris

To discover more about the history of Paris, including the Marais, visit the **Musée Carnavalet** ⑤① (www.carnavalet. paris.fr; Tue–Sun 10am–6pm; closed public hols) at 23 Rue de Sévigné. The area has retained a strong cultural identity and is the site of many special festivities. The house itself once belonged to Mme de Sévigné, 17th-century authoress and vicious gossip, whose *Letters* revealed the intricacies of aristocratic life at court. She was born, baptised and married in the Marais, where she also died.

Elegant Parisian interiors can be seen in the **Musée Cognacq-Jay** (Tue–Sun

A preserved shopfront in the Marais tells of times gone by.

The Colonne de Juillet with the Bastille opera house in the background.

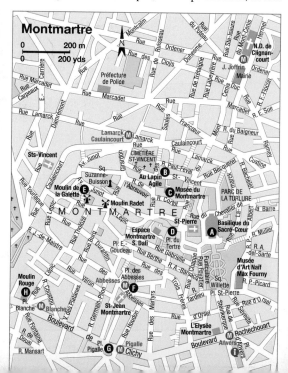

One of the elegant archways leading off the Place des Vosges.

10am–5pm; closed public hols), at 8 Rue Elzévir, the former home of La Samaritaine department store owner. Furnished as a private house, it contains paintings by Rembrandt and Canaletto.

Nearby, at Place Thorigny, the **Musée Picasso Paris** (www.musee picassoparis.fr; Tue–Fri 11.30am–6pm, Sat–Sun 9.30am–6pm, every 3rd Fri until 9pm, closed some public hols; charge) occupies the **Hôtel Salé**, built by a wealthy tax collector. Picasso's family donated a large collection of his works to the state, in lieu of huge inheritance tax payments due after the painter's death. The well-organised collection, comprising the world's largest of Picasso's work, is displayed in this beautiful Renaissance setting.

Behind the *hôtel*, down the Rue Birague, is charming 17th-century **Place des Vosges** , named after the first region to pay taxes to the new Republic. The rectangular *place*, the oldest in Paris, is where the writer Victor Hugo lived. You can visit his house, **Maison Victor Hugo** (www. maisonsvictorhugo.paris.fr; Tue–Sun 10am–6pm, closed public hols) at No.

6, where such literary luminaries as Balzac and Dumas used to visit, and see manuscripts and notes, and also his drawings and handmade furniture.

Bastille

The eastern limit of the Marais is marked by the **Place de la Bastille**. This was the site of the dreaded prison constructed in the 14th century, whose walls were about 11 metres (35ft) thick in some places, protected by high battlements and heavy artillery. Despite the apparently impregnable walls, the Bastille fell before the onslaught of the furious population on 14 July 1789. "Is it a revolt?" asked Louis XVI. "No sire," he was told, "a revolution." The hated jail was completely destroyed and in its place was eventually erected, in 1840, the towering **Colonne de Juillet** commemorating the victims of a second revolution in July 1830.

Dominating the Place de la Bastille is the **Opéra de Paris Bastille** , another monument to glass and concrete, opened in 1989. The "opera of the people" has been dogged by scandal and criticism, but has led to

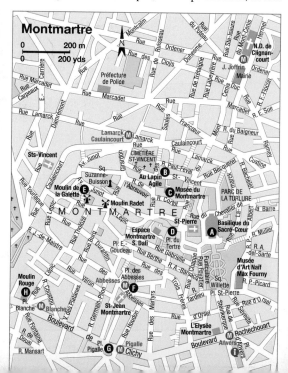

Montmartre

0   200 m
0   200 yds

legendary **Moulin Rouge**  is on Place Blanche, most recently immortalised in the Baz Luhrmann movie *Moulin Rouge!* (2001) starring Nicole Kidman and Ewan McGregor. The windmill is neon-lit now and most of the audience arrive by tour bus. Though they still perform a version of French can-can, the girls are more modestly clothed than in the Belle Epoque although champagne is still obligatory.

Pigalle is changing all the time which makes it a good place to find more dynamic and contemporary nightlife as new venues emerge from seedy pasts to become hip dance clubs and trendy bars and music venues. In fact, the area known as South Pigalle (or SoPi for the hipsters) is the latest trendsetting neighbourhood in the capital. Stroll down Rue des Martyrs and Rue Clauzel to discover the latest in coffee shops, cocktail bars and trendy fashion boutiques.

Further Out

An excellent transport system means that places outside the city centre are easy to reach, and can make a good half-day break.

Père Lachaise

East of the city centre is the **Cimetière du Père Lachaise** ①. This graveyard with streets and boulevards, aboveground monuments and regular visitors feeding the wild cats, is like a miniature city. You can buy a map of some of the many famous gravesites. These include the tombs of Abélard and Héloise, Rossini, Chopin, Edith Piaf, Gertrude Stein, Molière, Oscar Wilde, Sarah Bernhardt, Marcel Proust, Simone Signoret and Yves Montand, and The Doors' lead singer Jim Morrison.

The French who visit the cemetery usually make a point of seeing the **Mur des Fédérés**: in 1871, the last of the insurgents from the *Commune de Paris* took a stand among the sepulchres of the hilly cemetery. They were trapped and executed against the wall, which still bears the marks of the fatal rounds. Rumour was that some of the *communards* had escaped detection and were living in Père Lachaise

QUOTE

"I want my heart to be preserved in a pitcher of Vin de Beaujolais in the restaurant in Place du Tertre on the summit of Montmartre."

John Dos Passos

The Moulin Rouge – you can't miss it.

One of the most visited graves in Cimetière du Père Lachaise is that of Jim Morrison, which has become a shrine for his fans. Graffiti ensures you will not miss it and security has had to be implemented to protect it from further vandalism.

secretly. Even today, there are rumours of strange and unwholesome goings-on after nightfall.

La Villette

From Place de la Bastille it is possible to skirt the city centre by boat in a two-and-a-half hour trip along the **Canal Saint Martin**, through a tunnel and several locks, to Porte de la Villette. Here, the old slaughterhouses have been transformed into the high-tech **Parc de la Villette ❷**. The **Géode**, a huge geodesic dome covered with polished steel mirror surfaces, houses a hemispheric cinema screen that takes you on a journey from the galaxies to the depths of the oceans, while next door the **Cinaxe** uses flight-simulation techniques to show films in 3D.

The **Cité des Sciences et de l'Industrie** (www.cite-sciences.fr; Tue–Sat 10am–6pm, Sun 10am–7pm; charge) is a futuristic museum, celebrating human ingenuity with interactive exhibits.

In contrast, the solidly 19th-century **Grande Halle** on the other side of the canal seems a relic from the Iron Age. Next door is the new, Jean

Nouvel-designed **Philharmonie de Paris** (www.philharmoniedeparis.fr; Tue–Sat noon–6pm, Sun 10am–6pm; charge), with a museum of the history of music, plus concert halls and studios.

The Bois de Boulogne

Across the other side of Paris is the city's green lung, the **Bois de Boulogne ❸**, a lovely 872-hectare (2,500-acre) park on the western edge of Paris. The several lakes and the many paths through the woods as well as the **Longchamps Racetrack** are all popular with city dwellers. However, it is not a good place to wander around after dark because of crime and prostitution.

Especially beautiful is **Pré-Catelan** with an outdoor theatre, the **Jardin Shakespeare**. In this enchanted spot, gardeners have tried to plant every type of tree, bush and flower that the Bard spoke of in his plays.

Another favourite spot in the park is the **Parc de Bagatelle**, with a magnificent rose garden, where some 1,200 varieties bloom along the fragrant paths.

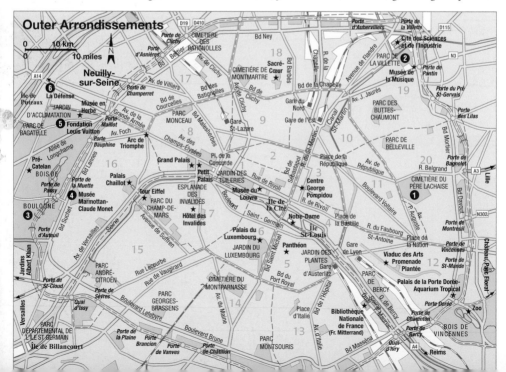

Outer Arrondissements

e St-Pierre. Not far from the *étangs* (ponds) lies pretty **Château de Pierre-fonds** ⓫ (May–Aug daily 9.30am–6pm, Sept–Apr Tue–Sun 10am–1pm and 2–5.30pm, closed public hols; charge). It is a strange monument: a medieval castle built in the 19th century. Architect Viollet-le-Duc undertook the restoration for Napoleon III, who used it for hunting and entertaining. At the fall of the Second Empire, the castle became government property.

Disneyland

At Marne-la-Vallée, 32km (20 miles) east of the city is **Disneyland Paris** ⓬ (www.disneylandparis.co.uk; daily from 10am, closing times vary throughout the year, for details call 0825 30 05 00; RER line A, or a TGV train from Roissy-Charles de Gaulle airport takes 15 minutes, or take a shuttle bus from Orly airport; charge). A little piece of America dropped into the French countryside it is built around a fun park divided into five themed areas: Main Street USA, Frontierland, Adventureland, Fantasyland and Discoveryland (high-tech wizardry). Alongside it is Walt Disney Studios Park with shows and activities about the business of film-making.

The best way to benefit fully from your time here is to decide what you want to do in order of priority and get there early, as, by midday, queues at the most popular rides can be up to 45 minutes long. You should also be aware that long-term closures do occur for refurbishment to attractions; check the website for further details when you travel.

Once through the turnstiles, you enter **Main Street USA**. City Hall, on the left, is the central information centre, a contact point for lost children and property. Here, too, is the Main Street station (possible closure Aug 2015–Aug 2016), from where the Disneyland train (possible closure Aug 2015–Feb 2016) circles the park. The station is often quite crowded, so it is a good idea to get on the train at one of the other stations en route.

What many small children love best is the daily parade of Disney characters, which goes round both parks each afternoon.

Frontierland, to the left of Main Street, evokes dreams of the Wild West.

Children can meet their animation heroes at Disneyland Resort Paris.

Thrills, hopefully without the spills, courtesy of Parc Astérix.

GETTING AROUND

The Ile de France has a good integrated transport system. Where the Métro gives out, the five lines of the RER (denominated A to E) take over and the two systems are integrated, sharing stations, making it easy to switch between the two. The RER network is extended by the SNCF's Transilien lines (lettered H, J, K, L, N, P, R, U), departing from the main stations to reach most places in the Ile de France and also parts of Normandy, Picardy and Centre region, giving you more than one choice for a journey. Ensure you have the right ticket. Fares jump once you get outside zones 1 and 2, and an ordinary "t+" Métro ticket will not do. You need a "billet Origine-Destination" for the specific journey. If you buy a *mobilis* ticket make sure it covers the zones you will be travelling to.

Nocturnal pyrotechnics, part of an equestrian display at Provins.

Château de Vaux-le-Vicomte.

Its centrepiece, **Big Thunder Mountain** (possible closure Nov 2015–Dec 2016), is a towering triumph of red rock reminiscent of every Western movie you have ever seen. **Adventureland** contains another top attraction, the **Pirates of the Caribbean** (possible closure Jan–June 2017), whose water ride through tropical swamp to the open sea is orchestrated by jovially barbaric Disney workers.

Le Temple du Péril, near Explorers' Club Restaurant, is a stomach-churning ride in carts that plunge through rainforest and turn upside down above a mock archaeological dig inspired by the *Indiana Jones* sagas.

The most popular land for younger children is **Fantasyland**, containing Sleeping Beauty's Castle – the centrepiece of the park – and Snow White and the Seven Dwarfs. **Discoveryland** provides an assortment of futuristic high-tech experiences.

Walt Disney Studios begins with **Front Lot**, an elaborate film set, with hundreds of movie props. **Animation Courtyard** is Disney's homage to the art of the cartoon. In **Production Courtyard**, shows and productions take place almost every day in the Walt Disney Television Studios.

Back Lot is where most of the thrills are: the special-effects facility, the music recording stages and the stunt workshops. The highlight of the Back Lot is the **Stunt Show Spectacular**. Staged up to five times a day, the live action trashes cars, motorcycles and jet skis in a crescendo of movie stunts performed in a Mediterranean village seaside set. New for 2014 Ratatouille: The Adventure, is a fun-packed 4D experience, when you are shrunk to rat-size and whisked away in a ratmobile, as you hurtle across the rooftops of Paris. Dropped into the kitchens you are chased by various huge chefs wielding enormous kitchen tools.

Provins

One of France's lesser known World Heritage sites is **Provins** ⑱, 95km (60 miles) southeast of Paris. The former capital of the Counts of Champagne has 58 listed monuments and received its citation for being a "town of medieval fairs". It looks down on the valley

of the Seine from a ridge and has formidable 12th- and 13th-century ramparts. It's most splendid monument is the castle keep, the Tour de César which, despite its name and the legend attached to it, was built more than a millennium after Julius Caesar passed this way.

Vaux-le-Vicomte

East of Paris the inspiration for Versailles can be seen at the wonderful house and gardens of the **Château de Vaux-le-Vicomte ⑭** (www.vaux-le-vicomte. com; early Mar–early Nov daily 10am–6pm; charge). It was commissioned by Nicolas Fouquet who was appointed treasurer to Sun King Louis XIV in 1653 and used his privileged position to amass a fortune. A patron of the arts, he supported Molière and Jean de la Fontaine, and organised extravagant parties that were the talk of the town. When he decided to build a country palace, he called on the finest designers: architect Le Vau and landscapist Le Nôtre.

They chose a site near the ancient town of **Melun** (by car on N6 or A5 or by train from Gare de Lyon). The park was Le Nôtre's first major work, and the elegant symmetry of the garden is echoed by the château. The blue water in the pools, the green velvet lawns and the sandy pathways set off to perfection the warm stone and slate-blue roofs of the building.

When it was completed in 1661 Fouquet organised a grand *fête* to celebrate the king's birthday. The fountains sprayed, musicians played and torches sparkled everywhere. A fantastic show, including dancing horses (some of them drowned in the moat), was given for the king's enjoyment. But Louis was not amused. He was outraged at the display of Fouquet's wealth and panache. His aide Colbert assured him that the treasurer's fortune had been stolen from the king's own coffers. Fouquet was arrested and imprisoned at Vincennes. But Louis' pride still wasn't satisfied. He ordered Le Vau and Le Nôtre to build another, bigger palace, sparing no expense. They did, and while Fouquet grew old and died in prison, the Sun King and his court shone at his new palace at Versailles. Visitors can relive the château's history

Medieval jousting re-enacted at Provins.

Weird and wonderful rock formations, beloved by climbers, are a feature of Fontainebleau forest.

The intricate carvings inside Chartres Cathedral.

in candlelit visits on Saturday nights from May to early October.

Fontainebleau

Melun, 50 km (40 miles) south of Paris, sits on the northern edge of the beautiful **Forêt de Fontainebleau**, 200 sq km (77 sq miles) of oak, beech, birch and pine, incorporating 300km (185 miles) of walking trails. There are weird giant rock formations in the forest, and local alpinists and climbers stay in shape by scurrying up them.

The station (reached from Gare de Lyon) is in the suburb of Avon, in the heart of the woods, and is a starting point for cyclists, picnickers, mushroom hunters and bird watchers. The centre of **Fontainebleau** ⓯ is dominated by the rambling **Château de Fontainebleau** (www.musee-chateau-fontainebleau. fr; Wed–Mon Apr–Sept 9.30am–6pm, Oct–Mar 9.30am–5pm, closed some public hols; charge). The first royal residence was erected in the 12th century and every subsequent royal inhabitant left his mark on the hunting palace. The most remarkable work was commissioned by François I in the 16th century.

In the long, airy gallery and ballroom, you can almost hear the swish of voluminous skirts, the satin dancing slippers and the music drifting out to mingle with the sounds of the forest.

The château bid *adieu* to regal splendour in 1814, when Napoleon I parted company with the Imperial Guards before going into exile in the aptly named **Cour des Adieux**. His **Throne Room** can be visited on guided tours.

The Barbizon school

Close by, **Barbizon** ⓰ is a village famed for its links with 19th-century artists, when landscape painters Rousseau and Millet settled here and formed the Ecole de Barbizon. The **museum** of the school is in the Auberge du Père Ganne (Wed–Mon 10am–12.30pm, 2–5.30pm, July–Aug until 6pm; charge), while Rousseau's studio is open for occasional exhibitions.

In **Milly-la-Forêt** ⓱, there is an impressive **marketplace** where people have been shopping beneath the massive wooden *halles* since 1479. Now the square is surrounded by high-priced antiques shops and property agents, none offering anything as beautiful as the rough-hewn beams of the simple shelter.

Another old tradition in the area is the cultivation of medicinal herbs and flowers. These plants, known as *simples*, were first grown around a 12th-century leprosarium. When it was demolished, only the **Chapelle St-Blaise-des-Simples** remained (May–Oct 10am–6pm, Mar–Apr 10am–12.30pm, 2–6pm, Nov–Dec Sat–Sun 2–5pm; charge) and it still stands today. Poet Jean Cocteau decorated the chapel in 1958. Flowers grow up the walls, around tiny stained-glass windows, and a frisky cat is poised to leap into the holy water font. Above the altar, Cocteau painted the resurrection of Christ in pure lines and delicate colours. In the woods outside Milly-la-Forêt stands **Le Cyclop** (for guided visits only Apr–mid-Nov Fri–Sun 2–6.30pm; charge), a massive kinetic iron and mirror sculpted

monster created by Jean Tinguely, which can be clambered over via a series of ladders and galleries.

Northwest of Fontainebleau, in the lovely *département* of Les Yvelines, is the summer home of the president of France, the ivy-clad **Château de Rambouillet** ⓲ (for guided visits only; daily Apr–Sept 10am, 11am, 2pm, 3pm, 4pm & 5pm; Oct–Mar 10am, 11am, 2pm, 3pm & 4pm ; closed public hols & during official residence; charge). The **Forêt de Rambouillet** is the region's richest hunting ground, reserved today for the *chasse à courre*, running with hounds.

Chartres

Another favourite day trip from Paris is to **Chartres** ⓳, 97km (60 miles) southwest of the city. The attractive medieval town sits upon a plateau hemmed in by wheat fields, on the banks of the Eure. The first glimpse of the lofty spires of the **Cathedral** (www.cathedrale-chartres. org; daily 8.30am–7.30pm; charge for tower) rising above the rich plain – exactly as 13th-century pilgrims must have seen them – is magical.

Begun in 1194, the cathedral took only 30 years to construct, lending it an architectural unity and an air of perfection. Before you enter, be sure to take a look at the intricate carvings on the door known as the **Portail Royal**. The 13th-century **stained-glass windows** represent the world's most remarkable collection, measuring a total of 2,499 sq metres (26,900 sq ft). The three large **Rose Windows** fill the cathedral with changing patterns of light and colour. An ancient labyrinth is inlaid in the nave floor. It is not known exactly what its use was but it is possible that penitents followed its serpentine path on their knees.

Parts of the crypt below date from the 9th century. Having plumbed the depths of this beautiful building, climb to the top of the tower, where sunlight and shadows will make your spirits soar.

The major restoration work taking place begun in 2009 is due for completion in 2017. The controversial project has been subject to criticism for its aim to restore the cathedral to its 13th-century origins, considered by some to be an impossible task.

FACT

Fontainebleau has been called "a rendezvous of châteaux" because it incorporates buildings of so many different periods.

The halles in Milly-la-Forêt's market-place.

The vineyards of Hautvillers, in the Champagne region.

THE NORTH

The north can be thought of as a frontier, since
it is greatly influenced by France's neighbours.
Where once battles were fought, now
international connections are being forged.

*An iron sign in the
Champagne region.*

The four regions that spread across France's porous
northern border with Belgium, Luxembourg and
Germany were on the front line in the 20th century's two world wars. Travelling from west to east, **Le
Nord** begins with the luminous Côte d'Opale, the coast
of the North Sea and English Channel, with Nord-
Pas-de-Calais and Picardy. The largest town here is the
Flemish industrial and commercial city of Lille, which
has reinvented itself with great flair as a euro-shopping
centre. It is hard to avoid the memories of the Somme
battlefield where hundreds of thousands of soldiers per-
ished during the Great War. Inspiring places to visit are Amiens with
its enormous cathedral, Arras and Douai.

Champagne is the most northerly wine-producing area of France,
though it started out producing red wines before it discovered fizz.
The capital, Reims, has an extraordinary Gothic cathedral that was the
traditional place of coronation for the kings of France.

Lorraine, next door, has always been an industrial
region but its two largest cities, Metz and Nancy are
packed with historical monuments. Less obvious sights
to see are Verdun, scene of historic resistance in 1916-
18 and the redundant forts of the Maginot Line built
between the wars.

Standing apart from the other regions for its cultural
cohesiveness is **Alsace**, squeezed between the Vosges hills
and the mighty Rhine river. Alsatian cuisine is highly
regarded, and the region produces fine white wines and
excellent beers. It has many pretty – almost too pretty –
towns and villages to explore.

World War I graves at Verdun.

Alsace is influenced by its associations with Germany,
although its capital city Strasbourg prefers these days to think of itself
as an international metropolis that happens to be in France. And this
attitude could easily symbolise the whole of the north.

LE NORD

First World War battlefields and war memorials recall
the region's beleaguered past but Gothic cathedrals
and handsome historic towns celebrate its glories.

Paris

Flanders (officially the region of Nord-Pas-de-Calais) and Picardy provide a first taste of France for visitors arriving across the Channel from Great Britain. The landscapes are mostly flat and arable but any drabness is compensated for by history and culture, and the lack of hills makes it easy to get around. Lille apart, towns and cities are mostly of modest size.

In the frontier region of the north influences of France and the Low Countries intermingle to create towns that are by turns cosy and elegant, with ornate Flemish brickwork interspersed with sober French classicism. Terraced cafés, chic shops and classical boulevards vie with Flemish gables and vaulted cellars, belfries and carillon concerts, rich tapestries and old masters. Beer, hearty stews and *moules-frites* are as acceptable as French fine wines and good cuisine. Progressing south, closer to Paris, Picardy is unmistakeably French as can be seen in the uncompromising architecture of its great Gothic cathedrals.

Around Dunkerque

The town closest to the Belgian border, and the only French port on the North Sea, **Dunkerque** (Dunkirk) ➊ is associated with the mass evacuation of British and French troops in May 1940. Having been driven back to the sea by the German Panzer division,

the British Expeditionary Force was cut off from the retreating French army. Some 337,000 soldiers, a third of them French, were taken off the beaches in a flotilla of 900 vessels. To the British, the evacuation was a miracle without which the war would have been lost. To the French, at the time, it represented defeat and the desertion of an ally. A brave rearguard of 30,000 French soldiers had to be left behind to the mercy of the Germans.

The city itself was virtually destroyed by bombardment in the same year

Main Attractions
Bergues
La Coupole
Côte d'Opale
Amiens
Somme battlefield
Arras
Le Cateau-Cambrésis
Douai
Lille

The docks at Dunkerque.

and there is not much of interest to see except the **Musée Portuaire** (daily 10am–12.30pm, 1.30pm–6pm; charge) in a hulking tobacco warehouse on Quai de la Citadelle, which is dedicated to the port's maritime past, with restored tall ships alongside it.

A short way inland is **Bergues ❷**. This fortified, partially moated wool town possesses a baroque gabled pawnshop, now a museum of Flemish and French treasures, and is crowned by medieval and Vauban fortifications. The place became famous in 2008 as the location for the comedy film *Bienvenue chez les Ch'tis* (*Welcome to the Sticks*) which either made fun of the people of the north, or fun of French stereotypes of them however you prefer to see it. The common nickname

for the people of Nord department, Ch'ti, supposedly derives from the local way of saying "*C'est toi? – C'est moi*": "*Ch'est ti? – Ch'est mi*".

Rocket bunker

Further inland, southwest of St Omer, is **La Coupole ❸** (www.lacoupole-france.co.uk; daily Jul–Aug 10am–7pm, rest of the year 9am–6pm; charge), a bunker from which V2 rockets were fired during the last months of World War II in a bid to destroy London or at least the morale of its inhabitants. The first long-range ballistic missile, and the first to reach the stratosphere, the V2 was the forerunner of modern rockets. Its speed and high trajectory made it invulnerable to anti-aircraft fire or fighter planes. The only

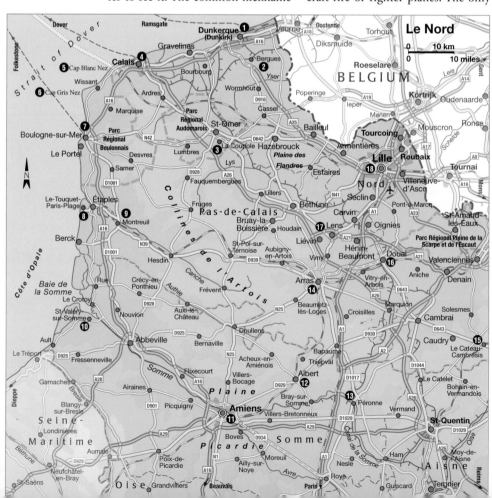

effective countermeasure was to find and destroy its launch facilities.

The Opal Coast

The dunes, beaches and cliffs of the Côte d'Opale (Opal Coast – named by a local painter because of its ever-changing iridescent light) stretch from Calais to the Bay of the Somme. Sangatte, just south of the port of **Calais** ❹ is the arrival point of the Channel Tunnel – really three tunnels joined to each other. With 38km (23.5 miles) running under the bed of the English Channel (La Manche in French), it is the longest undersea tunnel in the world. The first proposal to build a tunnel for horse-drawn carriages was put forward in 1802, and even when it became technologically possible, there was concern in Britain about establishing a fixed link with the Continent until the 1950s lest another Napoleon or Hitler would make use of it to invade Britain. After 150 years of dreams and unfeasible (or bankrupt) projects, the tunnel was built at great expense, in collaboration between Britain and France, and opened in 1994.

The most scenic parts of the Côte d'Opale are its two capes, **Cap Blanc Nez** ❺, 134m (440ft) chalk cliffs and the more prominent but lower **Cap Gris Nez** ❻, site of a radar station controlling ships in the Straits of Dover, the busiest shipping lane in the world. At this point the English Channel becomes the North Sea.

Boulogne ❼ is the most important fishing port in France, landing 30 percent of the national catch. The medieval walled upper town, later fortified by Vauban, is well preserved, with picturesque cobbled streets and a cluster of historic buildings. Finest of these is the **Château-Musée** (Wed–Sat 10am–12.30pm, 2–5.30pm, Sun 10–12.30, 2.30–6pm, closed at Christmas; charge), completed in 1231, the first castle to be built without a keep.

Apart from strolls along the ramparts, Boulogne offers edible pleasures in the form of a morning fish market,

good restaurants and an excellent cheese shop, **Philippe Olivier** (43 Rue Thiers). Near the port is **Nausicaá** (www.nausicaa.co.uk; daily Sept–June 9.30am–6.30pm, July–Aug 9.30am–7.30pm, closed Jan; charge), a marine centre with aquaria and games.

Le Touquet

The soubriquet "Paris-Plage," gives **Le Touquet** ❽ a touch of the city sophistication it once had, after it was created in the late 19th century by the founder of Le Figaro newspaper. The resort, bounded by the sea, sand dunes and lush pine woods, has a horse racing track, casino and an air of faded gentility. The rich and fashionable sought to outdo each other with their modern villas, and today there are architectural tours of the town.

Inland is **Montreuil** ❾, a hill-top market town with a medieval citadel and Vauban gate, cosy cottages and half-timbered inns.

The mouth of the Somme has an ornithological reserve on its northern shore. Across the river is **St-Valery-sur-Somme** ❿ where William the

Contrasting towers at the Abbey of St Winoc, Bergues.

The cliffs of the Côte d'Opale.

QUOTE

"Now all the roads lead to France. And heavy is the tread Of the living; but the dead Returning lightly dance..."

Edward Thomas, killed in action, Arras, 1917

Conqueror amassed his fleet in 1066 before setting sail for England. The town has a medieval quarter with a château and one of the oldest abbeys in France, founded in the 7th century.

Memories of war

Amiens ⓫, the capital of Picardy, was devastated during both world wars and retains little of its past as a wealthy cloth town. The exception is the **Cathédrale Notre-Dame**, the largest in the country and the most impressive 20th-century survivor. Twice the size of Notre-Dame in Paris, the cathedral displays a grandiose façade. As a bridgehead, Amiens bore the brunt of attacks in 1918 and was set ablaze in 1940, with 60 percent of the city destroyed. As a result, the only charming quarter left is **St Leu**, the renovated millers' area beside the banks of the Somme, dotted with bars and brasseries.

East and northeast of Amiens is the scene of one of the bloodiest battles of modern warfare, the Somme. The town of **Albert** ⓬ is a good place to orient yourself and start the **Circuit du Souvenir** (the Route of Remembrance).

THE BATTLE OF THE SOMME

World War I (1914–18) was for much of its duration a bloody stalemate with both sides dug into trenches stretching from the North Sea to the Swiss border. The most infamous attempt to end the impasse was the series of offensives launched by British and French forces between 1 July and 18 November 1916, which have become known as the Battle of the Somme. The battle is notable for the importance of air power and for the first use of the tank.

The aim was to break through enemy lines and relieve the pressure on beleaguered Verdun to the east which had been almost taken by the Germans during the previous months.

A week of bombardment was a prelude to the first of a series of suicidal attacks by British and French forces along a front between Albert and Péronne. On that first day alone, British troops suffered over 57,000 casualties including almost 20,000 dead. Altogether, more than a million soldiers died in the Somme for an Allied gain of 16km (10 miles) of territory and no end to the military deadlock.

It has been argued that German forces were weakened by the onslaught and that the Somme can therefore be regarded as the turning point of the war but the price in human life can be seen in the memorials and museums that now mark the battlefield particularly at Albert, Péronne and Thiépval.

There is also a museum here, **Musée Somme 1916** (www.musee-somme-1916.eu; daily Jun–Sept 9am–6pm, Oct–May 9am–noon and 2–6pm, closed Jan; charge). The two other essential visits to get to know the story of the battle are the **Historial de la Grande Guerre** (http://en.historial.org; Apr–Sept 9.30am–6, Oct–Mar Thu–Tue 9.30am–5pm; charge) besides the château in **Péronne** ⓭ and **Thiépval** (northeast of Albert), a memorial to the 73,357 men who died between 1915 and 1918 but have no known grave.

Arras ⓮, to the north, suffered from shelling because of its proximity to the front until 1917. However, civic pride ensured that the capital of Artois embarked on dignified post-war reconstruction. The **Grand' Place** is somewhat austere, with serried ranks of 17th- and 18th-century gabled mansions standing on arcaded sections. On **Place des Héros**, visitors can appreciate the Flamboyant neo-Gothic town hall and belfry before visiting **les boves**, the labyrinth of medieval limestone passages beneath the city (guided tours only, ask at the tourist information office). These provided refuge in times of strife, from the 11th century to the Great War.

Southeast of Arras you can leave the horrific memories of the Western Front behind and visit the small town of **Le Cateau-Cambresis** ⓯, birthplace of Henri Matisse (1869–1954) and home to the **Musée Matisse** (www.museematisse.lenord.fr, Wed–Mon 10am–6pm, closed some public hols; charge) located in the 18th-century Palais Fénelon. Established by Matisse himself in 1952, it contains 170 works by the artist.

Douai ⓰, northeast of Arras, is a historic, sober city that retains its 18th-century design despite devastation in 1940. Douai's pride and joy is a magnificent Gothic belfry encrusted with turrets and pinnacles, surmounted by the Lion of Flanders.

Northwest is the former mining town of **Lens** ⓱, home to the Louvre

Lens, a futuristic annexe of the Louvre in Paris opened in 2012 (www.louvre-lens.fr; Wed–Mon 10am–6pm).

Lille

The capital of Nord-Pas-de-Calais region is an old industrial and commercial city that has been reborn in the last decades, not least because of its Eurostar station making it the nearest Continental shopping centre to London. Like Dijon and Brussels, **Lille** ⑱ was a force in the Burgundian Empire before becoming part of the Spanish Netherlands. Finally French in 1667, the city retains a Flemish heart and a Franco-Flemish stomach, best appreciated in the *estaminets*, the traditional brasseries in Vieux Lille – the old town. Lille's driverless Métro system is an efficient means of exploring the rest of the city.

The Palais Rihour on place Rihour houses the tourist office in a Burgundian palace while Rue Rihour shows Flemish and classical influences. The neighbouring **Grand'Place** is lined with café terraces and gabled mansions, notably the **Vieille Bourse** Ⓐ, the former stock exchange. The Flemish flair for illusionistic design means that thin gabled houses can be slotted into narrow passages concealing improbably large interlocking courtyards. **Rue de la Monnaie** is an elegant street lined by chic shops and brasseries. Here too is the atmospheric **Musée de l'Hospice Comtesse** Ⓑ (Wed–Sun 10am–6pm; charge). This intimate medieval foundation contains the former hospital, framed by an upturned keel roof.

The **Palais des Beaux-Arts** Ⓒ (www.pba-lille.fr; Mon 2–6pm, Wed–Sun 10am–6pm, closed some public hols; charge) displays a fine collection of Flemish works, from Rubens to Van Dyck. However, the highlight is the vaulted cellars containing many Flemish medieval and Renaissance paintings and sculptures. In the northwest of the city is **La Citadelle** Ⓓ, the largest and best-preserved bastion in France. The star-shaped structure was designed in 1670 as part of France's defence against the Spanish Netherlands.

A modern addition to the city is **Euralille**, a glass and steel complex encompassing a shopping centre and Lille Europe, the railway station.

FACT

Vieux Lille is the ideal place to try hearty Flemish specialities – mostly a cuisine for committed carnivores, such as *carbonnade flamande* (beef in beer). Try, too, *waterzooi* (creamy vegetable and fish stew) and *tarte aux maroilles* (rich cheese tart).

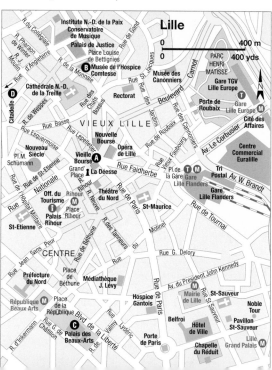

Elegant gabled roof in Lille.

CHAMPAGNE

This region, where there is always fizzy wine to celebrate, has the crowning glory of France – Reims, the cathedral city where the country's monarchs were crowned.

Main Attractions
Laon
Reims
Troyes
Half-timbered churches
Colombey-les-Deux-
 Eglises
Langres

The Cathédrale Notre-Dame at Laon.

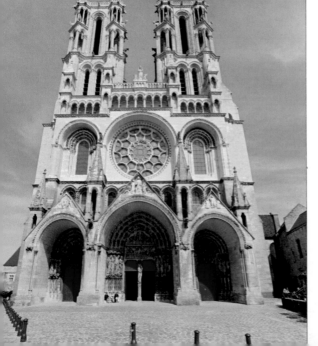

The significance of Champagne goes much further than celebratory drinks. This could be said to be the spiritual omphalos of the country. Every schoolchild in France is taught that the baptism of Clovis, chieftain of the Francs, in Reims on 25 December 496 was the first step in uniting France and thus is effectively the birthday of their country. From then on kings of France came to the city for their coronations in order to legitimise their regimes.

In the Middle Ages, Champagne was a prosperous region ruled over by a dynasty of counts who made good money during the 12th and 13th centuries by holding annual trade fairs which brought together merchants from the Low Countries and Italy and gave an impetus to Europe's developing economy.

In more recent times, Champagne has been one big battlefield. Nudging up to the Belgian border, it was strategically important during the three defensive wars fought by the French against invading German armies (in 1870, 1914–18 and in 1940). The region is consequently full of memorials, war museums and cemeteries.

Northeast approach

From the northeast, the best approach to Champagne is by way of the lovely old Picardy town of **Laon ❶**, whose historic **Ville Haute** (upper town) is completely separate from the modern Ville Basse and feels very remote from below. The best way to reach it is by the Poma "mini-metro" train which begins at the station. The view from the ramparts is best appreciated on a sunny day, but the town's main draw, **Cathédrale Notre-Dame**, is just as spectacular wreathed in mist. It is an early example of Gothic architecture, famed for the stone oxen which jut out of the towers.

Different in character is **Charleville-Mézières ❷** and its early 17th-century **Place Ducale**, a version of the

Place des Vosges in Paris, but on a far larger scale. The poet Arthur Rimbaud, who always claimed he hated his home town but continued to come back here, is honoured in the newly refurbished **Musée Rimbaud** (Tue–Sun 10am–noon and 2–6pm; charge), housed in an old water mill, and the **Maison Natale Arthur Rimbaud**, where he was born.

In the Ardennes hills, near the Belgian border, the memories of war are still fresh. **Sedan ❸**, which has one of the biggest castles in Europe, has a tragic history. In 1870, the Emperor Napoleon III and his army were surrounded here by the Prussians and forced to surrender, leaving the way clear for the invader to take Paris. In World War II Sedan was identified as the weak point in France's northern defences, the "hinge" between two defending armies, making it the principal target of Hitler's strategy to take France by pushing a column of armour through the Ardennes.

The royal city

The city of **Reims ❹** was largely destroyed by the fighting that raged around it in World War I and the magnificent **Cathédrale Notre-Dame**, begun in 1211, was left a hollow shell. Its restoration has been lengthy and meticulous. Though badly scarred, its west front is covered in 13th-century carvings – look for the Smiling Angel and attendants on the north portal. A further surfeit of statuary decorates the interior wall, and richly carved

QUOTE

"Champagne is the only wine which makes a woman more beautiful after drinking it."

Madame de Pompadour

DOM PERIGNON
1638 – 1715
CELLERIER DE L'ABBAYE D HAUTVILLERS
ET LE CLOITRE ET LES GRANDS VIGNOBLE
SONT LA PROPRIETE DE LA MAISON
MOËT & CHANDON

The statue of Dom Pérignon outside Moët et Chandon's cellars in Epernay.

Wine-producing lands.

friezes encircle the pillars in the soaring but otherwise simple nave. The stained glass is superb, from the 13th-century rose window to the 20th-century windows by Chagall in the ambulatory, with their luminous blues and purples. After Clovis set the trend with his baptism, 26 kings of France elected to be crowned in the city.

Next door, the former archbishop's residence, **Palais du Tau** (Tue–Sun 6 May–8 Sept 9.30am–6.30pm,9 Sept–5 May 9.30am–12.30pm, 2–5.30pm, closed public hols; charge), with precious objects and tapestries, was the residence of royalty during their sojourns in Reims. At the **Musée des Beaux-Arts** (Mon-Fri, 2–6pm, Sat 10am–noon, 2–6pm, Sun until 6.30pm, closed Tues/public hols; charge) you can re-live the coronation rites through the paintings hung in honour of the royal arrival.

Another interesting church is the early Gothic **Basilique de St Rémi**. Around it are some of the prestigious champagne houses, including the cellars of Taittinger and Champagne Pommery, which offer guided visits.

Vineyards of Champagne

The other main Champagne town is **Epernay ❺**. Here, Moët et Chandon gives guided tours of its cellars, and the town's museum has a section on champagne production. Nearby is **Hautvilliers**, home of the creator of Champagne, Dom Pérignon.

There are more wine producers in **Châlons-en-Champagne ❻** (called Châlons-sur-Marne until 1998 and still marked as such on some maps), which sits roughly in the middle of the region. It is a harmonious collection of preserved half-timbered houses that are at their best on Place de la République, the old market square. One good way to see the town is by boat on a canal that runs through the centre.

The **Monument National de la Victoire de la Marne** (museum open Jun–Sept Sun 3–6pm) at **Mondement ❼** northeast of Sézanne celebates the First Battle of the Marne in September 1914, an early turning point in the war. The Germans succeeded in advancing as far as Meaux, 40km (25 miles) from Paris. The tide of the battle is supposed to have been turned by the arrival of

---

MÉTHODE CHAMPENOISE

Champagne was allegedly created accidentally in the 17th century by Benedictine monk Dom Pérignon, who announced its genesis with the words, "Come quickly, I am seeing stars!". Today, the process is somewhat more technical, involving a double fermentation process to obtain the bubbles. The first fermentation of the base wine takes place in stainless-steel tanks, or sometimes in oak casks. The wine is then siphoned off and blended with other wines. At the same time that this blended wine is bottled a mixture of sugar, yeast and wine is added to trigger the second fermentation that produces the sparkle. The bottles are stored in chalky cellars *(crayères)* for about a year. Finally the deposit from the second fermentation is expelled by the *dégorgement* process and the cork is inserted.

The champagne vineyards are the northernmost in France, making them susceptible to frost, but also giving the wine its characteristic light acidic taste. Unlike most other wine regions, in Champagne there are "brand names" that are not designations of varietal or territorial origin, but those of the companies assembling and manipulating the wines. These large and famous Champagne houses buy the grapes from the growers, and after a first pressing at the harvest site, transfer the incipient wine to their cellars, concentrated in Reims and Epernay, which provide the necessary cool temperature for the optimum development

reinforcements ferried by Parisian taxis. Although the German army was driven into retreat, the two sides dug themselves trenches and a four-year war of attrition began. In the Second Battle of the Marne in July 1918 another German attack was followed by another French advance and this began the momentum that would lead to the armistice 15 weeks later.

Troyes and the lake

Troyes ❽ is a brilliant souvenir of the Renaissance period, with many half-timbered houses whose upper levels jut over the narrow streets. Nine churches contain marvels of stained glass and religious treasures. Next door to the cathedral, don't miss the **Musée d'Art Moderne** (Tue–Sun 10am–1pm, 2pm–6pm, closed public hols; charge), which has an exceptional collection of paintings by André Derain.

To the northeast of Troyes is Champagne's lake district, around **Lac du Der-Chantecoq**, the largest artificial lake in France. It is dotted with 10 quaint timber-framed churches built between the 15th and 18th centuries and looking like overgrown cottages. The tourist information office has a map but if you just want to see one, **Châtillon-sur-Broué** church ❾ is as picturesque as any.

East of Troyes, off the main road to Chaumont, a huge double-barred Cross of Lorraine in pink granite stands on a hilltop, visible from far across the rolling, chalky plain. It beckons the visitor to the village of **Colombey-les-Deux-Eglises** ❿, where Charles de Gaulle had his country home, La Boisserie (Apr–Sept daily 10am–6.30pm, Oct–Mar Wed–Mon 10am–1pm, 2–5.30pm; charge). His simple headstone marks his grave in the humble churchyard. At the foot of the cross however stands the newly constructed **Mémorial Charles de Gaulle** (May–Sept daily 9.30am–7pm; Oct–Apr daily 10am–5.30pm, closed Jan and first week of Feb; charge), an outstanding museum and cultural centre.

On an open plateau **Langres** ⓫, birthplace of encyclopaedist Diderot, has intact Roman ramparts that look over a valley where modern highways follow the line of Roman roads.

QUOTE

"I always thought I was Joan of Arc and Bonaparte. How little one knows oneself."

De Gaulle replying to the suggestion that he was like Robespierre, 1958

The Cross of Lorraine near Colombey-les-Deux-Eglises.

LORRAINE

Industrial towns contrast with unspoilt countryside in Lorraine, which hugs the slopes of the Vosges and extends north to the borders of Germany, Luxembourg and Belgium.

Main Attractions
Verdun
Hackenberg
Metz
Nancy
Vosges

The sombre bulk of Douaumont at Verdun, a town synonymous with World War I.

The territory now known as Lorraine was first demarcated in the Treaty of Verdun in AD843. It later became a duchy and was only finally incorporated into France in 1788. A century later, northern Lorraine was claimed by a united Germany along with neighbouring Alsace. Between 1871 and 1944, the two shuttled backwards and forwards between the rival states. Lorraine was a prized commodity because it was, and is, one of the industrial heartlands of France producing coal, iron and steel.

More romantically, Lorraine represents heroic resistance against the aggressor in two formative episodes of history. The first of these is the Hundred Years War, and a good a location to begin a tour of Lorraine is **Domrémy-la-Pucelle** 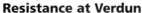. France's exemplary heroine Joan of Arc (Jeanne d'Arc) was born here in 1412. When she was 13 she left the village after having claimed to hear voices telling her to go and eject the English from France. The house where she was born, much modified, is freely open to the public. The national monument to her memory, half religious, half patriotic, is the **Basilique Du Bois-Chenu** near Domrémy.

Resistance at Verdun

In World War I, France successfully resisted invasion by the Germans. It was the town of **Verdun** ❷ that became the symbol of victory or defeat. Between 1916 and 1918, an estimated 800,000 men died on the battlefields on the hills above the River Meuse. A visit to the giant forts, the grassy remains of trenches, and the towering ossuary of **Douaumont**, is an immensely moving experience (www.verdun-douaumont. com; Feb, Nov Mon–Fri 9am–noon, 2–5pm, Sat–Sun 2–5pm, Mar Mon–Fri 9am–noon, 2–5.30pm, Sat–Sun 9am–noon, 2–5.30pm, Apr–June, Sept daily 10am–6pm, July–Aug daily 9.30am–6.30pm, Dec daily 2pm–5pm; charge). The Musée de la Citadelle Militaire presents life in the trenches. Today the

theme of Franco-German reconcilia-
tion dominates and Verdun has been
made World Centre for Peace and
Human Rights.

Land of Three Frontiers

The north is known informally as "the
land of the three frontiers" because Lorraine is the only region to have three
international borders – with Belgium,
Luxembourg and Germany. Near
the borders are the pretty village of
Rodemack ❸, with impressive 15th-
century ramparts that have caused it to
be called "the little Carcassonne of Lorraine", and **Sierck-les-Bains** ❹ where
the walls of its 11th-century château of
the Dukes of Lorraine still stand.

In the interwar years, this area
became one of the prime sections of

the Maginot Line. The experience of
trench warfare between 1914 and 1918
convinced military planners in the
early 1930s to build more permanent
fortifications. It was intended to act as
a deterrent and to give the French army
the two or three weeks it would need
to mobilise and reinforce the frontiers. The work was finished in 1935
and named after the Minister for War,
André Maginot.

The 58 great overages (fortresses), 400
casemates and assorted forward observation posts, tank obstacles, machine
gun nests, anti-tank gun emplacements
and infrastructure for supply and communications were built at enormous
expense; many were not subjected to
battle and are therefore in a good state
of conservation. The Maginot Line's

FACT

Joan of Arc's symbol
was the double-armed
Cross of Lorraine. It
became the symbol of
the Free French Forces,
under Charles de Gaulle,
during World War II.

FACT

The Route des Crêtes (route of crests) made by the French in World War I to transport materials through the Vosges, survives today as a fine mountain route with great views.

largest fortress is **Hackenburg**  (for guided visits only; Apr–mid-Nov Mon–Fri 2.30pm, Sat–Sun staggered between 2–3.30pm, mid-Nov–Mar Wed, Sat 2pm, ask about tours in English at the entrance; charge). It lies outside Veckring, and its access road is marked by a parked American tank. It is a complex of 10 km (6 miles) of underground galleries with a power station. Here, 1,000 battle-ready men could be kept self-sufficient for up to 3 months. The visit is aboard an electric train which was used for transporting munitions.

Metz

Lorraine's regional capital, **Metz**  has suffered from its reputation as an industrial city but it is going through a resurgence. Most emblematic of the change is the opening of a spectacular branch of the **Centre Pompidou** (www.centrepompidou-metz.fr; Mon, Wed–Fri 11am–6pm, Sat 10am–8pm, Sun 10am–6pm; charge). Its most conspicuous historic monument is the Cathédrale St-Etienne, which has the largest stained-glass windows in the world, some of them by Marc Chagall.

Less evident but no less interesting are the 4th-century St-Pierre-aux-Nonnains, and the diminutive 13th-century Chapelle des Templiers (usually kept locked), off one corner of the sprawling Place de la République. The lively Musées de la Cour d'Or (Wed–Mon 9am–6pm, closed public hols; charge) exhibit archaeological, architectural and fine-art collections.

Scy-Chazelles, in the outskirts of Metz, was the home of Robert Schuman (1886-1963), the former French prime minister who played an instrumental role in creating what is now the European Union and as such is known as "the father of Europe". His house is now a museum.

Hattonchatel , southwest of Metz, has a handsome château founded in the 9th century but destroyed in World War I and subsequently rebuilt.

Toul  is another historic town, with Roman roots and a fine Gothic cathedral. It produces *vin gris*: "grey wine", being white wine made from red grapes, in this case gamay and pinot noir. It also makes eau de vie flavoured with Mirabelle plums.

The Centre Pompidou in Metz.

KING STANISLAS

Stanislas Leszczynski, an Enlightenment philosopher, was born in Poland in 1677. He was placed on the Polish throne by Sweden in 1705 but was forced to abdicate in 1709. In 1725 his daughter Maria married Louis XV and he moved into the Château de Chambord in the Loire until in 1733, when he was placed on the Polish throne for a second time, by the French. In 1736 he abdicated again and as a consolation was given the Duchy of Lorraine with the proviso that it would revert to France on his death. While he was responsible for the beautifying of Nancy, he preferred to live 30km (20 miles) away in his palace at Lunéville surrounded by one of the last independent princely courts in Europe. In his last years he was engaged in scholarship and writing books. He died in 1788.

The seat of Nancy

Much more appealing as a city is **Nancy** , which owes its elegance to the dukes of Lorraine. The last of these, Stanislas, made his mark more than the others, although he didn't care to live here. The place to begin a tour of Nancy is the eponymous **Place Stanislas**. This pedestrianised 18th-century square is distinguished by gilded wrought-iron grillwork and the handsome buildings looking on to it: the town hall, a theatre, and the **Musée des Beaux-Arts** (Wed–Mon 10am–6pm; charge).

From the square, the redundant main street, the Grande-Rue, leads into the older part of town. The **Palais Ducal**, now the **Musée Lorrain** (Tue–Sun 10am–12.30pm, 2–6pm, closed public hols; charge) is a particularly fine building. Further in the same direction the Grande-Rue ends at the **Porte de la Craffe**, whose two towers and connecting bastion are impressive reminders of earlier fortifications.

Nancy is noted for its collection of Art Nouveau art and architecture. The tourist office publishes a map of examples but the best place to begin is the **Musée de l'Ecole de Nancy** (www.ecole-de-nancy.com; Wed–Sun 10am–6pm, closed some public hols; charge), even if it is a fair walk from the city centre.

A few kilometres east of the city is the basilica of **St-Nicolas-de-Port** ❿ dedicated to the patron saint of Lorraine, where pilgrims come in their thousands on the feast day, December 6.

The **Parc Régional de Lorraine**, near Sarrebourg, has forests that harbour wild boar and roe deer. Lorraine has several spas and the most well known of them is **Vittel** ⓫ to the south of Nancy.

The Vosges

In the southeast, Lorraine is joined to Alsace by the Vosges mountains (see page 172), rising to 1,424m (4,672ft) and popular with walkers. From the Lorraine side, the slopes rise quietly in dark green forests. From **Epinal**, a town with medieval fortifications, parks, gardens and an arboretum, the highway follows the Moselle River upstream to its source in the high Vosges.

Bussang ⓬ and **Gérardmer** ⓭, beside a beautiful lake, are hill resorts with fine skiing and hiking trails.

Looking through to Place Stanislas, Nancy.

Landscape of the Vosges.

ALSACE

Nestling between the Rhine and the Vosges, France's smallest region is cosy and compact, with picture-postcard prettiness, an excellent cuisine and fine wines.

France's smallest mainland region is a densely popular strip of land squeezed between the Vosges mountains in the west and the Rhine in the east. Alsace is famously conservative in its voting habits and also, appropriately for such a cultural crossroads, pro-European.

Small it may be but it is crammed with sights, particularly with exquisite, well-kept, flower-filled villages. A stay here is made all the more pleasant by the food, specialities of which include *choucroute* (*sauerkraut*), Munster cheese and the ubiquitous *tarte flambée*, a "flame-grilled" pizza. Unusually, the region produces both renowned wines (dry, white and fruity) and beers.

Two cultures

Although it is clear on any map which country Alsace belongs to, it hasn't always been so. The region has a long history of toing and froing between France and Germany, leaving it with an enchanting mix of the two rivals' cultures.

It was originally integrated into the Alemannic kingdom of Charlemagne's succession and did not become part of France until 1648. Meanwhile, its capital Strasbourg retained the right to levy its own taxes and finance a Protestant university. Then, following the French defeat in 1871, Alsace and part of Lorraine were annexed by Bismarck and not returned to France until the peace settlement of 1919.

In 1940, Alsace, along with part of Lorraine, was not so much occupied by the Nazis along with the rest of France as forcibly annexed to the Third Reich. In 1945 it reverted once again to France and its people are nowadays clearly turned towards Paris rather than Berlin. However, the influence of Germany is undeniable, as can be seen in the place names, architecture, cuisine and local patois.

Main Attractions

The Vosges
Hunspach
Strasbourg
Sélestat
Haut-Koenigsbourg
Alsace Wine Route
Parc de Cigognes, Hunawihr
Riquewihr
Colmar
Mulhouse

Petite France embankment, Strasbourg.

A mug for sale in Strasbourg sports a stork feeding its young motif, one of Alsace's emblematic sights.

Mist nestles down into the valleys of the Vosges.

The Vosges

The backbone of Alsace is the **Massif des Vosges**, a range of low mountains covered with mainly coniferous forests which separates the region from Lorraine. In many ways the massif mirrors the Black Forest on the other side of the Rhine. While the German range has its cherry *gâteau*, the restaurants of the Vosges invariably offer bilberry tart on their dessert menus.

Being gentle and not too high the Vosges is a favourite place for walking. The GR5 long distance footpath, linking the North Sea to the Mediterranean, runs north to south through the hills and intersects with the east-west running GR7. Altogether, there are 18,000km (11,180 miles) of footpaths signposted and maintained by enthusiasts of the Club Vosgien.

By car, the best way to get the flavour of the Vosges is to follow the **Route des Crêtes** (**Route of the Crests**) between Cernay and the Col de la Schlucht, along a road built to facilitate troop movements during World War I. The route skirts around the highest peak in the Vosges, the

Grand Ballon **⑭** (1,424m/4,672ft). The summit, which is topped by the white ball of a radar station, can be easily ascended on foot. Even more accessible is **Mt Hohnek** (1362m/4,468 ft), from where there are views over the Rhine Valley and into Germany.

The Route des Crêtes continues north, though not as scenically, to **Ste-Marie-aux-Mines ⑮** where the old silver mines have been converted into a museum, **Tellure** (July–Aug daily 10am–7pm, Apr–June and Sept–Oct Tue–Sun 10am–6pm), giving an impression of life for a miner underground in the 16th century.

Midway up the length of the Vosges is **Struthof**, the site of KL-Natzweiler, the only Nazi concentration camp in France. It was a labour camp, established in 1941 to hold political prisoners from all over Europe as well as Jews, gypsies and homosexuals; and was abandoned in 1944. Among those who came here were the rebels rounded up in the occupied territories under the "Nacht und Nebel" (Night and Fog) orders, the Nazis' infamous programme of "forced disappearance".

An estimated 52,000 deportees passed through the camp or its annexes and 22,000 of them died. The camp is now the **European Centre of Deported Resistance Members** (www.struthof.fr; daily Mar–mid-Apr and mid-Oct–23 Dec 9am–5pm, mid-Apr–mid–Oct 9am–6.30pm; charge), a museum and memorial to those who suffered, died or simply vanished.

The main town in the north of the range is **Saverne** 🛈 where the noble Rohan family built an extravagant and ostentatious **château** complemented by an immense rose garden. It houses a **museum** (Wed–Mon, closed some public hols, times vary tel: 03 88 91 06 28 for details; charge) investigating local archaeology and the château's history.

La Petite-Pierre 🛈 is the information centre for the **Parc Régional des Vosges du Nord**, where trails wander off through a wildlife reserve.

Lower Alsace

The north of Alsace is a land of ancestral forests and razed castles. The **Forêt de Haguenau** 🛈 shelters hamlets of wooden houses, renowned for their colourful festivities during which the women are coiffed with the giant starched bow of Alsatian folklore.

The most impressive of the ruined castles is, perhaps, **Fleckenstein** 🛈 (mid-Mar–June and Sept–Oct 10am–5.30pm, July–Aug 10am–6pm, Jan–mid-Mar Sun noon–4pm; charge), built in the 12th century, its crumbling masonry now blending into the rock outcrop it stands on.

More recently constructed fortresses mark the course of the Maginot Line (see page 167). The forts in Alsace never fired a shot in anger and they became a tourist attraction for the occupying German forces.

The most delightful village in the north, indeed one of the most beautiful in France, is **Hunspach** 🛈, a harmonious cluster of three- or four-storey high traditional black-and-white half-timbered houses. Many of the windows have rounded panes of glass to allow the occupants inside to see out without being seen themselves.

Two other places are worth visiting for souvenirs of traditional potteries: **Betschdorf** 🛈 and **Soufflenheim** 🛈.

This stork has chosen a chimney on which to build its nest.

STORKS IN DECLINE

Thousands of white storks *(Ciconia ciconia)* once spent the summer feeding in the fertile fields and raising their young, making them a symbol for Alsace. But their numbers declined throughout the 20th century and by 1976, the population had been reduced to five breeding pairs and an urgent programme was initiated, led by the Stork Reproduction Centre in Hunawihr. High-voltage electricity lines kill an estimated 15–20 per cent of the birds each year, while in their winter feeding grounds in Africa they are hunted as food and their food supply is reduced by pesticides. One objective of the programme is to suppress the migratory instinct of birds raised in captivity to encourage them to remain in the region over winter where they can be kept comparatively safe and assured of food.

FACT

Christmas markets are a big tradition in Alsace, with illuminations and stalls selling mulled wine, decorations, food specialities and hand-crafted gifts. The best-known are in Strasbourg, Colmar and Kaysersberg.

Betschdorf, which produces blue and grey pottery, has a ceramic museum (May–Sept Tue–Sat 10am–noon, 2–6pm, Sun 2–5.30pm; charge).

Hochfelden ㉓ is the lone outpost of Alsace's last independent brewery, Météor, which struggles to compete with the four giant breweries that supply half of the beer drunk in France. Beer is as respectable a drink in Alsace as wine and a favourite aperitif is beer with a shot of amer, a liqueur made from bitter herbs. Special beers are brewed in spring, drawing on the last barley harvest, and Christmas, when a strong rich ale is traditionally made to use up the brewery's leftover ingredients before beginning afresh.

Strasbourg

Sometimes known as the "Crossroads of Europe", **Strasbourg** ㉔ is enclosed in a series of basins and canals regulating boat traffic and flood waters. Within the outer rings of modern convention centres and genteel uncramped neighbourhoods is the nutshell of old Strasbourg, a small island formed by the **Ill River**.

Numerous bridges cross over the artificial arm of the river, channelled in its brick-lined bed.

The *quais* and cobbled lanes converge on **Cathédrale Notre-Dame** Ⓐ. The building, in rosy sandstone dappled with cream, is like an immense marble cake. When it was finished in the 15th century, the 142-metre (466ft) steeple was the highest in Europe although it looks somewhat forlorn without its missing twin. This is a cathedral laden with decoration, carrying the Gothic idea to its limit. Incessantly modified during its construction, the exterior is layered with lacy spires and innumerable statues. On the inside, the pulpit and the celebrated **Column of Angels** are flights of a sculptor's fancy. The **astronomical clock** was installed in the 16th century, a multi-faced mechanism tracing hourly, daily and yearly celestial movements. When it strikes at 12.30pm, figures of ancient and biblical mythology execute their ordained rounds. You can go up the 332 steps to the platform at an altitude of 66m (216ft) to see the view from the top (open daily; charge).

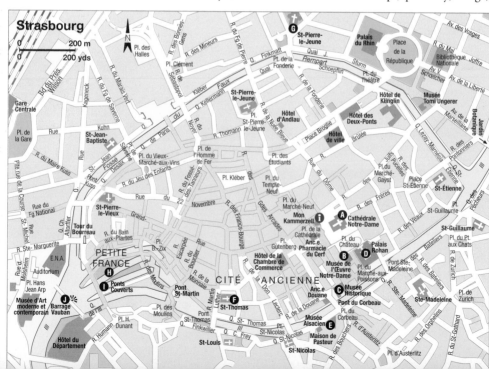

The **Musée de l'Œuvre Notre-Dame** B (Tue–Sun 10am–6pm, closed public hols; charge) was created during the 13th century to supervise the building of the cathedral, and has been in continuous existence since. Due to this unprecedented life-span, its **museum** has untold treasures. In a Renaissance mansion of lovingly polished wood, the displays range from a rare series of pre-14th century Jewish epitaphs to a superb collection of late medieval art, especially paintings of the Lower Rhine School. Most exceptional of all, this museum shows the original master plans for the cathedral. On 2-metre (6ft) scrolls of parchment the artists drew and coloured each section of the facades exactly as they were to appear.

The old city

The old neighbourhood is lively during the weekly flea-market. No two buildings on the evocatively named streets (like Old Fishmarket Street) appear exactly alike. The half-timbered houses seem to have been inflated to giant proportions. Above wide fronts to two or three storeys, the roofs carry up to five gabled windows, one above the other, diminutive in the distance. The **Ancienne Grande Boucherie**, or Great Butcher's shop, houses the **Musée Historique** C (Tue–Sun 10am–6pm; charge). The **Musée d'Art Moderne et Contemporain** (Tue–Sun 10am–6pm; charge), a superb glass building on the river with a fine modern art collection, is located in Rue Hans Jean Arp.

The **Palais Rohan** D (Mon and Wed–Sun 10am–6pm, closed public hols; charge) – which includes museums of fine art, decorative art and archaeology – amazes the eye with princely chambers of gilt and velvet.

Across the river on Quai St-Nicolas, the **Musée Alsacien** E (Mon and Wed–Sun 10am–6pm, closed public hols; charge) is installed in a typical 16th-century Strasbourg dwelling. The museum's 30 rooms display distinctive Alsatian artefacts, such as ovens made of green tiles, wooden furniture, ceramics and toys, which represent the traditions of various occupations including farming, wine-growing and arts and crafts.

Named after the legendary beast said to roam the Vosges some time between the 1970s and 90s, this amber ale is just as fierce at 8 percent proof.

On duty at the Musée Alsacien.

EAT

The hors d'oeuvre tarte flambée is the Alsatian equivalent of pizza, traditionally made with crème fraîche, cheese and onions, and baked in a wood-fired oven.

A town of liberal traditions, Strasbourg has prominent Jewish and Protestant minorities. Protestant congregations are numerous, and two of their churches are particularly notable. St-Thomas **F** has a cloister and the splendid mausoleum of the royal Marshal de Saxe, the 18th-century German who became Marshal of France. Across town, St-Pierre-le-Jeune **G**, founded in 1035, has a fine cloister and 14th-century frescoes.

Picturesque centre

The jewel of Strasbourg is the picturesque, traffic-free **Petite France** quarter **H**, a central knot of traditional houses that is impeccably maintained, with fresh paint and flowers applied regularly. In fact, it is so picturesque that it seems a little unreal, like a film set or an oversize doll's house.

Along the **Rue des Moulins**, where the river is divided into several channels for the running of mills, buildings have doors at water level. The **Ponts Couverts I** are no longer covered bridges as their name claims, but the square towers of the

14th-century fortifications still stand. Just upstream is the **Barrage Vauban J**, a dam designed to block river traffic, and offering a good view of the old city.

Strasbourg is one of the three non-capital cities in the world (along with New York and Geneva) to be the headquarters of major international institutions. Outside the old town, a purpose-built Euro-quarter of flagpoles and luxury hotels, inhabited by bureaucrats and interpreters, contains the seats of the Council of Europe and European Court of Human Rights, and is a regular host to the European Parliament, whose 751 members occupy the enormous **Palais de l'Europe** once a month.

Alsace wine route

Many of the towns and villages on the plain between the Vosges and the Rhine south of Strasbourg are stops on the Alsace wine route.

First of interest is **Molsheim 25**, a walled town enclosing preserved traditional houses. Particularly worth seeing is the **Metzig**, a beautiful Renaissance

The Petite France quarter of Strasbourg.

building with a double staircase and sculpted balconies.

Obernai ㉖ is distinguished by a central, covered market-place and an elaborate 16th-century fountain equipped with six buckets. A few kilometres from the town, on a winding road that leads into the Vosges, is **Mont Ste-Odile**. From pre-Christian times this spot was both sacred and strategically important, as the 10km (6-mile) long "pagan wall" attests. This presumably defensive installation (although no one knows what it was built for) continues almost without interruption through the forest, with views towards the remnants of surrounding fortresses. Two chapels remain from the 11th and 12th centuries.

Further south, **Sélestat** ㉗ is one of the old independent cities of Alsace that grouped themselves together as the Decapole to defend the privileges accorded them by the Holy Roman Emperor. A traditional market town, Sélestat has a medieval section including two city gates. The church of **Ste Foy** is of dusky yellow-pink stone with a slightly bulging central hexagonal tower. In the same stone is the Gothic **St Georges**. The city is proud of its **Bibliothèque Humaniste** (closed for reorganisation programme until spring 2017), one of the most important cultural treasures of Alsace. It houses the library of Beatus Rhenanus (1485–1547), a friend of Erasmus and leading light in Sélestat's influential humanist school. Illuminated manuscripts and rare tomes dating back to the 7th century are displayed alongside 15th-century carvings and *faïence*.

Medieval castles

Alsace's most visited tourist sight – it's also in the top league for the whole of France – is the castle of **Haut-Koenigsbourg** (www.haut-koenigsbourg. fr; daily Jun–Aug 9.15am–6pm, Apr–May, Sept 9.15am–5.15pm, Mar, Oct 9.30am–5pm, rest of the year 9.30am–noon, 1–4.30pm; charge). Standing on an outcrop of rock at an altitude of 757m (2,483ft), it may look from afar as every medieval castle should but it is not quite as authentic as it seems. The first fortress on the site was built

Resplendent interiors at the Mont Ste-Odile, site of a monastery complex.

The Palais de l'Europe.

TIP

The Alsace Wine Route is best trodden in autumn, just before the wine harvest, when the huge volume of tourists and tour buses has died down and the pretty villages are quiet once more.

in the 12th century. A rebuilt version was destroyed in 1633 by Swedish artillery during the Thirty Years War. It lay in ruins for two centuries until Kaiser Wilhelm II decided to restore the fortress to its original grandeur at the beginning of the 20th century – Alsace being in those days in the hands of the Germans. Although he let himself be guided by the historical and archaeological knowledge of his time there is evidently a large amount of his own taste in the finished product. It is also a political statement: **Haut-Koenigsbourg** is meant to look German. All the ingredients of a medieval castle are there – drawbridge, curtain walls, *cour d'honneur*, battlements – but there are also primly pointed turrets and touches of neo-Gothic fantasy.

Nearby **Château de Kintzheim** has been turned into the **Volerie des Aigles**, (www.voleriedesaigles.com; daily Apr–Oct, times vary tel: 03 88 92 84 33 for details) dedicated to the protection of birds of prey, where you can see eagles, condors and vultures in flight above the ruined medieval castle.

Crates of Alsace white wine.

Pretty wine towns

A string of beautiful wine towns begins to the south with **Ribeauvillé ㉘**. The town is stretched in a band along the Grand Rue, rising through the busy 18th-century new town to the tower guarding the medieval city. While cars continually climb up the main street, the few side streets are calm, with shaded, beamed houses. About halfway up, the half-timbered houses pull back from the street, forming a plaza of several Renaissance stone façades. The curve of an enclosed staircase, a dog's head carved on a beam end, a date set in the lintel over the door, are the details to look out for. At the end of the street an ancient fountain provides a few moments' rest. The perspective continues towards a ruined castle. One of three such châteaux, it is around an hour's walk on the marked path from town. From these high points away from the crowds, are splendid views both of the valley and the misty peaks above.

Hunawihr possesses a stork and otter rescue centre, the **Parc des Cigognes et des Loutres** (Mar–May, Sept Mon–Fri 10.30am–12.30pm,

FOLLOW THE WINE ROUTE

The Alsace Wine Route winds through the vineyards at the foot of the Vosges mountains for 170km (106 miles) from Marlenheim in the north to Thann in the south. It is well signposted with 103 stops at places of interest, mostly wineries but also churches, castles and picturesque views. Among the vineyards are orchards of cherries and plums destined for potent fruit brandies. Many producers are open for visits and tastings except during the harvest from late September until late October. Alsace is renowned for its white wines, which are divided into three *appellations d'origine protégée*. The bulk (83 percent of the total produced) is classed as AOP Alsace. Choicer wines made by 50 authorised producers come under the stricter AOP Alsace Grand Cru denomination. These stipulate the grape, vintage and producer on the label. AOP Crémant d'Alsace are the sparkling wines, which have become extremely popular in other parts of France. Alsace wines use only seven varieties of grape: Sylvaner, Pinot Blanc, Pinot Gris, Pinot Noir, Riesling, Muscat and the aromatic Gewurztraminer. The wines often smell sweet but in fact taste dry. They are intense with mouth-filling exotic fruit flavours. In the informal taverns known as *winstubs* they are served in attractive glasses with long green stems. The centre of the wine region is Colmar where there you can visit the Maison des Vins d'Alsace. (Mon–Fri 8am–noon, 2–5pm).

X.WYMANN
VITICULTEUR
RIBEAUVILLE (ALSACE)

X.WYMANN
VITICULTEUR
RIBEAUVILLE (ALSACE)

X.WYMANN
VITICULTEUR
RIBEAUVILLE (ALSACE)

2–5.30pm, Sat–Sun 10.30am–6.30pm, June–Aug daily 10am–6.30pm (first 3 weeks of Aug until 7pm), Oct Mon–Fri 2–5.30pm, Sat–Sun 10am–12.30pm, 2–5.30pm; charge), and a fortified church of thick crenellated walls overlooking the valley.

The best preserved and most stunning of this group of towns is **Riquewihr** . Enclosed in protective walls, the town is a tourist's heaven and to keep it that way cars are parked outside. Practically every house is a delight of colours, tiles, balconies and flower boxes. Many have cobbled courtyards multiplying the possibilities of little turrets or intricate woodcarvings. Riquewihr's most distinctive trait is its tradition of shop signs of forged iron. Old ones can be seen in the château's **Postal Museum** (Apr-1 Nov, Dec daily 10am–5.30pm; charge), modern ones in the streets. There are also plenty of wine cellars.

The town of **Kaysersberg** ㉚ is also seductive. Birthplace of Albert Schweitzer, Nobel Peace Prize winner, the old part has narrow streets typical of the region, enhanced by the River Weiss. Near the top of the town, the river traverses a circular plaza united by a fortified bridge and a stone altar, in the shadow of the castle keep perched on the mountain above. The 16th century houses in narrow alleys are served by Renaissance fountains, although the local wisdom is to choose wine over water. As well as Schweitzer's house, there is a small museum, **Centre Culturel Albert Schweitzer** (Apr–mid-Nov daily 9am–noon, 2–6pm, closed Wed Apr–June, Oct–Nov; charge).

Colmar

Centre of the wine route and the business centre for wine professionals, **Colmar** ㉛ is also Alsace's second-biggest tourist town and particularly pretty during the December Christmas market. The sculptor Bartholdi, creator of New York's Statue of Liberty, was born here, and his works are prominent in the town's parks. The old town is a large pedestrian zone of irregularly shaped plazas connected by short streets that wind around historic buildings and churches. The

Cast your eyes skywards to catch all the special touches to the old houses in Colmar's Petite Venise district, such as this carved figure.

Place de la Sinne, Ribeauvillé.

Wreaths of chewy dough studded with coarse salt make up a variety of bretzel (usually referred to in English as "pretzel").

Seeing Colmar the leisurely way.

Dominican church is the site of the altarpiece *Madonna with the Rose Bush* (1473), which hangs in the choir; it is an expressive masterpiece executed by 15th-century artist Martin Schongauer, a native of Colmar.

The **Musée d'Unterlinden** (www. musee-unterlinden.com; May–Oct daily 9am–6pm, Nov–Apr Wed–Mon 9am–noon, 2–5pm, closed some public hols; charge) is renowned for the works of Schongauer. Its highlight, however, is the phenomenal **Issenheim altarpiece** by Mathias Grünewald. The central tableau is surrounded by double panels, painted on both surfaces and emitting a strange glow rendering the saints' tortures and monsters as livid and fantastic as science fiction.

The stroll through Colmar leads to the quarter called **La Petite Venise**, in honour of the little River Lauch and adjacent canal where tanners once cleaned their pelts. Here, as throughout the city, the balconies are lined with flowers, and each half-timbered house has an individualistic touch, a gabled turret or unusual sculptures such as the heads on the **Maison des Têtes**. The **Ancienne Douane** or Koifhus is covered in glazed tiles arranged in patterns of green and yellow.

Around Colmar

Neuf-Brisach ㉜, southeast of Colmar, towards the Rhine, is a perfect piece of military town planning guarding the German border. The star-shaped citadel was designed by the great engineer Vauban, as explained in the museum in the Citadel's Porte de Belfort.

Back on the wine route heading south, **Eguisheim** ㉝ was the birthplace of the 11th-century Pope Leo IX. It is a lovely fortified town of concentric streets lined with half-timbered houses decorated with flowers.

In the hills behind **Guebwiller** is **Murbach** ㉞ a Benedictine monastery founded in AD727 but given a Romanesque church in the 12th century. This was partially destroyed in the 18th century to make way for a new church that was never built but the transept and two towers remain.

At the open-air **Bioscope Ecomusée d'Alsace** ㉟ (daily July–Aug 10m–6pm, Apr–Oct Tue–Sun 10am–6pm;

charge) at Ungersheim, shortly before Mulhouse, traditional timber-framed houses and farm buildings have been regrouped to form an Alsatian village, and rural farming and crafts are demonstrated.

Mulhouse and the Rhine

Mulhouse ③⑥ is an industrial city whose historical monuments from its time as an independent republic were erased by wartime bombing. To make up for this lack, it has become a city of museums with a technological focus.

The unique **Musée de l'Impression sur Etoffe** (www.musee-impression.com; Tue–Sun 10am–noon and 2–6pm, closed some public hols; charge) is devoted to techniques and arts of printed cloth and wall paperings. Another legacy of industrial wealth is the **Musée de l'Automobile** (www.citedelautomobile.com; daily Apr–Oct 10am–6pm, Jan Mon–Fri 1–5pm, Sat–Sun 10am–5pm, rest of the year 10am–5pm; charge), with a spectacular array of over 500 antique and rare cars (some 400 on display), while the **Cité du Train** railway museum (www.citedutrain.

com; daily Apr–Oct 10am–6pm, rest of the year 10am–5pm; charge) presents vintage locomotives.

A few miles east of Mulhouse is a Romanesque marvel, the octagonal church of **Ottmarsheim** ③⑦. This is one of the few points of interest on the Rhine, one of the defining rivers of Europe which forms the entire Franco-German border.

The section in Alsace is part of the Rhine rift valley although it is hard to get an idea of the natural river. Before 1800 it ran in so many rivulets and around so many islands that it was impossible to map. In the age of industrialisation, however, the river was straightened and confined to a single channel between dykes to prevent flooding. The development of river ports and the building of dams for generating hydro-electric power further transformed the Rhine.

The **Petite Camargue Alsacienne** ③⑧ wetland nature reserve and fish farm, south from Ottmarsheim, gives a hint of how the natural ecosystem of the Rhine was once and could perhaps be once again.

A brand of bitters, locally used to flavour beer.

The vineyards and villages of the Haut-Rhin.

FRANCE'S FESTIVALS

From ribald earthy fun to highbrow culture, France offers a busy programme of year-round festivities, particularly in summer when life is lived outdoors.

Every town and small village sets aside at least one weekend a year to be *en fête*, when families, friends and neighbours can eat a protracted lunch together and dance into the night to a local band. Even modest-sized towns, meanwhile, pride themselves on laying on grander celebrations and cultural events often featuring visiting international artists. While some concerts and shows require a ticket there is often plenty of atmosphere to enjoy in the streets and squares for free.

There are a host of cultural festivals, too, from the arts festivals and jazz festivals in the open air to classical concerts, film festivals and book festivals. The country has so many magnificent buildings that events like these are often the best way to appreciate them.

To get the most out of them, and to be sure you are not missing out, it's best to plan ahead. The local tourist information office will be only too pleased to tell you what is going on in the vicinity during your stay. The most popular events tend to get booked up well in advance and the same goes for accommodation in the neighbourhood. By the same token, festival time can make it difficult to see the sights as monuments and museums may be closed. But then, with so much life around you, why would you want to go looking for anything else?

A spot of nautical sea jousting sets aside the Festival de la St-Louis, held on the Canal Royal in Sète.

The Limoux three-month carnival, billed as the longest in the world.

An eye-catching street performer at the Avignon Theatre Festival.

Penitents in the Procession de la Sanch, a ceremony held in several towns in France on Good Friday, at the start of Easter week.

The Fête de la Musique, a nationwide event held yearly in June.

Beer festival in Villars-les-Dombes.

FÊTED FOODS

France reserves a special place in its heart for eating and drinking and many festivities honour local produce. Every wine producing town has its own celebration, particularly in the autumn after the grape harvest is in, when cellars are thrown open for tours and tastings. The most famous wine festival revolves around the Hospices de Beaune charity wine auction in late November. Similarly, Cognac, Armagnac, cider and other drinks are fêted in their respective domains.

Almost any edible harvest from land or sea, meanwhile, provides an excuse for a beanfeast and you can eat your way around France, hopping from food fête to food fête during the course of the year. There are almost as many cheese fêtes and fairs as there are cheeses; similarly for seafood, fish and meat. Celebrity foods include truffles, fêted in Lalbenque (Lot) in January; sea urchins in Carry-le-Rouet (Provence) in February; garlic in Beaumont-de-Lomagne (Gers) in July; oysters in Gujan-Mestras (on the Bay of Arcachon) in August; and red peppers in Espelette (Basque Country) in October.

Marion Cotillard, a hit on the red carpet and a Cannes Film Festival regular.

The seemingly endless geometric parterres at the Château de Villandry.

THE WEST

The green Atlantic seaboard is a place of enchanting extremes: from austere cliffs to the self-satisfied Renaissance châteaux of the Loire, from famous cities to the marshlands of the "Green Venice".

Coat of arms at the château of Azay-le-Rideau.

The western coast of France is given its characteristic shape by two peninsulas. The smaller and more northerly of them is **Normandy**, a land of mellow countryside producing cider apples and well-known cheeses such as Camembert. Its beaches are famous, too, not least for the Allied landings in 1944. The other essentials sights are Monet's gardens at Giverny and the island shrine of Mont-St-Michel.

The other peninsula is **Brittany**, protruding 200km (124 miles) into the Atlantic, and terminating in the dramatic cliffs of Finistère – literally, the end of the earth. A region rich in Celtic traditions, it is dotted with prehistoric menhirs and megaliths, notably at Carnac. Both these regions have magnificent coastal scenery with beautiful beaches and popular resorts for family holidays.

Brittany's southern border is marked by France's longest river, the Loire, whose lower valley is all many people want from France: easy travelling, a picturesque view at every turn and good restaurants to punctuate the day. **The Loire Valley** is the picture of sedate and beautiful rural France, and it is stuffed with history. Its prize possession is a string of splendid Renaissance châteaux bristling with beautiful architectural touches, striding proprietorially over watercourses or standing in magnificent formal gardens. As well as these stately homes, the Loire has historic towns and cities to explore, including Orléans, Tours, Angers and Nantes.

Yport beach huts.

Less well known is **Poitou-Charentes,** the region south of the Loire, which is worth visiting for a breath of Atlantic air and warmer weather to go with it. The towns and cities of La Rochelle and Rochefort on the coast, and Poitiers and Saintes inland, offer many historical monuments between them. Offshore, meanwhile, are the islands of Ré. Cognac has given its name to France's renowned brandy, and this is also the country's biggest oyster producing region.

The ever-popular Mont-St-Michel.

NORMANDY

A land of plenty first settled by Viking Norsemen, Normandy has an eventful history and embraces rich, pastoral farmland, a varied coastline, great monuments and thriving cities.

Normandy is one of the most pleasant and rewarding regions of France to tour in. Within easy reach of Paris and the Channel ports, it is a place with its own identity. It is extremely welcoming to outsiders, as are many places that have seen people come and go through their ports.

Settled by the Romans in the 1st century BC, the region came under the dominion of the Franks in AD497 who founded monasteries near the mouth of the Seine. In the 9th century it was overrun and settled by Vikings, the Norsemen who gave the region its name. They made Normandy an independent dukedom, and from the 10th to the early 13th century they built great monastic estates and blazed across Europe, to rule southern Italy and Sicily, while William, Duke of Normandy, took England's crown, his exploits beautifully retold in the Bayeux tapestry.

Ships came in the opposite direction on D-Day 1944, when Allied troops landed on the beaches of the north coast at great loss of life and began the work of liberating France.

Normandy is administratively split into Haute (Upper) and Basse (Lower) Normandie, which in turn are subdivided into five *départements*. It lives largely on fishing, farming and tourism. The seaside creates much of its interest: defiant cliffs, pretty fishing harbours, elegant resorts and the extraordinary tidal island of Mont-St-Michel. The countryside is often beautiful, with villages of thatch and timber cottages. Here, cows are grazed to make Normandy's famous butter and cheeses, such as Camembert, and apples are grown for cider and brandy.

Côte Fleurie

The beaches and resorts between the mouths of Normandy's two principal rivers, the Seine and the Orne, are known as the Côte Fleurie – the "Flowery Coast".

Main Attractions

Honfleur
Memorial, Caen
D-Day beaches
Bayeux
Mont-St-Michel
Giverny
Les Andelys
Rouen
Abbaye de Jumièges
Etretat

Fishing boats at Yport.

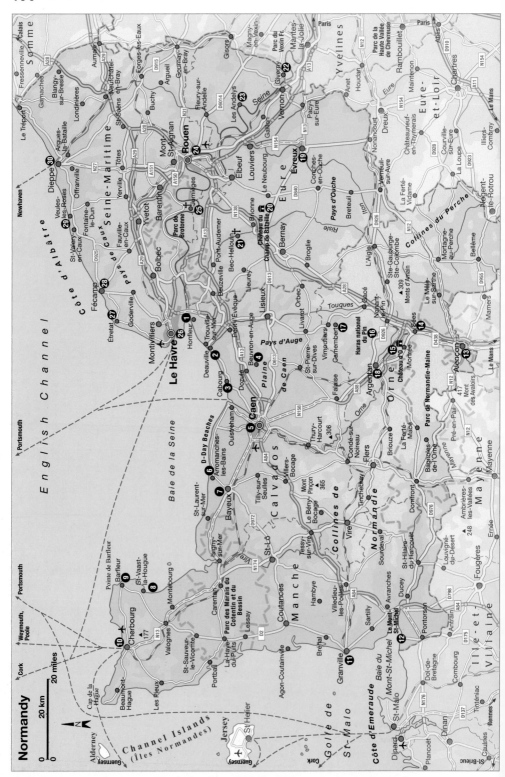

Normandy

At the mouth of the Seine is the delightful little port of **Honfleur ❶** home of the 19th-century painter Eugène Boudin whose attempts at capturing transient weather conditions prefigured Impressionism. Many of his works are hung in the **Musée Eugène Boudin** (mid-Mar–Sept Wed–Mon 10am–noon, 2–6pm, mid-Feb–mid-Mar, Oct–3 Jan Mon, Wed–Fri 2.30–5pm, Sat–Sun 10am–noon, 2.30–5pm; charge).

Trouville-sur-Mer, is an attractive fishing port on the River Touques, made famous in the 19th century by the Parisian literati, and you can take tours to follow in their footsteps. **Deauville ❷**, next door, soon overshadowed Trouville for fashionability, especially along the seafront catwalk, Les Planches, where striped deckchairs and tents retain a 1920s air. The large villas in the town still make it a stylish resort and it remains famous for its horse racing and polo ground. Its celebrity continues with the American Film Festival held each September.

In **Cabourg**, ❸ Marcel Proust sat down to compose his monumental *A la Recherche du Temps Perdu* (Remembrance of Things Past). He called the place Balbec, and likened the dining-room windows of its Grand Hotel to a giant aquarium.

Pays d'Auge

Normandy is at its most seductive in the **Pays d'Auge** the exquisite countryside of green meadows, lush shaded valleys and half-timbered villages and sedate manor houses inland from the Côte Fleurie.

Beuvron-en-Auge ❹, in particular, is filled with picturesque corners. As if the countryside were not enough, this is the major apple growing and cider making area. To get a flavour, you could always follow the cider route which leads you for 40km (25 miles) through **Augerons-de-Cambremer, Beuvron-en-Auge, Beaufour, Bonnebosq, Grandouet, Rumesnil, Victot-Pontfol, St Aubin-Lebizay, La Roque Baignard, Druval** and **Crèvecoeur-en-Auge**. Even better than cider is Calvados, an apple brandy which in Normandy is often drunk between courses to revive the appetite.

FACT

Tripes à la mode de Caen – tripe cooked in a local style – is said to have been William the Conqueror's favourite dish. He grew so fat that when he died he would not fit into his sarcophagus, and when attempts were made to push him in, his body exploded.

Honfleur.

AMERICAN FILM FESTIVAL

Franco-US international relations may wax and wane but Deauville American Film festival goes on regardless. During a week in mid-September, 100 films from Hollywood and from independent producers are screened in three cinemas the CID, the Cinéma du Casino and the Cinéma le Morny. Film-makers buzz around everywhere but the festival is as much open to the fan as the professional. A blue badge ticket entitles you to attend all daytime screenings. For evening ones you need to get an access card, subject to availability, available from 6pm on the day.

The festival always draws its share of stars, both household names and wannabes. Past visitors include Robert de Niro, Clint Eastwood, George Clooney, Harrison Ford, Tom Cruise, Sharon Stone, Al Pacino and Julia Roberts.

It may have a bomber suspended from the ceiling of its ticket hall, but the Caen Memorial stands for peace.

What's left of the Mulberry Harbour at Arromanches.

Caen

The city of **Caen** ❺, a short way inland down the Orne, represents the powerful, purposive side of Normandy: bustling, businesslike, forever arranging trade fairs and exhibitions, with a lively university and a chamber of commerce that draws attention to itself by flamboyant modern sculpture. William the Conqueror chose Caen as his base before going off to conquer England. A great builder (he built the Tower of London importing Caen stone), he is responsible for the château that now contains the **Musée des Beaux Arts** and the **Musée de Normandie** (Apr–Oct daily 9.30am–6pm, Nov–May Wed–Mon 9.30am–6pm; charge). After being excommunicated by the Pope for marrying his cousin, Mathilde, the pair made their reparations by founding an abbey each. His is the handsome **Abbaye aux Hommes** (guided tours daily at 10.30am, 11am, 2.30pm, 4pm, some extra tours in July–Aug, closed some public hols; charge) and hers is the nearby **Abbaye aux Dames** (daily 2–5.30pm, guided tours at 2.30pm, 4pm, closed some public hols; free entrance).

Caen was one of the principal objectives of D-Day but it cost the Allies a month of fighting to take the city which was all but destroyed by bombs. As a result, much of it has been rebuilt since the war. Among its modern buildings is a peace museum, the **Mémorial** (http:// normandy.memorial-caen.com; daily mid-Feb–mid-Nov 9am–7pm, rest of the year Tue–Sun 9.30am–6pm but closed Jan and some public hols; charge, free entry for World War II veterans).

D-Day Beaches

The Mémorial is a suitable way to prepare yourself for a journey along the **Plages du Débarquement**, the **D-Day Landing Beaches**. There are many museums and memorials, batteries and bunkers, to take in and, depending on your level of interest, you may just want to make for **Arromanches-les-Bains** ❻. At low tide you can still see the remains of the Mulberry Harbour, the portable dock that was towed across the Channel to unload heavy equipment now covered in green seaweed and mussels.

For a more detailed account of the events of this momentous day visit the **Musée du Débarquement** (www. musee-arromanches.fr; daily July–Aug 9am–7pm, the rest of the year opening times vary from month to month, for details call 02 31 22 34 31, closed Jan; charge) situated near the beach. At **Arromanches 360** (www.arromanches 360.com; daily, screenings at 10 past and 40 past the hour: June–Aug 9.40am–6.40pm, Apr–May, Sept–Oct 10.10am–5.40pm, Feb, Dec 10.10am–6.40pm, Mar, Nov 10.10am–5.10pm, closed Jan; charge) you are thrust right in the middle of the action. This is a wraparound 360-degree cinema with nine screens showing archive film footage by war correspondents shot in June 1944 combined with modern film of the same image.

Although most attention is focused on D-Day and its beaches, the landings were only the start of a campaign which continued for two-and-a-half

months and affected many parts of Normandy. Over 96,000 soldiers are buried in the region's 29 World War II cemeteries, 58,000 of them German, 19,000 British, almost 14,000 American, 5,000 Canadian and 650 Polish.

Bayeux and its tapestry

Bayeux ❼, set amid placid countryside, has a reminder of a very different battle. The celebrated **Bayeux Tapestry**, which is both an immortal work of art and an invaluable historical source, sets out in continuous form the story of Duke William's invasion of England in 1066, the defeat and death of the Anglo-Saxon Harold, and the subjugation of England by Normandy. Naturally, it tells the story from a Norman point of view.

After more than 900 years, the tapestry is still extraordinarily vivid and evocative, its colours hardly faded at all, its cartoon-like figures arresting and, behind the first impression of comicality, deeply moving. Housed in a special building, **Centre Guillaume-le-Conquérant** (www.tapisserie-bayeux.fr; daily Mar–Oct 9am–6.30pm, May–Aug

until 7pm, Nov–Feb 9.30am–12.30pm, 2–6pm, closed Christmas, Jan; charge), the tapestry has to be approached via an exhibition which prepares the visitor with the aid of a detailed audio-visual presentation.

Once you get to the tapestry, which is 70 metres (230ft) long, it is best to walk past it twice; once slowly, taking in the detail, and once at a normal walking pace. Above and below the narrative band are friezes depicting animals – some realistic, some mythological, and some on that intermediate ground between the two, a medieval European notion of what animals probably looked like.

The tapestry depicts 58 scenes in chronological order which can be divided into three parts: 1) Harold, who will later claim the English crown, visits Normandy in 1064-1066; 2) Edward the Confessor, the actual king of England, dies on 5 January 1066 sparking a crisis over who will succeed him leading the Normans under William the Conqueror to prepare to invade England during the spring of 1066; 3) William lands in

FACT

Bishop Odo of Bayeux, William's brother, joined the invading army and can be seen wielding a club in the tapestry. Clerics were not allowed to use sharp weapons.

The Bayeux Tapestry.

D-Day

The largest amphibian invasion in history has left its mark on the sandy beaches of Normandy – and across the countryside.

As dawn broke on 6 June 1944, a massive Allied fleet appeared off the coast of northern Normandy. The German defenders of the "Atlantic Wall" of France had been expecting an invasion for some time but it didn't know where or when it would come. It had been assumed that the Allies would choose the shortest sea route to the Pas de Calais rather than the more distant beaches of Calvados.

Both sides knew that the first few hours of the any landing would be decisive. Success in establishing a bridgehead was never guaranteed but several factors gave the Allies the upper hand, not least a favourable last minute break in the bad weather which had delayed the fleet in harbour for 24 hours. Almost miraculously, secrecy had been maintained during the lengthy and detailed planning of Operation Overlord, the

A corner of portable Mulberry Harbour at Arromanches, one of the D-Day Landing Beaches.

invasion of occupied Europe. A further piece of luck for the Allies was that even when the landings had started the German high command was slow to realise that the real invasion was upon them, not just some diversionary tactic meant to confuse them.

During the night before D-Day, parachutists and glider-borne troops landed behind the beaches to secure strategic objectives. Then in the first light of day, 135,000 American, British and Canadian men came ashore as best they could. Some drowned under the weight of their equipment without even reaching the shore. Those that did get out of their landing crafts had to struggle through obstacles placed in their way and race for what little safety there was at the top of the beach.

The five beaches used on D-Day are still known by their code names:

Utah, on the Cotentin peninsula, was allocated to the US army.

Omaha, also in the US sector, was an easy beach to defend and the high casualties earned it the epithet of "Bloody Omaha".

Gold, the middle beach was taken by the British who managed to get as far as Arromanches before nightfall.

Juno was given to Canadian troops who lost a quarter of their landing craft to submerged defences.

Sword was another British beach. During the preceding night, Pegasus bridge over the Caen canal had been taken by troops landed by glider. Ranville was the first village in France to be liberated. However, taking the Merville gun battery overlooking the beach had cost severe casualties.

D-Day was only the first 24-hours of a campaign which would become known as the Battle of Normandy. For the whole of July and August, the Allies made unexpectedly slow progress, taking Cherbourg and Caen only with some difficulty. By the middle of August, the German 7th Army was in full retreat eastward through the "Falaise pocket" (between Falaise and Argentan), a narrowing gap which was dubbed "the corridor of death" because of the vulnerability of the men filtering through it. The last German troops in Normandy surrendered on 22 August and the Allies were able to make quick progress to Paris which was triumphantly liberated on 25 August.

The events of the summer months of 1944 have left an indelible mark on the Normandy psyche and monuments, museums and above all cemeteries commemorate the main scenes of battle and those who died that summer.

England on 28 September 1066 and defeats Harold in the Battle of Hastings on 14 October 1066.

The tapestry is thought originally to have hung in the town's magnificent Cathedral, which was consecrated under William, by then King of England, in 1077.

Manche

At the northern end of D-Day's infamous Utah beach, on the Cotentin peninsula, is **St-Vaast-la-Hougue**  known for its oysters and its Vauban-built fortifications. Watch the brightly painted boats bobbing up and down in the harbour, or treat yourself to a memorable seafood lunch.

Barfleur ❾ is a hard-working fishing port with great grey stone houses facing the harbour, once the peninsula's chief port, used by the Vikings.

Anyone fascinated by ships will feel at home in the port of **Cherbourg** ❿. The quay of its deep-water harbour has the authentic smell of oil, seaweed and fish. A brief stroll from the waterside leads to the pedestrianised old town with its many shops and restaurants. Nearby green spaces are the town park and the botanical gardens. The largest attraction in Cherbourg is the **Cité de la Mer** (www.citedelamer.com; daily July–Aug 9.30am–7.30pm; the rest of the year opening times vary from month to month; for details call 02 33 20 26 69; charge), a submarine experience and aquarium dedicated to underwater life and exploration.

The largest town on the west coast of Cotentin is **Granville** ⓫, a port but also a quiet haven for family holidays, with smooth, golden sands and great stretches of butterscotch-coloured rock dotted with shallow rock pools, where generations of French children have played happily.

Granville's upper town is perched on a headland staring out at the Channel. The old houses, dominated by the magnificent church of **Notre-Dame**, from which one has a total perspective of the town, are solidly made of heavy blocks of stone, ready for any weather the sea may throw at them. They are roofed with dark grey slates as defence against torrential rain. Some houses have one wall slated against rain blasted horizontally at them from off the sea by the prevailing wind.

The childhood home of the legendary fashion designer Christian Dior, Villa les Rhumbs, in the suburbs of Granville, is now run as the **Musée Christian Dior** (www.musee-dior-granville.com; early June–Oct daily 10am–6.30pm; charge). Inside the house are exhibitions about the man and his work; outside is a clifftop garden.

From Granville, ferries sail to the **Iles Chausey**, a small archipelago of 52 islands (at high tide) 17km (11 miles) off the coast. Only Grand Chausey is populated, with about 30 people, who benefit from around 200,000 summer visitors. The islands are part of the **Channel Islands**, which, unlike their near neighbours, are British Crown dependencies. Off-season, when there is less traffic, it is possible to drive round the whole of the island of Jersey in a day, between the morning arrival and

Granville's port, dominated by Notre-Dame.

A brocante (flea market) in Granville.

afternoon departure (times depending on the tides) of the Granville ferry.

Mont-St-Michel

No one can come to Normandy without visiting **Mont-St-Michel** ⓬ (www.ot-montsaintmichel.com; daily May–Aug 9am–7pm, Sept–Apr 9.30am–6pm, closed public hols; charge). From a distance it cuts a striking silhouette: an abbey and its dependent village crowded onto a conical granite island rising out of a vast shallow bay that empties and refills with the tides twice a day, which race in and out with what Victor Hugo described as "the speed of a galloping horse". This is connected to the mainland near Pontorson by a new bridge, which will help the site cope with the increasing numbers of tourists, both secular and spiritual.

The first chapel on this site was built after the Archangel Michael appeared to Aubert, Bishop of Avranches in 708. By invitation of the Dukes of Normandy, Benedictine monks settled on the rock in AD966 and began raising a Romanesque abbey in the 11th century. Much of what can be seen today is a 13th-century Gothic extension called the Merveille (the Marvel), added as the fame of Mont-St-Michel as a pilgrimage destination grew. During the Hundred Years' War the village was fortified against attack by the English and withstood a 30-year siege.

In the wake of the Revolution, the shrine was abandoned by its spiritual garrison and turned into a prison. However, at the end of the 19th century, Mont-St-Michel was classed as a national monument and the gilded statue of the shrine's patron, the archangel St Michael placed on top of the spire. A ten-strong monastic community re-occupied the abbey in 1966.

The bottom part of the rock, the Grande Rue, is a brashly commercial gauntlet of souvenir shops and restaurants but the abbey has preserved much of its charm, even if it is essentially an empty shell of what it formerly was. In the summer months, it is wise to arrive as early or as late in the day as you can, to get some sense of the atmosphere. Another option is to take a guided walking tour of the bay at low tide. The Mont also has four museums.

The Mont-St-Michel.

Orne

Normandy's southernmost *département* is landlocked Orne. Its deeply rural nature is emphasised by the fact that much of its territory is covered by two regional nature parks, Normandie-Maine and the Perche.

The Orne's prefecture, **Alençon** ⑬, is a market town of 30,000 inhabitants on the Sarthe river which built its fortune on lacemaking in the 17th century as can be seen in its **Musée des Beaux Arts et de la Dentelle** (July–Aug daily 10am–noon, 2–6pm, rest of the year Tue-Sun 10am–noon and 2–6pm; charge), occupying a former Jesuit college. The streets of the old town also have some 15th century building including the Maison d'Ozé (now the tourist information office) and the Café des Sept Colonnes, former residence of the town's executioner.

The highest point in Normandy is just north of Alençon, the Signal d'Ecouves, which reaches an unspectacular 413m (1,355ft). All of the department's essential sights are roughly in this direction, too.

Sées ⑭ has a superb Gothic cathedral. The moated **Château d'O** ⑮ built in the 15th century, has trompe l'oeil frescoes inside it and beautiful gardens planted with old-fashioned varieties of vegetables in its grounds.

The **Haras national du Pin** ⑯ (www. haras-national-du-pin.com; daily Apr–Sept 10am–6pm, French school hols 10.30am–noon, 2–5pm, Oct Sat–Sun 2–5pm, rest of the year daily 2–5pm) is France's oldest state stud farm, built on the orders of Louis XIV. On Thursdays in summer it stages a musical equine parade. Lower Normandy has a long history of breeding horses for farm work, travel and war. Its stud farms produce, among other breeds, French trotters, which are often raced pulling two wheeled vehicles, and Percherons (named after the Perche region): grey or black heavy draught horses much appreciated in other countries including Britain and America.

Beyond the stud farm, heading back into the Pays d'Auge, is the undistinguished town of **Camembert** ⑰ which by historical chance gave its name to what has become the world's most recognisable cheese.

Argentan ⑱ is a historic town with a 12th-century remnant of its city wall and a reconditioned 14th-century château. Northwest of Argentan, continuing north towards Caen, is **Suisse Normande**, an attractive area of country, even if its name "Norman Switzerland" is an exaggeration.

Eure

The river Eure, flowing north into the Seine, marks the boundary between Normandy and the Ile de France. The *département* named after it is within an easy day trip of Paris. Its capital is **Evreux** ⑲, a modest-sized city and market town surrounding a Gothic cathedral.

Standing on the plain west of Evreux, near Le Neuborg, is the **Château du Champ de Bataille** ⑳ (July–Aug daily 3.30–5.30pm, Easter–Oct Sat-Sun, public hols only 3.30–5.30pm;

TIP

A spectacular time to visit "God's pyramid" is when very high tides flood round the island of Mont-St-Michel at new and full moon and, even better, during the spring and autumn equinox. Never be tempted to wander around on the mud of the bay without a guide. The tide can come in surprisingly fast.

State stud farm the Haras du Pin.

TIP

The SNCF runs a bicycle rental service (Train + Vélo) at many stations – when you buy your train ticket, reserve a bicycle, which you pick up at your destination. This is the best way to visit Giverny (from Vernon station). SNCF also runs a train/car hire service (Train + Auto).

charge). Despite its name, the castle on the battlefield, this is a 17th century country house sumptuously decorated inside and surrounded by French formal gardens.

The abbey of **Bec-Hellouin ㉑**, to the northwest, is a working monastery occupied by Benedictine monks. The first monastery on the site was founded in the 11th century but the majority of buildings, except for the outstanding 15th-century Anglo-Norman tower, date from the 17th and 18th centuries. After the revolution the abbey was used as stables by the cavalry and much of the church sold off as building stone.

Giverny and Les Andelys

Legions of art lovers descend annually on **Giverny ㉒** home of Impressionist painter Claude Monet until his death in 1926 (http://giverny.org; daily Apr–Nov 9.30am–6pm; charge). They come not to see paintings – there are only prints and copies in the house – but the garden, particularly the lily pond, crossed by a Japanese bridge, which so inspired the artist. Nearby is the **Musée d'Art Américain** (Apr–Oct

The Japanese Bridge at Giverny.

daily 10am–6pm; charge), which focuses on American Impressionist artists who settled in France.

Downstream from Giverny, the Seine forms a large loop guarded over by the ruins of **Château Gaillard**, built by Richard the Lionheart above the town of **Les Andelys ㉓** which once stood on the frontier between English and French domains.

Rouen Seine-Maritime

Describing another large loop further downstream, the Seine flows through the centre of **Rouen ㉔**, ancient capital of Normandy, which has an attractive skyline of steeples. Despite being over 80km (50 miles) from the sea, it is also one of France's busiest ports. The writer Gustave Flaubert was born here in 1821 and one scene towards the end of his most famous novel, *Madame Bovary*, serves as a guided tour of the 19th-century city.

The French heroine-saint, Joan of Arc was imprisoned and interrogated here, and subsequently burnt a witch on 30 May 1431 in what is now the **Place du Vieux-Marché Ⓐ**. The

west façade of the great late-Gothic **Cathédrale Notre-Dame** Ⓑ was captured at different times of day in a series of paintings by Monet. Among the treasures in the cathedral, which briefly in the 19th century was the tallest building in the world, is the heart of Richard the Lionheart.

The medieval church of **St-Maclou** Ⓒ contains some of the finest wood carving in France. Nearby is something more oppressive, however: the **Aître de St-Maclou** Ⓓ, a rectangular inner courtyard used as a mortuary during the plagues of the 16th century; carvings on the two-storey gallery display macabre motifs of skulls, crossbones and gravediggers' tools.

St-Maclou stands amid streets that match it in age. Arched over one of them is the golden-faced clock known as the **Gros Horloge** Ⓔ.

Rouen is also home to one of France's top art museums, the **Musée des Beaux Arts** Ⓕ (www.mbarouen.fr; Wed–Mon 10am–6pm, closed public hols; charge), with work from every European school, and including paintings by Velázquez, Rubens, and one of

Monet's famous west fronts of Rouen cathedral.

The Lower Seine

The Seine meanders west beneath the elegant ruins of the **Abbaye de Jumièges** ㉕. Along with Burgundy, Normandy was a pioneer of monasticism. The first abbey on the site was founded by St Philibert in the 7th century. It was rebuilt in the 10th century and the church consecrated in 1067 in the presence of the duke of Normandy, William the Conqueror.

Finally the Seine flows beneath the modern road bridge of the **Pont de Normandie** to join the English Channel (Manche in French) at **Le Havre** ㉖. Heavily bombed during World War II, this port city was rebuilt in exemplary modern architecture which earned it a place on Unesco's list of World Heritage sites.

In 1873, when Le Havre was still an atmospheric old maritime town, Claude Monet sat on the quay at sunrise to paint the boats in the misty harbour. He called his picture *Impression–Soleil Levant* (*Impression–Sunrise*)

One of Rouen Old Town's half-timbered houses.

The Pont de Normandie.

MADAME BOVARY

Gustave Flaubert knew that he would shock French society with his novel *Madame Bovary*, published in 1857. Set supposedly in the town of Ry northeast of Rouen, and in Rouen itself, it tells the story of the scandalous behaviour of Emma Bovary who dreams of more than the modest life her marriage to a provincial doctor can provide. Her adultery and profligate attitude to money – both at her naïve but adoring husband's expense – lead to her self-destruction and the ruin of her family. And yet Flaubert is coyly non-judgmental, leaving us to draw our own conclusions about small town rural society and his heroine's reaction to it. In its time the book was a bestseller and became regarded as a masterpiece. Today, it still reads like an ethical conundrum rather than a morality tale.

QUOTE

"Another time, [Monet] took hold of the scene of a shower on the sea with his both hands and threw it on the canvas. And thus he had truly painted rain, only rain veiling the waves, the rocks and the sky, which were hardly distinct under this flood."

Guy de Maupassant

One critic disparaged it as merely *impressionniste*, thus unwittingly giving a name to the art movement.

The Musée d'Art Moderne André Malraux or **MuMa** (www.muma-lehavre.fr; Mon, Wed–Fri 11am–6pm, Sat–Sun 11am–7pm, closed public hols; charge) is considered the second most important collection of works by the Impressionists in France after the Musée d'Orsay. It has six canvases each by Monet and Renoir, seven by Pissarro and three by Sisley as well as drawings by Degas, exhibited in rotation. There are also breezy paintings of the coast by Raoul Dufy. The town of **Harfleur** has been swallowed up as a suburb by Le Havre but it has a longer history. It was besieged by the English in 1415 and famously appears in Shakespeare's *Henry V*. The king, standing before the town which he is about to overrun, rallies his troops with: "Once more unto the breach dear friends…"

Côte d'Albâtre

The coast northwards from Le Havre is known as the Côte d'Albâtre or the Alabaster Coast after its brilliant white chalk cliffs. The best are at **Etretat** ㉗, which has inspired a string of creative people including Monet, Victor Hugo and the composer Jacques Offenbach.

The best cliffs, the Falaise d'Aval, are south of the town where there are two rock arches and an offshore spike called L'Aiguille (The Needle). Going north is the Falaise d'Amont, which gets fewer visitors and also makes for a good walk. A large white pointed sculpture marks the point where the French aviators Charles Nungesser (a World War I flying ace) and François Coli were seen heading out to sea on their attempt to make the first nonstop flight cross the north Atlantic aboard *L'Oiseau Blanc* (*The White Bird*) on 8 May 1927. They were sighted once more over Ireland but then never seen again. Two weeks later Charles Lindbergh flew solo nonstop from New York to Paris.

Etretat was the residence of the writer Maurice Leblanc (1864–1941) whose former home, **Le Clos Arsène Lupin** (daily Apr–Sept 10am–5.45pm Oct–Mar 11am–4.45pm; charge) is named after his most famous character, a gentleman burglar. Unlike other writers'

The Falaise d'Aval flanked by L'Aiguille.

residences, this one is not so much a shrine as a hunt for clues that mix biographical fact with literary fiction.

The port of **Fécamp** ㉘ is the source of Benedictine liqueur. The distillery is an extravagant 19th-century château and at times feels more like an art gallery than an industrial building. The abbey church of La Trinité seems too big for the town, but it was once the main pilgrimage site in Normandy.

The most attractive place on the Côte d'Albâtre is almost the smallest, **Veules-les-Roses** ㉙, which has what is claimed to be France's shortest river. No more than a stream, it is little over 1km (half a mile) from its source among beds of watercress until it joins the sea.

The second largest town on the Côte d'Albâtre, after Le Havre, is **Dieppe** ㉚ which has survived better than many other port-resorts. Between the 15th and 17th centuries, Dieppe made its living from trade and piracy. Jean Ango, shipbuilder to King François I led expeditions from here to capture galleons ships and their valuable cargoes. In the 19th century, as beach bathing became fashionable, Dieppe grew as a seaside resort and ferry port linked to Newhaven in England. Oscar Wilde arrived here after his release from prison in 1897.

In 1942, in what is now regarded as a trial run for D-Day. In Operation Jubilee 6,000 Allied soldiers, mainly Canadians, attempted to land and establish a beachhead in occupied France. They were beaten back by German defences and sustained heavy casualties.

Dieppe nowadays is a peaceful place with a pleasant atmosphere and some life in its waterfront restaurants and cafés. Other than its long beach, the main sight is its picturesque 15th-century **château**.

Pays de Caux

Inland from the Côte d'Albâtre is the **Pays de Caux** blending into the Pays de Bray to the east. There are several castles here but few other sights, although devotees of Flaubert's novel *Madame Bovary* make the pilgrimage to Ry to try to glimpse something of the mediocrity of provincial life that drove the eponymous protagonist to such desperate acts.

Farm-produced Normandy cider, sweet or dry, is the perfect partner for crêpes.

Enquiring cow, Pays de Caux.

*Château de Josselin on the
Nantes–Brest Canal.*

BRITTANY

The key to the Breton character is that the people are firstly Atlantic dwellers and secondly Celts. Along with endurance, they have a rich imagination and ready recourse to symbol and legend.

This is the rocky Celtic corner of France, a chunky finger pointing out into the Atlantic with, at its tip, Finistère, buffeted by the sea. Great tides wash clean the dramatic cliffs, clean its oyster beds and claw at its sandy shores. Like other corners of France, Brittany gives the impression that this is another country. Here, in what the Celts called Armorica, signs of the past come from megaliths and Arthurian legends, and a deep Catholicism keeps alive such pageants as the annual Pardons.

Brittany became part of France in the mid-16th century and though the Breton language may have died out, many customs remain.

Like its neighbour Normandy, Brittany is overwhelmingly a rural province, and if you want to get to know Brittany properly, do not linger long in the big towns. Wild and lonely, the Breton countryside bred a distinct way of life, so that well into the 20th century the local costume was distinctive – you'll see everywhere pictures of the elaborate lace head dresses for the women, known as *coiffes*, and for the men black jackets and trousers and wide-brimmed black hats. These have not entirely disappeared and are still worn on festive occasions.

The rugged coast, with many inlets and islands, is ideal for boating. But perhaps the best way to get to know Brittany is to travel, either by road or rail, from the main cities of Rennes or Vannes, and work outwards.

Regional capital

Rennes ❶ is the regional capital and the most dynamic city in Brittany. It provided the nation with useful experience in urban regeneration when most of the medieval town, apart from a few picturesque streets was consumed by fire in 1720. It was rebuilt in the elegant classical style of the time. To speed up housing, buildings were sold off in

Main Attractions

Rennes
Josselin
Vannes
Golfe du Morbihan
Carnac Standing Stones
Concarneau Ville close
Quimper
Brest, Oceanopolis
Parish Closes
Dinan
St-Malo

Happy to be Breton.

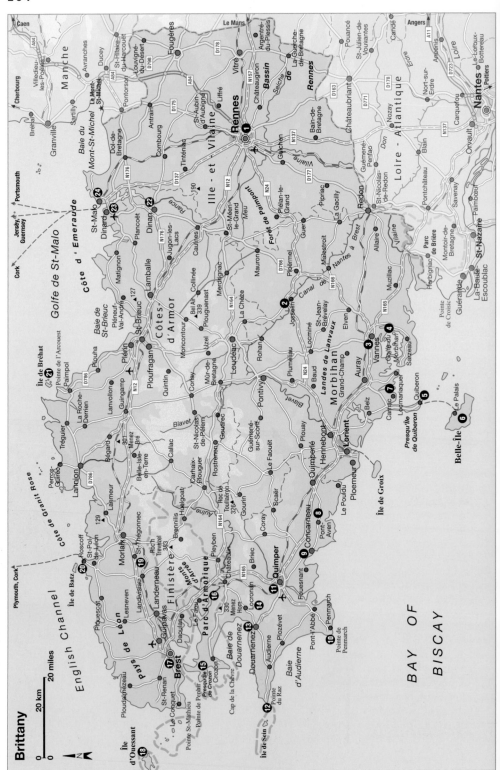

separate flats, two centuries before this became common practice.

Pre-fire half-timbered buildings can still be seen around Places des Lices, where there is a large Saturday morning market, and Place St-Anne, the lively heart of the old town, where inviting bars and *crêperies* are enlivened by students from the city's two universities.

The 17th-century parliament building also survived the fire, only to be severely burnt during fishermen's riots in 1994. Now restored and re-opened, it can be visited (guided tours only, contact the tourist office, tel: 02 99 67 11 11).

The **Musée de Bretagne** (www.musee-bretagne.fr; Tue noon–9pm, Wed–Fri noon–7pm, Sat–Sun 2–7pm; charge), on the quay by the Vilaine river, is the place to get a feel for the region. It has an ethnological collection, with an art museum attached containing work by Paul Gauguin and the Pont-Aven School.

Rural heartland

From Rennes head southwest, passing through a lush landscape that becomes rougher and more windblown, the houses lower, the agriculture more basic as you penetrate deeper into the peninsula.

Josselin ❷, in the heart of inland Brittany, is a pleasant place to spend a couple of days. This energetic little town, with one steep street running down to the river bank, half-timbering, busy Saturday morning street market and friendly, crowded local cafés, typifies rural Brittany.

The river that runs below the town is the Oust, canalised long ago to form part of the **Nantes-Brest Canal**. Its rippling waters reflect the dream-like **Château Josselin** of the Rohan family, the kind of castle that might illustrate a tale of chivalry and enchantment (www.chateaujosselin.com; mid-July–Aug daily 11–6pm, Apr–mid-July and Sept daily 2–6pm, Oct Sat–Sun 2–5.30 pm; charge). Across the river, perched on the opposite bank, is the unpretentiously lovely **Chapelle de Ste Croix**, which speaks of the other side of the Middle Ages – graceful piety.

The south coast

To the south lies **Vannes** ❸, on the coast – just. Its port has lost its

Josselin's main square.

TIP

Make a detour to the modern sculpture park, just 16km (10 miles) to the southwest of Josselin, at Kerguél-hennec. Works by European sculptors are displayed in the grounds of the 18th-century château. (July–Sept daily, rest of year Wed–Sun; charge).

importance partly through silting and partly through the increasing size of ships. But you can still sail there in a small boat to arrive at a yacht-basin opposite Place Gambetta under the fine ramparts, where there are many pavement cafés. Porte St-Vincent, just behind it, leads into the old town.

Vannes is a delightful place. The great **ramparts** are punctuated by fairy-tale round towers with tall conical slate hats. Beside the Porte Poterne are the *anciens lavoirs*, 17th century communal laundries.

Inside the walls, in the old town, are half-timbered houses, most built with jetties, each floor projecting a little beyond the one below, so that in a narrow street the topmost floors are almost touching.

The **Cathédrale St Pierre**, in the maze of winding streets that make up the medieval quarter, is noble and lofty outside, though lowering and forbidding in its interior, while the **Hôtel de Ville** is a striking example of the florid confidence of the late 19th century. In the open space in front is a swaggering statue of the Connétable

de Richemont, a 15th-century worthy who trounced the English and thereby put an end to the Hundred Years' War.

The ancient covered market on the Place St-Pierre, dating from the 13th century, once housed the Breton parliament and, until the 1950s, a theatre. Today it is the museum of fine arts, **La Cohue** (mid-June–mid-Sept daily 10am–6pm, mid-Sept–mid-June Tue–Sun 1.30–6pm; charge) displaying works from Delacroix, Corot and Goya, and contemporary artists such as Tal Coat and Soulages.

Golfe du Morbihan

Vannes is in the department of Morbihan. The name means "Little Sea" and the **Golfe du Morbihan ❹** is a vast inlet, effectively a seawater lake, fed by various channels from the Atlantic. It is 20km (12 miles) wide and from the open sea to the inner shore it reaches 15km (9 miles).

It is tidal and dotted with islands, of which the largest are **Arz** and **L'Ile aux Moines**, each of which supports a few hundred inhabitants. People who frequent the gulf do so by boat, mostly

Quiberon beach at high tide.

ARTHURIAN LEGENDS

The enchanted Forêt de Paimpont, southwest of Rennes, is steeped in legends of King Arthur and the Knights of the Round Table looking for the Holy Grail. This deep tangled forest covering over 7,000ha (17,300 acres) can be explored by marked footpaths, or by car on the Circuit de Brocéliande (information from Paimpont tourist office). In the north of the forest, the Château de Comper houses a visitor centre (Mar–June, Sept–Oct Thu–Mon 10am–5.30pm; July–Aug Thu–Tue 10am–7pm; charge) that relates through storytellers, exhibitions and guided walks the mysticism surrounding King Arthur. The legends extend throughout Brittany; the Golfe de Morbihan is said to have been filled by the tears of fairies chased from Brocéliande, and their fallen crowns became islands that dot the gulf.

to fish, kept company by the largest concentration of seabirds on the French Atlantic coast. The uninhabited island of **Méaban** at the entrance to the gulf, and the Duer marsh area of the **Presqu'île de Rhuys** are both excellent bird sanctuaries where you can spot oyster-catchers, crested cormorants, hooded mergansers, sandpipers, plovers, spoonbills and egrets. The islands of **Belle-Ile** and **Groix** are also of interest to bird-watchers. Information about the various boat trips around the gulf, stopping off at some of the islands, is available from Vannes; enquire at the tourist office on Quai Tabarly (tel: 0297 47 24 34).

Quiberon

The mouth of the gulf is guarded by a thin shell of land which makes safe haven for **Locmariaquer** and **Arzon**. Further out there is an even thinner finger of shore, running down from the summer resort of **Quiberon ❺** where there is a little harbour and lovely sandy beach.

A 45-minute car ferry ride due south from Quiberon brings you to Brittany's largest island, **Belle-Ile ❻**. It has a varied landscape of exposed highlands, sheltered valleys, rugged cliffs and golden beaches, and is ideal for walking and camping. Its port and capital is **Le Palais**, dominated by the Citadelle, a 16th-century fortress which houses the Musée Historique (daily; charge) with items relating to the island's past.

Mystical Carnac

The Quiberon peninsula provides shelter for magical **Carnac ❼**. This is one of the most important Celtic sites in Europe, the centre of a culture where a feeling of the past is so strong that in thousands of years it has not dispersed: the great stone circles and alignments of menhirs (single standing stones) and dolmens (hanging stones). This is where our ancestors of the Neolithic and Early Bronze Ages enacted their sacred rituals of death and the renewal of life.

Carnac's Standing Stones (daily, but times can vary, summer guided tours only, charge; winter, free access) consists of three groups of menhirs,

TIP

The best of Brittany's beaches lie on the south and north coasts. On the south, head for Bénodet, the Quiberon Peninsula, Carnac-Plage or Locmariaquer. On the north coast, try Trégastel, Tréstrignel, or Cap Fréhel, west of St-Malo.

Menhirs at Carnac.

Celtic-inspired souvenirs for sale in Carnac.

Sailing boats on the Aven, at Pont-Aven.

arranged in patterns of 10 to 13 rows, and also a series of long cairns covering funerary chambers. Time has not left the menhirs intact – it is probable that each row ended in a semi-circle of stones that are no longer standing – but still there are around 3,000 of them, and the effect is awe-inspiring.

Carnac has, of course, been carefully investigated and excavated, and many examples of fine workmanship have been taken away to museums. These include beautiful polished axes in jadeite. Objects made from jadeite have also been found in tombs of the ancient Chinese and of the Native Americans. There is also a **Musée de Préhistoire** (www.museede carnac.com; July–Aug daily, Apr–June, Sept–Oct 10am–12.30pm, 2–6pm (closes 5.30pm in Oct), Nov and Mar 2–5.30pm; charge), which sets Carnac's megaliths in the context of prehistory in an accessible way.

The Pont-Aven School

To the west lies **Pont-Aven 8** amid wooded river valleys and secluded coves that reveal the mellow side of Brittany. The Pont-Aven School of artists started coming here in the 1850s to escape Paris and find unspoiled surroundings. Today the town keeps up its artistic tradition with a collection of art galleries selling contemporary paintings. If you want to see Gauguin's work, you'll need to visit Rennes or Quimper.

When Gauguin returned here in the 1880s, he thought it had become far too touristy, and he escaped to the quiet little seaside resort of **Le Pouldu**, 16km (10 miles) to the southeast, the subject of several of his seascapes and harvest paintings.

The Southwest

West of Pont-Aven is **Concarneau 9**, whose granite-walled citadel, Ville Close, is built on a rocky outcrop in the bay, and tethered to the shore by a small bridge. The **Musée de la Pêche** (mid-Feb–Oct and Christmas school holidays daily; charge) traces the history of the industry from its earliest days.

Before retiring inland, take a trip out to **Pays Bigouden**, to the west.

Here the land falls flat to the sea, provoking thoughts of storms, shipwrecks and toiling seaweed gatherers.

From the top of the Eckmühl Lighthouse you can survey the **Pointe de Penmarch ❿** and the immense sweep of the Baie d'Audierne. Such great and majestic stretches of coast look much as they must have done 2,000 years ago. Even today, a primitive Brittany isn't difficult to imagine.

Finistère

Southern Finistère is known as **Cornouaille**, so named by the Celts who fled across the English Channel from Cornwall in the 6th century BC. Here Breton culture remains most evident.

Its capital, **Quimper ⓫**, from the Breton *kemper* meaning 'confluent', sits at the convergence of the rivers Odet and Steir. On the north bank of the River Odet the old streets clustered around the **Cathédrale St Corentin** have plenty of enticing *crêperies*. A *galette* (buckwheat pancake) with a savoury or sweet filling and a cup of cider will seem quite appropriate after visiting the city's **Musée des Beaux-Arts** (July–Aug daily 10am–7pm, Apr–June, Sept Wed–Mon 9.30am–noon, 2–6pm, Nov–Mar until 5.30pm and closed Sun am, closed public hols; charge), which houses an excellent collection of Breton paintings, including works by Paul Gauguin and the Pont-Aven School. With its strong Celtic identity you can find specialist shops selling Breton-language books, Quimper pottery (which has been made here since 1690) and *keltia musique*. The Festival de Cornouaille, held every July, is a celebration of Celtic music and culture.

Windswept promontories

Lunging out into the Atlantic Ocean the **Pointe du Raz ⓬** is a rocky promontory at the western edge of southern Finistère. At over 70m (230ft) high it is a dramatic spur of rugged rocks formed from the constant pounding of the waves. There are several footpaths weaving their way across the headland, including the long-distance path GR34, and on a clear day the **Ile**

FACT

A Breton legend concerns the founder of Quimper, King Gradlon: his coastal kingdom of Ys was engulfed by waves after his daughter was duped by the devil into opening the city gates. The king escaped on horseback with his daughter, but was ordered by God to jettison her, at which point the seas retreated.

Quimper's footbridges in bloom.

The lighthouse of the Creac'h (meaning "promontory" in Breton) on Ouessant is one of the island's five lighthouses.

The Crozon Peninsula, a rewarding landscape for ramblers.

de Sein and **Ar Men** lighthouse can be seen from the clifftop.

Continue along the coast, bordering the bay, to the pretty fishing port of **Douarnenez** ⑬. Once a leading sardine port, it was here that the canning industry was established in 1853. The best place to pick up a tin of sardines is at Penn Sardin, 7 rue Lebreton. This specialist shop, a few streets back from the Grand Port, has a vast range of tinned sardines, some even vintage.

The quays of **Port du Rosmeur** on the eastern side of the town are lined with fish restaurants and cafés, and the Port du Plaisance is notable for the **Le Port-Musée**, which charts the local seafaring history (July–Aug daily 10am–7pm, Apr–June, Sept–Oct (museum and boats) Tue–Sun 10am–12.30pm, 2–6pm, Feb–Mar and Christmas hols (museum only) 10am–12.30pm, 2–6pm; charge).

Inland from Douarnenez is the picture-postcard village of **Locronan** ⑭, which swarms with tourists in summer. The granite Renaissance houses in the cobbled square were built when the town was the centre of sail-cloth manufacture. Each July Locronan is the setting for the Petit Troménie, a pilgrimage held in honour of St Ronan an Irish monk who fervently worked, to convert the pagan Bretons.

The Crozon Peninsula

The landscape of the hammer-head shaped **Crozon Peninsula** ⑮ offers myriad delights, from wind buffeted cliffs to sandy coves with turquoise waters. The route from the mainland traces its way through wild moorland before arriving at the busy market town of **Crozon**. The main interest here is the Eglise St-Pierre, which has a magnificent 16th-century wooden altarpiece depicting the story of the Ten Thousand Martyrs.

Just down the hill is the pretty seaside resort of **Morgat**, with a modern marina and a sandy beach sheltered by trees. Originally a small fishing village it was made popular as a holiday resort in the early 20th century by the Peugeot family which built hotels here for their employees.

South of Morgat at **St Hernot**, housed in the old school building, is the **Maison des Minéraux** (July–Aug daily 10am–7pm, Apr–June, Sept–mid-Nov Mon–Fri 10am–noon, 2–5pm, Sun 2–5pm; charge). The highlight of the collection is a rare display of fluorescent rocks.

For spectacular seaviews from craggy outcrops head for the **Cap de la Chèvre, Pointe de Penhir** and the bleak **Pointe des Espagnols**.

A good chunk of this weather-beaten landscape now belongs to the **Parc Régional d'Armorique** ⑯ which extends westward from the granitic moorlands of the Monts d'Arrée, along the Crozon Peninsula and across the sea to Ile de Ouessant.

This is a wild region of desolate gorse-edged uplands and dense green woodlands, shot through with streams, lakes and rivers littered with huge boulders. The peaked crown of its highest point, **Roc'h Trévezel**, juts out of a windswept moorland plateau and provides magnificent views north to the coast and south past the Montagne St Michel to the Montagnes Noir.

Brest

Brest ⑰ is one of France's most important naval ports and the European capital of marine science and technology. Many of its attractions have a nautical theme.

The **Musée National de la Marine** (www.musee-marine.fr; Apr–Sept Wed–Mon 10am–6.30pm, Oct–Mar 1.30pm–6.30pm, open Tue during school hols, charge) is housed in the city's sturdy 12th-century castle.

A short way from the city centre at the Port de Plaisance lies Brest's biggest tourist attraction, the excellent **Océanopolis** (www.oceanopolis.co.uk; for times see website or tel: 02 98 34 40 40; charge), a futuristic sea centre covering three themes: polar, tropical and temperate.

Brest also has a rich cultural calendar including the tall-ship event that takes place every four years in July (2016, 2020). This is a gathering of over 2,000 sailing vessels arriving by sea at the tip of Brittany. During this festival chartered sailing trips around the coast are on offer.

Ile d'Ouessant

Known to the English as Ushant, **Ile d'Ouessant** ⑱ is the most remote of Brittany's islands – stormy and windswept in winter, besieged by migrating birds in spring and autumn, and pleasantly mild in summer. It is best explored by taking the rugged 45km (28 mile) coastal path. There is an air service from Brest, and a ferry, which takes 2.5 hrs, and a ferry from nearby Le Conquet at the end of the Crozon Peninsula, which takes 1.5 hours.

Back on the mainland the landscape becomes increasingly wild, rocky and stormy as you move towards Finistère, the End of the Earth. This is where you'll find the *enclos paroissiaux*, the parish closes of **northern Finistère**, of which perhaps **St-Thégonnec** ⑲ is the best-known example.

In a boarded up doorway, this mural of a Breton woman shows her proudly wearing the traditional Breton headdress.

The resort of Morgat.

TIP

Several walks follow the coastline on the old coastguards' paths, or Sentiers des Douaniers. Particularly recommended is the watchpath from Perros-Guirec to Ploumanach which leads past the rose-tinted rocks of the Côte de Granit Rose.

The north coast

The Channel ferry port of **Roscoff ⓴** once had a reputation for piratical corsairs and the shipowners grew rich from their booty. Their 16th and 17th century mansions show how much they profited. Marine memorabilia fills the church.

Expect onions to feature on restaurant menus – the town is known for them, and they have an Appellation d'Origine Protégée. It was from here that the first onion sellers, called Johnnies, got on their bikes and took their strings of onions to Britain. Their story is told in the Maison des Johnnies and there is an onion festival every August.

It's a 15-minute ferry ride from Roscoff to the **Ile de Batz**, where there is an exotic garden and a lighthouse you can climb.

Heading east, the coastline between Trébeurden and Paimpol is called the **Côte de Granit Rose** after its pink-hued cliffs. There are many fine, sandy beaches here, several of which, such as Trégastel, have rock pools and huge, bizarrely shaped granite boulders.

Well worth discovering is the delightful **Ile de Bréhat ㉑**, off the Côte de Granit Rose, which is easily accessible from the Pointe de l'Arcouest near Paimpol. It has a mild climate, and is a pleasure to wander round, as it is a car-free zone.

The stretch of coast between Pointe de Grouin and Val-André is known as the **Côte d'Emeraude** and it encompasses sweeping sandy bays, rocky headlands – such as Cap Fréhel with a lighthouse and carpet of spring flowers – secret inlets, meandering estuaries and pretty seaside towns.

Some 10 river-miles inland is the beautiful old town of **Dinan ㉒** Rue du Jerzual, rising steeply up the high bluffs that overlook the River Rance, is lined with fine old half-timbered houses, in many of which artists and crafts people live and work. And from the Jardin Anglais behind the stately church of **St Sauveur** there is a wonderful view of the river, crossed by a huge viaduct and a reconstructed Gothic bridge.

St-Malo intra-muros – aka the walled city.

A trip down river is rewarding. The banks are green and wooded, with fine houses to be glimpsed. Small cabins on stilts allow fishermen to sit right over the tidal flow of the river. On top of these cabins are crossed staves, which, when projected forward, make a square framework for a close-meshed net which they lower and bring up repeatedly with pulleys. The catch has to be something too small to be fished with a baited hook, but abundant enough to be caught in bulk, such as whitebait.

A hydro-electric dam crosses the estuary harnessing the tide.

Dinard and St-Malo

Dinard and St-Malo lie either side of the estuary and form an attractive holiday centre on the Côte d'Emeraude.

Dinard ㉓, "the Cannes of the North", is touched by the Gulf Stream, and its mild climate and wonderful stretch of beaches have made it a successful resort ever since resorts came into being. Here, from the 1890s, the well-to-do merchants of northern France built a wonderful

fantasy of clifftop mansions, with turrets and pillars and buttresses – Alfred Hitchcock based the house in Psycho on one of the houses here.

There are several grand hotels, a casino and sea water therapy centre. Palm trees line the Promenade du Claire de Lune, where piped music soothes summer strollers.

On the opposite side of the estuary, surrounded by wide, clean beaches, is the august, historic walled town of **St-Malo ㉔**. Ideally situated on what was once an island at the entrance to the English Channel, the town's corsairs could exact payment from passing traffic. Their story is told in the town museum in the keep of castle, and in the 1725 Privateer's House, which contains weapons and other memorabilia.

The best way to get a feel for the town is to walk along the top of the magnificent granite ramparts. Inside, the town is a delightful mélange of streets, with charming shops, *crêperies* and atmospheric restaurants that help make it the most visited place in Brittany.

FACT

Natives of St-Malo are Malouins, whose forefathers roamed far and wide. They settled in – and gave their name to – the Malvinas (Falkland Islands) and landed in Canada in 1534.

A bounty of oysters.

PARISH CLOSES

Born of an intense faith and spurred by a keen inter-parish rivalry, Brittany's parish closes (*enclos paroissiaux*) now stand in lichen-covered testimony to the fervour and superstition that once gripped the Breton soul. Begun in the mid-16th century and completed over the following 150 years, these are grandiose religious ensembles adorned with elaborate granite carvings, their churches, calvaries, ossuaries and triumphal arches absurdly large for the small rural communities that created them.

Morlaix is the closest town to the three most interesting parish closes, of which **St-Thégonnec** is the most complete, exhibiting all the traditional elements. Rivalry with neighbouring **Guimiliau** was intense: theirs is the most impressive of Breton calvaries with more than 200 figures carved between 1581 and 1588. **Lampaul-Guimiliau** has perhaps the simplest close complex, but its church has a marvellous canopy over the font, while in front of the choir, a rood beam spans the central nave. Christ on the cross can be seen on one side, and on both sides groups of figures depict the Stations of the Cross. To the left of the choir stand three altarpieces depicting St Miliau and the birth of the Virgin, a rare theme in Brittany.

Look for signposts to the Circuit des Enclos Paroissiaux.

LOIRE VALLEY

The wealth and beauty of this lush valley were once denied to all but a privileged few. Today, the private domains of the Loire are a public showcase of French civilisation.

Main Attractions
Chambord
Blois
Amboise
Chenonceau
Tours
Azay-le-Rideau
Villandry
Chinon
Fontevraud l'Abbaye
Saumur
Angers
Bourges

The Château de Sully-sur-Loire, a moated castle.

Once the setting for the French court, the Loire valley attracted counts and courtiers who wanted easy access to the king, and built their grandiose homes close to the royal palaces. Where all was once designed to exclude the many and please a few, today the visitor is welcomed in the châteaux and their parks. Between visits, you can enjoy the quiet pleasures of a beautiful, and little changed, landscape, and the rivers that define it.

Starting at the eastern end of the Loire Valley, the small town of **Gien**

❶ owes much of its beauty to Anne de Beaujeu, daughter of Louis XI. She was responsible for building the château, the bridge, the cloisters and church in the late 15th century. The château now houses a museum of hunting, the **Musée International de la Chasse** (closed for restoration until early 2016).

The red and black brick of the château, laid in geometric patterns, is one of the typical styles of the valley. The streets of this lively little Renaissance town are hung with flags and lined with flowers. Faïencerie de Gien (glazed earthenware), founded in 1821, is well known for its bright designs; the riverside factory can be visited only by request (write in advance or telephone 02 38 05 21 05, museum and shop Mon–Sat 10am–6pm; charge).

Castles and churches

About 23km (14 miles) downstream from Gien lies the château of **Sully-sur-Loire** ❷ (daily 10am–6pm, closed Jan; charge). Seemingly afloat along with the ducks and swans around it, the castle has two distinct parts: the early 14th-century fortress and the 17th-century wing added by the Duc de Sully, finance minister to Henry IV. In the older section, three vast rooms on succeeding floors tell of life in the Middle Ages. Furniture was reduced to large chests which served for storage, seating, even sleeping; dining tables were planks laid over simple trestles; the court slept as many as 12 to a bed.

The big draughty rooms were lined with tapestries, which were also used as hanging partitions.

The high, keel-shaped timber roof, made of chestnut, is 600 years old. The great tree trunks were soaked and salted, heated and bent, a process that took up to 50 years. In the 17th-century wing, the rooms are of more human proportions. The beams are hidden by ornamental ceilings and the floors panelled in wood. Sully-sur-Loire is a rare example of a château with the contrasting architecture of medieval fortress and Renaissance pleasure palace.

A little further downstream, pause to see not a château but a church: that of **St-Benoît-sur-Loire** ❸, one of the finest Romanesque buildings in France. Most remarkable is the square bell tower which forms the porch, embellished with three aisles of arches decorated with carved capitals. The crypt contains the relics of St Benedict, brought from Italy in the 7th century – a monastery was founded here in AD650.

Some 10 miles further along the river is **Germigny-des-Prés** ❹, a diminutive church dating from the time of Charlemagne (9th century, except for the 11th-century nave). It contains a wonderful Byzantine glass mosaic, also 9th century, which was uncovered in 1840. Glowing with colour, it depicts the Ark of the Covenant.

The Maid of Orléans

At the point where the Loire leaves its northward course to flow southeast stands **Orléans** ❺, a modern city whose heart was bombed out during World War II. Its soul, however, lives on in the cult of Joan of Arc; it was here that she successfully resisted the English Army before being burnt at the stake at Rouen. Deprived of its historic buildings except for the **Cathedral**, built and rebuilt in Gothic style over hundreds of years, Orléans is now strewn with memorials to her. In the handsome but desolate **Place du Martroi** there is an equestrian statue of the heroine, and the site where she stayed in 1429 has become the **Maison Jeanne d'Arc** (3 Place du Général-de-Gaulle, Apr–Sept Tue–Sun 10am–6pm, Oct–Mar 2–6pm, closed public hols; charge).

Jeanne d'Arc.

The Loire at Orléans.

FACT

Every year on 7–8 May, Orléans celebrates its liberation from the English by Joan of Arc with a pageant and a service of dedication in the cathedral.

Just 18km (11 miles) west of busy Orléans is quiet **Beaugency** ❻, where an 11th-century bridge provides a view of the river and town. The tiny streets still have a medieval feel. Market days, with local produce and handicrafts, the smell of roast meats and fresh bread, are particularly atmospheric.

The 15th-century **Château de Beaugency** (July–Aug Tue–Sun 10am–7pm, May–June, Sept–Oct Tue–Sun until 6pm, Mar–Apr Sat–Sun 2–6pm; charge), formerly Château Dunois, has remained unchanged, except for slight damage sustained during the French Revolution. After 11 years of internal restoration the renamed château reopened in October 2014, with 15 rooms refurbished to their former glory. Family entertainment and educational workshops are staged throughout the year.

Chambord and Cheverny

In the **Fôret de Chambord**, deer, boar and other wild animals roam the national game reserve freely, and observation towers have been set up for the public. In all, the park covers 5,463 hectares (13,500 acres), surrounded by the longest wall in France.

The **Château de Chambord** ❼ (daily Apr–Sept 9am–6pm, Jan–Mar, Oct–Dec 9am–5pm, closed public hols; charge) is the largest on the Loire, built for François I. It's an airy pleasure palace with such a fanciful array of chimneys and turrets that it has been called "the skyline of Constantinople on a single building". The most striking feature is the double-spiralled staircase in the centre of the castle, where lords and ladies played flirtatious games of hide-and-seek.

From Chambord to Blois, the traveller can take a delightful route past less grandiose châteaux of white tufa stone and slate. At the end of a long avenue of stately trees, **Cheverny** ❽ (www.chateau-cheverny.fr; daily Apr–Sept 9am–6.30pm, Jan–Mar, Oct–Dec 10am–5pm; charge) rises gracefully. Though it is still inhabited – by the same family since the early 16th century – visitors can tour the sumptuous 17th- and 18th-century rooms, richly hung with Aubusson and Flemish tapestries.

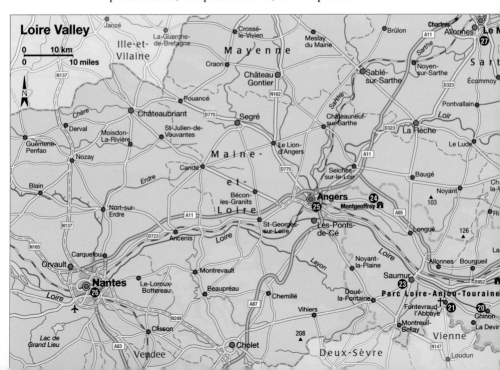

More intimate is the **Château de Beauregard** (www.beauregard-loire.com; July–Aug daily 10am–7pm, Apr–June daily 10.30am–6.30pm, Mar, Oct–Nov Mon–Fri 1.30pm–5pm, Sat–Sun 10am–5pm; charge) in the nearby village of Cellettes, with a 17th-century Galerie des Portraits, containing charmingly naive depictions of 327 famous men and women; the tiny Cabinet des Grélots, with marquetry of bells; and a lovely modern walled garden, which is at its best in May.

A short distance away is **Fougères sur Bièvre** ❾, a charming village off the tourist track, with a 15th-century feudal château, built for the treasurer of Louis XI (mid-May–mid-Sept daily 9.30am–12.30pm and 2–6.30pm, mid-Sept–mid-May Wed–Mon 10am–12.30pm, 2–5pm; charge).

Elegant Blois

To the north, the town of **Blois** ❿ was a central stage for courtly intrigue. Louis d'Orléans was assassinated in the **Château de Blois** (www.chateaude blois.fr; daily July–Aug 9am–7pm, Jan–Mar and Nov–Dec 9am–12.30pm

and 1.30–5.30pm, Apr–June and Sept–Oct 9am–6pm, closed some public hols; charge), as was Duc de Guise, suspected of plotting against Henry III. His mother, Catherine de Medici, gave up the ghost in the castle after a lifetime of power play; her gorgeous apartments are riddled with secret hidey-holes. Their stories are told in the spectral *son et lumière* (Apr–mid-Sept).

In the clear light of day, Blois is a pleasant, sunny place. The château's monumental octagonal staircase and its sculpted balconies are superb examples of early French Renaissance design. Though the town itself suffered during World War II, the reconstruction was all carried out in regional style, with slate roofs and brick chimneys. The pedestrian areas near the castle are paved in colourful stone.

The Loire at nearby **Chaumont-sur-Loire** ⓫ is very wide, and the round towers of the **Château de Chaumont** (daily 10am–5pm, longer hours in summer; charge) look down on it from the top of a wooded hill. Catherine de Medici acquired it in 1560 after the

The porcupine, carved into the stone of the Château de Blois, was the emblem of Louis XII.

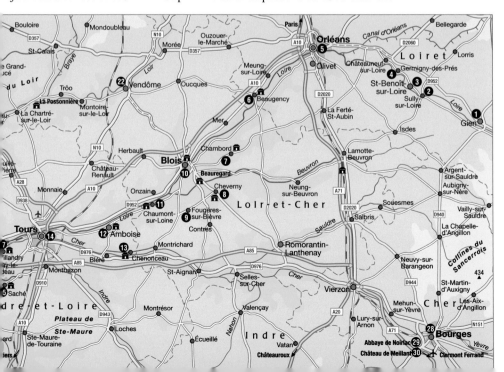

Taking shelter in the park at Chaumont.

death of her husband Henry II, when she forced his mistress, Diane de Poitiers, to leave her palace of Chenonceau and move here. Visiting the richly furnished rooms and the large, attractive gardens, it is hard to relate to Diane's distress. Today, however, Chaumont is known for its adventurous **International Garden Festival**, when experimental themed gardens by leading garden designers, architects and artists transform the grounds each summer.

As you cross the river at Chaumont, the park and the Loire form a lovely picture. Reaching the village of **Onzain**, you are in the **Vallée de la Cisse**, whose winding river flows through the pleasant rolling hills of Touraine-Mesland, many of which are covered with vineyards.

Leonardo's last home

Château de Chaumont.

Downstream, the town of **Amboise** ⑫ nestles around an impressive **château** (www.chateau-amboise.com; daily July–Aug 9am–7pm, Mar, Nov 9am–5.30pm, Apr–June 9am–6.30pm, Sept–Oct 9am–6pm, rest of the year 9am–12.30, 2–5pm, closes some public hols; charge). Rich in history, Amboise belonged to the Counts of Anjou and Berry before becoming a part of the French throne in 1434. Charles VIII died here of a concussion he inflicted on himself passing through a low doorway. Visitors take note – and duck.

The murderous Amboise Conspiracy of 1560 was no accident, however, and the cursed château fell from royal favour. Napoleon handed it over to politician Roger Duclos, who demolished two-thirds of it, and World War II damaged most of what was left. Only the facade facing the river reveals the original Renaissance charm. Nonetheless, the château is still beautiful and contains several unique features, notably the **Tour des Minimes**, with a spiral ramp for mounted horsemen, and the **Chapelle St Hubert**, where Leonardo da Vinci is buried.

The town seems a natural extension of the château. Rue Nationale is the colourful main market street, reserved for pedestrians. The essence of a provincial French town is captured in the sing-song of the merchants, the cafés, aromas and abundant fresh produce.

A short walk from the château is **Clos Lucé** (www.vinci-closluce.com; daily July–Aug 9am–8pm, Feb–June and Sept–Oct 9am–7pm, rest of the year it closes earlier 02 47 57 00 73; charge), the red-brick manor house where Leonardo spent the last three years of his life, invited to join the royal court by his patron and admirer, François I. The house is a museum now, displaying scale models of his precocious inventions, based on the master's drawings. Outside, the family-oriented **Parc Léonard de Vinci** (hours as Clos Lucé above; charge) is dotted with lifesize interactive maquettes of Leonardo's inventions, such as the helicoidal screw, the multi-barrelled cannon and the armoured car.

If you leave the banks of the Loire, and follow instead its tributary, the Cher, you will come to the **Château de Chenonceau** ⑬ (www.chenonceau.com; daily July–Aug 9am–8pm, June, Sept 9am–7.30pm, Mar–May 9am–7pm, rest of the year it closes earlier; charge). This is perhaps the most elegant of all the Loire valley jewels, renowned for the arches that carry it across the water. The building rests on pillars planted in the river bed, but might as well be floating on air, light and delicate as it is. The interior is worthy of the architecture. At night, a *son et lumière* recounts the story of Diane, Henry II's favourite, and his jealous wife, Catherine de Medici, who couldn't bear to see so much perfection and not own it.

The tumultuous events of the 20th century touched the château, when owner Gaston Menier set up a military hospital in the gallery during World War I. During World War II, a number of people benefited from the particular situation of Chenonceau village: the southern exit was in the free zone, while the château entrance was in German occupied territory.

Lily of the valley

Amboise and Chenonceau are on the eastern edge of the region called **Touraine**. The city of Tours is the centre of this "Garden of France" described by novelist Honoré de Balzac in *The Lily of the Valley*: "Each step in this land of enchantment allows a fresh discovery of a picture, the frame of which is a river or a tranquil pool in whose

TIP

Tours of Chenonceau are self-guided, so you can wander at will. Don't miss a visit to the kitchens, housed in the feet of the bridge, with their very effective waste-disposal system.

Exquisite stained glass displaying the coat of arms of Catherine de Medici.

TAKE A SLOW BOAT ON THE RIVER

The Loire river, together with its tributaries the Sarthe, Mayenne and Cher, and their associated canals, makes a boat the obvious way to get around. One of the best ways to get afloat is to take a trip on one of the traditional wooden boats, *gabares* (also called *chalands*) and their smaller versions, *toues*, sail-powered craft steered with an oar. Their flat shallow draft enables them to avoid being grounded on the sandbanks.

The Association Millière Raboton, based in Chaumont-sur-Loire offers trips in a *toue* for 12 passengers at a time (tel: 06 88 76 57 14 www.milliere-raboton.net). A Toue Loire operates *toues* and *gabares* out of Angers (tel: 06 80 08 13 03 www.atoueloire.com).

Other companies offer sightseeing trips in more conventional boats. La Ligérienne de Navigation at Rochecorbon sails along the River Loire (tel: 0247 52 68 88 www.naviloire.com). Bateaux Nantais is based in Nantes (tel: 02 40 14 51 14 www.bateaux-nantais.fr) and runs cruises lasting 1hr 45min up the River Erdre to the Château de la Gascherie. The *Gabare* and *L'Ambacia* sail from Chisseaux through the arches of the Château de Chenonceau. (tel: 02 47 23 98 64 www.labelandre.com).

If, on the other hand, you want to go as you please, a number of companies offer barges (*péniches*) and cruisers for hire, fully equipped with all mod cons.

Ceiling carving at the Château of Azay-le-Rideau.

A lesson in topiary at Villandry.

watery depths are reflected a château and its turrets, parks and fountains."

As you head towards the centre of Touraine, you pass **Château d'Artigny**, high above the Indre river valley. Designed by the perfumer François Coty in pure 18th-century style with spacious lawns and terraces, the château has been converted into a luxury hotel. Nearby, the 10th-century **Château de Montbazon** is mostly in ruins. The eccentric American painter Lillian Whittaker once lived here and fond tales of "La Dame de Montbazon" may be heard. A small crêperie at the foot of the ruins is pleasant for lunch.

Tours

The capital of the Loire-et-Indre department, **Tours** ⓮ is a thriving and lively university town with a number of interesting buildings. These include the **Cathédrale St Gatien** with a fine cloister and scriptorium (daily 9am–7pm, charge); the shrine of St Martin in the **Nouvelle Basilique St Martin**; and the **Musée des Beaux-Arts** (Wed–Mon 9am–12.45pm, 2–6pm, closed some public hols; charge) with its interesting collection of paintings and decorative arts. More quirky is the **Musée du Compagnonnage** (www.museecomgag nonnage.fr; 16 June–15 Sept daily 9am–12.30, 2–6pm, 16 Sept–15 June Wed–Mon 9am–noon, 2–6pm, closed public hols; charge), which is full of masterpieces from craft guilds ranging from slate-working to chocolate.

The medieval quarter, centred around **Place Plumereau**, has many picturesque half-timbered buildings. One important event occurred in Tours in the 5th century. Saint Martin had planted a vineyard in his monastery. One day monks discovered their errant donkeys had found a way into it and chewed off most of the tender young branches. The following year's harvest was the best ever, and *la taille* (pruning) has been practised ever since.

The River Indre

Deep in the **Indre valley** lies the river itself, "unravelling like a serpent in a magnificent emerald basin". Honoré de Balzac loved the valley dearly, and in the 1830s he passed his most prolific days in the **Château de Saché** ⓯

(www.lysdanslavallee.fr; July–Aug daily 10am–7pm, Apr–June and Sept daily 10am–6pm, Oct–Mar Wed–Mon 10am–12.30pm, 2–5pm, closed public hols; charge). The corpulent author of *La Comédie Humaine* series of 90 novels worked daily from 2am to 5pm when he stayed at Saché, which belonged to friends of his parents.

Inside, devotees will discover a wonderful collection of Balzac memorabilia, including letters and portraits of his lady loves, his manuscripts (which he edited at such length that typesetters refused to work on them more than one hour a day, and that at double pay) and his room, exactly as it was. The first-floor salon has also retained its character, in part due to the surprising optical illusion of the hand-painted wallpaper. The arrangement of the furniture and game tables makes it easy to imagine the drawing-room intrigues described in novels of the period.

Further along the Indre is **Azay-le-Rideau** 🆖, a small château of exquisite proportions (daily July–Aug 9.30am–7pm, Apr–June, Sept daily 9.30am–6pm, Oct–Mar 10am–5.15pm, closed some public hols; charge). The river forms a wide moat around this epitome of Renaissance grace and perfection. The influence of medieval defence architecture is clear, but at Azay all is designed for pleasure. The turrets are slim and elegant, the crenellations ornamental, and the outlook better for observing clouds reflected in the water than advancing enemies.

The River Cher

Touraine's fourth major river is the Cher, and not far from its banks stand the **Château de Villandry** 🆗 and its famous 16th-century **gardens** (www.chateauvillandry.fr; July–Aug 9am–6.30pm, rest of the year 9am–5.30/6pm, opening times are subject to change, phone Feb–mid-Nov daily for details 02 47 50 02 09, gardens open daily all year; charge). The three tiers of the garden (pond, decorative gardens and kitchen garden) can be viewed at once from the high terrace of the château. Planted with low boxwood and yew hedges enclosing flowerbeds, the gardens represent the four faces of love on one side, music on the other.

FACT

In Villandry's kitchen garden you will find many vegetables, both exotic and common, but no potatoes: they were not introduced until the 18th century.

Small but perfectly formed – Azay-le-Rideau.

Renaissance author François Rabelais, creator of the rambunctious and bawdy giants Gargantua and Pantagruel.

The kitchen gardens and herb garden were designed according to documents preserved by medieval monks. The kitchen garden is like something from *Alice Through the Looking Glass.* Each square describes a geometric design in contrasting colours that change from year to year in the course of crop rotation. The standard red roses sweetening the air represent the monks tending the vegetable plots.

Sleeping beauties

North of Villandry, on the Loire, the **Château de Langeais** ⓭ presents a much more severe image (www. chateau-de-langeais.com; daily July–Aug 9am–7pm, Feb–Mar 9.30am–5.30pm, mid-Nov–Jan 10am–5pm, rest of the year 9.30am–6.30pm; charge). Built in the 15th century by Louis XI as a defensive fortress on the site of a 10th-century stronghold, it has never been altered or added to. The last owner, Jacques Siegfried, oversaw the complete furnishing of the castle in wonderful period pieces before donating it to the Institut de France in 1904. Those who are particularly interested in the transition from

Fontevraud Abbey.

medieval to Renaissance life will enjoy the authentic interiors, the 15th-century Flemish and Aubusson tapestries and the unequalled collection of furniture, everything immaculately maintained.

In 1491, Charles VIII married Anne de Bretagne in the Langeais chapel. Her dowry was the realm of Brittany, which thus became united with France. Her reputation for piety is unsurpassed, and her humility and strength of character shine through the ages in the handsome wedding portrait of the couple as well as in her motto, which she had inscribed on the walls: "If God is with us, who can be against us?"

Cross the Loire and head down the D7, where the many turrets of a tall white castle loom up against the background of the tenebrous forest of Chinon. This is **Château d'Ussé** ⓯ (www.chateaudusse.fr; daily mid-Feb–Mar 10am–6pm, Apr–Sept 10am–7pm, Oct–mid-Nov 10am–6pm; charge), the castle which inspired Charles Perrault to write *Sleeping Beauty of the Woods.* The furnishings are in poor repair, but young children will want to visit the wax figures of fairy-tale characters.

THE RIVER LOIRE

There is a lot more to the Loire Valley than the stretch with the châteaux. At 1,012km (630 miles), the Loire is France's longest river, a *fleuve* in French, a river which meets the sea rather than a mere *rivière*, a tributary of another river. Until the railways came, it was one of the country's main highways.

It rises as a spring at the base of Mont Gerbier de Jonc near Sainte-Eulalie in the Ardèche, on the eastern edge of the Massif Central. From there it flows through 12 *départements*, draining a fifth of the land surface of France on the way, to meet the Atlantic at St-Nazaire. It is crossed by 165 bridges carrying roads, railways, pedestrians and even canals. The adjective for all things to do with the Loire is *ligerien(ne)*, from the ancient name for the river, the Liger.

Rabelaisie

On the other side of the dark forest lies Chinon on the River Vienne, in the heart of **Rabelaisie**, the name given to this locality in honour of the 16th-century humanist and author, François Rabelais. His satirical works, *Gargantua* and *Pantagruel*, are recommended for those who would appreciate a less stuffy perspective of the Renaissance. Particularly juicy passages of *Gargantua* describe rather unholy activities at the imaginary Thelème Abbey, where the entrance gate bore the motto: "Do What You Will!". You can visit the **Musée Rabelais**, his house in nearby **La Devinière** (daily July–Aug 10am–7pm, Apr–June, Sept Wed–Mon 10am–12.30 and 2–6pm, rest of the year it closes at 5pm, charge).

The immaculate town of **Chinon** ⓴ itself has an imposing, though largely ruined, 12th-century **château fort** (www.forteressechinon.fr; daily Apr–Sept 9.30am–7pm, Mar and Oct 9.30am–6pm, rest of the year 9.30am–5pm; charge) running along the top of a steep ridge above the well-preserved historic town, overlooking the River Vienne.

The English Plantagenet kings spent much time at Chinon, and Charles VII met Joan of Arc here in 1429.

Now turn back towards the banks of the Loire, passing by **Fontevraud l'Abbaye** ⓴ (www.fontevraud.fr; daily June–Aug 9.30am–6.30pm, Apr–May, Sept–Oct until 6pm, 23 Jan–Mar, Nov–Dec 10am–5pm, closed some public hols; charge). Part of the abbey has been converted into a cultural centre, luxury accommodation and restaurant.

In this rather over-restored 12th-century abbey lie the remains of the earliest Plantagenet kings. Four recumbent funeral effigies are the only decoration in the vaulted 90-metre (295ft) long church. Stone sculptures represent Henry II, his wife Eleanor of Aquitaine and their son Richard the Lionheart. Henry was buried here at his request, though English interests would have preferred that he rested closer to the heart of his kingdom. Eleanor had been the abbess and royal protector of Fontevraud. Richard, who succeeded his father to the English throne, also chose to be buried here, next to his beloved parents. The three polychrome

The recumbent effigies of Henry II, king of England from 1154 to 1189, and his spouse Eleanor of Aquitaine in Fontevraud Abbey.

Chinon, dominated by its château fort.

Saumur's tufa limestone caves.

Sampling the local Saumur wines.

sculptures lie side by side. The fourth figure is that of Isabelle of Angoulême, wife of King John Lackland (Richard's brother), and the oldest known wooden monument of this type.

Architecturally, the abbey is celebrated for its large Romanesque kitchens in the **Tour Evraud**, with 21 chimneys constructed entirely of stone, though the restoration here was completed with some disregard for historical accuracy.

The Loir valley

The River Loir runs to the north of the great Loire, stretching from Ile-de-France to Anjou. The two should not be confused: the Loir is far more tranquil, flowing slowly through a landscape of deep meadows and lines of poplars. Leaving for a time the mighty river, follow the valley of the Loir along the stretch from La Possonnière to Vendôme, where it is at its loveliest.

The manor of **La Possonnière**, birthplace of the poet Ronsard, is a beautiful Renaissance building of white stone (mid-June–mid-Sept daily 10am–6pm, Apr–mid-June, mid-Sept–Oct Thu–Sun 2-6pm; charge).

All around the Touraine region, cellars, terraces and dwellings have been carved out of the tufa, the chalky white stone used to construct most of the Loire châteaux. The village of **Trôo** is known for its maze of subterranean dwellings, called *habitations troglodytiques*. One or two are open to the curious, and the owners will show you how comfortably and snugly you can live underground.

Vendôme ㉒ is an attractive, sophisticated old town full of elegant shops and restaurants. Its centrepiece is the abbey church of **La Trinité**, which encompasses architectural styles from the 11th to the 16th century. The bell tower is the earliest part of the building; the most spectacular is the facade, with resplendent Flamboyant Gothic tracery.

At the crossroads

The D947 route from Fontevraud to **Saumur ㉓** sums up the Loire Valley. Besides the numerous châteaux perched above the majestic river, prehistoric dolmens, troglodyte wine cellars and

Roman churches and baths testify to a long history of human community in this region at the crossroads of Anjou, Poitou and Touraine. Saumur is mainly known for its **château** (July–Aug daily 10am–6.30pm, Apr–early Nov Tue–Sun 10am–1pm, 2pm–5.30pm; charge) and for the **Cadre Noir Cavalry School**; you can visit the school and its stables (www.cadrenoir.co.uk; mid-Feb–Oct for guided visits only 10–11.30am, 2.30–4pm, visits on the half hour mid-Apr–mid-Oct, on the hour in mid-Feb–mid-Apr, late Oct; charge) and maybe watch the morning training sessions.

The network of tufa limestone caves cut into the high cliffs set back from the river serve to age the fine wines of Saumur, and many of the *grandes caves* are open to the public for a tour and a taste. Another use of these cool, dark spaces is the cultivation of mushrooms. The Saumur region is the world's leading mushroom producer. Just outside Saumur in St-Hilaire-St-Florent, the **Musée du Champignon** (www.musee-du-champignon.com; mid-Feb–mid-Nov daily 10am–7pm; charge) offers guided visits of the underground galleries

where all the various uses of the caves are demonstrated.

As you continue towards Angers (along route D74), notice the distinguished 18th-century **Château de Montgeoffroy** ㉔ at Maze, and its long, tree-lined drive. The château, resplendent with Louis XIV furnishings, is still inhabited, but visitors are welcomed (www.chateaudemontgeoffroy.com; daily mid-June–mid-Sept 10am–6pm, mid-Mar–mid-June, mid-Sept–Oct 10am–noon, 2.30–5pm; charge).

Capital of Anjou

Angers ㉕ is the ancient capital of Anjou and fiefdom of the Plantagenets. The **Château** (daily May–4 Sept 9.30am–6.30pm, 5 Sept–Apr 10am–5.30pm; charge) took 100 years to build. The 17 turrets are built in local stone and slate in a striking striped pattern. Formidable from the exterior, the battlements have only a few small openings at the top. From inside the castle, the view of the grassy moat alongside the deer and flowers softens the image somewhat.

Angers is home to an impressive

Wood-carved figure in the facade of a Saumur house.

Château d'Angers.

The rooftops of Bourges.

Visiting the Château des Ducs de Bretagne.

tapestry collection. Most famous is the **Apocalypse of St John**, displayed inside the château in a specially constructed building. The world's largest tapestry is 107 metres (350ft) long and was commissioned by the dukes of Anjou in the 14th century. It is an astonishing show of complexity, technique and imagination. Each of the 75 detailed coloured panels reveals John, in a small Gothic structure, observing and reacting to his fantastic visions.

On the other side of the river, the **Musée Jean Lurçat** (June–Sept daily 10am–6.30pm, Oct–Mar Tue–Sun 10am–noon, 2–6pm; charge) holds that artist's reply to the Apocalypse, *Le Chant du Monde* (Song of the World). Woven at the Aubusson studios from 1957 to 1966, the 10 tapestries are on display in the nearby Gothic **Hôpital St Jean** built by Henry II Plantagenet in repentance for the death of Thomas Becket at Canterbury in 1170. Angers' **Musée des Beaux-Arts** (June–Sept daily 10am–6.30pm, Oct–May Tue–Sun 10am–noon and 2–6pm; charge) displays art from the 15th–20th century in a sumptuously restored Renaissance

house and other buildings.

Outside Angers is a botanical theme park, **Terra Botanica** (daily Apr–Sept 10am–6pm, with exceptions; charge).

Nantes

Near the mouth of the Loire stands the city of **Nantes** ㉖, emotionally and economically attached to Brittany but no longer officially part of it since local government re-organisation in 1972. The two main sights to see are the beautiful, austere **Cathédrale de St Pierre**, whose pale stone resembles that of Canterbury in England and does, in fact, come from the same source, and the **Château des Ducs de Bretagne** (www.chateaunantes.fr; July–Aug daily 10am–7pm, rest of the year Tue–Sun 10am–6pm; charge). The château was begun by Duke François II and continued by his daughter, the Duchess Anne, who married King Louis XII of France in its chapel in 1499, thereby uniting France and Brittany.

North of the River

To the north of the Loire Valley is **Le Mans** ㉗, which has lovely old streets

JULES VERNE'S INSPIRATION

As a young boy growing up in the busy port of Nantes, Jules Verne (1828–1905) was inspired by the sight of so many great ships arriving and departing for mysterious destinations. When he was 12 he stowed away on the *Coralie* bound for the West Indies but only got a short way down river before his father caught up with him. He is famously supposed to have decided as a consequence, "From now on I shall only travel in my imagination."

On leaving home he became a lawyer and stockbroker but his heart was always in writing. His first success was *Five Weeks in a Balloon* (1863) set in Africa and written at a time when aeronautics was still in its infancy. *A Journey to the Centre of the Earth* (1864) brought him further fame. In *Twenty-thousand Leagues Under the Sea* (1870) he returned to his nautical roots, envisaging a submarine, the Nautilus, powered by electricity several years before the electric motor had been perfected. *Around the World in Eighty Days* (1873) describes an attempt to circumnavigate the globe in what was then an impossibly short time. He wrote many more books but his later works are less well known.

Verne is often called the father of science fiction, but above all he was a writer of good adventure stories, some of which have proved to be highly accurate in their technological predictions.

lined with houses dating from the 15th and 16th centuries southwest of the Cathédrale St-Julien. The city is known for its 24-hour endurance car race.

Berry

Southeast of Orléans is **Bourges** ㉘, an architectural gem, and seat of the duchy of Berry. Its 13th-century Cathédrale de St Etienne is one of the finest Gothic buildings in France and visible from a long way away. Supported by majestic flying buttresses, its high, narrow nave is a symphony of vertical lines culminating in superb stained glass.

The finest example of the city's Renaissance domestic architecture is the 15th-century Gothic **Palais Jacques Coeur** (Rue Jacques Coeur, daily May–June 9.30am–noon, 2–6.15pm, July–Aug 9.45am–12.45pm, 2–6.30, Sept–Apr 10am–12.15pm, 2–6pm, Oct–Mar 9.30am–noon, 2–5.15pm, closed public hols; charge), named after its first occupant, a merchant and royal treasurer to Charles VII. More fine Renaissance residences line Rue Bourbonnoux, including **Hôtel Lallemant** (Tue–Sun July–Aug 10am–noon, 2–6pm, rest of the year it closes earlier; free entrance), which houses the Musée des Arts Décoratifs. Nearby is Place Gourdaine, with half-timbered medieval houses.

Further south still, heading towards the Massif Central, is the **Abbaye de Noirlac** ㉙ (daily Feb–Mar, Oct–Dec 2–5pm, Apr–Sept 10am–6.30pm, closed Jan; charge), located almost at the geographical centre of France. It is a rare example of a perfectly intact Cistercian abbey, and its 12th-century church of light-coloured stone conveys a powerful simplicity through a total lack of decoration, which the monks regarded as frivolous and distracting. For that reason it is an ideal setting for summer concerts.

Located in the lordly seclusion of its wooded grounds near St Amand-Montrond, the splendid **Château de Meillant** ㉚ (daily July–Aug 10am–6.30pm, May–June 10am–noon, 2–6.30pm, Apr, Sept–mid-Nov until 6pm, Mar 2–6pm; charge) is an example of how successfully the sophisticated Renaissance style could be grafted on to a medieval castle, with moat. Its courtyard is pure Renaissance and has a free-standing chapel.

FACT

In the third week of April, Bourges plays host to an excellent festival of music and dance, with a varied programme.

Cathédrale de St Etienne, Bourges.

CHÂTEAUX COUNTRY

"Chambord is truly royal – royal in its great scale, its grand air, its indifference to common considerations," wrote Henry James. It's a verdict that would have pleased French monarchs.

From the Middle Ages until the 17th century, the Loire was the seat of royalty. Government from the centre of the kingdom made good sense. Fine feudal châteaux and a soft and sensual landscape also swayed the balance. Orléans was France's intellectual capital in the 13th century, confirmed by the presence of the royal court. Under the dukes of Anjou and Orléans, the courts and castles of Angers and Blois took over Orléans' mantle, attracting artists, poets and troubadours. The reign of Charles VIII (1483–98) heralded a period of sustained château-building. This tradition was continued by Louis XII and François I, who transformed Blois into a splendid palace. Following the royal lead, the Renaissance élite used their profits from the silk trade and banking to indulge in château-building. The lovely Azay-le-Rideau, Chenonceau and Villandry date from this period. Azay and Chenonceau, the most romantic of the Loire châteaux, were built by noblewomen whose husbands were away in battle.

The accession of Henri II in 1547 marked the *apogée* of Renaissance excess with Diane de Poitiers, Henri's mistress, running Chenonceau as a pleasure palace. Catherine de Medici, Henri's wife, plotted Diane's downfall with the aid of her Italian astrologer in Chaumont. After the creation of Versailles, the Loire became a pleasant backwater, providing a racy salon for the literati and occasional hunting for Louis XIV. The Loire châteaux did not escape the Revolution unscathed but, thanks to the popularity of individual châtelains, many were spared, including Chenonceau, Cheverny and Chambord.

Stained glass at Chaumont.

Dove-grey domes and delicate cupolas mean Chambord can be likened to an Oriental town in miniature.

Villandry has Renaissance gardens, such as the geometric jardins d'amour (symbolising the different faces of love) to kitchen gardens.

Louis XIV, the self-proclaimed Sun King.

ROYAL CHAMBORD

Louis XIV loved hunting at Chambord, a château that began as a mere hunting lodge but finished as a sumptuous palace, with 365 fireplaces. Chambord was François I's bid for immortality, prefiguring Louis XIV's relationship with Versailles. Chambord also foreshadows Versailles in its scale of conception and sheer size. It represents a château in transition: Renaissance quicksilver poured into a Gothic mould. Almost 2,000 craftsmen worked on the site, producing a vast palace containing about 450 rooms, 365 windows and 70 staircases.

As the supreme Renaissance king, François presided over an airy palace partly designed by Leonardo da Vinci. Chambord was conceived as an escape from an unhappy marriage and the claustrophobia of court life in Blois. François chose the salamander as his enigmatic emblem, accompanied by the inscription: "I cultivate good and extinguish evil." After François' death, the court left for Chenonceau, while Chambord was inhabited fitfully.

Chenonceau is a sumptuous pleasure palace moulded by a series of female owners.

An ornate fireplace at Chaumont.

Royal plumbing comes with a difference – drainpipe at Blois, a château whose architecture represents more than four centuries' worth of influences.

POITOU-CHARENTES

Islands and oysters, Cognac, coastal wetlands, and little-known country churches: this is the region to visit if you want to compile an eclectic but fascinating itinerary.

Main Attractions
Cognac
Saintes
Talmont
Rochefort
La Rochelle
Marais Poitevin
Poitiers
Planète Futuroscope

Ile de Ré is just a skip away from La Rochelle, accessed by a toll bridge.

This largely rural region composed of four *départements*, with its capital at Poitiers, could claim to be the geographical, climatical and cultural meeting point of northern and southern France. Midway up the Atlantic coast, and bordered to the east by the Massif Central, it enjoys generally warm and sunny weather, but never gets as hot or dry as the Midi. Its coast is the sunniest part of the country outside the Mediterranean.

Two of its three regional dialects are derived from the *langue d'oil* (French)

and the third from the *langue d'oc* (the language of the south).

Comic Angoulême

During the 16th and 17th centuries, **Angoulême ❶** was famous for paper-making, which might partly explain why it has become the capital of the *bande dessinée* (BD for short). The English translations, "comic book" and "graphic novel", don't quite capture the spirit of what in France is considered a respectable art form for adult readers, although Tintin and Astérix are as revered as any other creations. The world of BDs is revealed in the **Cité Internationale de la Bande Dessinée et de l'Image** (July–Aug Tue–Fri 10am–7pm, Sat–Sun 2–7pm, Sept–June Tue–Fr 10am–6pm, Sat–Sun 2–6pm; charge). In January and February Angoulême holds a prestigious international festival in honour of all things to do with *bande dessinée*.

The other thing to do in Angoulême is visit the *ville haute* (upper city), to see the magnificent 12th-century **Cathédrale St Pierre**, which has an intricately detailed Romanesque facade and a 60-metre (216ft) high Romanesque bell tower rising from the north transept. The neo-Gothic **Hôtel de Ville** was built in the 19th century in place of the city's château, of which only two towers remain. From the medieval ramparts there is a splendid view of the Charente valley.

Brandy country

Cognac ❷ is the obvious place to enjoy a glass of brandy. Grapes grown in the region are first turned into wine, then distilled to make the famous Cognac. Curiously, Cognac is never "vintage", that is to say, the year it was made does not figure on the label. The age of a Cognac is determined by a series of highly regulated ageing "codes": *Trois Etoiles* from 2.5 to four years of age; VSOP (Very Superior Old Pale) from four to 10 years; XO, Napoléon, or Royal if over 10 years. Cognac is an ingredient of a local speciality, Pineau des Charentes, a fortified wine made by mixing Cognac with grape must. The result is a pleasantly sweet "wine" often served as an apéritif.

A number of private distilleries open their doors to visitors for tours and tasting sessions. One of the most spectacular is the **Otard** distillery (tel: 05 45 36 88 86), where the guided tour affords a chance to see the remains of the 13th-century Château de Cognac. At the back of the château the Rue Grande, lined with gracious 15th- and 16th-century buildings, leads towards the centre of the old town.

The **Musée des Arts du Cognac** (July–Aug daily 10am–6.30pm Sept–June Tue–Sun 2–6pm, closed some public hols; charge) gives a multi-media presentation of the town's star product. Next to the Hôtel de Ville the **Musée d'Art et d'Histoire** (July–Aug daily 10am–6.30pm, Tue–Sun Sept–June 2–6pm; charge), presents prehistoric, Gallo-Roman, and more recent artefacts and paintings.

West of Cognac, a Roman arch and remains of the amphitheatre prove that traffic-congested **Saintes** ❸ was once a thriving Roman metropolis. Once off the main road, it has some fine old houses along the Charente, while the church of the **Abbaye aux Dames** (www.abbayeauxdames.org; daily June–Sept 10am–7pm, Apr–May, Oct 10am–12.30pm, 2–7pm, Feb–Mar, Nov–Dec 2–6pm; charge) is a lovely example of the ornate local Romanesque style. The abbey is classified as a Trésor de Saintonge, one of the architectural treasures scattered around Saintes' hinterland. It has also become the focal point of music in the town.

Art by Yslaire painted on the side of an Angoulême building.

Angoulême in late autumn.

The Gironde Estuary

The *département* of **Charente-Maritime** is bordered to the south by the Gironde estuary. The most delightful place on its shore is **Talmont** 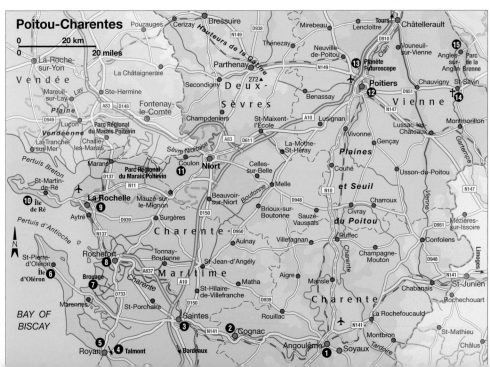 a village founded in 1284 by England's Edward I around a 12th-century church which stands on the edge of a cliff. Cars are excluded from the well-kept, flower-filled village centre.

Up the coast is the altogether different **Royan** ❺, a harbour town that was bombed in World War II leaving it with little old architecture. It is now a busy family holiday resort. Ferries from here sail across the estuary to Le Verdon-sur-Mer on the tip of the Médoc peninsula (see page 285). There are also boat excursions out to see an isolated lighthouse, the Phare de Cordouan, guarding the mouth of the Gironde. Next to Royan is the zoo of La Palmyre (www.zoo-palmyre.fr; daily Apr–Sept 9am–7pm, Oct–Mar, 9am–6pm; charge), home to 1,600 animals, some of them for the purposes of conservation programmes.

The river Seudre runs in an oblique line to the north of Royan feeding the extensive oyster beds around **Marennes**. Here, the Cité de l'Huître (daily July–Aug 10.30am–8pm, Apr–June, Sept 11am–7pm, closed Mon and Tue except during school hols, Oct Sat–Sun 11am–6pm;,charge) will tell you all you want to know about the cultivation of France's favourite shellfish. For an entirely different experience, in summer, a steam engine pulls the Train des Mouettes (Seagull Train) down the Seudre from La Tremblade (across the lagoon from Marennes) to Saujon 23km (14 miles) southeast.

The **Ile d'Oléron** ❻, France's largest Atlantic island, is reached by bridge from the mainland near Marennes. As well as forming part of the oyster producing area it is also popular for its sandy beaches. If you go no further on to the island, visit the citadelle in **Le Château** (always open, free entry).

Back on the mainland, **Brouage** ❼, north of Marennes, was founded in 1555 as a fortified port trading particularly in salt. It was occupied by Cardinal Richelieu during the siege of La Rochelle in 1627 but fell into decline. In the 18th century its harbour silted up making it redundant and the town migrated inland where it stands now, without a purpose. Its ramparts are still intact although overgrown in places and make for a good stroll.

Beguiling **Rochefort ❽** was created by Louis XIV's naval minister Colbert as a military port to defend the Atlantic coast from the marauding English, and was laid out according to a geometrical grid plan. The beautiful 17th-century **Corderie Royale** (www.corderie-royale. com; daily Apr–Sept 10am–7pm, mid-Feb–Mar, Oct–Dec 10am–12.30pm, 2–6pm; charge) looks far too elegant to have ever been a factory, but it was the royal rope manufacture – hence the building's long length because of the rope-turning machines it housed. Outside, you can see the *Hermione*, a replica of the frigate which carried General La Fayette to America in 1780 to assist the struggle for independence. South of the town is a transporter bridge, an unusual iron construction in which a suspended platform moves across the river carrying vehicles. It has been replaced by a motorway flyover and is operated only as a tourist attraction.

La Rochelle

Up the coast is **La Rochelle ❾**, one of France's loveliest ports, now a busy yachting centre. It was founded as a fishing port in the 10th century but grew in importance and was given a measure of autonomy over its affairs by the Dukes of Aquitaine. From the 13th to the 15th century it was the most important French port on the Atlantic. The Knights Templars used it as a base until the dissolution of the order in 1307. Legend has it that some Templars fled from the port in ships laden with fabled treasure.

During the Reformation, La Rochelle became a hothouse of Protestant rebellion, and because of this its submission became a priority for Henry III's chief minister, Cardinal Richelieu. He besieged the town for 13 months in 1627–8 and, despite assistance from the English, it was forced into ignominious surrender. As punishment its privileges were withdrawn and its ramparts demolished. La Rochelle recovered during the age of empire, trading with France's colonies in Canada and the West Indies. During World War II, the

FACT

In 1627 Cardinal Richelieu laid siege to the Huguenot stronghold of La Rochelle. When the siege finally ended, after 15 months, only 5,000 of the original 28,000 inhabitants were still alive.

Boat building the traditional way.

Street in St-Martin, Ile de Ré.

The bridge leading to Ile de Ré.

German navy sited a U-boat base here to feed submarines into the North Atlantic shipping lanes. La Rochelle was the last German garrison in France to surrender to the Allies, holding out until 8 May 1945.

Tour St Nicolas and **Tour de la Chaîne** face each other over the sheltered 13th-century port where a huge chain was drawn across to keep ships out. The **Tour de la Lanterne** was used as a prison, with graffiti carved here by English soldiers in the 17th and 18th centuries. Through the old gate at Place Barentin are many 15th-century houses with fine vaulted archways. On the main square is the high Gothic **Hôtel de Ville**, the town hall and, on Rue Dupaty, **Maison Henri II**, an intricately sculpted Renaissance residence. Museums include the **Musée du Nouveau Monde** (Oct–June Mon, Wed–Fri 9.30am–12.30pm, 1.45–5pm, Sat–Sun 2–6pm; July–Sept Mon, Wed–Sat 10am–12.30, 2–6pm, Sat–Sun 2–6pm; closed public hols; charge), dedicated to La Rochelle's connection with the New World. La Rochelle's most popular attraction,

though, is the huge **Aquarium** (www.aquarium-larochelle.com; daily July–Aug 9am–11pm, Apr–June, Sept 9am–8pm, Oct–Mar 10am–8pm; charge).

Ile de Ré

From La Rochelle, the **Ile de Ré ❿**, is reached by a toll bridge. Smaller than Oléron, "La Blanche" is 30km (18 miles) long. The dunes and beaches are made of white sand, giving Ré its nickname: "the White Isle".

At **St-Martin**, remains of Vauban's 17th-century fortifications surround the town and its 15th-century church. Ré can be visited in one day by bicycle, gliding through vineyards, oyster parks, cool woods and dunes, on the way to the salt marshes of **Ars-en-Ré**, with its long beaches and German bunkers.

Marshlands

North of La Rochelle is France's second largest area of marshland after the Camargue, **Le Marais Poitevin**, dubbed *La Venise Verte* – Green Venice. Eleventh-century monks took advantage of coastal dyke-building to dig 1,450km (900 miles) of waterways

OYSTERS FROM THE MARENNES-OLÉRON

Wild oysters harvested on France's Atlantic coasts have become exhausted. Now almost all oysters eaten in France are farmed, and 50 percent of them are raised in the Marennes-Oléron growing region where the River Seudre feeds flat, shallow basins with enough freshwater to keep the level of salinity low, just as the oysters like it.

It's a lengthy, painstaking process that begins with the oysters spilling millions of eggs into the sea. When these are fertilised the larvae attach themselves to supports which can be easily moved into "parks" that are submerged most of the time but exposed at low tide.

When they are between 18 and 24 months old the oysters are moved to metal cages or plastic boxes where they are regularly disturbed so that they grow round. In their fourth year the oysters are brought from the parks and placed in *claires* for fattening. These are shallow ponds connected to the sea by gullies. The algae "soup" in these *claires* gives the oysters a greeny colour which is considered attractive by gourmets, complementing texture and taste. Before going to market the oysters have to be purged by putting them in basins with pure water.

Oysters are found in seven growing regions of France from Normandy to the Mediterranean, particularly on in the Bassin d'Arcachon and Brittany but those from Marennes-Oléron are particularly highly prized.

which were filled up by the Sèvre Niortaise river. These now form a labyrinth of green channels that can be explored by boat, on foot or by bicycle.

At **Coulon** ⑪, Arçais and one or two other places, boatmen await passengers on their traditional, flat-bottomed wood boats guided by long forked poles. The Marais is a regional nature park, protecting its way of life as much as its wildlife, with 15,000 hectares (37,000 acres) of green silence and still waters covered with water lilies, under the dome of poplar and oak. Other ways to enjoy the Marais are to hire a boat or canoe, or join a horse riding trek.

Historic capital

The regional capital of **Poitiers** ⑫ is one of the oldest cities in France. It was just north of here that, in 732, Charles Martel stopped the Moorish invasion from Spain, eventually forcing their retreat from France. The architectural richness of Poitiers is outstanding. On the main square is **Notre-Dame-la-Grande**, with a magnificent Romanesque facade in the *poitevin* style and frescoes decorating the vault of the choir. During the *Polychromies de Notre-Dame* (21 June–21 Sept and over Christmas), the facade is spectacularly lit each evening to recreate the coloured appearance it would have had in the 11th century. More important still is the church of **St Hilaire-le-Grand**, unique in France for its seven naves.

At Jaunay-Clan, 7km (4 miles) north of Poitiers, is the extraordinary **Planète Futuroscope** ⑬ (www.en.futuroscope.com; daily, closed Jan, times vary tel: 05 45 36 88 86; charge) theme park, its futuristic architecture a setting for the latest in visual technology.

The eastern Interior

The abbey of **St-Savin** ⑭, some 40km (25 miles) east of Poitiers on the Gartempe river, is decorated with beautiful frescoes dating from the 12th century, depicting stories from the Old Testament.

To the north is the entrancing village of **Angles-sur-Anglin** ⑮. Castle ruins, a watermill, willows and water lilies make it a perfect setting.

TIP

At Coulon you can hire a punt (with or without a boatman), a canoe or a pedalo. If you are happier on dry land, you can hire a bicycle or take the tourist mini-train.

The IMAX theatre at Futuroscope.

The Montenvers train by the Mer de Glace glacier, Chamonix Valley.

Chamonix, an old-fashioned resort at heart.

CHAMONIX · MONT · BLANC

CENTRAL FRANCE AND THE ALPS

This is the heart of gastronomic France, the home of delicious wines and exceptional restaurants. The mountains and watery landscapes are perfect for outdoor activities, as are the ski slopes in the Alps. The less well-known Auvergne has a surreal beauty, strung with volcanoes and crater lakes.

Porcelain tea set by Royal Limoges.

The region defined as Central France encompasses Burgundy, the Rhône valley and French Alps, and Auvergne and Limousin; we also include in this section Franche Comté, which lies to the east of Burgundy rising from the Saône valley.

Burgundy is the land of wine, food and dukes that saw itself as the heart of Europe in medieval times. Modern Burgundians believe that paradise begins in the kitchen and ends in the wine cellar, and "better a good meal than fine clothes." Dijon is its main town, famous for its mustard.

The Lyonnais love their food no less than the Burgundians, and Lyon, principal city of the **Rhône Valley** and third city of France, is a gourmet's paradise, awash with fine restaurants. Never turning its back on its long and fascinating past, it is today a vibrant, modern city of culture and industry. Traditional crafts also thrive in these regions chiefly known for their wines. You can always be sure of a sympathetic *cave* open for a little wine tasting around the next bend.

In days gone by, the higher passes of the **French Alps**, dominated by Mont Blanc, the highest peak in Europe, were deserted when winter weather closed in; now the more remote the valley, the more likely it is to fill with skiers. Lower down, there are landmarks aplenty: Briançon, highest town in Europe, the monastery of Chartreuse, and of course Geneva and its elegant lake.

Cycling the Alps, for those who like a challenge.

Although in the very heart of the country, the **Auvergne**, hoisted high on the Massif plateau among a wild, volcanic landscape, and the beautiful countryside of **Limousin**, have rarely seized centre stage. Limousin, famous for its cattle, is a land of untouched towns, spas and shepherds, peacefully isolated in verdant valleys.

BURGUNDY

The "heart of France" is an opulent province, blessed with glorious architecture, bastions of gastronomy, world-renowned vineyards and a beautiful, lush landscape. Franche Comté is ideal for outdoor activities, offering cross-country skiing and walking trails, and crystal clear waters.

Main Attractions

Abbaye de Fontenay
MuséoParc Alésia,
   Alise-Ste Reine
Basilique Ste Madeleine,
   Vézelay
Dijon
Hôtel–Dieu, Beaune
Cluny
Besançon
Chapelle Notre-Dame-du-
   Hast, Ronchamp

Quartier de la Marine – the Marine Quarter – Auxerre.

Less than an hour from the roar of Paris traffic, the calm, bright Burgundian countryside comes as a welcome surprise to many a visitor travelling south from the French capital. North of Dijon, where the powerful dukes of Burgundy controlled an immense kingdom, the Yonne river winds its way to Sens through a peaceful valley where ancient glory still clings to the rich, unpretentious farmland of Bourgogne (Burgundy).

Here, canals offer the possibility of gentle waterborne holidays, with plenty to do, visiting châteaux, ancient abbeys and vineyards.

Gothic splendour

Until 1622, the Archbishop of **Sens** ❶ lorded over an area extending all the way to Paris. His palatial lodgings house two museums (Wed–Mon 10am–noon, 2–6pm, closed Oct–May Mon, Thu and Fri mornings, and public hols; charge) with collections devoted to local history showing a variety of artefacts from the Bronze Age to the 18th century, and the Collection Marrey, which includes 19th- and 20th-century ceramics and paintings.

The **Cathédrale St-Etienne** was the first in France to be built in the Gothic manner. Construction began in the 12th century and work was not completed until 500 years later. In the course of time, this monumental structure was embellished with intricate sculpture, high arches and an impressive series of stained-glass windows. In the adjoining buildings, the **Trésor de la Cathédrale St-Etienne** is remarkable for rare liturgical garments.

Auxerre ❷, the immemorial capital of northwestern Burgundy, resounds with history, being one of the oldest cities in France. Renaissance houses follow a semi-circular pattern around the 15th-century **Tour de l'Horloge**, which once guarded the ramparts. The unusual clock has two dials, one for the time and the other for tracking the movement of the sun and stars.

Two churches rival one another for attention. The **Cathédrale St-Etienne** is recognised by the sharp slope of its asymmetric facade. The medieval sense of Christianity is vivid in this church, from the tympanum's three-tiered life of Christ, to the lives of the saints depicted in jewel-like red and blue stained glass. The abbey church dedicated to **St Germain**, also Gothic, is built on an extraordinary hive of underground chapels. Parts of the church date from the time of Charlemagne and the **frescoes of St Stephen** go back to AD850. The ancient dormitory houses the **Musée d'Art et d'Histoire** (Wed–Sun 10am–noon, 2–6.30pm, Oct–May until 5pm; charge).

Southwest of Auxerre, the spires of the brick and stone **Château de St-Fargeau** ❸ (www.chateau-de-st-fargeau. com/en; Apr–Nov daily 10am–noon, 2–6pm, July–Aug until 7pm; charge) appear like minarets on the horizon. This is where the *Grande Mademoiselle*, Louis XIV's sister, once lived. Dating from the 15th century, the château was renovated in the mid-17th century by Le Vau, the architect of Versailles.

Nearby is **Guédelon**, an amazing construction site, where a medieval château (www.guedelon.fr/en; Easter–Nov Thu–Tue 10am–6pm, July–Aug daily until 7pm; charge) is being built by 35 craftsmen and women, using only 13th-century materials, techniques and equipment – the project, which started in 1997, is expected to last 25 years.

La Puisaye

St-Fargeau is situated in an area known as **La Puisaye**. This is rural Burgundy at its best. The hills shimmer in the early afternoon heat and tall trees line the banks of rivers such as the Loing. Gentle and watery, it is a perfect region to explore by bicycle or on foot. The area's most celebrated native daughter is the author Colette (1873–1953) whose writings remain popular in France and abroad and whose birthplace can be seen in Rue des Vignes in the centre of the little town of **St Sauveur-en-Puisaye** ❹. The **Musée Colette** (www.musee-colette. com; Easter–Nov Wed–Mon 10am–6pm; charge), housed in a beautifully furnished château, is dedicated to her.

Construction of a wall at Guédelon.

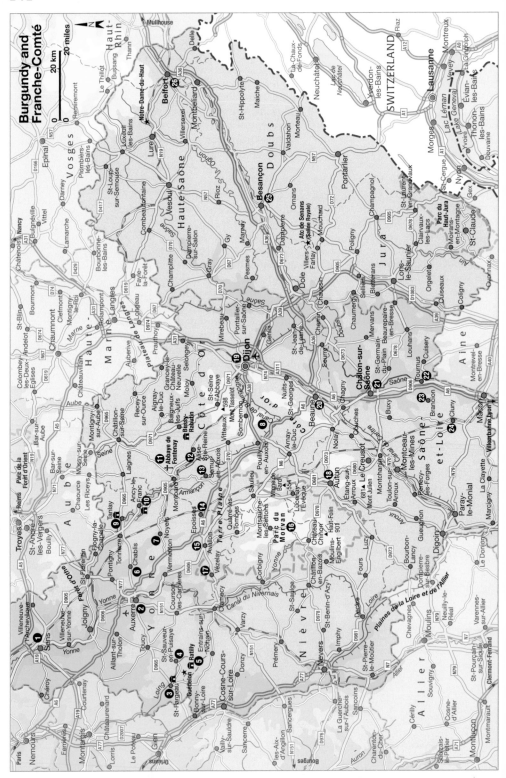

Burgundy and Franche-Comté

Through a network of farm villages, the back roads lead to **Ratilly ❺**. Here the superb 13th-century **Château de Ratilly** (mid-Mar–Oct Mon–Fri 10am–12.30pm, 1.30–5.30pm, Sat–Sun 10am–6pm, mid-June–Sept daily 10am–6pm; charge) lies hidden in a brambly wood. Inside the arched entrance a grassy courtyard opens onto a pottery school.

From Pontigny to Montréal, the **Serein** (Serene) **river valley** is a haven that merits its name. A major attraction is the small town of **Chablis ❻**, mainly because of its world-famous vineyards, stitched like patchwork quilts over the hills. Upstream, cradled in a bend of the river, the little town of **Noyers ❼** has preserved all the charm of its medieval history. The rampart wall is guarded by 16 towers circling the arcades of the central square.

Canal country

Beyond the Chablis vineyards is the **Canal de Bourgogne ❽**. Part of a countrywide network of waterways built for freight (see page 250), the canal is increasingly used by houseboats, and barges are rented by holidaymakers. Just the width of a single *péniche* (barge), the narrow channel is equipped with locks and wider basins for crossing traffic. Once on a canal, the rest of the world ceases to exist and one can drift down the tranquil waters visiting châteaux from **Tonnerre** to Bussy-Rabutin.

The **Château de Bussy-Rabutin** (http://bussy-rabutin.monuments-nationaux. fr/en; daily 9.15am–1pm, 2–5pm; charge) is Burgundy's most absorbing stately home. It was rebuilt in 1649 by Roger de Bussy-Rabutin, who was banished to the countryside by Louis XIV for his satirical commentaries on court affairs. In exile, he decorated the house with contemporary portraits: there are 25 women onlookers in his bedchamber, including Madame de Sévigné (his cousin) and Maintenon.

Passed along the way between Tonnerre and Bussy-Rabutin, the Renaissance **Château de Tanlay ❾** (Apr–mid-Nov Wed–Mon; charge) is a fine sight, ensconced in a series of moats, arcades and iron grilles. Another château gem, **Ancy-le-Franc**

CHABLIS
NUITS-ST-GEORGES
POMMARD
VOSNE-ROMANEE
GEVREY-CHAMBERTIN
MEURSAULT

The names every wine lover will savour are at the Musée du Vin de Bourgogne.

Château de Ratilly.

FACT

After the battle of Alésia, Vercingétorix was taken to Rome where he was imprisoned for five years, before being paraded in triumph and killed, probably by strangulation.

❿ (www.chateau-ancy.com/en; mid-Apr– mid-Nov Tue–Sun 10.30am–12.30pm, 2–5pm; charge) presents an austerely symmetrical exterior, but the inner courtyard and furnishings are of sumptuous splendour inspired by the Italian Renaissance.

Founded by Saint Bernard, the **Abbaye de Fontenay** ⓫ (www.abbayede fontenay.com/en; daily mid-Nov–Mar 10am–noon, 2–5pm, Apr–mid-Nov 10am–6pm; charge) is Burgundy's most complete ensemble of life in a medieval monastery. Solitary and independent at the bottom of a remote valley, all its buildings have been preserved. The church and cloister are examples of Cistercian simplicity; intended to be piously modest, without ornamentation of any kind, the bare paving stones and immaculate columns have acquired a look of grandeur.

Vercingétorix, Celtic hero

Just south of Fontenay is the site of a battle decisive in French history and of which it has been dramatically stated: "It is here that Gaul died and France was born."

Boeuf bourguignon is a favourite dish.

Mont Auxois, above the village of **Alise-Ste-Reine** ⓬, is generally accepted as the site of the battle of Alésia, where the Gauls under Vercingétorix were defeated by Julius Caesar. A monumental statue of Vercingétorix overlooks the Gallo-Roman city where excavations have been under way since 1906. Among the foundations uncovered are those of an early Christian church dedicated to the virgin martyr St Reine. Objects from the site are on display at the **MuséoParc Alésia** (www.alesia.com; Feb–Nov daily 10am– 5pm; charge), an interpretation centre and remains of the Roman city.

Travelling west, one arrives in **Semur-en-Auxois** ⓭, which retains the flavour of a medieval fortress town, guarded by imposing dungeon towers that overlook the peaceful Armançon river and the Pont July. The architecturally eclectic church of **Notre-Dame** (1218) offends purists but delights others. Beyond Semur lies **Epoisses** ⓮, less known for its medieval **château** (July–Aug Wed– Mon 10am–noon, 3–6pm; charge) and Renaissance houses than for its cheese.

BURGUNDY'S DIVINE FOOD

The Burgundians' near-religious devotion to food is long-established. To prove that the high quality of the region's cuisine is a result of their innate understanding of food, they will point to ancient culinary inscriptions in the Dijon archaeological museum and tell of their dukes, whose kitchens were vast and whose meals took on the aura of religious ceremonies, with hand-held torches lighting the dishes' way to the duke's table. They will also pointedly allude to the sacramental properties of bread and wine.

Dijon's two culinary specialities, mustard and *pain d'épice*, have long historical associations, as do some of the great cheeses of the region: Chaource and the brandy-washed Epoisses were first made in the abbeys of Pontigny and Fontenay, while delicately flavoured Cîteaux is still made only in its eponymous monastery. It is also the quality and variety of local ingredients that shape Burgundian cooking. Wild produce is prized: crayfish, snails, boar, quail, thrushes and woodland mushrooms, while Bresse chickens are reared on a special diet. Then there are the *charcuterie* from Morvan, pork dishes such as *jambon persillé, gougère* made with cheese, kidneys with mustard, and the great stews, such as the classic *boeuf bourguignon*, liberally doused in red wine. The beef comes from its fine native cattle, the cream-coloured Charolais.

Creamy, pungent and soft, its orange rind is washed with brandy *(marc de Bourgogne)* as it matures in the cellars. It's the region's finest cheese and is best enjoyed with a glass of red Burgundy.

The Black Mountains

A town of parks and cosy old houses, **Avallon ⓕ** is the gateway to the **Parc Régional du Morvan ⓖ**. These first spurs of the **Massif Central** are covered with dense forests, hence the Celtic name *Morvan*, meaning "Black Mountain". Once an inaccessible backcountry derided by its richer neighbours, the **Morvan** is now a popular weekend retreat. Fast streams churning in narrow gorges provide excellent fishing and canoeing.

Set on a high hilltop, **Vézelay ⓗ** offers a splendid view of the countryside and is one of Burgundy's most spectacular monuments. The majestic **Basilique Ste Madeleine** was founded in the 9th century as an abbey, and it was here that Bernard of Clairvaux launched the Second Crusade in 1146. The presence of Mary Magdalene's supposed relics in the basilica made Vézelay a place of pilgrimage. A winding road climbs through the town to the basilica. Clustered in the shadows of the narthex (entrance hall), medieval pilgrims could ponder the mysteries of the magnificent tympanum before flooding into the uplifting nave, flanked by black-and-white arches.

From the **Mont Beuvray**, an ancient wooded plateau, there's a lovely view east over the soft contours of the vineyards towards **Autun ⓘ**. This town, which celebrated its bi-millennial in 1985, has been an administrative centre since Augustus defeated the Gauls. Traces remain of Roman roads that led to the town, and the quadruple-arched gates of this small provincial city bear witness to its imperial past. The **amphitheatre** held up to 15,000 spectators. Medieval prosperity left behind the **Cathédrale St-Lazare**, whose white sculpted doorway contrasts with

the more rustic rock of the church. Opposite is the **Musée Rolin** (mid-Feb–Nov Wed–Mon 10am–noon, 2–5pm; charge), with seven rooms of Gallo-Roman archaeology and collections of medieval painting and sculpture. Behind the cathedral the remaining ramparts make a lovely stroll to the ancient Ursulines' keep.

Dijon

Northeast of Autun is the undisputed capital of Burgundy, **Dijon ⓙ**. The many old buildings are in the active city centre, particularly the monumental **Palais des Ducs ⓐ**. Arched passageways give access to its spacious courtyards where the light colour of the wide, regular paving stones echoes the pale facades. Housed in the palace, the **Musée des Beaux-Arts ⓑ** (Wed–Mon 10am–5pm, closed public hols), one of the finest in France, displays French, German and Italian statuary and art from the 14th–18th century. Much of the vast collection was acquired during the Revolution from the homes of local nobility, as well as churches and monasteries.

The Temple of Janus in Autun, where Roman remains can be seen.

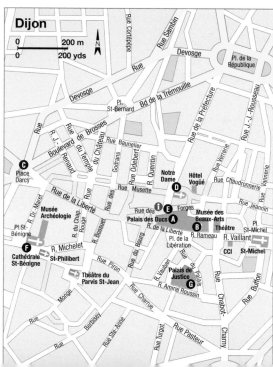

TIP

The Route des Grands Crus, (www.route-des-grands-crus-de-bourgogne. com) covers 60km (37 miles) from Dijon to Santenay and passes through 37 Burgundy wine-making villages. One of the largest vineyards at Clos de Vougeot has a small château which was built to house wine presses. Today it is the home of the Chevaliers du Tastevin.

Place de la Libération, Dijon.

The **Salle des Gardes** contains prized tombstones of three members of the ducal dynasty, sculpted in alabaster and black marble. The 14th-century **kitchen** has six huge fireplaces, recalling the splendour of banquets past.

A circular stroll from the palace to the **Place Darcy** ● and back takes in the old quarter of malls and tiny squares. **Notre-Dame** ● is a 13th-century Gothic church full of delightful curiosities, such as the family of figures animated by a clock mechanism. Idiosyncratic old facades line the narrow streets only a few feet from the church walls. Along the pedestrian shopping streets, elegant boutiques and antique shops have taken up residence, with lustrous, low-beamed ceilings and sculptures decorating the upper floors.

Rue des Forges ● was, until the 18th century, the main street of Dijon, named after the goldsmiths, jewellers and knife-makers who had workshops there. The **Hôtel Chambellan** is the most striking of a series of Renaissance residences that line the street, with elaborate balconies and staircases hidden in interior courtyards.

Further west, **Cathédrale Ste-Bénigne** ● draws the eye with its tall spire and multi-coloured octagonal towers. Behind it, in the former abbey, is the **Archaeological Museum** (Feb–Oct Wed–Mon 9.30am–12.30pm, 2–6pm, closed public hols; charge).

Coming full circle, the **Palais de Justice** ● and its neighbourhood are reminiscent of the days when the provincial parliament officiated under the painted and wainscoted ceilings.

Before leaving Dijon, be sure to sample the local *pain d'épice* (a honey-sweetened, aniseed-flavoured cake/bread) and buy a jar of the tangy mustard that has been produced here for more than 600 years.

Côte d'Or wine route

What name is more evocative than that of the *département* in which all the great vineyards are located, **Côte d'Or**, the "hills of gold"? Some say the name comes from the gold-coloured leaves that cover the hills in autumn, while others maintain that it is from the great wines or "bottled gold" they produce.

The vineyards are quite easy to visit since most of them line the western edge of the D974 that runs from Dijon to Châlon-sur-Saône. Here, the names of the towns evoke great wines: **Gevrey Chambertin**, **Vougeot**, **Vosne-Romanée**, **Nuits-St-Georges**, **Aloxe-Corton**, **Beaune**, **Pommard**. Roadside signs invite passers-by to stop and sample the wine; you will be expected to buy at least a few bottles if you taste.

Beaune

The jewel-like roof of the **Hôtel-Dieu**, made of multicoloured tiles, can be seen glimmering as one approaches is **Beaune ⑳**. Since the 18th century, the city has been the heart of the Burgundian wine trade, and the auction of the Hospices de Beaune in the Hôtel-Dieu, a charity hospital historically supported by the wine produced on lands donated by benefactors, is still the high point in the local calendar. Under its splendid multicoloured roof, the long ward contains the original sick beds. The halls off the courtyard house a collection of artwork and tapestries crowned by a painting of the *Last Judgement* by Roger Van der Weyden (daily 9–11.30am, 2–5.30pm; charge).

The wine culture in Beaune is all-pervasive. Every other shop peddles if not wine, then books on wine, cellar equipment or wine glasses; every other café or restaurant proclaims its loyalty to the vinous tradition. The big Beaune *négociants* (wine merchants) lure tourists into their cellars with free tastings. The **Musée du Vin de Bourgogne** (Apr–Nov daily; charge) is in the Hôtels des Ducs de Bourgogne, on Rue d'Enfer.

Beyond Beaune are the villages that produce the most reputed Burgundy whites. These humble stone cottages hardly suggest that here are some of the most sought-after vineyards in the world. It is here the Chardonnay grape shines to produce the succulent wines of Meursault and Montrachet.

Approaching **Châlon-sur-Saône ㉑**, vineyards are more scattered. Although an industrial centre, half-timbered houses still crowd around the **Cathédrale St-Vincent** in the

Detail of the Abbaye St Pierre-et-St-Paul.

The Hôtel-Dieu of the Hospices de Beaune.

WHERE

Louis Pasteur was born in Dole, southwest of Besançon, and his childhood home La Maison Natale (Apr–mid-Oct daily 10am–6pm, mid-Oct–6 Dec Tue–Sun 2–6pm; charge) displays artefacts from his youth, including his university cap and gown.

old quarter. Châlon is the birthplace of Nicéphore Niépce, the inventor of photography, and has a museum (Wed–Mon 9.30–11.45am, 2–5.45pm) dedicated to him.

The Saône Valley

Further south in the Saône valley, **Tournus** ¤ is the remarkably quiet site of one of Burgundy's greatest Romanesque churches. **St Philibert** owes its special beauty to its small irregular stones. The exterior has a forbidding, military appearance. Inside, massive columns of the same yellow stone carry three parallel systems of arches. This austerity is the hallmark of the church, cloister and surrounding monastery buildings (11th–12th century). Old streets lead to the river and from the bridge there's a splendid view of the church and its buildings.

Perched on a narrow crest of rock, **Brancion** ㉓ is a delightful feudal burg. Above the old quarter of the church and marketplace is the crumbling château, one of the few such examples in Burgundy where the

The Chardonnay grape, at home in Burgundy soil.

dukes' power countered individual fiefdoms.

Burgundy in the Middle Ages was marked by the great monastic orders whose fervour and ramified organisation revived a spiritual life while greatly influencing the politics of Christian Europe. The Benedictine rule radiated from **Cluny** ㉔, where the abbots were on equal footing with the Pope.

The remains of the Cluny monastery, the **Ancienne Abbaye St-Pierre-et-St-Paul**, founded in 910, only faintly suggest the power of this order. Five of 15 guard towers remain. The church that was for five centuries the largest in all Christendom was almost entirely destroyed after the French Revolution. The whole immense ensemble can be admired from the **Tour des Fromages** (check with the Tourist Office for opening hours; charge). The town's museum, **Musée d'Art et d'Archéologie** (Palais Jean de Bourbon; daily 9.30am–5pm, July–Aug until 7pm; charge), offers an overall view of Cluny's dramatic rise and fall.

CLUNY AND THE CISTERCIANS

There are two orders that express the greatness of Burgundian monasticism: Cluny and Cîteaux. The Cluniac order of Benedictine monks was founded in 910 by William I (the Pious), Count of Auvergne, at Cluny. The abbey was subject only to the pope's authority, and in the Middle Ages became the leading monastic institution in Europe. Hundreds of priories and abbeys were attached, all directly under the supervision of the abbey of Cluny. The Cluny order became the wealthiest in the western world permitting the monks to live an elaborate lifestyle. Cluniac zeal diminished in the 12th century and monastic reform was taken over by the Cistercians.

The Cistercian order of Benedictines was founded at Cîteaux 30km south of Dijon in 1098 by a small group of monks from the monastery of Molesme, which was under Cluny's control. They believed in simplicity and poverty and were the first order to directly manage and work its own land, including vineyards. They also pioneered the iron-smelting industry, evidence of this can be seen at Fontenay.

Cluny, which was the largest church in Christendom before St Peter's basilica in Rome, was heavily plundered in the years following the French Revolution, and little remains of its splendour today. Cîteaux was partially destroyed during the French Revolution, but it is still home to a small community of monks. Nothing remains of Molesme.

Franche-Comté

Rolling hills rise up from the Saône valley into Franche-Comté, heading east towards the forested Alpine mountains of the Franco-Swiss frontier.

The region's capital **Besançon** ㉕, in the crook of the Doubs river, developed into a major town because of its position on the Rhine-Rhône trade route. Formally a religious centre, and later a military stronghold, today it is reputed to be France's leading watch- and clock-making town. The **Musée du Temps** (Tue–Sat 9.15pm–6pm, Sun 10am–6pm, closed public hols; charge), housed in the Renaissance Palais Granvelle, exhibits an impressive collection of time-pieces. Another tribute to the trade is in the belltower of the Cathédrale St-Jean – the **Horloge Astronomique**. A magnificent astronomical clock with 57 faces and 62 dials which gives the time in 16 places in the world,

Sitting on a hilltop above the town is the **citadelle**, financed by Louis XIV and built by Vauban by 1711. Within the fortress walls there are 11 hectares (27-acres) of grounds with a zoo, an insectarium, a noctarium, an aquarium and two museums (www.citadelle.com/en; daily 9am–7pm, with exceptions; charge).

South of Besançon at **Arc de Senans** are the ambitious 18th-century royal salt works, now a World Heritage site.

To the northeast, the frontier military town of **Belfort** ㉖, with a mountain top citadel, is an ideal base for visiting the splendid **Chapelle Notre-Dame-du-Haut** at the former mining town of **Ronchamp**. Designed by Le Corbusier and completed in 1955, this building of curved white walls and vast swell of concrete roof is a masterpiece of contemporary architecture.

The deep forests, rivers, lakes and waterfalls of the region are worth exploring. Spring is the best time to see waterfalls in full splendour. The most spectacular are in the **Vallée du Doubs**, and further south in the **Région des Lacs** where the River Hérisson tumbles down the valley forming a series of waterfalls, most impressively the 65m (213ft) l'Eventail (the Fan).

Le Corbusier's unmistakeable Chapelle Notre-Dame-du-Haut.

THE GOLDEN AGE OF CANALS

The commercial heyday of the canals was the 19th century, since when working barges have given way to pleasure boats.

The French network of canals began during the reign of Plantagenet Henry II. Later, Henri IV (1589–1610) created a canal system that linked the Loire with the Seine and the Saône with the Rhône, to provide a flowing highway from the Channel to the Mediterranean. The Canal de Briare, created in 1604–42, was one of the first in the kingdom, and work continued in Louis XIV's reign. The canals represent notable technical achievements of their day: the Canal du Midi passes 115 locks and the first canal tunnel ever built; at Agen a series of four locks signals a 23-arched aqueduct crossing the Garonne. At Pouilly-en-Auxois in Burgundy, the canal vanishes underground for 3km (5 miles), an engineering feat that pre-dates Brunel.

Crossing the Landscape

Although the initial climatic contrast is between the lush northern canals and sun-baked southern ones, more subtle regional variations can be seen across the network. In Aquitaine, canal banks are planted with poplars and willows; in Languedoc, with pines and mulberries. In the south, oaks, elms and limes were planted to prevent the banks drying out; in the Mediterranean, cypress and olive trees thrive. The Canal du Nivernais crosses cheese and wine country and is the least-spoilt canal in northern France. The Canal du Midi embraces Cathar country and the Camargue. It forms part of the Canal des Deux Mers, linking the Atlantic and the Mediterranean, and is a Unesco World Heritage site.

An idyllic stretch of the Canal du Midi where lock-keeper's cottages, dating from the 17th century, also tend to be photogenic

A transit of the Canal St-Martin in Paris, near Place Stalingrad

Commercial barges have priority. Locks can be manual, automatic or operated by lock-keepers.

The canal at Deluz, in Franche-Comté.

CANAL CRUISING

The French waterways offer an array of possibilities, from narrow boats to cabin cruisers and floating hotels. Apart from the famous bateaux-*mouches* along the Seine in Paris, there are short city cruises in Strasbourg and Colmar in Alsace. Real canal-lovers can choose between houseboats *(bateaux habitables)*, *péniches* and *pénichettes* (narrow boats). *Péniches* act as floating hotels with attentive crews and dinner on board. As well as standard narrow boats, the Canal du Midi offers short pleasure cruises in a *gabarre*, a replica of the traditional canal boat that once plied the waterways. Or take a cruise on a 40-metre (131ft) solar-powered narrow boat along the Canal du Midi, between Béziers and Carcassonne.

There are canal-cruising opportunities in Alsace, Champagne, Burgundy, the Loire, Poitou-Charentes, Ardèche, the Dordogne, Aquitaine, the Midi-Pyrénées and Languedoc. Cruises along canals in the Loire, Burgundy, Bordeaux and the Midi can be combined with wine-tasting tours. Cruises from Avignon to Châteauneuf-du-Pape, for example, include visits to vineyards. For land-lovers, cycle routes often run parallel to the canals.

The Briare canal aqueduct (1897) across the Loire is a 610-metre (2,000-ft) Art Nouveau construction designed by Gustave Eiffel.

The Plan Incliné of Saint-Louis-Arzviller, effectively a boat lift allowing access in the Vosges.

The future of French waterways lies in pleasure cruising.

Lyon's *Vélo'v* bike rental scheme.

THE RHÔNE VALLEY

On its journey from the Alps to the Mediterranean, the
mighty Rhône flows through Lyon, France's vibrant
third city, a modern metropolis with a long history.

The transition between Burgundy and the Lyonnais can be seen at **Mâcon** where northern pointed roofs of slate meet the southern, red, rounded Roman tile. Although a sprawling urban town, there are interesting places to discover if you take the time to turn off the busy route that follows the quay.

In the Old Town, pedestrianised Rue Carnot is lined with shops, and there are a number of half-timbered buildings overlooking the market square, Place aux Herbes. One of these, the 16th-century Maison de Bois Doré, is decorated with bizarre figures. Nearby is the Musée Larmartine (Tue–Sat 10am–noon, 2–6pm, Sun pm; charge) which displays memorabilia of the Mâcon-born Romantic poet Lamartine. There is an interesting collection of sculpture and fine arts from French and Flemish schools at the Musée des Ursulines (Tue–Sat 10am–noon, 2–6pm, Sun pm; charge) in a 17th-century convent used a prison during the Revolution.

Just outside the city are the **Pouilly-Fuissé** vineyards. This buttery Chardonnay comes from five villages surrounding the Solutré rock, including **Pouilly** and **Fuissé**.

Stone Age hunting ground

The massive **Roche de Solutré** rears above the wavy line of hills like a listing ocean liner, giving its name to Solutrean Stone Age civilisations. Prehistoric man used this cliff as a hunting ground, herding deer and wild horses towards the summit and then frightening them into jumping over the edge. The bone yard below extends over 4,000 sq metres (almost an acre), and the excavations can be seen in the **Musée de Préhistoire** (daily Apr–Sept 10am–5pm, Oct–Mar until 5pm; charge).

The panorama, as one walks up the slope, encompasses the black and yellow patchwork of surrounding hills.

Main Attractions

Mâcon
Dombes
Pérouges
Lyon
Vienne
Hauterives, Palais Idéal du
    Facteur Cheval

Hiking through Burgundy.

SHOP

Much Beaujolais
Nouveau is poor quality.
When buying, steer clear
of all but the most
reliable *négociants* (such
as Pierre Ferraud,
Joseph Drouhin and
Georges Duboeuf).

Beaujolais Nouveau

Like taciturn troops guarding the vineyards, the **Monts du Beaujolais** are covered with sombre chestnut and pine forests, and there is a local wood industry. The bell-shaped vines reach high up the slopes, as do the typical farmhouses, with living quarters over the cellar.

Technically part of the Burgundy wine region, Beaujolais produces mainly red but also a little white and rosé wine. Red Beaujolais is made from the Gamay grape. The better wines come from single *cru* vineyards from 10 villages in the north, towards Mâcon. The famous Beaujolais Nouveau is produced by *macération carbonique*, which results in fresh fruity reds that are to be enjoyed relatively young.

In **Juliénas** the wine cellar is in a long-disused church. At the **Château de Corcelles** the former guard room is now a tasting room. **Belleville ❷** is the commercial centre of an area where the most serious wine-makers work at improving the quality of the traditional Beaujolais. The Beaujolais Nouveau "season" opens with a media bang in mid-November – on the third Thursday of the month – just a few weeks after the grapes have been harvested. At midnight preceding the date set for the first sale, luxury sports cars and private planes rev their engines for the race to be the first to bring the year's vintage to London, Dublin or New York.

On the opposite bank of the Saône is a land of solid farm traditions, whose products are the basis of the

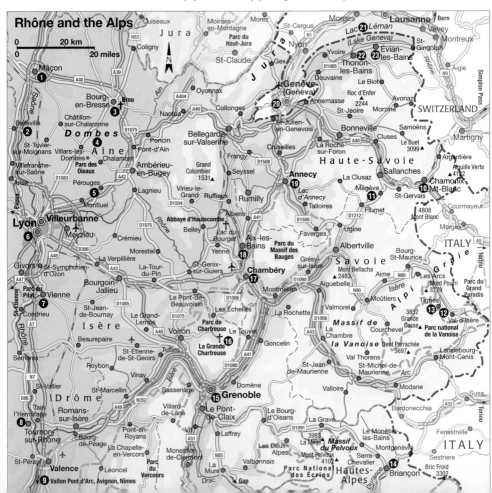

Rhône and the Alps

city dweller's cuisine. **La Ferme de la Forêt** in **St-Trivier-de-Courtes** (Apr–Oct Tue–Sun 10.30am–6pm, Apr–June, Oct weekends only; charge) is a farm museum where all activities were once concentrated in a single building combining stable, tool shed and dwelling. The "Saracen" chimney topped by a cowl is just one of the signs of the Bresse region. The rustic building materials and wood furniture used by generations of the same family are now relics of a lifestyle that died out in the 1950s.

Bresse capital

The capital of the former province of Bresse, **Bourg-en-Bresse** ❸, has a thriving speciality in farm-fattened chickens and capons. At the weekly poultry market, thousands of birds, specially prepared in a milk bath after slaughtering, are snapped up by professional buyers.

On the outskirts of town the church of the royal monastery of **Brou** is a splendid jewel of the Flamboyant Gothic style. It was commissioned by Archduchess Marguerite of Savoy as a memorial to her husband, who died

in 1504, aged 24. Inside, the triple-arched rood screen, one of the few left in France, is famous for its beautiful stone lattice-work. The entry to the choir is lined with 74 monks' stalls carved in dark oak. Finest of all the marble sculptures are those of the three royal tombs in the choir, exquisitely carved with small statuettes and life-size figures of the noble family.

Lakes and marshes

Southwest of Bourg-en-Bresse is the **Dombes** ❹, a marshy plateau with more than 100, mostly artificial, lakes. Large areas are private hunting grounds stocked with waterfowl and fish, while a network of channels and sluices drains water from one lake to another in a traditional system of rotating land use from fish to grain. The multitude of ponds and marshes make it a popular place for birdwatchers and anglers.

At the centre of the region at **Villars-les-Dombes** is the **Parc des Oiseaux**, the largest ornithological park in France with more than 400 different native and exotic species (www.parcdesoiseaux.com/uk; daily

An ariel toucan, all the way from Brazil to the Parc des Oiseaux in Dombes.

Theizé, in Beaujolais country.

FACT

Lyon is constantly
upgrading its river
banks, giving the city
back to pedestrians and
cyclists. You can hire a
"cyclopolitain" (a
high-tech rickshaw
propelled by both pedals
and an electric motor) to
take you around the city
centre (one hour €40 for
two people).

Mar–mid-Nov 9.30am–6.30pm, with exceptions; charge).

After the wildlife, **Pérouges** ⑤ is a return to urban bustle, albeit that of the Middle Ages. The entire town is medieval in character, and thrives on its past. Saved from destruction in the early 20th century, the houses and ramparts have been conscientiously restored and marvellously adapted to modern ideas of space and light. The stone-paved streets encourage a snail's pace for looking into a crooked passageway or window shopping in the boutiques devoted to traditional Bresse crafts, such as blue Meillonas ceramics.

Contemporary architecture reaches a high point at **Eveux**, near **L'Arbresle** 10km (6 miles) northwest of Lyon. Here, in a small vale, is the Dominican priory of Ste-Marie-de-la-Tourette (tel: 0472 19 10 90; guided tours Sun only). Considered to be one of the most important buildings of the late Modernist style, the priory was designed by Le Corbusier and Iannis Xenakis, and constructed between 1956 and 1960. The stark structural frame, resting on slim pillars, is of reinforced concrete with glass panes on three exterior faces.

Lyon

The high-speed TGV reaches **Lyon** ⑥ at La Part-Dieu station, just to the east of city centre, which can be reached by Métro or tram. With the Rhône on one side and the Saône on the other, the city centre is known as the Presqu'île (peninsula), and is ideal for walking.

Lyon was once a great silk manufacturing centre, and the **Musée Historique des Tissus et des Arts Décoratifs** ⓐ (34 Rue de la Charité; www.mtmad.fr; Tue–Sun 10am–5.30pm, closed public hols; charge) tells its story and covers the development of textile techniques from all over the world, with some of the rarest and most beautiful materials ever made. The **Musée des Beaux-Arts** ⓑ has an exceptional collection of French and European paintings (Palais St-Pierre, 20 Place des Terreaux; www.mba-lyon.fr; Wed–Mon 10am–6pm, closed public hols; charge).

Lyon was the first town to have a stock exchange and first to issue a cheque, and the **Musée de l'Imprimerie** ⓒ (13 Rue de la Poulaillerie; Wed–Sun 10am–6pm, closed public hols; charge) outlines the history of European commerce. East of the city centre, the **Musée Lumière** (25 Rue du Premier Film; Tue–Sun 10am–6.30pm; charge) celebrates another of Lyon's innovations, the invention of the cinema. The **Musée d'Art Contemporain** (www.mac-lyon.com; Wed–Sun 11am–6pm; charge) is fittingly housed in the ultra-modern **Cité Internationale** on Quai Charles-de-Gaulle, designed by Renzo Piano.

At the confluence of the rivers Rhône and Saône sits a bleak piece of industrial wasteland chosen as the site for an ambitious contemporary attraction, the **Musée des Confluences** ⓓ (Tue–Fri 11am–7pm, Sat–Sun 10am–9pm; charge). Opened in 2014, this futuristic steel and glass building, housing a science, technology and humanities museum, includes 10 exhibition rooms, cafés, restaurants and a riverside garden.

Just one of Lyon's multitude of bistros.

Along the Saône, a tree-lined *quai* extends a view over the wide water, with some bridges painted red. On the opposite bank lies the city's oldest quarter, **Vieux Lyon** Ⓔ. Typically, the Renaissance houses were constructed around a courtyard, which was reached from the street through a vaulted passage beneath a house. In each street a few courtyards had another vaulted passage at the back leading into the next street. These public passages, still in use, are called *traboules*.

A walk offers many discoveries. From the Rue Saint-Jean to the Place du Change, and further on to the Place du St-Paul, back down the Rue Juiverie and then the Rue Gadagne, is less than a kilometre altogether. The **Hôtel de Gadagne** Ⓕ is the finest Renaissance mansion in Lyon. It houses the **Musée d'Histoire de Lyon** and the **Musée des Marionnettes**, with a special collection of puppets from all over the world (www.gadagne.musees.lyon.fr; Wed–Sun 11am–6.30pm; charge). The **Cathédrale St-Jean** Ⓖ dates from the 11th–14th century. It contains a remarkable 14th-century astronomical clock, still in working order. The clock was designed to mark religious feast days right up until 2019.

The Roman city

The **Fourvière Hill** is reachable on foot by a steep climb, or by funicular cable cars. It is topped by a rococo **Notre-Dame de Fourvière** Ⓗ which has four towers, and a terrace overlooking the city. On the southern slope, the **Musée Gallo-Romain** Ⓘ (www.musees-gallo-romains.com; Tue–Sun 10am–6pm, closed public hols; charge) is unusual and well designed, built into the hill. From the upper entrance a spiral ramp glides gently down through artefacts. Windows look out onto two **Théâtres Romains** Ⓙ, still used for performances.

The other hill rising between the two rivers is **La Croix Rousse**, bastion of the *Canuts*, skilled workers in silk-weaving for generations. From the 15th century to the Industrial Revolution thousands of small workshops produced the richly coloured silks. A handful of craftsmen have maintained the tradition, furnishing the museums and palaces of Europe

EAT

The word *bouchon* in Lyon has its own particular meaning. Here it is not only a "bottle-stopper" or "traffic jam", but also a traditional restaurant serving regional dishes in a convivial atmosphere. The oldest, most authentic bouchon in Lyon is Comptoir Abel, rue Guynemer, 69002.

Notre-Dame-de-Fourvière dominates the city.

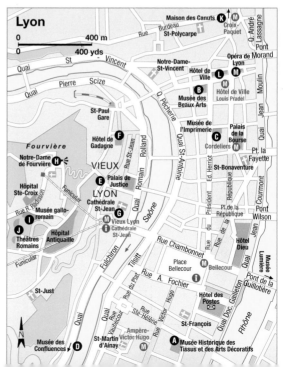

Lyon

FACT

Lyon's Fête des Lumières in early December marks the celebration of the city being saved from the plague. Re-introduced in 1989, the ceremony was rained off, so the citizens of Lyon lit candles in their windows. The event has been celebrated ever since and now around 4 million visitors come to see the annual festival of lights.

Bridge over the Rhône, Lyon.

with the brocades of a bygone era. **La Maison des Canuts** (http://maison descanuts.com; 10–12 Rue d'Ivry; Mon–Sat 10am–6.30pm, closed public hols; charge) gives demonstrations on different looms and patterns – Jacquard invented his silk loom here. From the **Place Bellevue**, a maze of passages and courtyards winds down to one of the town's most remarkable buildings, the **Hôtel de Ville** . Behind is the dramatic modern steel-and-glass addition to the **Opéra de Lyon** .

Gateway to Provence

The Rhône valley, gateway to Provence, is best seen off the main routes in places such as **Vienne** . The town is full of the echo of its distant glory as a Roman and then episcopal city.

Its restored **Théâtre Romain** is used for performances in summer. The **Temple d'Auguste et Livie** is, with the Maison Carrée at Nîmes, the best example of a Roman temple surviving in France. The corinthian columns were walled in during the 11th century when the temple was used as a church. The Musée des Beaux Arts et d'Archéologie (closed

for renovation until spring 2016) on Place de Miremont has Roman silverware and 18th-century ceramics.

The **Cathédrale St-Maurice**, built from the 11th–16th century, has a facade with three portals carved in the Flamboyant style, still remarkable though its statues were removed during the Wars of Religion. Across the river at **St-Roman-en-Gal** a Roman suburb of Vienne has been excavated. The adjoining museum (www.musees-gallo-romains. com; Tue–Sun 10am–6pm; charge) houses an impressive collection including murals and mosaics.

Staying on the right bank of the river, moving south, the traffic-laden RN86 passes through the wine villages of **Ampuis** and **Condrieu**. Though they don't look exceptional, they are noteworthy for wine connoisseurs. The neatly-trained vines grown on steep granite terraces overlooking the Rhône produce some of the best Northern Rhône wines: rich spicy red Côte Rôtie and delicately perfumed Condrieu. The local goat's cheese 'Rigotte de Condrieu' and a glass of Condrieu are perfect partners for a picnic.

Sunny orchards

Heading south, the landscape develops a Mediterranean feel with vast orchards of apricot, cherry and peach trees.

Tournon-sur-Rhône ❽, a lively little town, especially on Saturday mornings when the market is in full flow on the tree-lined quays, is worth a short visit. The imposing 11th-16th-century château has a small local history museum (Mar–Nov daily 2–6pm; charge).

Directly across the river is the town of Tain l'Hermitage, another wine-making centre, famous for its Hermitage wines. The town centre is unappealing with a constant flow of heavy goods traffic, but is a haven for chocolate lovers. Located in a chic boutique on the main street, is Valrhona's, one of the finest chocolate manufacturers in France.

The Ardèche

Situated on high plateaus on the west side of the Rhône, given to abrupt descents, lies the region known as the Ardèche, which marks the southern edge of central France. The Ardèche river, a tributary of the Rhône, which gives its name to the region, has carved its way through the limestone gorge to create a towering rugged landscape riddled with caves and tunnels. The caves at Grotte de la Madeleine and Aven d'Orgnac are both ornamented with impressive stalagmite and stalactite formations.

Canoeing, kayaking and white-water rafting are popular. The section beyond the village of Vallon Pont d'Arc ❾ is especially scenic. The river has dug extremely deep and formed large gorges that are equally spectacular when viewed from the river or from the road 400 metres (1,300ft) above.

At Pont d'Arc the river has pierced a passage through the rock and formed a beautifully symmetrical arch. For canoeists, the river runs at a good speed with challenging rapids. Descend before mid-July, after which the water is too low. In autumn the fast-flowing waters are unsuitable for beginners.

Canoes can be rented at many places around Vallon Pont d'Arc and return transport can be organised from St-Martin-d'Ardèche. A guided canoe trip along the river is the perfect way to enjoy the sheer-sided gorge and its secluded beaches.

WHERE

The Palais Idéal du Facteur Cheval (www.facteurcheval.com) in the village of Hauterives is a fantasy palace built by a postman called Ferdinand Cheval out of stones he picked up on his rounds. André Breton and Picasso have been among its admirers, and music concerts take place there today in summer.

Pont d'Arc, where canoeists can behold the spectacular scenery of the Ardèche.

GASTRONOMIC CAPITAL

In addition to its role as a serious business, banking and conference centre, Lyon is the undisputed gastronomic capital of France. As in Burgundy, food is a science and an art, even a religion. The city is stuffed with fine restaurants and bistros, and regional specialities abound: *rosette* and *Jésus* salamis, pâté cooked in pastry, *quenelles de brochet* (poached mousse of pike), *coq au vin, poulet de Bresse* and freshwater crayfish. The daily rhythm of life revolves around meal times, which are strictly observed: the mid-morning *mâchon*, specifically Lyonnais, is no snack but a meal of charcuterie, which might include sausages and rosette salamis as well as stuffed hocks and hams.

THE FRENCH ALPS

●Paris

A paradise for skiers and walkers, the old regions
of Savoie and Dauphiné roll south from Geneva
and its elegant lake across snow-capped
mountains, including magnificent Mont Blanc.

Main Attractions
Chamonix-Mt-Blanc
Megève
Briançon
Grenoble
Monastère de la Grande
  Chartreuse
Chambéry
Annecy
Evian-les-Bains

*Skiers negotiating the
lofty slopes of Mont
Blanc.*

Any account of the French Alps
should start with **Mont Blanc**,
the highest mountain in Europe
at 4,808 metres (15,780ft). Regarded
from any viewpoint, with its notable broad shoulders, the mountain
is quite magnificent. At the top, the
great chains of the Alps, stretching
from Italy to Austria, seem like tiny
mountain ridges far below. In the
spring, experienced climbers and
guides, with a bit of luck, climb the
mountain for two days on their skis
and spend their final night two hours

from the summit. Then they go to
sleep just as new snow begins to fall.
The next morning they climb to the
summit in the very early hours, and
spend the entire day skiing all the
way back down to the border town
of **Chamonix-Mt-Blanc** ❿ in fresh
deep-powder snow.

Mont Blanc comes down on the
town in the form of the **Glacier des
Bossons**, which may be seen quite
clearly at the entrance to the **Tunnel
du Mont Blanc**. At 11.5km (7 miles),
it was the longest road tunnel in the
world until 1978, and at its highest
point, the tunnel's roof reaches nearly
2,470 metres (8,100ft) in altitude. The
tunnel links Chamonix to the Italian
resort of **Courmayeur**, less than 20km
(12 miles) away. After a fire in 1999
that killed 39 people it was closed for
repairs until June 2002, and there were
angry protests by environmentalists
when it re-opened.

It is possible to take the same trip
to Italy and return via the spectacular
cable-car network which goes up from
Chamonix to the **Aiguille du Midi**
(3,800km/12,500ft), traverses the top of
the **Vallée Blanche** spring ski run and
the **Glacier du Géant** to the **Pointe
Helbronner**, popular with year-round
skiers, and then descends to the village
of **Entrèves**, near Courmayeur.

The trip is one of the most spectacular, if somewhat harrowing, voy-
ages of its kind in the world. For the
more sedentary, a train goes up from

Chamonix to **Montenvers** with a view onto the end of the Vallée Blanche and the **Mer de Glace** (Sea of Ice).

Sadly, cowbells are heard no more in the Chamonix region. The town has become a fully fledged year-round tourist resort, and the pastures and herds of cattle have been replaced by hotels, swimming pools and restaurants. In its centre, however, like most Alpine resorts, it remains an old-fashioned mountain town, with a sophisticated international clientele.

St-Tropez of the Alps

Not far from Chamonix is **Megève** ⓫, a summer resort set in pine forests frequented by the rich and famous. This old village with turreted houses has a very famous ski school.

Val-d'Isère ⓬ is one of the finest ski areas in Europe, together with the more recently developed **Tignes** ⓭, which was relocated here after the original Tignes was drowned making the Isère hydro-electric scheme. The whole ski area is called Espace Killy resort after Jean-Claude Killy, a champion skier who dominated the

sport in the 1960s, and who came from Val d'Isère.

The trails go up to 3,750 metres (12,300ft) and, as in Chamonix, skiing is possible all year round; the facilities are so extensive that you can ski for a week without ever taking the same lift twice. From both Megève and Val-d'Isère you can enjoy stunning views of the French and Italian faces of majestic Mont Blanc.

In summer, Val-d'Isère becomes a tourist centre focused on the **Parc National de la Vanoise**, one of the more important reserves of Alpine flora and fauna, and well worth the visit by cable-car up to **Mont Bochor** (2,070 metres/6,650ft).

Established in 1963 this was France's first national park, and now comprises five nature reserves. Marmots, chamois and the country's largest colony of Alpine ibexes wander carefree within the protected borders of the park. The sure-footed Alpine ibex that lives mainly above the tree line was on the verge of becoming extinct but conservation measures in the park have saved the population. Footpaths for hikers

FACT

The wildlife in Vanoise includes chamoix, marmot, blue hare and the splendidly horned Alpine ibex, and skyward, golden eagles and bearded, griffon and black vultures.

Alpine climbers descending a ridge.

An Alpine ibex makes an appearance in the Parc National des Ecrins.

Starting them off young.

lead through a wild and spectacular landscape. The Grande Tour de Haute Maurienne and La Tour des Glaciers are both five to six-day hikes into the world of the park's glaciers and high peaks. Be sure to be properly equipped for the terrain and the altitude.

Parc National des Ecrins

Further to the south is **Briançon** ⑭, a military town and home of the Chasseurs Alpins, the French Army's mountain brigade. At 1,320 metres (4,334ft) it is the highest town in Europe. Its old part is dominated by a fortress and it remains much as it was in the time of Louis XI, with narrow streets making automobile traffic virtually impossible.

Briançon is the gateway to the valley of **La Vallouise** and the **Parc National des Ecrins**. The national park stretches over an area of 91,800ha (226,847acres) between Gap, Grenoble and Briançon and is bounded by the river valleys of the Romanche, Durance and Drac and their impressive glaciers. It has more than a hundred mountain peaks over 1,000m (3,280ft) and the highest is the Barre des Ecrins (4,101m/13,455ft).

The core of the park can only be explored on foot, and there are plenty of well-marked paths to follow, including the GR54.

A good source of information about the park's geology, flora and fauna can be found at the Musée des Minéraux et de la Faune des Alpes (Wed–Mon pms, July–Aug daily; charge) at **Bourg d'Oisans**.

Spectacular scenery can be admired from the carriages of the Chemin de Fer de la Mure. Due to a landslide in 2010 the service was suspended but there are now plans to reopen the line at the end of 2015. This 1930s little red train winds its way on narrow-gauge tracks through deep gorges and tunnels and across majestic viaducts. The journey begins at **St-Georges de Commiers**, south of Grenoble, and terminates at **La Mure**.

The nearby purpose-built ski resort of **Alpe d'Huez** has the French Alps' longest black run, 'La Sarenne'.

Grenoble

The Alps' main city is **Grenoble** ⑮, in a wonderful mountain setting

WHERE AND WHEN TO SKI

The main ski season starts in December and finishes at the end of April. The busiest period is during the February school holiday in France, and best avoided if you can. One of the most popular winter sports regions is the vast **Trois Vallées**, with 600km of pistes. Its famous resorts include the glitzy **Courchevel**, a destination that draws the jet-set, smart but more traditional **Méribel**, **Les Menuires**, which is a popular destination for the French, and **Val Thorens**, the highest at 2,300m (7,500ft).

In addition, **Val d'Isère** has something to please everyone from serious snowboarders to families. **Tignes**, **Les Arcs** and **La Plagne** are all functional resorts, with hideous concrete architecture; Tignes however, at 2,100 metres (6,900ft), offers good snow conditions for most of the season. **Chamonix-Mont-Blanc**, site of the first Winter Olympics in 1924, is the oldest winter sports town and although sometimes lacking snow on the lower slopes there are some outstanding runs such as the off-piste **Vallée Blanche**. **Les Houches** and **Argentière** are its more affordable satellites.

Other favourites are **Morzine**, which has an old-world charm, situated on the Swiss border, modern **Avoriaz** with its wooden high-rise architecture, and **Albertville** home to the Winter Olympics in 1992.

where the River Drac joins the Isère. The birthplace of Stendhal, author of *The Red and the Black*, is an old and respected university town, though the campus is now in the suburbs.

The Winter Olympic Games of 1968 gave the town a push into the modern age and changed it forever. It is a many-faceted city, with chemical, computer and microchip industries, and all the noise and rush of modern traffic. But it also has a lively cultural life, as can be seen in the library and the modern sculptures that adorn the huge patio of the Hôtel de Ville.

To get an overview of Grenoble, take the cable car up to the **Fort de la Bastille**. There is a superb view of the layout of the city and the surrounding mountains.

A clutch of museums testify to a rich cultural heritage. The modern **Musée de Grenoble** (www.museedegrenoble.fr; Wed–Mon 10am–6,30pm; charge) has a painting collection from the 16th century onwards and includes works by Chagall and Matisse. The **Musée Dauphinois** (Wed–Mon 10am–7pm, 6pm in winter) in a former convent

gives an idea of the history of the region – Grenoble was the capital of Dauphiné, an independent county in the Middle Ages. The Musée de l'Ancien Evêché (Mon–Tue, Thu–Fri 9am–6pm, Wed, Sat–Sun closed am) has earlier artefacts from Celtic and Roman times.

The monks' liqueur

In 1084 the bishop of Grenoble dreamed of seven stars announcing the arrival of seven travellers, led by Saint Bruno, who had decided to live in complete isolation from the world. The good bishop then led them to the mountain chain of La Chartreuse, which gave its name to the Carthusian Order of monks. They built their famous **Monastère de La Grande Chartreuse** ⑯ there, far removed from all other human habitation, and to this day the monks of the monastery distill their well-known liqueur.

Living in solitude, they engage in religious devotion, study and manual labour. They meet three times a day in the chapel and eat together only once a week, on Sunday in the refectory. The

FACT

Spring and summer in the Alps are a prime time to discover the hundreds of plant species. Above the tree line Alpine juniper flourishes on south-facing slopes, while rhododendrons populate north-facing hillsides. Richly-coloured blue and yellow gentians, bellflowers, glacier buttercups and saxifrage thrive on the steep meadows.

The Grenoble cable car.

The Fontaine des Eléphants in Chambéry.

Waterskiing on the Lac du Bourget.

monastery was completely destroyed by an avalanche in 1132 and has been nearly destroyed by fire on eight different occasions. The present buildings date from 1688. Though the monastery is closed to visitors, there is a museum depicting the Order's history and the monks' daily life at its entrance, the **Musée de la Grande Chartreuse** (www.musee-grande-chartreuse.fr/en; Apr–Nov daily 10am–6.30pm, closed Apr, Oct–Nov Mon–Fri pm; charge). Of particular interest are the representations of the monks passing their solitary lives in prayer.

Nearby **Chambéry** brings the visitor back down to earth. It became the capital city of the dukes of Savoy in 1232 and remains a largish town defended by its fortress. Its best-known monument is the **Fontaine des Eléphants**, built in 1838 as a memorial to a town benefactor, the Count de Boigne, and his rollicking adventures in colonial India.

Adjoining the cathedral housed in the former Franciscan monastery is the **Musée Savoisien** (closed for restoration until further notice), which is devoted to local Savoyard history, archaeology and fine arts. The **Château des Ducs de Savoie**, now home to the Préfecture, was erected as the home of the first rulers of Chambéry and then the Savoie dukes. From the **Place du Château** there is a fine view of the old town centre.

Chambéry is associated with perhaps the most famous French romantic, the creator of the revolutionary social contract, Jean-Jacques Rousseau. In 1728, at the age of 16, Rousseau, then an apprentice engraver who had been badly treated by his employer, ran away from his Calvinist home in Geneva.

On the outskirts of Chambéry is **Les Charmettes**, the cottage, completely restored as it was in his day, which he shared for six years with his mistress, 28-year-old landlady Madame de Warens. She had been converted back to Catholicism from Calvinism and was working to re-convert others. As indicated in his *Confessions*, Rousseau was converted to Madame de Warens, if nothing else (890 Chemin des Charmettes; Wed–Mon 10am–5pm, closed public hols; charge).

Resort spas and baths

The neighbouring spa of **Aix-les-Bains** ⑱ is known for rheumatism treatment, and the remains of Roman baths testify to past fame and elegance, as does its name, derived from *aquae Gratianae* (Baths of Emperor Gratian). After the fall of the Roman Empire the baths fell into disuse but were rebuilt in 1779–83.

Today's resort has as its centre the **Thermes Nationaux** (National Thermal Baths), along with the **Parc Municipal** and the **casino**. It also has a superb small museum, **Musée Faure** (10 Boulevard des Côtes; Mar–Oct Wed–Mon 10am–6pm, Nov–Feb closed Mon also; charge), with works by Bonnard, Pissarro, Degas, Renoir and other Impressionists.

During the summer, there is much activity around the two ports and the beach on **Lac du Bourget**. The baths, which today receive more *curists* than any other French spa, are open all year with sulphuric waters and hot pools for the relief of aches and pains.

At the Grand Port boats sail across the lake (seasonal) to the Abbaye d'Hautecombe on the northeast side. This picturesque 12th-century abbey (Wed–Mon 10am–noon, 2–5pm; charge) founded by Benedictine monks was abandoned after the French Revolution, and was restored by the King of Sardinia in 1824. It houses the mausoleum of the Savoyard royalty.

Lake Annecy

The lake and small city of **Annecy** ⑲ are both associated with Jean-Jacques Rousseau. It was here, soon after his flight from Geneva, that he first met Madame de Warens. Like most cities around Lake Geneva on both the French and Swiss sides, Annecy was a town of lake-dwellers in prehistoric times. It derives its name from an ancient Roman estate, the *Villa Aniciaca*. Annecy developed in the 12th century, when its fortress was constructed. Its most famous citizen, Rousseau aside, was Saint François de Sales, who became a priest in 1593 and entered into the Wars of Reformation against the Calvinists.

Contemporary Annecy is a small industrial city involved in the manufacturing of ballpoint pens, razor blades and jewellery. The main street, the **Rue**

TIP

The 38km (23-mile) circuit of Lac d'Annecy can be driven, walked or cycled (bicycles are available for hire from several outlets located on the shores of the lake); or you could see the lake by taking a cruise. Details from the Annecy tourist office.

The Palais de l'Isle, dating from the twelfth century and once Annecy's old prison, squats in the Thiou canal.

Along the canal in Annecy's atmospheric Old Town.

The medieval castle of Yvoire on Lake Geneva.

Ste-Claire, is lined with ancient arcaded buildings intersected by canals. Cars are forbidden in parts. The 17th-century church of **St-François**, the **Palais de l'Isle** (12th century), originally a prison, the 16th-century **château** and the **Cathédrale St-François-de-Sales** constitute the major landmarks.

Geneva

Nearby **Geneva** ⑳ is no longer part of France – strictly speaking. But the city is the main aircraft entry point to the French Alps and figures prominently in the area's history and activities. People who live in Geneva tend to ski and go for excursions in France, and the offices of the busy city are filled with *frontaliers*, French citizens who cross the borders daily.

Lake Geneva ㉑ is Lac Léman in French, and the lake, 70km (45 miles) long, the largest entirely inland body of water in Europe, is shared between France and Switzerland. Two famous spas are on the French shore.

The road along the lake from Geneva passes by the picturesque French village of **Yvoire**, which juts out into the lake and is famous for its restaurants and its narrow streets of gabled houses. Part of the 14th-century ramparts still stand, as do many medieval houses bedecked with flowers. Here visitors must park their cars at the gates of the fortress wall and make their way down to the port on foot.

Taking the waters

Thonon-les-Bains ㉒ is a chic little spa town sitting on a cliff overlooking the lake, with a funicular that links the upper town to the harbour where boats can be hired. The spa waters have a high mineral content and they are used to treat intestinal disorders. Fill up your water bottles with Thonon mineral water for free at the Fontaine de la Versoie in the Parc Thermal.

On the Place du Château stood a fortress of the dukes of Savoy (from whom the *départements* of Savoie and Haute-Savoie take their name), which was destroyed by the French in 1589. The **Musée Chablais** (July–Aug daily, Sept–June Wed–Sun pm only; charge) is devoted to the folklore of the region. At the church of **St**

Hippolyte (12th–17th century), Saint François de Sales preached the return to Catholicism to the wavering believers in the area.

The Route des Grandes Alpes a 680km (425 mile) road tour to the Côte d'Azur, starts from here Thonon-les-Bains.

Evian-les-Bains ㉓ is the source of bottled Evian mineral water. Much of the construction along the lakeside here, including the casino, dates from 1865, when the city fathers shrewdly decided to develop "Evian water" and turn the small fortified city into a spa. The baths, fully renovated in 2012, are open daily (tel: 04 50 75 65 99; closed mid-Dec–mid-Jan; charge) and Evian churns out around 40 million bottles every month.

The **Jardin Anglais** (English Garden) fronts the lake near the port, where the Lake Geneva paddle-wheel steamers carry tourists to the towns all around the lake and make repeated journeys from Evian to **Lausanne** (on the Swiss side) to take French people who go to work daily in Switzerland.

In summer it is possible to make a complete tour of Lake Geneva from Evian. The steamers of the Compagnie Générale de Navigation link up over 38 ports on both the French and Swiss sides of the lake.

Gateway to the sun

The Lake Geneva area of the French Alps is called **Le Chablais**. The Swiss border, at **St-Gingolph**, is the gateway to **Les Portes du Soleil**, or the Gateway to the Sun, a ski area encompassing eight French and six Italian resorts, most notably **Morzine** and **Avoriaz**, and several other ski towns on both the French and Swiss (Champéry, Les Crozet) sides of the Alps.

Developed over the past 25 years, Les Portes du Soleil is a vast series of sun and snow bowls where downhill skiers can swoosh from one top-class ski area to another, cross-country skiers can trek to their heart's content, staying the night in different towns, and mountain climbers and hikers will be in heaven. From hundreds of look-out points throughout the Portes du Soleil area, visitors can catch a glimpse of Mont Blanc.

The Lake Geneva area, with the Dents du Midi mountain range visible in the background.

The Chapelle St-Michel-d'Aiguilhe,
Le Puy-en-Velay.

AUVERGNE

The Massif Central is the remote core of France, a
huge, rugged plateau of granite and rock. It
embraces the Auvergne, whose volcanic
landscape is dramatic yet serenely peaceful.

Paris

For centuries the **Massif Central** was largely cut off from the rest of France, whose history took place along its perimeter. It was a self-contained, mountainous region of isolated valleys, and its principal common denominator was its remoteness. But the map shows that numerous rivers, like the fingers of a hand, radiate out from the Massif Central's craggy heights and develop into mighty waterways that snake their way to the Atlantic and the Mediterranean.

Regional capital

Clermont-Ferrand ❶, the regional capital, originally consisted of two rival towns, Clermont and Montferrand, which merged in the 18th century. There is a startling contrast in Montferrand between the elegant Renaissance architecture of its old quarter and the sprawling Michelin tyre factory.

Clermont's **Basilique de Notre-Dame-du-Port** is one of a group of Auvergnat Romanesque churches that are the pride of the Puy-de-Dôme *département*. Hemmed in on all sides by the houses and narrow streets of the old quarter, the 11th- and 12th-century church takes one by surprise. Steps lead down into a dim nave formed by semicircular arches with fine capitals. Round chapels are arranged like lobes round the apse, and the theme of roundness is

repeated in the semicircular tiles of their almost flat roofs.

South of the city is the well-preserved village of **St-Saturnin ❷**. Its 12th-century Romanesque **church** of pale yellow stone bears carved figures of almost casual spontaneity on the outside. The interior is lit from above by windows with semicircular arches repeating the pattern of the nave.

On the square in front of St-Saturnin's medieval château is a remarkable Renaissance fountain: a large sculpted stone basin into which

Main Attractions
Clermont-Ferrand
St-Saturnin
Puy de Sancy
Thiers
Le Puy-en-Velay
Tournemire

Clermont-Ferrand.

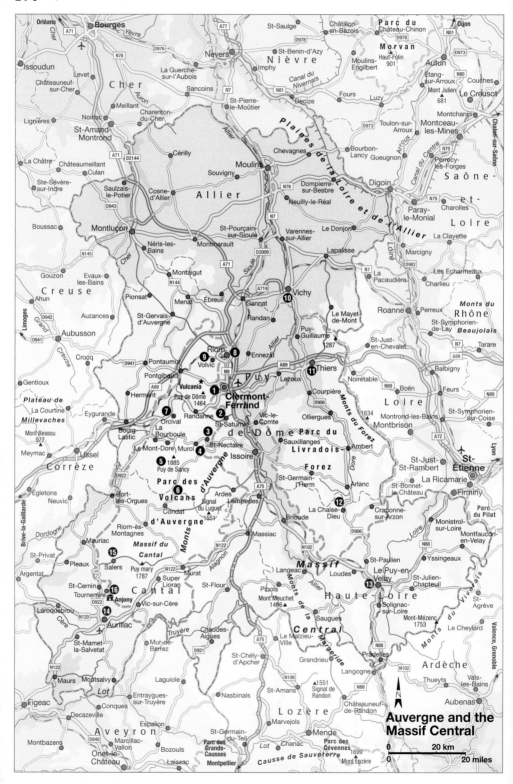

water flows from a central column. The **Château Royal de St-Saturnin** belonged to Queen Catherine de Medici and Queen Marguerite de Valois. In the 16th century it was given a roof of grey stone tiles *(lauzes)* that protected its main structural elements. Many other features suffered from the encroachment of the town, however restoration by volunteers has succeeded in recreating the illustrious past of a castle, which is now a hotel (Easter–mid-Nov).

Water worship

The sleepy town of **St-Nectaire ❸** is tucked in a hollow of greenery. It has numerous typically Auvergnat attributes. Its nutty-flavoured eponymous cheese is renowned all over France. The mineral water from its 40 springs, which inspired the Gauls' water worship, run along conduits deep below the streets. Worth visiting are the remains of the Roman baths at the Grottes du Cornadore, hand-hewn under the Mont Cornadore (daily mid-Feb–Oct 10am–noon, 2–6pm; charge). Today, late 19th-century

hotels cater for families looking for peace, and retired people coming to take the waters. Majestically set on a promontory above the town is the **church of St-Nectaire**, built in stone ranging in colour from a deep mossy green to a violet-tinged black. Its nave and choir contain 103 capitals, evoking miracles worked by St-Nectaire.

The partly ruined 13th-century **Château de Murol** (Apr–Sept daily 10am–6pm, Oct–Mar Sat and Sun until 5pm; charge) overlooking the village of **Murol ❹**, near **Lac Chambon**, is imposing. Its thick, copper-coloured walls enclose a complex of cellars, courtyards, staircases, two chapels and living quarters, an ideal setting for the themed historical events that take place here. Only those with a head for heights are advised to visit the rampart walk and watchtower.

A few kilometres to the south is situated the pretty mountain village of **Besse-en-Chandresse**. The traditional red-shuttered houses in the medieval centre are built of local volcanic stone – black lava and basalt. In the Middle Ages this was a thriving market town

The St-Nectaire, an AOP (Appellation d'Origine Protégée) semi-hard cheese with a distinctive brownish grey rind.

The Puy de Sancy.

FACT

Joseph Cantaloupe, a musicologist from the region, collected and orchestrated the traditional Songs of the Auvergne, which were first recorded by Madeleine Grey in 1930. Since then many sopranos, including Tiri Te Kanawa and Victoria de los Angeles, have sung these haunting tunes.

Funiculaire du Capucin (Le Mont-Doré), the Belle-Epoque funicular that is France's oldest.

renowned for its cheese – there are numerous St-Nectaire producers scattered on the surrounding mountain pastures. But cheese wasn't the only commodity on sale, there was meat, leather and cow horn used for the handles of traditional Laguiole knives.

There is also a small ski museum in the town and the nearby ski resort **Super Besse** is popular in winter.

Not far to the west, on the other side of a high pass inaccessible in winter, is the highest point in the Massif Central, the **Puy de Sancy** ❺, on whose slopes the River Dordogne rises. In winter, skiers from the nearby resorts of **Le Mont-Doré** and **La Bourboule** have an exhilarating time on the Puy de Sancy, while in summer it is visited for the unparalleled view it offers from the summit, encompassing the Monts du Cantal, the Puy de Dôme and, on a very clear day, the Alps. There is a cable car for those who don't want to walk.

Volcanic Park

In the heart of the **Parc Régional des Volcans** ❻, a major centre, Vulcania,

simulates volcanic activity in a state-of-the-art underground museum at **Saint-Ours-les-Roches** (www.vulcania. com; Apr–Oct daily 10am–6pm, with exceptions; charge).

A spectacular drive through mountainous terrain leads to **Orcival** ❼, where the 12th-century **Basilique de Notre-Dame** is another fine and remarkably homogeneous example of Auvergnat Romanesque. Behind the altar is a striking *Virgin and Child in Majesty*. Made of wood covered with silver and gold plaques, the sculpture shows the figures in a stiff, front-facing pose and is the object of several pilgrimages.

South of Orcival is the impressive **Col de Guéry**, part of the Massif du Sancy. From the summit there are splendid views, especially of the gigantic granite peaks of the **Roches Tuilière et Sanadoire**. Discover the wide variety of Auvergne's flora at the **Maison des Fleurs d'Auvergne** (mid-June–Sept daily 10am–7pm, May–mid-June Sat–Sun). Displays explain the fragile ecosystem that exists on the mountain slopes, whose volcanic

VOLCANOES AND LAKES

The Volcans d'Auvergne region consists of a chain of extinct volcanoes covering three areas: Monts Dômes or Chaîne des Puys, Monts Dorés and Monts du Cantal.

The **Chaîne des Puys** first erupted more than 70,000 years ago. But with the last eruption at a mere 8,000 years ago fresh volcanic activity is not completely ruled out. The chain of volcanoes extends more than 30km (18.6-miles) with around 80 domes. The domes are shorter and flatter than those of Monts du Cantal and Dorés since they are monogenic volcanoes – formed by one single short eruption. Regular volcanoes are formed by successive eruptions over a long period of time.

The **Monts Dorés** are older, created between 100,000 and 3 million years ago. The principal volcanoes are the **Puy de Sancy** (the highest in the Massif Central), **La Banne d'Ordanche**, and the lesser known **Puy de l'Aiguiller**.

The **Monts du Cantal** is a giant volcano that first erupted 13 million years ago. It is the largest strato-volcano in Europe, recognisable by its tall, conical shape formed by layers of hardened lava and volcanic ash.

The entire Auvergne volcanic region is also dotted with lakes. These were created in one of three ways: they occupy volcanic craters; they were created after a barrage of lava dammed a steam or river; or they are "glacial lakes" formed after the melt down of a glacier.

soils support plants and flowers such as gentian, veratrum, lilies and orchids.

Nearby, sitting in a volcanic crater, is the highest lake in the Massif Central, **Lac de Guéry**. Full of trout and perch, this is an ideal spot for fishing. The lake freezes over in winter, but around March, the *pêche blanche* season starts – fishing through holes made in the ice.

Second city

For centuries **Riom** ❽ was Clermont's fierce rival as administrative capital of the region. Its erstwhile importance can be judged from its numerous Renaissance townhouses built of dark volcanic stone. **Sainte Chapelle**, all that remains of the Duc de Berry's château, contains remarkable stained-glass windows. The main attraction of the church of **Notre-Dame-du-Marthuret** is its superb 14th-century Gothic statue, *Virgin with Bird*.

Mineral water towns

The little town of **Volvic** ❾ is best known for its mineral water, but it also gives its name to a highly resistant grey volcanic rock used locally as a building material. The **Maison de la Pierre** (www.maisondelapierre-volvic. com; Feb–Nov daily 11am–5pm with exceptions, closed Sat Feb-mid–Apr, Sept–Oct; charge), next to the spring, organises a slide-show and tours of the lava quarry.

Just to the north of Volvic, the half-ruined **Château de Tournoël** (July–Aug daily 10.30am–12.30pm, 4–6pm; charge) provides a fascinating insight into how people once lived. From the medieval keep to the *châtelaine*'s chambers with their secret entrance, all its elements evoke a precise period and activity.

Vichy ❿ came to prominence when it was chosen as the seat of the government that collaborated with the Nazi occupation forces. Today it is a pleasant town that has kept up with the times, unlike some of Auvergne's other spas, whose faded salmon-pink hotels are only a shadow of their former glory.

Remote and rugged

The last section of rugged terrain in the Massif Central driving northwards comes with the canyons of the River Sioule. They are succeeded by the rolling country of the **Bourbonnais**, which in turns flattens into a vast agricultural plain approaching the invisible frontier between northern and southern France.

Clinging to a hillside above the Gorges de la Durolle is **Thiers** ⓫ a city renowned for cutlery making since the Middle Ages, producing everything from pocket knives and tableware to guillotine blades. A vast collection of knives along with an explication of cutlery-making is found in the Musée de la Coutellerie (June–Sept daily 10am–noon, 2–6pm, Oct–May Tue–Sun; charge). The old town is riddled with steep streets lined with medieval houses, many with intricately carved wooden façades, notably Maison du Pirou on the Place Pirou. There is a stunning view from the ramparts of the Monts Dômes and Monts Dorés.

The road going south, heading in the direction of **Le Puy-en-Velay**,

Thiers, a town long synonymous with the cutlery industry.

The evocative outline of an extinct volcano.

FACT

In the third week of September, Le Puy holds the "Roi de l'Oiseau", a masked and costumed carnival that had its origins in the 16th century as a display of archery skills.

climbs through uninterrupted colonnades of pine forest to **La Chaise-Dieu** , where even in high summer a slight drizzle can begin to turn to sleet. This is the remote and rugged site of a grand 11th-century monastery, and the venue of a prestigious classical music festival in August.

In the choir of the abbey church of **St-Robert**, the marvellously carved monks' stalls are surmounted by an incomparably rich series of 16th-century tapestries. Contemplating these 11 tableaux, restored to their original luminous colours, is like walking into an illuminated manuscript. Each tapestry, a triptych representing scenes from the Old and New Testaments, is alive with a rich cast of vigorously and naturalistically portrayed characters, from urchins to executioners. Another drama is depicted in the grim *Danse Macabre* fresco, in which Death invites a succession of elongated figures to dance.

Lace and spindles

The town of **Le Puy-en-Velay** , in the heart of the **Velay** region, makes a spectacular sight with two huge,

Le Puy-en-Velay and its largest lava pillar.

almost vertical pillars of volcanic rock rising above its roofs. It was an important staging post for pilgrims on their way to Santiago de Compostela. Steep streets rise to the **Cathédrale Notre-Dame**, whose west facade, reached by a broad flight of steps, is a Romanesque mosaic of yellow, black and reddish stone that seems to float surreally against the sky. The lively geometric patterns of naturally coloured stone in the beautiful, Arabic-inspired cloister make this a delightful place.

Lacemaking is a traditional craft in **Le Puy-en-Velay**, and in its lace shops *dentellières* can be seen manipulating dozens of small spindles with incredible speed and dexterity. Work on an intricate tablecloth can take up to a year, so the mind boggles at the number of hours' work that must have gone into some of the lace collection in the **Musée Crozatier** (closed for renovations until end of 2015).

Perched on top of the largest lava pillar, looking almost as if it has grown out of it, is **Chapelle St-Michel-d'Aiguilhe** (www.rochersaintmichel.fr; mid-Mar–Sept daily 9.30am–5.30pm with exceptions, Feb–mid-Mar closed am; charge). The name Aiguilhe refers to the "needle" of rock, which is reached by a climb of 268 steps. The original sanctuary, the shape of a three-leafed clover, was just large enough for an altar. It was later enlarged by an asymmetrical ambulatory. The expressiveness of the tableau of saints over the doorway contrast with the simplicity of the rough-hewn interior.

Volcanic hills

The Cantal mountains, dating from the Tertiary period, formed the oldest and largest volcano in Europe with a diameter of 70km (45 miles). From the highest peaks, the **Plomb du Cantal** at 1,855 metres (6,086ft) and the **Puy Mary** at 1,787 metres (5,863ft), there are breathtaking views. Snaking up the slope of Puy Mary is France's highest road pass, the **Pas de Peyrol**, the summit of which has been crossed eight

times since 1947 by the gruelling Tour de France race.

At their southwestern extremity lies **Aurillac** , whose **Musée des Volcans** (mid-June–mid-Sept Mon–Sat 10am–6.30pm, Sun pm, mid-Sept–mid-June Tue–Sat pm only; charge) is an excellent source of information about the area's geological history and its natural park.

Extending from Aurillac to Clermont-Ferrand, this vast reserve of volcanic origin is crisscrossed by a network of signposted hiking paths (including one along the Compostela pilgrimage route) that wend their way through forests, grassy meadows dotted with wild flowers, and banks of heather and blueberry. These expanses of unspoilt natural beauty are still used as summer pastures for cows whose milk goes into the making of Cantal cheese and its higher-grade version, Salers. In the old days, a lone cowherd would stay up in the hills for the entire season. The low-slung stone huts called *burons* that dot the slopes would serve as bedroom, dairy and cellar for maturing the 40kg (88lb) cheeses. The cowherd's tasks covered every phase of cheesemaking, from gathering firewood to boil the water for sterilising the cheesecloths, to filtering the milk and pressing the curd.

Salers

Perched above the scenic valley that runs westwards from the Puy Mary is the striking little town of **Salers** ⓯, which has given its name to a breed of cow, a cheese and an apéritif made from the wild gentian that grows on the surrounding mountains. The lovely houses, notable for their *bartizans* (turrets), spiral staircases and stone window sashes, reflect the prestige the town earned by becoming a bailiwick in the 15th century. Housed in one of these Renaissance houses, once the former headquarters of the Order of Malta, is the local history museum (Apr–Oct Sat–Thu 10am–12.30pm, 2–5.30pm, closed Sat am; charge). The eclectic collection consists of furniture and household objects relating to everyday life in the Auvergne. One room is equipped as a pharmacy from 1890, another explains the making of Salers cheese and the local gentian-based apéritif. On the top floor is a small exhibition of contemporary art.

A few kilometres from Salers is the village of **Tournemire** ⓰ and the remarkable 15th-century **Château d'Anjony** (mid-Feb–mid-Nov daily 2–5pm, Jul–Aug am also; charge), overlooking a valley that was once administered by four feudal lords, each with his respective castle. It has survived almost intact and been tastefully restored. A miniature chapel tucked into one of the castle's four towers is frescoed from ceiling to floor with a vast anthology of biblical lore in deep reds and sombre blues. In the Salle des Chevaliers the walls tell the tale of the nine knights of legend, the Neuf Preux. The banner identifying King Arthur has been effaced, perhaps indicating disapproval of the English, who ravaged the region during the Hundred Years' War.

The Salers cow, distinguished by its long-haired, rather curly reddish coat and slender horns.

From the Pas de Peyrol, steps lead walkers up the Puy Mary.

LIMOUSIN

Limousin is a centre for the arts of fire – porcelain and enamel; and a land of water – rain and lakes. Still relatively unknown to tourists, the unspoilt landscape is rich with history and tradition with pretty medieval villages and ancient churches and bastides.

Main Attractions
Limoges
Oradour-sur-Glane
Aubusson
Arnac-Pompadour
Coussac Bonneval
Uzerche
Turenne
Collonges-la-Rouge

The distinctive red-hued buildings of Collonges-la-Rouge.

Many a bridal trousseau has been graced by delicate china from **Limoges ❶**, making it a household name. In this quiet, half-timbered country town there are more than 30 porcelain workshops of all sizes, many offering guided tours. The **Musée National Adrien Dubouché** (Wed–Mon 10am–12.40pm, 2–5.45pm; charge) has a collection of 10,000 pieces from all periods.

The capital of Limousin has many historic sights. Simple and graceful, the eight arches of the 13th-century stone

Pont St-Etienne over the Vienne river marry civil engineering with aesthetic qualities. The **Cathédrale St-Etienne** is a Gothic masterpiece, begun in the 13th century and continued in the Flamboyant style. The church of **St-Michel-de-Lions** is noted for its stained glass. Housed in a former episcopal palace, the **Musée des Beaux-Arts** (www.museebal.fr; Apr–Sept Wed–Mon 10am–5pm, Oct–Mar closed Sun am; charge) includes a collection of the brilliant enamel work for which Limoges has been famous since the 12th century.

In the summer the city hosts porcelain and enamel exhibitions.

Martyred town

A 20-minute drive southwest of Limoges will bring you to the village of **Oradour-sur-Glane ❷**, and the *Village Martyr*. Rusty carcasses of 1930s cars, the crumbling facades of burnt out buildings and long abandoned tramway lines bear testimony to the destruction that took place here on the afternoon of 10 June 1944. On this fateful day, just four days after the D-Day Normandy landings, the German SS 'Das Reich' Division rounded up and massacred 642 villagers, and then set fire to the whole town. The village has remained untouched since, and in the Centre de la Mémoire (daily Feb–mid-Dec 9am–5pm; charge) exhibitions and videos recount the event.

Lying about 86km (54 miles) to the east, **Aubusson ❸** is to tapestry what

Limoges is to porcelain. The industry grew here because of the clean waters of the Creuse. The **Centre Culturel Jean Lurçat**, named after the artist who revitalised the art of tapestry-making in the 1930s, includes the **Musée de la Tapisserie** (Wed–Mon 10am–6pm, July–Aug daily; charge), which has a permanent exhibition of both contemporary and traditional tapestry work. No longer sufficient for this extensive collection, a new museum is under construction in the former National School of Decorative Arts, which will triple the space and is due to open early 2016.

Horse country

For a change of element, the artificial **Lac de Vassivière ❹** east of Limoges offers a wide range of lakeside activities, including horse riding, which is popular in the region.

One of France's many national (as distinct from private) stud farms is south of Limoges in **Arnac-Pompadour ❺**, where the **château** evokes the Marquise de Pompadour, mistress of Louis XV (château terraces Apr–Oct daily, Nov–Mar Mon–Sat; charge). Horse races are held here from early July to the end of September.

One of the region's most spectacular castles (mid-June–mid-Sept daily 2.30–6pm; charge) is perched above nearby **Coussac-Bonneval ❻**. The exterior is that of a forbidding feudal fortress. Inside, the Renaissance courtyard is the reverse, with decoration intended to please, not subdue. And the interior is splendidly furnished.

Sheltered under impressive grey slate roofs and towers, **Uzerche ❼** is set high up on a crag above a loop in the River Vézère, crowned by the Romanesque church of St Pierre. There are fine views from the Esplanade de la Lunarde.

Take a free guided visit (Mon–Fri reservations only; tel: 05 55 20 08 89) of the celebrated accordion manufacturers at the Maugein Factory in **Tulle ❽**. The Nuits de Nacre music festival held here in mid-September focuses on accordion playing.

To the south, perched on a rocky spur rising from the River Dordogne is the picturesque village of **Turenne ❾**. Just two towers, a guard room and crumbling ramparts remain of the once imposing château (www.chateau-turenne.com; Apr–Oct daily 10am–noon, 2–6pm, Nov–Mar Sun pm; charge) dominating this hilltop village – the last independent feudal fiefdom of the Vicomtes de Turenne. The 11th-century Tour de César has an outstanding panoramic view that sweeps down from the Monts du Cantal across to the Dordogne and the Marches du Midi Toulousain.

The nearby village of **Collonges-la-Rouge** also profited from the protection of the Vicomtes de Turenne until it was sold to Louis XV to settle gambling debts. It's a striking village with distinctive crimson sandstone houses and pepperpot towers. On the main square stands St Pierre church. Over the door is a 12th-century white limestone tympanum representing the Ascension of Christ. Nearby is the old covered market with a communal bread oven that is used every August for the traditional Marché d'Antan (bread fair).

FACT

Early motorists in open cars used to have to wear heavy coats with hoods, like the shepherds of Limousin, who were out in the cold, wet winters. That is how smart cars came to be called limousines.

Parade in the traditional colours of the Basque country.

Brantôme, on the Dronne river.

THE SOUTHWEST

Green and rural, this corner of France is not always
in the limelight but it's a great place to tour if you
want to explore away from the crowds, enjoy good
wine, and breathe fresh mountain air.

Cave painting at the Grotte de Lascaux.

The two regions that make up the southwest of France, **Aquitaine** and **Midi-Pyrénées**, are framed by three natural frontiers: the Massif Central to the northeast, the Pyrenees to the south and the Atlantic coast to the west. Between them they cover an eighth of the surface area of metropolitan France and yet the population density of this corner of the country is only half the national average (falling to a quarter of it in some places) giving a clear indication that their landscapes are essentially rural.

There are few cities and only two large ones, the regional capitals of Bordeaux and Toulouse. Instead, most of the area is composed of farmed and forested hills dotted with hamlets, villages and small market towns.

The southwest is all the opposite of the intensively populated, industrialised north, and has preserved much of its heritage intact. And if it lacks the glamour of what is normally thought of as *the* south of France, Provence, it more than makes up for this with its space, peace and a slower pace of life to enjoy. It offers an unbeatable combination of usually good weather and invariably green scenery, thanks to slow green rivers such as the Lot and Dordogne, while the Canal du Midi runs across the flatter lands beneath the rising haunches of the Pyrenees. These are mountains par excellence, unbeatable for walking along routes that have been travelled for centuries by pilgrims and nature lovers, and where the Cathar heresy grew to frighten the papacy. Here the snow melts into crystal streams and spas heal the sick and provide indulgence.

The vibrant textiles of the South – apron for sale in St-Jean-de-Luz.

The region's history starts before everywhere else in France with extraordinary cave paintings date back 20,000 years. There is also a rich cuisine to discover, highlights being truffles and foie gras. As for wines, the legendary *crus* of Bordeaux are a reliable place to start but there are many good but unsung local wines to try.

St-Jean-Pied-de-Port, a lovely rest stop for pilgrims on their way to Santiago de Compostela.

AQUITAINE

World-famous Bordeaux wine châteaux, exquisite river valleys in the Dordogne, the immaculate villages of the Basque Country – there's a lot to see packed into this corner of France.

The name Aquitaine refers at once to a modern region of five diverse *départements* with its capital at Bordeaux and to an ancient, long-vanished realm. It began as a Roman province covering the southwest corner of Gaul. In 781, Charlemagne bequeathed it as a kingdom, from the Atlantic to the Rhône, to his third son, Louis le Débonnaire, who was then aged three. The kingdom demoted to two duchies in 877, Gascony and Guyenne, but three hundred years later these were reunited as one.

When Eleanor of Aquitaine married Henry II of England she took the dominion after which she is named with her and it became one of the principal battle grounds of the Hundred Years War, which ended in 1453 when Aquitaine reverted to the French crown.

Bordeaux

France's ninth-largest city and seventh-largest port, **Bordeaux ❶** proudly shows off its long-standing prosperity in the harmonious 18th-century style of its city-centre buildings. Some 1,810 hectares (4,472 acres) of the city are listed as an Unesco World Heritage Site.

The Romans first exploited its strategic position on the Gironde, the tidal estuary of the southwest's principal river, the Garonne, 80km (50

miles) from the sea. Later it grew rich on international trade, including slavery and commerce in sugar, coffee and spices with France's colonies.

Bordeaux calls itself "the wine capital of the world" and this is certainly one of the main attractions for visitors. In front of the tourist information office is the **Ecole du Vin ❶** (advance reservations only, tel 05 56 00 22 85 or follow the "wine school" link from www.bordeaux.com) offers two-hour wine tasting courses throughout the year.

Main Attractions
Bordeaux
Médoc wine châteaux
St Emilion
Lascaux II
Sarlat
Biarritz
Basque Country

Bordeaux's Grand Théâtre.

Just to the north of these two information centres is the city's most conspicuous landmark, the **Monument aux Girondins** ⑧, a 50-m (164ft) column with a statue of liberty on top, which commemorates the deaths of Bordeaux's parliamentarians who were executed in 1793 for being out of step with the French Revolution. It looks down on a broad dusty park, the Esplanade des Quinconces.

Going the other way down the street, you pass the **Grand Théâtre** ⓒ, a neoclassical monument of symmetrical columns and arches, and enter the city centre proper, a maze of pedestrianised shops and small squares bordered on one side by the riverbank and on the other by the **Cathédrale St-André** ⓓ and its adjacent Gothic belfry, the **Tour Pey-Berland**.

Other surviving remnants of pre-Englightenment Bordeaux are two 15th-century gateways, **Porte-Cailhau** ⑤ and **Grosse Cloche** ⑤, formerly the bell tower of the city hall.

Keep walking southeast, following the line of the river, and you come to two churches, the Flamboyant Gothic St-Michel ⑤ with a detached bell tower and, further on, the Romanesque **Sainte-Croix**.

Bordeaux has many fine museums but in the centre are three particularly worth visiting: the **Musée des Beaux-Arts** ⑪ (Wed–Mon 11am–6pm, closed public hols; charge), the nearby **Musée des Arts Décoratifs** (Wed–Mon 2am–6pm, closed public hols; charge) and the **Musée d'Aquitaine** ① (www.musee-aquitaine-bordeaux.fr; Tue–Sun 11am–6pm,closed public hols; charge) tracing the history of the region.

Another important museum is the **Musée d'Art Contemporain (CAPC)** ⑩ (www.capc-bordeaux.fr; Tue, Thu–Sun 11am–6pm, Wed 11am–8pm, closed public hols; charge). Its home is a fine 19th-century colonial warehouse to the north, beyond the Esplanade des Quinconces.

But don't get the idea that Bordeaux is all sobriety. On the river bank facing the city's most elegant square, the Place de la Bourse, is the long rectangular fountain **Miroir d'eau** ⑩ (Water Mirror), in which 2cm (1in) of reflecting

Bordeaux has a tram network.

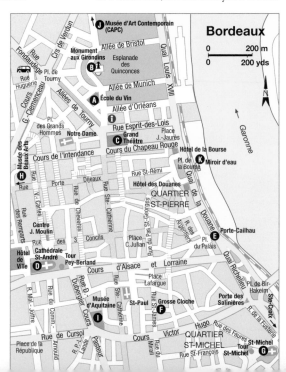

water cover a granite basin. Every so often, micro jets embedded in the fountain squirt a damp mist 2m into the air as people, children especially, run through them.

The Médoc

The city's hinterland is the *département* of the Gironde, which is practically synonymous with the Bordeaux wine region and with vines that begin in the suburbs and extend outwards in all directions. Each major town has a wine information centre and most wine producers (known here as châteaux, whether or not their headquarters are in a stately home) welcome visitors, although almost always by prior arrangement.

Many of the most prestigious wine estates are packed into the Médoc peninsula, where a narrow band of vineyards stretches northeast from the city along the coastline of the Gironde estuary. The Médoc is reclaimed marshland and the vines are grown on gravel ridges that are less waterlogged. At several points along the coast are sluice gates – not to irrigate the land but to drain off excess water, and prevent the tide from moving up the channels.

The largest town in the Médoc is **Pauillac ❷**, which has a wine information centre. On the way there, the D2 goes near to the châteaux of Siran and Margaux, the latter a 19th-century Neo-Classical mansion. Further on are Beychevelle, Beaucaillou and Latour.

Beyond Pauillac the trail of châteaux comes to an end with Lafite-Rothschild, Mouton-Rothschild and the oriental-style Cos d'Estounel.

St-Emilion

As an alternative to going back to Bordeaux, it is possible to cross the estuary by ferry from Lamarque to **Blaye ❸**, overlooked by a citadel, and continue touring the eastern reaches of the wine region.

Close to Libourne is one of Bordeaux's most renowned wine towns, **St-Emilion ❹**. Honoured by the English as the "king of wines", the quality has been supervised for eight centuries by an elected council of peers, known as Jurats. The deliberations of this brotherhood take place with

St-Emilion wine tasting.

St-Emilion.

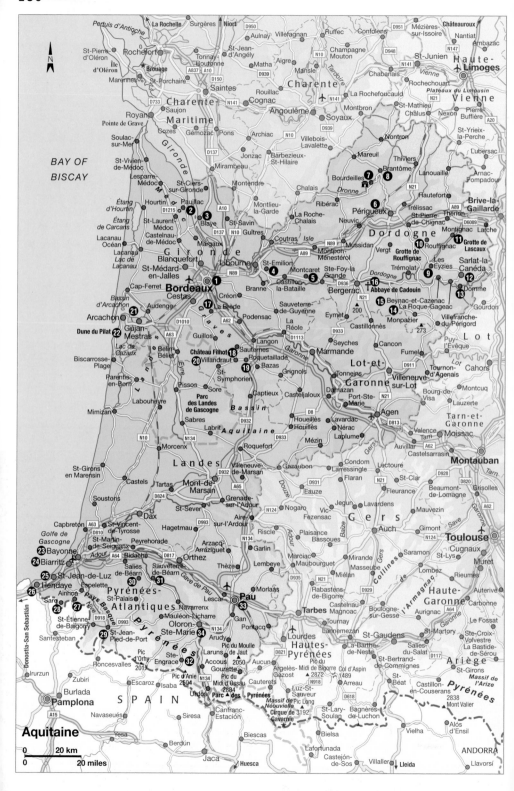

Aquitaine

0   20 km
0   20 miles

red-robed ceremony in one of the town's Gothic cloisters. The Maison du Vin, opposite the Tourist Information office, is a wine school which also sells wines from the region and can offer advice.

With two monasteries, St-Emilion offers a wealth of religious architecture. The most spectacular is a unique monolithic church. Tunnelled into the hillside in the 11th century, the steeple emerges at street level on the hill top.

Not far away is the superb Roman villa of **Montcaret** ❺ (near Lamothe-Ravel on the road to Bergerac). The extensive foundations of this house are visible, including ducts for a warm-air heating system, the baths and several complete mosaic floors.

Dordogne

The northeastern corner of Aquitaine is the *département* of the Dordogne, named after the river flowing through it, although sometimes known as its old name, Périgord.

Its capital is **Périgueux** ❻, built around the Cathédrale de St-Front which was founded in the 12th century but virtually razed and reconstructed in the 19th century – only the great bell tower was spared. The domed roof was rebuilt with five domes and 17 new towers and turrets. The result has a rather Oriental look about it, more like a large mosque than a Christian church. The surrounding quartier, Puy St-Front, is a conservation area. The cobbled streets are lined with Renaissance facades, here a doorway topped by a pointed stone arch, there a majestic staircase giving on to a tiny courtyard-foyer. Many buildings have been elegantly restored, and now house chic boutiques.

Despite these signs of prosperity, it is said that the modern-day city is not as wealthy as was the Gallo-Roman agglomeration, reminders of which can be seen in the **Musée d'Art et d'Archéologie** (www.perigueux-maap.fr; Oct–Mar Mon, Wed–Fri 10am–5pm, Sat–Sun 1–6pm, Apr–Sept Mon, Wed–Fri 10.30am–5.30pm, Sat–Sun 1–6pm; charge) which also has an extensive prehistoric collection.

Northwest from Périgueux is the **Château de Bourdeilles** ❼ on the River Dronne. The ensemble, which

FACT

Wild mushrooms are one of the delicacies of rural France and mushroom picking is a favourite pastime in the autumn. Especially numerous and prized by many chefs are cèpes (Boletus edulis) and the much-loved orange and yellow chanterelles (Cantharellus cibarius), also known as girolles.

Cathédrale de St-Front, Périgueux.

is in fact two castles – one feudal, the other Renaissance – is bordered by terraces overlooking the cliff edge. The square and crenellated silhouette is dominated by an octagonal keep. The elegance of the 16th-century facades and the regular spacing of the stone framed windows are complemented by luxurious interior furnishings and tapestries. (July–Aug daily 10am–7pm, rest of the year Wed–Mon 10am–1pm and 2–6pm; charge). Located at the foot of the château is the Lord's Mill, which is closed to the public.

At **Brantôme** ❽, upstream, a 16th-century abbot undertook the construction of an elbow-shaped canal that still hugs the town in the crook of its arm. On one of the banks is a green park with Renaissance gazebos, which was once the monks' garden. Leading to the grounds of the old abbey (now a hotel) is a right-angled stone bridge, designed to resist the weight of the water arriving from two directions at once. The abbey buildings include a cave chapel. The bell tower, separate from the church, is a fine example of 11th-century construction.

Prehistoric art

In a short stretch of the Vézère valley between **Montignac** and **Les Eyzies-de-Tayac** there is the world's most astonishing collection of prehistoric art. **Les Eyzies** ❾ styles itself as "the prehistoric capital of France", and a statue of Cro-Magnon man looks out, somewhat bewilderedly, from a ledge over the town's roofs. The **Musée National de Préhistoire** (http://musee-prehistoire-eyzies.fr; July–Aug daily 9.30am–6.30pm, Sept, June Wed–Mon 9.30am–6pm, Oct–May Wed–Mon 9.30am–12.30pm and 2–5.30pm; charge, get there early as tickets sell out fast), presenting archaeological discoveries, is located in a feudal fortress half built into a cliff that shows traces of where beams were inserted.

There are dozens of important prehistoric sites clustered around Les Eyzies. The tourist office organises excursions to many of them, which avoids long waits in queues. Just down the road is **Font-de-Gaume** (Sun–Fri mid-Sept–mid-May 9.30am–12.30pm and 2–5.30pm, mid-May–mid-Sept 9.30am–5.30pm, closed public hols;

Watersports-friendly Brantôme.

charge), decorated with paintings and engravings almost as stunning as Lascaux; the nearby **Grotte des Combarelles** (Sun–Fri mid-Sept–mid-May 9.30am–12.30pm and 2–5.30pm, mid-May–mid-Sept 9.30am–5.30pm, closed public hols; charge) contains engravings. The **Abri du Cap Blanc** (Sun–Fri mid-Sept–mid-May 9.30am–12.30pm and 2–5.30pm, mid-May–mid-Sept 9.30am–5.30pm, closed public hols; charge) is a prehistoric shelter (*abri*) containing a 13-metre (42ft) bas relief which includes six horses, a bull, a bison and other animals. At **La Roque St-Christophe** (daily Apr–Sept 10am–6.30pm, Oct–Mar until 5.30pm; charge) an immense, eroded limestone cliff provided cave dwellings for prehistoric man, and from the Middle Ages to the Renaissance it was a fort and town.

A bit further way is the **Grotte de Rouffignac** ❿ (daily Apr–June, Sept–Oct 10–11.30am and 2–5pm, July–Aug 9–11.30am and 2–6pm; charge), the channels of an ancient underground river that created 10km (6 miles) of tunnels. An electric train takes visitors

through the dimly lit galleries, the walls dotted with knobs of hard rock that resist erosion although show the marks of bears' claws. Although the caverns have been known for centuries, the drawings inside were not identified as prehistoric until 1956. Mammoths are the speciality, in a sequence depicting the confrontation of two groups.

Lascaux

The most famous of the caves in France, the **Grotte de Lascaux** ⓫, is up the valley from Les Ezyies. Dating from around 20,000 BC and perhaps associated with magical rites, its three-colour friezes (in black, yellow and red) representing a variety of animals including bulls, cows, deer, bison and horses, deploy a whole range of techniques to create the impression of perspective, texture and movement.

Closed off in prehistoric times, the cave was not rediscovered until 1940 during the search for a dog which had disappeared down a hole. Due to the preoccupations of the war and ensuing hardships, crowds only started flocking

Drawings from millennia past at the Grotte de Lascaux.

Dwelling caves within the cliffs, les Eyzies-de-Tayac.

CAVE ART

During the Old Stone Age, 30,000 to 10,000 years ago, early man or woman spent much time feverishly drawing, engraving and painting on the walls of caves in southwest France and northern Spain. When these paintings were first discovered, aesthetes of the time refused to believe that "primitive" people were capable of depicting their reality so expressively and accurately. Picasso and other modern artists have declared themselves in awe of their anonymous forebears' art.

The subjects depicted fall into three groups: animals (but not representing the diet of the people of the time), human beings (rare) and signs. The artists used a limited range of pigments extracted from minerals and must have illuminated the walls and ceilings with oil lamps, torches and fires lit especially for the purpose – although all of these would have given a dim light for such detailed and colourful work.

Academic debate continues about how the early artists were able to reach rock walls above stretching height from the cave floor, or paint in the almost inaccessible crevices where some images are placed. Even more of a mystery is why they went to so much trouble. Were the paintings part of some magical or religious ritual? In times of constant fear and hunger it is unlikely that they would have been undertaken merely as "art for art's sake".

EAT

The Dordogne is a rich source of culinary treats including walnuts, truffles (sniffed out under oak trees by pigs) and foie gras. The market in Sarlat is a good place to shop for all good things to eat.

to the site some years later. When, in 1963, it was realised that a green fungus was growing over the paintings the cave was immediately closed while restoration was still possible. In compensation, a partial copy, called **Lascaux II**, was created with great care and skill in the adjacent quarry, and is open to the public (Feb–Dec daily 9.30am–6pm, Nov, Dec, closed Mon; charge; tickets must be obtained in advance from the office in Montignac). Most of the paintings are reproduced, including a rare human figure visible only with difficulty in the cave itself because it is inside a well.

Sarlat and the Dordogne

The prime stretch of the Dordogne river is between Sarlat and Bergerac where magnificent views are combined with lovely villages and proud castles. **Sarlat-la-Canéda** ⓬ is a busy market town that could be the stage for a film set in the Renaissance, the church and episcopal palace creating a breathing space among the interlacing streets that run between the sculpted facades.

At Montfort begin the almost full-circle bends in the river called *cingles*. From **Domme** ⓭ the road plunges down to the river, and across the bridge, a few kilometres west, the village of **La Roque-Gageac** ⓮ is lodged on the steep slope between the river bank and the cliff edge. A walk through the streets, which alternate between staircase and pavement, provides an intimate view of local architecture. At the highest point metal bars jut from the cliff where once a staircase climbed to the plateau above.

At **Beynac-et-Cazenac** ⓯, the 13th-century château, perched above the town is a vision straight out of a medieval chronicle; the dizzying blank face of the tower keep is softened by the perspective of the surrounding towers and lower buildings.

Leaving the river for a moment, the **Abbaye de Cadouin** ⓰ (daily July–Aug 10am–7pm, Apr–June, Sept–Oct 10am–1pm, 2–6pm, rest of year Tue–Sun 10am–12.30pm, 2–5pm, closed Jan; charge), on the road from Le Buisson, is an ensemble of sober

Beynac-et-Cazenac.

architecture in an unusual style. The church of yellow stone presents a wide and sternly undecorated facade, the interior a flat transept. The 16th-century cloisters are rich with elaborately sculpted biblical characters. An excavated Romanesque chapterhall displays the coffer that contained the relic of the Holy Shroud that was Cadouin's glory – and source of considerable income – until it was proved to be a fake in 1934.

Graves and Sauternes

Returning to the city of Bordeaux, the landscapes of Aquitaine become entirely different as you travel south. The Graves wine region along the left bank of the Garonne starts up as soon as the suburbs give up. The name "Graves" refers to the gravelly nature of the soil, producing red and white wines, sometimes from the same vines.

La Brède ⑰ is not a wine-producing château but home of the 18th-century philosopher Montesquieu. The modest, partially furnished baron's castle is surrounded by a functioning moat,

stocked with carp (June–Sept Wed–Mon 2–6pm, Apr–May, Oct–Nov Sat–Sun 2–6pm; charge).

For wine, the best place to go is **Château Filhot** ⑱, which offers wine tasting and a friendly welcome (tel: 05 76 61 09; Mon–Fri 9am–noon and 2–6pm; by appointment at weekends).

Further on is **Roquetaillade** ⑲, the best preserved of a series of medieval fortresses built by Pope Clement V (July–Aug daily 10.30am–5pm, Sept–Oct daily 2.30–5pm, Nov–Easter Sun and public hols 2.30–4pm, Easter–June daily 2.30–4pm; charge). A line of four great towers form the facade, surprisingly austere among the sunny and placid vineyards. Another such fortress, in **Villandraut** ⑳ (daily May–Sept, Mar–Apr Sat–Sun)

All this is the Sauternais region, producing sweet white Sauternes and Barsac wines. Their intensity is caused by "noble rot", that is, allowing the grapes to ripen until attacked by a fungus which causes the grape to shrivel, but the sugar content to increase.

The Château de Puymartin, another in an area thick with châteaux.

Sights set on the château at La Roque-Gageac.

BORDEAUX WINE

More than just another wine region, Bordeaux is 57 varieties (appellation d'origine protégée) under one umbrella. There is no one single classification system governing all these wines – to devise one would cause no end of controversy – but many of the finest vintages are classified as *crus* or "growths", referring to growing environment of the vines, *premier crus* being the aristocracy in the oenological hierarchy.

For simplicity, however, the various wines are officially grouped into six AOP families. The classic labels, Bordeaux and Bordeaux Supérieur, account for half the wines produced in the region. The Médoc peninsula and Graves (on the left bank of the Garonne) contribute another 15 percent of the output, including many of the great châteaux. Côtes de Bordeaux, meanwhile, are aromatic reds of strong character. St-Emilion, Pomerol and Fonsac produce what are described as "more feminine reds", with an emphasis on the use of the Merlot grape. Dry white wines include those from Blaye and Bourg across the river from Bordeaux city and Entre-deux-Mers – between not two seas but two rivers, the Dordogne and Garonne. Among the sweet whites is Sauternes.

So why are they so great? An official publication says, "the combination of a selected, fine low yield grape variety, and poor growing conditions (the vine must struggle and suffer) and the work of man both in vineyards and the winery, lead to the production of a high quality wine."

Biarritz attracts a lot of surfers.

Bigger and better – the record-breaking Dune du Pilat.

Arcachon and the Landes

West from here, the vineyards cede to forests, which continue almost to the edge of the ocean.

The 100-km (6 mile) coast from the mouth of the Gironde estuary coast to the **Bassin d'Arcachon** ㉑ is effectively one long beach backed by sand dunes held down by scrub pine and with large lakes inland. While swimming is limited in the high surf, resort towns also offer horse riding and cycling in the pine forests. Arcachon and its bay are renowned for oysters, pleasure boating and birdwatching.

Just outside Arcachon is the **Dune du Pilat** ㉒, the highest sand dune in Europe. From here to Biarritz is another 100-km strip of beach served by small resorts catering for mainly domestic tourism. Behind it is the *département* of the Landes, a flat and otherwise featureless expanse of pine forest planted in the 19th century to hold the land.

The Pays Basque

The Pays Basque is the French part of the Basque Country that lies mainly in Spain. It is home to approximately 10 percent of Basques, a people who claim ancient roots and who have maintained a strong sense of their own independent identity. Cultural, social and economic links across the border are very close although some connections are less desirable ones: terrorists of the Spanish Basque militant group ETA have tended to use the French Basque country as a refuge and a base. Spanish Basques are strongly nationalistic, but those on the French side, while keen to keep their own culture and traditions, are happy to remain part of France although they would like greater autonomy, having to share a *département* with the Béarnais. An estimated quarter of Basques speak their traditional language, Euskara, but French is the lingua franca of day-to-day and official transactions.

Bayonne and Biarritz

Bayonne ㉓, the capital of the Basque Country, is sited at the confluence of the rivers Nive and Adour and is a remarkably intact ensemble of tall, timbered mansions, making it a pleasure to stroll around. The two main

sights are the Gothic **Cathédrale Ste-Marie** and the **Musée Basque** (Sept–June Tue–Sun 10am–6pm, July–Aug daily 10am–6.30pm, closed public hols; charge), which gives an excellent introduction to the history and traditions of this singular corner of France.

Without leaving the built-up area, you arrive imperceptibly in the very different town of **Biarritz ㉔**. "Discovered" in the mid-19th century by the Empress Eugénie and Napoleon III, it is still a charming and discreet resort of large houses and *salons de thé* (tea rooms). The beaches of Biarritz extend past the two advances of cliffs, the Pointe St-Martin and the Plateau de l'Atalaye, to the northern beach of Chambre d'Amour (love room), famous for its spectacular waves and the site of surfing competitions.

In the middle of the town are the **Promenades**, where steep cliffs fall to the ocean. The romantic alleys shaded by tamarisk trees lead the visitor to the **Rocher de la Vierge** (Rock of the Virgin), linked to the mainland by a frail footbridge. The sea rages among the jagged rocks below, but the white

Virgin Mary remains unperturbed. Much of the French Basque coast can be admired from this point.

St-Jean-de-Luz

Down the coast by main road or motorway is **St-Jean-de-Luz ㉕** a pleasing amalgamation of lively beach resort with a fishing port that once landed whale and cod but now supplies anchovies, sardines and tuna to the many restaurants in town.

Many of the narrow houses on the older streets are covered by overhanging roofs of red tiles and have exposed beams painted in the traditional colour of browny-red. Halfway along Rue Gambetta, a lively commercial street, stands the church of St-Jean-Baptiste. This is the largest and the most famous of Basque churches: externally quite severe with high walls and a massive tower; the splendid interior, with three tiers of galleries, creates a striking contrast. In 1660, Louis XIV came to St-Jean with the express purpose of getting married to Marie-Thérèse, daughter of the King of Spain. After the wedding the door that the

Wafer-thin slices of cured meat, a speciality of Bayonne.

A charcuterie in St-Jean-de-Luz.

THE PILGRIM ROUTE

France had several pilgrimage destinations of its own in the Middle Ages but the greatest of them all was Santiago de Compostela in northwest Spain, third in importance after Jersusalem and Rome. Four main routes to Santiago, collectively known as Les chemins de Saint-Jacques-de-Compostelle, cross the southern half of France to converge on two passes over the Pyrenees, at St-Jean-Pied-de-Port in the Basque Country and Somport, south of Pau.

These routes are now are used by latter-day hikers, some doing the whole route, others doing only sections of it. You can easily tell when you have stepped on to the pilgrimage route because it will be marked with the sign of the scallop shell of St James in the pavement, on a wall or on a modern signpost.

couple left the church by was closed up so that it would not be used by ordinary people. The king spent the night before his wedding in the **Maison Louis XIV** (www.maison-louis-xiv.fr; guided visits only, July–Aug 10.30am–12.30pm and 2.30–6.30pm, June, Sept visits only at 11am, 3pm, 4pm, 5pm, Easter and French bank hols only at 11am, 3pm, 4pm; visits take 30 to 40 minutes; charge) on Place Louis XIV at the end of Rue Gambetta.

St-Jean's fishing port is a beautiful chaos of fishing boats, masts and nets. Across it is the much smaller town **Ciboure**, birthplace in 1875 of the composer Maurice Ravel.

From here an attractive coastal drive sets off south along the *corniche basque*. It goes through **Socoa**, a small resort protected by an old fortress. The last 10km (6 miles) of the road are the most scenic. Atop high cliffs, the road teeters precariously close to the edge and the views are spectacular. The end of the drive is also the end of France. **Hendaye** ㉖, with a long sandy beach, looks across an estuary at the Spanish-Basque towns of **Irún** and

Bayonne with its Gothic cathedral just visible.

Hondarribia. It's easy to nip over the border for a change of food or to do some shopping. **San Sebastián** is only 20 minutes' drive down the motorway.

Inland

Inland, the Basque Country is for the most part neat and picturesque. Two small towns in particular, **Ainhoa** ㉗ and **Sare** ㉘, are worth a stroll around to get a feel of the local vernacular architecture dominated by stout old farmhouses with white walls and timbers painted dark red or green.

Above Sare looms the peak of **La Rhune**, which can be ascended on foot or by an old cog railway from the Col de St-Ignace. On the summit (905m/3,000ft) the only thing to do is cross the border into Spain and have a drink in a bar. The view reveals the entire Côte Basque as well as the hills of the backcountry. On a clear day you can also see the endless beaches of the Landes, north of Biarritz, a marvellous mix of white surf and golden sand.

The Pyrenees begin to gain a little altitude by the time you reach the historic town of **St-Jean-Pied-de-Port** ㉙

where pilgrims rest before crossing a pass into Navarra on their long way to the shrine of Santiago de Compostela in Spain. The old bridge leading up to one of the gateways to the town is particularly photogenic.

The Béarn

The Basque Country shares the *département* of Pyrénées-Atlantiques with the Béarn. The join is roughly marked in the lowlands by the two handsome towns of **Salies-de-Béarn** ㉚ where there are thermal baths, and **Sauveterre-de-Béarn** ㉛ where the river is injoyed by canoeists and bathers, and in the uplands by the quaint chapel of **Ste-Engrace** ㉜.

Pau ㉝, the departmental capital, was the birthplace of Henry IV (1589–1610), venerated king of France who managed to put an end to the bloody Wars of Religion during his reign only to be assassinated by a Catholic fanatic. The **Château de Pau** (daily mid-June–mid-Sept 9.30am–12.30pm and 1.30–5.45pm, rest of the year 9.30am–11.45pm and 2–5pm, closed public hols; charge) is a charming Renaissance palace, rare for the region, inside of which hang close to 100 Flanders and Gobelins tapestries. The château is at one end of the Boulevard des Pyrénées, from which there is a panoramic view of the range.

From the Béarn eastward the mountains start to disrupt communications but two great valleys carve clear north-south routes, each ending with a border crossing. The Valley d'Aspe begins in the historical town of **Oloron-Ste-Marie** ㉞, where there is an important Romanesque church with superb carvings. The upper valley is one of the last refuges of the Pyrenean brown bear.

The other valley is the Vallée d'Osau, which climbs steadily towards the Pic du Midi d'Ossau, a distinctive, isolated peak plunging spectacularly into its surrounding lakes. In Gabas, you can take the 15km (9-mile) footpath, or the cog train, up to the Lac d'Artouste, a lovely mountain lake above tree level, at an elevation of 1,989 metres (6,524ft). A spectacular drive heads east out of the valley over the Col d'Aubisque and into the region of Midi-Pyrénées.

FACT

Colourful stories about Henri IV abound, from his idyllic childhood (he was given Jurançon wine and garlic to taste at his baptism, and his tortoiseshell cradle is on display at Pau's Château) to his turbulent love life. He famously said that he wanted there to be a chicken in every peasant's pot every Sunday.

The old cog railway leading to La Rhune.

Rocamadour, to the north of the
Lot valley.

MIDI-PYRÉNÉES

From the drama of the Pyrenees to the bucolic charms of Gascony, the Tarn and the Lot, this region captures the essence of easy southern French living.

Main Attractions
Lourdes
Pont d'Espagne
Cirque de Gavarnie
Col de Tourmalet
Pic du Midi
Albi
Toulouse
Moissac
Rocamadour
Conques

rance's largest region – bigger than either the Netherlands or Denmark – straddles the watershed between the Atlantic and Mediterranean climate zones. It is a patchwork of eight very different *départements* that are all essentially rural and revolve around Toulouse, the regional capital and the only city of any size. These *départements* are connected by mountains – the highest part of the Pyrenees are due south – and a capillary network of beautiful rivers (chiefly the Lot, the Aveyron, the Tarn, the Ariège and the Baïse), which flow into the Garonne as it carves its broad corridor between Languedoc and Aquitaine.

The High Pyrenees

The Pyrenees form an unbroken barrier stretching for more than 400 km (250 miles) from the Basque Country on the Atlantic coast to French Catalonia on the Mediterranean, with the Franco-Spanish border following the summits. In the middle 250km (150 miles) there are only seven road passes across them and even the tamest can be blocked by snow.

Lower than the Alps they may be but the Pyrenees are still popular among winter sports enthusiasts. None of its 40-plus resorts is particularly large or glamorous but all of them are easily accessible from the lowlands. Some specialise in

cross-country skiing, with marked trails to follow through the woods. As well as snow, another resource is hot mineral water, which is pumped to the surface in numerous thermal spas. The Pyrenees' greatest asset, however, is its exceptional but fragile wildlife. To protect it, part of the range is covered by the Pyrenees National Park.

Outside the winter months, the most rewarding way to see the Pyrenees is to follow them on foot. The GR10 long distance hiking trail links the Atlantic to the Mediterranean. The whole

High-altitude grazers.

Midi-Pyrénées

route can take two months. Motorists can piece together a relatively low-level route along the mountains using the D918 and D618. Cyclists also use this route and many relish the challenging gradients up to the 2,000-metre (6,500ft) passes (cols) that are such a highlight of the Tour de France. For more leisurely sightseeing, the great beauty spots and viewpoints of the range are easily reached within day trips from the lowlands.

The shrine of Lourdes

The best approach to the Pyrenees is through **Lourdes ❶**, one of the most important Catholic shrines. The mountain surroundings and picturesque old town contribute to the climate of unrelenting hope and spiritual devotion. On the other hand, the thousands who crowd the streets each year in search of miracles and healings can create a grim atmosphere of despair.

In 1858 14-year-old Bernadette Soubirous first saw an apparition of the "beautiful lady" in a cave, the Grotte Massabielle, on her way to catechism. That year, the Virgin Mary appeared

The emblem of French automobile manufacturer Citroën, the first mass-production car company outside of the US.

Nuns in Lourdes.

Top of the world, or feels like it – the observatory crowning the peak of the Pic du Midi.

Hikers at Vignemale.

before Bernadette 18 times. The miracle drew crowds at once, and six years later a sanctuary, along with a statue of Notre Dame de Lourdes, was set up at the entrance of the cave. In 1871, a splendid basilica was built above it.

Non-religious sights include the château in the old town, which houses the excellent Musée Pyrénéen (www.lourdes-visite.com; daily June–Sept 9am–6.30pm, Oct–May 9am–noon, 2–6pm but closes 5pm on Fri; charge), devoted to local traditions and pioneering climbers.

Pont d'Espagne

Heading south into the mountains from Lourdes, beyond the spa of **Argelès-Gazost**, the valley forks. Both branches lead to extraordinary beauty spots that take time to explore.

Up the Vallée de St-Savin is the large, elegant thermal resort of **Cauterets ❷**, whose springs have been thought to benefit sterile women since Roman times. It has also been fertile in literary romance. Victor Hugo womanised there; Georges Sand discovered the thrills of

adultery; Chateaubriand, in a visit in 1829 to soothe his rheumatism, met the elusive young Occitan girl who was to haunt his life. There's not much to see in Cauterets itself but a few kilometres further on the road ends at the **Pont d'Espagne**, a stone bridge that spans stunning waterfalls, from where you can take a chair lift to the **Lac de Gaube** for a superb view of Vignemale (3298m/10,820ft), the highest peak in the French Pyrenees.

Cirque de Gavarnie

The other fork in the road takes you via **Luz-St-Sauveur** to the natural wonder of the **Cirque de Gavarnie ❸**. A mysteriously unreal "monument", Gavarnie has awed countless writers and painters. From the village of Gavarnie you can reach the cirque on horseback or by foot (which can take up to two hours). Some way after the Hôtel du Cirque, 5km (3 miles) up the trail, you will be greeted by a dazzling view of the mountain. Glacial erosion gouged out the magnificent natural amphitheatre, which is made up of three semicircular

THE TOUR DE FRANCE

The route of the Tour de France varies each year but a highlight is always its gruelling trek up and down a selection of the high passes *(cols)* of the Pyrenees. The high points are south of Tarbes and Pau. Portet d'Aspet, Peyresourde, Aspin, Tourmalet and Aubisque all provide famous tests of endurance and the advantage of seeing the cyclists climb up to these passes is that they travel relatively slowly – the first time it was included in the race was 1910, when bikes did not have multiple gears. Elsewhere, on a downhill stretch on the flat, the entire Tour and its *caravane* can whiz past before you have had a chance to register what is happening.

Out of season, the cols provide a challenge for cyclists who can get a "passport" stamped to their mettle in the saddle.

superimposed shelves, the top shelf being a succession of peaks, all above 3,000 metres (10,000ft). Waterfalls tumble from shelf to shelf. It is possible to walk to the bottom of the largest, the Grande Cascade, which, at 240 metres (790ft) is the longest in Europe. Up above, a vertical breach, the Brèche de Roland, slashes into the wall of mountain.

Pic du Midi

Retrace your steps down to Luz-St-Sauveur and turn right through Barèges to climb to the **Col du Tourmalet**, which at 2,114 metres (6,934ft) is the highest of the French Pyrenees and climax of the Pyrenean stage of the Tour de France.

As you descend, you reach the ski resort of **La Mongie** ❹. From here a cable car (daily 9.30am–4pm, longer hours in summer; departures every 15 minutes; charge) departs for the observatory, museum and restaurant on the **Pic du Midi** (2,872m/9,423 ft). It's only worth the trip if it is a reasonably clear day. To see a spectacular sunrise, stay in the hotel on the summit.

Arreau to St-Bertrand

Drop down from La Mongie and turn right at **Ste-Marie-de-Campan**, where another ascent begins, this time to the Col d'Aspin on the other side of which is pretty **Arreau** ❺. This is followed by the Col de Peyresourde, and a long descent to **Bagnères-de-Luchon** ❻, by far the most important spa in the Pyrenees. The Romans exploited the springs of Luchon in the 2nd–4th centuries AD, and excavations have revealed three large pools with marble floors. The 80-odd springs that feed Luchon yield water that is effective in the treatment of respiratory ailments, and the resort has attracted many rich and famous clients. Above the valley of the Lys is Luchon's ski resort of Superbagnères.

Continue north to the edge of the lowlands. Here, the attractive town of **St-Bertrand-de-Comminges** ❼ clusters around the Cathédrale Ste Marie-de-Comminges (daily Nov–Apr, Oct 10am–noon, 2–5pm, Sun pm only, May–Sept 9am–7pm, Sun pm only; charge), a fortified Romanesque-Gothic church standing proud of the

Cathédrale Ste-Cécile detail.

The other-wordly landscape of the Cirque de Gavarnie.

FACT

The greatest challenge for the engineers of the Canal du Midi was how to get over the Seuil de Naurouze, a watershed between the east and west drainage basins of the region. The solution was an ingenious hydraulic system drawing water from the Montagne Noir.

The dungeon of the château at Foix.

buildings around it. The pale facade is adorned by a beautifully sculpted portal, and the High Renaissance choir stalls are superbly carved: hounds, monkeys, cherubs and slathering figures clamber around the misericords and arm rests.

The Ariège

The first stop worth making in the Ariège is the quaint, historic village of **St-Lizier** ❽ which has a cathedral and bishop's palace, even though most of the populace moved down to the valley below in the 12th century to create the new town of St-Girons.

The main road from here leads to the departmental capital of **Foix** ❾ which is overlooked by the dramatically sited castle of the counts who bequeathed their name to the town when they ruled over large parts of southwest France in the Middle Ages. Up the valley from here at **Niaux** ❿, near Tarascon-sur-Ariège are some of France's best prehistoric painted caves (reservation required; for details and booking tel: 05 61 05 10 10 or email: info@grands-sites-ariege.fr; charge) which

have been kept open to visitors only by strictly controlling the number of people allowed to enter at any time.

Cathar country

This is now Cathar country, the haunt of a doomed 12th–13th century sect demonised by the Catholic Church and the French Crown but idolised by contemporary mystery hunters. The Cathars' dualist belief in the existence of a "good" God and an equally powerful evil one brought a crusade against them by nobles from northern France.

There are several ruined Cathar castles along the road between Foix and Quillan but the one that works most on the imagination is **Montségur** ⓫, which became the final seat of the beleaguered Cathar Church.

In May 1243, an army of crusaders and inquisitors lay siege to the castle, which held out until the following March when the Cathars agreed to surrender. Cathars who refused to recant were led meekly down the hill from the castle in chains and burnt to death on a giant bonfire below. This was effectively the end of Catharism, yet in

THE CATHAR HERESY

The Cathars (from the Greek *katharos* meaning 'pure') were a breakaway religious movement formed around the middle of the 11th century. The movement existed in a large part of western Europe but its home was the Languedoc where it gained a strong following. Cathars believed in the dualistic doctrine of good and evil: to be pure, they adhered to an austere lifestyle of poverty, chastity, non-violence and humility, and renounced meat. The material world was considered evil, and the Catholic Church was criticised for its immorality and wealth.

In 1208 Pope Innocent III launched a vicious crusade, promising reclaimed heretic lands to French noblemen willing to join in the persecution. In a reign of terror both nobles and common people were burnt alive at the stake, thrown to their deaths from high walls, or publicly humiliated and dispossessed of their lands. Major Cathar strongholds at Béziers, Carcassonne and Minerve were besieged and inhabitants slaughtered indiscriminately. Béziers was burnt to the ground and around 20,000 people, both Catholics and Cathars, were massacred. The abbot who led this siege called out "Kill them all. God will know his own". The Inquisition, in 1233, was established to purge Languedoc of the remaining Cathars, most of whom had taken refuge in the remote fortresses at Montségur, Quéribus and Peyrepertuse. These bastions were amongst the last to be taken.

some remote upland villages the heresy lingered on into the 14th century.

In the north of the Ariège is the *bastide* (see page 308) **Mirepoix** ⓬, which sheltered Cathars and withstood a siege in 1209. It has a charming main square of half-timbered houses with shady arcades beneath them. The Maison des Consuls has inscrutable medieval faces carved on its protruding beam ends.

The Canal du Midi

Emerging from the Ariège to the north, the landscape opens up, and the motorway and railway line take advantage of a broad corridor between Toulouse and the Mediterranean coast. They are joined by a much older artery of communication, the **Canal du Midi**.

The canal links the Garonne river (which empties into the Gironde estuary) at Toulouse with Sète on the Languedoc coast. It was the brainchild and life's work of one Pierre-Paul Riquet (1604–80) who sunk all his money and energy into the project but died six months before his vision was fully realised. With its 328 locks, bridges, aqueducts (including a modern one over Toulouse's motorway ring road) and other constructions, the canal is still a marvel of ingenuity and engineering. Barges and other boats are for hire in several places along its length but an even better way to enjoy it is to walk or cycle along the shady tow path.

There is a permanent exhibition on the Canal du Midi in a service area at **Port Lauragais** ⓭ (near Avignonet-Lauragais), off the A61 motorway between Toulouse and Carcassonne.

Albi and The Tarn

The Cathars are often referred to as the Albigensians, because of their supposed association with the city of **Albi** ⓮, capital of the *département* of the Tarn.

It was not until 1282, 30 years after the demise of the Cathars, that the bishop of Castanet started building Albi's Cathédrale Ste-Cécile. As a stern message to any aspiring heretics, it was conceived as a fortress, a style that characterises many Gothic cathedrals in Languedoc. Its barren walls of bright red brick dwarf

Poster by Toulouse-Lautrec advertising a show by can-can dancer La Goulue ("The Glutton").

Morning breaks over the Canal du Midi.

The five-storey-high octagonal bell tower of St-Sernin.

Cordes.

the old town. The interior is more ornate. The walls are all painted with religious scenes or intricate patterns; most admired are the 15th-century frescoes of *The Last Judgement*. Flamboyant Gothic arches enclose the choir in the middle of the nave.

Albi is now best known as the home of the painter Toulouse-Lautrec and adjacent to the cathedral is the old episcopal palace that houses the **Musée Toulouse-Lautrec** (www.museetoulouselautrec.net; Oct–Mar Wed–Mon 10am–noon, 2–5pm, Apr–June daily 10am–noon, 2–6pm, July–Sept daily 9am–6pm, closed public hols; charge). It contains the most complete collection of the artist's work, including many portraits, and has a delightful garden (free entry) at the rear overlooking the river.

Northwest of Albi, wrapped around a conical hill in a cloak of steep cobbled streets, mellow stone and mossy tiles, stands **Cordes-sur-Ciel** ⓯, a perfectly restored medieval town which grew prosperous from leather-working and weaving. Park at the bottom of the hill and walk up into the

pedestrianised town centre through the western or eastern gateway; both lead to the main street where some of the houses have sculpted facades.

The main road from Cordes leads to the Aveyron river and across it to **St-Antonin-Noble-Val** ⓰, a town with historic buildings from various periods. The Maison Romane on the Place de la Halle is thought to be France's oldest surviving civic building. On Rue Droite is the 15th-century Maison de l'Amour on the facade of which are carved the heads of a couple turning towards each other as if about to kiss.

Downstream, the Aveyron carves a small but picturesque gorge looked down upon by **Penne** ⓱ and the spectacularly sited ruins of a 13th-century castle. The gorge comes to an end shortly after another beautiful village with a castle, **Bruniquel** ⓲.

Small roads lead from here south through the Vallée de la Vère and Puyceli to **Gaillac** ⓳ founded around a monastery in 972 and thought to have been making its dry white wines almost as long.

TOULOUSE-LAUTREC

Henri de Toulouse-Lautrec was born in Albi in 1864 into a wealthy aristocratic family. Aged eight, he went to live with his mother in Paris, where he began to draw. While still a teenager he suffered two accidents that left him unable to walk properly. In 1881 he decided to become an artist and soon rejected the conventions of formal art in favour of his own forms of expression. He was particularly inspired by the low-life of Montmartre, and in 1896 produced a series of studies of a brothel, *Au salon de la rue des Moulins* (*At the Salon*). A heavy drinker, he died at the family's Château de Malromé in the Gironde on 9 September 1901, three months before he would have turned 37. After his death, his mother paid for his works to be displayed in the family's home town of Albi.

Toulouse

France's fourth-largest city, **Toulouse** ⑳, stands plumb between the Atlantic and Mediterranean. Resolutely southern in both climate and way of life, it can claim to be the de facto capital of that indefinable southern territory, the Midi. The only material yielded by the plain of the Garonne river, on which the city stands, is clay for brick-making which gives **Toulouse** the epithet of the *ville rose*, the "pink city".

Until the military campaigns against the Cathar heresy brought interference from northern France, the counts of Toulouse enjoyed great autonomy over their dominions in the southwest. Thereafter, Toulouse was relegated to a provincial city but it continued to prosper. In the 15th and 16th centuries profits from woad financed several mansions in the city centre.

Place du Capitole ⓐ, the main square, has numerous cafés and restaurants and is a convenient reference point from which to strike out and explore the city. It is overlooked by the neo-classical city hall, the **Capitole** ⓑ. Up the monumental staircase

is a suite of rooms including the Salle des Illustres, covered with frescoes and paintings.

From the square, the Rue du Taur leads north to the 11th-century basilica of **St-Sernin** ⓒ. The city does have a cathedral but it is outshone by this, the largest Romanesque church in France and an important halt on the pilgrimage route from Arles to Santiago de Compostela in Spain. It is distinguished by a magnificent octagonal bell tower five storeys high. Inside is a cavernous space ending in an ambulatory and the crypt-tomb of the eponymous St Saturninus, martyred by bulls around the year AD250.

Opposite the church is the city's archaeological museum, the **Musée St-Raymond** ⓓ (www.saintraymond.toulouse.fr; daily 10am–6pm; charge), which has a wealth of Roman sculpture and mosaics.

West of Place du Capitole is Toulouse's second most interesting church to visit, **Les Jacobins** ⓔ (Tue–Sun 10am–6pm; charge), in a Languedoc variant of Gothic. It, too, is a sepulchre, this time of the Italian

D'Artagnan of The Three Musketeers' fame.

Place du Capitole, Toulouse.

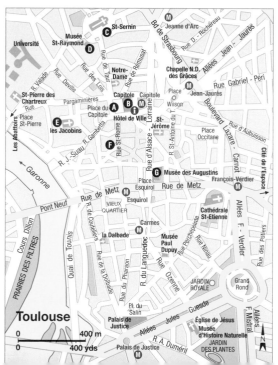

Toulouse

Bottles of Armagnac, a speciality of Eauze.

theologian St Thomas Aquinas. Look up in the nave to see the intricate fan vaulting sprouting from palm-like columns. Also note the modern stained glass windows by Max Ingrand and the restored cloister.

Continue in this direction and you reach the river Garonne, across which is a museum of modern and contemporary art, **Les Abattoirs** (www.lesabattoirs.org; Wed–Sun noon–6pm, until 8pm on Thu; charge), housed in the former slaughterhouse of the revitalised St-Cyprien district.

Returning to the Place du Capitole, the pedestrianised **Rue St-Rome** ❺ leads into a pleasant tangle of medieval streets lined with many small and interesting shops. Turn left when you strike Place Esquirol to reach the door of the **Musée des Augustins** ❻ (www.augustins.org; daily 10am–6pm, until 9pm on Wed, closed public hols; charge) a 14th–15th century monastery turned into a museum of paintings and sculptures from the early Middle Ages to the 20th century.

Build your own rocket at the Cité de l'Espace.

If you have children with you, you may want to limit your time in the city centre and spend the best part of a day in the **Cité de l'Espace** (in the eastern outskirts of the city, on the Castres road; www.cite-espace.com; daily end-July–Aug 10am–7pm, rest of the year 10am–6pm, with exceptions, closed Jan; charge). This science museum is dedicated to all things to do with space, extraterrestrial life included. It has a number of interactive displays and a few small theme park rides but all the while manages to impart a lot of information on everything from weather forecasting to distant nebulae. It's wise to plan your visit around the screenings in the planetarium and IMAX cinema.

Toulouse has a long association with the aviation industry, and next to the airport at the European aircraft consortium Airbus (which assembles the giant double-decker A380 passenger plane) is **Aeroscopia** (www.musee-aeroscopia.fr; daily 9.30am–6pm; charge), a fascinating aeronautical museum.

Gascony

Heading west from Toulouse you drive into one of France's least

populated *départements*, the Gers, the heart of the ancient province of Gascony. Although none of the towns, villages and monuments here stand out individually, together they make up a charming pastoral corner of the country where life seems slower than elsewhere. Winding backroads lead up and down hills, through small broadleaved woods, by fields of sunflowers, passing quaint country houses and opportunities to buy local wine. The Gers is also a good place to browse in local markets, and you can be sure of eating well on its favourite dishes derived from duck and goose, *confit de canard*, *magret de canard* and *foie gras*.

The compact and friendly capital of the Gers is **Auch ㉑**. Leaving the modern lower part of town, make instead for the old part which stands on a hill overlooking the River Gers. The **Cathédrale Ste-Marie** (daily 9.30am–noon, 2.30–5.30pm, until 7pm in summer, closed Sun am; charge) is remarkable for its interior decorations. The vivid stained glass, depicting some 360 individual figures, both mythical

and biblical, and dating from around 1513, is attributed to Gascon painter Arnaud de Moles. Equally exuberant are the oak choir stalls, vigorously and occasionally immodestly carved with over 1,500 figures. Bring a torch to see them to best effect.

Round the corner from the cathedral, a formidable staircase of 232 stone steps, the Escalier Monumental descends towards the river. On it stands a statue of d'Artagnan, the swashbuckling hero of Alexandre Dumas's *The Three Musketeers* (1844), who was based on a real Gascon, Charles de Batz.

Clockwise tour

To begin a clockwise tour of the Gers, take the D943 southwest of Auch to **Barran ㉒**, which has an unusual spiral church spire. Continue on the same road through the riverside l'Isle de Noë (Noah's Isle), and Montesquiou to **Bassoues ㉓**, Here, the main street cuts straight through the covered market hall which straddles it. A soaring tower at the bottom of the main street draws most attention

FACT

A lovely way to spend a sunny day is to take a picnic and hire a canoe on the River Célé. As the river does not have any locks with weirs it does not present great difficulties and children can go, too. Details from the tourist office in Cahors (tel: 05 65 53 20 65).

Auch high town.

TIP

The best view of Rocamadour is from the village of L'Hospitalet, across the Alzou gorge, and the best time to see it is in the early morning light.

– a splendid 14th-century four-storey keep, with wide views of the countryside from the top.

Tillac ㉔, a detour to the south, is a pretty *bastide* of one street, guarded at either end by fortified gates. If you are here the first two weeks of August, continue west to enjoy one of France's best jazz festivals in the small town of **Marciac** ㉕, which slumbers undramatically for the rest of the year. Concerts get booked up well ahead but during the day there is free music on the stage in the square.

From Bassoues, make your way north by little roads through Lupiac (where there is a lake with an artificial sandy beach for summer swimming) to **Eauze** ㉖. This part of the route takes you through two lesser known wine areas, Saint-Mont, which makes reds of growing reputation, and Armagnac, a brandy that connoisseurs consider to be on a par with Cognac. Eauze is proud of its horde of 3rd-century Gallo-Roman coins displayed in a converted bank vault (daily Mar–June, Sept–Nov 10am–noon, 2–6pm, July–Aug 10am–7pm; charge).

Strike northeast and just outside Montréal you will come across the Roman villa of **Séviac** ㉗ (daily Mar–June, Sept–Nov 10am–noon and 2–6pm, July–Aug 10am–7pm; charge), where mosaic floors have been excavated on top of a picturesque stand in a peaceful hilltop.

Many of the towns and villages in the Gers are *bastides* but the diminutive **Fourcès** ㉘, northeast of Montréal, is exceptional in being laid out to a circular rather than rectangular plan.

Condom

From here head towards Condom making a detour to **Larressingle** ㉙, part castle and part village, preserved but not over-prettified. In the 13th century the abbots of nearby Condom used it as a bolthole from the wars between the English and the French.

The main town of this corner of the Gers is **Condom** ㉚, on the banks of the River Baïse, which despite the name has nothing to do with contraceptives. At the heart of it is the superb Cathédrale St-Pierre, rebuilt in the 16th century in its original

Bastide at Tillac.

BASTIDES

Many small market towns in southwest France – and a few cities – are *bastides*, new settlements of the Middle Ages. They were built during the 13th and 14th centuries to tame tracts of wilderness and gather together the scattered habitants, making them easier to govern and tax. Most *bastides* are arranged on a grid plan, with a covered market standing on the arcaded main square in the middle and straight parallel and perpendicular streets leading away from it. Some *bastides* were named after foreign cities probably as souvenirs of their founders' exotic travels: Barcelonne (Barcelona), Cordes (Cordoba), Grenade (Granada), Bruges and Fleurance (Florence).

There is a Musée des Bastides in the town of Monflanquin in the Lot-et-Garonne between Montauban and Bordeaux.

late-Flamboyant Gothic style. Close by is the musty **Musée de l'Armagnac** (Apr–Oct Wed–Mon 10am–noon and 3–6pm, Nov–Mar Wed–Sun 2–5pm, closed public hols; charge).

From Condom take the main road towards Auch to visit the **Abbaye de Flaran** ❸ (daily July–Aug 9.30am–7pm, rest of the year 9.30am–noon and 2–6pm, closed public hols; charge) a well-preserved Cistercian monastery founded in 1151 although the existing buildings are mostly 17th- and 18th-century. It now serves as a cultural centre staging concerts and exhibitions.

Moissac and Montauban

Over the Garonne river from northern Gascony is the otherwise unprepossessing town of **Moissac** ❸ which is much visited for its abbey. The 12th-century south portal of this is a triumph of Romanesque stone carving portraying the *Vision of the Apocalypse According to St John*. The cloisters, entered through the tourist information office (daily 10am–noon, 2–5pm), also have some beautiful sculptures.

To the southeast is **Montauban** ❸, birthplace of the artist Jean-Auguste-Dominique Ingres (1780–1867), whose paintings can be seen at the **Musée Ingres** (July–Sept daily 10am–6pm, Nov–Mar Tue–Sat 10am–noon and 2–6pm, Sun 2–6pm, Apr–June, Oct Tue–Sun 10am–noon and 2–6pm, closed public hols; charge).

The Lot and the Célé

Apart from the Pyrenees, the most beautiful part of the Midi–Pyrénées region is the Lot. **Cahors** ❸, its capital, has a magnificent fortified bridge, the Pont Valentré. A good round trip to make from here is up the valley of the river Lot, stopping to stroll in the exquisite village of **St-Cirq-Lapopie** ❸, to the historic town of **Figeac** ❸, birthplace of Jean-François Champollion (1790–1832), who cracked the code of Egyptian hieroglyphs. A sign in the old town leads to the discreet Place des Ecritures which is paved with a reproduction of the Rosetta Stone.

The return trip is down the delightful valley of the Lot's tributary,

Place Nationale, Montauban.

the Célé, calling at **Espagnac-Ste-Eulalie** ❸❼ to see the church belfry; and at **Marcilhac-sur-Célé** ❸❽, where there is a ruined Benedictine abbey; and finally, in the wooded hills above Cabrerets, the **Grottes du Pech-Merle** ❸❾ (www.pechmerle.com; Apr–Oct daily 9.30am–noon and 1.30–5pm, rest of year days limited; booking recommended tel: 05 65 31 27 05; charge). This cave combines extraordinary rock formations with prehistoric paintings, including enigmatic dots, a negative image of a prehistoric hand outlined in red paint and a footprint.

Rocamadour

Across the austere *causses* (upland plateaux) to the north of the Lot valley are more picturesque sights, chief among them **Rocamadour** ❹❶. Since the body of St Amadour was found uncorrupted in its grave here in 1166, the site has been one of France's most important places of pilgrimage. Over the centuries it has grown as an accretion of crypts, chapels and shrines clustered like the cells of a beehive against the cliff. The

Conques.

complex is linked by lifts and flights of steps. The Black Madonna on the altar of the Chapelle Notre-Dame is the main object of veneration. The ancient ramparts, which overlook the valley, are all that remains of the 14th-century fortress that once defended the town.

The **Gouffre de Padirac** ❹❶, 15km (9 miles) from Rocamadour, is an enormous circular chasm or pot-hole, 99 metres (325ft) across and 103 metres (338ft) deep (www.gouffre-de-padirac.com; daily Easter–Oct 9.30am–6.30pm with exceptions; charge). Lifts and staircases take the visitor down to a remarkable system of underground rivers and lakes. The tour takes 1.5 hours and covers 2km (1.25 miles) including a stretch by boat across a spectacular lake.

The Lot department continues north of Rocamadour and Padirac to take in a stretch of the Dordogne around the picturesque town of **Carennac** ❹❷. The river is overlooked by the formidable **Château de Castelnau-Bretenoux** (daily July–Aug 10am–7pm, Apr, Sept 10am–12.30pm and 2–5pm, May–June 10am–12.30pm and 2–6.30pm, Oct–Mar Wed–Mon 10am–12.30pm and 2–5.30pm, closed public hols; charge). This château of bright red, rusty rock betraying iron ore is remarkably conserved. The long facade dominates the village from steep and unassailable foundations. From the massive wooden portal of the entry to the opposite tower commanding the valley, the evolution of architecture is visible. The interior furnishings are equally splendid.

There are good views of the whole area from the pretty village of **Loubressac** ❹❸. Its near neighbour **Autoire**, is similarly small but worth visiting.

Conques

Travelling up the Lot from Figeac, the landscape changes and the steeply rising wooded hills begin to give a feel of the Massif Central. A few kilometres southeast of the river is the charming village of **Conques** ㊹ and its magnificent church, the 11th- and 12th-century Ste-Foy, one of the most important shrines on the medieval pilgrimage route to Santiago de Compostela in Spain. Of Romanesque construction, Ste-Foy's simple barrel-vaulting is given the lofty proportions of a Gothic cathedral. The extraordinary weight of the building has caused the ground to subside and necessitated restoration. The tympanum above the west door was designed to strike fear into the medieval observer. On it, Christ the King presides over The Last Judgment. Of the 117 figures, the grimacing devils and tortured souls are far more amusing than the happy few elected to Paradise.

The church's treasury (daily Apr–Sept 9.30am–12.30pm and 2–6.30pm, Oct–Mar 10am–noon and 2–6pm, closed some public hols, charge) has many rare and beautiful objects. Standing out from the rest is the 10th-century **reliquary of St Foy**, a primitive statue covered with successive plaques of gold and decorated with precious stones and intaglios, some of which date from Greek and Roman times.

Millau

Away in the far eastern corner of the Midi-Pyrénées region, en route to the Gorges du Tarn (see page 322) and the Cévennes (see page 321) are a group of diverse attractions beginning with the **Viaduc de Millau** ㊺, which carries the A75 over the Tarn valley near Millau. This is not any old flyover but the world's tallest road bridge that has been attracting trippers since it was opened in 2004. Not only is it 2.5km (1.5 miles) in length but it is also curved and slightly sloping. There is a visitor's centre at the aire des Cazalous, on the D992 heading from Millau heading towards Albi.

Not far off the motorway, to the southeast of the viaduct, is **La Couvertoirade** ㊻, a remarkably compact, preserved medieval village founded by the Knights Templar and still enclosed by its walls and towers.

Roquefort ㊼, southwest of Millau, makes the famous tasty blue cheese that goes so well with a bottle of good red.

The Viaduc de Millau.

The plateau setting of Bonnieux, dominated by its church tower.

The ochre-hued, tumbledown lanes of Hyères.

THE SOUTH

From the border with Spain to Italy, this region is a melting pot of traditions and cultures. Cathar hideouts litter rugged Languedoc, Roussillon guards its Catalonian roots and Provence is captivating with lavender fields and hilltop villages, while the Côte d'Azur basks under dazzling blue skies.

An eye-watering cornet of chilis in Nice's Saleya market.

The Mediterranean coast of **Languedoc-Roussillon** has charming fishing ports such as the artists' haunt of Collioure, as well as a string of sparkling resorts, distinguished by their golden beaches and modern architecture. Inland, Languedoc is Cathar country, with ruined castles and defensive villages marked by years of religious struggle – most distinguished of these is the medieval theme park of Carcassonne. The Romans great architectural skills can be admired both at Nîmes and the extraordinary Pont du Gard while Montpellier, just a few hours by TGV from Paris is a lively modern city.

Provence is a cultural high spot: crowds flock to the theatre festival in Avignon, the bullfight *feria* in Nîmes and the gypsy pilgrimage to Saintes-Maries-de-la-Mer. France's finest Roman remains include the amphitheatre in Arles and the theatre in Orange. And Marseille was European Capital of Culture in 2013. Always in the background are the windswept mountain plateaus, river gorges and lavender terraces. The South is famous for its *villages perchés*, hamlets that cling to mountain crags. The region provides wonderful walking country from the dry maquis and sunbleached rocks of the Lubéron, to the many verdant river gorges of tumbling streams and rushing waterfalls.

The prow of a small boat sums up Marseille's inextricable links to the sea.

The South of France has been a glamorous holiday destination, both winter and summer, for more than a century and its enduring popularity accounts for millions of visitors every year. Along the southeast coast of the Mediterranean the star-studded names of the **Côte d'Azur** are strung like a glittering necklace: Cannes, Nice, Monte-Carlo, Antibes and St Tropez. Their plentiful pleasures include not only sun and sea but magnificent modern art museums and medieval architecture, glorious perfumes and exotic flower gardens, world-class yachts, casinos, and film and jazz festivals. It is a region best appreciated through the eyes of the many artists inspired by its luminous light.

LANGUEDOC AND ROUSSILLON

This region offers wide river valleys and rugged gorges as well as popular coastal resorts and regenerated cities that are centres of artistic activity and architectural innovation.

Main Attractions
St-Martin-du-Canigou
Collioure
Céret
Carcassonne
Sète
Montpellier
Gorges du Tarn
Nîmes
Pont du Gard
Uzès

St Martin-de-Canigou, a monastery that's inspiring in more ways than one.

Though it comprises half of the Languedoc-Roussillon administrative French region, **Roussillon** is most distinguished by its Catalonian identity. Local architecture, landscapes and lifestyles all have a largely Spanish flavour, and the language of Catalan is widely spoken here. Indeed, some of Roussillon's older inhabitants still stubbornly refer to Barcelona as their capital.

Coming from the Pyrenees and the Col de Puymorens, the road winds down steeply, passing the ski resort of **Font-Romeu ❶**, into a wide valley that separates France and Spain, and gives the impression of being already near sea level. Yet at the fortified town of **Mont-Louis ❷**, the road suddenly plunges into the steep and narrow **Gorges de la Carança**, and does not level off until it reaches **Prades ❸** at the foot of the **Pic du Canigou** and provide some of the best scenic and cultural treats of the region. The favoured town of the cellist Pablo Casals, who died in 1973 aged 97, Prades holds a commemorative summer music festival in the magnificent 11th-century abbey of **St-Michel-de-Cuxa ❹** (http://abbaye-cuxa.com; daily 9.30–11.50am, 2–5pm, closed public hols; charge) and other local churches and chapels.

Climbing to Canigou

Up the road, the **Vernet-les-Bains** spa is cooled by a vociferous mountain torrent. From nearby **Casteil** is the steep ascent (on foot) to the spectacularly sited abbey of **St-Martin-du-Canigou ❺** (http://stmartinducanigou.org/en; guided tour only; June–Sept daily, Oct–May Tue–Sun, closed Jan; charge), one of the finest examples of Romanesque architecture in the region.

The forbidding road to Canigou leaves from the **Col de Millières**. It is 16km (10 miles) to the **Refuge des Cortalets** where you have to leave the car for the two-hour walk to the top where, at 2,784 metres (9,132ft), the Canigou looks over the Pyrenees, towards the Mediterranean.

French Catalonia

Anyone falling from the sky and landing in the marble paved Place Arago in Perpignan ⬤, would be sure that they had dropped in on Spain. A city of moderate size and moderate touristic appeal, its streets are always lively. Approach it along the canal, through the Castillet medieval gate that opens onto its oldest streets. Straight ahead, the **Loge de Mer**, **Hôtel de Ville** (city hall) and the **Palais de la Députation** are three fine adjacent 15th-century facades whose inner courtyards have the ornate splendour of Spanish palaces.

The gem of the Catalonian coast, and inspiration of 20th-century painters such as Matisse, Braque and Picasso, is **Collioure** ⬤. Encased in a small, rocky bay by the Albères mountains, Collioure has escaped the development that has devoured the coast of Roussillon down to **Argelès-sur-Mer**, 10km (6 miles) away. The horseshoe-shaped bay is separated in two by the 13th-century **Château Royal** (daily 9am–5pm, July–Aug until 7pm; closed public hols; charge) of the king of Mallorca.

The rocky coast south of Collioure is scenic and refreshing, but suffers traffic jams in summer. The narrow road winds up and down across Port-Vendres and Banyuls, all the way to **Cerbère** ⬤, the last port before Spain.

Set on the Pyrenean foothills in the Tech valley, **Céret** ⬤ is a small Catalan town famous for early-cropping

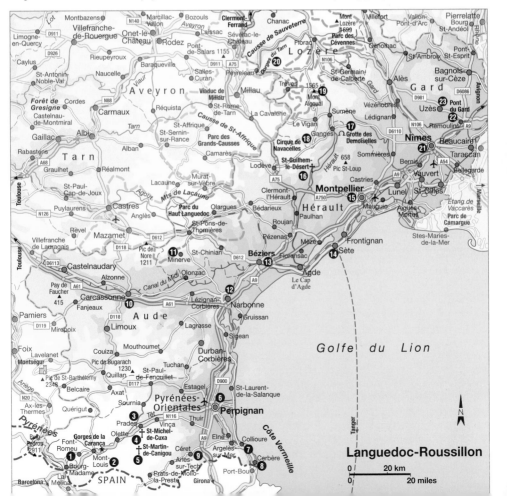

The blason, or coat of arms, of Carcassonne.

cherries and the excellent **Musée d'Art Moderne** (May–mid-Oct daily 10am–6pm, Wed–Mon mid-Oct–Apr; charge). This rural medieval enclave was the inspiration for Picasso and Braque during the Cubist period. Other famous 20th-century artists Masson, Gris, Herbin, Picabia and Chagall were captivated by the local landscape as well. There is a remarkable contemporary art collection in the museum consisting of around 50 works donated by Picasso, including a series of ceramics based on the corrida, and other works by Dalí, Miró and Matisse. The old town is lovely to stroll around with narrow streets, Spanish-style loggias and shady squares. However, the town still clings to its Catalan traditions, and the summer sees the *féria* with bullfights held in the local *arènes*, and the Festival de la Sardane which celebrates Catalan folk dance.

Languedoc

Re-enacting times past in Carcassonne.

The ancient region of **Languedoc** extends westerly from the Rhône valley to the Garonne and takes its name from its own language, Occitan, which gave the region its name: *langue d'oc*.

Strategically situated on what was once the border with Spain, and dominating the plain, **Carcassonne** ❿ is the only medieval monument of its kind in Europe. Local legend has it that after Charlemagne had besieged the city for five years, one Dame Carcas gathered all the remaining bits of grain in the starved-out city, fed them to a stray pig, and ordered the animal to be thrown over the ramparts. On landing, the stuffed beast burst, scattering grain at the feet of Charlemagne's army. Amazed at the abundance of food, Charlemagne called for negotiations, and Dame Carcas answered with victorious trumpet blasts: whence the name *"Carcassonne!"* (Carcas rings).

Aside from its romance, the uniqueness of Carcassonne lies in its two sets of intact fortifications, which surround a tiny town of 350 inhabitants overlooking the modern city. The first ramparts were built by the Romans in the 3rd and 4th centuries AD. They

WINES OF THE LANGUEDOC-ROUSSILLON

The vineyards extend throughout the region from south of Nîmes sweeping down to the plains of Languedoc, into the hillsides south of Carcassonne, and onto sun-baked terraces of Roussillon. This wine region, labelled Pays d'Oc with 16 *appellations*, is the largest in the world, accounting for around 40 percent of France's production. It formerly consisted of a lot of it cheap bulk wines produced by the local co-operatives. However, efforts have been made to improve the quality resulting in some very good respected wines. Red wine production dominates ranging from meaty red Costières de Nîmes, ripe juicy reds from the Côteaux du Languedoc, dark Côtes de Roussillon with its strawberry hints, to the *vins doux naturels* of Banyuls and Rivesaltes.

The most reliable Languedoc AOP wines come from Faugères, Chinian, Minervois, Corbières and Fitou. In the south the Roussillon reds are some of the best and the rosés are also delicious, while at Collioure there is a small amount of tasty rich red wine. Whites include the refreshing sparkling Blanquette de Limoux, and quality whites are produced near Narbonne. Most of the rosé is for local consumption and is best appreciated on a sunny terrace facing the sea.

The vineyards of the Languedoc are often referred to as 'patchwork' as so many grape varieties grow side by side, and most producers make blends instead of varietal wines.

were later improved upon in the 13th century under St Louis, for fear of a Spanish invasion.

During the Middle Ages, the town housed 4,000 inhabitants, and in periods of siege, up to 10,000 would take refuge inside the fortifications. The two sets of walls rendered the city absolutely impregnable; if a group of enemy soldiers managed to climb over the first set, they would only find themselves trapped between the two ramparts.

Early appreciation of Carcassonne's beauty in the 19th century by the author Prosper Merimée led to its restoration by the controversial 19th-century architect Viollet-le-Duc, who rebuilt it in what he considered to be medieval style, complete with dubious pepperpot towers.

After crossing the drawbridge, or **Porte Narbonnaise**, you reach the heart of the bustling little town, filled with cafés and restaurants, bakeries and antique shops. The medieval **Château Comtal** (daily 9.30am–5pm, until 6.30pm in summer, closed public hols; charge) is particularly impressive,

and during July a cultural festival is held here, using its fabulous amphitheatre for a stage. Walking between the ramparts, you can follow the entire perimeter of Carcassonne and admire the combination of Roman and medieval construction methods. The town is full of tourist shops and jam-packed with visitors in high season, but stunning nonetheless.

The plains

The journey between Carcassonne and Montpellier is a pleasant one, through fields of grapevines, along the banks of slow rivers and roads lined with plane trees. This is the growing region for the robust red Corbières and Minervois wines. In the south, standing out amongst the perfumed *garrigue*, are the impressive former Cathar strongholds of Peyrepertuse and Quéribus.

To the north of the region surrounded by a sea of vines, **Minerve** ⓫ is proud of its defiant past, when the Cathar town held out against Simon de Montfort in a siege that lasted seven weeks; 140 citizens were

Come buy your souvenir Crusader Knights.

The walled city of Carcassonne with its double layer of fortifications.

TIP

Although the facades lining the side streets around Montpellier's Rue de la Loge are quite austere, the curious visitor who pushes some of the heavy doors will step into magnificently elaborate courtyards.

Béziers.

burned at the stake when they refused to renounce their faith.

The roads in this region are often flanked by the **Canal du Midi**, which links the Mediterranean with the Atlantic via the Garonne River, and is a favourite playground for holiday-makers on rented houseboats.

Narbonne , once the capital of the Roman region of *Narbonensis Prima*, is today a shadow of its former self. Nevertheless, it is worth visiting for its well-restored medieval quarter, the excellent archaeological collection housed in the **Palais des Archevêques** (Archbishop's Palace; June–Sept daily 10am–6pm, Oct–May Mon–Sat 10am–noon, 2–5pm; charge) and next to it, the remarkable **Cathédrale St-Just**, which has a beautiful stained glass and tapestries and 14th-century cloisters. Note that despite its vast size, the cathedral today is only the choir of the gigantic structure originally planned.

The city of **Béziers** ⓭, 80km (50 miles) from Montpellier, prospered under the Roman occupation. However, the crusade against the Cathars in 1209 reduced the city to ruins. Since the 19th century, thanks to the growing wine market, Béziers has regained its vitality, and is today a quiet city typical of the Midi. Life is taken at an unhurried pace along the plane-tree shaded esplanades where the *Biterrois* (inhabitants of Béziers) play *pétanque* or sip pastis.

The coast

During the 1960s a major development programme on the Languedoc-Roussillon coast created a string of new resorts. Some, like Cap d'Agde and La Grande-Motte, came with dramatic (if controversial) modern architecture, but all were still interspersed with miles of windswept beaches.

Sète ⓮ stands out as the most authentic town along this coast, its bridges and canals reminiscent of Venice, and its unsurpassed seafood restaurants are particularly popular with the fishermen who still frequent the port.

Set a few kilometres inland from the Mediterranean, **Montpellier** ⓯ is the capital of the Languedoc-Roussillon region and one of the liveliest and youngest cities in the Midi. It was revitalised during the 1990s by a dynamic mayor and a programme of avant-garde public architectural developments. A further stimulus to the local economy was the launch in 2001 of the TGV Méditerranée, cutting journey times from Paris to Montpellier to 3 hours 20 minutes. The city has a large university, but most important is its medical school, the oldest in France, dating back to the early 13th century.

The old town of Montpellier is confined to the very centre of the city, which is the focal point for student and social life. The best starting point into this section is the **Place de la Comédie**, a large oval, often known as l'Oeuf (the egg), in front of the opera house. In the adjacent Esplanade Charles-de-Gaulle, a daytime market of fruit and meat, clothes and jewellery, operates until early afternoon.

The **Rue de la Loge** leads to the **Place Jean-Jaurès**, the liveliest city square, filled with tables from the surrounding cafés. In the evening, it is a popular meeting place.

Rue de la Loge soon meets with **Rue Foch** that, in turn, climbs to **Promenade du Peyrou** at the top of the hill. The Promenade consists of wide alleys lined by tall trees and flowerbeds, with an imposing statue of Louis XIV at its centre. From here, the sunset over the Cévennes mountains is splendid.

Across the boulevard from the 14th-century **Cathédrale St-Pierre** is the **Jardin des Plantes**, the oldest garden in France, founded in 1593 by Henry IV. And don't miss the **Musée Fabre** (Tue–Sun 10am-6pm, closed public hols; charge), a beautiful building that holds an excellent collection of art from 15th-century masterpieces to 20th-century modern art.

The Cévennes

The distant mountains of **Cévennes** offer some spectacular natural formations, along with the solitary peace of mountain trails. Among the large massifs are several *causses*, which are the elevated, extremely dry plateaux, divided by very deep gorges, through which flow some of the major rivers of Languedoc.

The Cévennes rise abruptly about 60km (36 miles) north of the Mediterranean. Considering the proximity to the sea, the climate is quite cool, with temperatures of just 18–21°C (65–70°F) in the summer, and chilly winds constantly blowing over the more elevated points. The winters can be harsh, with freezing winds and regular snowfalls. Protected as a national park, the Cévennes provide an ideal break in the summer from the torrid heat and the crowds of lower Languedoc.

En route from Montpellier is the once remote Romanesque abbey of **St-Guilhem-le-Désert** ⓰, tucked into the head of a ravine overlooking the gorge of the Hérault River. Close by, the caverns of the **Grotte des Clamouses** (www.clamouse.com/en; daily July–Aug 10.30am–6.20pm, June, Sept until 5.20pm, Feb–May,

FACT

In 1878 Robert Louis Stevenson, author of 'Robinson Crusoe', travelled through southwest France on a donkey called Modestine. The result was 'Travels with my Donkey in the Cévennes', one of the first great travel books. Follow his trail on GR70.

Place de la Comédie, Montpellier.

Street signs old and new in Nîmes.

The Roman amphitheatre in Nîmes.

Oct until 4.20pm; charge) can be explored. At the foot of the Cévennes the **Grotte des Demoiselles** (daily 10am–5.30pm; charge) is reputedly the most spectacular network of caves in the region. The central chamber, dubbed the cathedral, is 120 by 80 by 50 metres (395ft long, 262ft wide and 164ft high).

Following the flow of the River Hérault northward will lead to the looming **Cirque de Navacelles** , a huge natural amphitheatre 300 metres (1,000ft) deep and 1.6km (1 mile) in diameter created by the River Vis.

Continuing along the course of the Hérault, the pretty road ultimately leads to the highest peak of the Cévennes, **Mont Aigoual** (1,565 metres/5,140ft). From here the view is magnificent. On a clear day you can see the Alps to the east, the Mediterranean to the south, and the Pyrenees to the southwest.

The entire region surrounding Mont Aigoual is full of footpaths, marked by the code GR, followed by a number. These trails are well travelled in summer and have mountain lodges along the way. Further north, however, in the area known as **Lozère**, it is easy to lose one's bearings on the deserted paths.

Gorges du Tarn

West of Florac are the magnificent **Gorges du Tarn** ; the Tarn river carves extraordinary canyons through steep limestone cliffs. **Les Détroits** (the straits), the most impressive section of the gorges, start from the town of **Le Rozier**. Here the river is just a few metres wide with the cliffs towering more than 300 metres (1,000ft) above. Just a few kilometres upstream of the town of Les Vignes, where the river widens, is the **Point Sublime**.

The spectacular Millau Viaduct across the Tarn is the world's highest road bridge (see page 311).

Roman Nîmes

The 2,000-year-old Roman amphitheatre at **Nîmes** still echoes with thundering hooves and desperate cries, when summer bullfights draw

enormous crowds to this former gladiatorial arena. Nîmes is home to France's top bullfighting school and each May hosts the **Feria de Pentecôte** series of bullfights, one of the best-attended festivals in Europe.

In addition to the bulls, the arena (http://arenes-nimes.com/en; daily 9am–5pm with exceptions, closed for events; charge) is a summer venue for rock concerts and sporting events. Nearby, the ancient temple of the **Maison Carrée** (daily 10am–6pm; charge) is a fine example of Roman architectural flair with its delicate Corinthian columns. Opposite, the **Carré d'Art**, a modern tribute in glass and steel by British architect Lord Norman Foster, houses a contemporary art museum (daily 10am–6pm; charge). This is only one of many new buildings in Nîmes, a far-sighted city that successfully combines the old with the avant-garde. Among the old is the lovely **Jardin de la Fontaine** (daily), an 18th-century network of terraces, bridges and water pools.

Nîmes is also the spiritual home of blue jeans. Blue durable cloth was imported from Egypt by Nîmois tailors in the 17th century. In 1848 Levi-Strauss, a Californian, discovered the cloth in America, and used it to make work clothes for farmers. The cloth he used had the mark "de Nîmes", and "Denim" was born.

Pont du Gard

Twenty kilometres (12 miles) northeast of Nîmes is the **Pont du Gard** ㉒ (www.pontdugard.fr/en; daily 9am–6pm, longer hours in summer; charge), one of the finest remaining Roman aqueducts in the world. Spanning 1km (0.5 mile) over the River Gardon, its massive stones have stood for more than 2,000 years, and in 2002 withstood a devastating flood that turned the tranquil river into a raging torrent.

North of the Pont du Gard, in the rugged, scrub-covered hills of the *garrigue*, the town of **Uzès** ㉓ announces itself with a flourish of medieval towers. Its focal point is the central Place aux Herbes, with its arcaded buildings and colourful Saturday-morning market laid out under the trees.

FACT

There are three types of bullfight in Nîmes: *corridas* in which the bull is killed; *courses* where *cocards* are grabbed from the bulls horns, and *courses libres* when bulls run through the streets with *cocards*. In addition to the five-day Whitsun feria, bullfights feature at the Feria des Vendanges in September, when the bulls are driven through the streets.

The Pont du Gard.

WILDLIFE

An underpopulated countryside, mighty mountain ranges, broad rivers and a varied coast create habitats for all kinds of mammals, birds, insects, amphibeans and fish.

France stands at the crossroads of four biogeographical regions – Atlantic, Mediterranean, Alpine and Continental – creating a wide range of habitats for an extremely varied wildlife. There are more than 100 mammal species and more than 500 different kind of bird have been recorded on land or off the coasts.

Over 80 percent of the land surface of metropolitan France is countryside (farm or forest) and large swathes of it are protected in one way or another. There are seven national parks, 49 regional nature parks (managed for the benefit of biodiversity and traditional ways of life) and over 700 other, smaller nature reserves. In all these places, the aim is to protect threatened species from disturbance while giving the public access to non-endangered wildlife and providing information about it.

Large terrestrial predators are rare in France and almost impossible to see except in wildlife sanctuaries. The lynx and the wolf have been successfully reintroduced in the mountains of the east and their small populations are now considered established. Things don't look so good for the Pyrenean brown bear.

Other creatures are more common and conspicuous if you go to the right places, including flamingos in the Camargue and storks in Alsace and the mid-Atlantic seaboard.

The Camargue's briny ponds are the only place in France where the Greater Flamingo nests. The flamingos mainly eat plankton, and it is this which causes the birds' pink plumage.

Wolf conservation in France has proved a bone of contention between environmentalists, politicians and local communities.

A white stork (ciconia ciconia) in flight over Alsace carries nesting material in its beak. The bird is traditionally associated with fertility and luck, which it is said to bring to any home it nests upon.

Ursus arctos - one of the few remaining brown bears

THE FATE OF THE BEAR

Centuries ago, the brown bear *(ursus arctos)* was found in all the upland regions of France but it is an animal that need lots of space – particularly the male – away from the interference of man. Gradually, the spread of human habitation together with unlimited hunting reduced the bear population and by 1940 it was confined to the remote parts of the Pyrenees. At the start of the 1990s, there were less than ten bears left in France and they were separated into three groups, which made breeding difficult. Three Slovenian bears were released into the wild in 1996 and 1997 to boost the population but the killing of Cannelle, a female and the last surviving native Pyrenean bear, by a hunter in 2004 (claiming he did so in self-defence) was a blow to conservation efforts. Five more bears were released in 2006 but one of them, another female, died during the first summer. There are still only about 20 bears living in the Pyrenees and their survival is far from sure.

The wild boar, which tends to inhabit forests, is widespread in many parts of southern France although not commonly spotted.

The common dolphin, which normally lives in pods of 10–12 animals, can potentially be seen off much of the French coast.

The Club-Tail Dragonfly (gomphus vulgatissimus) adult female, with its club-shaped abdomen. Its natural habitat are clean, slow to moderate flowing rivers and creeks with sandy soil.

PROVENCE

This is the magical, light-infused world of the Mediterranean, where black cypresses bend in the breeze under an azure-blue sky, and the scent of pine and lavender hangs on the air.

rovence is a place where the myth of the French people comes alive: here, people are characteristically depicted as open-hearted, relaxed and full of *joie de vivre*. The passionate Provençal people have witnessed civilisation succeed civilisation over thousands of years and, although independent in character, have learned the advantage of accepting the influence of Italy, Spain and the Arab world. Vestiges of this past are scattered across the region. Stretching from the marshy Camargue to the Alpine foothills, most of Provence is dry but fertile, and pine forests are in constant danger of sweeping fires.

Northern Provence

This is a beautiful mix of rolling hills and woodland, much of which has national park status. Nature rules this wild countryside bringing the violent and sometimes destructive Mistral wind roaring down the Rhône valley.

Classified as the warmest city in France, **Orange ❶**, at the northwestern tip of Provence, was founded by Julius Caesar's Second Legion and became a thriving Roman settlement. It possesses a majestic Roman theatre (Théâtre Antique; www.theatre-antique.com/en; daily 9am–6.30pm with exceptions; charge), with a 3-metre (10ft) high statue of Emperor Augustus.

Vineyards near Mont Ventoux.

On the south end of town the original **Arc de Triomphe**, built in AD26, is another great Roman monument.

Surrounding Orange, the *département* of the **Vaucluse** is richly fertile. In May the sweet melons of **Cavaillon** are carried up to Paris for the French president's delectation. In early summer wild morel mushrooms, sweet tomatoes and peppers colour the fields; in October the grape and olive harvests begin. This is also home to the Provençal truffle: the dark, earthy fungus has a strong smell attractive to pigs, which are

Main Attractions
Orange
Avignon
Lubéron
St-Rémy-de-Provence
Arles
Camargue
Aix-en-Provence
Marseille

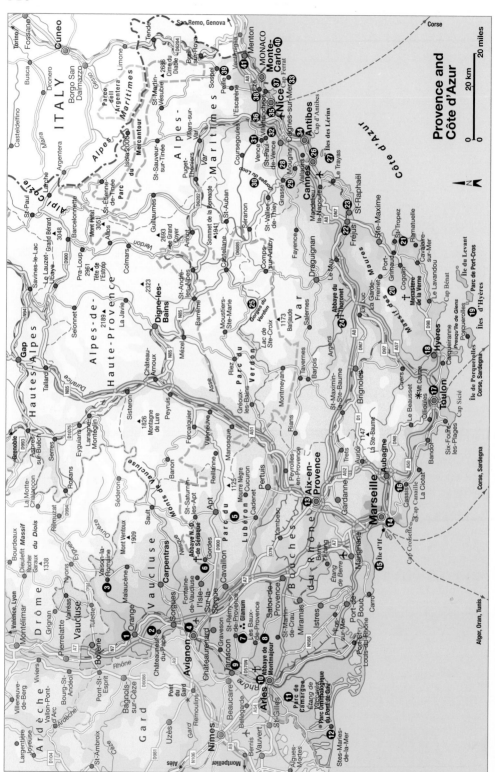

Provence and
Côte d'Azur

0   20 km
0   20 miles

trained to find them. The rich earth also nourishes some of prestigious vineyards, in particular those at **Châteauneuf-du-Pape ②**, renowned for their strong, full-bodied red and crisp white wines.

Situated on the northern edge of the Vaucluse straddling the capricious river Ouvèze is the Provençal market town of **Vaison-la-Romaine ③**. It's a short climb to the Haute-Ville dominated by the ruins of a 12th-century castle. The ancient belfry is the entrance to the medieval centre, which has considerable charm with narrow streets, fountains and stone houses.

Another era can be explored on the opposite bank of the river, which has a tendency to burst its banks. Here the remains of the Roman city, the largest archaeological discovery in France, have been uncovered (daily Apr–Sept 9.30am-6pm, Nov–Mar 10am–noon, 2–5pm, closed Jan; charge). There are two main sites: **La Villasse** and **Puymin**. At La Villasse retrace the steps of everyday Roman urban life by strolling among the ruins of shops, villas and public baths. The Théâtre Antique, which is still used for concerts, and the

archaeological museum are found on the other site at Puymin.

If you can brace the biting Mistral, the summit of nearby **Mont Ventoux**, the 'windy mountain', offers spectacular views over the Vaucluse and, in the other direction, the Alps.

Fields surrounding the hillside town of **Sault** are carpeted in mauve, blue and pink lavender hues during the flowering period in July and August. The highlight of the year is the Fête de la Lavande on 15 August.

The region's capital

At the confluence of the Rhône and Durance rivers, **Avignon ④** is a walled city packed with history and culture. The popes moved here from Rome in 1309 at the behest of King Philippe Le Bel (the Handsome). For 70 years Avignon was the centre of European religion, art and prostitution. The clerics and brothels are long gone, but the palace remains the most breathtaking sight in Provence.

The **Palais des Papes** (www.palais-des-papes.com/en; daily 9am–7pm with exceptions; charge) is superb inside

The Pont d'Avignon, or strictly speaking Pont St-Bénezet.

FACT

In 1377, Pope Gregory XI returned from Avignon to Rome. When an Italian was chosen to succeed him, the disaffected French faction within the church appointed Clement VII as the first of several antipopes to remain in Avignon.

and out with its silent cloisters, cavernous halls and imposing ramparts. A few paces north of the palace is the 13th-century **Petit Palais** (Weds–Mon 10am–1pm, 2–6pm; charge) Once home to bishops and cardinals it now houses a fine collection of early-Renaissance Italian paintings with works by Botticelli and Giovanni. **Place de l'Horloge** is the place to sip a *pastis* and wonder why the popes ever left. Among the many museums, **Musée Calvet** (Wed–Mon 10am–1pm, 2–6pm; charge) is worth visiting as much for the elegant architecture and gardens of the 18th-century *hôtel particulier* as the collection of mainly French works.

Take a step back from the bustle to discover one of the prettiest streets within the ramparts, Rue des Teinturiers. Tree-lined and cobbled, it borders the River Sorgue, which took its name from the 15th-century manufacturers of the brightly coloured fabrics called *indiennes*.

The famous "Pont d'Avignon", **Pont St-Bénezet** (www.avignon-pont.com/en; daily 9am–7pm with exceptions; charge), on which the nursery rhyme

Lavender field.

dances, is a disappointing four-arch ruin tumbling into the Rhône.

The Avignon Theatre Festival takes place in July, as well as a lively parallel fringe event Festival Off, but at any time the town offers a feast of museums and art galleries.

The Lubéron

To the east of Avignon lies the **Lubéron ❺**, the region described in Peter Mayle's 1991 bestselling book *A Year in Provence*. Still relatively untarnished, the Lubéron retains a mystical attraction.

Mayle lived in **Ménerbes**, but the villages of Cucuron and **Gordes ❻** have far more charm. Though besieged by tourists in the summer, Gordes remains one of the most picturesque hilltop villages in Provence. The streets are steep and cobbled, the ancient stone houses are perfectly restored and the view out over the valley spectacular.

About 5km north of Gordes is the much-photographed 12th-century **Abbaye Notre-Dame-de-Sénaque** (tel: 04 90 72 05 86; visits by appointment only), which provides the backdrop to an immense lavender field. In

LAVENDER ROUTE

Lavender thrives well throughout Provence. *Lavande vraie*, which produces the finest essence, grows at 600–1,200 metres (2,000–4,000ft) altitude, but plantings are increasing of the lower quality *lavande aspic* and a hybrid *lavandin*, which grow on lower slopes and yield more essence. Lavender is harvested from July to September, dried for several days and finally distilled for its essence. July and August, when it is in full flower, is the best period to visit. Suggested *Routes de la Lavande* are found on www.grande-traversee-alpes.com, with lists of producers, distilleries and boutiques. There is a Musée de la Lavande near Coustellet, the Le Coulets distillery at Apt, and a lavender festival in August at Sault.

keeping with Cistercian principles the interior is austere with pure lines, yet beautiful in its simplicity.

The pretty riverside village of **Fontaine-de-Vaucluse** has Europe's largest natural spring with a 400-metre (1,300ft) deep pool. Jacques Cousteau almost drowned here and nobody as yet has plunged to the bottom. The powerful flow of water is used to turn the Moulin à Papier, a restored papermill which uses traditional methods to make handmade paper.

Another gem is **Cucuron**, in the heart of Grand Lubéron, a village of medieval houses, narrow streets and ramparts. Not surprisingly it has been used as a film set more than once.

Here too is the moonscape of **Roussillon** and its incredible rock formations of red ochre. From the centre of the village follow the signposted Sentier des Ochres (daily depending on weather, closed Jan; charge) which leads you through the panorama of coloured rocks. In the 1990s the Lubéron became one of the most fashionable places to live in France: Brigitte Bardot and Sean Connery have houses here.

Vallée des Alpilles

At the foot of the rocky limestone hills of the Massif des Alpilles among the vines and olive groves is picturesque **St-Rémy-de-Provence** ➐. This thriving market town attracted the Provençal gentry who built the fine 17th- and 18th-century houses that line the streets from the Place Jean-Jaurès to the Vieille Ville. On the Place Favier, the Renaissance mansion Mistral de Mondragon is home to the eclectic **Musée des Alpilles** (Tue-Sun May–Sept 10am–6pm, Oct–Apr 1–5.30pm; charge). The most famous of St-Rémy's residents include Nostradamus, 16th-century astrologer and scholar, and Van Gogh who spent a year at St-Paul-de-Mausole mental hospital. These serene, isolated surroundings inspired Van Gogh to complete 150 works, such as *Irises, Starry Night and Olive Grove in the Evening*, and you can follow a trail

to the scenes he painted.

On the town outskirts are two marvellously sculpted monuments, the **Arc de Triomphe** and the **Mausolée**, known as The Antiques. They were the only vestiges of Roman occupation until the ruins of Glanum were unearthed in 1921. Established by the Celtic-Ligurian people, then the Greeks, it was the Romans who created a real city with baths, villas and temples. Little of the ancient city remains, but the visitors centre has an informative exhibition which traces its history (Apr–Aug daily 9.30am–6pm, Sept–Mar Tue–Sun 10am–4.30pm; charge).

Troubadours' town

The Alpilles plateau is punctuated only by the rock outcrop of **Les Baux-de-Provence** ➑, once famous for courtly love and the songs of its troubadours. The tortuous valley below this medieval citadel inspired Dante's view of hell in *Inferno*, and today it is known as one of France's most spectacular villages. Its windy summit provides an unforgettable panorama over the **Plaine de la Crau** to Arles, the Camargue

The mausoleum on the outskirts of St-Rémy.

Gordes.

Sunflower in the Vallée des Alpilles, a setting which inspired Van Gogh.

Café in St-Rémy.

and out towards the sea. The **Musée d'Histoire des Baux** (www.chateau-baux-provence.com/en; daily 10am–5pm with exceptions; charge), which serves as the entrance to the massive fortress, illustrates the history of the castle and its village through the centuries. There is also an exhibition of medieval siege machines, built from original plans, that includes a *trébuchet*, which is an enormous sling catapult that took 60 men to fire 100kg (220lb) stones. Demonstrations take place in summer. Stroll along the ancient cobbled streets, lined with souvenir shops and cafés, and stop to admire the lovely Renaissance town hall housing the Musée des Santons (Christmas crib figures). The 12th-century Eglise Saint-Vincent has 20th-century stained glass by Max Ingrand and the nearby Chapelle des Penintents Blanc is decorated with frescoes by Yves Brayer. The Musée Yves Brayer is a few steps away in a 16th-century mansion (Oct–Mar Wed–Mon 11am–12.30pm, 2–5pm, Apr–Sept daily until 6.30pm, closed Jan–mid Feb; charge).

Bauxite, named after the town, was discovered here in 1821. One of the disused quarries provides a vast backdrop for the Cathédrale d'Images. The 4,000-sq-metre (4,784 sq ft) stone walls provide an immense screen for projected images creating an awesome visual and musical display.

Tarascon

On the banks of the Rhône, between Avignon and Arles, at the crossroads leading to the Alpilles and the Camargue, lies the medieval town of **Tarascon** ❾. According to the legend, Ste Marthe rescued the inhabitants from Tarasque, a terrifying half-animal and half-fish monster that devoured children. An effigy of the Tarasque is paraded through the streets during the Fêtes de Tarasque on the last weekend of June. Tartarin, one of Alphonse Daudet's *héros*, is also associated with the town and tales of his adventures are enacted by mannequins at the Maison de Tartarin.

However, the main reason to visit Tarascon is to admire the almost perfectly intact Château (daily 9.30am–5pm, July–Aug until 6.30pm; charge). Built by King René of Provence in the

PROVENÇAL FABRIC

The origin of gaily coloured Provence material dates from the 17th century when fabric was imported from the Levant and India into the Port of Marseille. The demand for these colourful fabrics, called *indiennes*, reached the court of Louis XIV, and French manufacturers were quick to copy the Indian and Persian printing techniques. The original designs were gradually replaced by the classic Provençal motifs of lavender, olives, sunflowers, cicadas, mimosas and lemons. Colours were determined by local raw materials, such as the ochre from Roussillon, which ranges from saffron-yellow to ochre-red. Patterns are named after Provençal towns, some retain their Indian references like Raipur and Mangalore. At Tarascon, manufacturer Souleiado has a fabric museum (Mon–Sat 10am–6.30pm; charge).

15th century, it is one of the most outstanding examples of military architecture in Provence. In contrast, the
Flemish-Gothic Cour d'Honneur is
surprisingly flamboyant.

Other nearby places worth a detour
include the Romanesque **Abbaye de
Montmajour**, and the village of **Graveson** which has both a small museum
(daily; charge) of perfume and a
museum dedicated to Fauvist painter
Auguste Chabaud.

Arles

The soul of Provence lies in **Arles ⑩**.
In among the pretty nests of red roofs
and soft stone is the superbly preserved
and recently restored amphitheatre,
Les Arènes (daily; charge). Built to
hold 20,000 spectators who cheered
and jeered combatting gladiators, it is
nowadays regularly used for bullfights.
A few streets away is the superb church
of **St Trophime** with a Romanesque
tympanum and cloisters (daily; charge
for cloisters). The statue of Frédéric
Mistral, poet of Provence, responsible
for reviving the Provençal language
and traditions at the beginning of the

20th century, gazes down in the Place
du Forum. The Museon Arlaten, which
he founded, is undergoing major renovation and is due to re-open in 2018.

Above all, this is a place to wander
and sit, following in the footsteps of
Van Gogh who lost his sanity in the
sun-dappled cafés and neighbouring
heat-swirled fields. Newly restored
in 2014, the **Fondation Vincent Van
Gogh** (Tue–Sun 11am–7pm; charge)
only actually exhibits one of his paintings, but is instead a celebration of Van
Gogh's influence through the work of
modern artists.

Gauguin was Van Gogh's house
guest for two months at Arles, but
their friendship ended in a bitter
argument and a severed ear. Some
of Gauguin's works are on display in
the **Musée Réattu** (www.museereattu.
arles.fr; Tue–Sun 10am–5pm, Mar–
Oct until 6pm, closed some public
hols; charge), which is remarkable
for a display of 57 sketches by Picasso,
donated by the artist.

Outside the city centre on the
ancient site of a Roman chariot-racing
track stands the ultra-modern building

The flag of Provence.

Les Baux-de-Provence.

Post-Impressionists in the South of France

"The whole future of art is to be found in the South of France," declared Vincent Van Gogh, a northern artist with a southern sensibility.

While Impressionism emerged in Paris, Provence was the creative melting pot between in the last quarter of the 19th century and the first of the 20th. Claude Monet and Jean Renoir, two leading lights, were entranced by the seductive landscape and intoxicating southern light. In their footsteps came French and foreign post-Impressionists, from Vincent Van Gogh and Paul Gauguin to Paul Cézanne, the greatest of them all. It was in the south that Van Gogh (1853–90) abandoned the illusion of painting as an imitation of nature.

The wave of avant-garde artists continued, from Picasso and Braque in their Cubist incarnations, to Chagall, Matisse and Dufy. Van Gogh and Gauguin

The Village of Gardanne by Paul Cézanne, which dates from 1885–86.

are associated with Arles, Cézanne with Aix, while Signac and Matisse are linked to St-Tropez and Nice. The Nabis were post-Impressionists who styled themselves as followers of Gauguin. Bonnard (1867–1947), the painter of sensations, lived in a hillside villa above Cannes. His was a seductive Mediterranean idyll of dreamy southern interiors and sun-dappled light. Les Fauves, founded by Henri Matisse (1869–1954) in 1905, were dubbed "wild beasts" for their fondness for lurid colours. Other Fauves included André Derain, Dufy, Marquet, Maurice de Vlaminck and Georges Braque. After passing the winter of 1916–17 in Nice, Matisse settled there. One of his most important works is the chapel in Vence.

Pablo Picasso (1881–1973) lived on the Côte d'Azur, notably in Antibes and Juan les Pins, and worked on Cubism with Georges Braque (1882–1963) in Céret in 1911. Picasso dismissed Bonnard as painting in "a pot pourri of indecision" and failing to "go beyond his own sensibility". Picasso spent much of his life on the Mediterranean coast, and in 1946 he was given the keys of the Grimaldi Palace in Antibes to use as a studio. The château is now home to the Musée Picasso and contains a collection of more than 50 of his works. It was in Vallauris that Picasso began his experiments with ceramics, and produced his famous series of drawings and paintings of Sylvette David.

Another French artist, Jean Cocteau, came on holiday to Villefranche in 1925, and stayed to decorate the chapel of St Pierre, where you can still buy his prints, and the mayor's office in Menton.

At the end of the Second World War many artists were drawn to the South of France. Russian-born Marc Chagall settled in St-Jean-Cap-Ferrat in the spring of 1949, where the azure blue light and seascapes inspired the artist with new ideas. After seeing Matisse's painting at the chapel in Vence, he strove to find one of his own to decorate. His Bible-based works fill the Musée National Marc Chagall in Nice.

Nice was the base for a new school of artists in 1958, the Nouveaux Réalistes. The founders of this new movement – Yves Klein, Arman, Martial Raysse, César, Dufêne, Raymond Hains, Jean Tinguely, Jacques Villeglé, Spoerri and Italian-born Ben Vautier – advocated the use of objects taken from contemporary life. Nouveau Réalisme is often presented as the French version of Pop Art. Paint tubes, trash cans, packaging and industrial waste are united to create a material surface.

that houses the **Musée Départemental Arles Antique** (Wed–Mon 10am–6pm; charge). The collection traces the history of Arles through 1,300 archaeological finds from the Neolithic period to the end of the Roman era. Marvel at spectacular floor mosaics, paleo-Christian sarcophagi and a marble bust of Caesar recovered from the bed of the Rhône in 2008.

Stay around for the lively Saturday market in the town centre, when gypsies gather from surrounding villages with their guitars.

The Camargue

Arles is gateway to **La Camargue ⑪**, a wild place of lagoons, rice fields and cowboys. The *gardians* ride white horses and tend to the herds of black bulls that roam the marshes. These hardy cowboys used to live in the traditional thatched cottages that dot the landscape. Today the best way to experience the Camargue is still on horseback with an organised excursion.

In late May, **Saintes-Maries-de-la-Mer ⑫** becomes the Roma capital of Europe. Thousands of travellers flock to the village for the festival of the black Madonna, when a statue of the Virgin is carried into the sea surrounded by white horses. The statue is kept in the crypt of the village church, along with a terrifying effigy of a woman whose stare follows you around. The beach here is one of the longest in Provence: kilometres of white sand and shallow water.

In summer, thousands of flamingos congregate on the lagoons, turning the water pink. The protected wetlands also attract a further 500 species of visiting birds. Open all year the **Parc Ornithologique du Pont de Gau**, at 4km (2-miles) to the north of Saintes-Maries-de-la-Mer, is an ideal place to view birdlife from a series of discovery trails that weave through the marshlands. Along with a pair of binoculars be sure to arm yourself with plenty of mosquito repellent. A newly revamped museum (Wed–Mon Apr–Sept 9am–12.30pm, 1–6pm, Oct–Mar 10am–12.30pm, 1–5pm; charge) on the Camargue's history and ecosystems stands on the route between Arles and Saintes-Maries in an old sheep shed

FACT

The most important harvest of the Camargue is sea salt. The salt water lagoons evaporate under the summer sun and salt crystals pile up into mounds called *camelles* which can reach up to 8 metres (26ft) in height.

The white horses of the Camargue.

FACT

The Fontaine des Quatre Dauphins lies at the heart of the Quartier Mazarin in Aix-en-Provence. This aristocratic area, with its chequerboard street plan, was named after an archbishop of Aix, the brother of the famous cardinal.

Detail of the facade of Aix's Tribunal de Commerce, on the Cours Mirabeau.

at **Mas du Pont de Rousty**. Outside there is a nature trail which leads to an observation tower.

Taking the route over to the southeast corner of the Camargue, there is an *écomusée* that is worth a visit, the **Musée du Riz** at Le Sambuc.

Intellectual heart

Aristocratic **Aix-en-Provence** ⑬, city of fountains and tree-lined avenues, is the intellectual heart of Provence. Between 1487 and the Revolution the Supreme Court of France sat here, and Aix still possesses one of Europe's most prestigious universities. Its ancient streets, 17th-century residences and numerous squares are reminiscent of Paris and, like the capital, Aix adores its "beautiful people". A Sunday afternoon in a café on the **Cours Mirabeau** Ⓐ is a lesson in crafted chic. Adjust your sunglasses, pout and watch the world and his poodle go by.

Aix derives its name from the Latin for water, *aqua*. Water is everywhere and fountains trickle in every corner. The **Fontaine des Quatre Dauphins** is one of the most beautiful in a small

square of 17th-century townhouses. During the 19th century, novelist Emile Zola's father was the engineer responsible for building aqueducts to improve Aix's water circulation. Zola grew up in the city along with his friend, painter Paul Cézanne.

One of the best ways to see Aix is by taking the **Cézanne Trail**, shown in a free leaflet from the tourist office. Bronze plaques mark sites from the painter's life. North of the cathedral on Avenue Paul Cézanne, the **Atelier Paul Cézanne** (daily; reserve in advance at the tourist office; charge) preserves the artist's studio and house – his cape and beret hang where he left them.

Modern art is found at the **Fondation Vasarely** (4km/2 miles west; bus from Boulevard de la République; daily 10am–6pm; charge).

On Saturdays **Place de l'Hôtel de Ville** Ⓑ and **Place des Prêcheurs** Ⓒ are filled with stalls of garlic, tomatoes, beans, olive oil, spicy sausage and riotous flowers.

To the north of the centre is the **Cathédrale St-Sauveur** Ⓓ and behind is the **Musée des Tapisseries** Ⓔ

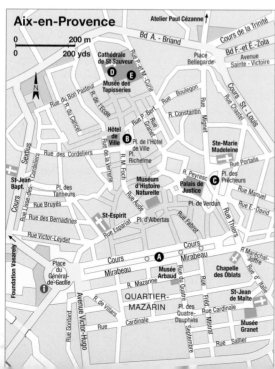

(Wed–Mon mid-Apr–mid-Oct 10am–12.30pm, 1.30–6pm, rest of year 1.30–5pm, closed public hols; charge).

Dominating Aix, the **Montagne Ste-Victoire** was depicted by Cézanne in over 60 of his paintings. Strikingly triangular when viewed from the picturesque hamlet of **Le Tholonet**, the mountain is a naked contortion of white rock. Cézanne collapsed on one of the paths leading to the mountain, and died in Aix in 1906. The magical light of Ste Victoire attracted numerous other artists – Picasso is buried under the shadow of the rock, at his former château in **Vauvenargues**.

Marseille

South of Aix, **Marseille** ⑭ is France's oldest and second-biggest city. Founded by Greek traders in 600 BC, the gateway to the Mediterranean, the Orient and beyond has been a busy port for centuries. Marseille's reputation as the "Chicago of France" was built on tales of the Mafia, financial corruption and drugs. In the 1960s and 70s this was the infamous "French Connection" providing drugs for the United States.

Marseille has done much to clean up its image and the TGV connection with Paris, the new tramway and the title of European Capital of Culture in 2013, has made it fashionable. Today the city is a vibrant, spicy concoction, worthy of its culinary gift to the world, the rich fish stew *bouillabaisse*.

The newly remodelled **Vieux Port** Ⓐ may have undergone a transformation in preparation for 2013, but the colourful fishmarket still survives and there are many seafood restaurants to choose from. Beautified pedestrian areas provide a very pleasant place to stroll, while Norman Foster's Ombrière – a giant mirror of polished metal – offers shade from the sun.

On the waterfront, the modern structures of the Villa Méditerraneé exhibition hall and the **MuCEM** Ⓑ (www.mucem.org; Wed–Mon 11am–7pm, until 6pm in winter; charge), a museum devoted to cultures of the Mediterranean, now dominate the J4 Esplanade. The old maritime station has been taken over by the Musée Regards de Provence (daily 10am–5.30pm; charge),

Norman Foster's l'Ombrière in Marseille's Vieux Port.

TIP

A 24- (€24), 48- (€31) and 72-hour (€39) Marseille City Pass is available from the tourist office or online at www.resamarseille.com. It gives you free access to several museums, free inner-city public transport, and a return boat trip to Château d'If and the Frioul Islands.

dedicated to classical, modern and contemporary art.

To the north of the Vieux Port is **Le Panier** the city's oldest *quartier*, a charming labyrinth of narrow steep streets, stairways and colourful tall houses with rickety shutters. Now home to artisan boutiques, this shantytown was where dockers, sailors and fishermen lived until the 1960s.

At the top of the hill is **La Vieille Charité ●**, a former hospice built by Marseillais sculptor Pierre Puget in the 17th century. Saved from demolition by Le Corbusier, it is now home to two museums: the **Musée d'Archéologie Méditerranéenne** and the **Musée d'Arts Africains, Océaniens et Amérindiens** (both Tue–Sun 10am–6pm; charge).

Le Panier's neighbour, **La Joliette**, is part of an urban regeneration project that has seen the area enhanced with cultural sites and commercial centres.

Running from the port is Marseille's most famous street, **La Canebière ●**. The boulevard is a human tide of different nationalities by day and the streets around the Canebière are lively at night,

with the **Opéra ●** a focal point for music-lovers.

The city has a thriving cultural scene and other fascinating museums in the centre include the **Musée Cantini ●** (Tue–Sun 10am-6pm; charge), with a fine Fauve and Surrealist collection; the Musée d'Histoire de Marseille (Tue–Sun 10am–6pm; charge), reopened in 2013 following a major facelift, now one of the largest of its kind in Europe; and the Musée des Docks Romains (Tue–Sun 10am–6pm; free), where you can see remains of the old Roman port.

South of the Vieux Port are elegant 17th-century townhouses. Climb to **Notre-Dame-de-la-Garde ●** the white church that is the spiritual home of the city. On top of the campanile of the basilica, looking seaward, is a statue of the Virgin Mary, entirely covered in gold leaf.

It's a 20-minute boat ride from the Vieux Port to **Ile d'If ⓯**, one of the cluster of islands that makes up the Frioul Archipelago. The imposing 16th-century fortress built on the island by François I to guard the harbour was never put to military use, and

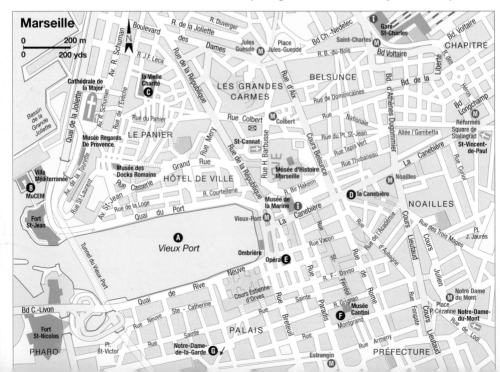

was converted into an escape-proof prison. Made famous by Alexandre Dumas' novel with the fictitious Count of Monte Cristo and Abbé Faria, real inmates were mostly political prisoners, especially Protestants and Republicans. A trip combining the other wild, windswept Frioul islands is easy to do in a day.

To the east of the city is the town of **Aubagne** whose rough white rock hills were home to Marcel Pagnol and his stories of Provençal lust and revenge: Jean de Florette prayed in vain for water in the parched fields and Manon des Sources stalked the herb-scented ravines.

Dramatic coastline

The least developed of a much-abused coastline lies between Marseille and Toulon. Here the shore is distinguished by **Les Calanques**, steep-sided fjords carved out of cliffs, best viewed by boat from **Cassis ⑯**. This charming little port is a chic resort of restored village houses with a popular golden beach. It is known for its fragrant white wine, which tantalises the palate with hints of the herbs that cover these hills. A little further down the coast is **Bandol**, home to another fine Provençal wine.

To the north, the high ridge of Le Gros-Cerveau (Big Brain) overlooks vineyards, orchards and fields of flowers – and on clear days, the distant harbour of Toulon. The D11, around Gros-Cerveau, leads into wilder country, through the **Gorge d'Ollioules**, a hill village with ruined basalt houses holding fast to the side of a long-extinct volcano.

Down the road **Mont Caume** has a panorama extending from **Cap Bénat** in the east to **La Ciotat** in the west. La Ciotat has long sandy beaches, a port and an old centre with attractive 17th- and 18th-century mansions, especially the Hôtel de Grimaldi-Regusse. It was here in September 1895 that the brothers Lumière, who came to La Ciotat regularly on family holidays, held the first public viewing of a film.

Returning to the coast, there is another terrific view from **Cap Canaille**, east of Cassis. The highest sea cliff in Europe (350 metres/1,000ft) has vistas across Cassis, the Calanques and the Mediterranean.

FACT

Cassis AOC wines come in three colours: red, white and rosé. The deeply coloured reds are gutsy wines, the whites have interesting herby aromas and the rosés are pleasant. Recommended producers: Château de Fontcreuse; Domaine des Quatre-Vents; Clos Val Bruyère.

One of the turquoise-blue inlets of Les Calanques.

SANTONS

Santons (derived from the Provencal word *santoùn* meaning "little saint") are hand-painted clay figurines used to depict the traditional Christmas nativity scene. Today made from clay, the very first santons were crafted using bread, papier-mâché or wood. A traditional crèche is a detailed tableau with 55 different characters symbolising all forms of village life – fishwife, baker, shepherd, lavender-seller, the blind man. Santons are 2.5–15cm high and are made in two halves that are stuck together then painted. Manufacturers continue to produce these figures at **Aubagne** and **Fontaine-de-Vaucluse**. A two-day fair, the Foire du Santonnier, is held in December at Aubagne, and the **Musée du Santon** at Marseille has a collection of 18th-and 19th-century santons.

The stylish fittings of a speedboat moored at St-Tropez.

THE CÔTE D'AZUR

Despite the crowds, the Côte d'Azur maintains
its allure and remains the classic image of a
summer holiday, while a rich artistic legacy
and unspoilt hinterland add to the heady mix.

ebate as to the precise definition of the Côte d'Azur continues to rage, especially among property developers anxious to claim some of the magic. This chapter follows the coast from Toulon to the Italian border, and samples the secrets of the interior.

The *préfecture* of the *département* of the Var, **Toulon** ⑰ is France's principal naval base and the headquarters of the Mediterranean fleet. An amphitheatre of limestone hills, covered with pine, screens its deep natural harbour, one of the Mediterranean's most attractive. The surrounding hills are crowned by the star-shaped forts built by Vauban, Louis XIV's great military architect and engineer. Toulon was badly damaged in World War II and much of the post-war building is ugly, especially along the quays, where boats depart for tours of the harbour and nearby islands.

Toulon is associated with the work of 17th-century sculptor Pierre Puget of Marseille, who began his career carving ships' figureheads, and two of his best works, the *Atlantes*, can be seen on the *quai*. Works by his followers stand in the **Musée National de la Marine** (www.musee-marine.fr; June–Sept daily 10am–6pm, Oct–May closed Tue; charge), along with models of the many ships once made in Toulon.

Quai Stalingrad separates the port from the old town, with plenty of bars

and cheap hotels in such streets as Place Puget and Rue d'Alger. The best time to visit is during the morning, when the market on Place Louis-Blanc is particularly lively.

Hyères and the islands

Modern **Hyères** ⑱, northeast of Toulon along the coast, is made up of a *vieille ville* (old town) and a newer area with modern villas and boulevards lined with date palms. This was an ancient and medieval port, but it is now 4km (2 miles) from the sea.

Main Attractions
St-Tropez
Fréjus
Cannes
Grasse
St-Paul-de-Vence
Antibes
Nice
Cap Ferrat
Monte-Carlo
Menton

Toulon.

Explore the backstreets and courtyards of Hyères, a modern town that retains its older core.

The Calanques at Porquerolles.

Hyères has long been a centre for the French *sportifs*, its sub-tropical climate encouraging sailing, scuba-diving, wind-surfing and water-skiing. The busy atmosphere of a modern town combines charmingly with its backdrop of faded Belle Epoque grandeur. The 14th-century château is built on the Casteou hill, above the old town's twisting medieval streets. Nearby is the 13th-century church of **St-Louis**, a marriage of Italian Romanesque and Provençal Gothic. In the old town, entered via a 13th-century gate, is the **Place Massillon**. The pedestrian streets nearby play host to the Saturday morning food market, which is good for Arab and Provençal delicacies.

The **Presqu'Ile de Giens**, which was once one of the **Iles d'Hyères** ⑲, is connected to the mainland by sand bars. The **Salins des Pesquiers** is the only salt marsh still worked on the Côte.

Most of the forest on **Porquerolles**, the largest of the three islands, and **Port-Cros** next to it, burned in the 1890s so that they now resemble rugged hilltops lushly planted with semi-tropical vegetation – which is, in fact, what they are; part of the very old mountain system to which the Maures and Estérel massifs belong.

The Iles d'Hyères and Massif des Maures are schistous rock, while the colourful Massif de l'Estérel is known for its blood-red porphyry rock. Sunlight reflected by mica in the rock is the origin of the name bestowed long ago, *Iles d'Or* or golden islands.

The navy bought **Ile du Levant**, the easternmost island, in 1892 for a firing range. Comparatively barren, it is used as a military testing centre. But also sharing Ile du Levant is a nature reserve and the well-known nudist colony, **Héliopolis**.

Massif des Maures

In the Middle Ages these islands and islets belonged to monks who were constantly at risk from pirate raids. Until the 18th century the shore opposite, the wild, wooded, hilly **Massif des Maures** ⑳, was almost deserted for fear of pirates. Only well-fortified hill and fishing villages like St-Tropez and its upland neighbours were inhabited. The demand for sea-and-sunbathing

accommodation transformed the Maures coast into a lively strip of resorts – some less spoiled than others – and traditional local industries like bottle-cork and briar-pipe manufacturing took second place to tourism.

The Maures' uncrowded inland roads pass through charming villages, ravines with waterfalls, and forests of cork-oak and chestnut. Visitors are rewarded with glimpses of the sea; a semi-ruined 18th-century monastery, **Chartreuse de la Verne**; a medieval town, **La Garde-Freinet**, built around ruins of a Saracen castle with gardens designed by André Le Nôtre; and a market town, **Draguignan**, centre of commercial wine production in the Maures (red and rosé).

The damage from forest fires, which particularly raged in the summer of 2003, is noticeable from the **Corniche des Maures**, the spectacular coastal road from **Le Lavandou** (a pleasant fishing village, whose name evokes its fields of lavender, which is protected by the Cap Bénat) to **La Croix Valmer**, a resort that produces one of the better Côte-de-Provence wines.

The ultimate resort

At the eastern end of the Maures, **St-Tropez** ㉑ looks north across the Golfe de St-Tropez. Thus the quayside cafés receive the golden evening light and the bay's stunning sunsets. Today this once tiny fishing village increases its population by about 10 times in summer, becoming a sort of Mediterranean extension of the Left Bank of Paris, with all that this implies for parking and prices.

The writer Colette and other Parisians complained as early as the 1920s that "St-Trop'" was too crowded. Today even the yachts number in the thousands. French painters and writers had discovered it by the late 19th century and kindly recorded their findings. Paintings by these artists, some showing the unspoiled village, are in the **Musée de l'Annonciade** (Wed–Mon 10am– 1pm, 2–6pm, closed Nov; charge), a converted 16th-century chapel.

Head for the hills to get away from holidaymakers who assemble to watch celebrities and each other. Several villages in the Maures have their own elaborate way of preparing *marrons*

The St-Tropez quayside.

ST-TROPEZ BEACHES

The beaches of St-Tropez are mostly occupied by private concessions or "clubs", although there are small stretches of free public beaches. The private clubs range from bamboo shacks with sun loungers and parasols to designer bars, discos and spas, depending on your budget. To the west of the town at **La Bouillabaisse** beach there are a few beach clubs, but one of the best is the trendy **Pearl Beach**. Within walking distance of the citadel is **Plage des Graniers**, and to the east the larger **Plage des Canebiers**, and the more crowded **Plage des Salins**. The legendary **Plage de Pampelonne**, with 5km (3 miles) of golden sand, has fashionable, showbiz-frequented beach clubs. The favourites are **Nikki**, **Tropicana**, **Key West Beach** and **Tahiti**.

FACT

Bikinis struck the beaches of St-Tropez at the end of World War II. In 1957, director Roger Vadim filmed Brigitte Bardot, wearing even less on the beach, starting the national craze for St-Tropez. (Vadim is now buried in the Cimetière Marin.)

glacés, the delicious sugary chestnuts that comes foil-wrapped, and a tour could be built around them. Alternatively, since this is the place for posing, you could squeeze into discos and onto the beaches, shop in designer boutiques, admire the eclectic Hôtel Byblos, try to get a table somewhere and order a white Cassis, the best Côte white wine, or one of M. Ricard's anisettes, and watch the mob. There are motorboat tours of the port and of Port Grimaud.

Port Grimaud is a modern resort designed to look like a local village, except that each house has its own waterfront and boat mooring. Built by architect François Spoerry in 1966, this Provençal Venice has its detractors, but has nevertheless proved popular, contributing to the purported future of the Var as the "Florida of Europe".

Inland on the peninsula, towering above the lower vineyards slopes and woodland, are the hilltop villages of **Ramatuelle** and **Gassin**. These pretty villages with winding streets and alleys, have spectacular views of the gulf. Ramatuelle is also the venue for lively

summer festivals. The lower slopes of the peninsula are covered with prime vineyards. The signposted Route des Côtes de Provence (http://routedesvins-deprovence.com) leads you to the most important wineries, such as Château Minuty and Château de Barbeyrolles, near Gassin. At La Foux, near Port Grimaud, Les Maîtres Vignerons de St-Tropez is an ideal place to taste a range of local co-operative wines.

Roman ports

Fréjus ㉒ and **St-Raphaël ㉓**, grown together, divide the Massif des Maures from the Massif de l'Estérel. Fashionable St-Raphaël has a casino and a **Musée Archéologique** (Tue–Sat 9am–noon, 2–6pm; charge), where the substantial collection of amphorae has mainly been collected from the sea by teams of divers. The plateau of Fréjus, like Hyères, used to lie on the sea. Its name derives from *Forum Julius*; it was founded by Julius Caesar as one of the important trading centres of Transalpine Gaul. At Fréjus, Augustus built the galleys that decisively defeated Mark Antony at the Battle of Actium in Greece. Here there

Fréjus.

are important Roman ruins, including the 10,000-seat arena where Picasso liked to watch bullfights.

Two-hour-long tours (tel: 04 94 51 83 83) are available of both the Roman city and the episcopal city, which has an outstanding 5th-century baptistry, 12th-century cloisters and cathedral, certain sections of which date back as far as the 10th century.

The Estérel

The Romans built with porphyry rock taken from the Massif de l'Estérel that lies between the Golfe de Fréjus and Golfe de Napoule, where strata of yellow, green, blue and purple run together with the famous red. Ragged red cliffs, occasional red beaches, lichen-covered rocks and islets contrast with the intense blue of sea and sky. The **Corniche de l'Estérel** follows the promontories and long, deep indentations of the coast, linking beach resorts and isolated panoramic view points. The **Pic du Cap Roux**, a 452-metre (1,483ft) peak visible 48km (30 miles) out to sea, and **Pic de l'Ours** inland provide highly rated views.

The Aurelian Way *(Via Aurelia)* that connected Gaul to Rome, one of the triumphs of civil engineering in which southern France abounds, passed through the Estérel. Early on, escapees from galleys and other criminals hid in its gorges and dense forest.

Smaller in area than the Massif des Maures, the Estérel is even wilder and more rugged. Highwaymen and a weird, unwelcoming landscape discouraged visitors until the 19th century, when Charles Lenthéric, an engineer, wrote: "To the geologist and the botanist it is a most remarkable upheaval of eruptive rocks, whose mineral wealth and remarkable flora call for minutest investigation. To the traveller and the artist it is a piece of nature's most wonderful scene painting."

Verdon valley

For fewer crowds and more countryside, head inland to the vine-fringed villages of the **Haut-Var** with their legends of flying donkeys and fire-breathing dragons. The **Abbaye du Thoronet** ❷ is a beautiful 12th-century monastery hidden in the hills

FACT

The hills above Fréjus contain moving reminders of the last days of French colonialism and World War I: a mosque built by Sudanese soldiers and a cemetery with a Buddhist shrine where 5,000 Annamite (Vietnamese) soldiers are buried.

The Lac de Ste-Croix, largest of the Verdon lakes.

Moustiers pottery, one of the town's claims to fame.

Moustiers-Sainte-Marie.

on the way to the **Gorges du Verdon** ㉕, France's Grand Canyon. The Verdon cuts through limestone cliffs that Iles des Lérins plunge to the torrent 600 metres (2,000ft) below.

The two main places to explore are the villages of **Castellane** and **Moustiers-Sainte-Marie**. Built along part of Napoleon's route from Golfe Juan, Castallane is dominated by an immense limestone rock crowned by the tiny Notre-Dame-du-Roc from where you can see the machicolated Tour Pentagonale and the remains of ramparts. The town centre is pleasant to wander around and has a 14th-century bell tower, La Tour de l'Horloge. Moustiers-Sainte-Marie is famous for its pottery and the silver star hanging from a chain suspended from two peaks above the town, said to have been put there by a crusader.

From the gorges stretch the **Alpes-de-Haute-Provence**, a wild landscape leading up into the French Alps.

Cannes and its islands

In 1834 Lord Brougham "discovered" **Cannes** ㉖ at the eastern end of the Estérel, when it was one of the most insignificant fishing villages on the coast; in his wake arrived wintering British and Russian royals and aristocrats and a few rich Americans, attracted by the temperate climate and lovely setting.

Competition for the *Palme d'Or* at the international film festival, rebranded in 2002 as the Festival de Cannes, begun in the late 1940s to rival the competition held in Venice, consolidated its reputation for glamour. One of the most fashion-conscious seaside promenades in the world, palm-lined **Boulevard de la Croisette** divides a long row of luxury hotels, galleries, boutiques and other expensive speciality shops from the sweep of beach.

Cannes should be viewed from the **Pointe de la Croisette** at the eastern end of the promenade (where the original "Palm-Beach" is located) and from the *vieille ville*, known as **Le Suquet**, just west of it.

The **Iles des Lérins** ㉗, located off Cannes, are called **St Honorat** and **Ste Marguerite** after the 4th-century monk and his sister who founded a monastery

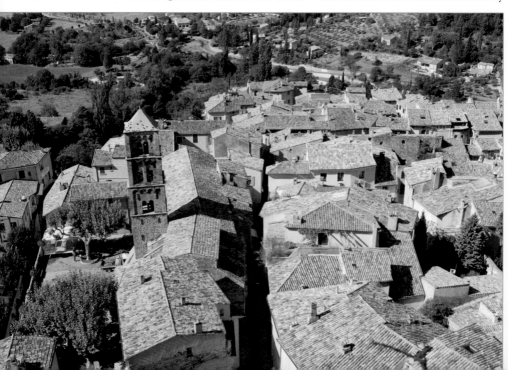

and a nunnery on each. The monastery declined due to pirate attacks, and by the 18th century had become a "monks' galley" for disgraced priests. Cardinal Richelieu built a fort on Ste Marguerite, which was improved by Vauban. It is a melancholy place where the "Man in the Iron Mask", whose story was told by Alexandre Dumas, was imprisoned from 1687 to 1698.

Picasso country

Two of the 20th century's most important artists spent their last years above Cannes (see page 334): Pierre Bonnard (1867–1947) at **Le Cannet**, and Pablo Picasso (1881–1973) at **Mougins ㉘**. From Mougins, in 1937, Picasso first visited nearby **Vallauris**. Returning in 1947, he combined his gifts for painting and sculpture by fashioning and decorating thousands of ceramics at the Galerie Madoura, where originals are still on view. Picasso revitalised the village industry, living there until the mid-1950s. He gave one of three bronze castings of his *Man with a Sheep* to Vallauris on the condition that it be placed in the square.

In the barrel-vaulted, deconsecrated 12th-century chapel where the ceramicists gave Picasso a 70th birthday banquet, he painted the *War and Peace* with War on one wall and Peace opposite, a controversial work conceived during the Korean War and installed in 1959. To complete it, he isolated himself in his vast studio on **Rue de Fournas** in Vallauris for two months. He was moved by the dim light and atmosphere in the austere chapel and he even suggested the chapel be visited by torchlight like the cave paintings at Lascaux.

Just outside the little walled village of **Biot** to the north, also renowned for its glassworks, is the **Musée Fernand Léger** (Wed–Mon May–Oct 10am–6pm, Nov–Apr until 5pm; charge), with gigantic ceramic panels and mosaics on the exterior walls of the building, a spectacularly colourful sight burnished by the strong sun of the Midi.

Beyond is the plain of Valbonne, the vast **Sophia-Antiopolis** technology park, and above it, **Grasse ㉙**, a sheltered retreat of pink villas and palm trees. This was the home of another

Glass vase and plate from Biot.

Cannes seafront.

FACT

The Fragonard museum, surrounded by a charming formal garden, contains copies of his masterpiece – *The Progress of Love*, panels painted for Mme du Barry, now in the Frick Collection, New York.

Flower petals used in the manufacture of perfume at the Molinard distillery.

important artist, Jean-Honoré Fragonard. Here he lived in the 17th-century country house that is now the **Villa-Musée Fragonard** (currently closed for restoration). There have been perfume distilleries in Grasse since the 16th century. Two of them, Fragonard and Molinard, give tours that explain the difference between *enfleurage*, extraction and distillation, methods of obtaining the essences that are sent to Paris. At the **Musée International de la Parfumerie**, housed in an elegant 18th-century mansion, you can observe the history of perfume manufacture, see a remarkable collection of perfume bottles and Marie-Antoinette's travelling case. Best of all, smell the perfumed plants themselves in a rooftop greenhouse (www.museesdegrasse.com; Apr–Sept daily 10am–7pm Oct–Mar Wed–Mon 10am–5pm; charge). The city of Grasse and the perfume industry are evoked in Patrick Süskind's imaginative novel, *Perfume*.

Gorges du Loup

To the northeast of Grasse are the dramatic **Gorges du Loup** ㉚ which

have a number of interesting villages to discover, especially for walkers. At **Le-Bar-sur-Loup** is a 16th-century castle, and a Gothic church with an extraordinary 15th-century painting of *La Dance Macabre* (The Dance of Death) in the nave. The tourist office has details of the local walks.

At the south end of the Gorges du Loup is another good walking centre, the village of **Pont-du-Loup**, which is surrounded by spectacular mountain scenery marred only by the ruins of a mighty viaduct blown up by the Germans in 1944.

Climbing high above Pont-du-Loup is the stunning perched village of **Gourdon**. The majestic château at the entrance to the village, which dates back to the Middle Ages, has beautiful ornate gardens (tel: 04 93 09 68 02; gardens only Apr–Sept; guided tour by appointment). There are three styles of gardens; a trim Le Nôtre, a romantic Italianesque, and an apothecary garden of medicinal plants.

Tourrettes-sur-Loup is strategically situated between two ravines. To the west of the village are troglodytes

THE PERFUMES OF GRASSE

The gentle climate, rich soil and cradle of mountains that protect it from the north wind make Grasse ideal for flower production almost all year round. Golden mimosa blooms in March. By early summer, there are many acres of fragrant roses, ready to be picked. Jasmine appears in the autumn. And, high above the town, the mountains are terraced with row upon row of lavender.

The perfume industry in Grasse originated from immigrant Italian glovemakers in the 16th century. These glovemakers discovered the wonderful scents of the area and began perfuming their soft leather gloves at a time when the odour of the populace definitely required some masking.

Today, Grasse is better known for improving raw materials imported from other countries. Nonetheless, you can still see flowers waiting to be processed each morning. The flowers must be picked early, when the oil is most concentrated, and delivered immediately. It takes enormous quantities of the blooms to produce even the tiniest amounts of "absolute" perfume: about 750 kilos of roses for just one kilo of rose "absolute", about 4,000 kilos to produce one kilo of "essential oil". The highly-trained "noses" can identify and classify hundreds of scents.

Parfumerie Galimard in Grasse runs workshops at its Studio des Fragrances, where you can learn to create your own perfume.

dwellings carved into the rock. The narrow twisting streets of the old village have some art galleries and craft shops, especially around the Grande Rue but not enough to spoil its quaintness. To the north of the village the Chapelle St-Jean has some naïve frescos.

Matisse's masterpiece

"Au fond," Picasso said about one of his Côte d'Azur neighbours, *"il n'y a que Matisse."* ("After all is said and done, there is only Matisse.") And Matisse (1869–1954) considered his **Chapelle du Rosaire** (Tue, Thu 10am–11.30, 2–5.30pm; Mon, Wed, Sat pm only, closed mid-Nov–mid-Dec; Mass Sun 10am; charge), painted for the Dominican nuns at **Vence** ③, northeast of Grasse on the D2210, his masterpiece. In the Villa La Rêve nearby, the bedridden artist was in the habit of making large wall drawings with a thick, long-handled brush and Indian ink. These became the mural-sized black line drawings on the white tiles of the chapel, completed in 1951.

In another mode, Matisse had begun to make gouache-painted *papiers découpés* (paper cut-outs). He called this "drawing in colour" with his scissors, and it is the method he used to design the windows and vestments. He created green, red, violet, rose, black and white chasubles, which were worn by the priest according to the liturgical calendar. The nuns' habits were black and white. It is only during Mass, therefore, that Matisse's colour scheme can be fully appreciated. His designs are on display in a gallery next to the chapel.

St-Paul-de-Vence to Antibes

Artists who worked along the Mediterranean were attracted by the quality of the light, which has, by all accounts, always been especially fine at **St-Paul-de-Vence** ③ directly south of Vence. A walled town with 16th-century ramparts almost intact, St Paul was "discovered" by artists (among them, Signac and Bonnard) in the 1920s.

La Colombe d'Or at the entrance to the village, an exclusive hotel and restaurant patronised by well-known entertainers, has developed from the

A golden dove welcomes you to La Colombe d'Or in St-Paul-de-Vence.

St-Paul-de-Vence.

FACT

Juan-les-Pins was practically invented by the US millionaire Frank Jay Gould, who made it a sought-after resort between the wars. Here was the "bright tan prayer rug of a beach" that F. Scott Fitzgerald spoke of in his novel *Tender is the Night*.

café where pre-war painters gathered to view the Mediterranean or the Alps over terraced hillsides, enjoying the healing warmth and fresh air. Today the hotel has a priceless collection of works donated by visiting artists; in the garden are Léger mosaics, a Calder mobile and an exquisite Braque dove (best seen by visiting the restaurant, an expensive but memorable experience).

St-Paul is a perfectly formed hill village with walls ideal for strolling round and admiring the vista of swimming pools, villas and cypresses as far as the eye can see. It is, however, extremely popular, and its narrow winding main street becomes jammed with visitors.

Just outside the village the **Fondation Maeght** (daily; charge) occupies a white concrete and rose-coloured brick structure designed by Spanish architect J.L. Sert. In addition to the 20th-century paintings in the building itself, there are several outdoor sculpture areas among the pines with works by Giacometti, Calder, Miró, Arp and others. Inside you can see works by

Braque, Bonnard, Kandinsky and Chagall, whose huge, colourful *La Vie* expresses joy in all aspects of life.

Cagnes

Auguste Renoir spent the last 12 years of his life at **Cagnes-sur-Mer** ❸❸ where his home, now the **Musée Renoir** (Wed–Mon 10am–noon, 2–5pm. closed public hols; charge), remains almost exactly as it was when he died.

The old town, **Haut-de-Cagnes**, is squeezed tightly into its walls and is crowned by its 14th-century château. Inside the ramparts are many splendid Renaissance houses with arcades. At the top of the town is the Château-Musée Grimaldi with a wonderful crenellated tower (Weds–Mon 10am–noon, 2–5pm; charge). At the entrance to the castle there is an arcaded courtyard with a grand staircase leading to the galleried loggia. The ground floor explains the history of the olive tree, while the former Marquise's boudoir has 40 paintings of thirties cabaret artist Suzy Solidor. And the Musée d'Art Moderne Méditerranéen is on the top floor.

The beach at Promenade des Anglais, Nice.

Antibes

Antibes ❸ and **Cap d'Antibes** face Nice and St-Jean-Cap-Ferrat across the Baie des Anges (Bay of Angels). Here, sandy French beach turns into Italian shingle.

The "Antiopolis" of the Greeks, Antibes was a Roman arsenal and, until 1860, the first French port west of the Var. Today **Port-Vauban** is the centre of Mediterranean yachting, sheltering some of the world's most expensive yachts. Remains of the Vauban-built ramparts now constitute the sea wall and the imposing Fort Carré can still be seen to the north. On a terrace overlooking the sea is the 12th-century Grimaldi château, reconstructed in the 16th century and now home to the magnificent **Musée Picasso** (Tue–Sun 10am–6pm, closed public hols; charge). It contains a remarkably unified collection of more than 50 works Picasso painted here in 1946 when offered the château to use as a studio.

Juan-les-Pins, south of Antibes, has an active nightlife, with many of the clubs open until 4am. Expensive villas and hotels are hidden by high walls and vegetation; but take the D2559 around **Cap d'Antibes** for the coastal views, the sailor's offerings at the **Sanctuaire de la Garoupe**, and the **Jardin Thuret** (Mon–Fri), named after the horticulturist who acclimatised a number of the tropical plants that give the Côte what the French call its "African" appearance. At the southern tip is the glamorous **Hôtel du Cap-Eden-Roc** ("Hôtel des Etrangers" in F. Scott Fitzgerald's novel *Tender is the Night*).

Nice, capital of the Côte

Prefecture of the Alpes-Maritimes, and France's fifth-largest city, **Nice** ❺ was a resort by the mid-18th century. The style of its architecture, from medieval to early 20th-century, is Genoese but it was the British who created the **Promenade des Anglais**. Today the promenade is a 3km (2-mile) traffic-clogged boulevard leading to the **Quai des Etats-Unis**. Near this area of town, behind the Hôtel Negresco, is the **Musée Masséna** (Wed–Mon 10am–6pm; charge). The collection in a sumptuous Belle Epoque villa

Old absinthe bar sign, Antibes.

Overlooking Nice from the hill of Le Château.

FACT

Sports enthusiasts will enjoy reliving great moments at the Musée National du Sport (off A8 west of Nice). Founded in 1963, this is one of the world's largest collections of sports memorabilia, which didn't have a permanent home until it opened at the Stade Allianz Riviera in June 2014. Legends' rackets, cycles, skis and clothing bring to life great moments of French sporting history from the 16th century to the current day.

Nice's Cours Saleya.

relates Nice's history from Bonaparte's Empire to the late 19th century.

Nice is divided by what remains of the Paillon river, now a mere trickle and covered over with promenades and hanging gardens, dominated by the **Acropolis** convention centre and the **Musée d'Art Contemporain** (www.mamac-nice.org; Tue–Sun 10am–6pm; charge) with a collection of modern works, especially the Nice School of Klein, Raysse, César and Arman.

To the south is the **vieille ville**, a maze of winding streets and pastel-coloured houses. Head for Cours Saleya, the site of the colourful morning market and many terrace cafés. Rue Droite has workshops of young French artists, and is also where you will find the Genoese style **Palais Lascaris** (Wed–Mon 10am–6pm; charge), now a museum with 18th-century pharmacy, Flemish tapestries, frescoes and Baroque furniture.

Dominating the old town is the **Cathédrale Ste-Réparate**, dedicated to the city's patron saint. Admire the stucco facade and the coloured ceramic tiles of the belfry and roof.

To the north of the old town you'll find the **Musée National Marc Chagall** (Avenue du Docteur-Ménard; Wed–Mon 10am–6pm; charge), which houses Chagall's masterpiece, *Le Message Biblique*, a series of 17 paintings based on themes from the Old Testament. This affluent suburb of **Cimiez** has excavated Roman ruins, including baths and an amphitheatre often used for festivals. Here also is the **Musée Matisse** (www.musee-matisse-nice.org; Wed–Mon 10am–6pm; charge), which contains many of the artist's drawings and all of his bronzes.

The Riviera Corniches

Until 1860, when France annexed Nice, the Var river was the French border. The **Var Corniche** (Avenue Auguste-Renoir from Cagnes) follows the west bank of the river, tamed since the 19th century. A once controversial motorway (the A8), completed in 1980, runs along the opposite bank a few miles north from Nice before turning east to tunnel through several mountains.

The **Alpes-Maritimes** east of Nice plummet down to the sea, producing some of the most spectacular scenery along the coast. For those prepared to explore, a whole new world awaits in the hinterland of the Alpes-Maritimes; high mountain peaks, plunging gorges, clear sparkling rivers and crowning the most inaccessible craggy peaks, the *villages perchés* (perched villages).

Three corniches, one above the other, traverse the 30km (20 miles) from Nice to Italy. The *grande corniche*, highest and most breathtaking, follows the military road built by Napoleon in 1806. After Nice the coastline changes dramatically, with wide bays giving way to towering craggy cliffs.

Here, **Villefranche-sur-Mer ❸** is a surprisingly unspoilt little town, built round one of the deepest harbours in the world, used by both French and US warships. It is well restored with a huge 16th-century citadel, and lovely pastel-painted Italianate houses on the seafront. Here there are lively bars, and on the Quai Courbet is the 14th-century **Chapelle St-Pierre** (Wed–Mon, closed mid-Nov–mid-Dec; charge) with an interior decorated by poet and dramatist Jean Cocteau (1889–1963), who spent his childhood in Villefranche. In the walls of the citadel are two museums. The former navy barracks house the **Musée Goetz-Boumeester** with a collection of engravings and paintings by Henri Goetz and his wife Christine Boumeester, along with about 100 minor works by artists that they had hung out with like Picasso, Picabia and Miró. Sculptor Antoniucci Volti lived at Villefranche-sur-Mer, and a good collection of his work can be found displayed both inside the **Musée Volti**, and outside in the main courtyard of the citadel (both museums Wed–Mon, closed Sun am and Nov).

Luxurious enclave

Beyond Villefranche-sur-Mer is the refuge of the seriously rich, **Cap Ferrat ❸**, though the 10km (6-mile) drive around the perimeter offers only glimpses of celebrity villas and glorious gardens secreted behind security

The villa that houses the Fondation Ephrussi de Rothschild.

TROPICAL GARDENS OF THE RIVIERA

Most of the exotic botanical gardens on the Riviera were designed during the Belle Epoque, many of them by foreigners who came to live in the mild climate. Some were created for scientific purposes, others as the setting for flamboyant villas. Countless new species of tropical and subtropical plants were introduced, including dark tropical ferns, majestic palms, cacti and succulents, mimosa and the brightly coloured bougainvillea. Villa Ephrussi at **Cap Ferrat** has a series of themed gardens including a formal French garden with musical fountains, a lapidary garden, and a Japanese garden ornamented with shrines. The gardens at Domaine de Rayol in **Rayol-Canadel-sur-Mer** in the Var, range from desert to jungle to underwater. With the mildest climate along the coast, **Menton** has a cluster of wonderful gardens: Serre de La Madone has romantic pools, parterres and pergolas; Jardin Botanique du Val Rahmeh an amazing variety of fruit trees, and Jardin des Colombières an authentic Provençal allure. At **Monaco** the Jardin Exotique, high on a cliff, has a stunning hanging garden of cacti and succulents.

The **Route des Jardins de La Riviera** proposes extensive lists of gardens, parks and villas. The **Route du Mimosa** suggests garden and nurseries between **Bormes-les-Mimosas** and **Grasse**. Details from local tourist offices.

Lotus flower at the Serre de la Madone, one of Menton's myriad gardens open to the public.

Eze.

systems. The **Fondation Ephrussi de Rothschild** (www.villa-ephrussi.com; daily 10am–6pm, July–Aug until 7pm, Nov–Feb Mon–Fri pm only; charge) gives a hint of the lifestyle: huge, whimsical gardens spread right along the crest of the Cap with views on all sides and fine gardens. The pink and white villa was built to house the art collection of Baroness Ephrussi de Rothschild and includes magnificent 18th-century furniture, porcelain, carpets and paintings, with ceilings designed to accommodate her Tiepolo paintings.

Just the other side of the Cap is **Beaulieu-sur-Mer**, which lays claim to the best climate on the coast, protected from the north wind by a great rock face. It is thus a popular retirement town, with many elegant rest homes and genteel hotels, surrounded by softly waving palm trees. It also has some of the best hotels on the Riviera. Worth a visit is the **Villa Kérylos** (www.villa-kerylos.com; daily 10am–6pm, July–Aug until 7pm, Nov–Feb Mon–Fri pm only; charge), a complete reconstruction of an ancient Greek villa with cool courtyards open to the sea, and housing a large collection of mosaics, frescoes and furniture.

The tiny village of **Eze 38**, perched high above the sea, is restored to the last stone: a bijou museum of medieval detail, with charming features to be seen at every turn – medieval chimneys, Romanesque windows and tiny rooftop gardens. But its current prosperity belies its troubled past. For most of its history Eze has been nothing but a charred ruin, razed successively over several centuries, enslaved by Saracens, its citizens regularly tortured and burned. What little remains of the château is surrounded by the **Jardin Exotique** (daily; charge), with a fine collection of cacti and succulents.

High up on the *grande corniche* beyond Eze there is a dramatic view of Monaco from the Roman monument at **La Turbie**. The name La Turbie comes from the Latin, *tropaea*, meaning trophy, and the village is named after the vast monument erected to commemorate the conquest of the 45 Alpine tribes who had been attacking Romanised Gaul. It was built between 13 and 5 BC, probably using enslaved tribes as labour. The names of the tribes are inscribed on the monument – the longest intact Roman inscription to have survived into modern times.

Perched Villages

Perched villages are medieval fortified towns built on strategic hilltops to stave off invaders. A few, like Eze, are actually only a short drive from the coast, and can provide a cool break from the busy seaside resorts. Not far from the urban sprawl of Nice are two splendid examples of *villages perchés*, clinging to craggy outcrops above the Paillon river valley. **Peille 39** is the most remote and least-known of these two villages that date from the Middle Ages. The centre is charming with narrow streets and small squares; Place du Mont-Agel has particularly fine stone

houses. Leaving the square you pass the 17th-century Palais Lascaris, and a path takes you to a war memorial, where there is a magnificent view to Cap d'Antibes.

Nearby **Peillon**, considered to be the most stunning perched village, appears as a cluster of houses clutching onto a rocky spur among olives and pines. The narrow streets, often ending in steep stone steps, wind through low-vaulted arches. The main feature is the Chapelle des Pénitents-Blancs, which contains lovely 15th-century frescos.

Ste-Agnès and **Gorbio** are less charismatic, and more tourism-led, but they both have charm. Further into the hinterland are the picturesque villages of **Utelle**, **Lantosque** and **Lucéram**.

High rollers

Between the 1870s and 1930s, **Monte-Carlo** ⓯ was the roulette capital of Europe, and the wintering place of the very rich and of mothers with eligible daughters. The late Prince Rainier III diversified his economic base by

turning the tiny country of **Monaco** into the Miami of the Mediterranean.

Sea, skyscrapers and mountains form concentric circles around the tiny headland that is Monaco. Tourism in Monaco doubled within a few years of Grace Kelly's 1956 televised wedding in the **Cathédrale St-Nicholas** on Le Rocher, alongside the **Musée Océanographique** (www. oceano.mc; daily 10am–6pm with exceptions; charge) and the **Palais des Princes**, Prince Albert II's official residence (daily Apr–Oct 10am–5.30pm, Jul–Aug until 6.30pm; charge). From the Palace, where a daily changing of the guard is still performed, a stroll through the old quarter leads to the cathedral and **Jardin Exotique** (www. jardin-exotique.mc; daily 9am–5pm with exceptions; charge).

Further along the coast, **Menton** ⓰, pretty and well-protected, was the home of a large British colony until 1914 and remains more reserved than its Côte neighbours. It has a good beach and several exotic gardens and in the two weeks around Shrove Tuesday, it hosts a lively lemon festival.

Palace guard at the Palais des Princes.

The legendary Casino de Monte-Carlo.

CORSICA

The least populated but perhaps the loveliest of the larger Mediterranean islands has a flavour as much Italian as French, a proud people and an astonishingly varied landscape.

Main Attractions
Filitosa
St-Florent
Ajaccio
Bonifacio
Sartène
Calvi
Bastia

Calvi, one of Corsica's most popular seaside resorts.

The rugged island of Corsica, with a turbulent history to match, looks like a mountain thrust from the sea, pointing an accusatory and gnarled northern finger, Cap Corse, towards the Genoan Riviera. Its wild and often surprising scenery is its chief glory, ringed by a 960km (600-mile) coastline of world-class sandy beaches, quiet coves, fishing villages, jagged headlands and tumbling rocks. The interior comprises an extraordinary variety of landscapes. There are snow-capped mountains, rocky peaks and clear pools and streams, forests of chestnut and *laricio* pine (used by the Romans for masts), vineyards, olive and orange groves, tropical palms, even a region of arid desert.

Almost two-thirds of the interior is covered with the thick tangle of scented shrubs and wild flowers, known as *maquis* and renowned for concealing bandits; *maquis* was also the name given to World War II French Resistance fighters. Though friendly and welcoming to tourists, traditionally Corsicans are depicted as being fiery by nature.

Early settlements

Evidence of Corsica's earliest occupation by man can be seen in the mystical, majestic granite menhirs at **Filitosa ❶** (www.filitosa.fr/en/; Easter–Oct daily 8am–sunset; charge), carved into the shapes of warriors by megalithic man around 4,000 years ago. Since then, centuries of oppression have dogged the island. Excavations have uncovered Roman remains at **Aléria ❷** (daily; charge), where Greek invaders before them had established a prosperous trading port.

Between the 11th and 13th centuries, Corsica was ruled by the Italian city state of Pisa, resulting in a crop of small, perfectly proportioned Tuscan Romanesque churches. One lies outside the sophisticated yachting centre of **St-Florent ❸**: **Cathédrale de Santa Maria Assunta**, the only remaining vestige of the ancient city of Nebbio. The other is **St-Michele** at nearby **Murato**, where swirling green and white walls dazzle the eye. West of St-Florent, the parched landscape of the **Désert des Agriates** stretches along the coast.

Brief independence

In 1284 the Genoese finally crushed their Pisan enemies in a decisive sea battle, and took Corsica. They were to rule for 484 years: many of their coastal watchtowers can still be seen, such as the one on the promontory at Porto, a wonderful place to watch the sunset. For 15 short, but deeply felt years in the 18th century, Corsica tasted independence under the leadership of Pasquale Paoli.

He was born in **Castagniccia ❹**, a beautiful region of rocky crests and valleys covered in chestnut groves, which was once the island's most prosperous area but is now all but deserted. Tourists outnumber locals by six to one in high season; many Corsicans seek work in mainland France, particularly in government service jobs.

In 1769, Corsica was annexed by Louis XV and it has belonged to France, without ever becoming quite French, ever since. Militant separatist groups continue to dog the island with sporadic violent attacks against the authorities. Most prominent is the Front Libéral National Corse (FLNC), but it was apparently an obscure breakaway group that ordered the assassination, in early 1998, of the chief French government official on the island. Subsequent political scandals involving French officials have maintained support for the nationalists.

Mainland connections

Two boat companies, SNCM and Corsica Ferries, service the island from mainland France with crossings all year from Toulon, Marseille and Nice arriving at the ports of Ajaccio, Bastia, Calvi, L'Ile-Rousse and Porto Vecchio. The main airport is at Ajaccio, while more minor ones are located at Bastia, Calvi and Figari.

Visitors who want to explore Corsica are hard-put to do so without a car – notably one that will easily negotiate the many narrrow, twisting inland roads.

The Corsican flag depicts the head of a Moor, once blindfolded but whose bandana was pushed back above his eyes in the eighteenth century – a change symbolic of a new clarity of direction for the island.

Eyeing up the souvenirs.

Corsica

0   20 km
0   20 miles

TIP

A wonderful way to see the island is by taking the narrow-gauge railway between Ajaccio and Bastia by way of Corte. The little train called 'Trinighellu' is a really convenient and fast way of getting around Corsica.

Built to be impregnable – Bonifacio old town.

Ajaccio and Corse-du-Sud

Ajaccio , with palm-lined boulevards and a wonderful morning market, is Corsica's capital and the birthplace of Napoleon Bonaparte, who had to learn French when he went to military school on the mainland, since he spoke only Corsican, a dialect of Italian. Visit his baptismal font in the **Cathédrale Notre-Dame-de-la-Miséricorde** and his childhood home, **Maison Bonaparte** (Rue Saint-Charles; Tue–Sun Apr–Sept 10.30am–noon, 1.15–5.50pm, rest of year until 4pm; charge). Most interesting though, is the renovated **Palais Fesch**, built by Napoleon's uncle, Cardinal Fesch, who amassed a notable collection of early Italian paintings during the Italian campaign and displayed them here (50 Rue Fesch; Wed–Mon 10am–5pm, closed Thur, Fri, Sun am; charge).

Ajaccio heralds the island's southern *département*, Corse-du-Sud, whose coastline is studded with sandy bays and long white beaches, **Plage de Palombaggia** and **Plage de Pinarello** near the busy holiday resort of **Porto-Vecchio** **6**.

At the southern tip is **Bonifacio** **7**, with superb seaward views as far as Sardinia, and a fortified old town crowning the hilltop, and bustling harbour, where you can dine at one of the many seafood restaurants lining the quay.

Inland, **Sartène** **8** is an austere medieval town of grey granite where each Good Friday a re-enactment of Christ's walk to Calvary takes place in a procession called Catenacciu.

Quenza **9** is an attractive hill village with a fine church; nearby is the well-known beauty spot, **Col de Bavella**.

The west coast

North of Ajaccio, from **Porto** **10** to Calvi, the coastline is at its wildest and loveliest, no more so than at the **Golfe de Porto**, where the red cliffs of the **Calanche** plunge a sheer 300 metres (1,000ft) into the sea below.

The Porto River, calm where it reaches the sea, can be followed inland to the point where several mountain torrents form the **Gorges de Spelunca**. The old mule track to the mountain

village of **Evisa** passes through these gorges, and a walk in the lowest part gives a good idea of what the island's former "road system" used to be like.

Mountainous interior

Further inland is the island's highest mountain, the 2,706-metre (8,877ft) **Monte Cinto ⑪**, on the slopes of which, at **Haut-Asco**, you can ski. This is the **Niolo** region, the one part of Corsica where the husbandry of sheep and goats still provides the main income.

At the island's centre is **Corte ⑫**, Pasquale Paoli's capital during independence, and still the 'spiritual capital' of the island. It is seat of Corsica's university and home to the **Musée de la Corse** (July–Sept daily 10am–8pm, Apr–June and Oct Tue–Sun until 6pm; Nov–Mar Tue–Sat until 5pm; charge). A steep climb up to the old town brings you to the ancient citadel which houses the museum. The collection relates the history of the island and people, from the discovery of the island to present day.

The north

Moving back to the coast, still in sight of Monte Cinto, is one of Corsica's major seaside resorts, **Calvi ⑬**, where Admiral Nelson lost an eye during an attack on the town in 1794. Although besieged by tourists in summer – there's a good jazz festival in June – and reminiscent of a kitsch copy of the resorts along the Côte d'Azur, it does have some charm. The 15th-century citadelle, a splendid Genoese fortification overlooking the marina, is a base for France's crack Foreign Legion. You can take a pleasant stroll through its cobbled streets, deserted in low season.

To the southwest are the **Restonica** and **Tavignano** gorges.

Bastia ⑭ is the principal town of Haute-Corse, the island's northern *département*, and a major commercial port. It has a colourful, Mediterranean flavour, with a lively square and Vieux Port, and a 16th-century citadel. From there you could head north and explore remote **Cap Corse ⑮**, particularly the west coast, where the lovely port of **Centuri** lies near the tip. Allow time on the narrow, twisting road.

A western Mediterranean cruise, perhaps encompassing Sardinia and the Italian Riviera, is one way to take in Corsica's sights.

Sailing off the coast of Corsica.

FOOD AND DRINK SPECIALITIES

The island's *maquis* and forests are rich with game in season, and wild pigs that feed mainly on acorns and chestnuts. Corsica is famed for its *charcuterie* such as *prisutta* (smoked ham), *salamu* (smoked cured sausage) and *salsiccia* (spicy cured sausage). Avoid the mass-produced *charcuterie* and opt for small-scale traditional producers. Local meat dishes include *cabrettu*, a pork stew; Sartène tripe and Corsican veal. Other game includes pigeon, partridge and blackbirds traditionally stuffed with myrtle.

Fish and seafood are abundant. Corsica's equivalent to *bouillabaisse* is called *aziminu*. Mussel and oyster cultivation takes place on the east coast. Cheese is mainly made from ewe's and goat's milk. The most popular are the goat's cheeses from Sartène, and ewe's cheeses from Niolo and Alta Rocca. Other good cheeses include those of Venachese, Calinzana and Bastilicacciu. Brocciu, a fromage blanc, is used a lot in cooking as a filling for pasta, tarts and omelettes.

Although not a fine wine region the island's AC wines are good; and a decent beer made from chestnuts is produced at the brewery "La Pietra" – sweet chestnut flour, used to make bread, is mixed with the malt during mashing. Corsica produces quantities of fine olive oil and honey, both of which have AOP status.

TRAVEL TIPS
FRANCE

Transport

Getting There 362
  By Air 362
  By Sea 363
  By Rail 363
  By Bus 363
  By Car 363
Getting Around 364
  Airport Transfers 364
  Paris Métro and RER 364
  By Bus 364
  By Train and Tram 364
  By Air 365
  Taxis 365
  Driving 365
  Motorbikes and Mopeds 366
  Hiring Bicycles 366
  Segway Tours 366
  On Foot 366
  Hitchhiking 367
  Inland Waterways 367

Eating Out

How to Choose 368
Wine – Reading the Label 368
Restaurant Listings 368
Paris 369
Around Paris
  (Ile de France) 371
Le Nord 371
Champagne 371
Lorraine 372
Alsace 372
Normandy 373
Brittany 373
Loire Valley 374
Poitou-Charentes 375
Burgundy and
  Franche-Comté 376
Rhône Valley and the Alps 376
Auvergne 378
Aquitaine 378
Midi-Pyrénées 379
Languedoc and Roussillon 380
Provence and Côte d'Azur 381
Corsica 382

Activities

The Arts 383
  Live Entertainment 383
  Theatre, Dance and Opera 383
  Popular Music 384
  Music Venues 385
  Cinema 385
Festivals and Events 385
Nightlife 386
  Where to Go 386
  Paris 386
  Côte d'Azur 387
Shopping 387
  Where to Shop 387
  Clothing Sizes 387
  Opening Hours 388
  Market Shopping 388
  Shopping by Area 388
  Buying Direct 388
  Export Procedures 389
Sport 389
  Water Sports 389
  Fishing 389
  Air Sports 389
  Cycling 390
  Horse Riding 390
  Golf 390
  Walking 391
  Health and Beauty 391
  Winter and Mountain
    Sports 391
  Potholing 392
Children's Activities 392

A – Z

Admission Charges 393
Budgeting for Your Trip 393
Children 393
Climate 394
Crime and Safety 394
Customs Regulations 394
Disabled Travellers 394
Electricity 395
Embassies and Consulates ... 395
Etiquette 395
Gay and Lesbian Travellers 395

Health and Medical Care 395
Lost Property 396
Maps 396
Media 396
Money 397
Opening Hours 397
Pets 398
Postal Services 398
Religious Services 398
Student Travellers 398
Telephones 399
Tourist Information 399
Visas and Passports 400
Websites 400

Language

Basic Rules 401
Language Study 401
Words and Phrases 401
Emergencies 402
On Arrival 402
On the Road 402
Shopping 402
Sightseeing 402
Dining Out 402
  Breakfast and Snacks 403
  La Viande – Meat 403
  Poissons – Fish 403
In the Café 403
Time 403
Days and Months 403
  Days of the Week 403
  Seasons 403
  Months 403
On the Telephone/Internet 403
Arts and Architecture 404

Further Reading

History and Social
  Commentary 404
Belles Lettres 404
French Literature 404
Classics by Date 404
Food and Wine 404
Living in France 404
Other Insight Guides 404

TRANSPORT

GETTING THERE AND GETTING AROUND

GETTING THERE

By Air

The boom in low-cost airlines has transformed air travel to France, with over 25 airports serviced directly from the UK. If you are flexible on when you fly, prices can be low, but at high season they can rise dramatically, at which point the no-frills angle becomes less attractive. The following airlines currently fly regularly to France, but the situation is constantly changing.

From the UK

Air France has regular flights to 14 airports, including Bordeaux, Lyon, Marseille, Nice, Paris and Toulouse.
British Airways flies from various destinations in the UK to Bordeaux, Lyon, Marseille, Nice, Paris and Toulouse, and to Angers and Quimper (summer only), Chambéry and Grenoble (winter only).
Easyjet flies to Bordeaux, Biarritz, Grenoble, Marseille, La Rochelle, Lyon, Montpellier, Nice, Paris, Nantes, Brest and Toulouse.
Jet2 flies from Manchester, Bradford, East Midlands and Newcastle to Chambéry, with flights also from Bradford to Bergerac, Nice and Paris, and from Manchester to Nice, Grenoble and Toulouse.
Ryanair flies to Beauvais, Bergerac, Béziers, Biarritz, Bordeaux, Brive, Carcassonne, Dinard, Lourdes, Grenoble, La Rochelle, Clermont-Ferrand, Limoges, Deauville-Normandy, Marseille, Montpellier, Nîmes, Perpignan, Poitiers, Rodez, Toulon and Tours.
Flybe flies to over 20 airports including Paris, Bordeaux, Nice, Toulouse, Lyon and Avignon.

From the US

Travellers from North America can obtain direct flights to Paris and major destinations in France, such as Nice and Lyon, via Air France and other national airlines. American Airlines, United Airlines and Delta also fly to France. Delta has a daily flight to Nice from New York.

Paris Airports

Paris has two airports:
Roissy–Charles de Gaulle, 23km (15 miles) north of the city via the A1 or RN2.
Orly, 14km (9 miles) south of the centre via the A6 or RN7; tel: 3950, or from overseas 01 70 36 39 50 www.aeroportsdeparis.fr for both airports.

See page 364 for details on travelling to and from (as well as between) the two airports.

Airline Numbers

UK
Air France
Tel: 0870 142 4343
www.airfrance.com
British Airways
Tel: 0844 493 0787
www.britishairways.com
Easyjet
Tel: 0330 365 5000
www.easyjet.com

Jet2
Tel : 0800 408 1350
www.jet2.com

Ryanair
Tel: 0871-246 0000
www.ryanair.com

France
Air France
Tel: 3654

The Channel Tunnel

The Channel Tunnel offers fast, frequent rail services by Eurostar between London (St Pancras) and Ashford in the UK to Lille (1 hour 30 mins), Paris (Gare du Nord – 2 hours 30 mins, and Disneyland Resort), and since May 2015 direct routes to Lyon and Marseille. Tel: 09432-186186, www.eurostar.com in the UK.

Eurotunnel takes cars and their passengers from Folkestone to Calais on a simple drive-on-drive-off system. The journey time through the tunnel is about 35 minutes. Reservations are not needed – you just turn up and take the next service. However, it is advisable to reserve in advance if you wish to travel at peak times. Eurotunnel runs 24 hours a day, all year round, with a service at least once an hour through the night. The cost varies widely between peak and off-peak hours, so you can save money by travelling late at night or in the early morning. Good deals are often available through the website. Enquiries in UK, tel: 0870-535 3535, www.eurotunnel.com.

British Airways
Tel: 08 25 82 54 00
Ryanair
Tel: 871 246 0002

USA
Air France
Tel: 1-800-237 2747
British Airways
Tel: 1-800-AIRWAYS
Delta
Tel: 1-800-221 1212

By Sea

There are several ferry services operating from the UK, the Republic of Ireland and the Channel Islands to the northern ports of France. All of them carry cars as well as foot passengers. The ports of Boulogne, Calais and Le Havre offer direct access by motorway to Paris; there is almost direct motorway access via Dunkerque and Caen.

Brittany Ferries sail from Portsmouth to Saint-Malo, Le Havre and Caen, Plymouth and Cork (Eire) to Roscoff, and from Poole to Cherbourg (May–Oct only). Tel: 0871 244 0744, www. brittany-ferries.com.

DFDS Seaways sail from Dover to Dunkerque and Calais and Newhaven to Dieppe Tel: 0871 574 7235, www. dfdsseaways.co.uk.

P&O Ferries operate crossings from Dover to Calais and Hull to Zeebrugge. Situated 56km (35 miles) from the French border, Zeebrugge has good motorway access to the Paris region. The overnight services offer entertainment. Tel: 0871 664 5645, www.poferries.com.

MyFerryLink sails from Dover to Calais. Tel: 0844 2482 100, www. myferrylink.com

Corsica Ferries operate crossings from Toulon and Nice to Corsica. Tel: 0825 095 095 (France); www.corsica-ferries.fr. And SNCM sails from Toulon, Marseille and Nice to Corsica. Tel: 3260 (France); www.sncm.fr.

By Rail

France has a fast, efficient rail network operated by the SNCF (Société Nationale des Chemins de Fer de France). Its much-praised TGV programme is developing all the time, offering comfortable express services via Paris and Lille to many destinations across France and into other European cities. For visitors travelling from Paris, the train is a comfortable way to reach any major destination in France, with most express services offering refreshments (and even play areas for young children). There are six main stations serving the provinces from Paris, so check which one you need before setting off. Getting across country by rail is less easy. Car and bicycle hire is available at most main stations (see www.bikes. sncf.com).

Tickets and Information

Tickets may be booked for through journeys from outside France.

In the UK, tickets, including ferry travel, can be booked from larger National Rail stations. National Rail travel centres can supply details of continental services or contact **Voyages-SNCF**, 193 Piccadilly, London W1J 9EU, tel: 0844-848 5848, uk.voyages-sncf.com. If you are a student, under 26 years old, or over 60 don't forget to ask about discounts.

In France, SNCF has a central reservation office in Paris, tel: 3635; www.voyages-sncf.com.

Rail Passes

There are several rail passes available to foreign visitors, which must be purchased before leaving for France.

In the UK, an Interrail Pass offers unlimited rail travel in France on a specified number of days (from three to eight) within a month for EU citizens. This pass is available online at www.interrail.eu or http://uk. voyages-sncf.com.

In the US, visitors have a wider choice of passes, including France Railpass, Saverpass and Eurail Select. The France Rail 'n' Drive pass offers a flexible rail and car-rental package. Various companies offer these passes; try the following websites:
www.railfrance.com
www.euroilways.com

By Bus

Eurolines is a consortium of around 30 coach companies, operating in France and throughout Europe. They operate services from London (Victoria) to many major French destinations. Some (such as Paris) are daily, others are seasonal and some have services several times a week throughout the year.

This is one of the cheapest ways of reaching France, and there are discounts available for young people and senior citizens. The ticket includes the ferry crossing (via Dover). **National Express** coaches have connections from most major towns

Validating Tickets

Rail tickets bought in France must be validated using the orange automatic date-stamping machine at the entrance to the platform. Failure to do so may incur a fine. These machines are marked *compostez votre billet.*

in the UK that link up with the London departures.

For details, contact Eurolines UK, 52 Grosvenor Gardens, Victoria, London SW1W 0AU, tel: 08717-818181, www.eurolines.com.

By Car

Almost all the motorways in France are privately owned and subject to tolls (credit cards are usually accepted). The trip from the northern ports to the south of France costs around €100 in tolls one-way. The benefits of paying for the use of the motorway can be seen in the high standards of maintenance of the roads and the frequent rest areas, picnic sites and catering facilities.

Free motorway maps are often available at motorway service stations and are useful as they mark the position and facilities of all the rest areas en route. Note that petrol at these stations is more expensive than at supermarkets.

If speed is not of the essence and you intend to make the drive part of your holiday, follow the green holiday route signs (BIS) to your destination – these form part of a national network of *bison futé* routes to avoid traffic congestion at peak periods. You will discover parts of France you never knew existed and are more likely to arrive relaxed. The first and last *(rentrée)* weekends in August and the public holiday on 15 August are usually the worst times to travel, so avoid them if you can. (For Driving, see page 365) For motorway information, visit www. autoroutes.fr.

Road signs at Chambord.

GETTING AROUND

Airport Transfers

From Charles de Gaulle Airport

Rail
The TGV-SNCF train station is located between Terminals 2C, 2D, 2E and 2F for other Terminals take the free shuttle bus to the train station. From there take the RER to Métro station Gare du Nord, St Michel or Châtelet, from where you can change onto most Métro lines. The RER runs every 10–20 minutes from 5am to 11.45pm. The average journey time is 30–40 minutes.

Bus
Roissy Bus shuttles between Roissy/ Charles de Gaulle Etoile and Rue Scribe, near Place de l'Opéra from Terminals 1, 2A, 2B, 2C, 2D, 2E and 2F and 3D. Buses run every 15–20 minutes 5.15am–midnight, journey time 60–75 minutes.
Air France Bus (to Métro Porte Maillot or Charles de Gaulle Etoile) leaves from Terminal 2 or Terminal 1 arrival-level Gate 34. The bus runs every 30 minutes 5.45am–11pm; journey time 50 minutes.
The night bus Noctilien leaves from Terminal 3 to Paris Gare de l'Est every 60 minutes from midnight to 5.30am.
There is a shuttle bus service to **Disneyland Paris**, which departs every 30–45 minutes.

Taxi
By far the most expensive but unquestionably the easiest solution, especially for those laden with bags or children. The cost will be clearly indicated on the meter, although a small supplement is charged for each large piece of luggage, pushchairs, and pets.
It is customary, though not required, to tip the driver – usually about 10 percent of the fare.

From Orly Airport

Rail
Take the shuttle from Orly Sud or from Orly Ouest to the Orly train station, Pont de Rungis RER Line C. The RER stops at Austerlitz, Pont St-Michel, and the Quai d'Orsay. It runs every 15–20 minutes from 5.40am–10.40pm. The journey takes about 40 minutes.
Orlyval is an automatic train that runs between Antony (the nearest

RER to Orly) and Paris about every 5 minutes from 6am–11pm. The journey takes about 20–30 minutes.

Bus
Orlybus goes to Place Denfert-Rochereau and leaves from Orly Sud Gate H, or Orly Ouest arrival-level Gate G. This bus runs every 10–15 minutes from 5.35am–midnight.
Air France Bus goes to Invalides and Gare Montparnasse, leaving from Orly Sud Gate L, or Orly Ouest arrival-level Gate D. It runs every 30 minutes from 6am–11pm. The journey takes about 30 minutes.
A bus service to **Disneyland Paris** runs every 45 minutes.
As of 2013, a tram runs between Orly and Villejuif–Louis Aragon, which connects to the subway. The tram runs every 6 minutes and the journey takes about 35 minutes.

Between Airports

In addition to the above services, an **Air France bus** links Charle-de-Gaulle and Orly, leaving each airport every 15–20 minutes 5.45am–11pm.

Paris Métro and RER

The Paris Métro is one of the world's oldest subway systems and some of its stations are almost historic monuments. Despite that, it is quick and efficient. The Métro operates roughly 5.30am–12.40am; its comprehensive map and signage make it virtually impossible to get lost; the lines are identified by number and the names of their terminals. It operates in conjunction with the RER, suburban regional

The Strasbourg tramway.

express trains, which operate on five lines, identified as A–E.
Flat-fare tickets are valid for both the subway and the bus, but a book *(carnet)* of 10 gives a considerable saving. Buy them at bus or Métro stations and some *tabacs*.
Another option is the Paris-*visite* card, which is valid for 1–5 consecutive days on the Métro, bus and railway in the Paris/Ile de France region, in zones 1–3, and 1–5. It also gives discounted entry to various tourist sites; available from main Métro and SNCF stations and the airports. For shorter stays, buy the *Mobilis* card, which allows an unlimited number of trips in any one day on the Métro, bus and suburban trains and the night buses (zones 1–5). Buy it from Métro offices or mainline train and bus stations. Information on all passes is available from RATP, tel: 3246, www. ratp.fr, or Hello Paris in the UK (see page 383).

By Bus

Details of bus routes and timetables are generally available free from bus stations *(gares routières)*, which are often close to railway stations, or tourist offices. They will also give details of bus tours and sightseeing excursions.

By Train and Tram

Information on services is available from stations *(gares SNCF)*. If you intend to travel extensively by train it may be worth obtaining a rail pass before leaving home (see page 363). Always check on any

discounts available, e.g. the *Carte Enfant+* if you are travelling with children. Children under 4 travelling free can't have their own seat unless you pay a small extra fee. Four to 12 year olds travel for half fare. People travelling in groups of six or more can also obtain discounts (of 20–40 percent depending on numbers). Many large towns have efficient tramway networks that service the city centre, and some suburbs. The main towns are Bordeaux, Lyon, Clermont-Ferrand, Lille, Lyon, Marseille, Nancy, Nantes, Nice and Rouen. This form of transport is popular and is expanding throughout France. Tickets can be obtained from automatic machines at Métro stations, or ticket offices at train and tramway stations.

By Air

Air France operate the majority of flights within France but they face stiff competition from the budget airlines that now fly from the UK to many provincial airports. Using France's excellent train service to get around the country is cheaper and more comfortable than flying.

Taxis

Taxis are most readily available at airports and railway stations. In Paris there are almost 500 taxi ranks, but be careful in the capital to hail only a genuine taxi (with a light on the roof); other operators may charge exorbitant fares.

Taxi drivers in Paris operate on three tariffs:
Tariff A 10am–5pm Mon–Sat
Tariff B 5pm–10am Mon–Sat and all day Sunday from 7am–midnight.
Tariff C at night in the suburbs and during the day in the outlying districts of Hauts-de-Seine, Seine Saint-Denis and Val-de-Marne, when the taxi has no client for the return journey.

A 10 percent tip to the driver is usual. Any complaints about Paris taxis should be addressed in writing to the **Service des Taxis**, Préfecture de Police, 36 Rue des Morillons, 75015 Paris, tel: 08 21 00 25 25.

Roads in France

Motorways (*Autoroutes*) are designated "A" roads, National Highways (*Routes Nationales*) "N" or "RN" roads. Local roads are known as "D" routes.

Priorité à Droite – Give Way to the Right

On main roads, traffic on the major road normally has priority, with traffic being halted on minor approach roads with one of the following signs.
Cédez le passage – give way
Vous n'avez pas la priorité – you do not have right of way
Passage protégé – no right of way
    But care should be taken in towns, and in rural areas where there may not be any road markings (watch out for farm vehicles), in which case you will be expected to give way to traffic coming from the right.

If an oncoming driver flashes their headlights it is to indicate that he or she has priority – not the other way around.

Priority is always given to emergency services and also to vehicles from public utility (eg gas, electric and water) companies.

A yellow diamond sign indicates that you have priority; the diamond sign with a diagonal black line indicates you do not have priority.

Driving

Licences

European Union, US, Canadian and Australian licences are all valid in France. Foreigners cannot drive on a provisional licence.

Insurance

You should always carry your vehicle's registration and insurance documents and personal identity papers.

Additional insurance cover, which can include a get-you-home service, is offered by several organisations including the **British Automobile Association** (tel: 0800-085 7253, www.theaa.com).

Information

Automobile Club Association, 14 rue Paul Baudry, 75008 Paris, tel: 01 40 55 43 00, www.automobileclub. org. Co-ordination with automobile clubs from other countries, mainly assistance with breakdown. They don't hire out cars but can give local numbers, etc.

For information about road conditions see www.bison-fute.gouv. fr or tune in to local radio stations (frequencies are often indicated on signs beside roads and motorways).

Online Information

www.mappy.fr provides maps and itineraries for all European journeys. www.autoroutes.fr suggests routes on French motorways and gives information on tolls, weather, safety, etc.
www.infotrafic.com.provides up-to-date information on road conditions.

Petrol

Sans plomb is unleaded petrol (gas); leaded petrol is no longer available. Petrol is generally slightly less expensive than in the UK, while diesel (*gazoil*) is about 20 percent cheaper. Fuel on the *autoroutes* is the most expensive; most French drivers fill up at supermarkets.

Car Hire

Hiring a car is expensive and some fly/drive deals work out well if you're only going for a short visit. French Railways offers a good deal on its combined train/car rental bookings. Weekly rates work out better than daily hire and it can be cheaper to arrange hire through an agent in your own country before leaving for France. The minimum age to hire a car is 21. Some firms will not rent to people under 26 or over 60. The hirer must have held a full licence for at least one year.

The central offices of the major car hire companies are listed below. Car hire in France can be arranged through them or online or through your airline at the same time as you book your ticket. To hire a car locally, check telephone directories or ask at tourist offices.
Avis, tel: 08 21 23 07 60
www.avis.com
Budget, tel: 08 25 00 35 64
www.budget.com
Europcar, tel: 08 25 35 83 58
www.europcar.co.uk
Hertz, tel: 08 25 80 09 00
www.hertz.com

Rules of the Road

The **minimum age** for driving in France is 18.
Britons must remember to drive on the right: extra care should be taken when crossing the carriageway or when emerging from a junction – when it is easy to end up on the left side without thinking.

Full or dipped **headlights** must be used in poor visibility and at night; sidelights are not sufficient unless the car is stationary. Beams must

Scenic Routes

Following a designated tourist route is a sure way of getting to see the major sights of a region. Tourist offices will help with suggestions. Another source of ideas is **Demeure Historique**, 57 Quai de la Tournelle, 75005 Paris, www. demeure-historique.org.

be adjusted for right-hand-drive vehicles, but yellow tints are not compulsory.

The use of **seat belts** (front and rear) in cars, and crash helmets on motorcycles is compulsory. Children under 10 are not permitted to ride in the front seat unless the car is fitted with a rear-facing safety seat or has no rear seat.

The French **drink-driving** limit is 0.5 mg alcohol per litre of blood. This can mean that just two small glasses of wine or beer can take you up to the limit. Since 2013, carrying a breathalyzer in the car has been obligatory although there is no penalty for not observing this law.

Speed Limits

Speed limits are as follows, unless otherwise indicated: 130kph (80mph) on toll motorways; 110kph (68mph) on other motorways and dual carriageways; 90kph (56mph) on other roads except in towns where the limit is 50kph (30mph). There is also a minimum speed limit of 80kph (50mph) on the outside lane of motorways during the day and on level ground. Speed limits are reduced in wet weather as follows: toll motorways 110kph (68mph), dual carriageways 100kph (62mph), other roads 80kph (50mph).

Fines may be levied for speeding: on toll roads the time is printed on your ticket when you enter and can be checked on exit. If you pay on the spot the fine will be lower than if you delay payment, when a surcharge will be added. Nearly all *autoroutes* (motorways) are toll roads.

It is an offence to hold and use a mobile phone while driving.

Accidents and Emergencies

It is compulsory to carry a luminous reflecting jacket to wear, and a red triangle to place at least 30 metres (100ft) behind the car in case of breakdown or accident for all vehicles.

In an emergency, call the police (tel: 17) or use the free emergency

telephones sited every 2km (1 mile) on motorways. If another driver is involved, lock your car and go together to call the police.

It is useful to carry a European Accident Statement Form (obtainable from your insurance company) which will simplify matters in case of an accident.

Motorbikes and Mopeds

Rules of the road are largely the same as for car drivers. The minimum age for driving machines over 80cc is 18 years. Home-country plates must be shown and crash helmets are compulsory. Dipped headlights must be used at all times.

Hiring Bicycles

Bicycles *(vélos)* are readily available for hire. Local tourist offices keep information on hire facilities. Bikes can be carried free on buses and on some trains *(autotrains)*. On other, faster, services you will have to pay.

Travelling by a combination of bike and bus or train can be an excellent way of touring and relieves you of some of the legwork (see page 390).

Self-service public bicycle services, such as Vélo'+ (www. agglo-veloplus.fr), are becoming more and more popular in big towns and cities. Bicycles can be hired out and dropped off at stations, at very low cost using a credit card. Bike network maps are often provided by the local tourist office or see www. bikes.sncf.com for interactive guides for cyclists. Cyclopolitain is a cycle taxi service (www.cyclopolitain.com) available in Bordeaux, Grenoble, Lyon, Nantes, Nice, Orléans, Paris, Reims, Rennes, Toulouse and Tours. The 'taxis' are electric trikes, driven by '*cyclonautes*', which transport you around the city.

Segway Tours

One of the best ways of seeing Paris is to glide around the streets on a Segway Tour (tel: 01 82 88 80 96, http//:paris.citysegwaytours. com). Day tours leave all year round at 9.30am and 2pm and last approximately 3 hours. The night tour (Apr–mid-Oct) leaves at 6.30pm and last around 2 hours. Participants must be over 12 years (under 18s must be accompanied by an adult) and weigh at least 45kg (100lb). All tours start from the Segway office at 24 rue Edgar Faure, 75015 Paris; the nearest metro is Dupleix, line 6).

On Foot

There are countless opportunities for exploring France on foot; given the time, you could cross the whole of France north-south or west-east by following footpaths. All the main footpaths in France form part of the national network of long-distance footpaths (*Sentiers de Grandes Randonnées* or GR). The routes are numbered for easy identification, e.g. the GR1 takes you around Paris and the Ile de France, covering 630km (395 miles).

The French Ramblers' Association, Fédération Française de la Randonnée Pédestre (FFRP), publishes Topo-guides (guidebooks incorporating IGN 1:50,000-scale maps) to all France's footpaths but they are available only in French. For information contact the FFRP, Centre d'Information Sentiers et Randonnées, 64 Rue Dessous des Berges, 75013 Paris, tel: 01 44 89 93 93, www.ffrandonnee.fr. These guides are available in good bookshops in France, as well as abroad. The IGN Blue series maps, at a scale of 1:25,000, are ideal for walkers.

There are also many opportunities for guided walks to be found in cities and towns throughout France. For themed walks of Paris check out http//:en.parisinfo.com, and for a free tour every day try Sandemans (www.newparistours.com). For other city and regional walks check with the local tourist office (see page 399).

Walking Tours and Holidays

Each *département* has its own ramblers' organisation (operating under the FFRP umbrella), which arranges a variety of activities throughout the year: guided walks taking a day, a weekend or more, as well as walks with a particular theme, such as flowers or wildlife. Tourist offices will give information about local clubs.

Various walking holidays with accommodation either in hotels or under canvas are available. Some are organised through tour operators in the UK, others are bookable through the French tourist offices and local organisations.

Independent travellers can take advantage of low-priced accommodation offered in *gîtes d'étapes*, hostels offering basic facilities, which are to be found on many of the GR routes and in mountain regions. For more information contact the Gîtes de France organisation (tel: 0871 277 0399; http://en.gites-de-france.com).

A few of the UK operators are:
Headwater Holidays
Old School House, Chester Road,
Northwich, Cheshire CW8 1LE
Tel: 01606-828560.
www.headwater.com
Holidays in the Creuse, Dordogne,
Provence, and other areas.
Ramblers Holidays
Lemsford Village, Welwyn Garden City,
Herts AL8 7TR
Tel: 01707-331133.
www.ramblersholidays.co.uk
Range of tours, including the Alps,
Cévennes, Pyrénées and Corsica.
Sherpa Expeditions
1B Osiers Road, Wandsworth, London
SW18 1NL
Tel: 0800 008 7741
www.sherpaexpeditions.com
Independent guided walking and
cycling for a fortnight or just a
weekend.

Hitchhiking

Hitchhiking is not generally
recommended, but if you take
sensible precautions it is an
inexpensive way to get around. It is
difficult to get a lift out of the Channel
ports, so it may be worth taking a
bus or train for the first leg of your
journey. Hitching is forbidden on
motorways, but you can wait on slip
roads or at toll booths. **Allostop** is a
nationwide organisation that aims to
connect hikers with drivers (you pay
a registration fee and a contribution
towards the fuel), www.allostop.net.

Inland Waterways

One of the most pleasant ways of
exploring a small corner of France is
on board a narrowboat or one of the
other craft that can be hired on many
of the country's navigable canals and
rivers. Holidays on inland waterways
are very popular, with choices ranging
from piloting your own hired boat to
enjoying the luxury of "hotel barges",
where the navigation and catering is
all taken care of for you.

Even if you have never navigated
before, you are likely to feel very
confident after just a minimum of
instruction (foreigners require no
permit or licence). Several companies
offer package holidays afloat,
including the following:

UK

Abercrombie and Kent
St George's House, Ambrose Street,
Cheltenham, Gloucestershire GL50
3LG
Tel: 01242 855 856

www.abercrombiekent.co.uk
Organises a range of canal and river
barge holidays in Alsace-Lorraine,
Burgundy, Charente, Loire, Provence,
South of France.
Le Boat
DST House, St Marks Hill, Surbiton,
Surrey KT6 4BH
Tel: 0844 273 8277
www.leboat.co.uk
Offers a wide range of cruisers on all
the main waterways.
European Waterways
35 Wharf Road, Wraysbury, Middx
TW19 5JQ
Tel: 01753 598555 (from the US, dial
1-800 394 8630)
www.gobarging.com
Holidays in Alsace-Lorraine,
Armagnac/Southwest, Burgundy,
Loire, South of France.
Hoseasons
Lowestoft, Suffolk NR32 2LW
Tel: 0844 8471 356
www.hoseasons.co.uk
Operates on the canals in Alsace-
Lorraine, Burgundy, Loire, Lot and
Baise, South of France.
France Afloat
Tel: 0870 0110 538
www.franceafloat.com
Boating holidays on canals and rivers
in Alsace-Lorraine, Brittany, Burgundy,
Loire, South of France.

US

Abercrombie and Kent
1411 Opus Place, Executive Towers
West II, Suite 300, Downers Grove,
Illinois 60515-1182
Tel: 800-554 7016
www.abercrombiekent.com
Destinations as for Abercrombie and
Kent in the UK.
French Country Waterways
PO Box 2195, Duxbury,
Massachusetts 02331
Tel: 800-222 1236
www.fcwl.com
Holidays in Alsace-Lorraine, Burgundy,
Champagne, Loire.

Booking Direct

If you prefer to book direct in France,
try the tourist offices in the individual
départements or contact one of the
following companies (this is just a
small selection of the many operators
available).
Bateaux2Bourgogne
48 rue André Henriat, 89220 Rogny-
les-Sept-Écluses
Tel: 03 86 74 56 34
www.bateaux2bourgogne.com
This company acts as an agent for
many smaller operators.
Le Boat
93 N Park Place Boulevard,

Clearwater, Florida 33759-3917
Tel: 1-800-734-5491
Locaboat
BP 150, Quai du Port-au-Bois, 89303
Joigny
Tel: 03 86 91 72 72
www.locaboat.com
The following operators offer holidays
on luxury hotel barges. These trips are
not cheap but you are pampered and
the cuisine is usually excellent.
Hotel Barges
Bowers Wharf, Skipton, BD23 2PD
Tel: 01756 706512
www.hotelbarges.co.uk
Paris Canal
Bassin de la Villette, 19–21 Quai de
la Loire, 75019 Paris
Tel: 01 42 40 96 97
www.pariscanal.com
SONAFHO
Château La Chassagne, 21410 Pont-
de-Pany
Tel: 03 80 49 76 00
www.chassagne.com

Navigation Aids

If you are navigating for yourself,
a map or guide to the waterway is
essential. These are often provided as
part of a package deal, otherwise you
will need to take your own. Le Boat
produces an App with maps, points
of interest and other information,
which can be downloaded from their
website. Chagnon map-guides are
very good, with detailed mapping
showing routes and locks and some
colour photography.

France by Boat

Burgundy is particularly favoured
by internal waterways; the longest
is the Canal de Bourgogne, which
connects the river Yonne in the
north to the Saône in the south.
Devotees of canal architecture
can use the aqueduct at Briare.
This masterpiece of engineering,
whose foundations were laid by
the engineer Eiffel's company, was
constructed in 1896 to connect the
Briare and the Loire lateral canals,
to allow freight to be carried all
the way from the Channel to the
Mediterranean. Other popular
options for boating holidays are
the Canal du Midi, the Nantes-
Brest canal in the southwest and
the little Rhône-Sète canal that
finishes on the Mediterranean
coast. The mysterious green
waterways of the Marais Poitevin,
just inland from La Rochelle, have
a unique charm and are ideal for
day trips.

EATING OUT

RECOMMENDED RESTAURANTS, CAFÉS AND BARS

HOW TO CHOOSE

France is full of wonderful restaurants, from the grand classics to the tiny *auberge* (inn) serving perhaps only one menu of home-grown food. The French pay very serious attention to their food and fast foods are not so prevalent in French supermarkets; the high streets in large cities though have succumbed to the international burger chains. It may be argued, however, that the French have always enjoyed convenience foods provided by their splendid *pâtissiers* (bakers), *traiteurs* (delicatessens) and *charcutiers* (butchers), where you can pick a selection of their prepared dishes for dinner or a delicious picnic.

Each region has its own specialities: the creamy sauces of Normandy, the traditional *confits* of duck and goose in the southwest, *choucroute* (sauerkraut) in the east, *coq au vin* (chicken in red wine sauce) in Burgundy and wonderful seafood all around the coast. (See page 402 for help on deciphering French menus.)

Eating out in France is excellent

Restaurant Law and Lore

Smoking is now banned in public places in France, including restaurants. The rule is generally respected, except in some bars.

Menus must be displayed by law outside any establishment. Most places will offer a *prix fixe* menu – a set meal at a particular price. Otherwise you order separate items from *La Carte*. The set menu is usually excellent value for money, unless you really only want one dish.

value for money, and it is still difficult to get a bad meal, except occasionally in Paris or on the Côte d'Azur. It is always worth seeking out the local regional food; it is likely to be freshest and most skilfully cooked and is the best way to get the flavour of a region, complemented by the local wine. French regional cooking is in fashion these days and many of the most popular restaurants in Paris specialise in the cuisine of the provinces. Vegetarianism hasn't really taken off yet in France and non-meat eaters may find their choices limited.

WINE – READING THE LABEL

Wines are graded according to quality, and this is shown on the label. In 2012 the classification system was changed and reduced to three from four official categories – there is now no category known as VDQS. The grades are as follows:
Vin de France: a table wine category replacing Vin de Table, which allows the consumer to know much more information about the wine.
IGP (Indication Géographique Protégée): an intermediate category replacing Vin de Pays, which offers producers myriad of choices as there are no restrictions on grape varieties.
AOP (Appellation d'Origine Protégée): the highest category basically replacing AOC wines.

Other terms on the label you might come across are:
Mis en bouteille au château: bottled at the vineyard. Also indicated by the words, *récoltant* or *producteur* around the cap.
Négociant: a wine that has been bought by a dealer and usually bottled

away from the estate. However, this is not necessarily to the detriment of the wine.

The French are fiercely proud of their wines and keen to educate visitors about their production. In all the regions of wine production you will find roadside signs offering visits to cellars *(caves)* open to the public for tours, tastings and the sale of wine.

For further information on wine-tastings or visits to châteaux, contact the local tourist office.

RESTAURANT LISTINGS

The following is a selection of some of the best restaurants in the regions, worth looking out for or even making a special detour. Most specialise in the food of their region, cooking local ingredients with traditional skill and sometimes a more modern twist.

The restaurants below are listed by region in the same order as in the Places section of this book, and then alphabetically by town.

The formule, or set-price menu.

PARIS

L'Arpège
84 Rue de Varenne, 75007
Tel: 01 47 05 09 06
www.alain-passard.com
Fashionable restaurant near the
Musée Rodin with svelte modern
decor, highly creative cooking focused
on vegetables, fish and poultry, and
a good wine list. Closed Sat and Sun.
Book in advance. €€€€

Auberge Etchegorry
41 Rue Croulebarbe, 75013
Tel: 01 44 08 83 51
www.etchegorry.com
This restaurant facing a park near
the Place d'Italie has a pretty flowery
facade. It specialises in the cuisine
of the Basque Country and the
Southwest. Closed Sun and Mon. €€

Au chien qui fume
33 Rue du Pont Neuf, 75001
Tel: 01 42 36 07 42
www.auchienquifume.com
Porcelain dogs and pictures of dogs
decorate this popular and friendly
Parisian restaurant founded in 1740.
It serves traditional French cuisine,
particularly seafood, and has a
terrace for outdoor dining. €€

Au Pied de Cochon
6 Rue Coquillière, 75001
Tel: 01 40 13 77 00
www.pieddecochon.com/
Venerable Les Halles brasserie open
around the clock for onion soup, pigs'
trotters and seafood. €€

Aux Lyonnais
32 Rue St-Marc, 75002
Tel: 01 58 00 22 06
www.auxlyonnais.com
This pretty vintage bistro, under the
wing of superchef-entrepreneur Alain
Ducasse, offers a modernised take on
Lyonnais cooking. Closed Sat lunch,
Sun, Mon. €€€

Brasserie Bofinger
5–7 Rue de la Bastille, 75004
Tel: 01 42 72 87 82
www.bofingerparis.com
Hugely popular brasserie with
exquisite Belle Epoque decor serving
specialities that include foie gras,
oysters and choucroute. Reserve in
advance, especially if you want to sit
beneath the beautiful glass dome.
€€€

Café Beaubourg
43 Rue Saint Merri, 75004
Tel: 01 48 87 63 96
http://cafebeaubourg.com/
This trendy café is next to the
pedestrian square beside the Centre
Pompidou, which means that you can
eat while watching street entertainers
perform. It's popular with locals and

tourists alike and it serves brunch at
any time of the day. €€

Café de la Paix
5 Place de l'Opéra, 75009
Tel: 01 40 07 36 36
www.cafedelapaix.fr
This beautiful café/brasserie with
decor by Charles Garnier is classified
as a historic monument; great people-
watching from the terrace. €€

Le Chalet des Iles
Lac Inférieur du Bois de Boulogne, Porte
de la Muette 75016
Tel: 01 42 88 04 69
A beautiful and secluded restaurant,
inaugurated in 1880, on the edge
of a lake in the Bois de Boulogne. It
is reached by a short ride in an old-
fashioned boat and it is the perfect
location for a romantic summer
evening. €€€

Chartier
7 Rue Faubourg Montmartre, 75009
Tel: 01 47 70 86 29
www.bouillon-chartier.com
This Parisian institution decorated
with brass, glass, mirrors and plain
wood, was founded in the late 19th
century and has preserved much of
its original character, including the
waiters' costumes. €€

Le Cinq
31 Avenue George V, 75008
Tel: 01 49 52 71 54
www.restaurant-lecinq.com
Le Cinq, located in the grandiose
Four Seasons Hotel, is elegance
personified. Recent arrival Breton
chef Christian Le Squer heads up this
outstanding team at the two-starred
Michelin dining experience. You'll find
artistry on a plate, with flavours to
match. Reservations essential. €€€€

La Closerie des Lilas
171 Boulevard du Montparnasse, 75006
Tel: 01 40 51 34 50
www.closeriedeslilas.fr
Cocktail bar and brasserie once
the haunt of Joyce and Hemingway
and still popular with artists and
intellectuals, plus smarter restaurant.
Reservations essential. €€€

Chez Georges
273 Boulevard Péreire, 75017
Tel: 01 45 74 31 00
Authentic Parisian brasserie dating
back to 1926. The Art Nouveau décor
with leather banquettes, silverware,
wood and copper radiate a warm
atmosphere in which enjoy refined
bourgeois cuisine. €€€

**Le Comptoir du Relais Saint
Germain**
9 Carrefour de l'Odéon, 75006
Tel: 01 44 27 07 97

www.hotel-paris-relais-saint-germain.com
The tiny restaurant of the Hôtel du
Relais is a brasserie by day which
transforms itself into a gourmet
restaurant serving specialities from
the Southwest in the evening. €€€

Costes
239 Rue St-Honoré, 75001
Tel: 01 42 44 50 00
www.hotelcostes.com
Relaxed restaurant in a luxury hotel
serving fashionable dishes including
light snacks. €€€

La Coupole
102 Boulevard du Montparnasse, 75014
Tel: 01 43 20 14 20
www.lacoupole-paris.com
Popular Art Deco brasserie
that serves good choucroute,
Châteaubriand and huge platters of
seafood. €€

Dans le Noir
51 Rue Quincampoix, 75004
Tel: 01 42 77 98 04
http://paris.danslenoir.com
Be prepared for a new dining
experience in this restaurant
where you eat in pitch darkness to
appreciate both the flavours of the
food and what it is like to be blind.
Book well in advance. €€€

Le Dôme
108 Boulevard du Montparnasse, 75014
Tel: 01 43 35 25 81
Along the road from the other famous
café, La Coupole, this is one of the
grandest seafood restaurants in
Paris. Try the bouillabaisse (fish stew).
€€€

Epicure
112 Rue du Faubourg Saint-Honoré,
75008
Tel: 01 53 43 43 40
www.lebristolparis.com
Considered one of the top restaurants
in the world, Epicure can be found
in the opulent Le Bristol Paris hotel.
Renowned chef Eric Fréchon has
been awarded three Michelin stars for
his superb interpretation of modern
French classics. It's ultra-expensive
but unforgettable. €€€€

La Fontaine de Mars
129 Rue Saint Dominique, 75007
Tel: 01 47 05 46 44
www.fontainedemars.com

PRICE CATEGORIES

Price categories are per person for
a three-course meal:
€ = under €30
€€ = €30–60
€€€ = €60–100
€€€€ = more than €100

Opened in 1908, this is one of Paris' oldest bistros. The white and red chequered table cloths, napkins and curtains give it a homely atmosphere in which to enjoy a good value lunch. €€€

Le Fouquet's Barrière
46 Avenue George V, 75008
Tel: 01 40 69 60 00
www.fouquets-barriere.com
Luxury brasserie-dining in the Champs-Elysées, in the restaurant of the Hôtel Fouquet's Barrière. The prices include the pleasure of people watching. €€€

Le Grand Véfour
17 Rue de Beaujoulais, 75001
Tel: 01 42 96 56 27
www.grand-vefour.com
This exquisite 18th-century restaurant, headed up by Michelin-starred chef Guy Martin, has been catering for artists, writers and politicians for more than two hundred years. Closed Sat, Sun and Aug. €€€€

L'Hôtel
13 Rue des Beaux-Arts, 75006
Tel: 01 44 41 99 01
www.l-hotel.com
The gourmet restaurant of this hotel in which Oscar Wilde died in 1900 is located on a quiet back street, set back from the bustle of St-Germain-des-Prés. It has been awarded a Michelin star. Sun and Mon breakfast only. €€€€

Lucas Carton
9 Place de la Madeleine, 75008
Tel: 01 42 65 22 90
www.lucascarton.com
A beautiful Art Nouveau setting where perfect service and refined cooking is always delivered. The extravagant can choose the *carte* with its suggested wine for each dish, but there's also a superb lunch menu. Advance

reservation essential. Closed Sun and Mon. €€€€

Le Meurice
228 Rue de Rivoli, 75001
Tel: 01 44 58 10 55
www.dorchestercollection.com/paris/le-meurice
Very good "revisited" classical cooking, overseen by Alain Ducasse, is presented in flamboyant style in this grand hotel dining room. A place for a special occasion under a blowsy rococo painted ceiling. Closed Sat lunch, Sun and two weeks mid-Aug. €€€€

Polidor
41 Rue Monsieur Le Prince, 75006
Tel: 01 43 26 95 34
www.polidor.com
A traditional Left-Bank restaurant, popular amongst students and tourists alike, who don't mind sharing the long tables with strangers. It has a good choice of grilled meats. €€

Le Réservoir
16 Rue de la Forge Royale, 75011
Tel: 01 43 56 39 60
www.reservoirclub.com
A trendy restaurant with an eclectic selection of dishes on its menu. It also stages live music. Open for dinner only. Closed Sun and Mon. €€

Rôtisserie du Beaujolais
19 Quai de Tournelle, 75005
Tel: 01 43 54 17 47
www.larotisseriedelatour.com
A country-style bistro with a homely atmosphere, serving good-quality regional cuisine. €€

Seb'on
62 Rue d'Orsel, 75108
Tel: 01 42 59 74 32
www.seb-on.com
A popular, charming bistro in the middle of Montmartre, serving quality French food. The delicious menu,

handwritten on the blackboard, is changed weekly and consists just of three choices of starters, mains and desserts. Closed Mon–Thu lunch, Sun–Tue dinner. €€

Le Sixième Sens
43 Rue de la Roquette, 75011
Tel: 09 83 88 63 52
www.restaurant-sixieme-sens.fr
Here Guillaume Poupard is your dedicated chef, host and waiter. The small menu might offer a fish starter, a main of roasted lamb with thyme followed by his own version of tiramisu. Dinner only; closed Sun and Mon. €€

La Tour d'Argent
15–17 Quai de la Tournelle, 75001
Tel: 01 43 54 23 31
www.latourdargent.com
The ultimate in luxury, established in the 16th century, celebrated both for duck and its views over the Seine; the ground floor has a museum of gastronomy. Closed Sun and Mon. €€€€

Le Train Bleu
Gare de Lyon, Place Louis-Armand, 75012
Tel: 01 43 43 09 06
www.le-train-bleu.com
An extravagantly and luxuriously decorated restaurant on the first floor of the Gare de Lyon train station, with painted ceilings, gilded mouldings, mirrors and solemn waiters. €€€

Le Troquet
21 Rue François-Bonvin, 75015
Tel: 01 45 66 89 00
Creative modern bistro fare with a Basque tinge in an animated, friendly setting. Closed Sun and Mon, and three weeks in Aug. €€€

Violon d'Ingres
135 Rue St-Dominique, 75007
Tel: 01 45 55 15 05
www.maisonconstant.com/violon-ingres
Fashionable restaurant serving traditional cooking with a modern twist. €€€

Ze Kitchen Galerie
4 Rue des Grands-Augustins, 75006 Paris
Tel: 01 46 33 00 85
www.zekitchengalerie.fr
Successful modern fusion fare mixing fine French ingredients with exotic vegetables, using plancha grilling and Oriental sushi and tempura techniques, all produced in a tiny open kitchen. Closed Sat and Sun. €€

A classic Parisian brasserie calls for waiters in traditional livery.

PRICE CATEGORIES

Price categories are per person for a three-course meal:
€ = under €30
€€ = €30–60
€€€ = €60–100
€€€€ = more than €100

AROUND PARIS (ILE DE FRANCE)

Auvers-sur-Oise
Sous le Porche
Place de la Mairie, 95430 Auvers-sur-Oise
Tel: 01 30 36 16 50
www.sousleporche.com
This welcoming restaurant, in the heart of a village associated with Van Gogh, is decorated in contemporary style and serves a creative cuisine. It often has live music. €€

Chartres
La Passacaille
30 Rue Sainte-Même, 28200 Chartres
Tel: 02 37 21 52 10

www.lapassacaille.fr
A cheerful Italian restaurant, located in the centre of Chartres, which serves up a good selection of pizzas and fresh pastas, as well as salads, carpaccios and grills. €€

Fontainebleau
Au Moulin du Flagy
2 Rue du Moulin, 77940 Flagy
Tel: 01 60 96 67 89
www.aumoulin.fr
On the banks of the Orvanne, 20 minutes from Fontainebleau, is this converted 18th-century flour mill. Enjoy adventurous cooking by candlelight in winter or dine by the river in summer. €€€

Versailles
Gordon Ramsay du Trianon
1 Boulevard de la Reine, 78000 Versailles
Tel: 01 30 84 50 18
www.trianonpalace.fr/gordon-ramsay
The celebrity Scottish chef directs this restaurant in the Trianon Palace in Versailles. The decor is elegant and intimate and the innovative food inspired by French tradition. Closed Sun, Mon and lunch Tue–Thu. €€€€

LE NORD

Amiens
Le Bouchon
10 Rue Alexandre-Fatton, 80000 Amiens
Tel: 03 22 92 14 32
www.lebouchon.fr
A simple and modern restaurant serving gourmet dishes prepared with fresh seasonal ingredients. €

Calais
Le Channel
3 Boulevard de la Résistance, 62100 Calais
Tel: 03 21 34 42 30
www.restaurant-lechannel.com
A well-established family-run restaurant in which the Crespo

brothers harmonise quality menus with well-chosen wines. Closed Tue and Sun dinner. €
La Diligence
Hôtel Meurice, 5 Rue Edmond Roche, 62100 Calais
Tel: 03 21 19 57 07
In part of the Hôtel Meurice, although not part of the set-up, this small restaurant's set menus are very good and great value for money. Closed Sun and Mon. €€

Lille
A l'Huîtrière
3 Rue des Chats Bossus, 59800 Lille

Tel: 03 20 55 43 41
One of the city's best restaurants, serving seafood as well as other traditional dishes; beautiful tiled Art Deco interior in the old section of Lille. Excellent wine list. Closed Sun dinner and Aug. €€€
Le Compostelle
4 Rue St-Etienne, 59800 Lille
Tel: 03 28 38 08 30
www.lecompostelle.fr
A stone's throw from the Grand'Place is this refined restaurant in a beautiful Flemish Renaissance building. It serves mainly Mediterranean cuisine but also some regional dishes. €€

CHAMPAGNE

Charleville-Mézières
La Clef des Champs
33 Rue du Moulin, 08000 Charleville-Mézières
Tel: 03 24 56 17 50
www.laclefdeschamps.fr
Located in a charming 17th-century building in the centre of Charleville, this restaurant with rooms prides itself on sophisticated cuisine of a high standard, utilising local ingredients such as truffles and venison. Traditional French cooking with an innovative twist. Closed Sun. €€€

Colombey-les-Deux-Eglises
Restaurant Natali
Hostellerie La Montagne, 52330 Colombey-les-Deux-Eglises
Tel: 03 25 01 51 69
www.hostellerielamontagne.com
In this restaurant on the first floor of the Hostellerie La Montagne,

garlanded chef Jean-Baptiste Natali serves gourmet seasonal cuisine using mainly produce sourced from local farmers. The fish comes fresh from Roscoff once a week. Closed Mon and Tue. €€€

Laon
La Petite Auberge
45 Boulevard Brossolette, 02000 Laon
Tel: 03 23 23 02 38
www.zorn-lapetiteauberge.com
A stylish restaurant where chef Willy-Marc Zorn prepares a creative cuisine in line with market availability and the seasons. He also bakes his own bread. €€€

Reims
Les Crayères
64 Boulevard Henry-Vasnier, 51100 Reims
Tel: 03 26 24 90 00
www.lescrayeres.com

Haute cuisine in a luxurious château with an excellent selection of vintage champagnes to accompany the gourmet dishes. There is a large terrace giving onto the garden. For a slightly cheaper and less formal option try La Brasserie Le Jardin, in the château's garden, which is decorated in a more modern style and specialises in regional cuisine. Reservation essential. Closed Mon, Tue and August. €€€€

Troyes
Brasserie de la Paix
52 Rue du Général-de-Gaulle, 1000 Troyes
Tel: 03 25 73 15 26
Facing the central market, this 1930s-style restaurant specialises in mussels, sautéed potatoes, tripe and home-made terrines. It has a small and flowery inner patio. Closed Sun. €

LORRAINE

Nancy

Le Capucin Gourmand
31 Rue Gambetta, 54000 Nancy
Tel: 03 83 35 26 98
www.lecapu.com
This restaurant in the city centre
is a meeting point for the city's
gourmets. There is a good value set
menu at lunchtime. Cooking courses
are held on Saturdays. Closed Sun.
€€€€

Excelsior
50 Rue Henri-Poincaré, 54000 Nancy
Tel: 03 83 35 24 57
www.brasserie-excelsior.com
Nancy's finest historic brasserie,
decorated in Art Nouveau style and
specialising in oysters. €€

Metz

A Côté
43 Place de Chambre, 57000 Metz
Tel: 03 87 66 38 84
www.restaurant-acote.fr
Looks just like a trendy wine bar with
an energetic vibe, but Eric Maire also
serves up good innovative food to
match. The bouillabaisse is amazing.

and the veal beautifully tender.
Closed Sun and Mon. €€

Brasserie Flo
2 bis, Rue Gambetta, 57000 Metz
Tel: 03 87 55 94 95
www.flo-metz.fr
A very pleasant brasserie outside
the train station, decorated in Belle
Epoque style, with mirrors and plush
velvet. Perfect for a drink or a bite
before or after the opera or theatre.
€€€

La Table de Pol
1 Rue Grand Wad, 57000 Metz
Tel: 03 87 62 13 72
www.latabledepol.fr
Very popular restaurant in Metz
where chef Pol Nivoix prepares his
cuisine inspired by available market
produce. In the dining room, his wife
Sylvie offers a good choice of wines
to accompany the food. Closed Sun
and Mon. €€

Verdun

Le Chantaco
Avenue de la Victoire, 55100 Verdun
Tel: 03 29 86 36 36

www.coq-hardi.com
Part of the Verdun institution that is
the Hôtel Le Coq Hardi, which has
been operating since 1827, this
contemporary brasserie has a young
chef whose specialities include snails
on toast and frog soup. €€

The Excelsior.

ALSACE

Colmar

A l'Echevin
Quartier Petite Venise, Place des Six-
Montagnes-Noires, 68000 Colmar
Tel: 03 89 41 60 32
www.hotel-le-marechal.com
The cosy restaurant of the hotel Le
Maréchal occupies a converted a
16th-century inn on the waterside
in Colmar's "Little Venice". It serves
gourmet cuisine, combining regional
dishes with modern flair. Try the
*pigeon from Alsace stuffed with foie
gras.* €€€

Maison des Têtes
19 Rue des Têtes, 68000 Colmar
Tel: 03 89 24 43 43
www.la-maison-des-tetes.com
Authentic 17th-century brasserie
with a magnificent facade; the place
to go for Alsatian classics such
as *choucroute* (sauerkraut with
sausage). Closed Sun dinner, Mon
and Tue lunch and Feb. €€

Gérardmer

Hostellerie de Bas Rupts
181 Route de la Bresse, 88400 Gérardmer
Tel: 03 29 63 09 25
www.bas-rupts.com
Whether you choose the *casserolette
d'escargot*, the filet mignon, or the

daily delivered fresh fish in this Relais
& Château hotel and restaurant you
can be sure the presentation will be
exquisite. €€€

Kaysersberg

Chambard
9-13 Rue du Général-de-Gaulle, 68240
Kaysersberg
Tel: 03 89 47 10 17
www.lechambard.fr
The Nasti brothers are at the head
of this hotel restaurant, called 64°
Le Restaurant, where the delicious
gourmet dishes are accompanied by
the best Alsatian wines. There is also
a winstub serving more affordable
fare. €€€

Marlenheim

Le Cerf
30 Rue du Général-de-Gaulle, 67520
Marlenheim
Tel: 03 88 87 73 73
www.lecerf.com
Upmarket village inn makes a good
place to try Alsatian dishes and game.
Closed Tue and Wed. €€€€

Mittelbergheim

Winstub Gilg
1 Route du Vin, 67140 Mittelbergheim

Tel: 03 88 08 91 37
www.hotel-gilg.com
Traditional half-timbered winstub
(restaurant) on the Alsace wine route
where you can complement wine
tasting with a range of fish dishes.
Closed Tue and Wed. €€

Strasbourg

Au Crocodile
10 Rue de l'Outre, 67000 Strasbourg
Tel: 03 88 32 13 02
www.au-crocodile.com
An elegant restaurant near the
cathedral, in the historic part of
town, which serves a refined and
sophisticated cuisine. Closed Sun
and Mon. €€€

Buerehiesel
4 Parc de l'Orangerie,
67000 Strasbourg
Tel: 03 88 45 56 65
www.buerehiesel.fr

PRICE CATEGORIES

Price categories are per person for
a three-course meal:
€ = under €30
€€ = €30–60
€€€ = €60–100
€€€€ = more than €100

This reconstructed Alsatian farmhouse in Strasbourg's Orangerie Park is home to one of the city's best restaurants. Closed Sun and Mon. €€€
Maison Kammerzell
16 Place de la Cathédrale, 67000 Strasbourg
Tel: 03 88 32 42 14

www.maison-kammerzell.com
Excellent food and wine in one of the oldest houses in Strasbourg, next to the cathedral. Dishes range from the signature *fish sauerkraut* to *baecheoffe with three meats*. €€
L'Eveil des Sens
Rue des Dentelles,

67000 Strasbourg
Tel: 03 88 32 81 01
www.eveil-des-sens.com
Friendly restaurant in Petite France, which is decorated in Alsatian style with paintings on the walls. It's the culinary fief of chef Antoine Huart. There is an intimate dining room upstairs. €€

NORMANDY

Caen

A Contre Sens
8 Rue des Croisiers, 14000 Caen
Tel: 02 31 97 44 48
www.acontresenscaen.fr
Chef Anthony Caillot has earned a Michelin star for his inventive cooking using local seasonal produce to fine effect. Smoked eel, foie gras with black pudding and tripe are among the local specialities. Closed Tue lunch, Sun and Mon. €€€

Cherbourg

Café de Paris
40 Quai Caligny, 50100 Cherbourg
Tel: 02 33 43 12 36
www.restaurantcafedeparis.com
Founded in 1803, this popular brasserie faces the fishing port of Cherbourg, and specialises in fresh fish and seafood. It also serves some creative dishes. Closed Sun. €€

Clécy

Au Fil de l'Eau
La Cambronnerie, 14570 Clécy
Tel: 02 31 69 71 13
www.au-fil-de-leau-normandie.fr
Delightful views can be had from this restaurant overlooking the river. Come here for some good-value set menus or choose à la carte. House specialities include smoked salmon, rabbit terrine and desserts featuring salted butter caramel. €€

Dieppe

Auberge Clos Normand
22 Rue Henri IV, 76370 Martin-Eglise

Tel: 02 35 40 40 40
www.closnormand.fr
Farmhouse restaurant outside Dieppe. In summer, food can be eaten in the orchard by the trout stream. All very good value (some rooms available too). Closed mid-Nov–mid-Dec. €€

Gaillon

La Closerie
Château Corneille, 17, Rue de l'Eglise-Vieux-Villez, 27600 Gaillon
Tel: 02 32 77 44 77
www.chateau-corneille.fr
A gourmet restaurant located in the stables of an 18th-century château. It is well located for visiting the D-Day beaches, Giverny and Rouen and has a big, welcoming fireplace for relaxing in the evening. €€

Honfleur

L'Assiette des Mondes
39 Chemin de la Croix Rouge, Equemauville, 14600 Honfleur
Tel: 02 31 81 52 11
www.assiettedesmondes.fr
Friendly service and good value makes this an excellent choice in a village just outside Honfleur. Traditional Normandy fare comes with interesting Asian and European twists. Mains could include wok of veal with cream and cider or homemade fish stew. €€

Mont-St-Michel

A l'Abri du Saunier
La Chaussée, Saint-Léonard, 50300 Vains

Tel: 02 33 70 88 60
www.alabridusaunier.com
Located in a pretty village on the bay of Mont-St-Michel, this restaurant uses mainly fresh produce to prepare its traditional cuisine that varies with the seasons. It has a terrace for summer dining. Closed Tue and Wed except in Jul and Aug. €€
La Mère Poulard
Grande Rue, 50170 Mont-St-Michel
Tel: 02 33 89 68 68
www.merepoulard.com
Visitors come from afar to sample the cuisine du terroir (regional food), particularly the celebrated omelettes at this traditional inn and hotel. Other specialities include lobster and pre-salted lamb. €€€

Rouen

La Couronne
31 Place du Vieux Marché, 76000 Rouen
Tel: 02 35 71 40 90
www.lacouronne.com.fr
One of the oldest auberges in France, on the square where Joan of Arc was burned. An elegant interior and excellent regional cooking. €€

Trouville-sur-Mer

Les Vapeurs
160 Quai F. Moreaux, 14360 Trouville-sur-Mer
Tel: 02 31 88 15 24
www.lesvapeurs.fr
Fashionable place for seafood, close to the fish market, with good fresh dishes available at all times. €€

BRITTANY

Brest

La Maison de l'Océan
2 Quai de la Douane, 29200 Brest
Tel: 02 98 80 44 84
www.restaurant-fruit-mer-brest.com
Seafood delights served up in a marine atmosphere down on the quay in Brest. Start with freshly caught mussels or oysters and follow with a

seafood platter. Carnivores are not forgotten and for cheaper options try the set menus. €€€

Concarneau

Crêperie des Remparts
31 Rue Théophile-Louarn, Ville Close, 29900 Concarneau
Tel: 02 98 50 65 66

You can eat your fill of crêpes and *galettes* in this crêperie, which is situated in the middle of the ancient walled town of Concarneau. Closed Wed low season. €

Dinard

Le Balafon
31 Rue de la Vallée, 35800 Dinard

TRANSPORT
EATING OUT
ACTIVITIES
A – Z
LANGUAGE

La Mère Poulard, celebrated for its omelettes.

Tel: 02 99 46 14 81
www.lebalafon-restaurant-dinard.fr
This is a small unpretentious restaurant with a discerning menu, which utilises fresh produce from the nearby market. Starters might include shrimp ravioli, mains salmon risotto or beef tenderloin, and desserts rum cake with roasted pineapple mousse and passion fruit. €€

Quimper

L'Ambroisie
49 Rue Elie-Fréron, 29000 Quimper, Southern Finistère

Tel: 02 98 95 00 02
In one of the small streets of the old town, this pretty restaurant proposes regional cuisine with a contemporary touch. Closed Sun dinner, Mon. €€

Rennes

Auberge St-Sauveur
6 Rue St-Sauveur, 35000 Rennes
Tel: 02 99 79 32 56
www.restaurant-lesaintsauveur.fr
A half-timbered building in the old town that survived the great fire of 1750. Traditional cuisine includes

Breton lobster, fish and shellfish. Closed Sun, Mon lunch and Aug. €€

Riec-sur-Belon

Chez Jacky
Port de Belon, 29340 Riec-sur-Belon
Tel: 02 98 06 90 32
www.chez-jacky.com
Great place to eat exquisite Belon oysters and other seafood with Muscadet wine, right on the water's edge. Closed Nov–Easter, Mon in low season. €€

Ste-Anne-de-Palud

Hôtel de la Plage
La Plage, 29550 Ste-Anne-de-Palud, Southern Finistère
Tel: 02 98 92 50 12
www.plage.com
Near Douranenez, facing the sea, the menu at this hotel restaurant focuses mainly on seafood, which is meticulously prepared with a touch of imagination. Closed Mon–Wed and Fri lunch. €€€

St-Malo

La Gouesnière
Le Limonay, 35350 Ste-Méloir-des-Ondes
Tel: 02 44 10 11 52
www.tirel-guerin-restaurant.fr
Friendly family-run restaurant in the Hôtel Tirel Guerin, with specialities of blue lobster and poached oysters of Cancale. Closed Mon. €€€

LOIRE VALLEY

Blois

Le Médicis
2 Allée François 1er, Route d'Angers, 41000 Blois
Tel: 02 54 43 94 04
www.le-medicis.com
A friendly restaurant and hotel near the Château de Blois where chef Grégory Boussard prepares his ingenious cuisine which is given exotic touches from the different countries where he has worked. Closed Sun dinner and Mon from Oct–June. €€

Chinon

L'Ardoise
42 Rue Rabelais, 37500 Chinon
Tel: 02 47 58 48 78
In his restaurant in the centre of Chinon, chef Stéphane Perrot prepares high-quality cuisine and serves an excellent three-course lunch in a friendly atmosphere. €€

Au Chapeau Rouge
49 Place du Général-de-Gaulle, 37500 Chinon

Tel: 02 47 98 08 08
www.auchapeaurouge.fr/
This traditional restaurant, in the town centre, at the foot of the château, serves gourmet cuisine using local and seasonal produce, including wild fish from the Loire river, saffron and truffles. €€€

Fontevraud

La Licorne
Allée Sainte-Cathérine, 49590 Fontevraud l'Abbaye
Tel: 02 41 51 72 49
www.restaurant-gastronomique-licorne.fr
This restaurant is housed in an 18th-century house standing in the middle of a pretty garden. It is the perfect place to sample Loire specialities, some of which are cooked in local wine. Closed Sun dinner, Mon and Wed in winter, and two weeks in Jan. €€€

Lamotte-Beuvron

Hôtel Tatin
5 Avenue de Vierzon, 41600 Lamotte-

Beuvron
Tel: 02 54 88 00 03
www.hotel-tatin-lamotte-beuvron.fr
This was where *tarte tatin*, the now ubiquitous caramelised apple tart, was invented, so it is always on the menu along with local game and fish. Closed Tue lunch and Mon. €€€

Nantes

L'Atlantide
16 Quai Ernest-Renaud, 44100 Nantes
Tel: 02 40 73 23 23
www.restaurant-atlantide.net
A spacious and bright restaurant offering panoramic views of the Loire from its big bay windows. The specialities combine French cuisine with traditional Asian dishes. Closed Sat lunch and Sun €€€

La Cigale
4 Place Graslin, 44000 Nantes
Tel: 02 51 84 94 94
www.lacigale.com
This historic Nantes café is decorated in exuberant Belle Epoque style and serves excellent fish and seafood. €

Le Un
1 Rue Olympe-de-Gouges, 44000 Nantes
Tel: 02 40 08 28 00
www.leun.fr
An original restaurant near the town centre and not far from the Loire river, serving a good selection of tapas and main dishes at reasonable prices. On Saturday mornings there are cooking workshops given by the chefs and on this day it is closed at lunchtime. €

Orléans

La Chancellerie
27 Place du Matroi, 45000 Orléans
Tel: 02 38 53 57 54
www.restaurant-chancellerie.fr
Popular brasserie with outside tables in centre of Orléans, always full at lunchtime for good local dishes with Loire wines. €€

Le Lift
Place de la Loire 45000, Orléans
Tel: 02 38 98 01 47
www.restaurant-le-lift.com

Cancale oysters.

Refined, contemporary and creative cuisine is the hallmark of Philippe Bardau's restaurant. It's located in a modern building and is divided into different spaces. The tables on the terrace have great views of the city and of the Loire river. Brunch is served between noon and 2.30pm on Sun. Closed Sun dinner. €€

Saumur

Auberge St Pierre
6 Place St Pierre,
49400 Saumur
Tel: 02 44 10 10 74
www.aubergesaintpierre-saumur.fr
This charming little restaurant is not far from the château in the old town; try the delicious fish stew or *boeuf bourguignon*. €€

Saumur/Rou-Marson

Les Caves de Marson
1 Rue Henri Fricotelle,
49400 Rou-Marson
Tel: 02 41 50 50 05
www.cavesdemarson.com
For the total troglodyte experience head for this restaurant near Saumur with its rooms carved out of limestone caves. Try the *fouaces*, wheat pancakes cooked in an old wood-fired oven and stuffed with a variety of fillings. Closed Mon and mid-Dec–late Jan. €€

Solesmes

Grand Hôtel de Solesmes
16 Place Dom-Guéranger, 72300 Solesmnes
Tel: 02 43 95 45 10
www.grandhotelsolesmes.com
Comfortable dining room in this hotel serving excellent fish, seafood and regional classics. Closed Sat lunch and Sun dinner in winter, end Dec–early Jan. €€€

Tours

Les Hautes Roches
86 Quai Loire, Rochecorbon, 37210 Tours
Tel: 02 47 52 88 88
www.leshautesroches.com
The Loire's fanciest troglodyte hotel has a fine restaurant on a terrace overlooking the Loire. Closed Sun dinner, Mon, Tue and Wed lunch. €€€€

L'Odéon
10 Place du Général-Leclerc, 37000 Tours
Tel: 02 47 20 12 65
www.restaurant-lodeon.com
A creative and refined gourmet regional cuisine is served in this modern restaurant decorated in Art Deco style. Closed Sat and Mon lunch, Sun and two weeks Aug. €€

Le Petit Patrimoine
58 Rue Colbert, 37000 Tours, Indre et Loire
Tel: 02 47 66 05 81
This tiny, brightly coloured bistro is very popular for its fresh, market-inspired daily menu and regional favourites. Closed Sun and Mon. €

Villandry

Le Cheval Rouge
9 Rue Principale, 37510 Villandry
Tel: 02 47 50 02 07
www.lecheval-rouge.com
A conveniently located restaurant and hotel near the château serving local specialities. It has a terrace for dining al fresco. €€

Vouvray

Château de Noizay
Promenade de Waulsort, 37210 Noizay
Tel: 02 47 52 11 01
www.chateaudenoizay.com
A 16th-century château converted into a four-star hotel in its own park, with a superb restaurant featuring a seasonal menu complemented by local wines. Closed mid-Jan–mid-Mar. €€€

POITOU-CHARENTES

Cognac

Les Pigeons Blancs
110 Rue Jules Brisson, 16100 Cognac
Tel: 05 45 82 16 36
www.pigeons-blancs.com
A gourmet restaurant in an ancient coaching inn, with elegantly laid tables and lighting carefully arranged to make the most of chef Jacques Tachet's tasteful and imaginative cuisine. €€€

Ile de Ré

Le Bistrot de Béné
1 Quai de la Criée,
17590 Ars-en-Ré
Tel: 05 46 29 40 26
www.bistrotdebene.com
Reliable cooking in a stylish setting on the quayside with a large patio. Popular with the Ile de Ré yachting crowd. Closed Mon lunch. €€

Le Grenier à Sel
20 Rue de la Baie, 17590 Ars-en-Ré
Tel: 05 46 29 08 62
www.grenierasel.fr
A pleasant bistro serving a simple but original cuisine that combines local ingredients with Chinese, Thai and Mexican touches. Enjoy a 'dish of the day' on the lovely patio. Closed Sun dinner and Mon. €€

Poitiers

Alain Boutin
65 Rue Carnot, 86000 Poitiers

PRICE CATEGORIES

Price categories are per person for a three-course meal:
€ = under €30
€€ = €30–60
€€€ = €60–100
€€€€ = more than €100

Tel: 05 49 88 25 53
www.alainboutin.com
Alain Boutin's welcoming gourmet restaurant near the Blossac gardens specialises in regional cuisine prepared using seasonal market produce. Closed Mon lunch, Sat lunch and Sun. €€
Le Poitevin
76 Rue Carnot, 86000 Poitiers, Vienne
Tel: 05 49 88 35 04
www.lepoitevin-fr
This rustic bistro specialises in local dishes such as guinea fowl in foie gras cream or deer steak with chestnuts. Closed Sun dinner, two weeks in July, and Christmas–New Year. €€

La Rochelle
L'Entracte
35 Rue Saint-Jean-du-Pérot, 17000 La Rochelle
Tel: 05 46 52 26 69
www.lentracte.net

A Grégory Coutanceau restaurant serving more traditional recipes and classics of French cuisine such as sautéed veal kidneys in cognac sauce. €€
Les Flots
1 Rue de la Chaîne, 17000 La Rochelle
Tel: 05 46 41 32 51
www.les-flots.com
Grégory Coutanceau – son of top La Rochelle chef Richard Coutanceau – runs a contemporary, experimental kitchen bringing in cosmopolitan influences. €€€

Rochefort
Le Marydiane
72 Rue Jean-Jaurès, 17300 Rochefort
Tel: 05 46 99 07 11
www.le-marydiane.com
This gem of a restaurant serves traditional local food using the best of seasonal produce. Highlights include such delights as cream of porcini mushrooms and walnut

cream. Good-value set menu available. €€

Saintes
Clos des Cours
2 Place du Théâtre, 17100 Saintes
Tel: 05 46 74 62 62
www.closdescours.com
French and foreign light cuisine, creatively prepared by chef Jean-Luc Bonedeau, are served in this modern and bright restaurant in the historic part of town. Closed Sun €€
Le Parvis
12 Quai de l'Yser, 17100 Saintes
Tel: 05 46 97 78 12
www.restaurant-le-parvis.fr
A sophisticated, yet friendly restaurant producing elegantly presented seasonal fare. The chef is renowned for his macaroons and foie gras. High quality food served in nice surroundings, including a garden dining room. Closed Sun dinner and Mon. €€€

BURGUNDY AND FRANCHE-COMTÉ

Beaune
La Bouzerotte
21200 Bouze-lès-Beaune
Tel: 03 80 26 01 37
www.labouzerotte.fr
Dine on the sunny terrace or beside the cosy fire according to the season. Regional cuisine with a range of menu options of varying prices. Closed Mon and Tue. €€
Ma Cuisine
Passage Ste-Hélène, 21200 Beaune
Tel: 03 80 22 30 22
The daily menu revolves around the wine list, which has over 800 different wines listed. Small city centre restaurant, reservation advised. Closed Wed, Sat, Sun, and Aug. €€

Besançon
L'O à La Bouche
9 Rue du Lycée, 25000 Besançon
Tel: 03 81 82 09 08
Delightful restaurant in an old vaulted stone cellar. The menu offers fine regional cuisine making the best

of local produce, such as Morteau sausage. Closed Mon dinner, Sat lunch and Sun. €€

Dijon
Pré aux Clercs
13 Place de la Libération, 21000 Dijon
Tel: 03 80 38 05 05
www.jeanpierrebilloux.com
Rich traditional Burgundian cuisine cooked with panache by father and son team, Jean-Pierre and Alexis Billoux, and served with a delectable choice of highly prestigious wines. Closed Sun dinner, Mon and 10 days in Aug. €€€€

Puligny-Montrachet
La Table Olivier Leflaive
Place du Monument, 21190 Puligny-Montrachet
Tel: 03 80 21 37 65
www.olivier-leflaive.com
A wine tasting, of 10 or 14 different wines, accompanies the dishes in this typical stone built Burgundy house

situated in this world famous wine village. Closed Sun and Jan. €€

Saulieu
Côte d'Or
2 Rue Argentine, 21210 Saulieu
Tel: 03 80 90 53 53
This acclaimed restaurant and hotel inspired by the late Bernard Loiseau serves innovative cuisine, beautifully accompanied by an equally fine range of wines. Closed Tue, Wed and mid-Jan–mid Feb. €€€€

Vézelay
L'Espérance
St-Père, 89450 Vézelay
Tel: 03 86 33 39 10
Booking is essential at chef Marc Meneau's celebrated hotel/restaurant, with its glass conservatory/dining room that feels like part of the garden. Exceptional cuisine based on traditional Burgundy ingredients. Closed Mon, Tue, Wed lunch, and Jan–Feb. €€€€

RHÔNE VALLEY AND THE ALPS

Chaintré
La Table de Chaintré,
72 Place du Luminaire,
71570 Chaintré (9km/6 miles southwest of Mâcon)
Tel: 03 85 32 90 95
www.latabledechaintre.com

Popular with the local wine producers, this excellent restaurant is housed in an old stone building. One unique menu, which changes each week according to the seasonal produce bought at the market. Good choice of wines.

Closed Sun dinner and Mon–Tue. €€€

Chambéry
L'Essentiel
183 Place de la Gare, 73000 Chambéry
Tel: 04 79 96 97 27

In Lyon's historic centre.

Acclaimed as one of the best in Savoie where gastronomic specialities are superbly cooked. Closed Sat, Mon lunch and Sun. €€

Chamonix Mont-Blanc

La Calèche
Rue Dr Paccard,
74400 Chamonix
Tel: 04 50 55 94 68
www.restaurant-caleche.com
Traditional family-run restaurant serving Savoyard specialities. The decor evokes a bygone era with old skis, Swiss clocks and a bobsleigh from the 1924 Winter Olympics. Good Savoie wines. €€

Courchevel

Chabichou
73120 Courchevel
Tel: 04 79 08 00 55
www.chabichou-courchevel.com
One of the most popular restaurants in Courchevel, this Michelin-star hotel restaurant serves imaginative dishes and has fabulous mountain views. €€€€

Grenoble

La Mas Bottero
168 Cours Berriat,
38000 Grenoble.
Tel: 04 76 21 95 33
http://lemasbottero.com
Gourmet food at this city centre restaurant where the chef prepares traditional Lyon produce with a Mediterranean influence. Summer

dining does indeed takes place under the *glycine* (wisteria). Good selection of Rhône wines. Closed Mon, Sun and weeks in Aug. €€€

Juliénas

Taverne du Coq
Place du Marché, 69840 Juliénas
Tel: 04 74 04 41 98
www.taverneducoq.com
Sit on the terrace of this traditional Beaujolais bistro and enjoy the best of regional cuisine, not least its very own *coq au vin*. Closed Sat, Sun dinner, Thu and Dec–Mar. €€

Mâcon

Restaurant Pierre
7 Rue Dufour, 71000 Mâcon
Tel: 03 85 38 14 23
www.restaurant-pierre.com
Chef Christian Gaulin has earned a Michelin star for his impressive menus. All the finest ingredients of France are beautifully prepared and complemented by an excellent regional wine list. Closed Tue lunch, Sun dinner and Mon. €€€

Lyon

Cazenove
75 Rue Boileau, 69006 Lyon
Tel: 04 78 89 82 92
www.le-cazenove.com
It is service with a smile at this elegant brasserie. Competent French cooking delivers dishes such as roast squab confit and roasted monkfish with bouillabaisse broth. Closed Sat, Sun and Aug. €€

Pierre Orsi
3 Place Kléber,
69006 Lyon
Tel: 04 78 89 57 68
www.pierreorsi.com
One of Lyon's top chefs runs this luxurious bourgeois restaurant with a charming courtyard for summer dining. Closed Sun and Mon. €€€€

Brasserie Georges
30 Cours Verdun, 69002
Tel: 04 72 56 54 54
www.brasseriegeorges.com
Open non-stop from lunch to late at night every day, this brasserie is a Lyon icon. Splendidly preserved Art Deco dining room serving a wide variety of dishes, including Lyonnais specialities. €€

Saint-Agrève

Domaine de Rilhac
07320 Saint-Agrève
Tel: 04 69 00 13 05
www.domaine-de-rilhac-restaurant.fr
Magnificent mountain views and a rustic setting in an old Ardèche farmhouse. Traditional country dishes cooked with style. Closed Wed. €€

St-Martin-de-Belleville

La Bouitte
St Marcel, 73440 St-Martin-de-Belleville, Savoie
Tel: 04 79 08 96 77
www.la-bouitte.com
Traditional Alpine chalet hotel, situated in the Trois Vallées, where inventive dishes are created with care and talent, using local mountain herbs. Tempting desserts and a good selection of cheese and wines. Closed May–June, Sept–Nov. €€€€

Vienne

L'Estancot
4 Rue Table Ronde, 38200 Vienne
Tel: 04 74 85 12 09
Friendly city centre bistro frequented by the locals. Good value menus serving regional dishes. The house speciality is *criques*, which is the local equivalent of a potato rösti. Selection of mainly Rhône wines. Closed Sun, Mon and Christmas–mid-Jan. €€

PRICE CATEGORIES

Price categories are per person for a three-course meal:
€ = under €30
€€ = €30–60
€€€ = €60–100
€€€€ = more than €100

TRANSPORT

EATING OUT

ACTIVITIES

A – Z

LANGUAGE

AUVERGNE

Aurillac

La Scala
19 Rue G. de Veyre, 15000 Aurillac
Tel: 04 71 48 26 46
www.lascala-aurillac.fr
Popular restaurant that is excellent
for tasting the authentic flavours of
Italy, with a nice terrace and cosy
atmosphere. Desserts are to die for.
Closed Sun. €€

Clermont-Ferrand

Avenue
10 Rue Massillon, 63000 Clermont Ferrand
Tel: 04 73 90 44 64
www.restaurant-avenue.fr
This sleek, intimate restaurant is
really worth a visit. The inventive
menus might feature a starter of
crème brûlée with goat's cheese, a
main of duck ravioli with miso soup,
plus a dessert of chocolate mousse
with caramelised spices. Closed Sun
and Mon. €€

Pavillon Lamartine
17 Rue Lamartine, 63000 Clermont-
Ferrand
Tel: 04 73 93 52 25
www.pavillonlamartine.com

Stylish contemporary restaurant
with a terrace where you can sample
cuisine gastronomique. Closed Mon,
Tue dinner, Sun, and first half of Aug.
€€

Limoges

Les Petits Ventres
20 Rue de la Boucherie,
87000 Limoges
Tel: 05 40 26 13 08
www.les-petits-ventres.fr
A medieval building with a charming
terrace; the place to try the local
specialities (offal features heavily).
Closed Sun and Mon. €€

Le Puy-en-Velay

Tournayre
12 Rue Chênebouterie, 43000 Le Puy-en-
Velay
Tel: 04 71 09 58 94
Vaulted ceilings, stone walls and
frescoes create the setting for
this restaurant which is housed in
an ancient 16th-century chapel.
Generous Auvergne cuisine featuring
top-quality produce. Closed Wed,Sun
dinner, Mon and Jan. €€

Sarpoil

La Bergerie de Sarpoil
63490 St Jean en Val, Sarpoil (10km east
Issoire)
Tel: 04 73 71 02 54
http://labergeriedesarpoil.com
Popular local restaurant oocupying
a 16th-century inn. Various set
menus offer a great selection of
meat and fish dishes from talented
chef Cyrille Zen. In winter there is a
cosy fire in the dining room, and in
summer a shady terrace. Reservation
recommended. Closed Tue, Wed and
Sun dinner. €€

Vichy

La Table de Marlène
Boulevard de Latter-de-Tassigny, La
Rotunde, 03200 Vichy
Tel: 04 70 97 85 42
Ultra-modern glass and chrome
building sitting on the Lac d'Allier.
The restaurant La Table (closed Mon,
Tue), on the first floor, has a wonderful
view and serves fine contemporary
cuisine; La Rotonde (closed Mon), on
the ground floor with a terrace, has a
more traditional menu. €€

AQUITAINE

Arcachon

Chez Yvette
59 Boulevard du Général Leclerc, 33120
Arcachon
Tel: 05 56 83 05 11
Excellent fresh fish and seafood is
showcased in such specialities as
a seafood platter; seasonal catches
include sole, turbot, mullet and
oysters. €€

Barcus

Hôtel Chilo
64130 Barcus
Tel: 05 59 28 90 79
www.hotel-chilo.com
Friendly, family-run hotel in small
village near the Spanish border,
serving exceptional food – imaginative
Basque specialities are made with
fresh local produce. Closed Mon. €€

Bayonne

Auberge du Cheval Blanc
68 Rue Bourgneuf, 64100 Bayonne
Tel: 05 59 59 01 33
www.cheval-blanc-bayonne.com
A family-run restaurant in Petit
Bayonne that has been serving
classic regional cuisine for more than
50 years. Chef Jean-Claude Tellechea
has been awarded a Michelin star.
Closed Sat lunch, Sun dinner and
Mon. €€€

Biarritz

Le Galion
17 Boulevard du Général-de-Gaulle, 64200
Biarritz
Tel: 05 59 24 20 32
Located in a wonderful position with
a terrace overlooking the beach, Le
Galion offers well-prepared seafood
with a Basque flavour. €€

Bordeaux

L'Absinthe
137 Rue du Tondu, 33000 Bordeaux
Tel: 05 56 96 72 73
An authentic Belle Epoque bistro
with an open-air terrace in summer,
which is enclosed in winter so it can
still be used. Try the veal kidney with

Jambon de Bayonne, the ham from Bayonne.

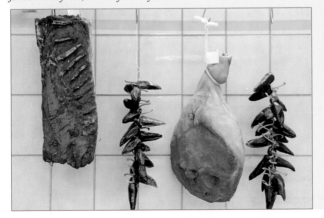

absinthe or smoked duck breast with peaches. Closed Sat lunch, Mon dinner and Sun. €€
Le Chapon Fin
5 Rue Montesquieu, 33000 Bordeaux
Tel: 05 56 79 10 10
www.chapon-fin.com
Head for this Bordeaux restaurant, with original Art Nouveau decor, to sample dishes such as yellow-ink cuttlefish, veal sweetbreads and rack of lamb. Closed Sun and Mon. €€€
Le Croc-Loup
35 Rue du Loup, 33000 Bordeaux
Tel: 05 56 44 21 19
www.crocloup.fr
Located in the old town, this small restaurant serves some good wholesome cuisine. Highlights include cuttlefish ravioli with coriander and a pyramid of iced nougat and raspberry coulis. Closed Sun, Mon and Wed. €€
Le Jardin de Burdigala
115 Rue Georges-Bonnac, 33000 Bordeaux
Tel: 05 56 90 16 16
www.burdigala.com
The gourmet restaurant of the Hôtel Burdigala has a glass roof and a statue of Bacchus in the centre to set the tone for its excellent selection of vintage Bordeaux wines. *Terrines de magret fumé* or *pigeons marinés* are amongst dishes that feature but the menu makes use of seasonal produce and changes regularly. €€€

Brantôme
Le Moulin de L'Abbaye
1 Route de Bourdeilles, 24310 Brantôme
Tel: 05 53 05 80 22
www.relaischateaux.com
A beautiful old mill with a peaceful terrace overlooking the River Dronne, where you can sample traditional Périgord dishes with a modern touch. Excellent Bergerac wines and good service. Closed Mon–Wed lunch, Mon dinner in May, Tue–Thu lunch, Wed dinner in Apr, and Nov–Feb. €€€

Domme
L'Esplanade
Rue Carral, Le Bourg, 24250 Domme

Tel: 05 53 28 31 41
www.esplanade-perigord.com
Wonderful views of the Dordogne from this hotel perched above the River Domme. Try trout, salmon or rack of lamb. Closed Nov–mid-Dec, mid-Jan–Feb. €€

Espelette
Euzkadi
285 Karrika Nagusia, 64250 Espelette
Tel: 05 59 93 91 88
www.hotel-restaurant-euzkadi.com
The house has a half-timbered façade hung with clusters of Espelette peppers in the autumn and the cuisine captures the best of Basque traditional food. €€

Eugénie-les-Bains
Les Prés d'Eugénie
40320 Eugénie-les-Bains
Tel: 05 58 05 06 07
www.michelguerard.com
Michel Guérard, inventor of *cuisine minceur* (haute cuisine for the figure-conscious), proposes three styles of menu here. Slimming Cuisine: healthy eating with great style; 3-Michelin-Star Cuisine: classic gastronomic; and La Ferme aux Grives: very reasonably priced country-style lunches and dinners. Reservations essential. €€€€

Pau
Le Jeu de Paume
1 Avenue Edouard VII, 64000 Pau
Tel: 05 59 11 84 00
Gourmet restaurant in the ultra-chic Hôtel Park Beaumont, near the Boulevard des Pyrénées. Sober, spacious and with a modern decor, it specialises in regional cuisine. Reservations essential. €€€

Saint-Jean-de-Luz
Donibane
4 avenue Laiatz, 64500 Saint-Jean-de-Luz
Tel: 05 59 26 21 21
www.hotel-donibane-saintjeandeluz.fr
In summer, there are excellent views of the mountain of La Rhune from this hotel restaurant. Chef Maxime

Lacombe specialises in dishes derived from Basque cuisine. €

St-Emilion
Le Clos du Roy
12 Rue de la Petite Fontaine, 33330 Saint-Emilion
Tel: 05 57 74 41 55
www.leclosduroy.fr
A classy restaurant in the old town, with two dining rooms and a terrace, serving refined French cuisine. Closed Mon and Tue. €€
Hostellerie de Plaisance
Place du Clocher, 33330 St-Emilion
Tel: 05 57 55 07 55
www.hostellerieplaisance.com
Splendid views of the medieval town of St Emilion and surrounding vineyards as you dine on local cuisine and local wine in the heart of wine country. Closed for lunch (except on Sat), Sun, Mon, and mid-Dec to first week Feb. €€€€

Sauternes
Le Saprien
11 Rue Principale, 33210 Sauternes
Tel: 05 56 76 60 87
www.restaurantlesaprien.fr
This restaurant in a village house has a terrace with tables set facing the vineyards in summer. It serves carefully prepared regional and seasonal cuisine, including filet mignon of pork chorizo and smoked Scottish salmon. Closed Sun dinner and Mon. €€

Valence-sur-Baïse
La Ferme de Flaran
Bagatelle
Maignaut Tauzia, 32310 Valence-sur-Baïse
Tel: 05 62 29 39 83
www.fermedeflaran.com.
A rustic-style restaurant serving regional dishes including *foie gras*, confit and *magret de canard* at their best. It has also a good selection of Armagnac brandies to give the final touch to your meal. There is a terrace for summer dining. Closed Sun dinner and Mon. €€

MIDI-PYRÉNÉES

Albi
L'Esprit du Vin
1 Quai Choiseul, 81000 Albi
Tel: 05 63 54 60 44
A gourmet restaurant in an old building in the centre of the city, in which the decoration successfully combines local and modern style. In

the same way, the dishes combine tradition with originality. Closed Sun and Mon. €€€

Auch
La Grande Salle
L'Hôtel de France, Place de la Libération, 32000 Auch

PRICE CATEGORIES

Price categories are per person for a three-course meal:
€ = under €30
€€ = €30–60
€€€ = €60–100
€€€€ = more than €100

TRANSPORT
EATING OUT
ACTIVITIES
A - Z
LANGUAGE

Tel: 05 62 61 71 71
www.hoteldefrance-auch.com
Just a couple of minutes' walk from
the cathedral, the hotel's restaurant
is true to its regional roots. Foie gras
and duck dishes feature strongly. For
more modern dining try the brasserie
(open daily). Closed Sat lunch, Sun
dinner and Mon. €€
La Table d'Oste
7 Rue Lamartine, 32000 Auch
Tel: 05 62 05 55 62
www.latabledoste.com
This restaurant near the cathedral
has a small terrace for al fresco
dining. It specialises in duck dishes,
and other regional recipes using
ingredients from local farmers. Closed
Sun and Mon lunch. €€

Castres
Le Victoria
24 Place 8 Mai 1945, 81100 Castres
Tel: 05 63 59 14 68
www.le-victoria-restaurant.com
Located in the vaulted cellars of a
17th-century convent near the Musée
Goya, this restaurant specialises in
regional cuisine. Closed Sat lunch
and Sun dinner. €€

Condom
La Table des Cordeliers
1 Rue Cordeliers, 32100 Condom
Tel: 05 62 68 43 82
www.latabledescordeliers.com
Restaurant housed in a 13th-century
chapel with a terrace in the summer.
Innovative cuisine with regional
ingredients. Closed Sun and Mon.
€€€

Conques
Hotel Ste-Foy
Rue Principale, 12320 Conques

Tel: 05 65 69 84 03
www.hotelsaintefoy.com
One of Aveyron's best hotels, a
charming stone and timber building
beautifully restored with intimate
dining room and flowery courtyard.
Inventive cooking and menu
changed daily. Closed Nov–Easter.
€€

Cordes
Bistrot Tonin'ty
Hostellerie du Vieux Cordes, Haut de la
Cité, 81170 Cordes-sur-Ciel
Tel: 05 63 53 79 20
www.vieuxcordes.fr
The restaurant of the historic
Hostellerie du Vieux Cordes has a
charming patio under a 100-year-old
wisteria. There are wonderful views
from the terrace in summer. €€

Figeac
La Belle Epoque
Le Coustal Camboulit, 46100 Camboulit
Tel: 05 65 40 04 42
www.domainelabelleepoque.com
Located 6km (4 miles) outside
Figeac, this restaurant forms part
of a rural holiday complex. It has a
shady terrace under plane trees and
a swimming pool. It serves mainly
traditional regional dishes. €€

Najac
Relais Mont Le Viaur
La Croix Grande, 12270 Najac
Tel: 05 65 65 08 68
www.montleviaur.fr
This charming hotel-restaurant
delivers a consistently high standard,
using regional produce and blending
traditional recipes with imaginative
touches. Eat in the elegant dining
room or on the terrace. Closed

Sun–Tue dinner and mid-Dec–mid-
Jan. €€

Rocamadour
Beausite
Cité Mediévale, 46500 Rocamadour
Tel: 05 65 33 63 08
www.bw-beausite.com
You can sample regional gourmet
cuisine here while enjoying the view
over the Alzou valley from the terrace
of this hotel-restaurant. Try the duck
foie gras terrine with mango chutney
and the local Cahors wine. €€

Toulouse
La Bohème
3 Rue Lafayette, 31000 Toulouse
Tel: 05 61 23 24 18
A romantically vaulted restaurant in
a street near the Place du Capitole,
specialising in cassoulet, magret de
canard and other regional dishes.
Closed Sat lunch and Sun. €€
Brasserie Flo les Beaux-Arts
1 Quai de la Daurade, 31000 Toulouse
Tel: 05 61 21 12 12
www.brasserielesbeauxarts.com
A lively and popular brasserie on the
quayside that blends Art Deco with
Belle Epoque. The oysters here are
especially recommended. €€
Michel Sarran
21 Boulevard Armand Duportal, 31000
Toulouse
Tel: 05 61 12 32 32
www.michel-sarran.com
Michel Sarran's elegant manor
house, with its classy interior
decoration, is one of Toulouse's best
restaurants. It has two intimate dining
rooms where Sarran, one of France's
most celebrated chefs, serves his
highly creative cuisine. Closed Wed
lunch, Sat, Sun and Aug. €€€€

LANGUEDOC AND ROUSSILLON

Bouzigues
Côte Bleue
34140 Bouzigues
Tel: 04 67 78 30 87
www.la-cote-bleue.fr
Large family restaurant overlooking
the Bassin de Thau, the best place to
sample mussels, langoustines, and
the local Bouzigues oysters. Closed
Wed. €€

Carcassonne
L'Escargot
7 Rue Violet-le-Duc, 11000 Carcassonne
Tel: 06 89 76 07 95
www.restaurant-lescargot-carcassonne.fr
Lovely little French tapas bar with a
quirky ambience, warm welcome and

an enthusiastic owner who personally
looks after his customers. It's right in
the heart of the walled citadel. Closed
Wed. €

Céret
L'Atelier de Fred
Rue Saint Férreol, 66400 Céret
Tel: 04 68 95 47 41
http://atelier-restaurant-ceret.com
Fred himself offers true hospitality
in contemporary surroundings. The
great-value Mediterranean-style
menu changes daily and everything
is cooked to perfection. The pretty
courtyard is smashing on a warm
evening. Closed Mon and Sun
dinner. €

Collioure
Les Templiers
12 Quai de l'Amirauté,
66190 Collioure
Tel: 04 68 98 31 10
www.hotel-templiers.com
Restaurant and hotel famous for
the many artists who stayed here,
Matisse and Braque among them;
fish and seafood feature on the
menu. Closed Jan–mid-Feb. €–€€

Narbonne
La Table de St-Crescent
68 Avenue du Général-Leclerc,
11100 Narbonne
Tel: 04 68 41 37 37
www.la-table-saint-crescent.com

Elegant contemporary dining room in ancient oratory. Inventive cuisine from the sea and Languedoc hinterland. Excellent regional wines. Vine-covered outdoor terrace. Closed Mon, Tue, Sun (Jan–June and Oct–Nov) and Sun, Mon dinner (Jul–Sept, Dec). €€€

Nîmes

La Patio Littré
10 Rue Littré, 30000 Nîmes
Tel: 04 66 67 22 50
www.lepatiolittre.fr
Just down the road from the covered food market you can be sure the produce is fresh in this friendly bistro. Interior courtyard for

summer meals. Closed Mon and Tue. €€

Perpignan

Casa Sansa
2 Rue Fabrique d'en Nadal, 66000 Perpignan
Tel: 04 68 50 48 01
Lively Catalan restaurant in the old town, very popular with locals. €€

Sète

La Palangrotte
Quai de la Marine, Rampe Paul-Valèry, 34200 Sète
Tel: 04 67 74 80 35
The blackboard announces the dishes of the day based on the

catch of the day. Some of the best seafood on the coast, with super fresh oysters and shellfish. Closed Mon. €€

Villefranche-de-Confluent

Auberge Saint-Paul
7 Place de l'Eglise, 66500 Villefranche-de-Confluent
Tel: 04 68 96 30 95
www.auberge-st-paul.fr
In a 13th-century chapel this charming restaurant has sophisticated dishes, served in a rustic dining room or on a shady terrace. Excellent choice of Roussillon and Burgundy wines. Closed Mon and Jan. €€

PROVENCE AND CÔTE D'AZUR

Aix-en-Provence

Les Deux Frères
4 Avenue de la Reine Astrid, 13090 Aix-en-Provence
Tel: 04 42 27 90 32
www.les2freres.com
Provençal dishes in a trendy bistro with attractive terrace. Expect dishes such as poached cod and braised rabbit leg. Closed Sun dinner. €€

L'Esprit de la Violette
10 Avenue de la Violette, 13100 Aix en Provence
Tel: 04 42 23 02 50
http://lespritdelaviolette.com
Dining here is not just about the inventive cuisine artistically presented by Chef Marc Passorio – attentive but unobtrusive service and the stylish subdued surroundings also leave you wanting more. Closed Sun and Mon. €€€€

Antibes

Restaurant de Bacon
Boulevard Bacon, 06160 Cap d'Antibes
Tel: 04 93 61 50 02
www.restaurantdebacon.com
Restaurant famous for its fish dishes, in particular its spectacular *bouillabaisse*. Closed Mon, Tue lunch and Nov–Mar. €€€

Arles

Le Criquet
21 Rue Porte de Laure, 13200 Arles
Tel: 04 90 96 80 51
Not far from the Arènes, this rustic restaurant proposes dishes in the traditional style of The Camargue. Look out for sea bass with rosemary sauce and carré d'agneau. Closed Mon and Tue. €€

Avignon

La Vieille Fontaine
Hôtel d'Europe, 12 Place Crillon, 84000 Avignon
Tel: 04 90 14 76 76
www.heurope.com
This grand 16th-century town house has a charming courtyard and terrace, a perfect setting for the unusual cuisine. Closed Sun, Mon and Jan. €€€

Les-Baux-de-Provence

Oustaù de Baumanière
13520 Les-Baux-de-Provence
Tel: 04 90 54 33 07
www.oustaudebaumaniere.com
Well-known gourmet restaurant in a 16th-century building in the spectacular fortress town of Les Baux. The favourite dishes are truffle ravioli and *rack of suckling pig*. Closed Jan, Feb, and Tue, Wed and Thu lunch rest of winter. €€€€

Biot

Les Terraillers
11 Route du Chemin Neuf
Tel: 04 93 65 01 59
www.lesterraillers.com
Elegant restaurant in the vaulted room of an ancient pottery. Richly flavoured dishes feature local produce, such as truffles and herbs from the nearby hills. The selection of Provence wines is good. Attractive terrace. €€€

Cannes

L'Affable
5 Rue Lafontaine, 06400 Cannes
Tel: 04 93 68 02 09
Contemporary bistro with glass, marble and wood decor. The open kitchen dishes out classic dishes

and delicious desserts with an individual twist. Particularly good value lunch menu. Closed Sat lunch and Sun. €€

Marseille

L'Epuisette
158 Rue du Vallon de Auffes, 13007 Marseille
Tel: 04 91 52 17 82
www.l-epuisette.fr
Built on a craggy rock out over the sea, the views around this restaurant are amazing. Dishes reflect top cooking skills, a sense of art and the local catch of the day. Closed Sun and Mon. €€€€

Menton

Mirazur
30 Avenue Aristide-Briand, 06500 Menton
Tel: 04 92 41 86 86
www.mirazur.fr
Reputed to be the best restaurant in Menton. The chef Mauro Colagreco creates sophisticated dishes with inventive combinations of ingredients. Panoramic terrace overlooking the sea. Closed Mon and Tue. €€€€

Monaco

Café de Paris
Place du Casino, 98000 Monte-Carlo
Tel: 377 98 06 76 23

PRICE CATEGORIES

Price categories are per person for a three-course meal:
€ = under €30
€€ = €30–60
€€€ = €60–100
€€€€ = more than €100

TRANSPORT

EATING OUT

ACTIVITIES

A – Z

LANGUAGE

This wonderful brasserie in the Belle Epoque-style is one of the sights of Monte-Carlo and a great way to sample the glamour without breaking the bank. €€

La Mérenda
4 Rue Raoul Bosio, 06300 Nice
http://lamerenda.net
This little bistro tucked away in the old town has a big reputation; cognoscenti drop in to make a reservation, since there is no phone. It is celebrated for its classic Niçoise cuisine, cooked by renowned chef Dominique le Stanc. Closed Sat–Sun, Easter, 31 July–20 Aug, Nov–Christmas, and public hols. No credit cards. €€

Auberge de la Madone
2 Place Auguste-Arnulf, 06440 Peillon
Tel: 04 93 79 91 17
www.auberge-madone-peillon.com

Mountain views guaranteed from the terrace of this delightful inn. Excellent regional cuisine offering a good choice of both meat and fish dishes. Closed Wed and Nov–Feb. €€€

Le Sloop
Port de Plaisance, 06230 St-Jean-Cap-Ferrat
Tel: 04 93 01 48 63
Superb choice of fish and seafood dishes at this restaurant overlooking the harbour. Try grilled lobster and stuffed squid. Closed Wed and Tue dinner. €€

Colombe d'Or
Place du Général-de-Gaulle, 06570 St-Paul-de-Vence
Tel: 04 93 32 80 02
This is an exquisite small hotel and restaurant, full of artworks donated by Picasso, Braque, Miró and many more when they came to what was then a

village café in the 1920s. The large terrace is open in summer. Closed Nov–Christmas. €€€

La Fontaine
19 Boulevard Mirabeau, 13210 St-Rémy-de-Provence
Tel: 04 32 60 16 89
Original salads, simple tasty grilled meat and home-made pasta are the specialities of this delightful restaurant. And the desserts are superb, with over 40 different flavours of ice-cream to choose from – all made with local produce. Closed Thur; Nov–Feb. €

Le Gireliers
Quai Jean-Jaurès, 84100 St-Tropez
Tel: 04 94 97 03 87
www.legirelier.fr
One of the best-value restaurants in St-Tropez. High-quality fish dishes prepared in the midst of the hustle and bustle of the port. €€

CORSICA

Le Bistrot d'Emile
6 Rue de L'Assomption, 2000 Ajaccio
Tel: 04 95 51 00 81
A great find tucked down a narrow alley near the main square, where good cooking skills and interesting combinations are evident in the tasty food. Closed Mon. €€

Aux Coquillages de Diane
Etang de Diane, 20270 Aléria
Tel: 04 95 57 04 55
www.restaurant-coquillagesdediana-aleria.com
Floating restaurant on the vast lake, a source for the oysters, mussels and fish on the menu. Large terrace with views out over oyster beds. Next door you can buy fresh oyster and mussels direct from the producer. Closed Fri lunch, Sat dinner and Jan €€

L'Ardoise
4 Place de l'Hôtel-de-Ville, 20200 Bastia
Tel: 04 95 35 17 11
Intimate bistro with tables on the square offering superb quality Corsican food. The hot-stone experience or fish fondue are a welcoming novelty. Closed Mon, Wed dinner and Tue. €

Stella d'Oro (Chez Jules)
23 Rue Doria, near the church of St-Jean-Baptiste
Tel: 04 95 73 03 63
www.restaurant-stelladoro-bonifacio.com
Try Bonifacio's showpiece *merrizzane* here – aubergine stuffed with brocciu cheese, tomatoes and herbs, baked in a wood-fired oven. Closed Nov–Apr. €€€

L'Abri Côtier
Quai Landry, 10 Rue Joffre, 20260 Calvi
Tel: 04 95 65 00 04
Panoramic view from this quayside restaurant. The menu has a range of well-presented dishes to please the International set, with Corsican dishes alongside more cosmopolitan choices. Closed Jan–Mar. €€

U Rasaghiu
Port de Plaisance, 20130 Cargèse
Tel: 04 95 26 48 60
Succulent grilled seafood platters, rock lobster and copious pizzas at quayside restaurant, with a lovely terrace overlooking the sea. Live Corsican music in summer. Closed Nov–Mar. €€

A Macciotta (Chez Sker)
Behind the harbour
Tel: 04 95 35 64 12
Seafood fans shouldn't pass up the chance to eat at this tiny restaurant in an old fisherman's cottage. Sea bass, anemones and lobster are on the *menu poisson*. Closed Nov–Apr. €€

A Cantina di L'Orriu
5 Cours-Napoléon, 20137 Porto Vecchio
Tel: 04 95 25 95 89
Cosy Old Town restaurant with an open fireplace for winter, and a pretty terrace for outdoor eating. Favourites include sautéed veal, home-made ravioli and generous Corsican cold meats. Closed Mon, Tue lunch and Jan–Mar. €€

Price categories are per person for a three-course meal:
€ = under €30
€€ = €30–60
€€€ = €60–100
€€€€ = more than €100

TRANSPORT

ACTIVITIES

EATING OUT

THE ARTS, FESTIVALS AND EVENTS, NIGHTLIFE, SHOPPING AND SPORT

THE ARTS

Live Entertainment

There is a huge variety of live entertainment in France, much of it taking place in Paris and other major cities. In the summer, many of these major cities (and even small towns) present a programme of events, including music and drama festivals, featuring a variety of street theatre and other live outdoor performances, which are often free.

A programme listing all major festivals and *fêtes* throughout the country is published annually. The

Ticket Booking

To book tickets from London

Hello Paris
4 Elmwood, Crockford Lane,
Chineham Road, Basingstoke,
RG24 8WG
Tel: 01256 521003
www.helloparis.co.uk
Cabaret shows, sightseeing tours,
museum and monuments passes,
Paris Visite travel card.
Liaisons Abroad
1 Warwick Row, London SW1E 5ER
Tel: 020 7808 7330
www.liaisonsabroad.com
Cultural festivals, sports.

Paris booking

Ticketac
14 Boulevard Haussmann, 75009
Paris
www.ticketac.com
Theatre, opera, sports, etc.
Branches of **Fnac** have ticket offices
for concerts, theatre, etc. Also
available online on www.fnac.com

programme is available from French Government Tourist Offices around the world. Note that theatre and opera seasons generally run from September to June, with many theatres and concert halls closed in July and August, when cultural activity turns to the prestigious summer arts festivals in the regions.

Son et lumière displays still exist at some châteaux and historic monuments but are now in decline because they are very expensive to present. Performances normally begin at around 9 or 10pm, and there are often several shows a night in July and August.

For information and reservations contact the local tourist offices. A national guide of historical shows is published annually and is available from the **Fédération Nationale des Fêtes et Spectacles Historiques**, 15 Impasse Croix de Régnier, 13004 Marseille, tel: 09 55 30 60 67; www.fffsh.eu.

Theatre, Dance and Opera

In Paris

The theatre and opera companies of the Comédie Française and the Opéra National de Paris perform at major venues and are most famous for their classical productions, but there is a good choice of theatre, concerts, opera and ballet for all tastes to be enjoyed in the capital, with the Théâtre de la Ville, Théâtre National de la Colline and Théâtre National de Chaillot catering for more modern tastes in theatre and dance. Just a short train ride from the city centre, the Centre National de Danse has mainly contemporary dance performances. The following are some of the major venues:

Comédie Française
2 Rue de Richelieu, 75001 Paris
Tel: 0825 101 680
www.comedie-francaise.fr
Opéra National de Paris
Opéra Bastille, 2bis Place de la
Bastille, 75012 Paris
Palais Garnier, Place de l'Opéra,
75009 Paris
Tel: 08 92 89 90 90
www.operadeparis.fr
Théâtre du Châtelet
1 Place du Châtelet, 75001 Paris
Tel: 01 40 28 28 00
www.chatelet-theatre.com
Théâtre National de Chaillot
1 Place du Trocadéro, 75116 Paris
Tel: 01 53 65 30 00
www.theatre-chaillot.fr
Théâtre National de la Colline
15 Rue Malte-Brun, 75020 Paris
Tel: 01 44 62 52 52
www.colline.fr
Théâtre Palais Royal
38 Rue de Montpensier, 75001
Paris
Tel: 01 42 97 40 00
www.theatrepalaisroyal.com
Théâtre de la Ville
2 Place du Châtelet, 75004 Paris
Tel: 01 42 74 22 77
www.theatredelaville-paris.com
Centre National de Danse
1 Rue Victor Hugo, 93507 Pantin
Tel: 01 41 83 98 98
www.cnd.fr

Outside Paris

Other major cities also have excellent opera, theatre and dance venues. Here are some of the main regional venues.
Grand Théâtre
Place de la Comédie, 33000
Bordeaux
Tel: 05 56 00 85 95
www.opera-bordeaux.com

ACTIVITIES

A – Z

LANGUAGE

The Palais Garnier, home to the Paris Opera.

Théâtre National de Bordeaux en Aquitaine
Place Renaudel, 33000 Bordeaux
Tel: 05 56 33 36 80
www.tnba.org
Grand Théâtre
Place du Ralliement, 49000 Angers
Tel: 02 41 24 16 40
www.nta-angers.fr
Opéra de Lille
2 Rue des Bons-Enfants, 59001 Lille
Tel: 03 28 38 40 50
www.opera-lille.fr
Opéra National de Lyon
Place de la Comédie, 69001 Lyon
Tel: 04 69 85 54 54
www.opera-lyon.com
Opéra Municipal de Marseille
20 Rue Beauvau, 13001 Marseille
Tel: 04 91 55 11 10
http://opera.marseille.fr/en
Opéra du Rhin
19 Place de Broglie, 67000
Strasbourg
Tel: 03 88 75 48 00
www.operanationaldurhin.eu
Opéra de Rouen Haute-Normandie
7 Rue du Docteur Rambert, 76000
Rouen
Tel: 02 35 98 74 78
www.operaderouen.fr
Grand Opéra de Tours
34 Rue de la Scellerie, 37000 Tours
Tel: 02 47 60 20 00
www.operadetours.fr
Opéra de Monte-Carlo
Place du Casino, 98000 Monaco
Tel: 377 98 06 28 28
www.opera.mc
Opéra Comédie
11 Boulevard Victor-Hugo, 34000
Montpellier
Tel: 04 67 60 19 99
www.opera-orchestre-montpellier.fr
Centre Chorégraphique National
Boulevard Louis-Blanc, 34000
Montpellier
Tel: 04 67 60 06 70
www.mathildemonnier.com
Théâtre Graslin
1 Rue Molière, 44000 Nantes

Tel: 02 40 69 77 18
www.angers-nantes-opera.com
Opéra de Nice
4 Rue St-François-de-Paul, 06300 Nice
Tel: 04 92 17 40 00
www.opera-nice.org
Théâtre du Capitole
Place du Capitole, 31000 Toulouse
Tel: 05 61 63 13 13
www.theatre-du-capitole.fr

Popular Music

The French popular music scene is diverse ranging from rock, acoustic, jazz and techno to World music. The national music festival, Fête de la Musique, held annually on 21st June, is the best event to discover the different genres of music in France. The former Minister of Culture Jack Lang inaugurated the first Fête de la Musique in 1982, and each year professionals and amateurs alike give performances throughout France, all night long.

Pop music in France reflects the International scene, and much of what you hear will be the same as anywhere else. In more remote corners of France traditional styles of music have survived, notably in the Basque country, Corsica and Brittany.

Jazz Clubs

Jazz, which became popular in the 1920s in Paris, is still strongly represented. You are sure to find a choice of jazz clubs in main towns, and there are several major jazz festivals throughout the year. Some of the best jazz clubs in Paris are:
Au Duc des Lombards
42 Rue des Lombards, 75001 Paris
Tel: 01 45 33 22 88
www.ducdeslombards.com
Attracts a high standard of jazz artists who entertain a savoir-faire crowd in an intimate space. Dinner can be enjoyed at the same time.

Caveau de la Huchette
5 Rue de la Huchette, 75005 Paris
Tel: 01 43 26 65 05
www.caveaudelahuchette.fr
Famous jazz club with a funky contemporary programme that attracts a huge crowd. Concerts start around 9pm and carry on until the early morning hours.
Jazz Club Etoile
81 Boulevard Gouvin-Saint-Cyr, 75017 Paris
Tel: 01 40 68 30 42
www.jazzclub-paris.com
Close to the Champs-Elysées. Live concerts Thu–Sat 9.30pm–1am.
New Morning
7–9 Rue des Petites Ecuries, 75010 Paris
Tel: 01 45 23 51 41
www.newmorning.com
All the greats have played here – from Chet Baker to Stan Getz and Miles Davis. Sets generally start around 9pm.
Le Petit Journal Montparnasse
13 Rue du Commandant Mouchotte, 75014 Paris
Tel: 01 43 21 56 70
www.petitjournalmontparnasse.com
Small, intimate club with performances from top jazz musicians.
Sunset/Sunside
60 Rue des Lombards, 75001 Paris
Tel: 01 40 26 46 60
www.sunset-sunside.com
The Sunset offers two jazz clubs in one: electric jazz and World music on the ground floor and acoustic jazz in the more intimate cellar.
And following is a selection of jazz clubs in other major towns:

Lyon
Hot Club
26 Rue de la Lanterne, 69001 Lyon
Tel: 04 78 39 54 74
www.hotclubjazzlyon.com
Jazz concerts Wed–Sat from 9.30pm.
Bec de Jazz
19 Rue Burdeau, 69001 Lyon
Tel: 06 69 38 74 17
Jazz-piano bar in the Croix-Rousse district. Wed–Sat 11pm–5am
Le Clef de Voûte
1 Place Chardonnet, 69001 Lyon
Tel: 04 78 28 51 95
www.laclefdevoute.fr
Intimate jazz club in the city centre.
Wed–Sat from 9pm; Sun 5pm.

Grenoble
Jazz à la Soupe
7 Route de Lyon, 38000 Grenoble
Tel: 04 76 87 05 67
www.jazzalasoupe.fr
All jazz styles are represented. Tue–Sat from 9pm.

Bordeaux
Le Comptoir du Jazz
59 Quai de Paludate, 33000
Bordeaux
Tel: 05 56 49 15 55
www.portdelalune-comptoirdujazz.com
Jazz bar and restaurant, jazz concerts;
closed Sun and Mon.

Nice
La Cave Romagnan
22 Rue Angleterre, 06300 Nice
Tel: 04 93 87 91 55
Jazz on Saturday nights.

Toulouse
Le Mandala
23 Rue des Amidonniers, 31000
Toulouse
Tel: 05 61 21 10 05
www.lemandala.com
Early evening jazz sessions on the
terrace in summer. Concerts Thu–Sat
from 9pm.

Music Venues

Music venues range from sport
arenas and modern concert halls
to *antiques théâtres* and *arènes*. In
Paris the main venues include Bercy,
a glass-covered pyramid hosting
sporting events, music concerts and
shows; Le Zénith, a modern concert
hall considered to be the best Paris
venue by top artists; Le Bataclan,
a concert hall hosting international
musicians from rock, to jazz to World
music; and the restored Salle Pleyel,
popular for jazz.
There are several purpose-built
Le Zénith venues throughout France
in major town such as Toulouse,
Dijon, Nantes and Montpellier. Other
main concert halls include the Halle
Tony Garnier in Lyon and Le Dôme at
Marseille.

The Fête de la Musique in full swing in Strasbourg.

Cinema

Cinema programmes in France
change every Wednesday. Films
marked V.O. *(version originale)* are
screened in the original language, not
dubbed into French. Watch out for
listings of V.O. films at mainstream
cinemas in major cities. Although
more uncommon in smaller towns,
cinemas may offer some films in
V.O., usually at a late night *séance*.
Many regional cinemas run mini-
festivals for film aficionados. During
the summer months open-air
cinemas are a regular sight. Aside
from Cannes, there are excellent
but lower-profile festivals: American
Film Festival at Deauville; Festival
du Film Britannique, Dinard; Festival
International du Film, La Rochelle,
Festival du Film Péplum, Arles.
In Paris, cinemas along the Champs-
Elysées (8th *arrondissement*) and
around Odéon in St-Germain-des-Prés
(6th *arrondissement*) often show recent
releases in their original language, as
do the Latin Quarter arts cinemas (5th
arrondissement) for old movies. The
following are repertory cinemas, with
interesting themed seasons, often
in V.O. But unfortunately these are
becoming rarer to find:
Cinémathèque Française
51 Rue de Bercy, 75012 Paris
Tel: 01 71 19 33 33
www.cinematheque.fr
Forum des Images
2 Rue du Cinéma, Forum de Halles,
75001 Paris
Tel: 01 44 76 63 00
www.forumdesimages.fr

Lyon
Institut Lumière
25 Rue de 1er Film, 69008 Lyon
Tel: 04 78 78 18 95

www.institut-lumiere.org
Cinéma Opéra
6 Rue Joseph-Serlin, 69001 Lyon
Tel: 04 78 28 80 08

Lille
Le Métropole
26 Rue des Ponts-de-Comines,
59000 Lille
Tel: 03 20 54 70 88
www.lemetropolelille.com

Nantes
Le Cinématographe
12 bis, Rue des Carmélites, 44000
Nantes
Tel: 02 40 47 94 80
www.lecinematographe.com

Bordeaux
Utopia St Siméon
5 Place Camille-Jullian, 33000
Bordeaux
Tel: 05 56 52 00 03

Dijon
Cinéma Eldorado
21 Rue Alfred-de-Husset, 21000 Dijon
Tel: 03 80 66 51 89

Marseille
Les Variétés
37 Rue Vincent-Scotto, 13001
Marseille
Tel: 0892 68 05 97

Nice
Cinéma Rialto
4 Rue de Rivoli, 06000 Nice
Tel: 0892 68 00 41

Strasbourg
Le Star Saint-Exupery
16 Rue du 22 Novembre, 67000
Strasbourg
Tel: 03 88 22 73 20

FESTIVALS AND EVENTS

Listed here are brief details of the
main annual events; there are
hundreds more taking place in the
smaller towns and villages. For more
specific information, contact the local
tourist offices or visit www.france-
voyage.com and www.viafrance.com,
where you can search events in France
by month, location and category.
January: Angoulême international
strip-cartoon festival; Monte-Carlo
International Circus Festival; La Folle
Journée classical music festival,
Nantes; St-Vincent Tournante wine
fête, Beaune.
February: Menton Lemon Festival;
Nice Carnival; Les Hivernales dance

TRANSPORT

EATING OUT

ACTIVITIES

A–Z

LANGUAGE

386 ◆ TRAVEL TIPS

festival, Avignon; Dunkerque Carnival; Fêtes de Mimosa at Bormes-les-Mimosas.
March: Omnivore Food Festival, Paris.
April: Monte-Carlo Printemps des Arts; European Film Festival, Lille; Paris Marathon.
May: Cannes Film Festival; Grasse international rose show; Mâcon wine festival; Monaco Grand Prix Formula 1 race; Nîmes *Féria* de Pentecôte bullfighting fiesta; French Tennis Open, Paris; La Bravade, St Tropez; Gypsy Pilgrimage, Saintes-Maries-de-la-Mer.
June: Calvi Jazz, Corsica; Chartres Music Festival; Noirlac Music Festival; Fête de la Musique (France-wide, 21 June); Festival d'Anjou theatre festival; Festival de St-Denis (Paris) classical music and dance; Les 24 heures du Mans car race; Fête de la Tarasque, Tarascon; Paris Jazz Festival; Gay Pride, Paris street parade, performances and parties; Les Voiles d'Antibes, Antibes yacht regatta; Festival de Marseille.
July: Jazz à Vienne (Vienne) jazz festival; Tour de France cycle race (France-wide); Francofolies de La Rochelle popular music festival; Montpellier Danse; Festival de Radio-France classical music, Montpellier; Orange Chorégies opera festival; Lorraine Air Ballons hot-air balloon festival (bi-annual event, next one in 2017); Aix-en-Provence International Opera Festival; Jazz à Juan (Antibes) jazz festival; Avignon Festival; Bastille Day – celebrated throughout France on the 14th; Fêtes de Cornouailles, Quimper; OENO Music Festival, Dijon.
August: Fêtes d'Arvor, Breton culture festival in Vannes; Antibes International Fireworks Festival; Fête du Lac Annecy, annual lake festival; Lorient Inter-Celtic Festival; Marciac Jazz Festival; Menton Music Festival; Flower Festival, Bagnères de Luchon; International Piano Festival, Roque d'Antheron (Provence); Rencontres Internationales Photographiques d'Arles photography festival; Paris Quartier d'Eté, Pottery Festival, Vallauris; St-Malo Route du Rock.
September: Fête de la Lumière, Chartres; Journées du Patrimoine (France-wide, third weekend in Sept); Strasbourg Music Festival; American Film Festival, Deauville; Grande Braderie de Lille; Festival d'Automne, Paris; Printemps de Toulouse contemporary art/photo festival; Piano aux Jacobins, Toulouse; Les Voiles de St-Tropez, St Tropez sailing boat regatta.
October: Planètes Jazz Tourcoing (Lille); Paris Motor Show; Montmartre

Wine Harvest, Paris; FIAC Paris contemporary art fair; Nuit Blanche in Paris; Nancy Jazz Pulsations; Fête d'Art Sacré religious music festival, Festival du Film Policier, Cognac (Crime Drama festival); Jazz in Touraine.
November: Dijon International Gastronomy Fair; Paris-Photo, Paris; Beaujolais Nouveau celebrations; Beaune Wine Auction; Dijon Gastronomic Fair.
December: Transmusicales de Rennes rock festival; Fête de la Lumière, Lyon; Paris Boat Show; Christmas markets, Strasbourg, Colmar, Kaysersberg; Critérium International de la Première Neige, Val d'Isère, first ski competition of the season; Foire aux Santons, Fréjus, Provençal craftsmen exhibit *santons* (small clay crib figures).

NIGHTLIFE

Where to Go

Paris offers excellent nightlife, with a huge choice of venues and entertainment; in the provinces you need to be in the major towns to find a similar standard. Many towns now organise festivals that run through the summer for both local people and tourists. If you are staying on a farm or in a country area, you may be invited to join in local festivities. Almost every town and village has its own *fête* during the summer; these range from simple *boules* competitions with a dance, hosted by an enthusiastic (sometimes excruciating) band, playing traditional music (or, if you're unlucky, ancient pop songs), to a full-blown carnival with street theatre, fireworks and sophisticated entertainment.

Information about nightclubs, cinemas and other entertainment in the provinces is available from tourist offices, or at your hotel.

The Moulin Rouge, where to head for cabaret.

Paris

The clubbing action in Paris is fast moving. Bars and clubs are all over the city, but particularly in the central areas around the Louvre, the Grand Boulevards, Marais, Bastille, Montmartre, Pigalle and the Latin Quarter. They are no longer called *boîtes* or discos however; most people refer to *soirées* or *clubs*. Refer to the listings magazine *Pariscope*. Find out more on www.novaplanet.com. For national information try www.cityvox.com or www.citegay.fr. Some of the most famous and popular nightspots in Paris include:

Cabaret

Bal du Moulin Rouge
82 Boulevard de Clichy, 75018 Paris
Tel: 01 53 09 82 82
www.moulin-rouge.fr
The classic can-can girls with lots of feathers.
The Crazy Horse Saloon
12 Avenue George V, 75008 Paris
Tel: 01 47 23 32 32
www.lecrazyhorseparis.com
Sexiest and most skimpily dressed of the big cabarets.
Le Lido
116 bis Avenue des Champs-Elysées, 75008 Paris
Tel: 01 40 76 56 10
www.lido.fr
Cabaret glamour with countless costume changes.
La Nouvelle Eve
25 Rue Pierre-Fontaine, 75009 Paris
Tel: 01 48 74 69 25
www.lanouvelleeveparis.com
A genuine Pigalle music hall, but without the vulgarity.

Nightclubs

Concrete
69 Port de la Rapée, 75012 Paris
www.concreteparis.fr

Opened in 2011, this floating venue has shaken up the Paris nightlife scene with its all-day parties,
La Machine
90 Boulevard de Clichy, 75018 Paris
Tel: 01 53 41 88 89
www.lamachinedumoulinrouge.com
Nightly from 11pm. Huge, popular nightclub with three dance floors.
Rex Club
5 Boulevard Poissonnière, 75002 Paris
Tel: 01 42 36 10 96
www.rexclub.com
A techno and house stalwart with big name DJs.
Red Light
34 Rue du Départ, 75014 Paris
Tel: 01 42 79 85 49
www.leredlight.com
House music plays to a mixed clientele.
Showcase
Port des Champs-Elysées, 75008 Paris
Tel: 01 45 61 25 43
www.showcase.fr
Slick joint with vaulted ceilings beneath the Pont Alexandre III. High-profile headliners have included will.i.am.
Social Club
142 Rue Montmartre, 75002 Paris
Tel: 01 40 28 05 55
In the centre of Paris, painted completely black with neon lights, and an eclectic mix of music.
Zig Zag
32 Rue Marbeuf, 75008 Paris
Tel: 06 35 25 03 61
http://zigzagclub.fr
Huge dance floor surrounded by a mezzanine, mixing house and techno.

Côte d'Azur

The Côte d'Azur is the place to mingle with the beautiful people, either on the terraces of chic café-bars, at beach clubs or trendy night clubs. Here is a selection of a few of the places to be seen:

Bars/Nightclubs

Antibes
Pam Pam
137 Boulevard du Président Wilson
Tel: 04 93 61 11 05
www.pampam.fr
Tiki huts, palm trees, bamboo, cocktails and live entertainment set the party scene.

Cannes
Bar 4U
6 Rue de Frères Pradignac
Tel: 04 93 39 71 21
Attracts a stylish crowd who sip cocktails and listen to funky house music.

Zanzibar
85 Rue Félix Faure
Tel: 04 93 39 30 75
Well-known gay bar and club.

Monaco
Jimmy'z
Avenue Princesse Grace
Tel: 377 98 06 36 36
Chic, expensive nightclub.

Nice
Le Relais
37 Promenade des Anglais
Tel: 04 93 16 64 00
Glamorous bar in the Hôtel Negresco.
Jam
8-10 Rue du Commandant Raffalli
Tel: 04 22 16 55 29
Great little bar with live music most nights.

Ste-Maxime
Café de France
Place Victor Hugo
Tel: 04 94 96 18 16
www.lecafedefrance.fr
Classic people-watching bar.

St-Tropez
Bar du Port
9 Quai de Suffren
Tel: 04 94 97 00 54
High-tech spot right on the port; light show and DJ booth.
Le Papagayo
Résidence du Port
Tel: 04 94 97 95 96
A favourite place to spot the famous.
Le VIP Room
Résidences du Nouveau Port
Tel: 04 94 97 14 70
One of St-Tropez's most fashionable clubs.

Casinos

Casinos are very much a part of the nightlife on the Côte d'Azur, although restricted to those aged over 21.

Antibes
La Siesta
Route du Bord de Mer
Tel: 04 93 33 31 31
www.joa-casino.com
Large nightclub and casino.

Cannes
Casino Barrière de Can2nes Croisette
1 Espace Lucien Barrière
Tel: 04 92 98 78 00
Open daily 10pm to 3am.

Monte Carlo
Casino de Monte Carlo
Place du Casino
Tel: 377 98 06 21 21
www.casinomontecarlo.com

ID card or passport required. Open daily weekdays from 2pm, weekends midday.

Nice
Casino Ruhl de Nice
1 Promenade des Anglais
Tel: 04 97 03 12 22
Open daily 9am–4am.

SHOPPING

Where to Shop

Since the 1980s most major towns in France have made the sensible decision to keep town centres for small boutiques and individual shops. Many of these areas are pedestrianised and very attractive, although beware – some cars ignore the *voie piétonne* (pedestrianised road) signs. The supermarkets, hypermarkets, furniture stores and do-it-yourself outlets collect on the outskirts of town, mostly designated as *Centres Commerciaux*.

These centres, although aesthetically unappealing, are fine for bulk shopping for self-catering or for finding a selection of reasonably priced wine to take home. But for gifts and general window-shopping the town centres are far more interesting. It is here that you will find the individual souvenirs with a particularly local flavour, alongside the beautifully dressed windows of delicatessens and patisseries. Markets are also a good source of handmade regional goods.

Clothing Sizes

Most shops are happy to let you try clothes on (essayer) before buying.

Market Etiquette

In a market all goods have to be marked with the price by law. Prices are usually by the kilo or by the *pièce*, that is, each item priced individually. Usually the stallholder (marchand) will select the goods for you. Sometimes there is a serve-yourself system – just observe everyone else. If you are choosing cheese, for example, you may be offered a taste to try first, *pour goûter*. Here are a few useful words:
bag *le sac*
basket *le panier*
flavour *le parfum*
organic *biologique*
ripe *mûr*
tasting *la dégustation*

Children's sizes, in particular, tend to be small compared with British and US age ranges. Hypermarkets are very good for inexpensive children's clothes, especially clothing for skiing.

Opening Hours

Food shops, especially bakers, tend to open early; boutiques and department stores open from 9am, but sometimes not until 10am. In most town centres, just about everything closes from noon until 2.30 or 3pm, but in Paris and other major tourist areas, some shops stay open. Most shops close in the evening at 7pm. Out of town and in areas frequented by tourists, hypermarkets are usually open all day until 8 or 9pm; in more remote areas they close for lunch and often shut at 7pm.

Many shops are closed Monday mornings and a considerable number close all day Monday.

Market Shopping

The heart of every French town is its market, and shopping for fresh produce there is one of the real pleasures of holidaying in France. The markets usually start early in the morning and close at midday, although some bigger ones are open in the afternoon too. The French themselves usually visit early to get the best of the produce. Markets are a riot of colour and bustle; the best have all kinds of stalls from flowers to domestic animals (do not be deceived – these are for the pot). Local cheeses, honey, wine, pâté and other specialities are often offered for tasting to encourage browsers to buy.

Antique or second-hand (brocante) markets are found all around the provinces, as well as flea markets

(marchés aux puces), which are fun to look around – you may even find a genuine bargain antique amongst all the old junk. The most famous of these, indeed the biggest flea market in the world, is **Les Puces de St-Ouen** north of Paris at Porte de Clignancourt, open Saturday to Monday 9am–6pm. There are also vide greniers, which are the equivalent of car-boot sales.

Look out for special fairs held all over the country at various times throughout the year, such as harvest times; check with the local tourist office for details.

Shopping by Area

The different regions of France are famous for particular products, for example Breton lace, Limoges porcelain, Provençal fabrics, perfume from Grasse, to name but a few.

Paris, naturally, has a fascinating range of shops from the fashion houses in the 8th arrondissement, particularly around the Faubourg St-Honoré, to the more affordable, but still chic department stores, such as **Galeries Lafayette** and **Printemps**, both of which are on the Boulevard Haussmann, 75009 Paris.

The giant underground **Les Halles** shopping centre (undergoing restoration) in the 1st arrondissement and Carrousel du Louvre are also worth a visit. The Marais is a focus for youthful fashion boutiques and quirky gift shops. Don't ignore the famous Champs-Elysées for shopping, where the options are surprisingly quite diverse.

At **Grasse** purchase your perfume direct from the boutiques within the perfume factories:
Fragonard
20 Boulevard Fragonard

Tel: 04 93 36 44 65
www.fragonard.com
Galimard
73 Route de Cannes
Tel: 04 93 09 20 00
www.galimard.com
Molinard
60 Boulevard Victor Hugo
Tel: 04 92 42 33 28
www.molinard.com

For everyday household goods the best places to shop are the chain stores Ikea, Alinéa, Habitat and Cèdre Rouge. For more exclusive tableware head for a specialist boutique like Baccarat, in Paris, Verrerie de Biot and Royal Limoges.
Baccarat
11 Place des Etats-Unis, 75116 Paris
Tel: 01 40 22 11 22
Verrerie de Biot
Chemin des Combes, 06410 Biot
Tel: 04 93 65 03 00
Royal Limoges
54 Rue Victor Duruy, 87000 Limoges
Tel: 05 55 33 27 30

Buying Direct

Around the country, you may be tempted by all the signs you see along the road for dégustations (tastings). Many wine producers and farmers will invite you to try their wines and other produce with an eye to selling you a case, or maybe a few jars of pâté. This is a good way to try before you buy and sometimes includes a visit to a wine cellar. Farm produce can be more expensive to buy this way than in the supermarkets – but do not forget that it is home-produced and not factory-processed, and it will be a lot fresher.

When buying wine direct from the vineyard or co-operative expect to pass a convivial moment tasting before you choose a bottle or two to take home. Many champagne houses, and Bordeaux châteaux offer guided tours and tastings – be prepared to pay for this. A list of domaines open to the public for organised visits is usually available from the local tourist office. A Maison des Vins is a local wine shop stocking wines from the neighbouring producers. This gives a good opportunity to purchase from a range of regional wines by the bottle.

Standard Fare

AOP, Appellation d'Origine Protegée, is a legal regulation for cheeses, poultry and other food items such as lentils and walnuts as well as wines, and it ensures the products conform to a particular standard.

Brocantes and marchés aux puces are heaven for bargain hunters.

Export Procedures

On most purchases, the price includes TVA (VAT or value added tax). There are four rates in France, but the standard rate is currently 20 percent. Non-EU visitors can claim back TVA on certain products – called *détaxe*; this is worth doing if you spend in one place more than around €175 in the same shop. Ask the store for a *bordereau* (export sales invoice). This must be completed and shown, together with the goods, to customs officers on leaving the country. It is wise to pack the items separately for ease of access. You then mail the form back to the retailer who will refund the TVA in a month or two. Certain items purchased (e.g. antiques) may need special customs clearance.

If you have a complaint about any purchase, return it in the first place to the shop as soon as possible. You will need your till receipt as proof of purchase. In the case of a serious dispute, contact the local Direction Départementale de la Concurrence et de la Consommation et de la Répression des Fraudes (see www. economie.gouv.fr/dgccrf).

SPORT

In general, sports facilities are first-rate throughout France. Most towns have swimming pools and even small villages often have a tennis court, but you may have to become a temporary member to use it – enquire at the local tourist office or *mairie* (town hall), which will also be able to provide details of other local sporting activities.

Many companies offer sporting and activity holidays in France; these are often organised by the tourist offices in individual *départements*; contact the regional tourist office in the destination of your choice (see page 399).

Water Sports

All over France water sports can be enjoyed at a *base de loisirs*. These centres, found not just on the coast, but inland on lakes and quiet river stretches, offer various leisure activities – not just water sports. They usually have a café or bar, maybe even a restaurant, as well as picnic areas.

Many such centres offer tuition in the various sports available – canoeing, windsurfing, etc; fees are usually charged at an hourly or half-hourly rate. Where boating and

Walking and Hiking

There are scores of walking guides to France, but a good basic guidebook for serious walkers is Bruce Lefavour's *France on Foot*. Cicerone publishers produce a series of guidebooks for walkers, which cover a wide selection of places in France such as the Pyrenees and Mont Blanc. Websites for general information about walking in France include: www.randosbalades.fr Online version of a French bi-monthly magazine about walking in France. www.distantjourneys.com A US company offering point-to-point guided walks in France and elsewhere in Europe. www.abc-of-hiking.com A listing of websites about walking with links to

windsurfing is permitted, equipment is often available for hire, or bring your own.

The following addresses are the central offices of the various water sports organisations in France; they will supply you with addresses of regional clubs.

Canoeing
Fédération Française de Canoe-Kayak et des Sports associés en Eau-Vive
87 Quai de la Marne, 94340 Joinville-le-Pont
Tel: 01 45 11 08 50
www.ffcanoe.asso.fr

Sailing
Fédération Française de Voile
17 Rue Henri Bocquillon, 75015 Paris Cedex 16
Tel: 01 40 60 37 00
www.ffvoile.fr

Rafting
Société AN Rafting
Les Iles de Macot, 73210 Macot La Plagne
Tel: 04 79 09 72 79
www.an-rafting.com

Underwater Sports
Fédération Française d'Etudes et de Sports Sous-Marins
24 Quai de Rive-Neuve, 13284 Marseille
Tel: 04 91 33 99 31
www.ffessm.fr

Surfing
Fédération Française de Surf
123 Boulevard de la Dune, 40150 Soorts-Hossegor

blogs and discussion forums. www.ffrandonnee.fr French Federation of Hiking, for a list of the French- and English-language trail guides in print and a downloadable app. www.onfootholidays.co.uk General and regional information on planning your walking holiday. www.meteo.fr/temps A detailed French site for the weather in France. www.parcs-naturels-regionaux.tm.fr/ France's regional parks online. www.sentiersdefrance.com A commercial site offering a wide variety of pre-planned but unguided walks in France. www.gr-infos.com A comprehensive list of the GR long-distance footpaths throughout France.

Tel: 05 58 43 55 88
www.surfingfrance.com

Kitesurfing
Fédération Française de Vol Libre
7 Rue de Suisse, 06000 Nice
Tel: 04 97 03 82 82
http://kite.ffvl.fr

Fishing

With its wealth of waterways and lakes, France is ideal fishing country. To book fishing holidays (a weekend or longer) with accommodation, try the regional tourist offices (see page 399). A permit *(permis)* is usually required for coarse fishing; enquire at local tourist offices. Sea fishing trips are widely available – look out for sign boards on quaysides advertising trips. For regional fishing information contact the **Union Nationale pour la Pêche**, tel: 01 48 24 96 00, www.federationpeche.fr; Fédération Française de Pêche Sportive au Coup, tel: 02 37 22 25 87, www.ffpsc.fr; and for fly fishing Fédération Française de la Pêche à la Mouche et au Lancer, www.ffpml.fr. For deep-sea fishing contact Fédération Française des Pêcheurs en Mer, tel: 05 59 31 00 73, www.ffpm-national.com.

Air Sports

There are small airfields on the outskirts of most French towns that offer flying, gliding or parachuting. Paragliding *(parapente)* is also very popular. Beginner flights can usually be booked at a reasonable fee; the following organisations will have further information.

Canoeing on the sea at Etretat.

Details of events can be obtained from the nearest tourist office, or from national organisers of events. Some of the better-known competitive events are the Tour de France, a 22-day, 4,000km (2,500-mile) bicycle race in July; the 24-hour car race at Le Mans in June; the Monaco Grand Prix in May and the Monte Carlo Motor Rally in January. May in Paris sees the Roland Garros Tennis Tournament. The Prix de Diane-Hermès, the French Derby, is held at Chantilly in June.

Fédération Française de Vol Libre
4 Rue de Suisse, 06000 Nice
Tel: 04 97 03 82 82
www.ffvl.fr
Fédération Française de Vol à Voile
55 Rue des Petites Ecuries, 75010 Paris
Tel: 01 45 44 04 78
www.ffvv.org

Cycling

Taking your own bicycle *(vélo)* to France is easy from the UK – they are carried free on most ferries and trains – or you can rent cycles for a reasonable cost; main railway stations usually have them for hire and you can often arrange to pick up at one station and leave it at another. Alternatively, try bicycle retailers/repairers or ask at the local tourist office.

Some youth hostels rent cycles and also arrange tours. For more information, contact the Fédération Unie des Auberges de Jeunesse (tel: 01 44 89 87 27, www.fuaj.org).

Cycling Holidays

Cycling holidays are offered by various organisations, with campsite or hotel accommodation and the advantage that your luggage is often transported for you to your next destination. Some operators are listed below:
Fédération Française de Cyclotourisme
12 Rue Louis-Bertrand, 94207 Ivry-sur-Seine
Tel: 01 56 20 88 88
www.ffct.org
More than 60 guided tours offered each year, all over France, covering 60–100km (40–60 miles) per day. Bring your own bike.
Cyclists Touring Club
Parklands, Railton Road, Guildford, Surrey GU2 9JX
Tel: 0844 736 8450
www.ctc.org.uk

Headwater Holidays
Old School House, Chester Road, Northwich CW3 1LE
Tel: 01606-822674
www.headwater.com
Hotel accommodation, and your luggage transported.
Susi Madron's Cycling for Softies
Norwood House, 53 Brighton Grove, Manchester M14 5JT
Tel: 0161-248 8282
www.cycling-for-softies.co.uk
Cycling holidays in many regions, with comfortable accommodation. Well-established with a good reputation.
French Cycling Holidays
56 Rosslyn Crescent, Harrow HA1 2SZ
Tel: 020 8861 5888
www.frenchcyclingholidays.com
Organised cycling tours.

Information and Tips

It is advisable to take out insurance before you go. The normal rules of the road apply to cyclists (see page 364). Advice and information can be obtained from the Touring Department of the Cyclists Touring Club in the UK (address above). Their service to members includes competitive cycle and travel insurance, free detailed touring itineraries and general information sheets about France. The club's French counterpart, Fédération Française de Cyclotourisme offers a similar service. The publication France en Vélo by John Walsh is a useful companion, and the IGN Cyclists' Map No. 906 *France Vélo* carries a mass of information.

Cycling Clubs

Such is the French passion for cycling that local clubs organise many trips lasting a day or more and visitors are often welcome to join in. Lists of clubs and events are available from local branches of the Fédération Française de Cyclotourisme. They also produce leaflets giving suggested cycle tours for independent travellers, ranging

from easy terrain to very hard going for the more experienced cyclist, with details of accommodation, cycle repairers and other facilities en route.

Mountain Biking

This sport is extremely popular in France. Many of the organisations listed under Cycling Holidays offer mountain bike holidays.
Mountain bikes (in French VTT – *Vélo Tout Terrain*) and protective gear can be hired locally. Try the local tourist office, or cycle shops/repairers.

Horse Riding

Riding holidays in France come under the umbrella of the **Fédération Française d'Equitation**, 81 Avenue Edouard-Vaillant, 92100 Boulogne Billancourt, tel: 02 54 94 46 00, www.ffe.com. Contact them for regional or local branches which can provide information about marked bridleways, maps, riding centres and insurance.

Treks lasting a day or more and longer holidays on horseback can be organised locally. Information can be obtained from the organisations mentioned above or, from tourist offices (see page 399).

Golf

The local tourist office will give you details of all the courses in their area. Information can also be obtained from regional tourist offices (see page 399) or **Fédération Française de Golf**, 68 Rue Anatole France, 92306 Le Vallois-Perret, tel: 01 41 49 77 00; www.ffgolf.org.
Golf packages combining all-day golfing with a luxury hotel are an ideal choice for the serious golfer. Following is a small selection of prestigious hotels with renowned golf courses nearby.

TRANSPORT

Evian Resort
South Shore Lake Geneva, 74500 Evian
Tel: 04 50 26 85 00
www.evianresort.com
18-hole Evian Masters golf course.
Royal Mougins
424 Avenue Roi, 06250 Mougins
Tel: 04 92 92 49 69
www.royalmougins.fr
Luxury hotel with spa and golf course.
Golf Hotel Grenoble Charmeil
38210 Saint Quentin sur Isère
Tel: 04 76 93 67 28
www.golfhotelgrenoble.com
Nearby is the Grenoble International golf course.
Saint-Malo Golf Resort
Domaine de Saint Yvieux, 35540 Le Tronchet
Tel: 02 99 58 96 69
www.saintmalogolf.com
27-hole golf course.

Walking

France has more than 60,000km (38,000 miles) of long distance walkways – Grandes Randonnées (GR), the most famous are the Chemin de Stevenson GR70 in the Cévennes, and the mythic Chemin de Saint-Compostelle GR65, the oldest in France. There is also a series of Petites Randonnées (PR). The walks vary in difficulty, the toughest is claimed to be the GR20 across the rugged mountains of Corsica.

Topo Guides (guides books with IGN 1:50,000-scale maps), published by the Fédération Française de Randonnée Pédestre (see box), provide details of the footpaths, places to stay and transport. There is also a series of guidebooks in English published by Robertson-McCarta called *Footpaths of Europe*, which includes the IGN maps. As well as this most rural communes have signposted walks and the *mairie* usually has details of these. Always wear appropriate footwear, a hat in hot weather, and take plenty of water too.

Health and Beauty

Thalassotherapy – sea-water based therapy – was invented by the French and centres are dotted along the French coastline. Centres can also be found at springs inland – Vichy, Evian and Aix les Bains all have major water therapy centres. Thalassotherapy and spa treatments are a great way to pamper yourself, the centres are often linked to luxurious hotels. The company Algoterm (www.algotherm.fr) specialises in chic upmarket establishments including spas at Deauville and Chamonix, and thalassotherapy centres at the four-star Exedra Hotel in Nice, and Grand Hôtel Intercontinental in Paris.

Les Sources de Caudalie (Chemin de Smith-Haut-Lafitte, 33650 Martillac; tel: 05 57 83 83 83; www.sources-caudalie.com) is a spa centre with a difference, near Bordeaux, offering vinotherapy – a series of treatments based on wine and its by-products. These include a grape facial, Cabernet scrub, Sauvignon massage and Merlot wraps.

Winter and Mountain Sports

Snow Sports

With the highest slopes in Europe, famous resorts and state-of-the-art facilities, France offers plenty of scope for skiers of all abilities and all ages. The newer resorts make an effort to keep the activity as environmentally friendly as possible.

France Montagnes is the major winter sports body in France, covering over 100 resorts and providing accommodation reservations. It also offers an on-line ski bulletin from mid-December to mid-April at www.france-montagnes.com. For information, contact them at 24 Rue Saint-Exupéry, Francin 73800, tel: 04 79 65 06 75.

Other useful addresses are the **Fédération Française de Ski**, 50 Rue des Marquisats, 74000 Annecy Cedex, tel: 04 50 51 40 34, www.ffs.fr (website in French only); and **Ecoles du Ski Français**, 6 Allée des Mitaillères, 38246 Meylan, tel: 04 76 90 67 36, www.esf.net, for information about schools.

You can also log on to http://en.ski-france.com, a British commercial site offering loads of information plus package deals on skiing in France.

Although the most famous and popular ski resorts are located in the Alps, the sport is also available in the Pyrenees and the Massif Central. The peak period for winter sports is February, although in some resorts it is still possible to ski in May.

The various forms of skiing are practised at most resorts, including cross-country skiing, monoskiing and snowboarding. Other popular activities are snowshoe walking, which needs no particular skills, climbing frozen waterfalls (which does), and dog-sleigh driving (mushing), now recognised as a competitive sport. Information on these is available from tourist offices.

The Mountains in Summer

The mountains are not just for skiing. France Montagnes also provide information on many activities that can be enjoyed in the summer in the same resorts, such as climbing, hiking, glacier skiing, mountain biking, horse riding, as well as white water and airborne activities. For further information, log on to: http://summer.france-montagnes.com.

Beaches

Sandy beaches are a major feature of France's coastline. There are many fine, sandy beaches on the northern coast of Normandy and Brittany, but don't expect the water temperatures to rise much above 17°C (62°F) even in the summer months. Some of best beaches include Le Touquet, Dinard, Perros-Guirec, Sables-d'Or-les-Pins, St-Michel-en-Grève and Brignogan Plage. In southern Brittany Bénodet and Quiberon have the best beaches, but get packed. Carnac is a quieter option.

The Atlantic coast has wide sweeping sandy beaches, the most popular situated south of Arcachon. The waves here can be powerful, and the current strong so take care with young children, and watch carefully for the coast-guards flag. There are several naturism beaches along this stretch of coast.

In Languedoc-Roussillon the beaches are sandy, especially at Narbonne Plage and Valras Plage. Sitting the western edge of the Mediterranean the wind can whip up to a frenzy around here. Along the Côte d'Azur the famous Pampelonne beach is the place to head, not only for its 5km (3 miles) of golden sands, but also to experience some of 'private' beach clubs that range from the bamboo shack to the designer restaurant with cocktail bar and disco. The favourites, which follow the whim of fashion, include the showbiz stomping ground The Tahiti, The Nikki Beach, Key West and Tropicana. Although much of the bay has been taken up with private concessions, there are small public beaches.

Corsica has a varied coastline; the west coast tends to have more wind, and therefore waves, while the beaches around Porto Vecchio, Calvi and St-Florent are the best.

EATING OUT

ACTIVITIES

A - Z

LANGUAGE

Mountain boarding and mountain scootering are two recent additions to the sporting agenda in the mountains in summer. Mountainboards, part snowboard and part skateboard, are used to slide down the mountain slopes on wheels, essentially snowboarding on grass. Further information can be found on the website www.mountainboard.fr. The mountain scooter is a non-motorised vehicle that is pulled up by the ski-lifts to the higher mountains slopes, from where you scoot down.

Mountain Climbing

The following agents are useful for organising mountain climbs or hikes at various locations in France:

France
Fédération Française de la Montagne et de l'Escalade
8–10 Quai de la Marne, 75019 Paris
Tel: 01 40 18 75 50
www.ffme.fr (in French only)
UK
Sherpa Expeditions
1b Osiers Road, Wandsworth, London SW18 1NL
Tel: 020-8875 5070
www.sherpaexpeditions.com
Specialists in mountain walking holidays; escorted and self-guided walks all over France.

Potholing

For information on potholing in France write to:
Fédération Française de Spéléologie
28 Rue Delandine, 69002 Lyon
Tel: 04 72 56 09 63
www.ffspeleo.fr

CHILDREN'S ACTIVITIES

France offers a wide range of activities for families travelling with children. Rural France is a great place for children to explore and offers outdoor activities all year round; the coast has wonderful beaches that are popular destinations for families, but be aware of strong currents in some regions; and cities are packed with places that provide amusement for the whole family.

The remarkable city parks and gardens can be a great source of inexpensive entertainment. The **Jardin d'Acclimatation** (www.jardindacclimatation.fr) at the Bois de Boulogne in Paris is an extensive amusement park featuring a menagerie, museum, a mini-golf, pony rides, a house of mirrors, and a puppet theatre. The largest inner city park in France is **Parc Tête d'Or** in Lyon, covering over 100 hectares (247-acres), with a zoo, botanical gardens, a lake and carousels.

Disneyland Paris (www.disneyland paris.co.uk), in the countryside east of Paris, attracts millions of visitors each year. Other major themed amusement parks include the **Parc Astérix** at Plailly (www.parcasterix.fr; closed winter), which has stomach-churning rollercoaster and water rides, and live shows. There are also the popular **Walibi Parks** (www.walibi. com), one situated in the Rhône-Alps region between Lyon and Chambéry, and the other near Agen in the Aquitaine region.

In the centre of France, near Poitiers the leisure park **Futuroscope** (http://en.futuroscope.com; closed Mon–Fri mid-Nov–mid-Dec, and Jan–early Feb) offers a range of attractions exploring the moving image and high-tech visual effects in a futuristic architectural environment. The **Cité des Sciences** (www.cite-sciences.fr; closed Mon) at the Porte de la Villette in Paris is another super place for children to discover science through play. Uncover the mechanics of volcanoes through games and hands-on activities at the state-of-the-art **Vulcania Centre** (www.vulcania.com; closed mid-Nov–late Mar) in the Auvergne region. And for those more artistically inclined the **Centre Pompidou** in Paris proposes interactive expositions and workshops for children.

In the summer months water parks are great fun if the weather is fine. **Aqualand** (closed Oct–mid-June) is a chain that has water parks at the coastal resorts of St Cyprien, Port Leucate, Cap d'Agde, St-Cyr-sur-Mer, Ste-Maxime and Fréjus. There are several outdoor adventure parks in France that offer thrills for those who enjoy swinging from tree to tree attached to a cable.

Aquariums are fun all year round, whatever the weather, and France boasts several ultra-modern aquariums. The **Aquarium de Paris** (http://cineaqua.com) houses over 15,000 fish, and 4 cinemas; **Océanopolis** (www.oceanopolis.com) at Brest takes you on a voyage through the oceans from warm climate to icy waters, and at Boulogne-sur-Mer discover the many facets of marine life at the impressive **Nausicaá** (www.nausicaa.fr) aquarium.

Zoos, themed animal parks, ornithological parks and botanical gardens are well-appreciated by children and addresses can be obtained from local tourist offices. Some exceptional sites are listed below:
Parc Ornithologique Pont de Gau, Camargue. Tel: 04 90 97 82 62; www.parcornithologique.com
Le Parc des Oiseaux, 01330 Villars des Dombes, northeast of Lyon. Tel: 04 74 98 05 54; www.parcdesoiseaux.com
Le Village des Tortues, Quartier Les Plaines, 83590 Gonfaron, on the northern edge of the Maures (all year). Tel: 04 94 78 26 41; www.villagetortues.com
Terra Botanica, Route de Cantenay Epinard, 49106 Angers. Ultra-modern botanical gardens (closed Oct–Apr). Tel: 02 41 25 00 00; www.terrabotanica.fr
Parc des Landes de Gascogne, Sabres, Les Landes, (closed Oct–Apr). Tel: 05 58 08 31 31; www.parc-landes-de-gascogne.fr

Circus entertainment is widespread in France and ranges from the small, family-run circuses that travel around rural France to the grand traditional circus companies such as **Arlette Gruss**, **Pinder**, **Bouglione** and **Franconi**, and the contemporary circuses like **Plume** and **Eloïse**. The main circus festival of the year is held in January at Monte-Carlo, but the Cirque de Demain held in Paris at the end of January is also a spectacular event celebrating the art.

Zip wire activities for Children in the Auvergne.

TRANSPORT

EATING OUT

A – Z

A HANDY SUMMARY
OF PRACTICAL INFORMATION

A

Admission Charges

The entrance fees for visiting museums, galleries and monuments generally fall between €5–15 per adult, with free admission for children – check on the qualifying age, for some places it is under 18 and others 12 or 7 years old. Since 2009 access to the permanent exhibitions of any state-owned museum or monument is free for those under 26, who are resident in the EU. There are also special rates for students, over 60s and families of five or more.

Major towns often have special city passes that can be bought at the local tourist office, or the participating museums. For example the Paris Museum Pass allows access to around 60 museums and monuments over a 2, 4 or 6 day period (cost is from €42–69); Lyon has a similar scheme called the Lyon City Card for 1, 2 or 3 days which allows free access to 22 museums and also includes free travel on public transport in the city (cost from €22–42).

B

Budgeting for Your Trip

Low cost budget chain hotels start from around €50 for a room, mid-range hotels range from around €90 for a double in low season to upwards of €200 for more upmarket lodgings at a busier period. Prices can triple during the peak holidays seasons, which are from July to August in the summer, and for the ski resorts from December to February.

Eating out depends on the style of the establishment. Eating out at a crêperie or pizzeria will cost around €15–20, while a three-course meal in a family-style restaurant costs around €25–40. In more stylish restaurants look at paying €40–60 for a fixed price menu, and if you opt for luxury, the sky is the limit with Michelin-starred restaurants easily reaching to upwards of €100.

Transport by train: full fare return tickets from Lyon or Bordeaux to Paris costs around €75, Nantes to Paris about €50, and Nice to Paris around €130. Ask about special passes and reduced rates at the ticket office. Car hire varies depending on the type of car and the rental period, but the average price is around €55 per day.

C

Children

Restaurants

In France generally, children are treated as individuals not nuisances. It is pleasant to be able to take them out for a meal (even in the evening) without heads being turned in horror. It has to be said, however, that French children, being accustomed to eating out from an early age, are on the whole well behaved in restaurants, so it helps if one's own offspring understand that they can't run wild.

Many restaurants offer a children's menu; if not, they will often split a *prix-fixe* menu between two children. If travelling with very young children, you may find it practical to order nothing specific at all for them but just to request an extra plate and give them tasty morsels to try from your

own dish. It is a good introduction to foreign food for them, without too much waste. French meals are usually generous enough to allow you to do this without going hungry.

Another option is to order a single simple, inexpensive dish such as an omelette, which most children will happily eat.

Hotels

Most hotels have family rooms so children do not have to be separated from parents, and another bed or cot *(lit bébé)* can often be provided for a small charge, although it is a good idea to check availability if you are booking in advance.

Holiday Centres

It is possible to organise activities for unaccompanied children, including stays in *gîtes d'enfants* or on farms, or activity holidays. Naturally, children would only be happy to be left if they have a reasonable command of French, but it is quite common in France, as in the US, for children to spend a part of their summer holiday at a holiday centre. PGL (tel: 0844 371 0101; www.pgl.co.uk), otherwise known as 'Parents Get Lost', arrange summer camps and activity holidays for groups of kids aged 7 to 17.

Camping

There is a good choice of campsites in France, which offer a great alternative when travelling with children. Many sites offer opportunities for sports such as windsurfing; often with the equipment and instruction included. The regional tourist offices (see page 399) each produce their own lists of all recognised sites, with details of star ratings and facilities. The French Federation of Camping and

ACTIVITIES

A – Z

LANGUAGE

CLIMATE CHART

Paris

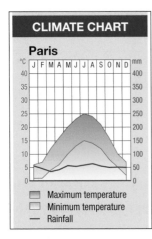

- ▨ Maximum temperature
- ☐ Minimum temperature
- — Rainfall

Caravanning guide (ffcc; tel: 01 42 72 84 08, www.ffcc.fr) lists sites nationwide, and indicates which have facilities for disabled campers. Members of the Camping and Caravanning Club of Great Britain (www. campingandcaravaningclub.co.uk) can make use of their booking services.

Packaged camping holidays are very popular with British families and are very convenient, as all the camping paraphernalia is provided on the site. Many companies now offer this type of holiday, usually with ferry travel included in the price. Camping Reservation Services can be found at Alan Rogers Travel Service, tel: 01580-214 4000, www.alanrogers. com.

Climate

The French climate is varied and seasonal.

In the north, it is similar to that of southern England and springtime is often suggested as the best time to see the capital. However, be prepared for showers. In the autumn, mornings can be quite sharp, but by midday the skies are usually clear and bright.

In the south, summers are dry and temperatures can frequently rise to over 30°C (86°F). However, watch out for occasional heavy thunder and hailstorms. Winters are mild (the temperature rarely falling below 10°C/ 50°F on the Mediterranean coast) and often wet; spring is even wetter.

Many areas of France have quite distinct micro-climates and the weather can change rapidly. The Midi has its own particular *bête noire*, the fierce wind known as the *Mistral*, which blows from the northwest, mainly in winter and spring, leaving clear blue skies in its wake.

Be prepared for seasonal differences; in summer only light clothes will be needed except in coastal and mountainous areas, where a warmer outer layer will be required for evenings. Sunglasses and sunscreen are needed both in the summer months, and at high altitude all year round.

Crime and Safety

Sensible precautions with personal possessions are all that should really be necessary when visiting France. Theft and other crime exist here as elsewhere.

However, you should be particularly vigilant in the Paris Métro, as gangs of pickpockets tend to congregate in certain stations in the city centre. Don't travel alone on the Métro at night.

Drivers should follow the rules of the road (see page 365). Heavy on-the-spot fines are given for traffic offences such as speeding, and drivers can be stopped and breathalysed during spot checks. Speeding offences can attract on the spot fines of up to €375 and immediate fines of up to about €4,200 can be levied for drink-driving offences (if you do not have enough cash, you will be required to pay a deposit). Police are fairly visible on the main roads of France during summer.

Customs Regulations

All personal effects may be imported into France without formality. It is forbidden to bring into the country any narcotics, pirated books, weapons and alcoholic spirits that do not conform to French legislation. In theory, there are no customs barriers within Europe for alcoholic drinks and tobacco. However, there are still recommended allowances, as shown below.

The CRS, or French riot police, on duty.

The following quantities can be exceeded, provided proof is shown that the goods bought are for personal consumption (for example, a family wedding) and not for resale. If in doubt, check with your local customs office. In the UK, contact HM Revenue and Customs, tel: 0300 200 3700 or (44) 2920 501261 from outside the UK; www.hmrc.gov.uk

Customs allowances for each person over 17 years of age are: 10 litres of spirits or strong liqueurs over 22 percent vol. 20 litres of fortified wine 90 litres of wine (of which no more than 60 litres may be sparkling wine) 200 cigars, or 400 cigarillos or 3,200 cigarettes or 1 kg tobacco 110 litres of beer

Non EU-visitors can bring in €10,000 in currency. For goods from outside the EU (note that this applies to Andorra, which is outside the EU), the allowances are: 200 cigarettes or 100 small cigars, 1 litre of spirits and 4 litres of wine, and 60cc/ml of perfume.

D

Disabled Travellers

Initiatives in France to improve provision for handicapped people include a series of special signs for specific disabilities, such as impaired mobility, mental disability, blindness and deafness, which direct people and carers to help points.

Parking: The international blue scheme applies. Ensure you have all the documentation with you.

Reduced tolls: People with vehicles adapted for the disabled pay reduced toll prices on motorways.

Accommodation: The French Tourist Office publishes a list of hotels with facilities for the disabled. However, you should always check directly for specific facilities.

Association Tourisme et Handicaps, 43 Rue Marx-Dormoy, 75018 Paris, tel: 01 44 11 10 41, www.tourisme-handicaps.org publishes a download-able brochure in English that gives a wide range of information for disabled travellers.

Michelin's Red Guide France for hotels and its Camping-Caravanning – France both include symbols for disability-friendly accommodation. The website www.disabledholidays4u.com provides a wide range of accessible holiday services.

Disabled Youth

Mobility International USA, www.miusa.org organises exchange schemes for disabled people.
Society for Accessible Travel and Hospitality, www.sath.org offers information and resources relating to travel in the US and overseas. The following website offers lists of facilities in France: www.mobile-en-ville.asso.fr

Organisations in the UK

Disability Rights UK, 49-51 East Road, London N1 6AH, tel: 020-7250 8181, http://disabilityrightsuk.org offers information for disabled travellers.
Access Project, 39 Bradley Gardens, West Ealing, London W13 8HE, www.accessinparis.org produces a free guide called Access in Paris.
Travel For All, 7A Pixel Mill, 44 Appleby Road, Kendal, Cumbria LA9 6ES, tel: 0845 1249971, www.tourismforall.org.uk is a national charity providing travel information for disabled people.

E

Electricity

220/230 volts. Visitors from the US will need a transformer for shavers, hairdryers and other equipment;

Emergencies

All emergency services **112**
Ambulance (SAMU) – dial **15**
Police – dial **17**
Fire (sapeurs-pompiers) – dial **18**
In case of a serious accident or medical emergency call the Service d'Aide Médicale d'Urgence (SAMU), or the police or fire department. The sapeurs-pompiers are also trained paramedics, and they and the police work in close contact with the SAMU.

visitors from the UK just need an adaptor plug.

Embassies and Consulates

In France
Australia: 4 Rue Jean-Rey, 75724 Paris, tel: 01 40 59 33 00, www.france.embassy.gov.au
Canada: 35 Avenue Montaigne, 75008 Paris, tel: 01 44 43 29 00, www.canadainternational.gc.ca
Ireland: 12 Avenue Foch, 75116 Paris. tel: 01 44 17 67 00, www.dfa.ie/irish-embassy/france
UK: 16 bis Rue d'Anjou, 75008 Paris, tel: 01 44 51 31 00, www.gov.uk/government/world/france
US: 2 Avenue Gabriel, 75008 Paris, tel: 01 43 12 22 22, http://france.usembassy.gov

Outside France
French Consulate, 21 Cromwell Road, London SW7 2EN, tel: 020-7073 1200, www.ambafrance-uk.org
Visa section: 6a Cromwell Place, London SW7 2EW, tel: 0845 7300 118.
French Embassy, 58 Knightsbridge, London SW1X 7JT, tel: 020-7073 1000, www.ambafrance-uk.org

Etiquette

When greeting people shake the hand of every person present, close friends and family kiss lightly on the cheek. You are also expected to say 'bonjour' or 'bonsoir' when entering and leaving a shop. Always address people using 'Monsieur' or 'Madame', and use the more formal 'vous', as 'tu' is used among family and friends.

When invited to eat at a French person's home it is customary to arrive with a gift – usually flowers. At the table don't start eating until the host, or hostess says 'bon appétit'.

G

Gay and Lesbian Travellers

General information is available from Radio FG (98.2 MHz), www.radiofg.com and national magazines Têtu and Curve. A good source of listings of bars, clubs and associations is the Queer Resource Directory, www.france.qrd.org; www.gay-sejour.com is also useful for listings of bars, clubs and beaches. For further information contact Centre LGBT Gai et Lesbien, 63 Rue Beaubourg, 75003 Paris; tel: 01 43 57 21 47; www.centrelgbtparis.org.

H

Health and Medical Care

EU Citizens
EU nationals should check before leaving home that they qualify for subsidised treatment in France under EU rules. Most British nationals do – check with the Department of Health and ask for the European Health Insurance Card (EHIC) form from the post office, or download a form from www.dh.gov.uk. The EHIC is valid for 3–5 years and partially covers the cost of medical treatment on the same basis as a resident in France. Note that it does not cover the full cost of any treatment or medicines and a contribution will be necessary, so it may be worthwhile taking out private insurance as well.

IAMAT
The International Association for Medical Assistance to Travellers (IAMAT) is a non-profit-making organisation that anyone can join free of charge. Benefits include a membership card (entitling the bearer to services at fixed IAMAT rates by participating doctors) and a traveller clinical record (a passport-sized record completed by the member's own doctor prior to travel). A directory of English-speaking IAMAT doctors on call 24 hours a day and advice on immunisation is published for members. IAMAT is at:
US: 1623 Military Road, Suite 279, Niagara Falls, NY 14304, tel: 716-754 4883.
Canada: 67 Mowat Avenue, Suite 036, Toronto M6K 3ES, tel: 416-652 0137 or 2162 Gordon Street, Guelph, Ontario N1L 1G6; www.iamat.org.

Medical Services
For minor ailments, in the first instance it is worth consulting a pharmacy (recognisable by its green cross sign), which have wider prescribing powers than those in the UK or US. They are also helpful in cases of snake or insect bites and identifying fungi.

If you need to see a doctor, expect to pay around €25 for a simple consultation, plus a fee for whatever medicine or treatment is issued by prescription. On each visit present the European Health Insurance Card (EHIC) to the doctor or pharmacist. This will enable you to claim back the majority of the cost (around 70 percent) under the EU agreement. Information on applying for the EHIC is available at UK post offices and on www.dh.gov.uk (see page 395).

The standard of treatment in French hospitals is generally high, and you should be able to find someone who speaks English to help you. You may prefer to go to an English-speaking hospital; the American Hospital at 63 Boulevard Victor-Hugo, 92200 Neuilly, tel: 01 46 41 25 25, is a private hospital that is not subsidised by the French or US government. Rates are more expensive than French state hospitals; or the British Hospital Hertford, 3 Rue Barbès, 92300 Levallois, tel: 01 46 39 22 01, both just outside Paris.

L

Lost Property

If you lose something on a bus or the Métro, first try the terminus to see if it has been handed in. In Paris, after 48 hours, you can go to the Bureau des Objets Trouvés, 36 Rue des Morillons, 75015 Paris, tel: 08 21 00 25 25 (in English). You must pay a small percentage of the value of any item reclaimed.

To report a crime visit the local police station (gendarmerie or commissariat de police). Telephone numbers are given at the front of local directories, or in an emergency, dial 17. If you lose a passport, report

first to the police, then to the nearest consulate.

If you are detained by the police for any reason, ask to telephone your consulate, which should be able to offer advice or assistance.

M

Maps

A first essential in touring any part of France is a good map. The Institut Géographique National (IGN) is the French equivalent of the British Ordnance Survey and their maps are excellent. For route planning, IGN 901 is ideal at a scale of 1:1,000,000 or 1 cm:10km (1 inch:16 miles); the **Michelin 911** at the same scale shows just motorways and main roads, with good clear presentation if you do not intend to stray far off the beaten track.

Berlitz Motoring Maps are a series of excellent maps to France, with clear, detailed mapping, a guide to road signs and driving regulations, and useful French words and phrases to help you on the road.

For more detailed maps, the **IGN Blue Series Top 25** (1:250,000, 1cm:2.5km) covers the country at a good scale for touring. Michelin also produces regional maps at a similar scale (1:200,000, or 1 inch:3 miles approx.). These sheets are also available bound as a Motoring Atlas including route-planning maps, a Paris area map and several town

plans. Collins also produces a good atlas based on the IGN's regional maps.

The **IGN Top 100** (1:100,000, 1cm:1km (or 1inch:1.6 miles) are more detailed local maps that cover the whole of France on 74 sheets. These are useful for travellers with a single main destination, and also quite good for walking. The Top 75 Recreational series has highly detailed maps for serious walkers and cyclists. Other specialist maps for walkers and climbers are produced by **Didier Richard** (Alpine maps), while the IGN produces detailed maps of the Pyrenees and the national parks.

Michelin publishes town plans, but local tourist offices often give away their own town plans free.

Shopping for Maps and Books

In France, most good bookshops and **Maisons de la Presse** should have a range of maps, but they can often be bought more cheaply in **supermarkets** or **service stations**. Motorway maps can often be picked up free of charge at rest areas.

Stockists in the UK are:
Stanfords International Map Centre, 12–14 Long Acre, Covent Garden, London WC2E 9LP, tel: 020-7836 1321, www. stanfords.co.uk
Dash4it, Unit 2 Barncoose Industrial Estate, Redruth, Cornwall TR15 3RQ, tel: 01209 310768, http://dash4it. co.uk
Michelin Maps and Guides, Hannay House, 39 Clarendon Road, Watford, Herts WD17 1JA, tel: 01923 205240, http://travel.michelin.co.uk
Nicolson Maps, 3 Frazer Street, Largs, Ayrshire KA30 9HP, tel/fax: 01475-689242, www.nicolsonmaps. com

Media

Newspapers

Regional newspapers, as in the US, contain national and international as well as local news, and are often read in preference to the national press. The main national dailies are Le Monde (good for a liberal overview of political and economic news), the more conservative Le Figaro and the left-wing papers, Libération and L'Humanité. Le Point, Le Nouvel Observateur and L'Express are the major weekly news publications. British and American dailies – including The Times, The Daily Telegraph and the International Herald Tribune – are widely available in major towns.

In big cities, you'll often find a map of the local area near transport hubs.

TRANSPORT

Television

All of France was converted to Digital Video Broadcasting (DVB) in 2011, which is called 'la télévision numérique terrestre' (TNT) in France.) There are over 60 free channels including the main national channels: TF1 (commercial) and France 2 (state-owned but largely financed by advertising); as well as France 3, which offers regional programmes, and France 4 covering mainly music, sport and films. Arté is a Franco-German channel showing cartoons during the day and arts programmes and documentaries in the evening. M6 shows mainly American films and serials (dubbed into French).

Radio

France Inter is the main national radio station (87.8 MHz); it broadcasts English-language news twice a day in summer (usually 9am and 4pm). During the peak holiday period, other local stations sometimes put out English bulletins. In some areas the BBC's Radio 4 can be received on longwave (198 kHz). The BBC World Service broadcasts in English on various wavelengths during the day and evening. Radio Traffic (107.7 FM) is useful when driving and gives regular bulletins of traffic situations in English.

Money

Currency

The French currency is the euro (€). It is divided into 100 cents. The coins used are 1¢, 2¢, 5¢, 10¢, 20¢, 50¢, €1, €2. The notes are €5, €10, €20, €50 and €100.

Changing money

Banks displaying a Change sign will exchange foreign currency and, in general, give the best rates; you will need to produce your passport in any transaction. If possible, avoid hotel or other independent bureaux de change, which may charge a high commission.

Credit and debit cards

Credit and debit cards are widely accepted. Visa and Access MasterCard/Eurocard) are the most common. American Express is not very popular.

Credit and debit cards issued from most European banks can be used as payment in many shops and restaurants. Check the validity of the card with your bank before departure,

Leave a small tip.

and the charges for using the card overseas. You will need to know your PIN for both debit and credit cards when paying, and often another form of identity will be requested, such as a passport. Although most establishments possess card readers that accept foreign cards with a valid PIN, sometimes the card might be rejected. In this case suggest to the retailer that the card has a magnetic strip and that the transaction needs to be signed for instead of using a PIN.

If your cash withdrawal card carries the European Cirrus symbol, withdrawals in euros can be made from bank and post office automatic cash machines bearing the same symbol. The specific cards accepted are marked on each machine, and most give instructions in English. Credit card companies and banks charge a fee for cash advances, but this still sometimes works out better value than paying the bureaux de change commission, and is much more convenient.

Ring your credit card company before your journey – increased fraud means that payment may not be authorised if spending deviates from the norm.

Lost Credit Cards

For lost credit cards, it is important to notify the authorities right away on the following numbers:

Visa
Tel: 08 00 90 11 79
American Express
Tel: 08 00 83 28 20
MasterCard
Tel: 08 00 90 13 87
National reporting centre for lost and stolen bank cards (Service Interbancaire),
tel: 0892 705 705

Traveller's cheques

Traveller's cheques are becoming less popular now that ATMs are so widespread. Some hotels will accept

them as payment but not all banks will cash them. In remote rural areas, where bank personnel are rapidly being replaced by ATMs, you may have difficulty finding anywhere to cash traveller's cheques.

Tipping

Most restaurant bills include a service charge, and this is generally indicated at the foot of the menu. If in doubt, ask: *Est-ce que le service est compris?* In any case it is common to leave a small additional tip for the waiter if the service has been good. Remember to address waiters as *Monsieur*, never as *Garçon*; waitresses are *Mademoiselle* or *Madame* according to age. It is customary to tip taxi drivers 10 percent, though this is not obligatory.

O

Opening Hours

Office workers normally start early – 8am is not uncommon – and often stay at their desks until 6pm or later. This is partly to make up for the long lunch hours (from noon or 12.30pm for two hours), which are still traditional in banks, shops and other public offices.

Outside the major towns, even large supermarkets and petrol stations shut for a couple of hours over lunch, operate shorter hours than is usual in the UK and US, and may close on Sundays and public holidays. Many shops in smaller towns and villages close on one day in the week, although you can usually find a bakery open in the morning. So plan your shopping carefully to avoid being caught without food or fuel.

Many companies are beginning to change to shorter lunch breaks as employees appreciate the advantages

Public Holidays

It is common practice, if a public holiday falls on a Thursday or Tuesday, for French business to *faire le pont* (bridge the gap) and have the Friday or Monday as a holiday too. Details of closures should be posted outside banks and other major institutions a few days before, but it is easy to be caught out, especially on Assumption day in August, which is not a UK holiday. Major public holidays are:

1 January (New Year's Day)
Easter Monday (but not Good Friday; March/April)
Whit Monday (Pentecost)
Labour Day (Monday closest to 1 May)
Ascension Day (May/June)
8 May (to commemorate the end of World War I)
14 July (Bastille Day)
15 August (Assumption Day)
1 November (All Saints Day)
11 November (Armistice Day)
25 December (Christmas Day, but not Boxing Day)

of getting home earlier to families in the evening.

Banks are normally open Monday–Friday 9am–noon and 2pm–5pm, but these hours may vary slightly, especially in rural areas.

P

Pets

It is possible to take your pet to France and re-enter Britain with your pet without quarantine. You will need an EU pet passport (or a valid PETS certificate). For further information on requirements for issuing the pet passport go online at www.gov.uk/take-pet-abroad; call the Pet Travel Scheme helpline, tel: 0370 241 1710; or contact the French embassy in London (tel: 020-7073 1000, www.ambafrance-uk.org). Once in Europe, travelling between countries requires only a valid PETS certificate or pet passport.

Postal Services

Provincial post offices – *postes* or PTTs (pronounced *pay-tay-tay*) are generally open Monday–Friday 9am–noon and 2–5pm, Saturday 9am–noon (opening hours are posted outside); in Paris and other large cities they are generally open continuously from 8am–7pm. The main post office in Paris is open 24 hours every day, at 52 Rue du Louvre, 75001 Paris.

Inside major post offices, individual counters may be marked for different requirements. If you just need stamps, go to the window marked *Timbres*. If you need to send an urgent letter overseas, ask for it to be sent *priorité* or by *Chronopost*, which is faster, but expensive.

Stamps are available at tobacconists *(bureaux de tabacs)* and sometimes also at other shops selling postcards and greetings cards. Standard-weight letters within France require a €0.76 stamp (first class) and most of the EU a €0.95 stamp.

For a minimal fee you can arrange for mail to held at any post office, addressed to *Poste Restante, Poste Centrale* (main post office), then the town's post code and name, e.g. 16000 Angoulême. A passport is required as proof of identity when collecting mail.

Many post offices have coin-in-slot photocopying machines.

R

Religious Services

Some of the most impressive buildings in France are its cathedrals, churches and chapels. They are popular tourist attractions and it is sometimes easy to forget that they are places of worship. France is traditionally a Catholic country and main religious services are held Sunday mornings. However, in small villages the services will be less frequent. The times of the masses are usually posted at the church.

S

Student Travellers

Students and young people under the age of 26 can benefit from cut-price travel to France and rail cards for getting around the country. If you wish to spend a prolonged stay in the region, it may be worth finding out about an exchange visit or study holiday. Several organisations provide information or arrange such visits.

Those with decent French can approach one of the UK-based camping holiday operators who often employ students as site couriers during the holidays.

Organisations in the US include: American Council for International Studies Inc., 343 Congress Street, Suite 3100, Boston MA 02210, toll free (USA) tel: 800-888 ACIS, www.acis.com.

Youth for Understanding International Exchange (YFU), 2141 Wisconsin Avenue, Suite D2, Washington DC 20007, www.yfu.org.

Volunteers are welcome at the camps organised on several of the archaeological sites in Burgundy (mainly in summer). Although unpaid, this is a good way to meet other young people of all nationalities and to learn French.

Once in France, students will find that a valid student ID card is useful in obtaining discounts on all sorts of activities, including admission to museums, cinemas, etc. If you do not have your ID card with you, reductions may be allowed by proving your age with a passport.

The Centre d'Information et de Documentation de Jeunesse (CIDJ), based at 101 Quai Branly, 75015 Paris, tel: 01 44 49 12 00, www.cidj. com, is a national organisation that issues information about youth and student activities.

Youth Hostel Association card holders may stay in any French

Reservations

Many *départements* now offer a central booking facility for accommodation (sometimes including *gîtes*) and for activity holidays and other services. Contact:

the relevant Comité Regional du Tourisme (CRT)
your local French Government Tourist Office

Gîtes de France, 59 Rue St-Lazare, 75009 Paris, tel: 01 49 70 75 75, www.gites-de-france. com. They provide addresses of the individual Relais Départementaux who each produce a list of all the gîtes in their département. Gîtes can get heavily booked in high season, so reserve well in advance.

Fédération Internationale des Logis, 83 Avenue d'Italie, 75013 Paris, tel : 01 45 84 70 00, www.logishotels.com. Logis is Europe's biggest hotel-restaurant network, acting as a type of quality-control stamp, where you can obtain a handbook direct or make a hotel or restaurant booking.

hostels run be either of two separate organisations: Fédération Unie des Auberges de Jeunesse (www.fuaj.org) and the Ligue Française pour les Auberges de Jeunesse (www.auberges-de-jeunesse.com). In the UK: British Youth Hostel Association (tel: 0800-019 1700; www.yha.org.uk). In the US: Hostelling International-USA (tel: 202-783 6161; www.hiusa.org).

Telephones

The French telephone system is one of the most efficient in the world. That is not to say that you can be guaranteed to find telephone boxes (cabines publiques) that are always operational, but most are.

Land-line Telephone numbers all have ten figures, given in sets of two, e.g.: 01 23 45 67 89. Note that numbers will be given in pairs of figures, unless you ask for them to be given chiffre par chiffre (singly). The only additional codes necessary are for dialling overseas. French mobile phones also have ten figures starting with either 06 or 07.

For directory enquiry services, there are now a score of private operators, whose charges vary widely. They all have six-figure numbers starting with 118. For example Le Numéro-France 118 218; France Télécom 118 712.

Public Telephones

There are still some coin-only public telephones in France but most have been converted to card or card/cash phones. These are simple to use, and it is worth purchasing a phone card (une télécarte) if you are likely to use a public call box several times. Cards are available from post offices, stationers, railway stations and tobacconists.

Cheap Rates

The cheapest times to call are weekdays 9pm–9am and at weekends after noon on Saturday.

Information

Internet access is widely accessible in main post offices, public libraries and main tourist offices. A lot of city hotels have Wi-Fi, and Internet access. Internet cafés have not really taken off in France and are mostly only found in large cities. A growing number of cities now offer free Wi-Fi hotspots.

Telephoning Abroad

To make an international call, lift the receiver, insert phone card, dial 00, then dial the country code, followed by the area code (omitting the area code prefix 0) and the number. For Monaco tel: 00 377 plus an eight-figure number.

International dialling codes

International Dialling Code 33
UK 44
US 1
Canada 1
Ireland 353
Australia 61

Regional Codes

All French telephone numbers have 10 digits, which include the regional prefix:
Paris, Ile de France: 01
Northwest 02
Northeast 03
Southeast and Corsica 04
Southwest 05.

All 10 digits must be dialled even when calling from within the same region. When dialling from outside the country, omit the initial 0.

US Credit Phone Cards

If you want to use a US credit phone card, dial the company's access number.
at&t 0800 99 00 11
MCI 0800 99 00 19

Tourist Information

Regional Tourist Offices

Tourist information is available from the office of the Syndicat d'Initiative, often attached to the town hall (hôtel de ville) in smaller places. There are also regional tourist offices (Comité Regional du Tourisme, or CRT), which you may want to contact before leaving home.
Alsace
20a Rue Berthe Molly, 68005 Colmar, tel: 03 89 24 73 50, www.tourisme-alsace.com
For Bas-Rhin and Haut-Rhin.
Aquitaine
4/5 Place Jean-Jaurès, 33074 Bordeaux, tel: 05 56 01 70 00, www.tourisme-aquitaine.fr
For Dordogne, Gironde, Landes, Lot-et-Garonne and Pyrénées-Atlantiques.
Auvergne
Parc Technologique La Pardieu, 7 Allée Pierre de Fermat, CS 50502, 63178 Aubière Cedex, tel: 04 73 29 49 49, www.auvergne-tourisme.info

Time Zone

GMT +1 (GMT +2 Apr–Oct). When it is noon in France, it is 6am in New York. Note that France uses the 24-hour clock.

For Allier, Cantal, Haute-Loire and Puy-de-Dôme.
Brittany (Bretagne)
1 Rue Raoul Ponchon, 35069 Rennes Cedex, tel: 02 99 28 44 30, wwwtourismebretagne.com
For Côtes d'Armor, Finistère, Ille-et-Vilaine and Morbihan.
Burgundy (Bourgogne)
5 Avenue Garibaldi, 21000 Dijon Cedex, tel: 03 80 28 02 80, www.bourgogne-tourisme.com
For Côte-d'Or, Nièvre, Saône-et-Loire and Yonne.
Champagne-Ardennes
15 Avenue du Maréchal Leclerc, BP 319, 51013 Chalons-sur-Champagne Cedex, tel: 03 26 21 85 80, www.tourisme-champagne-ardenne.com
For Ardennes, Aube, Marne and Haute-Marne.
Corsica
17 Boulevard Roi Jérôme, 20181 Ajaccio Cedex 01, tel: 04 95 51 77 77, www.visit-corsica.com
Franche-Comté
4 Rue Gabriel Plançon, 25000 Besançon, tel: 03 81 25 08 08, fax: 03 81 83 35 82, www.franche-comte.org
For Doubs, Jura, Haute-Saône and Territoire-de-Belfort.
Paris Ile-de-France
11 Rue du Faubourg Poissonnière, 75009 Paris, tel: 01 73 00 77 00, www.visitparisregion.com
For Seine-et-Marne, Yvelines, Hauts-de-Seine, Seine-St-Denis, Val-de-Marne and Val-d'Oise.
Languedoc-Roussillon
954 Avenue Jean Mermoz, 34000 Montpellier Cedex 2, tel: 04 67 20 02 20, www.destinationsuddefrance.com
For Aude, Gard, Hérault, Lozère and the Pyrénées-Orientales.
Limousin
30 Cours Gay-Lussac, CS 50095, 87003 Limoges Cedex 1, tel: 05 55 11 06 09 www.tourismelimousin.com
For Corrèze, Haute-Vienne and Creuse.
Loire Valley
Centre-Val de Loire: 37 Avenue de Paris, 45000 Orléans, tel: 02 38 79 95 00, www.visaloire.com
For Cher, Eure-et-Loir, Indre, Indre-et-Loire, Loir-et-Cher and Loiret.
Pays de la Loire: 1 Rue de la Loire, 44966 Nantes Cedex 9, tel: 02 28

TRANSPORT

EATING OUT

ACTIVITIES

A – Z

LANGUAGE

20 50 00, www.paysdelaloire.fr
For Loire-Atlantique, Maine-et-Loire, Mayenne, Sarthe and Vendée.

Lorraine
Abbaye de Prémontrés, BP97, 54704 Pont à Mousson Cedex, tel: 03 83 80 01 80, www.tourisme-lorraine.fr
For Meurthe-et-Moselle, Moselle, Meuse and Vosges.

Midi-Pyrénées
15 Rue Rivals, 31685 Toulouse Cedex 6, tel: 05 61 13 55 55, www.tourisme-midi-pyrenees.com
For Ariège, Aveyron, Haute-Garonne, Gers, Lot, Hautes-Pyrénées, Tarn and Tarn-et-Garonne.

Nord/Pas-de-Calais
3 Rue du Palais Rihour, 59026 Lille, tel: 03 20 14 57 57, www.tourisme-nordpasdecalais.fr
For Nord and Pas-de-Calais.

Normandy
14 Rue Charles-Corbeau, 27000 Evreux, tel: 02 32 33 79 00, www.normandie-tourisme.fr
For Calvados, Eure, Manche, Orne and Seine-Maritime.

Picardie
3 Rue Vincent Auriole, 80011 Amiens Cedex 1, tel: 03 22 22 33 66, www.picardietourisme.com.
For Somme, Aisne and Oise.

Poitou-Charentes
15 Rue de L'Ancienne Comédie, 86021 Poitiers Cedex, tel: 05 49 55 77 41, www.poitou-charentes-vacances.com.
For Charente, Charente-Maritime, Deux-Sèvres and Vienne.

Provence (Alpes/Côte-d'Azur)
61 La Canebière, 13231 Marseille Cedex 1, tel: 04 91 56 47 00, www.tourismepaca.fr
For Alpes de Haute Provence, Hautes Alpes, Bouches du Rhône, Var and Vaucluse.

Rhône-Alpes
8 Rue Paul Montrochet, 69002 Lyon, tel: 04 26 73 31 59, http://en.rhonealpes-tourisme.com
For Ain, Ardèche, Drôme, Isère, Loire, Rhône, Savoie and Haute-Savoie.

Riviera/Côte d'Azur
455 Promenade des Anglais, BP 602, 06011 Nice Cedex, tel: 04 93 37 78 78, www.cotedazur-tourisme.com
For Alpes-Maritimes.

UK

French Government Tourist Office
Lincoln House, 300 High Holborn, London WC1V 7JH; tel: 09068-244123, http://uk.rendezvousenfrance.com

French Institute, 17 Queensberry Place, London SW7 2DT, tel: 020-7871 3515, www.institut-francais.org.uk

Monaco Government Tourist Authority, 7 Upper Grosvenor Street, Mayfair, London W1K 2LX, www.visitmonaco.com, tel: 020-7352 9962.

US and Canada

French Government Tourist Office
US: http://us.rendezvousenfrance.com
Canada: http://ca.rendezvousenfrance.com

France

Air France
45 Rue de Paris, 95747 Roissy CDG Cedex, tel: 01 41 56 78 00 .
French Tourist Office, www.francetourism.com

Visas and Passports

European Union citizens only require a valid passport to visit France.

Citizens of Australia, Canada, New Zealand and the US, and certain other countries with which France has an agreement, do not require visas. If in any doubt, check with the French consulate in your country, or visit www.diplomatie.gouv.fr, as the situation may change from time to time. If you intend to stay in France for more than 90 days, then you should have a *carte de séjour* (again from the French consulate) – this can also apply to certain EU citizens.

Websites

Tour Operators and Travel Agents

www.enfrancetours.com US based company organises tours of France in small groups
www.frenchentree.com Range of activity holidays including motor sport, water sport, trekking, canoeing, photography and pottery
www.hotelsabroad.com will offer a bed and breakfast service that can include ferry bookings if desired. It will book accommodation at your chosen destination and overnight stops en route
www.allezfrance.com Organises short breaks, self-catering and theme park holidays
www.holidayfrancedirect.co.uk specialises in French holidays in independently owned properties
www.centralholidays.com has some interesting cookery and wine themed holiday packages, and Mediterranean cruises
www.ernalow.co.uk offers a range of ski holidays
http://winetours.co.uk Arblaster & Clarke is a reputable company that organises wine tours
www.stevenreedfrance.com organises residential painting holidays with expert tuition
www.yourfrenchholidays.com has a comprehensive list of tour operators and lots for information for planning a holiday in France

Weights and Measures

France uses metric for all weights and measures, although old-fashioned terms such as *livre* (about 1lb or 500g) are still used by some shopkeepers.

An Office de Tourisme or a Syndicat d'Initiative will provide tourist information.

LANGUAGE

UNDERSTANDING THE LANGUAGE

Everyone in France speaks French, but regional languages still exist in Brittany (Breton), Alsace (Alsatian) and the western Pyrenees (Basque); in some parts of the eastern Pyrenees Catalan is spoken.

French is the native language of more than 90 million people and the acquired language of 180 million. It is a Romance language descended from the Vulgar Latin spoken by the Roman conquerors of Gaul. People often tell stories about the impatience of the French towards foreigners not blessed with fluency in their language. In general, however, if you try your best to communicate in French, no matter how badly, people will be helpful. Moreover, many French people enjoy practising their English on visitors.

Since much English vocabulary is related to French, thanks to the Norman Conquest of 1066, travellers will recognise many words, such as *hôtel*, *café* and *bagages*. You should be aware, however, of some misleading "false friends" such as *le car* for a long-distance bus.

BASIC RULES

Even if you speak no French at all, it is worth trying to master a few simple phrases.

Pronunciation is the key; people really will not understand if you get it very wrong. Remember to **emphasise**

Non, Non, Garçon

Never use the word *garçon* (boy) for waiter, as this is considered highly insulting; say *Monsieur* or *Madame/Mademoiselle* to attract the waiter or waitress's attention.

each syllable, but not to pronounce the last consonant of a word as a rule (this includes the plural "s"), and always drop your "h"s.

Whether to use "**vous**" or "**tu**" is a vexed question; as society generally becomes less formal the familiar form of "tu" is used more and more. However, always use "vous" when speaking to adults you don't know; "tu" is acceptable when talking to children. It is better to use "vous" if in doubt. It is very important to be polite; always address people as **Madame** or **Monsieur**, and address them by their surnames until you are confident first names are acceptable. When entering a shop always say, "Bonjour Monsieur/Madame," and "Merci, au revoir," when leaving.

LANGUAGE STUDY

There are many study tours and language courses available. For information contact the following organisations:
Centre des Echanges Internationaux, 1 Rue Gozlin, 75006 Paris, tel: 01 43 29 13 39, www. cei4vents.com, for sporting and cultural holidays and educational tours for 15–30 year olds. Non profit-making.
Alliance Française, 101 Boulevard Raspail, 75270 Paris, tel: 01 42 84 90 00, www.alliancefr.org. A non profit-making, highly regarded French-language school, with beginners' and specialist courses. Centres throughout France.
UK Socrates-Erasmus Council, tel: 029 2092 4311; https://erasmusplus. org.uk, . Scheme for students studying within the European Union to spend a year in a French university.
Lists of private language schools

are obtainable from regional tourist offices (see page 399).

WORDS AND PHRASES

What is your name? *Comment vous appelez-vous?*
My name is... *Je m'appelle*...
Do you speak English? *Parlez-vous anglais?*
I am English/American *Je suis anglais(e)/américain(e)*
I don't understand *Je ne comprends pas*
Please speak more slowly *Parlez plus lentement, s'il vous plaît*
Can you help me? *Pouvez-vous m'aider?*
I'm looking for... *Je cherche*
Where is...? *Où est...?*
I'm sorry *Excusez-moi/Pardon*
I don't know *Je ne sais pas*
Have a good day! *Bonne journée!*
That's it *C'est ça*
Here it is *Voici*
There it is *Voilà*
Let's go *On y va. Allons-y*
See you tomorrow *A demain*
See you soon *A bientôt*
Show me the word in the book *Montrez-moi le mot dans le livre*
yes *oui*
no *non*
please *s'il vous plaît*
thank you *merci*
(very much) *(beaucoup)*
you're welcome *de rien*
excuse me *excusez-moi*
hello *bonjour*
OK *d'accord*
goodbye *au revoir*
good evening *bonsoir*
here *ici*
there *là*
today *aujourd'hui*
yesterday *hier*

TRANSPORT

EATING OUT

ACTIVITIES

A – Z

LANGUAGE

tomorrow *demain*
now *maintenant*
later *plus tard*
this morning *ce matin*
this afternoon *cet après-midi*
this evening *ce soir*

EMERGENCIES

Help! *Au secours!*
Stop! *Arrêtez!*
Call a doctor *Appelez un médecin*
Call an ambulance *Appelez une ambulance*
Call the police *Appelez la police*
Call the fire brigade *Appelez les pompiers*
Where is the nearest telephone? *Où est le téléphone le plus proche?*
Where is the nearest hospital? *Où est l'hôpital le plus proche?*
I am sick *Je suis malade*
I have lost my passport/purse *J'ai perdu mon passeport/porte-monnaie*

ON ARRIVAL

I want to get off at... *Je voudrais descendre à...*
What street is this? *A quelle rue sommes-nous?*
Which line do I take for...? *Quelle ligne dois-je prendre pour...?*
How far is...? *A quelle distance se trouve...?*
Validate your ticket *Compostez votre billet*
airport *l'aéroport*
train station *la gare*
bus station *la gare routière*
Métro stop *la station de Métro*
bus *l'autobus, le car*
bus stop *l'arrêt*
platform *le quai*
ticket *le billet*
return ticket *aller-retour*
hitchhiking *l'autostop*
toilets *les toilettes*
This is the hotel address *C'est l'adresse de l'hôtel*
I'd like a (single/double) room... *Je voudrais une chambre (pour une/deux personnes)...*
....with shower *avec douche*
....with a bath *avec salle de bain*
....with a view *avec vue*
Does that include breakfast? *Le petit déjeuner est-il compris?*
May I see the room? *Je peux voir la chambre?*
washbasin *le lavabo*
bed *le lit*
key *la clé*
lift/elevator *l'ascenseur*
air conditioned *climatisé*
swimming pool *la piscine*

to book *réserver*

ON THE ROAD

Where is the nearest garage? *Où est le garage le plus proche?*
Our car has broken down *Notre voiture est en panne*
I want to have my car repaired *Je veux faire réparer ma voiture*
I think I must have put diesel in the car by mistake *Je crois que j'ai mis du gasoil dans la voiture par erreur*
the road to... *la route pour...*
left *gauche*
right *droite*
straight on *tout droit*
far *loin*
near *près d'ici*
opposite *en face*
beside *à côté de*
car park *parking*
over there *là-bas*
at the end *au bout*
toll *le péage*
speed limit *la limitation de vitesse*
petrol *l'essence*
unleaded *sans plomb*
diesel *le gasoil*
water/oil *l'eau/l'huile*
puncture *un pneu crevé*
wipers *les essuies-glace*
Sat-Nav *GPS*

SHOPPING

Where is the nearest bank (post office)? *Où est la banque/Poste/PTT la plus proche?*
I'd like to buy *Je voudrais acheter*
How much is it? *C'est combien?*
Do you take credit cards? *Est-ce que vous acceptez les cartes de crédit?*
I'm just looking *Je regarde seulement*
Have you got...? *Avez-vous...?*
I'll take it *Je le prends*
I'll take this one/that one *Je prends celui-ci/celui-là*
What size is it? *C'est de quelle taille?*
size (clothes) *la taille*
size (shoes) *la pointure*
cheap *bon marché*
expensive *cher*
enough *assez*
too much *trop*
each *la pièce (eg ananas, €2 la pièce)*
chemist/pharmacy *la pharmacie*
bakery *la boulangerie*
bookshop *la librairie*
library *la bibliothèque*
department store *le grand magasin*
butcher's *la charcuterie*
fishmonger's *la poissonnerie*
delicatessen *le traiteur*

Slang

branché **trendy**
une copine/un copain **friend/mate**
un ami **friend**
petit(e) ami(e) **boyfriend (girlfriend)**
un truc **thing, "whatsit"**
pas mal **not bad, good-looking**
la frangine **sister**
le frangin **brother**
un pot/une pote **friend**
un mec/un gars **bloke**
une gonzesse/une meuf **woman**
un gamin/môme **kid**
une bagnole **car**
un bled **village**
bosser **to work**
un boulot **work**
bourré **drunk**
chouette **nice**
un flic **policeman**
le fric **money**

grocery *l'épicerie*
tobacconist *le tabac*
market *le marché*
supermarket *le supermarché*

SIGHTSEEING

town *la ville*
old town *la vieille ville*
abbey *l'abbaye*
cathedral *la cathédrale*
church *l'église*
hospital *l'hôpital*
town hall *l'hôtel de ville/la mairie*
nave *la nef*
stained glass *le vitrail*
staircase *l'escalier*
tower *la tour (La Tour Eiffel)*
walk *le tour*
country house/castle *le château*
Gothic *gothique*
Roman *romain*
Romanesque *roman*
museum *le musée*
tourist information office *l'office de tourisme/le syndicat d'initiative*
free *gratuit*
open *ouvert*
closed *fermé*
every day *tous les jours*
all day *toute la journée*
all year *toute l'année*

DINING OUT

Table d'hôte (the "host's table") is one set menu served at a set price. **Prix fixe** is a fixed price menu. **A la carte** means dishes from the menu are charged separately.
breakfast *le petit déjeuner*
lunch *le déjeuner*

dinner *le dîner*
meal *le repas*
first course *l'entrée/les hors d'œuvre*
main course *le plat principal*
dessert *puddings*
vegetables *légumes*
fruit *fruits*
drink included *boisson comprise*
wine list *la carte des vins*
fork *la fourchette*
knife *le couteau*
spoon *la cuillère*
plate *l'assiette*
glass *le verre*
napkin *la serviette*
bill *l'addition*
I am a vegetarian *Je suis végétarien(ne)*
I am on a diet *Je suis au régime*
What do you recommend? *Qu'est-ce que vous recommandez?*
Do you have local specialities? *Avez-vous des spécialités locales?*
I'd like to order *Je voudrais commander*
That is not what I ordered *Ce n'est pas ce que j'ai commandé(e)*
Is service included? *Est-ce que le service est compris?*
Enjoy your meal *Bon appétit!*

Breakfast and Snacks

pain bread
beurre butter
poivre pepper
sel salt
sucre sugar
confiture jam
oeufs eggs
assiette anglaise cold meats
potage soup

La Viande – Meat

bleu very rare
saignant rare
à point medium
bien cuit well done
grillé grilled
agneau lamb
bifteck steak
canard duck
farci stuffed
jambon ham
lapin rabbit
poulet chicken
poussin young chicken
rognons kidneys
veau veal

Poissons – Fish

anchois anchovies
bar (or loup) sea bass
barbue brill
cabillaud cod
calmars squid

coquillage shellfish
crevette shrimp
daurade sea bream
flétan halibut
hareng herring
homard lobster
huître oyster
limande lemon sole
lotte monkfish
raie skate
saumon salmon
thon tuna
truite trout

IN THE CAFÉ

drinks *les boissons*
coffee *café*
...with milk/cream *au lait/crème*
...decaffeinated *déca/décaféiné*
...black/espresso *noir/express*
...American filtered coffee *filtre*
tea *thé*
...herbal infusion *tisane*
...camomile *verveine*
hot chocolate *chocolat chaud*
milk *lait*
... full cream *entier*
... semi-skimmed *demi-écrémé*
... skimmed *écrémé*
mineral water *eau minérale*
sparkling/still *gazeuse/non-gazeuse*
fresh lemon juice served with sugar *citron pressé*
freshly squeezed orange juice *orange pressée*
fresh or cold *frais, fraîche*
beer *bière*
...bottled *en bouteille*
...on tap *à la pression*
white wine with cassis (blackcurrant liqueur) *kir*
kir with champagne *kir royale*
with ice *avec des glaçons*
neat *sec*
red *rouge*
white *blanc*
rosé *rosé*
dry *brut*
sweet *doux*
sparkling wine *crémant/vin mousseux*
house wine *vin de maison*
local wine *vin de pays*
pitcher *carafe/pichet*
...of water/wine *d'eau/de vin*
cheers! *santé!*
hangover *gueule de bois*

TIME

Note that the French generally use the 24-hour clock.
At what time? *A quelle heure?*
When? *Quand?*
What time is it? *Quelle heure est-il?*

DAYS AND MONTHS

Days of the week, seasons and months are not capitalised in French.

Days of the Week

Monday *lundi*
Tuesday *mardi*
Wednesday *mercredi*
Thursday *jeudi*
Friday *vendredi*
Saturday *samedi*
Sunday *dimanche*

Seasons

spring *le printemps*
summer *l'été*
autumn *l'automne*
winter *l'hiver*

Months

January *janvier*
February *février*
March *mars*
April *avril*
May *mai*
June *juin*
July *juillet*
August *août*
September *septembre*
October *octobre*
November *novembre*
December *décembre*

ON THE TELEPHONE/ INTERNET

How do I make an outside call? *Comment appelle-t-on à l'extérieur?*
I'd like an alarm call for 8 tomorrow morning *Je voudrais être réveillé(e) à huit heures demain matin*

Numbers

0 *zéro*	17 *dix-sept*
1 *un, une*	18 *dix-huit*
2 *deux*	19 *dix-neuf*
3 *trois*	20 *vingt*
4 *quatre*	21 *vingt-et-un*
5 *cinq*	30 *trente*
6 *six*	40 *quarante*
7 *sept*	50 *cinquante*
8 *huit*	60 *soixante*
9 *neuf*	70 *soixante-dix*
10 *dix*	80 *quatre-vingts*
11 *onze*	90 *quatre-vingt-dix*
12 *douze*	
13 *treize*	100 *cent*
14 *quatorze*	1,000 *mille*
15 *quinze*	1,000,000 *Un million*
16 *seize*	

TRANSPORT

EATING OUT

ACTIVITIES

A – Z

LANGUAGE

FURTHER READING

ARTS AND ARCHITECTURE

Châteaux of the Loire, by Jean-Marie Perouse De Montclos.
Nineteenth-Century French Art: From Romanticism to Impressionism, Post-Impressionism and Art Nouveau, by Henri Loyrette and Sébastien Allard.
The Private Lives of the Impressionists, by Sue Roe. Get behind the artists as they struggle for recognition and an insight of life of the times.

HISTORY AND SOCIAL COMMENTARY

Athénais as new edition: the Real Queen of France: Athénais and Louis XIV , by Lisa Hilton.
France in the New Century, by John Ardagh.
France Since 1945, by Robert Gildea.
Madame de Pompadour, by Christine Pevitt Algrant.
Marie-Antoinette, by Antonia Fraser.
Paris: After the Liberation, by Antony Beevor and Artemis Cooper.
The French Revolution: A Very Short Introduction, by William Doyle.

BELLES LETTRES

The Discovery of France, by Graham Robb. A humerous and enlightening tour as Robb cycles 22,530km (14,000 miles) around France, meeting all manner of French citizens.
A Little Tour in France, by Henry James.
A Moveable Feast, by Ernest Hemingway. The life of the artist in Paris.
Travels With A Donkey by Robert Louis Stevenson.

Satori in Paris, by Jack Kerouac. *Satori* is Japanese for "sudden illumination". Ten days of travel as the author searches for his French roots.
Two Towns in Provence, by M.F.K. Fisher. A tribute to Aix-en-Provence and Marseille.

FRENCH LITERATURE

The Oxford Companion to French Literature, by Peter France.

CLASSICS BY DATE

La Chanson de Roland, c.1100.
Rabelais, *Gargantua et Pantagruel*, 1532–64.
Molière, *Tartuffe*, 1669.
Racine, *Phèdre*, 1677.
Voltaire, *Candide*, 1759.
Hugo, *Nôtre-Dame-de-Paris*, 1831.
Balzac, *Eugénie Grandet*, 1833.
Flaubert, *Madame Bovary*, 1857.
Zola, *Germinal*, 1885.
Proust, *Du côté de chez Swann*, 1913.
Camus, *La Peste*, 1957.

FOOD AND WINE

French Country Cooking, by Elizabeth David.
The French Kitchen: A Cookbook, by Joanne Harris and Fran Warde.
My Paris Kitchen – Recipes and Stories, by David Lebovitz.
Raymond Blanc's Simple French Cookery, by Raymond Blanc.
Wine Atlas of France, by Hugh Johnson and Jancis Robinson. Best-selling work on wine and vineyards.
The Little Paris Kitchen, by Rachel's Khoo.

LIVING IN FRANCE

Buying a Home in France, by David Hampshire.

Buying a Property in France: An Insider Guide to Realising Your Dream by Clive Kristen.
Living and Working in France, by David Hampshire.

OTHER INSIGHT GUIDES

Insight Guides and Insight City Guides covering France include *Insight Guide Provence & the French Riviera*, *Northern France*, *Southwest France* and *Paris*. Insight Explore Guides deliver self-guided walks and tours to *Paris* and *Nice & the French Riviera*.

Send Us Your Thoughts

We do our best to ensure the information in our books is as accurate and up-to-date as possible. The books are updated on a regular basis using local contacts, who painstakingly add, amend and correct as required. However, some details (such as telephone numbers and opening times) are liable to change, and we are ultimately reliant on our readers to put us in the picture.

We welcome your feedback, especially your experience of using the book "on the road". Maybe we recommended a hotel that you liked (or another that you didn't), or you came across a great bar or new attraction we missed.

We will acknowledge all contributions, and we'll offer an Insight Guide to the best letters received.

Please write to us at:
Insight Guides
PO Box 7910
London SE1 1WE
Or email us at:
hello@insightguides.com

CREDITS

Photo Credits

akg-images 30
Alamy 96/97B, 97ML, 141L
Amanda Slater 77TR
austinevan on flickr 250MR
AWL Images 236/237, 238, 260
Cité de l'Espace 306B
Corbis 11R, 44, 45, 47, 48, 49, 50, 51, 130, 334
dynamosquito on flickr 289B
Everett Collection/Rex Features 66
FLPA 325BR, 325TR
Fotolia 19T, 76BR, 148B, 150B, 169T, 172B, 195T, 203, 208B, 209, 210T, 211T, 211B, 215T, 226T, 227, 240, 241, 243B, 245, 246, 250/251T, 251ML, 251BL, 255T, 262T, 263, 265, 266B, 268, 269, 271T, 271B, 274, 275T, 275B, 284, 297, 300B, 302, 303B, 307, 309, 316, 320, 342B
Getty Images 4/5, 42, 46, 95, 142, 182BR, 182/183T, 183BR, 183TR, 210B, 215B, 231B, 251TR, 257, 264B, 276, 282, 287, 311, 324/325T, 324BR, 337, 344, 347B, 355B
Ilpo Musto/Apa Publications 7ML, 14/15, 19B, 90, 116, 117, 120, 124T, 131B, 133, 135, 386, 397L
iStock 6B, 6TR, 7MR, 7TL, 8B, 31, 52, 77ML, 137, 145, 150T, 198, 199T, 199B, 214, 229ML, 239B, 244, 249, 253, 255B, 261, 262B, 266T, 267, 325ML, 325BL, 357T, 359B, 404
Jean-Christophe Benoist 301B
Jean-Pierre Dalbéra 372
Jesus Abizanda 300T
Julien Magne 148T, 149

Kevin Cummins/Apa Publications 26/27, 56, 57, 61, 62R, 63R, 64, 65, 72, 80, 83R, 84, 88L, 89, 97TR, 115T, 118T, 119, 121T, 126, 127T, 128, 131T, 134T, 134B, 136T, 138, 139T, 140BL, 141R, 143, 362, 368B, 370, 384, 396
Les Sources de Caudalie 69
Ming Tang-Evans/Apa Publications 62L, 70, 71R, 74, 102/103, 108, 109T, 109B, 112, 113, 114, 115B, 118B, 121B, 122, 123, 124B, 125, 127B, 129, 132, 136B, 139B, 140/141T, 360, 401
Mirazur 75
Myrabella 151
Opinel 96/97B
PA Picselect/Icon Home Entertainment 67
Parc Astérix 9MR, 147B
Parc du Futuroscope 235
Phonogalerie by J.G.Aro 96BL
Photoshot 348
Public domain 28T, 28B, 29, 140BR, 140MR, 222T, 229TR, 264T, 303T
Scala Archives 32, 33, 34, 35, 37, 38, 39, 40, 41, 43, 85, 86, 87L, 87R
Shutterstock 273T
Sipa Press/Rex Features 53, 183ML
SuperStock 197, 324BL
Sylvaine Poitau/Apa Publications 1, 6ML, 6MR, 7BR, 7TR, 9TL, 9BR, 10B, 11L, 12/13, 16/17, 18, 20, 21, 22, 23R, 24, 25, 54/55, 58R, 58L, 59, 60R, 60L, 63L, 68, 71L, 73, 76/77T, 76BL, 77BR, 77BL, 78, 79, 81L, 81R, 82, 83L, 91, 92, 93L, 93R, 94, 98/99, 100/101, 105B,

152/153, 154, 155T, 155B, 156, 157, 159B, 159T, 161, 162, 164B, 164T, 165, 166, 168, 169B, 170, 171, 172T, 173, 175T, 175B, 176, 177B, 177T, 178, 179T, 179B, 180T, 180B, 181T, 181B, 182BL, 183BL, 184/185, 186, 187T, 187B, 188, 189, 191, 192B, 192T, 193, 194, 195B, 196, 200, 201T, 201B, 202, 205, 206, 207, 208T, 212, 213, 217, 218T, 218B, 219, 220T, 220B, 221, 222B, 223T, 223B, 224T, 224B, 225T, 225B, 226B, 228BL, 228BR, 228/229T, 229BR, 229BL, 230, 231T, 233, 234T, 234B, 239T, 243T, 247T, 247B, 248, 250B, 251BR, 252, 256, 258, 259, 272, 273B, 278/279, 280, 281T, 281B, 283, 285T, 285B, 288, 289T, 290, 291T, 291B, 292B, 292T, 293T, 293B, 294, 295, 296, 299T, 299B, 301T, 304T, 304B, 305T, 305B, 306T, 308, 310, 315T, 318T, 318B, 319T, 319B, 321, 322B, 323, 326, 327, 329, 331B, 333T, 340, 343, 347T, 350, 351T, 351B, 352, 353, 354B, 354T, 355T, 356, 357B, 358, 359T, 363L, 364, 368T, 374, 375L, 377L, 378, 383, 385L, 388, 390, 392, 394, 400
The Art Archive 36, 97BR
Tran's World Productions 349T
Wadey James/Apa Publications 7ML, 8T, 10T, 23L, 88R, 96/97T, 104, 105T, 312/313, 314, 315B, 322T, 330, 331T, 332T, 332B, 333B, 335, 336, 339, 341, 342T, 345, 346T, 346B, 349B, 393
Walt Disney Corporation 146, 147T

Cover Credits

Front cover: Pont de Valandre *Shutterstock*
Back cover: Place de la Concorde *Ming Tang-Evans/Apa Publications*
Front flap: (from top) walk *Fotolia*; boat *Fotolia*; houses *Fotolia*; more

houses *Wadey James/Apa Publications*
Back flap: 2CV *Wadey James/Apa Publications*

Insight Guide Credits

Distribution
UK
Dorling Kindersley Ltd
A Penguin Group company
80 Strand, London, WC2R 0RL
sales@uk.dk.com

United States
Ingram Publisher Services
1 Ingram Boulevard, PO Box 3006,
La Vergne, TN 37086-1986
ips@ingramcontent.com

Australia and New Zealand
Woodslane
10 Apollo St, Warriewood,
NSW 2102, Australia
info@woodslane.com.au

Worldwide
Apa Publications (Singapore) Pte
7030 Ang Mo Kio Avenue 5
08-65 Northstar @ AMK
Singapore 569880
apasin@singnet.com.sg

Printing
CTPS-China

All Rights Reserved
© 2015 Apa Digital (CH) AG and
Apa Publications (UK) Ltd

First Edition 1986
Sixth Edition 2015

No part of this book may be reproduced, stored in a retrieval system or transmitted in any form or means electronic, mechanical, photocopying, recording or otherwise, without prior written permission from Apa Publications.

Every effort has been made to provide accurate information in this publication, but changes are inevitable. The publisher cannot be responsible for any resulting loss, inconvenience or injury. We would appreciate it if readers would call our attention to any errors or outdated information. We also welcome your suggestions; please contact us at: hello@insightguides.com

www.insightguides.com

Editor: Carine Tracanelli
Authors: Nick Inman, Lyn Parry, Jackie Staddon, Hilary Weston
Head of Production: Rebeka Davies
Update Production: AM Services
Picture Editor: Tom Smyth
Cartography: original cartography Stephen Ramsey, updated by Carte

Contributors

This new edition of *Insight Guide France* was updated by **Jackie Staddon** and **Hilary Weston**. Both have combined their skills as travel writers, updaters and editors for over 15 years and in that time have produced a host of guidebooks on destinations from around the world.

They have travelled extensively in France, visiting Paris on many occasions and have a particular love of the south of France.
    This edition builds on a previous edition written by **Nick Inman** and **Lyn Parry**.

About Insight Guides

Insight Guides have more than 40 years' experience of publishing high-quality, visual travel guides. We produce 400 full-colour titles, in both print and digital form, covering more than 200 destinations across the globe, in a variety of formats to meet your different needs.
    Insight Guides are written by local authors who use their on-the-ground experience to provide the

very latest information; their local expertise is evident in the extensive historical and cultural background features. All the reviews in **Insight Guides** are independent; we strive to maintain an impartial view. Our reviews are carefully selected to guide you to the best places to eat, go out and shop, so you can be confident that when we say a place is special, we really mean it.

Legend

City maps

	Freeway/Highway/Motorway
	Divided Highway
	Main Roads
	Minor Roads
	Pedestrian Roads
	Steps
	Footpath
	Railway
	Funicular Railway
	Cable Car
	Tunnel
	City Wall
	Important Building
	Built Up Area
	Other Land
	Transport Hub
	Park
	Pedestrian Area
	Bus Station
	Tourist Information
	Main Post Office
	Cathedral/Church
	Mosque
	Synagogue
	Statue/Monument
	Beach
	Airport

Regional maps

	Freeway/Highway/Motorway (with junction)
	Freeway/Highway/Motorway (under construction)
	Divided Highway
	Main Road
	Secondary Road
	Minor Road
	Track
	Footpath
	International Boundary
	State/Province Boundary
	National Park/Reserve
	Marine Park
	Ferry Route
	Marshland/Swamp
	Glacier / Salt Lake
	Airport/Airfield
	Ancient Site
	Border Control
	Cable Car
	Castle/Castle Ruins
	Cave
	Chateau/Stately Home
	Church/Church Ruins
	Crater
	Lighthouse
	Mountain Peak
	Place of Interest
	Viewpoint

INDEX

Main references are in bold type

A

abbeys
architecture 92
aux Dames (Caen) 192
aux Dames (Saintes) 231
aux Hommes (Caen) 192
Bec-Hellouin 198
Brou 255
Cadouin 290
Chartreuse de la Verne 343
Cîteaux 32, 248
Flaran 309
Fontenay 244
Fontevraud 223
Jumièges 199
Montmajour 333
Mont-St-Michel 32, **196**
Murbach 180
Noirlac 227
Notre-Dame-de-Sénaque 330
Ste-Marie-de-la-Tourette 256
St Guilhem-le-Desert 321
St Martin-du-Canigou 316
St-Pierre-et-St-Paul (Cluny) 248
St Savin 235
Thoronet 345
Abri du Cap Blanc 289
admission charges 393
Agincourt, Battle of 33
agriculture 21, 62
Ainhoa 294
air travel 364
Aix-en-Provence 336
Aix-les-Bains 265
Ajaccio 358
Albert 160
Albi 9, **303**
Alençon 197
Aléria 356
Algeria 47
Alise-Ste-Reine 244
Alpes-Maritimes 353
Alps. See French Alps
Alsace 11, 41, 43, 44, 80, 83, 155
Amboise 218
Amiens 160
Angers 225
Angles-sur-Anglin 235
Angoulême 230
Anjou 225
Annecy 265
Antibes 9, **351**
anti-semitism 45, 52, 64
Antonin-Noble-Val 304
Aquitaine 281, **287**
Arc de Senans 249
Arc de Triomphe (Orange) 327
Arc de Triomphe (Paris) 126
architecture 91
Ardèche 259
Arènes de Lutèce (Paris) 119
Argentan 197
Ariège 302
Arles 333

Armagnac 9
Arnac-Pompadour 277
Arras 160
Arreau 301
Arromanches-les-Bains 192
art 85, 200, 289, 334. See
  also museums and galleries
Arthur, King 206
Attila the Hun 31
Aubagne 339
Aubusson 276
Auch 307
Au Lapin Agile (Paris) 135
Aurillac 275
Autoire 310
Autun 245
Auvergne 239, **269**
Auvers-sur-Oise 9, **145**
Auxerre 240
Avallon 245
Avignon 33, **329**

B

Bagnères-de-Luchon 301
Balzac, Honoré de 39, 126, 219,
  220
bandes dessinées (comic books)
  230
Bandol 339
banlieues 53, 58
barbarian invasions 31
Barbizon 150
Bardot, Brigitte 66, 344
Barfleur 195
Barran 307
Basques 25
Bassin d'Arcachon 292
Bassoues 307
Bastia 359
bastides 308
Bastille (Paris) 38, **135**
Bateau Lavoir (Paris) 136
Baudelaire, Charles 39
Bayeux 10, **193**
Bayonne 292
beaches 391
Béarn 295
Beaugency 216
Beaujolais 80, 83
Beaulieu-sur-Mer 354
Beaune 247
Beauvais 145
Beauvoir, Simone de 48
Belfort 249
Belle-Ile 207
Belleville 254
Bergues 158
Berry 227
Besançon 249
Besse-en-Chandresse 271
Betschdorf 173
Beuvron-en-Auge 191
Beynac-et-Cazenac 290
Béziers 302, **320**

Biarritz 293
Bibliothèque Humaniste
  (Sélestat) 177
birds. See wildlife
Black Death 33
Blaye 285
Blois 217
Blum, Léon 45
boat trips 117, 367
Bonaparte, Napoleon 39, 115,
  123, 358
Bonifacio 358
Bordeaux 80, 81, 83, **291**
borders 22, 167
Boucher, François 86
Boudin, Eugène 191
Boulogne 159
Bourbon dynasty 40
Bourg-en-Bresse 255
Bourges 227
Brancion 248
Brantôme 288, 379
Braque, Georges 88, 318, 334
Brasserie Lipp (Paris) 121
Brest 211
Breton, André 89
Briançon 262
Brittany 23, 31, 187, **203**
Brouage 232
Bruniquel 304
Bruni-Sarkozy Carla 52
budgeting 393
Buffon 36
Buren, Daniel 89
Burgundy 9, 80, 81, 239
Bussang 169
bus travel 363, 364

C

Cabourg 191
Caen 192
Caesar, Julius 31, 244
Café de la Paix (Paris) 131
Café Flore (Paris) 121
Cagnes-sur-Mer 350
Cahors 309
Calais 159
Calvi 359
Camargue 10, 24, **335**
Canal de Bourgogne 243
Canal des Deux Mers 250
Canal du Midi 250, 251, **303**, 320
canals 251, 367
Canal St Martin (Paris) 135, 138
Cannes 346
canoeing and kayaking 259
Cap Bénat 339
Cap Blanc Nez 159
Cap Canaille 339
Cap Corse 359
Cap d'Antibes 351
Capet, Hugh 32
Cap Ferrat 353
Cap Gris-Nez 159

Carcassonne 8, 302, **318**
Carennac 310
car hire 365
Carnac 10, 31, **207**
Cassis 339
Castagniccia 357
Castellane 346
Catalans 25, 318
Cathars **302**, 319
cathedrals
  Chartres 151
  Evreux 197
  Notre-Dame (Amiens) 160
  Notre-Dame-de-la-
    Miséricorde(Ajaccio) 358
  Notre-Dame (Laon) 162
  Notre-Dame (Le Puy-en-Velay) 274
  Notre-Dame (Paris) 114
  Notre-Dame (Reims) 163
  Notre-Dame (Rouen) 199
  Notre-Dame (Senlis) 146
  Notre-Dame (Strasbourg) 174
  Orléans 215
  Santa Maria Assunta (St Florent)
    356
  St-André (Bordeaux) 284
  St-Corentin (Quimper) 209
  Ste-Bénigne (Dijon) 246
  Ste-Cécile (Albi) 303
  Ste-Marie (Bayonne) 293
  Ste-Marie (St-Bertrand-de-
    Comminges) 301
  Ste-Réparate (Nice) 352
  St-Etienne (Auxerre) 241
  St-Etienne (Limoges) 276
  St-Etienne (Sens) 240
  St-François-de-Sales (Annecy)
    266
  St-Gatien (Tours) 220
  St-Jean (Lyon) 257
  St-Just (Narbonne) 320
  St-Lazare (Autun) 245
  St-Maurice (Vienne) 258
  St-Pierre (Angoulême) 230
  St-Pierre (Montpellier) 321
  St-Pierre (Nantes) 226
  St-Pierre (Vannes) 206
  St-Sauveur (Aix-en-Provence) 336
  St-Vincent (Chalon-sur-Saône)
    247
Catherine de Medici 35, 219
Catholicism 64
Cauterets 300
Cavaillon 327
caves 10, 25
Célé River 309
Celts 31
Centuri 359
Cerbère 317
Céret 317
Cévennes 321
Cézanne, Paul 85, 87, 88, 334, **336**
Chablis 243
Chagall, Marc 334, 352
Chaîne des Puys 272
Châlons-en-Champagne 164
Chalon-sur-Saône 248
Chambéry 264
Chamonix 260, 262
Champagne 82, 155

Champ de Mars (Paris) 124
Champs-Elysées (Paris) 126
Channel Tunnel 362
Chantilly 146
Charlemagne 32, 283, 318
Charles Martel 32, 235
Charles VI 33
Charles VIII 35
Charles X 40
Charleville-Mézières 162
Chartres 151
Châteauneuf-du-Pape 329
châteaux 93, **228**
  Amboise 218
  Ancy-le-Franc 243
  Angers 225
  Anjony (Tournemire) 275
  Artigny 220
  Azay-le-Rideau 93, **221**
  Beaugency 216
  Beauregard 217
  Blois 93, **217**
  Bourdeilles 287
  Bussy-Rabutin 243
  Castelnau-Bretenoux 310
  Chambord 93, 228, **216**
  Champ de Bataille 197
  Chantilly 146
  Chaumont 93, **217**, 228
  Chenonceau **219**, 228
  Cheverny **216**, 228
  Chinon 223
  Comper 206
  Comtal (Carcassonne) 319
  Ducs de Bretagne (Nantes) 226
  Ducs de Savoie 264
  Ecouen 145
  Filhot 291
  Fontainebleau 151
  Gaillard (Les Andelys) 198
  Guédelon 241
  Haut-Koenigsbourg 177
  Josselin 205
  Kintzheim 178
  Langeais 222
  Meillant 227
  Montbazon 220
  Montgeoffroy 225
  Murol 271
  O (Sées) 197
  Peyrepertuse 302, 319
  Pierrefonds 147
  Quéribus 302, 319
  Rambouillet 151
  Ratilly 243
  Royal (Argelès-sur-Mer) 317
  Royal de St-Saturnin 271
  Saché 220
  Saumur 225
  Saverne 173
  St-Fargeau 241
  Sully-sur-Loire 215
  Tanlay 243
  Ussé 222
  Vaux-le-Vicomte 149
  Versailles 37, **143**
  Villandry 221
Châtillon-sur-Broué 165
Chaumont-sur-Loire 217
cheeses **76**, 197, 311

Cherbourg 195
Cher, River 221
children 8, 392, 393
Chinon 223
Chirac, Jacques 48, 49
Christianity 32
churches. See
  also abbeys;cathedrals
  Basilique de Notre-Dame-du-Port
    (Clermont-Ferrand) 269
  Basilique de Notre-Dame (Lyon)
    257
  Basilique de Notre-Dame (Orcival)
    272
  Basilique de St-Rémi (Reims) 164
  Basilique du Bois-Chenu (near
    Domrémy) 166
  Basilique du Sacré-Coeur (Paris)
    135
  Basilique St-Denis 145
  Basilique Ste-Madeleine (Vézelay)
    245
  Chapelle de Ste-Croix (Josselin)
    205
  Chapelle du Rosaire (Vence) 349
  Chapelle Notre-Dame-du-Haut
    (Ronchamp) 249
  Chapelle St-Blaise-des-Simples
    (Milly-la-Forêt) 150
  Chapelle St-Michel-d'Aiguilhe (Le
    Puy-en-Velay) 274
  Chapelle St-Pierre (Villefranche-
    sur-Mer) 353
  Dominican Church (Colmar) 180
  Germigny-des-Prés 215
  Guimiliau 213
  La Madeleine (Paris) 131
  Lampaul-Guimiliau 213
  La Trinité Vendôme 224
  Les Jacobins (Toulouse) 305
  Notre-Dame-de-la-Garde
    (Marseille) 338
  Notre-Dame (Dijon) 246
  Notre-Dame-la-Grande (Poitiers)
    235
  Sainte-Chapelle (Paris) 117
  St-Benoît-sur-Loire 215
  Ste-Engrace (Béarn) 295
  Ste-Foy (Conques) 311
  St-Etienne-du-Mont (Paris) 119
  St-Germain (Auxerre) 241
  St-Germain-des-Prés (Paris) 121
  St-Hilaire-le-Grande (Poitiers) 235
  St-Julien-le-Pauvre (Paris) 119
  St-Maclou (Rouen) 199
  St-Michele (Murato) 356
  St-Pierre-le-Jeune 176
  St-Robert (La Chaise-Dieu) 274
  St-Sernin (Toulouse) 305
  St-Séverin (Paris) 119
  St-Sulpice (Paris) 121
  St-Thégonnec 213
  St-Thomas (Strasbourg) 176
cider 191
Cimetière du Montparnasse
  (Paris) 121
Cimetière Père Lachaise (Paris)
  137
cinema 53, **67**, 191
Cirque de Gavarnie 11, **300**

Cirque de Navacelles 322
Clémenceau, Georges 44
Clement V, Pope 132
Clermont-Ferrand 269
climate 22, 394
Clovis, King 32, 145
Cluny 32, **248**
Cocteau, Jean 150, 334, 353
Cognac 9, 231
Col du Tourmalet 301
Colette 241
Collioure 317
Collonges-la-Rouge 277
Colmar 178, **179**
Colombey-les-Deux-Eglises 165
colonialism 48, 64
Comédie Française 129
Compiègne 146
Concarneau 208
Conciergerie (Paris) 117
Condom 308
Conques 311
constitution 48, 49
cookery courses 70
Corderie Royale (Rochefort) 233
Cordes-sur-Ciel 304
Corniche de l'Estérel 345
Cornouaille 209
Corsica 10, 25
Corte 359
Côte d'Albâtre 200
Côte d'Azur 24, 315, **349**
Côte de Granit Rose 212
Côte d'Emeraude 212
Côte d'Opale 159
Côte d'Or 246
Côte Fleurie 189
Coulon 235
Courchevel 262
Coussac-Bonneval 277
credit cards 397
crime 394
Crozon Peninsula 210
cruises, canal 251
Crusades **32**, 93
Cubism 88
Cucuron 330
cuisine 74
customs regulations 394
cycling 198, 366

D

Dalí, Salvador 136
David, Jacques-Louis 85, 86
D-Day beaches 10, 45, 192, **201**
Deauville 191
Degas, Edgar 88
de Gaulle, Charles 45, 48, 165
Delacroix Eugène 86, 121
Désert des Agriates 357
design 96
Deux Magots (Paris) 121
Diana, Princess of Wales 126, 129
Diane de Poitiers 219
Diderot 36
Dieppe 201
Dijon 245
Dinan 212
Dinard 213

Disneyland Resort Paris 9, **147**
Dombes 255
Domme 290
Domrémy-la-Pucelle 166
Dordogne 25, **287**
Douai 160
Douarnenez 210
Douaumont 166
Draguignan 343
Dreyfus affair 43
driving 365
Dune du Pilat 11, **292**
Dunkerque 157

E

Eauze 308
economy 49
Eguisheim 180
Eiffel Tower (Paris) 11, 43, **125**
Eleanor of Aquitaine 32, 223, 283
embassies and consulates 395
emergencies 395
Epagnac-Ste-Eulalie 309
Epernay 164
Epinal 169
Epoisses 244
ethnicity 63, **64**
Etretat 11, **200**
Eure 197
European Union 47, 48, 50, 168, 176
Evian-les-Bains 267
Evisa 359
Evreux 197

F

fashion 130
Fauvism 88
Fécamp 201
festivals and events 182, 385
Fifth Republic 47
Figari 357
Figeac 309
Filitosa 356
First Republic 41
fishing industry 23
Flaubert, Gustave 198, **199**, 201
Fleckenstein 173
flora 262, 272
Foix 302
Fontainebleau 150
Fontaine des Quatre Dauphins (Aix-en-Provence) 336
Fontaine-de-Vaucluse **331**, 339
Font-de-Gaume 288
Fontevraud l'Abbaye 223
Font-Romeu 316
food and drink **69**, 244, 258. *See also* cheeses;wine
foreign policy 49
Fôret de Chambord 216
Forêt de Haguenau 173
Forêt de Paimpont 206
Forum des Halles (Paris) 131
Fougères-sur-Bièvre 217
Fouquet, Nicolas 149
Fourcès 308
Fourth Republic 47

Fragonard, Jean-Honoré 86, 348
Franche-Comté 249
François I 229
Franco-Prussian War 41
Fréjus 344
French Alps 10, 23, 239, **266**
French Revolution 37, **39**, 117

G

Gaillac 304
Gascony 307
Gassin 344
Gauguin, Paul 145, 208, 334
Gauls 31
gay and lesbian travellers 395
Geneva 266
geography 24
Gérardmer 169
Géricault, Théodore 86
German occupation 45
Gers 307
Gide André 44
Gien 214
Gironde 232, 285
Giscard d'Estaing, Valéry 48
Giverny 9, **198**
Golfe de Porto 358
Golfe du Morbihan 206
Gorbio 355
Gordes 330
Gorge d'Ollioules 339
Gorges de Spelunca 358
Gorges du Loup 348
Gorges du Tarn 10, 311, **322**
Gorges du Verdon 346
Gouffre de Padirac 310
Gourdon 348
Gradlon, King 209
Grand Ballon 11, **172**
Grande Arche de la Défense (Paris) 95, **139**
Grand Mosquée de Paris 120
Grand Paris 114
Granville 195
Grasse 347
Graves 291
Graveson 333
greetings 60
Grenoble 262
Grotte de Lascaux 10, 25, **289**
Grotte des Clamouses 321
Grotte des Combarelles 289
Grotte des Demoiselles 322
Grottes de Rouffignac 289
Grottes du Pech-Merle 310

H

Hackenburg 168
Harfleur 200
Hattonchatel 168
Haut-de-Cagnes 350
health 395
Hemingway, Ernest 120, 129
Hendaye 294
Henri II 35
Henri IV **35**, 115, 295
Henry II of England 32, 223

Henry VI of England **33**, 115
Henry V of England **33**, 200
hitchhiking 367
Hochfelden 174
Honfleur 191
Hôtel des Invalides (Paris) 122
Hôtel de Ville (Paris) 132
Hôtel-Dieu (Beaune) 247
Hôtel Ritz (Paris) 129
Hugo, Victor 39, 109, 114, 119, 123, 134, 196
Huguenots 35
Hunawihr 178
Hundred Years' War **33**, 283
Hunspach 173
Hybert, Francis 89
Hyères 341

I

Ile de Bréhat 212
Ile-de-France 143
Ile de la Cité (Paris) 114
Ile de Ré 234
Ile d'If 338
Ile d'Oléron 232
Ile d'Ouessant 211
Iles Chausey 195
Iles des Lérins 346
Iles d'Hyères 342
Ile St-Louis (Paris) 118
immigration 51, 53, 63
Indochina Wars 47
Indre, River 220
Ingres, Jean-Auguste 85, 86, 309
inland waterways 367
Islam 63, 64

J

Joan of Arc **33**, 167, 198, 215
Jospin, Lionel 48, 49
Josselin 205
Juan-les-Pins 350
July Monarchy 40
Jura 23

K

Kaysersberg 179
Klein, Yves 89, 334
Knights Templars 132, 133, 233

L

La Brède 291
Lac Der-Chantecoq 165
Lac de Vasivière 277
La Chaise-Dieu 274
La Ciotat 339
La Closerie des Lilas (Paris) 120
La Coupole (near St Omer) 158
La Couvertoirade 311
La Défense (Paris) 139
La Garde-Freinet 343
Lake Geneva 267
La Mongie 301
Landes 292
landscapes 21
Langres 165

language 61, **401**
Languedoc 318
Languedoc-Roussillon 82, 315
Laon 162
La Petite-Pierre 173
La Possonnière 224
La Puisaye 241
La Rhune 11, **294**
La Rochelle 233
La Roque-Gageac 290
La Roque St-Christophe 289
Larressingle 308
La Sorbonne (Paris) 119
Latin Quarter (Paris) 118
La Turbie 354
lavender 330
Le-Bar-sur-Loup 348
Leblanc, Maurice 200
Le Brun, Charles 85
Le Cannet 347
Le Cateau-Cambrésis 160
Le Corbusier **95**, 249, 256
Le Havre 199
Le Mans 227
Le Nord 155, **158**
Le Nôtre, André 127, 144, 149
Lens 160
Leonardo da Vinci 35, 219, 218
Le Pen, Jean-Marie 50
Le Pouldu 208
Le Procope (Paris) 109, 118
Le Puy-en-Velay 273, **274**
Le Rozier 322
Les Andelys 198
Les Baux-de-Provence 331
Les Calanques 339
Les Eyzies 288
Les Portes du Soleil 267
Leszczynski, Stanislas 168
Le Touquet 159
liberalism 62
Lille 8, **161**
Limoges 276
Limousin 239, **277**
literature 39
Locronan 210
Loire, River 23, 219, **223**
Loire Valley 83, 187
Loir River 224
Lorrain, Claude 85
Lorraine 41, 43, 44, 155, **169**
lost property 396
Lot 310
Lot, River 25
Loubressac 310
Louis IX (St Louis) **33**, 117
Louis Napoleon 40
Louis-Philippe's 40
Louis XI 35
Louis XIII **36**, 116
Louis XIV **37**, 116, 143, 149, 293
Louis XV 37, 168
Louis XVI **38**, 134
Louis XVII 133
Louis XVIII 145
Lourdes 299
Lozère 322
Lubéron 330
Lumière, Auguste and Louis 66, 256, 339

Luz-St-Sauveur 300
Lyon 8, 31, **256**

M

Maginot Line 44, 167, 173
Maison Carrée (Nîmes) 323
Maison Louis XIV (St-Jean-de-Luz) 294
Malraux, André 44
Manche 195
Manet, Edouard 87
maps 396
Marais (Paris) 132
Marais Poitevin 10, **234**
Marciac 308
Marcilhac-sur-Célé 310
Marennes 232, 234
Marie-Antoinette, Queen 38, 117, 143, 144
markets 71, 174, 387, 388
Marne, Battle of the 164
Marne-la-Vallée 147
Marseille 8, **337**
Massif Central 24, 245, 269
Massif des Maures 342
Matisse, Henri 88, 160, 334, 349
May **1968** 48
Mazarin, Cardinal 36
media 396
medical care 395
Médoc 285
Megève 261
Melun 149
Mémorial de la Shoah (Paris) 133
Ménerbes 330
Menton 355
Méribel 262
Metro (Paris) 125, 364
Metz 168
Midi-Pyrénées 24, 281, **311**
Mignard Pierre 85
Millet, Jean-François 86, 150
Milly-la-Forêt 150
Minerve 302, **319**
Mirepoix 303
Mitterand, François 48, 95
Mitterrand, François **49**, 61
Moissac 309
Molay, Jacques de 132
molecular cuisine 74
Molsheim 176
Monaco 355
Monastère de La Grande Chartreuse 263
monasticism 32, 248. *See also* abbeys
Monet, Claude 87, 139, 198, 199, 334
money 397
Mont Aigoual 322
Montauban 309
Mont Blanc 23
Mont Bochor 261
Montcaret 287
Monte Carlo **355**
Monte Cinto 359
Montesquieu 36
Montgolfier brothers 36
Montignac 288

Mont-Louis 316
Montmartre (Paris) 9, **135**
Montparnasse (Paris) 120
Montpellier 320
Montreuil 159
Monts du Beaujolais 254
Monts du Cantal 272
Montségur 302
Mont Ste-Odile 177
Mont-St-Michel 32, **196**
Mont Ventoux 329
Monument aux Girondins (Bordeaux) 284
Morgat 210
Morlaix 213
Mougins 347
Moulin de la Galette (Paris) 136
Moulin Rouge (Paris) 137
Moustiers-Saint-Marie 346
Mulhouse 181
Murol 271
museums and galleries
   Atelier Brancusi (Paris) 132
   Atelier Paul Cézanne (Aix-en-Provence) 336
   Bioscope Ecomusée d'Alsace (Ungersheim) 180
   Centre Culturel Albert Schweitzer (Kaysersberg) 179
   Centre Guillaume-le-Conquérant (Bayeux) 193
   Centre National d'Art et de Culture Georges Pompidou (Paris) 95, **132**
   Centre Pompidou (Metz) 89, **168**
   Château-Musée (Boulogne) 159
   Cité de l'Architecture et du Patrimoine (Paris) 125
   Cité de l'Espace (Toulouse) 306
   Cité des Sciences et de l'Industrie (Paris) 9, **138**
   Cité du Train (Mulhouse) 181
   Cité Internationale de la Bande Dessinée et de l'Image (Angoulême) 230
   Espace Dalí Montmartre (Paris) 135
   European Centre of Deported Resistance Members (Struthof) 173
   Fondation Ephrussi de Rothschild (Cap Ferrat) 354
   Fondation Maeght (St Paul-de-Vence) 350
   Fondation Vasarely (Aix-en-Provence) 336
   Fondation Vincent Van Gogh (Arles) 333
   Historial de la Grande Guerre (Péronne) 160
   Jeu de Paume (Paris) 127
   La Ferme de la Forêt (St Trivier-de-Courtes) 255
   La Maison des Canuts (Lyon) 258
   L'Atelier Paul Cézanne (Aix-en-Provence) 87
   La Vieille Charité (Marseille) 338
   Le Clos Arsène Lupin (Etretat) 200
   Le Port Musée (Douarnenez) 210
   Les Abattoirs (Toulouse) 306

Les Egouts de Paris 126
Maison Bonaparte (Ajaccio) 358
Maison de Balzac (Paris) 126
Maison des Minéraux (St Hernot) 211
Maison Natale Arthur Rimbaud (Charleville-Mézières) 163
Maison Victor Hugo (Paris) 134
Mas du Pont de Rousty 336
Memorial (Caen) 192
Musée Alsacien (Strasbourg) 175
Musée Archéologique (St-Raphaël) 344
Musée Basque (Bayonne) 293
Musée Calvet (Avignon) 330
Musée Cantini (Marseille) 338
Musée Carnavalet (Paris) 133
Musée Chablais (Thonon-les-Bains) 266
Musée Christian Dior (Granville) 195
Musée Cognacq-Jay (Paris) 133
Musée Colette (St Sauveur-en-Puisaye) 241
Musée Condé (Chantilly) 146
Musée d'Aquitaine (Bordeaux) 284
Musée d'Armagnac (Condom) 309
Musée d'Art Américain (Giverny) 198
Musée d'Art Contemporain (Bordeaux) 284
Musée d'Art Contemporain (Lyon) 256
Musée d'Art Contemporain (Nice) 352
Musée d'Art et d'Archéologie (Cluny) 248
Musée d'Art et d'Archéologie (Périgueux) 287
Musée d'Art et d'Histoire (Cognac) 231
Musée d'Art et d'Histoire du Judaïsme (Paris) 133
Musée d'Art Moderne (Céret) 318
Musée d'Art Moderne de la Ville de Paris 126
Musée d'Art Moderne et Contemporain (Strasboug) 175
Musée d'Art Moderne (Troyes) 165
Musée Dauphinois (Grenoble) 263
Musée de Bretagne (Rennes) 205
Musée de Grenoble 263
Musée de la Corse (Corte) 359
Musée Delacroix (Paris) 121
Musée de la Grande Chartreuse 264
Musée de la Marine (Paris) 125
Musée de la Mode et du Textile (Paris) 128
Musée de l'Annonciade (St-Tropez) 343
Musée de la Pêche (Concarneau) 208
Musée de la Publicité (Paris) 128
Musée de l'Armée (Paris) 122
Musée de l'Armistice (Compiègne) 146

Musée de l'Automobile (Mulhouse) 181
Musée de l'Homme (Paris) 125
Musée de l'Hospice (Lille) 161
Musée de l'Impression sur Etoffe (Mulhouse) 181
Musée de l'Imprimerie (Lyon) 256
Musée de l'Oeuvre Notre-Dame (Strasbourg) 175
Musée de l'Orangerie (Paris) 127
Musée de Montmartre (Paris) 135
Musée de Normandie (Caen) 192
Musée Départemental Arles Antique 335
Musée Départemental de la Tapisserie (Aubusson) 277
Musée de Préhistoire (Carnac) 208
Musée de Préhistoire (Mâcon) 253
Musée des Arts Décoratifs (Bordeaux) 284
Musée des Arts Décoratifs (Paris) 128
Musée des Arts du Cognac 231
Musée des Augustins (Toulouse) 306
Musée des Beaux-Arts (Angers) 226
Musée des Beaux-Arts (Bordeaux) 284
Musée des Beaux-Arts (Caen) 192
Musée des Beaux-Arts (Dijon) 245
Musée des Beaux-Arts et de la Dentelle (Alençon) 197
Musée des Beaux-Arts (Limoges) 276
Musée des Beaux-Arts (Lyon) 256
Musée des Beaux-Arts (Quimper) 209
Musée des Beaux-Arts (Reims) 164
Musée des Beaux-Arts (Rouen) 192
Musée des Beaux-Arts (Tours) 220
Musée des Confluences (Lyon) 256
Musée des Marionettes (Lyon) 257
Musée des Tapisseries (Aix-en-Provence) 336
Musée des Volcans (Aurillac) 275
Musée d'Histoire des Baux 332
Musée d'Orsay (Paris) 122
Musée du Champignon (St-Hilaire- St-Florent) 225
Musée du Cheval (Chantilly) 146
Musée du Compagnonnage (Tours) 220
Musée du Débarquement (Arromanches) 192
Musée du Nouveau Monde (La Rochelle) 234
Musée d'Unterlinden (Colmar) 180
Musée du Quai Branly (Paris) 123
Musée du Vin de Bourgogne (Beaune) 247

Musée Eugène Boudin (Honfleur) 191
Musée Faure (Aix-les-Bains) 265
Musée Fernand Léger (Biot) 347
Musée Gallo-Romain (Lyon) 257
Musée Goetz-Boumeester (Villefranche) 353
Musée Historique des Tissus et des Arts Décoratifs (Lyon) 256
Musée Ingres (Montauban) 309
Musée International de la Chasse (Gien) 214
Musée International de la Parfumerie (Grasse) 348
Musée Jean Lurçat (Angers) 226
Musée Lorrain (Nancy) 169
Musée Marmottan-Claude Monet (Paris) 139
Musée Masséna (Nice) 351
Musée Matisse (Le Cateau-Cambrésis) 160
Musée National Adrien Dubouché (Limoges) 276
Musée National d'Art Moderne (Paris) 132
Musée National de la Marine (Toulon) 341
Musée National de la Renaissance (Château d'Ecouen) 145
Musée National de Préhistoire (Les Eyzies) 288
Musée National des Arts Asiatiques – Guimet (Paris) 125
Musée National d'Histoire Naturelle (Paris) 119
Musée National du Louvre (Paris) 127
Musée National du Moyen Age/Thermes de Cluny (Paris) 119
Musée National Marc Chagall (Nice) 352
Musée Océanographique (Monte Carlo) 355
Musée Picasso (Antibes) 351
Musée Picasso Paris 134
Musée Portuaire (Dunkerque) 158
Musée Pyrénéen (Lourdes) 300
Musée Réattu (Arles) 333
Musée Renoir (Cagnes) 350
Musée Rimbaud (Charleville-Mézières) 163
Musée Rodin (Paris) 87, **123**
Musée Rolin (Autun) 245
Musée Savoisien (Chambéry) 264
Musée Somme (Albert) 160
Musée St-Raymond (Toulouse) 305
Musée Toulouse-Lautrec (Albi) 304
Musée Zadkine (Paris) 120
Palais des Beaux Arts (Lille) 161
Philarmonie de Paris 138
Postal Museum (Riquewihr) 179
Sculpture Park (Kerguélhennec) 206
Villa-Musée Fragonard (Grasse) 348

N

Nancy 8, **169**
Nantes 226
Nantes-Brest Canal 205
Nantes, Edict of 37
Napoleonic Wars 38
Napoleon I, Emperor. See Bonaparte
Narbonne 320
national parks 22
  Ecrins 262
  Pyrenees 297
  Vanoise 261
Nazi regime 45
Nerval, Gérard de 120
Neuf-Brisach 180
Niaux 302
Nice 9, **351**
nightlife 386
Nîmes **323**
Normandy 23, 187, **189**
Normans 32, 192
Notre-Dame (Paris) 114
Noyers 243

O

Obernai 177
Oloron-Ste-Marie 295
opening hours 388, 398
Opéra de Paris Bastille 134
Opéra National de Paris 131
Oradour-sur-Glane 276
Orange 327
Orcival 272
Orléans 215
Orne 197
Ottmarsheim 181
oysters 232, **234**

P

palaces. See also chateaux
  Grand Palais (Paris) 127
  Palais de Chaillot (Paris) 125
  Palais de Justice (Dijon) 246
  Palais de Justice (Paris) 116
  Palais de l'Elysée (Paris) 127
  Palais de l'Europe (Strasbourg) 176
  Palais des Archevêques (Narbonne) 320
  Palais des Ducs (Dijon) 245
  Palais des Papes (Avignon) 329
  Palais des Princes (Monaco) 355
  Palais des Rohan (Strasbourg) 175
  Palais de Tokyo 126
  Palais du Luxembourg 120
  Palais du Tau (Reims) 164
  Palais Fesch (Ajaccio) 358
  Palais Garnier – Opéra National de Paris 131
  Palais Idéal du Facteur Cheval (Hauterives) 259
  Palais Jacques Coeur (Bourges) 227
  Palais Lascaris (Nice) 352
  Palais Royal (Paris) 129

Petit Palais (Avignon) 330
Petit Palais (Paris) 127
Panthéon (Paris) 119
Paoli, Pasquale 357
Paris 25, 31, 40, 44, 45, **109**
  eating out 118, 369
  fashion 130
  nightlife 386
  shopping 388
  the arts 383
Paris Commune 41, 135
parish closes (Brittany) 213
parks and gardens. See also national parks; regional parks; theme parks
  Bois de Boulogne (Paris) 138
  Jardin Anglais (Evian-les-Bains) 267
  Jardin de la Fontaine (Nîmes) 323
  Jardin des Plantes (Montpellier) 321
  Jardin des Plantes (Paris) 119
  Jardin des Tuileries (Paris) 127
  Jardin du Carrousel (Paris) 127
  Jardin du Luxembourg (Paris) **120**, 121
  Jardin du Palais Royal (Paris) 129
  Jardin Exotique (Eze) 354
  Jardin Exotique (Monaco) 353, 355
  Jardin Thuret (Juan-les-Pins) 351
  Parc de la Villette (Paris) 138
  Parc Léonard de Vinci (Amboise) 219
  tropical gardens of the Riviera 353
  Versailles 143
  Villandry 222
Pasteur, Louis 248
Pau 295
Pauillac 285
Pays Basque 292
Pays Bigouden 208
Pays d'Auge 191
Pays de Caux 201
Pei, I.M. 95, 127
Peille 354
Peillon 355
Penne 304
people 57
Pepin the Short 32
performing arts 383
perfume 348
Périgueux 287
Péronne 160
Pérouges 256
Perpignan 317
Pétain, Marshal 45
Petit Pont (Paris) 118
pets 398
Philip II (Augustus) 32
Philip IV the Fair 33, 132
Piaf, Edith 67
Piano, Renzo 95, 132, 256
Picasso, Pablo 88, 134, 136, 318, 334, 337, 347, 351
Pic de l'Ours 345
Pic du Canigou 316
Pic du Cap Roux 345
Pic du Midi 11, **301**

Pigalle (Paris) 136
Pissarro Camille 88
Place Charles de Gaulle-Etoile (Paris) 126
Place de la Concorde (Paris) 127
Place des Abbesses (Paris) 136
Place des Vosges (Paris) 134
Place Ducale (Charleville-Mézières) 162
Place du Tertre (Paris) 135
Place Vendôme (Paris) 129
Pointe de Penmarch 209
Pointe de Raz 209
Poitiers 32, **235**
Poitou-Charentes 187
politics 48, 49, 51, 62
Pompidou Centre (Paris) 95, **132**
Pompidou, Georges 48
Pont-Aven 208
Pont d'Espagne 300
Pont du Gard 323
Pont-du-Loup 348
Pont Neuf (Paris) 118
Pont St-Bénezet (Avignon) 330
Port-Grimaud 344
Port Lauragais 303
Porto 358
Porto-Vecchio 358
postal services 398
Pouilly-Fuissé 253
Poussin, Nicolas 85
Prades 316
Proust, Marcel 44, 191
Provence 24, **329**
Provins 148
public holidays 398
Puy-de-Dôme 11
Puy de Sancy 272
Puy Mary 11
Pyrenees 11, 25, 294, 309

Q

Quenza 358
Quiberon 207
Quimper 209

R

Rabelaisie 223
rail travel 363, 364
Ramatuelle 344
Ratilly 243
reform agenda 51
Reformation 35
regionalism 58
regional parks
    d'Armorique 211
    de Lorraine 169
    des Volcans 272
    de Vosges du Nord 173
    Morvan 245
regions and départements 22, 24
Reims 163
religion 63, **64**
religious services 398
Renaissance 35, 93
Rennes 203
Renoir, Jean 66, 334
Renoir, Pierre-Auguste 87, 88, 350

republicanism 60
reservations 398
Resistance 45
restaurants cafés and bars 73, 69
Restoration 40
Rhine, River 23, 171, 181
Rhône delta 24
Rhône Valley 23, 24, 239, **258**
Ribeauvillé 178
Richard the Lionheart 198, 199, 223
Richelieu, Cardinal 36, 119, 129, 232
Rimbaud, Arthur 163
Riquewihr 8, **179**
Robespierre 38
Rocamadour 8, **310**
Roche de Solutré 253
Rochefort 233
Rodemack 167
Rodin, Auguste 87, **123**
Rogers, Richard 95, 132
Romans **31**, 91, 244, 245, 258
Romanticism 39
Roquefort 311
Roquetaillade 291
Roscoff 212
Rouen 8, **198**
Rousseau, Henri 136, 150
Rousseau, Jean-Jacques 36, **39**, 119, 265
Roussillon 316
Route des Crêtes 168, **172**
Royan 232
Ry 199, **201**

S

safety 394
Saintes 231
Saintes-Maries-de-la-Mer 335
Salers 275
Santiago de Compostela **293**, 295
Santons 332, 339
Saône Valley 249
Sare 294
Sarkozy, Nicolas 50, 53, 114
Sarlat 290
Sartène 359
Sartre, Jean-Paul 48, 120
Satie, Erik 135
Sault 329
Saumur 224
Sauternes 291
Sauveterre de Béarn 295
Schuman, Robert 168
Schweitzer, Albert 179
Scy-Chazelles 168
sea travel 363
Second Empire 40
Second Republic 40
Sedan 163
Sées 197
Seine, River 114, 117, 198, 199
Sélestat 177
Semur-en-Auxois 244
Senlis 146
Sens 240
Serein river valley 243
Sète 320

Seven Years' War 37
Séviac 308
sexual attitudes 61
shopping 387
Sierck les Bains 167
skiing 262, 267
social issues 53, 58
Socoa 294
Somme, Battle of the 10, 44, **160**
Soufflenheim 173
sport 389
Stade de France (St-Denis) 145
St Bartholomew's Day Massacre 35
St-Bertrand-de-Comminges 301
St-Cirq-Lapopie 309
St-Denis 145
Ste-Agnès 355
Ste-Marie-aux-Mines 172
Ste-Marie-de-Campan 301
St-Emilion 8, **285**
Stendhal 39
Stevenson, Robert Louis 321
St-Florent 356
St-Germain-des-Prés (Paris) 121
St-Germain-en-Laye 144
St-Jean-de-Luz 293
St-Jean-Pied-de-Port 294
St-Malo 213
St-Michel-de-Cuxa 316
St-Nectaire 271
St-Nicolas-de-Port 169
St-Paul-de-Vence 8, **349**
Strasbourg 174
St-Rémy-de-Provence **331**
Struthof 172
St-Saturnin 269
St-Sauveur-en-Puisaye 241
St-Tropez 343
student travellers 398
student unrest 48
St-Vaast-la-Hougue 195
St-Valèry-sur-Somme 159
Suisse Normande 197
Sully-sur-Loire 215
Superbagnères 301

T

Tain l'Hermitage 259
Talmont 232
Tarascon 332
taxi 364
telephones 399
Temple d'Auguste et Livie (Vienne) 258
Théâtre Antique (Orange) 327
Théâtre Romain (Vienne) 258
Théâtres Romains (Lyon) 257
The Louvre (Paris) 95, 127
theme parks
    Disneyland Resort Paris 9, **147**
    Parc Astérix 9, **146**
    Planète Futuroscope (near Poitiers) 9, **235**
    Terra Botanica (near Angers) 226
Thiépval **160**
Thiers 273
Third Republic 45
Thirty Years' War 36

Thonon-les-Bains 266
Tignes **261**, 262
Tillac 308
time zone 399
Tinguely, Jean 151, 334
Tonnerre 243
Toul 168
Toulon 341
Toulouse 8, 25, **304**, 305
Toulouse-Lautrec Henri de 304
Touraine 219
Tour de France 299, **300**
tourist information 399
Tour Montparnasse (Paris) 120
Tournemire 275
Tournon-sur-Rhône 259
Tournus 248
Tourrettes-sur-Loup 348
Tours 220
Trocadéro (Paris) **124**, 125
Trôo 224
Trouville-sur-Mer **191**
Troyes 165
Tulle 277
Turenne 277

U

Universal Expositions 43
Utrillo, Maurice 135
Uzerche 277
Uzès 323

V

Vaison-la-Romaine 329
Val-d'Isère **261**, 262
Valée de la Cisse 218

Vallauris 347
Vallée des Alpilles 331
Vallon Pont d'Arc 259
Van Gogh, Vincent 136, 145, 331, 333
Vannes 205
Var Corniche 352
Vaucluse 327
vegetarian food 74
Vence 349
Vendôme 224
Vercingétorix 31, 244
Verdun 44
Verne, Jules 226
Vernet-les-Bains 316
Versailles 37, **143**
Veules-les-Roses 201
Vézelay 245
Viaduc de Millau 95, **311**, 322
Vichy 273
Vichy Regime 45, 47
Vienne 258
Villa Kérylos (Beaulieu-sur-Mer) 354
Villandraut 291
Villefranche-sur-Mer 353
Villepin, Dominique de 51
visas and passports 400
Vittel 169
Voltaire 36, 109, 119
Vosges mountains 169, 172, 177
Vulcania 9

W

walking 11, **366**
Waterloo, Battle of 40
Watteau, Jean-Antoine 85

websites 400
weights and measures 400
Wilde, Oscar 131
wildlife 324
    Alpine 261
    Aquarium (La Rochelle) 234
    bears 325
    Cadre Noir Cavalry School
        (Saumur) 225
    Cité de la Mer (Cherbourg) 195
    Haras national du Pin 197
    Nausicaá (Boulogne) 159
    Océanopolis (Brest) 211
    Parc des Cigognes et des Loutres
        (Hunawihr) 178
    Parc des Oiseaux (Villars-les-
        Dombes) 255
    Parc Ornithologique du Pont de
        Gau 335
    Petite Camargue Alsacienne 181
    storks 173
    Volerie des Aigles (Kintzheim) 178
William the Conqueror 160, 191, 192, 193
wine 9, 22, **79**, 164, 291
World War I 10, 44, 160, 172
World War II **45**, 116, 158, 163.
    See also D-Day; Dunkerque

Y

Yvoire 266

Z

Zadkine, Ossip 121
Zeldin, Theodore 61
Zola, Emile 44, 85, 119

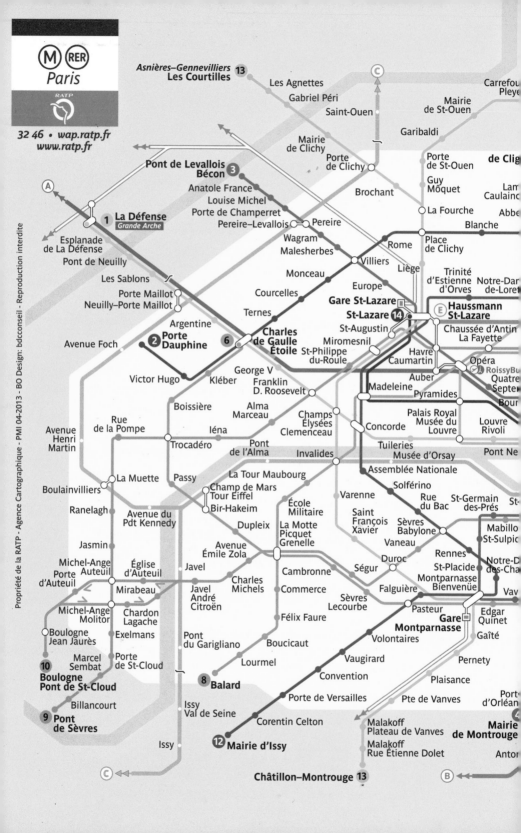